TITLES & EMOLUMENTS
IN SAFAVID IRAN

*A Third Manual Of
Safavid Administration*

By

MIRZA NAQI NASIRI

Translated and Annotated By

Willem Floor

MAGE
PUBLISHERS

Copyright © 2008 Willem Floor

All rights reserved.
No part of this book may be reproduced
or retransmitted in any manner whatsoever,
except in the form of a review, without the
written permission of the publisher.

Cover illustration of *farman* courtesy of Abolala Soudavar

Library of Congress Cataloging-in-Publication Data

Nasiri, 'Ali Naqi, 18th cent.
[Alqab va mavajib-i dawrah-'i salatin-i Safaviyah. English]
Titles & emoluments in Safavid Iran : a third manual of Safavid administration / by Mirza Naqi Nasiri ; translated and annotated by Willem Floor.
-- 1st ed.
p. cm.
Includes bibliographical references and index.
ISBN 1-933823-23-2 (alk. paper)
1. Iran--History--Safavid dynasty, 1501-1736. 2. Social status--Iran--History. 3. Iran--Officials and employees. I. Floor, Willem M. II. Title. III. Title: Titles and emoluments in Safavid Iran.
DS292.N3713 2008
955'.03--dc22
2007051518

Printed and Manufactured in the United States

Mage books are available at bookstores,
through the internet, or directly from the publisher:
Mage Publishers, 1032 29th Street, NW, Washington, DC 20007
202-342-1642 • as@mage.com • 800-962-0922
visit Mage Publishers online at
www.mage.com

CONTENTS

INTRODUCTION 7
TRANSLATION 17
    Category Five 20
    Category Six 45
    Category Seven 47
    Category Eight 52
    Category Nine. 56
    [Category Ten] 81
COMMENTARY 123
    Alphabetical List of Governorships. 136
GLOSSARY 307
BIBLIOGRAPHY 310
INDEX 317

INTRODUCTION

When Afghan and Seystani rebel troops led by Mahmud Khan Ghilzay invaded the heart of the Safavid kingdom in 1721 they probably believed that this was just another foray of plunder and rapine just as the one they had made in 1719. However, all that changed when they unexpectedly took Isfahan in October 1722 and deposed Shah Soltan Hoseyn. As a result of this victory, it was Mahmud Khan who commanded much of the Safavid kingdom as of October 21, 1722. However, although the capital city had fallen and the royal family, except for Tahmasp Mirza, had fallen into his hands, Mahmud Khan still did not feel secure, because opposition was still strong. He therefore focused on securing his hold on the country by eradicating his enemies. By the time that his cousin Ashraf Khan succeeded Mahmud by deposing and killing him in April 1725, it was clear that the Afghans aimed to stay to rule Iran, for Tahmasp Mirza, who had rallied the remaining Safavid supporters was unable from his position in Northern Iran to expel or even attack the Afghan forces. Because the Afghans had destroyed most of the archives of the Safavid administration in November 1722, while in June 1723 Mahmud Khan had thousands of its leadings officials killed, there was not much institutional memory available to Ashraf Khan when he wanted to rule his kingdom.[1] To provide guidance to the fledgling Afghan administration two manuals were written (between 1725 and 1727) that outlined how the Safavid state had been organized. Both manuals (the *Tadhkerat al-Moluk* and the *Dastur al-Moluk*, hereafter referred to as TM and DM) provide details about the main officials of the central government, their task and responsibilities, their remuneration and other details. It has been suggested by the late Mohammad Taqi Danesh-pazhuh that these two manuals relied on an earlier mother text, which provided the same information, but in more detail. The reason for this supposition is that both manuals, although covering the same ground, partly provide the same information and partly complementary data, while both were written in great haste. The latter would explain the alleged pick-and-choose method from that mythical mother-text, which resulted in two texts with partly overlapping, partly differing texts.[2]

---

1 On these events see Willem Floor, *The Afghan Occupation of Safavid Persia* (Paris, 1998).
2 On these issues see Willem Floor and Mohammad Faghfoory, *Dastur al-Moluk* (Costa Mesa: Mazda, 2006); *Tadhkirat Al-Moluk - A Manual of Safavid Administration*. Translated and explained by V. Minorsky (London: Luzac, 1943) [reprint Cambridge, 1980].

It was not only the leaders of the Afghan invaders who wanted to know how Iran had been governed, however. The lack of knowledge about the functioning of the bureaucracy also prevailed after the ouster of the Afghan invaders in the end of 1729 among some Safavid officials such as Mohammad Zaman Beyg (Mhamed Zamoen Beek) from Shiraz, who came to visit the Dutch Agent in Isfahan, Nicolaas Schorer, to ask him how the governorship of Lar and Gamron (Bandar 'Abbas) and the *shahbandar*ship had been organized in the past. Schorer told him that normally Lar and Gamron had been under one governor, while the *shāhbandar* was responsible for the collection of the import and export duties of both Gamron and Kong. At his request Schorer wrote a note about this for the elucidation of Tahmaspqoli Khan (the later Nader Shah) and Mirza Mohammad Taqi Shirazi, who was the latter's main adviser.[3] This shows that the need for information on how to manage the Safavid state was indeed felt at the highest levels of government. In 1731, the secretary of the royal council (*majles-nevis* or *vaqāye'-nevis*), therefore, completed a manual outlining the organization, functions, titles and remuneration of the Safavid bureaucracy, of which an incomplete text has survived and which has been published and edited by Yusof Rahimlu under the title of *Alqāb va Mavājeb Dowreh-ye Salātin-e Safaviyeh* (Mashhad, 1371/1992).

The original text of the manuscript, offered in English translation here, is kept in the National Library at Tabriz and was part of a donation of manuscripts by the late Hajj Hoseyn Aqa Nakhjevani. Because the manuscript has no title, Hajj Hoseyn Aqa Nakhjevani in view of its contents had given it the title of *Alqāb va Mavājeb-e Dowreh-ye Salātin-e Safaviyeh*, which Rahimlu adopted for his published text. A comparison with the contents of the other two manuals of the Safavid administration (the TM and DM) suggests that the current text probably represents only about one-third of the original text, according to Rahimlu.[4] It is, however, a moot question whether the *Alqāb* drew upon the same mother text as the other two manuals may have done. Since all three texts aim to provide information on the organization and functioning of the Safavid administration through entries of its most important officials, their manner of remuneration and nature of their work they all three cover the same ground. However, the *Alqāb* sometimes provides detailed information on offices that the DM and the TM do not or less so. Cases in point are the offices of the *majles-nevis* and the *khalifeh al-kholafā* where the *Alqāb* adds very useful information that is not found elsewhere. This may have been due to the fact that the offices concerned were so regularly held by a succession of the author's relatives that he claimed that they were almost hereditary in his family. However, he also provides an entry on the function of *vakil*, which neither the DM nor the TM do. The listing of the *vakil* suggests that the author was not slavishly copying from an existing text, but that he had done so, because the office had been revived for a while (in 1726) by Shah Tahmasp II after almost 100 years. The author further indicates that he had consulted archival material to find whether other officials had held the same office, given their importance, but he could neither find their appointment diplomas nor what their titles had been. He did the same in the case of some other officials, indicating that the author did some independent research to write his treatise. The *Alqāb* is further also different in that neither the DM nor the TM provides information on the official titles of the various office holders. This maybe due to the idiosyncrasy of a writing *majles-nevis*, but at the same time it is evidence that the author seems to have followed his own ideas rather than those of a pre-existing model text.

---

3   Nationaal Archief (NA or National Archives, The Hague), VOC 2168, Schorer to de Cleen (30/03/1730), f. 207-08.
4   Yusof Rahimlu ed. *Alqab va Mavajeb-e Dowreh-ye Safaviyeh* (Mashhad, 1371/1992), p. eighteen.

Although we do not know the original title of the treatise, we do know who wrote it. The author of this third manual of Safavid administration is, as is clear from the text, **Mirza Naqi Nasiri**, the *majles-nevis*. Since he further mentions that Mirza Mohammad Rahim had been appointed as grand-vizier, which occurred in October 1730 and because the Dutch report that Mirza Naqi's death had occurred exactly one year later[5] the manual must have been completed by the summer of 1731. The author himself has noted that his family was a prominent bureaucratic family from Ordubad (Azerbaijan), which had been able to obtain quasi hereditary and almost exclusive control over some of the most important offices in the Safavid state. Although the family claimed to be descended from Naser al-Din Tusi there does not seem to be any evidence for this. The first known member of the family was **Malek Bahram Ordubadi**, who had served the Aq-Qoyunlu kings and had to retire from government service when Shah Esma'il I (r. 1501-1524) acceded to the throne. Like other officials in a similar position he had sought refuge abroad. When Shah Esma'il passed through Ordubad he was taken aback by the decay of the beautiful homes. One of the shah's confidantes told him that this was due to the exodus of people like Malek Bahram. The latter was a kinsman of the shah's secretary (*monshi*) **Khvajeh 'Atiq**, the first man to affix his endorsement (*toghrā*) to Esma'il's letters after his departure from Gilan to make his bid for power. Shah Esma'il I, therefore, invited Malek Bahram back to Iran. Because his return had a positive impact on the situation at Ordubad Shah Esma'il I appointed him *kalāntar* of Ordubad, where he regularly hosted the shah when he came hunting and fishing in the area.

The Ordubadi or Nasiri family, as they were also called, continued to receive royal favors. Under Shah Tahmasp I (r. 1524-1576), **Mirza Kafi** (d. 1561-62) was appointed *monshi al-mamālek*, because he was a kinsman of Malek Bahram. The latter had died around 1550 en route to Mecca; he had five surviving sons. The eldest son, **Mirak Beyg**, was one of the retainers of Ma'sum Beyg Safavi, the grand vizier (1553-1568) of Shah Tahmasp, whom he served as *monshi* and *lashkar-nevis*. He later became vizier and ended his career as *majles-nevis* under Shah Tahmasp I. The second son was **Adham Beyg**, who became *mostowfi* and later vizier of Soltan Mostafa Mirza. When the latter was killed in 1576 he was unemployed for a while, but in 1578 he was appointed *kalāntar* of Tabriz by Shah Mohammad Khodabandeh. Because he could not get along with the governor of Tabriz he resigned and withdrew to Ordubad. When in 1584, the new governor of Tabriz asked him to return he once again accepted the function of *kalāntar* of Tabriz and subsequently became the governor's vizier. Under Shah 'Abbas I, Adham Beyg became vizier of the keeper of the seal. He became tired of wordly life, however, and resigned and first stayed at the shrine at Ardabil and later at Shiraz, where he died in 1608. The third son was **Hatem Beyg**. He had succeeded his father as *kalāntar* of Ordubad, but because of local disagreements he resigned and went to the royal court. He became vizier of the governor of Khoy and when the latter was dismissed from his post Hatem Beyg was unemployed and he retired to Ordubad and later to Ardabil. Under Shah 'Abbas I he became vizier of the governor of Kerman and later the shah appointed him *mostowfi al-mamālek*. He held the post for six months after which he was promoted to the post of grand vizier, and event which he owed to his youngest brother Abu Taleb Beyg, the fifth son of Malek Bahram. The fourth son, **Abu Torab Beyg** was employed under Shah Tahmasp I as *mostowfi* and later as vizier

---

5 "Mirza Naqi, the vakanevies (*vaqāye'-nevis*) has died, but no successor has been appointed for the time being. It was said that he had died in Qazvin of his wounds suffered in battle against the Turks. Also, that the grand vizier had been dismissed." VOC 2255, van Leijpsigh to de Cleen (03/11/1731), f. 1867. Later the news of his death was confirmed. VOC 2255, van Leijpsigh to de Cleen (28/12/1731), f. 1891-92. Mirza 'Ali Naqi had a successor, for in 1733 it was reported that "Miersa Takie, the vakanevies," was appointed vizier of Resht. VOC 2322, van Leijpsigh to Koenad (22/03/1733), f. 389.

of the governor of Mashhad, which function he held until his death. **Abu Taleb Beyg**, the fifth son, was serving first as *mostowfi* and later as vizier to the governor of Herat, 'Aliqoli Khan Shamlu, to whom he was related. He was sent as an envoy to 'Abdollah Khan, ruler of the Uzbegs, during the latter's grueling siege of Herat in 1587-1588. 'Abdollah Khan was not interested in negotiations and to show how serious he was he had Abu Taleb Beyg blown from the mouth of a cannon. As a result, Shah 'Abbas I took Hatem Beyg Ordubadi under his wings. He first appointed him *mostowfi al-mamālek* and in 1591 Shah 'Abbas made him his grand vizier, a function that he occupied until his death in 1610. Because of the Ordubadi family's loyalty to his house and because of the Hatem Beyg's services to him, Shah 'Abbas I then appointed Hatem Beyg's 10-year old son **Mirza Abu Taleb** as his father's successor. He remained in office as grand vizier from 1610-1621 when "he was dismissed as the result of committing various acts inevitable in a young man and inseparable from the arrogance of office and position." His career seemed to be over, but he was employed as *majles-nevis* by Shah Safi I (r. 1629-1642), who had succeeded his grand-father, Shah 'Abbas I in 1629, and when the new shah dismissed Khalifeh Soltan as grand-vizier in 1632, he called on Mirza Abu Taleb Ordubadi to become grand vizier for a second time. The latter remained in office until 1634, when Shah Safi I had him killed for unclear reasons.

This reversal of fortune had no consequences for other members of the Ordubadi family. Adham Beyg had a son, **Mirza 'Abdol-Hoseyn** who later became *monshi al-mamālek* and who is the author of a book on correspondence called *Tohfat-e Shāhi*, which he dedicated to Shah Safi I in 1034/1624-25, when he was in his sixties. He had two sons, **Mohammad Reza**, who became *majles-nevis* and **Mirza Zeyn al-'Abedin** who became *monshi al-mamālek*. Mohammad Reza also was an author and wrote a book entitled *Kafsh al-Ayāt-e Qor'ān-e Karim* and had wanted to write another book, which he was not able to finish, however. He had two sons, **'Abdol-Jamil** and **Mohammad Taqi**, about whom no details are known. When Mohammad Reza died he was succeeded as *majles-nevis* by his brother Mirza Zeyn al-'Abedin.

Another member of the family was **Mohammad Ebrahim Nasiri**, the author of the *Dastur-e Shahryārān*, a history of the early years of the reign of Shah Soltan Hoseyn. He also left a miscellany (*jong*) dealing with historical and administrative subjects. Mohammad Ebrahim was born in 1641-1642. He began his career as vizier of the governor of Astarabad in 1680. Later he became custodian of Shah Safi's tomb, vizier of Azerbaijan and finally *monshi al-mamālek*. Because of the back-biting of enemies at court he was dismissed from his post, which setback he did not like. However, he soon was received back in favor again, which probably occurred in 1699-1700, when he was appointed as *majles-nevis*. Mohammad Reza Nasiri has suggested that Mohammad Ebrahim may have had a son named **Mohammad Rabi'**, who was *moharrer-e sarkār-e tofangchiyān* under Shah Soleyman. He was sent as ambassador to the court of Siam and wrote a book about his embassy entitled *Safineh-ye Soleymāni*. It is not known when Mohammad Ebrahim died, but he apparently was still alive in 1714.[6]

---

6 For these biographical details I have drawn upon Monshi, Eskander Beyg. *Tarikh-e 'Alamara-ye 'Abbasi*. Iraj Afshar ed. 2 vols. (Tehran 1350/1971), vol. 2, pp. 387, 419-21, 723-27, 827, 804-05, 1091; Savory, Roger M. *History of Shah 'Abbas the Great* (translation of Monshi) 2 vols. (Boulder, 1978), vol. 2, pp. 913-17, 1320-21; Valeh Qazvini, Mohammad Yusef. *Iran dar zaman-e Shah Safi va Shah 'Abbas Dovvom* ed. Mohammad Reza Nasiri (Tehran, 1380/2002), pp. 109, 320, 347, 349; and in particular on Nasiri, Mohammad Ebrahim b. Zeyn al-'Abedin, *Dastur-e Shahriyan*. ed. Mohammad Nader Nasiri Moqaddam (Tehran 1373/1995), pp. xlv-lii. For an English translation of the *Safineh-ye Soleymāni* see John O'Kane, *The Ship of Sulaiman* (New York, 1972).

Unfortunately, Mirza Naqi Nasiri, the author of the *Alqāb*, does not provide any information about his parents and it is therefore not known to whom of the above-mentioned Nasiri relatives he was closest related. The same holds for the other members of the Nasiri family that he mentions such as Mirza Kafi, the last *khalifeh al-kholafā*. However, from his enumeration of posts that family members, who were contemporaries of his, occupied as well as from the position that he himself held it is clear that the Nasiri family was still one of the leading bureaucratic families in Safavid Iran in 1731.

This is also an image that the author of the *Alqāb* wants the reader to have. He claims that his family held the office of *monshi al-mamālek* since the beginning of the Safavid dynasty, although this is not borne out by the facts. It is true that a number of members of the Nasiri family held that office, but members of other families, notably those of the Jaberi Ansari family, likewise were appointed to that dignitiy. The author has a better claim where the office of *majles-nevis* is concerned where members of the Nasiri family indeed dominated among its office holders, but which they also had to share with others on occasion. Some family members also were *mostowfi al-mamālek*. Hatem Beyg, before he became grand vizier in 1591 held that post and Mirza Abu'l-Hoseyn Beyg Ordubadi held the office between 1629 and 1632. Furthermore, the family held the office of governor of Qarajehdagh and that of custodian of Sheikh Shehab al-Din's tomb, which is located in Ahar (both in Azerbaijan), as a hereditary right, but this was a recent acquisition. Furthermore, after 1650 the family also regularly supplied the holder of the office of *khalifeh al-kholafā*, including the very last one. In short, this shows that not only was Mirza 'Ali Naqi Nasiri a scion of a very powerful bureaucratic family, but per force also was a very well informed official, because he could draw upon not only his own experience, but also on his family's institutional memory.

This text of the *Alqāb* contains much information about the workings of the Safavid state that is not available elsewhere, not even in the other two published state manuals (the *Tadhkerat al-Moluk* and the *Dastur al-Moluk*). Unfortunately, the Persian text, which was published in 1992, is hardly known outside Iran.[7] I became only aware of the existence of this publication in 2000 and it was through the kind offices of Dr. 'Abdol-Karim Mashayekhi (director of the Bushire branch of the Institute of Iranology) that I was able to obtain a copy. In 2005, when I visited the University of Mashhad, which had pubished the text, I was told that all copies of the book had been sold and that none were available anymore. Because of all these reasons I decided to translate this text and make it available to those interested in the history of Safavid Iran.

The text seems to have been divided into a number of categories (*tabaqeh*), each of which represents a particular and distinct category of members of the Safavid government administration. It is not known what exactly the organizing principle was, because the text abruptly begins at the end of a sentence, somewhere in what possibly is the fourth category. The text then continues with categories five, six, (possibly seven), eight and nine. The last part of the text may have been part of category [?] ten [?]; it deals with the governors of provinces and districts and also ends abruptly and clearly is incomplete as many jurisdictions are missing from this part of the text. This is a very important part of the text, because we have yet another, be it incomplete, inventory of the administrative jurisdictions of the Safavid state, which, together with a similar inventory in the TM, thus provides a better insight as to extent of its territory and its administrative structure.

---

7 A search via the Karlsruhe Virtual Catalogue as well as of a sample of major US university library catalogues showed that only the British Library, the Bavaria State Library and Princeton University have a copy, which means that practically all of the major American and European universities that offer Middle Eastern studies, in particular Iranian studies, do not have a copy of this important text.

The organization of the material clearly was aimed to provide the higher echelons of the Safavid government with easy access to quick-to-read short write-ups on each major government office as well as on some that had existed.[8] This is clear from the fact that throughout the text the author has maintained the same structure to present his information. Each entry starts with the official name of the office. This is followed by the normal titles (*alqāb-e ma'muli*) of the office holder and in important cases variants thereof. This is followed by his source of income or emoluments (*mavājeb*). Then follows information on his subordinates (*tābinān*), thereafter his place (*makān*) in the royal council, and finally details about his work or function (*shoghl*) are provided.

The information is slightly different in case of category [ten?] officials, the governors of provinces and districts for in that case the information offered also concerns the name of the office, the titles of the office holder, his emoluments and, this is different, the number of his retainers (*molāzemān*). Moreover, although this is not made explicit, the governors are listed by province (*eyālat*). For the presentation of category [ten?] officials is per province under a governor-general (*beygler-beygi*) and his subordinate emirs, who were in charge of districts (*olkā*) and/or tribal groups. Unfortunately, like the other parts of the text this part is also defective, because many jurisdictions are missing from the list of governors-general and their subordinate governors. This listing is, however, a good start to make an analysis of the number of governates in Safavid Iran and the changes therein over time.

The organization of the information in this systematic fashion allowed the shah and his close advisers, who held the highest offices in the state, to easily see to which category a certain office holder belonged, what his titles were, his place in the royal council (if he had one), his claims on the state's revenues, the nature of his work and, in case of the governors, how many regular men they were supposed to keep on a permanent basis. All of this were essential inputs to the government of Iran and provided it with an idea about the size and scope of is executive apparatus, the required skills level or capacity (in case of the governors) of the office holders and its cost.

Because the author of this text was himself secretary of the royal council and a scion of a bureaucratic family that for decades had occupied high offices in the Safavid administration it comes as no surprise that the entry that provides the most detailed information about the office holders is that of the secretary of the royal council and other offices held by members of his family (*khalifeh al-kholafā* and governor of Qarajehdagh). Also, the fact that all entries list the proper titles (and their historical variants, depending on whom held the office) is a clear indication of the author's nature of employment, because as secretary of the royal council his office wrote all the royal appointment diplomas for the office holders in the Safavid administration.

I have kept the commentary on the text to a minimum as most of the offices presented here have already been discussed by me in other publications. Except in a few cases, I have therefore also refrained from making comments on the text, in particular when some aspect, in my view, provides incomplete or even wrong information. Instead, I have provided footnotes to each entry (except for the list of governors), which refer the reader to more detailed published information on the various government offices, its staff, operations and development. The same holds for the seating and standing arrangements of those officials who were member of the royal council, which are also mentioned in the two earlier state manuals (TM and DM) and to which the reader is referred. I have made an exception with regards to the list of governors as it is both incomplete and

---

8   This suggests that there was an ongoing discussion about whether to reinstate some of these old functions such as that of *vakil* or regent.

an unresearched field. To facilitate the understanding of this list and of Safavid administrative provincial organization I have added to the translation of this text a list of all jurisdictions known to me as well as the names of the governors and their years in office, where possible.

To other aspects of the text, such as fiscal terminology, I have not provided any reference either. Under the heading of emoluments (*mavājeb*), the author uses terms such as *hameh-sāleh*, *ma'āfi*, *an'ām*, *soyurghāl*, *eqtā'*, *talab*, *tankhvāh*, *vazifeh*, *pishkesh* and others, which are all explained in my book *A Fiscal History of Iran in the Safavid and Qajar Period* (New York: Bibliotheca Persica, 1999). Therefore, I have not explained or discussed these terms, but refer the reader to this publication. The information offered as to the sources of income of the various officials should be compared with that contained in the other two state manuals, the *Tadhkerat al-Moluk* (TM) and the *Dastur al-Moluk* (DM) to determine whether there are major differences and if so, whether that is of historical significance or not.

An issue that is of great interest for further study is that of the titles that the various officials were honored with. These and their variants provide an insight in the nuances of bureaucratic ranking and thus may allow us, if many more of such titles are available over a historical period, to determine the relative changes in importance of certain offices. For example, the following six titles were found to be the usual honorifics that were given to *soltān*s, or third-level governors. The simplest title given to the lowest ranking *soltān* was that of 'Asylum of the emirate' (*emārat-panāh*), which in the text is then followed by the words *Folān Soltān* or Soltan So-and-so. The more important the *soltān* was the more words were added to this basic title, while the first words were repeated after the 'center-piece' word of 'he who adorns' (*nezāman*), but now with the preposition *l'el*. If it so happened that the *soltān* also held in addition other offices, such as that of custodian (*motavalli*) of a tomb, then this was reflected in his titles.

> Asylum of the emirate So-and-so Soltan.
>
> Asylum of the emirate and government So-and-so Soltan.
>
> Asylum of the emirate and government, he who adorns So-and-so Soltan.
>
> Asylum of the emirate and government, he who adorns emirate and government So-and-so Soltan.
>
> Asylum of the custodianship, emirate, government and excellence, he who adorns custodianship, emirate, government and excellence So-and-so Soltan.

The same system of the titles of the *soltān* was also applied to higher ranking officials. For example, those governors who held the higher rank of *khān* were always rewarded with titles that contained the word *eyālat*. Also, instead of the base case of *emārat-panāh* as was the case for *soltān*s, *khān*s were indicated by the words 'Asylum of authority' (*showkat-panāh*). In rare cases, titles peculiar to a *khān* were also conferred on a *soltān* as a personal royal favor. The more important the *khān* the more words were added to the titles, which were repeated, but preceded by a proposition, after the 'center-piece' word *nezāman*, or in a few cases 'he who illuminates' (*shamsan*).

Asylum of the province and authority, he who adorns So-and-so Khan.

Asylum of the province and authority, pomp of the administration, he who adorns So-and-so Khan.

Asylum of the province and authority, pomp of the administration, he who adorns province and authority So-and-so Khan.

Asylum of the province and authority, pomp of the administration, who illuminates majesty and authority So-and-so Khan.

Asylum of the province and authority, pomp of the administration, His Excellency, he who adorns province and authority So-and-so Khan.

Asylum of the province and authority, pomp and majesty of the administration, he who adorns province and authority So-and-so Khan.

Asylum of the province and authority, pomp and majesty of the administration, His Excellency, he who adorns province and authority So-and-so Khan.

Asylum of the province and authority, pomp and majesty of the administration, His Excellency, he who adorns province, authority, majesty and felicity So-and-so Khan.

Asylum of the province and authority, pomp and majesty of the administration, His Excellency emir of emirs, he who embellishes the province, authority, majesty and felicity So-and-so Khan (Ziyadoghlu Qajar the Associate).

Beygler-beygis (governors-general) all seem to have had the same title, which like that of the lower-ranking and subordinate governors also was characterized by symmetry, with the 'center-piece' word of *nezāman* separating the simple words from the repeated words with the preposition 'Asylum of the province and authority, pomp and majesty of the administration, He emir of emirs, he who adorns province, authority, majesty and felicity So-and-so Khan.

Individuals, of course, were awarded 'upgraded' variants of the usual basic titles, because of that particular person's influence with the court. Also, if the office holder also was, for example, custodian (*motavalli*) of a tomb then this was reflected in his titles as was the case for the governor of Shirvan: Asylum of custodianship, province and authority, pomp and majesty of the administration, He emir of the emirs, he who adorns custodianship, province, authority, pomp, majesty, and felicity So-and-so Khan, custodian of the many splendored tomb of the Lord of the Sufis and Pole of the mystics Soltan Joneyd.

The same principle (choice of words, relative importance and order of these words, and the number of words, repeated in symmetry after a 'center-piece' word) also applied to the titles of the officials of the central government.

Finally, some observations on the translation. I have tried to stick as close as possible to the original text without, I hope, sacrificing readability. I have kept the occurrence of Persian terms to a minimum, but have added a glossary at the end of the translation to allow those readers who do not have access to the original Persian text to learn what the Persian technical terms are that have been used. For easy reference to the published Persian text I have inserted in bold typeface the page numbers of the Persian published text into the translated text. The different shahs are mostly indicated by their so-called *post-mortem* titles. Thus, Shah 'Abbas I is referred to as *sāheb-qerāni* or as *giti-setān*; Shah Soleyman as *towbi-āshyān*, but also as *rezvān makān*; and Shah Soltan Hoseyn as *mālek-e reqāb*. Shah Tahmasp II, who was still alive when this text was written, is refered to as *abad-e tow'amān*, which I have translated as Your Majesty.

Also, I have indicated the short 'a' by 'a' and the long 'a' in transliterated words by ā, which the readers may find useful. In the Commentary part I have made no difference between the short and the long 'a' in transliterated words. Otherwise, a long 'u' is a 'u', a short one is an 'o', and a long 'i' is an 'i' and a short 'i' is an 'e'.

Finally I want to thank Mohammad Faghfoory and Hasan Javadi for their comments on the translation of some parts of the text and John Emerson for his bibliographical support. I hope that the translation of this important text will contribute to further studies on the society and administrative organization of Safavid Iran.

TRANSLATION

[MISSING TEXT][1] His Majesty can go. If His Majesty wants something or something to be done he gives the order to a senior female harem attendant, who also stands in high regard and trust. The person concerned, having arrived at the gate of the harem, informs the eunuch and guard who are taking turns at guard duty, and they alert the senior officer of the harem. He, having come to the senior female harem attendant, hears the royal command from her and takes care of the execution of the said service. When later His Majesty says: 'well done',[2] then this is the sign of dismissal. If the senior officer of the harem has a request of his own or on behalf of the great emirs he, having come into the presence of His Majesty, then has the courage to make that request. In the days of *abu'l-baqā navvāb* Shah Esmā'il [I], may God's compassion be on him, and of the *jannat-makān* Shah Tahmāsp [I], when having eunuchs was not as yet so customary, mostly old women came to and fro outside [the harem] and passed on the shah's orders. In the days of the reign of His Majesty the world conqueror [i.e. Shah 'Abbas I], when the rules of kingship became fixed and permanent, many black and white eunuchs were acquired.[3] Also, a regiment was formed of them as part of the ranks of the royal household musketeers. A *quruqi* hat[4] with a silver belt was prepared for each one of them, and two centurions from among them were appointed for that group and a strong building was allotted to them inside the harem.[5] Its gate was made of iron and was named the Iron Gate. A unit of eunuchs had to guard it. It is well-known that His Majesty the world conqueror has said repeatedly that "we have a secret army that nobody knows of and we have acquired a treasury that is unknown to everybody." His Majesty meant [1] the secret army of the group of eunuchs and

---

1 Assuming that the beginning of the text presents material from category four it means that the missing text most likely must have been comprised of an introduction, categories one, two, three and the remainder of category four.

2 The term used, *fahwa*, is a contraction of *fa huwa*, which itself is an abbreviation of *fa huwa'l-ma'mul morād*.

3 For a discussion of these isssues see Willem Floor and Mohammad Faghfoory, *Dastur al-Moluk* (Costa Mesa: Mazda, 2006), pp. 175-77.

4 A hat worn by royal servants who went out in front of the shah and his women and declared the route that the shah took was 'out of bounds' or *quruq* to all males.

5 For more details on these musketeers see Floor-Faghfoory, *Dastur al-Moluk*, pp. 153-54. See also Willem Floor, *Safavid Government Institutions* (Costa Mesa: Mazda, 2003), pp. 213-16.

the incomparable treasure of the trees of the *Chahār Bāgh* and its [adjacent] gardens, whose value is equal to significant sums.[6] Among them 400 persons were musketeers; another unit was [formed by] the royal accouterment guards, the harem sentinels, the elephant keepers, the lion tamers, the cheetah keepers, the hunters, the sailors, the cooks and the musicians. Some of this group lived in holy Mashhad and Mazandaran, where they were occupied in the service of the holy shrine of the eighth Imam p.b.u.h. and in supervising the palaces of paradisiacal Mazandaran. In the days of His Majesty Shah Soltān Hoseyn there were about 500 eunuchs and each one had a considerable salary. There were even eunuchs brought from the outer-harem.

ROYAL ARMORER
Jabbehdār-bāshi

TITLES
The same[7]

EMOLUMENTS
First, his salary is 300 *tuman*s and later another hundred *tuman*s have been added so that it amounts to 400 *tuman*s. This office is also bestowed on others than on eunuchs, whom they call *selahdār-bāshi*. His post consists in the management of all royal arms, of whatever kind they may be, such as war, battle, and siege equipment. All of these are his responsibility as well as the staff of the arsenal who are needed by the armory. All of them were his subordinates and underlings and without his permission and confirmation none of the staff of the arsenal may be given a revenue assignment,[8] wages and a regular salary and none may serve in the ranks of this group. The word *qur* [in Turkish] means arms and therefore the place where arms are stored is called *qur-khāneh*.[9]

STEWARD OF THE MOSQUE OF HOLY MASHHAD
nāzer-e masjed-e Mashhad-e moqaddas-e mo'allā

TITLES
Asylum of super-intendancy, exaltedness and felicity, his excellency, the companion of the Khaqan, he who adorns the super-intendancy, exaltedness and felicity, So-and-so Beyg, servant and lamp holder of the holy, many-splendored and blessed Shrine of Imam Reza, may a thousand salutations be on its overseers and superintendent of Holy Mashhad.

---

6 On these gardens see Floor-Faghfoory, *Dastur al-Moluk*, pp. 67-68, 238-39.

7 This refers to the titles of the office holder immediately preceding the royal armorer of which the text is missing.

8 *Teyul*, a temporary or lifetime royal grant of a revenue assignment to officials or supporters as a salary or income.

9 For more details on this official see Floor-Faghfoory, *Dastur al-Moluk*, pp. 44-45, 181-82; Floor, *Safavid Government*, p. 147.

EMOLUMENTS

Because the stewardship of the endowments of the great mosque of Holy Mashhad, whose builder was Gowharshād Beygom, the wife of Shāhrokh,[10] is in the charge of eunuchs, who are appointed by His Majesty, it is not really clear how much the fee of the stewardship of the said mosque's trusts, which the aforementioned [builder] had entrusted to the said mosque, [2] amounts to per year. In accordance with the account of its agents, it amounts to 300 up to 500, 600 *tuman*s. The entire management of the affairs of the said mosque was in the hands of the above mentioned steward. The said steward has total authority over the endowments, its servants, staff, workers, and agents. The said steward always had to live in Holy Mashhad to watch over the endowments and the flourishing of the above mentioned mosque.

TUTOR OF THE [YOUNG] ROYAL SLAVES
Laleh-ye gholāmān

TITLES

Asylum of exaltedness and sublime matters, glory and excellence of the administration, the Confidante of the Khaqan, he who adorns exaltedness and sublime matters, Aqa So-and-so.

EMOLUMENTS

Consist of salaries and revenue assignments that are received from places located in the Komreh governate, 180 *tuman*s.

The royal slaves of the royal household who are not yet bearded, who are also called the 'trainee' royal slaves[11], are all his subordinates. They are taught proper behavior etiquette and how to serve the king in public and private; once they have reached the level of competence [to perform] royal services they take turns among the royal household slaves and execute services in His Majesty's presence. Formerly this group had ringlets of hair, but His Majesty Shah Soltan Hoseyn had their ringlets cut off and he made it a rule that henceforth ringlets would not be allowed any more. Once they [i.e. the young royal slaves] grew beards they were excused from serving in His Majesty's presence. Then they were entrusted to the groups of hundred, i.e. when they were [assigned to] the centurions of the royal slaves.[12]

---

10 Sharokh Mirza, king of most of Persia and Transoxiania (r. 1405–1447). The mosque built by his wife was completed in 1418. On the steward's role also see Floor-Faghfoory, *Dastur al-Moluk*, pp. 5-7.
11 It is not clear why these young royal slaves were known as *gholāmān-e anbār*. Perhaps the origin of the use of the term *anbār*, meaning "dung, manure, storehouse and reservoir", among other things, is due to the fact that, according to Chardin, *Voyages*, vol. 8, p. 38, the young royal slaves were housed in the *khāneh-ye gāv* or the cow stable. Elsewhere, Chardin calls the place where the young royal slaves were fed the *anbār-e gholāmān*, which perhaps is the origin of this qualification of these young slaves. Ibid, vol. 7, p. 388.
12 See also Floor-Faghfoory, *Dastur al-Moluk*, p. 47; Floor, *Safavid Government*, pp. 167-69.

OTHER EUNUCHS
sāyer-e khvājehsarāyān

TITLES

Asylum of exaltedness and sublime matters, he who adorns, So-and-so Beyg and So-and-so Aqa.

For each of those who among them stood in high esteem was written, in addition to the said titles, *moʿtamad al-khavāss*.

[EMOLUMENTS]

They have different emoluments. The rule is that the white eunuchs are called So-and-So *Beyg* and So-and-So *Āqā*. The word *āqā* is put behind his name such as Ebrāhim Āqā. Those who are black put the word *āqā* before [3] their name, such as Āqā Kamāl so that one may distinguish between black and white [eunuchs]. The word *beyg* is not written for the black eunuchs. Some of this group are the subordinates of the two centurions that have been mentioned before, and some are the subordinates of the senior officer of the harem and each one has a special place and function.

CATEGORY FIVE

Titles, revenue assignment, emoluments, regular salaries, and perquisites of the emirs of the royal court and what the functions of the subordinates and their sitting place of each of that group are in the paradisiacal gatherings.

GRAND VIZIER
vazir-e divān-e aʿlā

TITLES

Titles were written in different ways for the grand vizier in each period.
Before the function of regent was abolished the grand viziers did not have that much independence, because the affairs of the realm and kingdom were in the hands of the regent and were managed in a manner as he saw fit. Therefore, viziers were of very minor importance and consideration.[13] Apart from the *divān* taxes they had no involvement with the other affairs of the kingdom to such an extent that when Morshedqoli Khān Ostājalu held the office of regent, he himself removed the chief-vizier and gave the post to one of his kinsmen.[14] Because the office of regent was held by Turks, His Majesty Shah ʿAbbas I spent most of his time dealing with revolts and rebellions. After Morshedqoli Khān Ostājalu's death he abolished the function of regent. Because the collection of *divāni* taxes and the management of the kingdom's affairs did not progress without great authority and independence he sustained the grand viziers with total respect and cooperation.

---

13 For a discussion of the development of the office of grand vizier see Floor, *Safavid Government*, pp. 23-39; see also Ibid., "A Note of the Grand Vizierate in Seventeenth Century Persia," *ZDMG* 155 (2005), pp. 435-81.

14 On the role of Morshedqoli Khān Ostājalu see Monshi, *Tārikh*, pp. 350-72, 399-405.

This group mostly consists of Tajiks, and if some of them committed evil and rebellious deeds, the shah was content with their dismissal or reprimand due to the circumstance that they did not have an army or a tribe [of their own] to rebel against the shah and make him without any say in the affairs of the kingdom, and it was therefore that after the initial period of Morshedqoli Khān that the grand viziers were given full authority and power. Later shahs [4] also gave full consideration to this group and maintained them in a position of total esteem and respect. The office of vizier in effect has become the office of regent and the management of all affairs is in the charge of the viziers.

Because the office of vizier is mostly bestowed upon people of the class of the pen, scribes and Tājiks, in each period when it was not given to that group this resulted in great corruption during that time. Therefore it is clear to people of intellect that the nature of those who are not Tājik makes them mostly desirous to cause oppression, violence, injustice, collection of irresponsible imposts, and destruction to the subjects, while these kinds of conditions are fewer among the group of the Tājiks. Apart from this, writing skills, understanding, knowledge and maturity are all requirements for this function and Tājiks use their time to these ends, those not of this group use their time mostly in warfare and pillaging; meanwhile these two groups are totally different from one another.

The essence of the function of vizier is understanding, comprehension and maturity. For example, some theologians and *mojtaheds* consider the Friday prayers a general obligatory (*'eyni*) obligation, while some consider it an optional obligation (*vājeb-e takhyiri*) and some consider it forbidden. Each time that somebody wishes to choose one of them so as to decide which one [obligation] to perform, it is required that one of the senior *mojtaheds* examines this matter so that he may do that one that he prefers. It should not be common usage that this matter is examined by a common camel driver who apart from camel grazing does not do anything else. Writing, accounting, short-hand calculating, auditing of accounts and examination of the daily ledgers are sciences in all its forms. The supervision of these activities were in the hands of the grand viziers and every hour each of the clerks fell into the hands of the grand vizier for the examination of these activities; each time that the grand vizier was illiterate and uninformed these activities were not performed. What answer can be given and in what way can this clerk's problem be resolved? It was like asking the question concerning Friday prayer from a common illiterate camel driver.

Furthermore, the basis of the handling of Islamic law is this that each time, for example, when a person buys a house at the price of three *tuman*s, until the deed of that house has acquired the seal of the Islamic judge and of the knowledgeable olama of that time its deed is without authority and nobody will pay attention to it [5]. Each time that a poor clerk, seated behind a file, is copying and recording and confirms that emir so-and-so owes three thousand Tabrizi *tuman*s in *divān* taxes, which the *divān* has not collected, at that very moment the leading accountants, the grand vizier and His Majesty will give [pertinent] orders and a royal decree on this matter will be issued [stating] that since from the files it has been confirmed that emir so-and-so owes three thousand *tuman*s in *divān* taxes, collector so-and-so should go quickly to collect this amount. Each time proper attention has to be paid, for until a three-*tumān* house has obtained the seal of the great olama nobody will have confidence in it. As soon as a clerk writes one word that three thousand *tuman*s has to be taken from emir X the shahs without investigation appointed a tax collector who collects this amount with the application of the sticks and whip. Therefore the respect for this group in customary matters is greater than that of the olama. Consequently, the grand vizier, who is the head of this group, must be totally pious and virtuous, has always to keep foremost in his mind that he has to please the creator and the good-fortune of his own master as well as the comfort and kind treatment of the subjects. This attitude was mostly present among the Tājik group, although in the belief of some it was lacking, but it was not totally absent. However, among the non-Tājik group and the common people this kind of attitude is absent and they do nothing but grabbing and whipping.

In discussing these matters I have gone beyond the confines of my discourse and thus its intent has been lost. Therefore I begin with the subject such as I have [expounded] above [...]

In such a manner it has been decreed that as he is the most important pillar of the eternal state, the trust and confidant of the well-founded kingdom, therefore the great emirs should not go beyond what he has said.

Mirzā Mohammad Tāher was formerly secretary of the royal council and during the reign of His Majesty Shah Soleymān and after Sheikh 'Ali Khān was elevated to the post of [grand] vizier, he, in the reign of His Majesty Shah Soltān Hoseyn, also became grand vizier.[15] His titles were written in the following way:

Asylum of the vizierate, authority and felicity, magnificence, pomp and majesty of the administration, his excellency, the peerless, lofty, high, and royal E'temad al-Dowleh, the Asaf-like radiant E'tezad al-Saltaneh, he who illuminates the vizierate, authority, magnificence, pomp and majesty.

Mohammad Mo'men Khān Beygdeli Shāmlu who was chief royal mace-bearer in the reign of His Majesty Shah Soltān Hoseyn [**6**] was then promoted to the post of grand vizier.[16] His titles were as follows:

Asylum of the vizierate and authority, magnificence and majesty in administration, awakener of bravery and valor, the highest pillar of the eternal government, Confidante of the Kingdom, foundation of the rampart, descendant of inveterate Sufis of notable family, his excellency the radiant, royal E'tezad al-Saltaneh, the Asaf-like high, excellent and royal E'temad al-Dowleh, he who illuminates the vizierate, authority, majesty and felicity.

Shahqoli Khān Zanganeh was the son of Sheikh 'Ali Khān and in the reign of His Majesty Shah Soltān Hoseyn he was commander of the royal household troops, after which he was elevated to the post of grand vizier.[17] His titles were written as follows:

Asylum of the vizierate, authority and felicity, magnificence, pomp and honor of the administration, awakener of bravery and valor, the highest pillar of the eternal government, the greatest support of the royal throne, the foundation of the kingdom, his excellency the radiant, royal E'tezad al-Saltaneh, the Asaf-like lofty, excellent and royal E'temad al-Dowleh, he who adorns of the vizierate, authority, magnificence, pomp, majesty, bravery and felicity.

Fath 'Ali Khān was commander of the royal slave corps in the reign of His Majesty Shah Soltān Hoseyn and thereafter he was elevated to the post of grand vizier.[18] His titles were as follows:

---

15 He was *majles-nevis* from 1642-1679 and grand vizier from 1691-1699.

16 He was *ishik aghasi-bashi* from 1696-1698 and grand vizier from 1699-1707.

17 He was *qurchi-bashi* from early 1700 until 1707 and grand-vizier from 1707-1715.

18 He was *qollar-aghasi* from 1713 until 1715 and grand vizier from 1715-1720. On his career see Willem Floor, *Commercial Conflict between Persia and the Netherlands 1712-1718* (Durham, 1988), and Rudi Matthee,

Asylum of the vizierate, authority and felicity, magnificence, pomp and honor of the administration, awakener of bravery and valor, the highest pillar of the eternal government, the greatest support of the royal throne, the foundation of the kingdom, his excellency the radiant, royal E'tezad al-Saltaneh, the Asaf-like lofty, excellent and royal E'temad al-Dowleh, he who adorns of the vizierate, authority, magnificence, pomp, majesty, bravery, valor and felicity.

Mohammadqoli Khān Beygdeli Shāmlu was the son of Mohammad Mo'men Khān the former grand vizier. He was commander of the royal household troops in the reign of His Majesty Shah Soltān Hoseyn and then was elevated to the post of grand vizier.[19] His titles were as follows: Asylum of the vizierate and authority, magnificence and honor of the administration, awakener of bravery and valor, the highest pillar of the eternal government, Confidante of the Kingdom, foundation of the rampart, descendant of inveterate Sufis of notable family, his excellency the radiant, royal E'tezad al-Saltaneh, the Asaf-like high, excellent and royal E'temad al-Dowleh, he who illuminates the vizierate, authority, magnificence, honor, glory, bravery, valor, and felicity.[7]

Rajab 'Ali Beyg who was elevated to the office of grand vizier in the time of His Majesty [i.e. Shah Tahmāsp II]. Because during his vizierate this slave was not secetary of the royal council it was mentioned that the titles of his vizierate were written as commanded for Mohammadqoli Khān Shāmlu without the title of 'descendant of inveterate Sufis of notable family.'

Farajallah Khān 'Abdallu who was commander of the royal household troops in the time of His Majesty then became deputy of the grand vizier; he was dismissed and a short time after the death of Mohammad 'Ali Khān Mokri, who had become grand vizier, he became grand vizier in his own right. His titles were written in the same way as those ordered for Rajab 'Ali Beyg.

Mohammad 'Ali Khan Mokri who was commander of the royal musketeer corps in the time of His Majesty was elevated to the post of grand vizier in Azerbaijan. He occupied that function for ten to twenty days when he passed away. No royal decree for his vizierate was written. Therefore his titles were not specified.

Mirzā 'Abdol-Karim who was accountant of the royal domains in the days of His Majesty Shah Soltān Hoseyn after having come to Azerbaijan and having made the royal foot-kiss was appointed as deputy of the grand vizier. His titles were written as follows: 'Asylum of deputyship, nobility, exaltedness and excellence, glory and loftiness of the administration, Companion of the Khaqan inveterate scion of slaves, he who illuminates exaltedness and loftiness.' After he had been dismissed as deputy this function was bestowed upon Mirzā Mohammad Hoseyn. After the dismissal of Mirzā Mohammad Hoseyn once again Mirzā 'Abdol-Karim was honored with this function in his own right. Because the royal decree of his appointment as vizier was not written his titles were not specified.

Mirzā Mohammad Hoseyn who was accountant of the state domains during the days of Your Majesty. His titles have been recorded as follows:
Asylum of nobility, vizierate, authority, and felicity, magnificence, pomp and glory, descendant of inveterate Sufis of notable family, highest pillar of the eternal

---

"Blinded by Power: the Rise and Fall of Fath 'Ali Khan Daghestani, Grand Vizier under Shah Soltan Hoseyn Safavi (1127/1715-1133/1720)," *Studia Iranica* 33 (2004), pp. 179-220.

19 He was *qurchi-bashi* from 1716-1720 and grand vizier from 1720-1721.

government, well-wishing and devoted loyal slave, his excellency the radiant, royal E'tezad al-Saltaneh, the Asaf-like high, excellent and royal E'temad al-Dowleh, he who perfects nobility, vizierate, authority, magnificence, pomp, majesty, courage, valor and felicity.

Mohammad 'Ali Khān was high steward during His Majesty's reign. After the dismissal of Mirzā [**8**] Mohammad Hoseyn he became twice deputy of the grand vizier. The titles of his stewardship that he held have been recorded on the back of the royal decrees.

Mohammad Rezā Khān 'Abdallu had been elevated to the rank of commander of the royal household troops in the time of His Majesty and the deputyship of the grand vizier was also bestowed upon him. His titles as commander of the royal household troops were recorded on the back of royal decrees and orders.

Mirzā 'Abdallu was the former custodian of the Holy Shrine of Mashhad and attained the rank of grand vizier in Astarabad. The royal decree appointing him grand vizier was not issued so that in fact his titles are not distinctive. In the end, his titles were written as follows on the back of the royal decrees:

Asylum of sovereignty, learning, vizierate, and felicity, guidance and glory of the administration, awakener of bravery and valor, progeny of sayyeds and the highest nobles, his excellency the radiant, royal E'tezad al-Saltaneh, the Asaf-like high, excellent and royal E'temad al-Dowleh, he who resembles sovereignty, vizierate, guidance, nobility, magnificence, pomp, bravery, valor, and felicity.

Mirzā Mo'men Hoseyni son of Mirzā Qavām al-Din Hoseyn who, after the killing of Fath 'Ali Khān,[20] at the request of Tahmāspqoli Khān [the later Nāder Shah] had received the office of commander of the royal household troops, became deputy of the grand vizier. His titles were written as follows on the back of the royal decrees: Asylum of vice-regency and nobility, learning and guidance of the administration, scion of sayyeds, Companion of the Khaqan, he who illuminates vice-regency, nobility, learning and guidance.

Mirzā Mohammad Rahim who was accountant of the state domains in the time of His Majesty has now been elevated to the office of deputy grand vizier.[21] His titles, in addition to the word '*niyābat*', are written as follows: Asylum of nobility, vice-regency, exaltedness and felicity, his excellency, Companion of the Khaqan, he who illuminates nobility, vice-regency, exaltedness and felicity, Mirza Mohammad Rahim, deputy grand vizier and hereditary chief accountant.

---

20 Fath 'Ali Khan Qajar was killed in October 1726.
21 According to Nicolaas Schorer, the Dutch Agent at Isfahan, Tahmaspqoli Khan, the later Nader Shah, strengthened his own position by appointing Mirza Rahim as grand-vizier, who until then had exercised this function provisionally. Mirza Rahim was 45 years at that time and a very good friend of presents, Schorer wrote. NA, VOC 2253, Memorandum Schorer, f. 658. On October 2, 1730 the Dutch congratulated the grand vizier with his appointment. Mirza Rahim's macebearer was Tahmurath Beg (Tamoeras Beek). VOC 2255 (28/01/1731), f. 2260, 2271. He was still in function in October 1732, for Mohammad Rahim Khan together with Tahmaspqoli Khan [the later Nader Shah] and Mirza Kafi, the *khalifeh al-kholafā* received the Russian envoy in Isfahan. NA, VOC 2322 (28/10/1732), f. 307vs-309. In 1733 (the same or another?) Mohammad Rahim Khan was with Tahmaspqoli Khan at Baghdad, but the latter later demoted him and sent him to Khorasan. VOC 2322 II. Joseph Sahid (royal camp Baghdad) to van Leijpsigh (Isfahan) (16/06/1733), f. 16, 20, 37-41.

From the beginning of His Majesty's accession until now, which is Rabi' II 1141 (November 1728), which makes seven years,[22] he has appointed 13 grand viziers and deputies, including Mirzā Mohammad Rahim.

EMOLUMENTS OF THE GRAND VIZIER

Emoluments are collected in the form of a chancery fee, fees and fixed payments [9] in accordance with the regulations of the reign of His Majesty the world conqueror the late Shah 'Abbas [I] on account of what he collects from the revenue assignments of the senior emirs, to wit 300 *dinar*s per *tumān*; on account of what he collects from the regular salaries of the emirs to wit 220 *dinar*s per *tumān*; on account of the original amount of the revenue assignments of the royal companions and yeomen, viz. 330 *dinar*s per *tumān*; on account of what he collects from the regular salaries of the royal companions and yeoman, viz. 220 *dinar*s per *tumān*; on account of what he collects from the cash salary of the royal companions and yeomen, viz. 110 *dinar*s per *tumān*; on account of what he collects from the stipends of the emirs and those that are not retainers, viz. 660 *dinar*s per *tumān*; on account of what he receives from the stipends of the royal companions and yeomen, viz. 660 *dinar*s per *tumān*; on account of what he receives for confirming and fixing wages, revenue assignments, stipends, regular salaries and cash payments of the [members of the] victorious government staff, such as royal household troops, royal slaves, royal gunners. With this meaning that this group during the times that they are in attendance are given stipends that each one of them, whose wages, regular salaries and revenue assignments are regularized and confirmed [and] that were given, he receives per *tumān*, for the determination of wages and stipends 50 *dinar*s and of regular salaries and cash payments, 10 *dinar*s. On account of wages and a user fee of provincial fiscal officials that he collects, in that the viziers, accountants, army accountants and *kalāntar*s that are appointed in the outlying districts collect from the salaries of that group, viz. 660 *dinar*s per *tumān*. On account of rents he collects, what they call *haqq al-qarār*, i.e. the special royal areas that are given in lease to somebody, who each year pay a rent to the royal household department, viz. 500 *dinar*s of *haqq al-qarār* per *tumān*. On account of tax exempt land grants, landed fiefs and exemptions of which he collects 660 *dinar*s per *tumān*. On account also in the form of the vizier's fee. In some provinces they give a specified amount, which they give in the form of a vizier's fee; for example, from Lahejan they give 200 *tuman*s each year. On account of what he receives each year from the royal workshops in the form of life necessities. The acquiring of these aforementioned products is done to determine whether the products that the royal household department buys as life necessities are good or bad, so that he has the information. Fath 'Ali Khān estimated the price of these aforementioned products and each year collected 400 *tuman*s based on their price. [10]

All emoluments of the grand vizier such as these have been detailed per year are estimated at 12,000 *tuman*s.

His place in the royal council is higher than that of all other office holders; he is one of the war council emirs[23] and sits on the left side [of the shah].

The expenditure of one *dinar* or one *mann* of weight from the property of the royal household, be it from the royal treasury, be it from outside of that, cannot be transacted without his knowledge and seal. One cannot take one *dinar* [with] any file that is without his seal and his note in

---

[22] This must be a mistake, for 1141 A.H. or 1728 C.E. does not add up to seven years of reign by Tahmāsp II, who claimed the kingship in late 1723 or 1136 A.H. Adding seven years to that starting date results in Rabi' II 1143 A.H. (October 1730), which tallies with the month and year in which Mirzā Mohammad Rahim became grand vizier, which event the author refers to.

[23] On the *jānqi* council see Floor, *Safavid Government*, pp. 29, 32, 57-58, 184.

whatever manner it may be. The authority that the vizier has with regards to the shah's treasury not even the shah himself has.

In all matters the vizier has the total right to interfere, but without the confirmation and knowledge of the department head nothing should be undertaken and each department head and supervisor should not be without a say in his own work. For example, the wages, revenue assignments, regular salaries, and cash payments of the [entire] government staff are not given without the confirmation and approval of the chiefs [concerned] and the royal decrees and orders do not pass the grand vizier[ate's office] without the seal and endorsement (*toghrā*) of the department heads [concerned] and the bureaucratic documents are not valid without the seal of the chief accountant of the state domains and the heads of the royal secretariat. Total importance is given that each one in his own work is fully authorized and that royal dignity and its honor are preserved, because the office of vizier is very important. When no attention is paid to the other department heads and that each one is without a say in his own work this group is [then] in a status of lowered esteem, this of necessity will give rise to contempt among them and they will behave towards him in an impolite manner and treat him without respect. When the grand vizier has become undignified in their minds and the emirs because of the grand vizier's bad behavior also have become without authority this [causes] disrespect for the Crown.

The authority to appoint, change and dismiss the chiefs of the royal secretariat, the clerks, viziers, accountants, and army accountants that are at the frontiers are all with the vizier who may appoint, dismiss and demote them at his discretion. He can make any kind of appropriation that he wants concerning the *divān* taxes and give it into the possession of or rent it to whomever he wants.

COMMANDER OF THE ROYAL HOUSEHOLD TROOPS WHO IS ONE OF THE EMIRS OF THE WAR COUNCIL[24]
qurchi-bashi

USUAL TITLES

Asylum of the custodianship, exaltedness and felicity, glory and honor of the administration, his excellency, Companion of the Khaqan, senior of the highest emirs, he who adorns the custodianship, exaltedness, glory and felicity, So-and-so Khan custodian of the many-splendored tomb of the late khaqan Shah Safi may God's pleasure preserve it.

The custodianship of the *Khāqān*'s tomb [i.e. of Shah Safi I] is always the responsibility of the commander of the royal household troops. Whenever [the office of] commander-in-chief, army commander, governor-general or a province has been added to his post his titles then are also changed and are written taking into account that position. Several titles have been written for the commanders of the royal household troops.

Mortezaqoli Khān Bijerlu who was commander of the royal household troops in the reign of His Majesty Soleymān.[25] His titles were as follows:

---

24 For a discussion of the royal household guards and their commander, the commander of the royal household troops, see Floor, *Safavid Government*, pp.138-66.
25 He was commander of the royal household troops from 1698-1699.

Asylum of the province and authority, custodianship, pomp and glory of the administration, his excellency, emir of emirs, adorning the province, custodianship, authority, majesty and felicity, Mortezaqoli Khan Bijerlu, commander of then royal household troops and custodian of the many-splendored tomb of the late khaqan and governor-general of Adherbaijan.

Shahqoli Khān Zanganeh who had been elevated to the office of commander of the royal household troops in the reign of Shah Soleymān and His Majesty Shah Soltān Hoseyn.[26] His titles were as follows:

Asylum of the province, authority and felicity, magnificence, pomp and glory of the administration, awakener of bravery and valor, his excellency, senior of the highest emirs, he who adorns the custodianship, province, authority, magnificence, pomp, majesty, bravery, valor, and felicity, Shahqoli Khan Zanganeh, commander of the royal household troops and governor of Kolhar, Sonqar and Kermanshahan.

Mohammadqoli Khān Beygdeli Shāmlu and Sheikh 'Ali Khān Zanganeh son of Shahqoli Khān who both were commander of the royal household troops in the reign on His Majesty Shah Soltān Hoseyn.[27] Their titles were written without the word province (*eyālat*), at the orders of Shahqoli Khān [the grand vizier].

Mohammad Reza Khān 'Abdallu who was commander of the royal household troops in the time of Your Majesty. His titles were written in accordance with the normal titles of commanders of the royal household troops. After he had become army commander and governor-general of Azerbaijan at the orders of Shahqoli Khān Zanganeh in addition to his titles 'our inveterate scion of devoted royal slaves' (*gholām-zādeh-ye qadimi gholām-e yek-rang-e mā*) was written.

EMOLUMENTS

On account of a revenue assignment of the district of Kāzerun, which has been assigned to him, estimated at 3,000 *tuman*s per year. On account of the custodian fee of the [tomb] of His Majesty Shah Soleymān, which is collected from the Qom districts, 100 Tabrizi *tuman*s. On account of the original amount of the revenue assignments and the determination and approval of salaries and stipends of royal household troops he collects 500 *dinar*s per *tumān*. On account of the regular salaries and cash payments of the aforementioned group [**12**] he collects 100 *dinar*s per *tumān*.

His total emoluments per year are estimated at an amount of 7,000 *tuman*s.

SUBORDINATES

In all periods [their number] varied. In the reign of His Majesty the world conqueror the late Shah 'Abbās [I] the number of the royal household troops was 12,000 men and their revenue assignments and regular salaries [amounted to] 31,000 *tuman*s. In the days of the other late kings that number was sometimes higher and sometimes lower. In the time of His Majesty Shah Soltān Hoseyn their number was 8,019 men and the amount of 48,763 and odd *tuman*s was for the revenue assignments, regular salaries, and administrative wages of that group.

---

26 He was commander of the royal household troops from 170?-1707.
27 They were commander of the royal household troops respectively from 1716-1720 and 1721.

PLACE

His sitting place in the royal council is on the left side of His Majesty and lower than the grand vizier. If it happened that the *sadr-e 'ammeh* or *khāsseh*[28] were present in the royal council these were seated without ado behind the grand vizier and the commander of the royal household troops was seated lower than the *sadr*s.

FUNCTION

His function was that of chief of all the royal household troops, tribesmen and nomads of the kingdom, be it whether the aforementioned group had an emir or department head, be it that they had no office that was subordinate to the commander of the royal household troops. The retaining of the royal household troops and the giving of revenue assignments, salaries and regular salaries was subject to his approval. Unless the commander of the royal household troops approved it not even one person could be retained and not one person could be given a salary. To each of the aforementioned group whenever he would be given an office or honor the commander of the royal household troops had to be present during his foot-kiss so that he might introduce him. In the battlefield he stands at the right of the king with his subordinates and his standard is green of color. His authority in the management of the army and tribes as well as the ordering of the army is greater than that of the grand vizier.

Before the reign of His Majesty the world conqueror, when the function of the commander of the royal slaves had not as yet been created he enjoyed total dignity and power, he was the equal and the substitute of the regent. After the creation of the aforementioned office until the reign of Shah 'Abbās II, when Jāni Khān the commander of the royal household troops had Sāru Taqi the grand vizier killed, the abovementioned [king] in retaliation had him also killed,[29] while 'Isā Khān[30] and Sāru Khān[31] [both] commanders of the royal household troops also were killed and gradually his [i.e. the commander of the royal household troops] power suffered a decline and he gave up those ambitions and rebellious inclinations, which made the holder of that office also the equal of other office holders.

In effect, the office of commander of the royal household troops was an important function and out of esteem for [his] chieftainship of all tribes and nomads it always has had total power, authority and control [**13**] and the kings have been very considerate towards that group.

---

28 These two officials were the heads of the Safavid religious administrative structure and in charge, among other things, of the religious endowments. One was in charge of these endowments that were situated in the royal domans (*sadr-e khāsseh*) and the other of those situated in the state domains (*sadr-e 'ammeh*). For more information see Willem Floor, "The sadr or head of the Safavid religious administration, judiciary and endowments and other members of the religious institution," *ZDMG* 150 (2000), pp. 461-500.

29 On these events see Willem Floor, "The rise and fall of Mirza Taqi, the eunuch grand vizier (1043-55/1634-45)," *Studia Iranica* 26 (1997), pp. 237-66.

30 'Isā Khān b. Sayyed Beyg Safavi was commander of the royal household troops from 1612-1631; he was killed at the orders of Shah Safi I.

31 Sāru Khān Sahandlu was commander of the royal household troops from 1682-1691 and was killed at the orders of Shah Soleymān.

COMMANDER-IN-CHIEF OF IRAN
WHO IS ONE OF THE EMIRS OF THE WAR COUNCIL[32]
sepahsālār-e Irān

USUAL TITLES

Asylum of the province, authority and felicity, magnificence, pomp and glory of the administration, awakener of bravery and valor, his excellency, senior emir of emirs, he who adorns the province, authority, magnificence, pomp, glory, courage, valor and felicity, So-and-so Khan commander-in-chief.

The office of governor-general of the province of Azerbaijan and sometimes the office of commander of the royal musketeers are also in addition bestowed on the commander-in-chief.

EMOLUMENTS

Tabriz as well as a revenue assignment is given to the commanders-in-chief of Iran, estimated at 12,000 tumans per year.

PLACE

His sitting place in the royal council is on the right hand side of His Majesty and it is higher than of anybody else and opposite that of the grand vizier. If it happens that he is seated in the rows of the emirs of the left hand his place is lower than that of the commander of the royal household troops.

FUNCTION

His function is that during the day of battle he has total command of the army, be it the royal army, be it that of the emirs, which was completely his and nobody had the right to interfere.

During war, if the king would be present, because the real ruler is His Majesty, whatever he would command would be executed. When the king leaves it to the commander-in-chief he does whatever he deems fit. Whenever the king is not present, the army sent to serve is under his command and nobody might interfere. The positioning of the army and the determination of the place of battle is entirely his affair as well as to decide on whatever change and modification that he considers necessary and nobody had the authority to do anything that is contrary to his orders.

It is customary that in the decree of the commander-in-chief they write: "whenever any of the governors-general and emirs neglects the services concerned he may punish, castigate and dismiss them, and he may request [to grant] the office [of the dismissed person] to anybody whom he wants so that we send his royal [appointment] decree."

---

32 On this official see Floor, *Safavid Government*, pp. 17-23.

COMMANDER OF THE ROYAL SLAVES
WHO IS ONE OF THE EMIRS OF THE WAR COUNCIL[33]
qollar-āghāsi

USUAL TITLES

Asylum of exaltedness and felicity, glory, honor of the administration his excellency Companion of the Khaqan, he who adorns exaltedness and felicity, So-and-so Beyg.

Some of the commanders of the royal musketeers have been honored with the title *mosāheb* (associate).[34] If [**14**] the office of commander-in-chief, army commander, and governor-general of a province are added to the aforementioned office the titles are also changed to reflect these offices and are appropriately written.

Allahverdi Khān who was commander of the royal slaves in the time of the late Shah Safi.[35] His titles were as follows:

Asylum of the province, authority, and felicity, magnificence, pomp and glory of the administration, awakener of bravery and valor, his excellency, emir of emirs nezaman the province, authority, magnificence, pomp, majesty, glory, and felicity, Allahverdi Khan, associate, commander of the royal slaves, master of the hunt, and governor-general of Kuhgiluyeh and general of the victorious army.

Aslamas Khān who was promoted to the function of commander of the royal slaves in the days of Shah Soleymān.[36] His titles were in accordance with the usual titles of the commander of the royal musketeers.

Musa Khān[37] and Fath 'Ali Khān[38] were commander of the royal slaves and governor-general of Shirvan in the days of His Majesty Shah Soltān Hoseyn and the titles were written in the same manner for each of them. His Majesty Shah Soltān Hoseyn gave Fath 'Ali Khān in addition the title of associate trained at the succoring, royal sun (*mosāheb-e tarbiyat-kardeh-ye khorshid-e 'enāyat-e shāhenshāhi*).

EMOLUMENTS

on account of a revenue assignment that had been assigned to him from the province of Golpeygan 2,011 Tabrizi *tumans*. On account of the fixing and assigning of wages and stipends of the royal slaves he collects 500 *dinars* per *tumān*. On account of the regular salaries and cash salaries of the royal slaves he collects 100 *dinars* per *tumān*.

His total income per year is estimated at 6,000 *riyāls*.

---

33 On the royal slaves and their commander the commander of the royal musketeers see Floor, *Safavid Goverrnment*, pp. 166-76.
34 On other examples of honoring courtiers with such special honorifics, a custom that was pre-Islamic in origin, see Floor, *Safavid Goverrnment*, p. 92.
35 He held the office from 1655-1663 not during Shah Safi I, but during Shah 'Abbās II's reign.
36 Aslamas Khān held the office from 1693-1695.
37 Musa Khān held the office from 1701-170?.
38 Fath 'Ali Khān Dāghestāni held the office from 170?-1715.

SUBORDINATES

in each period they were different. In the time of His Majesty ʿAbbās I their number was 7,000 men and 20,000 *tuman*s for their revenue assignments and royal slaves. In the time of His Majesty Shah Soltān Hoseyn, 6,263 men and an amount of 41,252 *tuman*s and 3,368 *dinar*s for the revenue assignments, regular salaries and the administrative wages of that group.

PLACE

His sitting place in the royal council is on the left side of His Majesty; lower than the commander of the royal household troops. If it happens that the commander-in-chief is seated among the emirs of the left side the commander of the royal slaves is seated lower than the commander-in-chief [**15**]

FUNCTION

His function is that of senior officer of all slaves of the royal household wherever they may be. If from this group there are those that are seconded to the emirs and governors of provinces they still remain the subordinates of the commander of the royal slaves. If somebody of the group of royal slaves has been honored with an office, stipend or prize and they bring him into the royal presence for the foot-kiss this had to be done when the commander of the royal slaves was in attendance to His Majesty to introduce him. Without his approval nobody of his subordinates can be given a salary and stipend [or] can be employed.

During the day of battle and war he is located with his subordinates on the left hand of the king; his banner is white.

The office of commander of the royal slaves was created and established by the world conqueror the late Shah ʿAbbās. For the greater royal glory of his kingship, ʿAbbās II formed 700 royal slaves as slaves and he dressed them all in gold-woven velvet with brimmed *quruqi* hats on their heads, and for each one broad silver belts and they became the subordinates of the commander of the royal slaves. It was the rule that during the days that His Majesty was riding they would go on the right side of His Majesty's stirrup. In truth, the pomp and glory of the shah is peerless, which is evident to the onlookers.[39]

As the tribes [supplying] royal household troops were very riotous and involved in rebellions and riots most of the time His Majesty wanted to have a group as a counter-balance to that company to bring an end the unruliness of that corps. Therefore, His Majesty the world conqueror established the office of commander of the royal slaves and formed a regiment of royal slaves as his subordinates and made him the equal of commander of the royal household troops. Gradually his esteem grew and now he is one of the great emirs and after the office of commander of the royal household troops there is not a more important emir.

---

39 These are the *jazāyer* slaves referred to on the first page of the translated text.

CHIEF ROYAL MACE-BEARER
HE IS ONE OF THE EMIRS OF THE WAR COUNCIL[40]
ishik āghāsi-bāshi-ye divān-e aʿlā

USUAL TITLES

Asylum of the province and authority, pomp and majesty of the administration, he who adorns the province, authority, pomp, majesty and felicity.

To those of Mohammad Mo'men Khān Beygdeli Shāmlu, who [later] became grand vizier, the title 'scion of a longstanding and notable Sufi family' (*sufi-zādeh-ye qadim khāndān-e velāyat-neshān*) in addition was granted.

EMOLUMENTS

On account of the province of Rey and Shahryār[41] he collects a revenue assignment [16] of 2,675 *tuman*s and 1,000 and odd *dinar*s. Nine hundred of that total is his fixed salary and the remainder is the salary of 150 regular retainers there. The chief royal mace-bearers were always entitled to 6,000 *tuman*s annually from the said province for themselves. On account of fixed presents that are brought to the royal household he receives 10 per cent. annually; from fixed presents [that he receives] from the estimates from accountants an amount of 7,600 *tuman*s. On account of the branding of camels he collects, i.e. when they bring grazing camels as presents for the royal household, when the camels are branded, one from each lot of fifty is his. On account of the shoulder [?] meat of sheep that are branded in the royal household he has fees; when 1,500 plates of food have been prepared in the royal kitchen per day [he receives] per weight of Tabriz five *mann* of shoulder [?] mutton and the price of that is 1,000 *dinar*s per day, [or] 36 Tabrizi *tuman*s per year. On account of presents to the royal household that are not usual and fixed New Year's presents, but are brought as gifts and presents from ambassadors and others during the year, this has been estimated by the senior accountants to amount to 12,000 *tuman*s per year, of which he receives ten per cent. Per year this is an amount of 1,200 *tuman*s. On account of fixing and assigning the wages and stipends of the squires of the royal council and the mace-bearers of the royal secretariat and the senior yeomen and his own subordinates he receives 500 *dinar*s per *tuman* [assigned]. On account of the regular salaries and the cash payments of the said group he collects 500 *dinar*s per *tuman*. On account of the wine that is taken by the royal household from the winery about one *mann* per day. His total income per year is estimated at 6,000 *tuman*s.

SUBORDINATES

In each period they have been different. During the reign of Shah Soltān Hoseyn, in the days that Mohammad Salim Khān Shāmlu was chief royal mace-bearer the total of his subordinates consisting of senior squires and mace-bearers of the royal secretariat and yeomen, squires, porters, public criers, was 2,670 persons and the amount in revenue assignments, regular salaries and administrative wages was 33,700 *tuman*s per year. [17]

PLACE

He does not sit in the royal council. If a royal command is issued specially with regards to his sitting he sits on the left side of His Majesty and lower than the commander of the royal musketeers.

---

40 For more details on this official see Floor-Faghfoory, *Dastur al-Moluk*, pp. 140-71.
41 Shahryar is one of the districts of Rey. See Mohammad Mofid Mostoufi, *Mohktasar-e Mofid*. 2 vols., edited Seyfeddin Najmabadi (Wiesbaden, 1989) pp. 120–21.

FUNCTION

His function is to stand in the paradisiacal council opposite the shah with his studded staff in his hands that has a value of 7,000 *tuman*s and is adorned with gems and jewels.

He makes each of the senior squires and the mace-bearers of the *divān*, who have been elevated to the rank of the above-mentioned services, to prostate himself in the royal councils opposite His Majesty in a special manner. Having put the resplendent headgear on their head, he hits them three times with the wooden stick and at the first hit he says with a loud voice, Allah, at the second hit, Mohammad, and at the third one, 'Ali. After they have been hit three times the person that has been hit arises. The chief royal mace-bearer then gives the stick to him, with which he has hit that person. The latter takes the stick, kisses it and then begins with his service. In this manner it is a way of guidance given by the shah.

It is customary that they bring the petitions to him that come from all parts of the kingdom to the royal court. He immediately sends them to the chief mace-bearer of the royal harem. The chief mace-bearer of the royal harem having given it to the senior officer of the honored harem, the latter takes it to His Majesty. Whenever His Majesty goes outside he takes it himself to the most holy presence for the sun-like attention. This does not apply to petitions of emirs of the court, which are not within the jurisdiction of the chief royal mace-bearer, [for] the emirs send these themselves to the most holy presence.

During royal travels he rode before His Majesty to [ensure]: order of the ranks during the riding and of order and rule in the royal councils, have each person taken to his place and location, the distribution of gold and silver to the emirs and others on the occasion of the passing of the New Year, the performance of the kissing of His Majesty's foot by the retainers of the royal court during council meetings and travels, the distribution of the food and comestibles at the councils and the *divān* and the maintenance of order in the guard-house, the lifting of the coverlets of the special food plates for His Majesty when the royal household eats outside and the declaiming of the word *Fāteheh*[42] with a loud voice after the food has been eaten and the reciting by the grand vizier of the *Fāteheh*, all of this was his responsibility.

His office is important and powerful. No other emir has such authority as he has in the councils, the special and common meetings with His Majesty and the administration in the guard-house. **[18]**

Until he has seen them, he does not release the presents, which come from all parts of the kingdom for the royal household, to be brought to the attention of His Majesty.

The giving of salaries and regular salaries and revenue assignments to the senior squires and the mace-bearers of the *divān*, the leading yeomen, porters, squires and general subordinates and the retaining of that group is subject to his approval.

During war he is standing with his leading yeomen and common subordinates in His Majesty's [army] unit. His banner is Karbala white and blue. If an army unit is attacking or on the move then the chief royal mace-bearer customarily rides before His Majesty. The aforementioned office always was bestowed on [somebody from] the group of royal household troops, mostly on [somebody from] the Shāmlu tribe, although at one time it was bestowed on Manuchehr Beyg Gholām.

---

42 First chapter of the Koran.

COMMANDER OF THE ROYAL MUSKETEERS
HE IS ONE OF THE EMIRS OF THE WAR COUNCIL[43]
tofangji āghāsi

USUAL TITLES

Asylum of exaltedness and felicity, glory and honor of the administration his excellency, Companion of the Khaqan, he who adorns exaltedness and felicity.

If the office of commander-in-chief or other offices were in addition [bestowed] the titles also were changed appropriately as befitted the office.

EMOLUMENTS

on account of the province of Aberquh that has been assigned to him, it is estimated at 700 *tuman*s and it was mentioned that his tax officials even raised 1,500 *tuman*s. On account of the fixing and assigning of wages and stipends of the musketeers he receives fees as follows: 500 *dinar*s per *tuman*. On account of regular salaries and cash payments of the aforementioned group he receives fees 100 *dinar*s per *tuman*. His total income per year is estimated at an amount of 5,500 *tuman*s.

SUBORDINATES

In each period they were different. In the time of His Majesty the world conqueror the late Shah 'Abbas [I] up to 2,000 men and less and in the time of His Majesty Shah Soleymān they were up to 12,000 men. In the time of His Majesty Shah Soltān Hoseyn there were 7,390 men and all the commanders of one thousand, musketeers, axe-bearers, mallet-bearers, and ushers of the royal household generally were his subordinates.

PLACE

His sitting place in the royal council is on the right-hand side of His Majesty. If [19] it happens that he sits in the row of the emirs of the left he sits lower than the commander of the royal slaves and if the chief royal mace-bearer was also seated in the council than he was also placed lower than him.

FUNCTION

His function is one where he and his subordinates take position in front of His Majesty during the days of war. His banner is white with a red border.

The office of commander of the royal musketeers is a very powerful one and His Majesty the world conqueror created the aforementioned office. Previously Mir Fattāh Beyg Esfahāni was the commander of one thousand of that group. When His Majesty the world conqueror had created this office he wanted that the wages of the army be provided by itself[44], [so that] it had no business with the troops of the emirs. A large group entered the ranks of the musketeers of the royal household and are the subordinates of the commander of the royal musketeers.

During travels they go in front of His Majesty and during the day of battle they take up position in front of His Majesty. In truth, among the army there are no more colorful soldiers than the musketeers, in particular at the time when all of them are dressed in velvet, with broad silver belts,

---

43 The orthography of *tofangji* is in the original, although in the remainder the more normal orthography of *tofangchi* is used. For a discussion of the *tofangchi*s and their commander, the *tofangchi-āghāsi*, see Floor, *Safavid Government*, pp. 176-87.

44 Meaning that they had their own sources of income, which, in this case, were assignments on crown properties.

on their heads felt caps and colored vanes attached to their muskets that they carry on the shoulder and in this manner they go in front of His Majesty. The pomp and glory of the crown has increased [and] in the regard of foe and friend it adds more splendor.

The aforementioned office is also very important and [its occupant] is one of the powerful emirs of the shah, who enjoys total respect and position.

HIGH STEWARD OF THE ROYAL HOUSEHOLD
HE IS NOT ONE OF THE EMIRS OF THE WAR COUNCIL[45]
nāzer-e boyutāt-e sarkār-e khāsseh-ye sharifeh

USUAL TITLES

Asylum of super-intendancy, exaltedness and felicity, glory and honor of the administration, his excellency, Companion of the Khaqan, he who adorns super-intendancy, exaltedness and felicity, So-and-so Beyg.

Mohammad 'Ali Khan was high steward of the royal household in the time of Your Majesty (*abad-e tow'amān*). His Majesty bestowed upon him titles as follows:

Asylum of super-intendancy, exaltedness and felicity, glory and honor of the administration, his excellency Companion of the Khaqan, descendant of royal slaves of the lion-like Shah, scion of loyal Sufis, who is a pure Sufi, he who adorns super-intendancy, exaltedness, glory and felicity, Mohammad 'Ali Khan, servant of the holy, illuminated and blessed shrine of Imam Reza, may a thousand salutations be on its overseers and the chief steward of the royal workshops.

EMOLUMENTS

On account of the regular salary that in the time of Shah Soltān Hoseyn was collected mostly by the royal treasury [20] an amount of 500 *tuman*s. On account of the used clothes and other items of His Majesty that he receives from the department head of the royal treasury. His excellency Mohammad 'Ali Khan also had a royal order issued especially in this matter, [to wit] turban: one; belt: one; overcoat: one garment; surcoat: one garment; *kordi*: one garment; *kātebi*: one garment; *kheftān*: one garment; hose belt: one pair; shoes: one pair; boots: one pair; rope tied under the arm-pits: one garment; trousers of English cloth: one garment; hose: one pair; puttees: one pair; capped hat (*kolah-e tablak*): one pair; *quruqi* hat: one; scull-cap: one; blanket: one; cushion cover: one; pillow cover: one; mattress cover: one; leather cover: one. At one time his regular salary was 700 *tuman*s and lately he received 1,500 *tuman*s from the taxes of Kerman. His total income with his fees based on the records that have been taken into account was half of that of the grand vizier and annually 6,000 *tuman*s.

SUBORDINATES

All the department heads of the workers of the 33 departments and workshops of the royal household and of the workers of the royal buildings and gardens of Isfahan and its dependencies and of Mazandaran, Qazvin and the workers of the studs and others are all his subordinates. The number of that group was different in each period. In the time of Shah Soltan Hoseyn the number of all

---

45 For more details on this official, his establishment (*boyutāt*) and his staff, see Floor-Faghfoory, *Dastur al-Moluk*, pp. 210-29.

of the groups amounted to 5,940 persons of which 589 persons were workers of the buildings and gardens of Mazandaran. All revenue assignments, regular salary, and administrative wages of that group came to an an amount of 21,254 *tuman*s and 1,178 *dinar*s.

PLACE

His sitting place in the Eden-like council was on the left of His Majesty and lower than his excellency the commander of the royal slaves. If it happened that he was seated next to the commander of the royal musketeers that he was seated lower than he.

In the days of His Majesty Shah Soltan Hoseyn, when the office of the high steward was with Mahmud Beyg,[46] who was among the leading courtiers, it was granted to him that he might sit higher than the commander of the royal musketeers. In the end Mahmud Beyg became one of the group of emirs and was seated on the right with the chief royal physician at the edge of the council. [21]

FUNCTION

His function was very important and he had to be very close and have total loyalty towards His Majesty. Every morning and evening he was present at the gate of the royal palace; the individual pages of the journals of the royal workshops were submitted to him daily for his view and seal, which he examined as required and acted upon and he repeatedly considered the requests of the workshops and did not allow that the department heads of the royal workshops and others committed fraud and corruption with the government revenues. He has to spend his time on providing His Majesty with food, drinks and clothes such that he not neglect his duty one moment, day-and-night. Giving salaries, regular salaries, and employing workers of the royal workshops is totally subject to his approval and without the confirmation of the high steward of the royal household none of that group could be retained and their cash salaries could not be collected. All the department heads of the royal workshops had to be audited so that the government revenues that he received would not go astray.

The office holder had to be totally trustworthy, loyal, and pious, and had to be knowledgeable with any kind of good and product. Whenever he was not knowledgeable it is possible that he would be deceived. The appraisers and purveyors would sell every product at double prices to the royal household and this would be the cause of the deficit of the *divān*'s budget. The Tājiks also have become the supervisors of this post.

---

46 He was high steward around 1716.

LORD HIGH JUSTICE
HE IS NOT ONE OF THE EMIRS OF THE WAR COUNCIL[47]
divān-beygi

USUAL TITLES

Asylum of exaltedness and felicity, glory and honor of the administration, his excellency Companion of the Khaqan, he who adorns exaltedness and felicity, So-and-so Beyg.

To Shahqoli Khān and Khosrow Khān[48] who each were *divān-beygi* and out of consideration that both were Georgians in addition to abovementioned titles the title of *khalaf al-salātin al-'ozzām* was given.

EMOLUMENTS

on account of fines, crimes, as well as court that he held every day he had full benefits. His total income was annually an estimated 6,000 *tuman*s. [22]

SUBORDINATES

It is not fixed how many persons they are, except that from among the squires of the *divān*, ushers and [other] retainers of the royal household there is a group that are his subordinates who perform the government services that are pertaining to this group.

PLACE

The place of sitting in the Eden-like council is on the right side of the *qeblah*[49] of the two worlds [the shah] and behind the commander of the royal musketeers. If it happens that he is seated in the row of emirs of the left he is seated lower than the high steward of the royal household.

FUNCTION

His function is this that he is seated together with the two chiefs of the religious authority (*sadr*s) in a guardhouse that has been assigned to him where he presides over the special and general court. The Lord Justice has to execute every verdict that the *sadr*s give and he appoints collectors who execute [them] accordingly.

His Majesty the world conqueror also created the aforementioned office, because prior to that it had been the rule that the kings themselves sat in court each day and rendered firm justice and with their precious spirit oversaw the judging and the thorough investigation of the common man's cases. When travels and campaigns occurred taking care of other royal business also was required and he did not have the time to take care of it, i.e. to devote time to the nitty-gritty of the kingdom's affairs himself. Therefore, owing to the pressure of time and His Majesty's welfare, the Lord High Justice was appointed to act as deputy to His Majesty to take care of the people's court affairs, each time when His Majesty as to these aforementioned matters was unable to take care of them. For this reason the office holder has acquired great authority, as much as he wants. The great emirs and the companions of the court, that is the glory of the world, have been deputized on behalf of His Majesty to their own court to thoroughly investigate and administer justice.

---

47 On this official and the judicial system see Willem Floor, "The Secular Judicial System in Safavid Persia," *Studia Iranica* 29 (2000), pp. 9-60.
48 They were Lord High Justice during the first decade of the 18th century, between 1701 and 1712.
49 That part to which the Moslems direct their prayers.

The decisions and verdicts were written [i.e. sent] to all parts and corners [of the kingdom] to summon every one whom he wants. The requests of the people to lift oppression are given to him and wherever he is requested in the provinces in accordance with the writ of the Lord High Justice a sensible order is given embellished with the sun-like seal to administer justice.

In short, he has full authority over court matters as well as over wages and cash payments and the like.

COMMANDER OF THE ROYAL GUNNERS
HE IS SOMETIMES ONE OF THE EMIRS OF THE WAR COUNCIL AND SOMETIMES HE IS NOT[50]
tupchi-bāshi

USUAL TITLES

Asylum of exaltedness and felicity, his excellency, Friend of the high and excellent State, he who adorns exaltedness and felicity, So-and-so Beyg.

EMOLUMENTS

on account of a revenue assignment that has been assigned to him from the district of Shaft [in Mazandaran], an amount of 659 *tuman*s and 2,900 Tabrizi *dinar*s. On account of the original amount of the revenue assignment and the fixing and assigning of the salaries and stipends of the gunners he receives a fee, viz. 500 *dinar*s per *tuman*. On account of the regular salaries and cash payments of the abovementioned group he had fees viz. 100 *dinar*s per *tuman*. His total income per year is estimated at 2,659 *tuman*s and 2,900 *dinar*s.

SUBORDINATES

these were different in each period, sometimes they were 9,000, sometimes they were less. In the time of His Majesty Shah Soltan Hoseyn they were 4,990 persons.

PLACE

His place of seating is on the right of His Majesty and lower than the Lord High Justice. If it happens that he is seated in the row of emirs of the left he is seated lower than the high steward of the royal household.

FUNCTION

On the day of battle his function is, after he had arranged the gun carts that had been fastened together in front the army, to stand behind the guns, before the commander of the royal musketeers, with all the gunners that are his subordinates. The commander of the royal gunners has to wear a felt helmet, to have sandals on his feet and to busy himself with the placement of the guns. His banner is green with a white rim.

The said office is also one of the creations of His Majesty the world conqueror and it is equal to the commander of the royal musketeers and he is the chief of all the gunners.

---

50 For more details about the gunners and their commander, the *tupchi-bāshi*, see Floor, *Safavid Government*, pp. 188-98.

CHIEF OF THE ROYAL HUNTSMEN
HE IS NOT ONE OF THE EMIRS OF THE WAR COUNCIL[51]
amir shekār-bāshi

USUAL TITLES

Asylum of exaltedness and felicity, his excellency, Companion of the Khaqan, he who adorns exaltedness and felicity, So-and-so Beyg.

EMOLUMENTS

[On account of] a revenue assignment that has been assigned to him from the district of Abhar, 1,000 *tuman*s. On account of the fixing and assigning of salaries and stipends of his subordinates he receives a fee, viz. 500 *dinar*s per *tuman*. On account of regular salaries and cash payments of the said group he collects as a fee, viz. 100 *dinar*s per *tuman*. On account of the new [fees, introduced] in the days of His Majesty Shah Soltān Hoseyn at the time when Ja'farqoli Āqā Khvājeh was chief of the royal huntsmen. These new fees are two of a kind: one is according to a royal decree and the other by writ and that which [24] is collected in accordance with the royal decree has been established such that they collect from the governor-generals of the frontier areas 50 *tuman*s and from the governors of the [other] provinces each year an amount in the form of a fee in accordance with their income. Royal decrees have been issued in this regard. From among the group of falconers collectors are appointed and gradually they collect this amount in addition to a 10 per cent. [surcharge]. Sometimes these are granted to the falconers and sometimes for the use by others.

The other part that was [collected in accordance with] a writ was like this that the chief of the royal huntsmen wrote himself documents and papers and gave these to the group of falconers to collect this amount from the viziers, accountants, *kalāntar*s, and tax officials of the border areas as a falcon fee. But there was no falcon. The falconer took a feather with him and after his arrival at the location he collected that amount by force and oppression in addition of 10 per cent. [surcharge]. Sometimes it happened that they took by force 12 *tuman*s with the 10 per cent from the *kalāntar* of a locality whose total income was not more than five *tuman*s on the basis of the writ of the chief of the royal huntsmen.

Apart from the two invented fees there were other fees such as when people brought a falcon for the royal household as a present. In most cases, the falconers rejected that falcon, because it was not fitting, although it was an excellent present. Then, in stead, three to five *tuman*s were taken from the person who had brought the falcon as a present and this amount was taken by force from him.

SUBORDINATES

in each period these were different. Some of the royal slaves also were regularly among that group and they were in attendance separately. In the time of Shah Soltan Hoseyn the total number of that group was 1,833 persons and the revenue assignment, salaries and administrative wages was an amount of 6,358 *tuman*s and somewhat.

---

51 For more details on this official, his staff and activities, see Floor-Faghfoory, *Dastur al-Moluk*, pp. 185-99.

PLACE

His place of seating in the Eden-like council is on the left side of His Majesty and lower than the high steward. If it happened that he was seated to the right of His Majesty he was seated lower than the commander of the royal gunners.

FUNCTION

His function was that he was the chief of all falconers, cameleers, cheetah keepers, hunters, and dog-keepers. Employing them and giving the aforementioned group regular salaries and cash payment was totally subject to his approval. [25]

As his subordinates constitute an army, His Majesty the world conqueror most of the time was hunting with this group and neglected to attack the enemy and to punish rebels.

The holders of this office mostly were intimates of the king and had his total trust. At the time of war he and his subordinates were in the king's army unit.

MASTER OF THE ROYAL STABLES
amir ākhur-bāshi-ye jelow[52]

He is different from the master of the royal herds, who will be mentioned separately among the royal companions; he is not one of the emirs of the war council.

USUAL TITLES

Asylum of exaltedness and felicity, his excellency, Companion of the Khaqan, he who adorns exaltedness and felicity, So-and-so Beyg.

EMOLUMENTS

On account of a revenue assignment, an amount has been assigned to him from the district of Darazjin and Asadabad in Hamadan [province] as follows: the original assessment 180 *tuman*s and its estimate, an amount of 800 *tuman*s. On account of horses and mules that are presented to the royal household as gifts he receives a fee, which is divided between his excellency himself, the chief royal mace-bearer of the *divān*, the inspector and the department head, and the workers of the royal stables, viz. 3,000 *dinar*s per head.

SUBORDINATES

All horse breakers, fore-runners, equerries, and muleteers of the royal household are his subordinates and their number has been different per period.

PLACE

His seating place: in the royal council he sits to the left of His Majesty below the chief of the royal huntsmen.

FUNCTION

His function is that he was responsible for the horses and mules of the royal household; each horse and mule that was donated as a present was shown to His Majesty and given the royal brand. The royal brand was encased in gold. In stead of a belt he had a dagger at his waist; he rides any [of the horses] of the royal household stables and the special horses of the king that he wants.

---

52 For more details on this official and his staff, see Floor-Faghfoory, *Dastur al-Moluk*, pp. 199-209.

SECRETARY OF THE ROYAL COUNCIL
HE IS ONE OF THE EMIRS OF THE WAR COUNCIL[53]
majles-nevis-e mahfal-e behesht-ā'in

USUAL TITLES

Asylum of learning, nobility, exaltedness and felicity, his excellency, Companion of the Khaqan, he who adorns exaltedness and felicity, So-and-so Beyg. [26]

Formerly each of the secretaries of the royal council was given a special title. Mirza Ahmad, secretary of the royal council, Mirzā Sādeq, Mirzā Mehdi son of Mirzā Ahmad aforementioned were [all] honored with the title of 'Loyal scion of royal slaves.' The titles of this slave are:

Asylum of learning, nobility, exaltedness and felicity, his excellency, Companion of the Khaqan, shining scion of royal slaves and good-fortuned slave, he who adorns learning, nobility, exaltedness and felicity, Mirza 'Ali Naqi Nasiri, servant of the holy, illuminated and blessed shrine of Imam Reza, may a thousand salutations be on its inspectors and the secretary of state of the paradisiacal council.

EMOLUMENTS

on account of a regular salary that has been assigned to him from the district of Dasht-sar in Mazandaran, to wit, an amount of 300 *tuman*s. On account of fees which have been bestowed upon the secretary of the royal council by royal commands of past kings, viz. 200 *dinar*s per *tuman*.

From the great emirs, governor-generals, governors, tax officials, *dārugheh*s, and retainers of the royal household that have been appointed. When writing their appointment and investiture diploma whenever it concerns a salary and emolument he receives 200 *dinar*s per *tuman*. As to royal orders that are submitted for His Majesty's signature, the kings have also bestowed [upon him the right] that he does not to draw the *toghrā* on anyone's appointment and investiture diploma as long as [the person concerned] has not given the secretary of the royal council his fees.

His total income per year is estimated at 3,000 *tuman*s.

SUBORDINATES

Formerly, when not many royal orders were written he had three subordinates. During the reign of His Majesty Shah Soleymān and His Majesty Shah Soltān Hoseyn when most of the royal commands were changed to royal orders [the number of] his subordinates were increased. Lately he had 30 persons, of which some were charged with writing royal orders in the royal secretariat that were issued by the *khāsseh* department; they [also] prepare the blank royal orders and record each of them.

FUNCTION

His function was to be present in all public and private councils. He submits each request and petition that they sent to His Majesty from all parts. Those about which a royal decision has been taken he, on that basis, would write the royal orders [concerned]. The other department heads of the supreme *divān* are seal holders, and the seal of each one is authoritative. The signature of the secretary of the royal council was [also] authoritative, for what he writes on behalf of His Majesty is without the royal sun-like seal, [but] the court and provincial emirs and the [27] department

---

53 For a discussion of the development of the office of *majles-nevis* see Floor, *Safavid Government*, pp. 55-58.

heads of the royal secretariat considered it as officially documented by his signature, on the basis of which questions and answers that are necessary are made.

The aforementioned office was created by His Majesty the world conqueror the late Shah 'Abbas. Prior to that the royal documents passed through the secretariat, the department heads put their seal on the back and submitted it for the endorsement (*toghrā*) of the *monshi al-mamālek*. When during the reign of the world conqueror the borders were in turmoil and every moment petitions came from all over the God-protected realm to the royal court it was [found] necessary that an answer be written and to write those in the secretariat took too long and required at least a couple of days before the department heads of the royal secretariat had sealed on their back and submitted it for the [drawing of the] chief of the royal correspondence's (*monshi al-mamālek*) endorsement (*toghrā*) after which it was submitted for the royal seal. This matter was the cause of delay in [the handling of] royal affairs and of quite a lot of information about how things stood [in the country]. For this reason His Majesty the world conqueror created this office and because it was His Majesty's intention that he also should have a minister-at-large, so that when he moved and had not moved the secretariat matters of state would not remain neglected. He therefore took a piece of the office and function of the grand vizier, the chief accountant of the state domains, the *monshi al-mamālek* and the [first] clerk of the royal secretariat and bundled them together and gave them to one person and gave that person the title of secretary of the royal council.

The grand viziers, due to the fact that His Majesty the world conqueror had abolished the office of regent, had become very powerful like the regent and some matters that were in the jurisdiction of the regent of the *divān* were given for execution to their attention. The secretaries of the royal council also have become like the vizier; that which pertained to the grand viziers was transferred to him.

Gradually the grand vizier became the regent, and the secretaries of the royal council became [like the] vizier. Because of that, His Majesty the world conqueror, in defense of the Crown, was not pleased about the greater power of some of the emirs and he did not want that anybody other than the king was ruler and that for everyone there should be an opposite person, so that there would not be any excuses. He therefore created this office so that there would be someone opposite the grand vizier.

Furthermore, most of the time His Majesty the world conqueror and [the later] kings were occupied with amusements and [**28**] merry-making, although they could not neglect the situation of the kingdom and therefore they wanted someone who had special trustworthiness and who most of the time was present in the service of His Majesty and the handling the royal correspondence and who was not the cause of a delay of royal affairs and [therefore] there had to be from each group a trustworthy person. During the reign of each [subsequent] king the holders of that office gradually became the king's boon companion, confidante and trustee.

The holder of that office has to be completely reliable, pious, and truthfull [as well as] the keeper of secrets and documents and [have] complete competence in the art of writing and secretariat, the rules and regulations of governance, poetry and style so that the king whatever kind of writing that he commands him to do would not be deprived of them (i.e. these skills), [because] he is able to write it.

Because the secretaries of the royal council are the kings' tongue and the correspondence they write is on behalf of His Majesty, it is the rule that first attention is paid to the shah's might and glory, then the royal affairs are written in elegant phrases and metaphors so that royal awe, hope, law and order are always evident and clear and that from reading his correspondence the royal signs are self-evident, so that, although it may not be compared with God's majesty, justice, and unity that is evident in the Holy Koran, the writings and royal decrees demonstrate that the king has unlimited authority. Such a fact, viz. the requirements of kingship and governance is also demonstrated by the royal correspondence. During discussions, if there is apprehension it does not matter much, because words cannot be recorded, [but] writings are all recorded and documented.

Notwithstanding the bestowal of this office on this slave, to highlight this office and emphasize the importance of this post was disagreeable [to me], because this text concerns the general occupations of the emirs and the nature of the office of each one, and this will be made clear.

The royal orders for the office of court emirs, governors-general, governors, viziers, accountants, tax officials, provincial *kalāntar*s as well as answers to petitions and documents of that group [of officials] are all written by the secretary of the royal council with an endorsement (*toghrā*) drawn in black. Every kind of royal chancellery order that is issued by the royal secretariat and whose back is submitted for the seal of the department heads of the royal secretariat the secretary of the royal council likewise has to draw the *toghrā* [on them]. As to royal orders concerning the service of the victorious government staff, although, if [**29**] the secretary of the royal council writes them then it is not like when a mistake was made and that, there is interference with his office, [for] in every period these were written by the secretaries of the royal council. However, it is proper and in accordance with justice that royal orders of everybody of that group are written by the viziers concerned, in a manner that will be mentioned at its own place, who receives his own government fees. For example, the vizier of the the royal household troops has to write the royal orders for the service of the royal household troops.

CHIEF ROYAL MACE-BEARER OF THE ROYAL HAREM
ishik āghāsi-bāshi-ye haram-e ʿoliyeh-ye ʿāliyeh

He is not one of the emirs of the war council.[54]

USUAL TITLES

Asylum of exaltedness and felicity, his excellency, Companion of the Khaqan, he who adorns exaltedness and felicity, So-and-so Beyg.

For some of the chief royal mace-bearers of the royal harem different titles were written. Shahverdi Beyg Chuleh'i: Asylum of exaltedness and felicity, his excellency, Companion of the Khaqan, scion of a faithful family of royal slaves, he who adorns exaltedness and felicity, Shahverdi Beyg Chuleh'i, servant of the holy, illuminated and blessed shrine of Imam Reza, may a thousand salutations be on its overseers and the secretary of state of the paradisiacal council.

EMOLUMENTS

on account of a regular salary 400 *tuman*s. On account of the usual ration that he receives from day to day from the royal household; one plate per day and one plate per night, estimated 70 *tuman*s per year.

SUBORDINATES

All mace-bearers of the harem are his subordinates and their number is different in each period.

---

54 For more details on this official and his staff, see Floor-Faghfoory, *Dastur al-Moluk*, pp. 171-75.

PLACE

His place of sitting is at the gate of the harem. He does not sit in the royal council and he does not have a fixed place there.

FUNCTION

His function is to be present day and night at the gate of the harem in a guard-house that has been assigned to him. He does not move from that place. Petitions that the court emirs send to him and that come from all parts of the country all of them the chief royal mace-bearer of the *divān* sends to him. If His Majesty were present in the harem he, through the intermediary of the chief of the harem [eunuchs], sent them to His Majesty. The answer that he gives to him he forwards to each one.

It is the rule that in the guardhouse of the harem, which is his prerogative, a felt carpet had been laid out for him, on which he sits. Each of the great emirs, who goes to the aforementioned guard-house, [30] was not given his place. Whenever His Majesty comes to the guardhouse he sits in his place.

The guarding of the harem gate and not to allow anyone who has no business there to be in its surroundings as well as [maintaining] law and order in the streets of the entire palace is his responsibility just like the chief royal mace-bearer is the master of the outside he has full authority of the gate of the honored harem.

***

Because the description and circumstances of the situation of the court emirs has been concluded now will be described how some of them are member of the war council.

According to the regulations there were seven war council emirs.

One, the grand vizier; two, the commander of the royal household troops; three, the commander-in-chief; four, the commander of the royal slaves; five, the chief royal mace-bearer of the *divān*; six, the commander of the royal musketeers; seven, the secretary of the royal council.

The rule is that when His Majesty has given orders [concerning] a special issue that the emirs have to form the war council. These seven emirs have to sit in the guard-house of the chief royal mace-bearer of the royal harem or in the guard-house of the grand vizier or in the room of the chamberlain or in whatever place where they have been summoned. [Its] environs and surroundings are declared out-of-bounds and prohibited to outsiders and it is not allowed that anyone be in those areas. After this has been taken care of, they all form a circle. These emirs together deliberate the matter that His Majesty has commanded and on behalf of the emirs of the war council the secretary of the royal council writes the memorandum [summarizing] that which all of them have reflected upon and have thought wisest. If any of the great emirs has a different opinion than the other emirs then the secretary of the royal council writes the opinion of that emir separately and all of them put their own seal on the back of that memorandum. The secretary of the royal council, because he himself has written the memorandum and is not speaking for its contents, does not seal it. After that the grand vizier seals the top of that memorandum and it is given to the chief royal mace-bearer of the royal harem, who hands it to the chief of the harem [eunuchs] to be sent to His Majesty. For a while, the emirs remain on the place where they are seated, until the answer arrives. After the answer comes from [the harem] in whatever form it has been commanded [31] it is executed.

In this way, the consequence for the welfare or destruction of Iran keeps the emirs aforementioned cloistered in the guard-house. It is necessary that the emirs are totally knowledgeable, wise, well-meaning and upright and are not ignorant and crazy. First, in every case the interests of God, the holy Islamic Law, the holy refuge of prophethood [i.e. the prophet Mohammad] p.b.u.h. and piousness must be observed, thereafter the interests of His Majesty himself needs to be considered as a matter of loyalty.

CATEGORY SIX

The emirs who from the days of the late kings until the time of His Majesty the world conqueror the late Shah 'Abbās held important functions and which in the time of His Majesty aforementioned were abolished.

REGENT
vakil-e divān-e a'lā

He handled the management of the kingdom's and the realm's affairs completely as he saw fit. Without his approval, none of the emirs had any say in the affairs of the kingdom. In all periods he had total authority and power. The appointment to offices and services of each of the royal slaves, servants and retainers were entirely done to his liking and wishes. As His Majesty did not interfere that much in matters and affairs, the reins of the Crown's authority were totally in the grip of that person's authority and power. Most of the time, the royal seal was also with the *vakil* and hung around his neck. Royal orders and commands were written in the manner that he deemed fit and he put the royal seal on them.[55]

His Majesty the world conqueror after the initial period of Morshedqoli Khān Ostājalu abolished the office of regent and he did not give it to anybody thereafter. Although after Morshedqoli Khān, Farhād Khān Qarāmānlu,[56] on whom His Majesty had bestowed the title of 'son', had become very powerful so that [his power] neared that of the regent, but there is no document that remains which provides proof of his being a regent. [32] From that date until now the aforesaid office was abolished and was not given to anybody. His Majesty when he came to Astarabad bestowed on Fath 'Ali Khān Qavānlu Qājār, who was governor-general of Astarabad, the following titles.

[TITLES]

Asylum of the vice-regency, province, authority and felicity, magnificence, pomp and glory of the administration, awakener of courage and valor, firm pillar of the everlasting kingdom, foundation of the vice-regent, trusted of the strong pillared state, loyal slave, his excellency, radiant, royal Mo'tamen al-Saltaneh, Asylum of felicity, high and excellent, royal vice-regent, he who adorns vice-regency, province, authority, magnificence, pomp, honor, courage, valor, glory and felicity Fath 'Ali Khan Qavanlu Qajar, vice-regent of the supreme divan and governor-general of the Abode of the Faithful Astarabad.[57]

---

55 For a discussion of the office of *vakil* see Floor, *Safavid Government*, pp. 6-17.
56 On this courtier see Monshi, *Tarikh*, vol. 1, pp. 460-64.
57 See Lockhart, *Nadir Shah*, pp. 14-16, 24-27 on this person.

THE EMIR OF THE DIVĀN
amir-e divān

He is like the vizier of the chancellery [i.e., the grand vizier] Just like the grand vizier was appointed to the *divān*, prior to that time also the emir [of the divan] was [also] appointed. The power of the emir was greater than that of the vizier and this office was mostly given to important princes and was of great authority. They sealed the back of the royal commands such as Shah Tahmāsp who bestowed the aforementioned office on one of his own children and sent him to Herat and he made Mohammad Khān Sharaf al-Din-ughlu his tutor. When Homayun the emperor of India came to Iran he sent a royal command to the abovementioned prince and his tutor especially about the etiquette concerning the entertainment of the aforementioned king.[58]

CHIEF JUSTICE
divān-beygi bāshi

The justices were numerous in the outlying parts [of the kingdom] and they occupied themselves with the people's court. The justice [was] appointed and the district justices were his subordinates. Wherever an error was committed by the district justices the chief justice came to correct and investigate the matter.[59]

CHIEF ARMY MUSTERER
tovāchi-bāshi

The aforementioned office was of the jurisdiction of the chief royal mace-bearer of the *divān*. His function was to alert the army when expeditions and campaigns took place. He [**33**] appointed his own agents and sent them to inform and summon the army, viz. that all had to be mobilized. In time of war, he chose the place to give battle and he instructed the army as to the rules of warfare. He determined the place of each of the fighters and warriors, where they had to be. It was his exclusive responsibility to observe the best and record the young ones, who are like fighters for the faith during battle. After the end of battle he brought that record to the attention of the king. A reward and prize owed to the heroes were given by the king to each one based on the report of the chief army musterer. The aforementioned post is of great esteem.[60]

LORD OF THE SEAL
amir-e mohr

He is also one of the emirs. The royal edicts, diplomas and documents that have to be submitted to the royal sun-like seal, all of them had come to the Lord of the Seal. He took the aforementioned

---

58 For the translated text of this royal order see below. The *Mir Divān* occurs from the very beginning and frequently in the Safavid administration, see, e.g., Shamlu, Valiqoli b. Da'udqoli. *Qesas al-Khaqani*, 2 vols., ed. Hasan Sadat Naseri. (Tehran, 1371/1992), vol. 1, p. 395; Valeh Qazvini, *Iran*, pp. 39, 63-64, 77, 580-81; Mohammad Taher Vahid Qazvini, *Tarikh-e Jahanara-ye 'Abbasi*. ed. Sayyed Sa'id Mir Mohammad Sadeq (Tehran, 1383/2005), pp. 84, 388, 411, 616; al-Qomi, Qadi Ahmad b. Sharaf al-Din al-Hoseyn al-Hoseyni. *Kholasat al-Tavarikh*, 2 vols., ed. Ehsan Eshraqi. (Tehran, 1363/1984), vol. 1, pp. 83 (in 909/1503), 364.

59 This function had not been abolished; see Floor, "Secular Judicial."

60 On this official see Floor, *Safavid Government*, pp. 242-45.

documents to the seal bearers, ink holders and secretaries and distributed them appropriately and he gave them to each one of the persons concerned. He also had some troops who when there was war were in attendance.

REGISTRAR OF THE SEAL
vazir-e mohr

He is the [registrar] of the blessed royal seals and keeps their records. He had to read, record, and register each royal edict, fair copy and office memorandum, etc. that was submitted for the royal blessed seal after which he gave them to the Lord Chancellor to receive the royal seal, unless, God forbid, something was lost or neglected in the meantime.[61]

His Majesty the world conqueror the late Shah 'Abbas gave the aforementioned post to the forebears of this slave by way of a blank royal order.

The aforementioned office holders each had an establishment and considerable emoluments and a group of subordinates and they were completely independent and powerful. As at present all [these functions] are abolished I have not detailed them, [only] a summary of each one has been written in eloquent style for information. [34]

CATEGORY SEVEN

CHIEF LIEUTENANT
khalifeh al-kholafā

Various titles were written for him.[62]

USUAL TITLES

Asylum of the exaltedness and high places, glory and excellence of the administration, the *khalifeh al-kholafā*, the Companion of the Khaqani, he who adorns the lieutenancy, exaltedness and excellence, So-and-so Beyg.

For Mohammad Rezā Khān Kangarlu, who was governor of Nakhjevan and recently became *khalifeh al-kholafā*, [in addition the title of] His Excellency (*ālijāh*) was written.

As the custodianship of the Sheikh Shehāb al-Din tomb, situated in Ahar, Azerbaijan, who was the teacher of Sheikh Safi al-Din, may God bless his grave, was with the government of the province of Qarāchehdāgh, [which] mostly was held by the *kholafā* and by the Nasiri clan. When Mohammad Qāsem Soltān Nāsiri was *khalifeh al-kholafā'i* and governor of Qarājehdāgh his title was written as follows: Asylum of the custodianship, emirate and government, glory and excellence of the administration, khalifeh al-kholafā, Companion of the Khaqan, he who lights up the custodianship, emirate, government, glory and excellence Qasem Soltan, custodian of the many

---

61 This office had not been abolished; see Floor, *Safavid Government*, pp. 74-76.
62 For a discussion of the origin and development of this office, see Willem Floor, "The khalifeh al-kholafā of the Safavid sufi order," *Zeitschrift der Deutschen Morgenländischen Gesellschaft* 153 (2003), pp. 51-86.

splendored tomb of the Lord of the Sufis and Pole of the Mystics, Sheikh Shehab al-Din Ahari and governor of the district of Qarachehdagh.

Emāmqoli Beyg Suklan: formerly he was seal bearer of the royal seal and thereafter he became *khalifeh al-kholafā* and the usual titles were written for him.

Mohammad Amin Khān Nāsiri. He was the brother of Mohammad Qāsem Soltān *khalifeh al-kholafā* who was mentioned above. At the time when His Majesty was in Azerbaijan he bestowed upon him the following titles: Asylum of the custodianship, province and authority, lieutenancy, pomp and majesty of the administration, his excellency, Companion of the Khaqan, *khalifeh al-kholafā*, he who illuminates the custodianship, province, authority, lieutenancy, pomp, majesty and felicity Mohammad Amin Khan, custodian of the many splendored tomb of the Lord of the Sufis and Pole of the Mystics, Sheikh Shehab al-Din Ahari and governor of the district of Qarachehdagh. Mirzā Mohammad Kāfi Nāsiri, who is now *khalifeh al-kholafā*.

TITLES

Asylum of nobility, exaltedness and felicity, his excellency, Companion of the Khaqan, scion of royal slaves of old, he who illuminates exaltedness and felicity Mirza Mohammad Kafi, custodian of the many splendored tomb of the Lord of the Sufis and Pole of the Mystics, Sheikh Shehab al-Din Ahari and governor of the district of Qarachehdagh.

EMOLUMENTS

On account of the governate of Qarāchehdāgh: 359 *tuman*s and [35] 6,000 and odd *dinar*s have been allotted to him. After [payment] of the wages of 100 regular retainers of the aforesaid governate, 300 Tabrizi *tuman*s remain for him. On account of the tax exempt land grant, which he collects from the aforementioned governate, the original amount of 24 *tuman*s and the estimate thus comes to 100 *tuman*s. On account of the revenue assignment, which he has from the Kamareh [?] area, [he receives] 400 *tuman*s. Together with the fees and votive offerings, which people bring to the chantry the total comes to approximately 1,000 *tuman*s per year.

SUBORDINATES

All chanters and Sufis from all parts of the kingdom are his subordinates.

PLACE

His seat in the royal council is on the right side of His Majesty, and he is seated lower than the chief accountant of the state domains, as will become clear, in what follows, when [we discuss] the function of chief accountant of the state domains in the ranks of the highest office holders.

With the Sufi hat and baton on his head, his task is to come to the chantry with the chanters and Sufis to be engaged in invocations on Thursday evenings. Of the Sufis who come to him from the [various] parts [of the kingdom], whoever has the aptitude for the office of *khalifeh* and for providing guidance, he appoints to the office of *khalifeh* and has his Sufi diplomas written by the chief of the royal correspondence (*monshi al-mamālek)* and confirmed by the great royal seal. This [decree] contains several conditions, indicating how to provide guidance to the people and to enjoin the good and ban the evil in a manner that will be made clear in what follows. It is the rule that every one to whom an office or service in the palace or the provinces has been granted, has brought votive offerings to the chantry out of devotion and Sufi spirituality in the form of cash, kind, and sweetmeats. What is brought, after he has deducted his fees, is divided among the Sufis and pious immediate neighbors of the chantry. Two hundred *dinar*s of that amount is put in the golden skimmer and given to the *khalifeh* of the chantry so that he may bring it to His Majesty as a blessing. He has to instruct the leading emirs of the royal court to come on Thursday evenings to the chantry with their glorious hat and to remain in his circle of recitation for one hour and recite the *Fāteheh* for His Majesty's well-being. To everyone who is negligent in coming, he sends the *qurchi*s (royal lifeguards) to remind them. If then he does not show up, [the *khalifeh al-kholafā*] appoints a fee collector who collects a certain amount, which is divided among the Sufis. He does not allow anybody to enter the chantry armed. He opposes the expulsion from the chantry of any criminal and the like who seeks sanctuary there, provided there is no order from His Majesty to make him leave. [36] If someone stands at the palace gate for a claim or a grievance he [i.e. the said officer] must immediately inform His Majesty of his grievance. After having been dismissed [by His Majesty] the said officer takes the man away from the palace gate and satisfies his grievance.

The ritual of staying at the palace gate consist of this: every time that injustice has befallen someone or when he himself has a request that he wants to be heard by His Majesty, he, with the Sufi hat on his head, positions himself at the entrance of the king's palace or at a place that he selects at random, and stands on his feet with his face towards the *qeblah*. He spreads his prayer-mat, because, after he has become incapable to stand any longer, he will commence to pray so that, in doing his genuflections and prostrations, he may nevertheless find total peace of mind. He does not speak at all; he does not answer any one who puts a question to him, unless to the *khalifeh*s who have been sent by the king. In this manner, [even] if he has to make his stand three days and nights, and nobody has been sent on behalf of His Majesty to release him, he does not say a word, he does not eat at all, he does not go anywhere, and he does not sit down, save in prayer.

Having observed this situation, the Sufis and the onlookers inform His Majesty about this. [His Majesty] charges the *khalifa al-kholafā* to go to that person and make him speak and ask him what his grievance is. The said official does as ordered, and after investigation of his grievance, submits it to His Majesty Once the grievance of that person is satisfied, he inevitably leaves the palace gate and is released. Otherwise, it is the rule that he stands at the palace gate until his grievance is met. If, without his grievance being met, he walks away from the palace gate and goes elsewhere, the Sufis, after having taken this man, punish and fine him, because he has violated the rules of the palace gate by not having respected its sanctity.[63]

---

63 This description is borne out by actual practice. Eskandar Beyg Monshi reports that in 1571 Bektash Beyg had been found to be guilty of "dereliction of duty, and he fell from favor of his spiritual director (*morshed-e kāmel*). As a result, the Sufis endowed with pure faith did not allow him to cross the threshold of the palace gate. The accused man did not go home; for three months he stayed outside the palace gates like any old beggar, in the bitter cold of winter, enduring rain and snow, imploring forgiveness for his sins. Finally when the month of Ramazan arrived, at the intercession of *seyyeds* and *'olama*, the Shah forgave his sins and gave him leave to go to his house. On the feast of the breaking of the Fast, Bektash Beyg came, in accordance with prescribed Sufi ritual, to postrate himself before his spiritual director. But the Shah still felt resentment against him and he received no mark of favor. After the death of Shah Tahmasp, Bektash Beyg was put to death by the Takkalus." Roger M. Savory, *The History of Shah 'Abbas the Great*. 2 vols (Boulder, 1978), vol. 1, p. 188, see also pp. 300, 304.

MASTER OF THE OF THE ROYAL HERDS
amir ākhur-bāshi-ye sahrā

USUAL TITLES

Asylum of exaltedness and excellence, glory and loftiness of the administration, Companion of HM, he who adorns exaltedness and excellence, So-and-so Beyg.

To some instead of Companion of HM (*moqarrab al-hezrat*) [the title of] Companion of the Kingdom (*moqarrab al-khāqān*) was granted. After 'Abdollah Beyg Zanganeh, the brother of Shahqoli Khān the grand vizier in the days of His Majesty Shah Soltān Hoseyn, was elevated to the rank of [37] the aforementioned post out of respect for his brother his titles were written as follows:

Asylum of exaltedness and felicity, Companion of the Khaqan, he who resembles exaltedness and felicity.

EMOLUMENTS

Revenue assignment, 100 *tuman*s. With fees this aforementioned post is estimated to get 2,000 *tuman*s annually.

PLACE

His place of seating in the Eden-like council is on the left side of His Majesty and lower than the seal bearer of the royal seal, who will be mentioned later among the seal bearers.

SUBORDINATES

all district heads, herders, horse trainers, and equerries of the royal household, which group is in charge of the young royal foals.

FUNCTION

His function is the approval of the hiring as well as of the assigning of the salaries and regular salaries of the aforementioned retainers. Every year he has to inspect the royal household herds and to see to it that all foals and young animals are branded. His establishment is very large and his office is important.[64]

MINT MASTER
mo'ayyer al-mamālek

USUAL TITLES

Asylum of exaltedness and excellence, glory and loftiness of the administration, Companion of the Khaqan, he who adorns exaltedness and excellence, So-and-so Beyg

EMOLUMENTS

On account of official fees which he has from the refined dust; the aforementioned dust is made from gold. The rule is this that the Jewish group buys the refined dust from the mint master on the basis of one *mann* at shah weight at 1,600 *dinars*. The refined dust is made into the form of non-watered bricks with salt and some saltpeter. On account of his fees from processed [?] dust, which

---

64 For more details on this official and his staff, see Floor-Faghfoory, *Dastur al-Moluk*, pp. 207-09.

is taken from the silver. Lead the mint master has to supply himself. It is customary that whenever miscellaneous silver is brought for coining to the Mint, at a weight of 1,000 *methqāl*s, the mint master supplies 2,000 *methqāl*s of lead, which is twice as much as that silver, to melt it and 2,400 *methqāl*s of its processed [?] dust he keeps and holds for himself. From each 1,000 *methqāl*s he [thus] gets 200 *methqāl*s of additional processed dust [?]. Thereafter, the processed dust [?], that [**38**] is treated this way is melted. After the deduction of these expenditures, from each *mann* at shah weight, which is 1,200 *methqāl*s, 1,303 Tabrizi *dinar*s are produced, which belong to the mint master. On account of his official fees [which are] 1/16th. It is such that whenever gold, silver and copper is being carried from the royal household to the royal Mints the mint-masters record and coin that. From every 16 Tabrizi *tuman*s, which is government property, one *tuman* is for the mint master, which amount the minter-masters record and treat as their expenditure. On account of usual fees, which are not official, that is when a piece of silver is put into a mould so that it reaches the state of unadulterated silver, most commonly they made that piece of silver into [a weight of] 50 *methqāl*s or 5,000 *methqāl*s. From each piece he receives an amount of 50 *dinars*. On account of his normal fees that he receives from rings. It is thus that they use rings to make silver thread, gold-thread and one-tenth thread.[65] Each ring has to be of a weight of 200 *methqāl*s, be it whether this ring is to make gold-thread or silver thread. From each ring he receives 50 *dinars* in fees. On account of his usual fees from the refining [process] and it is thus that silver at a weight of 200 *methqāl*s which is repeatedly refined and finally made into rings for [making] gold-thread he has his 20 *dinars* of fees from each refining. On account of his usual fees, it is thus that that when gold is brought from the melting [crubicle] gold coins will be made from it, he receives on the basis of one *methqāl* 25 *dinars*. Also, his usual gold fees, the result of the refining [process] to make [gold] plating, silver thread and gold thread, are 50 *dinars* per *methqāl*. On account of his usual fees for making copper coins; of each *mann* at shah weight he receives 30 *dinars*, and for silver he has no fees. On account of the usual fees for copper pieces, which are taken to the Mint to strike copper coins when it reaches each workshop. The workers of the workshop concerned of the Mint receive as per standard operation an amount and another amount of 30 *dinars* on the basis of one *mann* of shah weight is the share of the mint master, which he receives from the abovementioned copper. His total income is estimated to be 2,000 *tuman*s per year if not higher.

SUBORDINATES

All the assayers, coiners, and workers of the Mint of Isfahan and of the God protected kingdom [**39**] are all his subordinates.

PLACE

His place of seating in the royal council is on the left side of His Majesty and lower than the master of the royal herd.

FUNCTION

His function is that he has to maintain the Mints of the God protected kingdom in total splendor and order, that the assayers, coiners, and expert workers are completely trustworthy and that he has to appoint and manage of all them, and that he does not allow that they waste the *divān*'s money. The employing and the giving of cash salaries to the workers of the Mint are subject to his approval and confirmation. He has to pay attention that gold is not counterfeited and falsified and that the assay is perfect. All the coined copper and the output of the Mint that is made he has to record for the royal household and the inspectors and the coiners have to send the individual files of the

---

65 *Dah-yek* means that this thread or wire contains 10% of silver.

daily ledgers to the royal secretariat. Each year, during the passing of the New Year, an amount of 12 Tabrizi *tuman*s, that since the time of His Majesty the world conqueror Shah 'Abbās had been fixed as his pension together with seven *tuman*s and 5,000 Tabrizi *dinar*s separately that had been established in the time of His Majesty Shah Soltān Hoseyn, has to be ready in the royal council at the moment of the change [of the year] to be submitted to His Majesty as well as to have ready all that is necessary for the service and office proper and in order in all respects.[66]

ROYAL STIRRUP HOLDER
qurchi-ye rekāb[67]

USUAL TITLES

Asylum of exaltedness and excellence, glory and loftiness of the administration, Companion of HM, he who adorns exaltedness and excellence, So-and-so Beyg.

EMOLUMENTS

He has an amount of 50 Tabrizi *tuman*s and a salary paid in drafts and 100 *tuman*s regular salary from the district of Esfaharān-e Lenjān of Isfahan and 50 other *tuman*s as regular salary from Kashan. His total income is 200 *tuman*s per year.

His seating place in the royal council is on the right side of His Majesty and lower than the mint master (*mo'ayyer al-mamālek*).

FUNCTION

His function is that on the days that His Majesty rides at the moment that he mounts and at [**40**] the time that he dismounts from his horse he has to grab the blessed stirrup and secure it so that His Majesty mounts auspiciously. The aforementioned service most of the times is given to [someone of] the Zanganeh tribe.

CATEGORY EIGHT

The titles, revenue assignments, regular salaries, salaries, emoluments and subordinates of the physicians, astrologers and their seating and standing places in the royal council and their work.

---

66 For more details on this official and his staff, see Floor-Faghfoory, *Dastur al-Moluk*, pp. 247-53.
67 On this official see Floor-Faghfoory, *Dastur al-Moluk*, pp. 63, 81, 91, 203.

CHIEF ROYAL PHYSICIAN
hakim-bāshi[68]

USUAL TITLES

Asylum of sovereignty, nobility, learning and excellence, ingenuity, glory and loftiness of the administration Galenus of the Age, Companion of the Khaqan, he who adorns sovereignty, nobility, learning, ingenuity and loftiness, Mirza So-and-so.

In the days of His Majesty Shah Soltān Hoseyn [the additional title of] '*ālijāh* was written for Mirzā Mohammad Bāqer, chief royal physician and sometimes it was not written.

EMOLUMENTS

On account of the royal treasury he receives every year 100 *tuman*s. On account of a regular salary that has been established for him from the revenues of Isfahan and Fars he had 300 *tuman*s annually. On account of rations on a daily basis he has one plate, which has an estimated value of 1,000 Tabriz *dinar*s and per year an amount of 33 *tuman*s.

SUBORDINATES

All physicians of the royal household are his subordinates.

PLACE

His place of sitting is on the right of His Majesty and below the *khalifeh al-kholafā* and in the days of His Majesty Shah Soltān Hoseyn he was removed from the sitting rows and with Mahmud Āqā the high steward he was placed closer to the olama at the edge of the council.

FUNCTION

His function is to watch over His Majesty's health and all that His Majesty eats and drinks and to ban all food and drinks that are unfit. He always has kept the king healthy with physicks and scientific wisdom and on a daily basis the pulse of His Majesty is felt and he does not allow it to go out of normal balance. [41] When the king falls ill, in accordance with the saying, 'a sick person's judgement is indisposed' the king's judgement likewise became very troubled, for he [the king] has to distinguish between right and wrong in accordance with reality and this has led to major abuses, and the foundations of the kingdom were shaken. When His Majesty Shah Soleymān's disposition exceeded the normal balance he did not pay attention to his health and therefore he became sicker day by day. His mental state deteriorated and he was not able to pay attention to the affairs of the kingdom. Therefore, the condition of the kingdom began to decline and gradually became prone to be overthrown to the extent that the Afghans came to Iran and conquered it. The first [sign] of Iran's ruin was the sickening of and not paying attention to the kingdom's affairs by His Majesty Shah Soleymān.

SUBORDINATES

All physicians of the royal household were his subordinates. Without his permission none in the ranks of physicians could be retained and no salaries and regular salaries could be given to anyone.

The rule is that whenever there is illness among the royal relatives he has to get herbs from the apothecary of the royal household. The recipe for the medicine has to be sealed by the chief

---

68 For more details on this official and his staff, see Floor-Faghfoory, *Dastur al-Moluk*, p. 242.

royal physician. The royal apothecary on that basis takes action and charges it to his own account. Without the seal of the chief royal physician he gives no medicine to anybody.

Mirzā Moʿezz al-Din chief royal physician, whom they called the junior [chief] royal physician.[69]

USUAL TITLES

the same as the chief royal physician without [the title of] Galenus of the Age (*Jālinus al-Zamān*) and the word His Excellency (*ʿālijāh*).

EMOLUMENTS

On account of the regular salaries from the province of Fars each year an amount of 400 *tuman*s. On account of the revenue of 50 bales of tobacco, which has been settled and bestowed upon him as a tax-exempt [emolument] so that nothing is demanded from him, viz. per bale one *tuman* in accordance with the *divān*'s share, annually 50 *tuman*s. On account of rations on a daily basis one plate of which the value is 1,000 *dinar*s and the annual share is 36 Tabrizi *tuman*s per year. His total income is annually 486 *tuman*s.

PLACE

His place of sitting is next to the chief royal physician. [42]

PHYSICIAN OF THE ROYAL HAREM
hakim-e haram[70]

USUAL TITLES

Asylum of wisdom, ingenuity and learning, benefit, abundance, nobility and perfection of the administration, he who adorns ingenuity and learning, benefit, abundance, nobility, Mirza So-and-so.

When Mirzā Jalālā became physician of the royal harem, because he had complete knowledge, it was ordered that for him [the additional title of] Galenus of the Age (*Jālinus al-Zamān*) would be written. After him Mirzā Sharif, son of Mirzā Jalālā was elevated to [the office of] physician of the royal harem and the title *moqarrab al-khāqān* was further added and written for him.

In the time of Your Majesty, Mirzā Esmāʿil, son of Mirzā Sharif was made physician of the royal harem, because of his expertise and closeness to His Majesty. The title of chief physician of the lofty harem (*hakim-bāshigari-ye haram-e ʿoliyeh*) was also bestowed on him. Now for Mirzā Mohammad Taqi, his brother, it is written in the same way: Asylum of wisdom, ingenuity and learning, benefit, abundance, nobility and perfection of the administration, he who adorns ingenuity and learning, benefit, abundance, nobility Mirza Mohammad Taqi, chief physician of the honored and lofty harem.

EMOLUMENTS

On account of a regular salary from the revenues of Isfahan [he has] 400 *tuman*s per year. On account of rations one plate on a daily basis. It value is 36 *tuman*s [per year]. His total income per year is 436 *tuman*s.

---

69 This title was already in use in the 1570s, if not earlier. Mohammad Yusof Valeh Esfahani, *Khold-e Barin* ed. Mir Hashem Mohaddeth (Tehran, 1372/1993), p. 697 (Abu'l-Fath Tabrizi *hakim-e kuchek*); Shamlu, *Qesas*, vol. 1, p. 168; Monshi, *Tarikh*, vol. 1, p. 301.

70 For more details on this official and his staff, see Floor-Faghfoory, *Dastur al-Moluk*, p. 242

PLACE

His place of sitting. At first he was not sitting in the council, but was in the standing rows. When Mirzā Sharif became physician of the royal harem it was established that he would sit to the right of His Majesty and below the junior chief royal physician.

FUNCTION

His function is to watch over the health of the inmates of the harem and the royal children who fall ill in the harem and to heal them. When any of the inmates of the harem falls ill the eunuchs come and bring him inside the harem for medicines, while the harem is not declared out-of-bounds. If it required that the holder of this office on account of the fact that he goes to the royal harem had total trust, and has to be aged, experienced, competent and knowledgeable and that he is not young and inexperienced. [43] On account of the fact that some physicians who outside [the harem] are engaged in healing it may happen that they treat and heal a sick person, but the special physician of the harem is one person, no other person can go into the harem.

When a sickness occurs, it is the rule that he writes the recipe for the medicine and the food [as to] what medicines and food [the patient] consumes. He seals it and gives it to the sick person, who, after having it sent to the royal apothecary, receives the medicine. When the royal apothecary, who is the department head of the apothecary, has recorded himself the recipe he, accordingly, dispenses it charging it to his own budget.

ROYAL ASTROLOGER
monajjem-bāshi[71]

USUAL TITLES

Asylum of nobility, exaltedness and excellence, learning, glory and perfection of the administration, Companion of the Khaqan, Ptolemy of the Age, king of the astrologers, he who adorns nobility, exaltedness and excellence, Mirza So-and-so.

EMOLUMENTS

On account of a regular salary, 400 *tuman*s. On account of the bread that he receives from the royal bakery one piece. On account of the goods that the commander of the royal household troops brings as alms on the birthday of His Majesty; it is the rule that these are sent to the royal astrologer who forwards them to the needy but most of them he keeps for himself.

PLACE

His place of sitting is on the right side of His Majesty below the junior chief royal physician.

FUNCTION

His function is to determine the auspicious and inauspicious hours and communicate these to His Majesty. Every year he writes the calendar for that year and sends it to His Majesty and he also writes each month a monthly calendar and indicates the auspicious and inauspicious hours and sends it each month to His Majesty to be acted upon, so that on bad hours he does not give an order. [44]

---

71 For more details on this official and his staff, see Floor-Faghfoory, *Dastur al-Moluk*, pp. 244-45.

CATEGORY NINE

The titles, revenue assignments, regular salaries, salaries, perquisites and subordinates of the office holders, department heads of the royal secretariat and the ministers, accountants, and people of the pen, their seating and standing places in the royal council and a summary of their work.

CHIEF ACCOUNTANT OF THE STATE DOMAINS
mostowfi al-mamālek[72]

USUAL TITLES

[Asylum of] exaltedness and felicity, his excellency Companion of the Khaqan, meritorious chief accountant, he who adorns exaltedness and felicity, Mirza So-and-so.

The word *bi'l-erth* (hereditary) was not written for any chief accountant of the state domains on account of the fact that *bi'l-erth* has the meaning that the function of chief accountant of the state domains, apart from the clan of the person of which the word *bi'l-erth* was written, will not go to anyone else, [because] it is hereditary in that clan. This office was bestowed on any of the clans of the men of the pen. Lately, it was written for Mirzā Abu'l-Hasan, chief accountant of the state domains and Mirzā Mohammad Hoseyn who thereafter was elevated to [the rank of] grand vizier and Mirzā Mohammad Rahim, chief accountant of the state domains.

EMOLUMENTS

His regular salary and wages are not known to this slave, except that he has fees. On account of the original assessment of the revenue assignments of the great emirs he receives 45 *dinars* per *tuman*. On account of the regular salaries of the great emirs he receives 30 *dinars* per *tuman*. On account of the original assessment of the revenue assignments of the royal companions he receives fees of 45 *dinars* per *tuman*. On account of the regular salaries of the yeomen he receives fees of 15 *dinars* per *tuman*. On account of the cash wages of the great emirs he receives 15 *dinars* per *tuman*. On account of the stipends of the companions and yeomen he has fees of 90 *dinars* per *tuman*. On account of the stipends of the great emirs and of some who are not retainers of the *divān* he has a chancery fee of 90 *dinars* per *tuman*. On account of the salaries and the user fee of the tax officials he receives 90 *dinars* per *tuman*. From the court emirs, governors-general, provincial governors he also has fees and he also has the total amount of the accountancy fee of each group. [45]

His total income is estimated to be per year 5,000 Tabrizi *tuman*s.

SUBORDINATES

All the staff of the royal secretariat, except for its department heads, are his subordinates.

PLACE

His place of seating. In the royal council he sits on the right of His Majesty and immediately below the commander of the royal gunners. If it happens that he is seated in the row of the emirs of the left hand he is seated below the secretary of the royal council.

---

72 For a discussion of this official's tasks, see Floor, *Safavid Government*, pp. 41-42; see also Floor, *Fiscal History*, pp. 72-73.

FUNCTION

His function is to come every day to the royal secretariat; he had the responsibility to see to it that all staff and scribes charged with the recording and registration of the *divān* revenues do so with total diligence. The authority of the handling of the *divān* revenues and the giving of cash payments to [members of] the government staff was totally in his hands. All tax payers, renters and those with whom the *divān* revenues are were summoned by him. After he has cleared the accounts of that group, whenever something is left behind with the said group, he collects and receives it completely. He does whatever is required for the proper collection of revenues.

The authority that the chief accountant of the state domains has over the *divān* taxes, the grand vizier does not have in the same way. Without his seal and writing there can be no transaction of even one *dinar* of the *divān* taxes. The royal orders, commands and notes that are to be obeyed and are issued by the royal secretariat with the administrative files and accounts of totals all have to be sealed by him. After all the department heads of the royal secretariat have put their seal on the back the chief accountant of the state domains also puts his seal on the back, [once] having received the endorsement (*toghrā*) of the secretary of the royal council and the chief of the royal correspondence (*monshi al-mamalek*) then thereafter the grand viziers seals [them]. If an administrative falsification occurs then the chief accountant of the state domains examines it. In short, the authority of the chief accountant of the state domains concerning the *divān* finances and the secretariat is greater than before and whenever something is not related to the account and there is a deficit for the *divān*, if the grand vizier and the king have given orders [to pay], he has the authority not to execute this and to examine the finances of the *divān*. [46]

The holder of this office has to be completely competent in writing, to have total knowledge of short-hand accounting, writing of bills, and all kinds of *divān* accounts and regulations and has to be extremely upright, truthfull and pious so that all clerks attest to his competence and knowledge.

CHIEF ACCOUNTANT OF THE ROYAL DOMAINS
mostowfi-ye khāsseh[73]

USUAL TITLES

Asylum of exaltedness and excellence, glory and loftiness of the administration, Companion of the Khaqan, he who adorns exaltedness and excellence, Mirza So-and-so.

When Mirzā Rabi' became chief accountant of the royal domains the title of scion of longstanding adherents (*bandeh-zādeh-ye qadimi*) was written for him,[74] which now also is written for the chief accountant of the royal domains.

EMOLUMENTS

A revenue assignment of 40 *tumans* and its estimate is valued at an amount of 700 *tumans* per year. All his revenues with authorized fees are estimated to be annually 4,000 *tumans*.

---

73 For this official see Floor, *Safavid Government*, pp. 43-45; see also Floor, *Fiscal History*, pp. 73-74.
74 He became chief accountant of the royal domains in 1701.

SUBORDINATES

The clerks and scribes of the royal domains department are all his subordinates.

His place of seating in the Eden-like council is on the right of His Majesty below the chief royal physician.

FUNCTION

His function: the management of the revenues of the royal domains department is his. Because His Majesty the world conqueror the late Shah 'Abbās during his reign made many constructions and buildings in each province, in particular in Isfahan and Mazandaran he gave his full attention by building mosque[s], the *Meydān-e Naqsh-e Jahān*, and bazaars in Isfahan and the *Chahār Bāgh*. Sometimes, the army argued that "the revenues used for palaces and buildings is the army's pay and our pay is being used for construction, which is contrary to [proper] ruling" and it wanted the world conqueror to put his income separately so that every expenditure that he wanted to make would stop the army's tongue wagging. Therefore, Isfahan, Mazandaran, the Gilans,[75] Qom, Kashan and the other provinces that were in the environs of Isfahan were set aside for the expenditures of the royal household and the transactions of the revenues of the said provinces were made his responsibility and he became the equal of the chief accountant of the state domains (*mostowfi al-mamālek*). [47]

VIZIER OF ISFAHAN
vazir-e isfahan[76]

USUAL TITLES

Asylum of the vizierate, exaltedness and excellence, glory and loftiness of the powerful administration, he who adorns exaltedness and excellence, Mirza So-and-so.

EMOLUMENTS

Annually with wages and a regular salary [blank] *tuman*s.

PLACE

His seating place in the royal council is on the right side of His Majesty and below the chief accountant of the royal domains and the vizier of the endowments.

FUNCTION

All transactions with the revenues of Isfahan and the appointment of tax officials, tax collectors and lease-holders for the collection of the said revenues and the keeping of the files thereof, the repairs of the royal buildings and gardens and that which concerns Isfahan is completely his responsibility. Every year he had to collect the said revenues so that nothing of the taxes is wasted and lost.

---

75 The province of Gilan traditionally was divided into Gilan-e biyeh-pas (the western part around Resht) and Gilan-e biyeh-pish (the eastern part around Lahejan).
76 For more details on this official see Floor-Faghfoory, *Dastur al-Moluk*, pp. 65-67.

VIZIER OF THE ENDOWMENTS OF THE FOURTEEN INFALLIBLE ONES P.B.U.T.
vazir-e mowqufāt-e chahārdeh ma'sum salavāt-e allah 'aleyhom ajma'eyn[77]

USUAL TITLES
Asylum of the vizierate, exaltedness and excellence, glory and loftiness of the administration, he who adorns exaltedness and excellence, Mirza So-and-so.

EMOLUMENTS
What the world conqueror has commanded is that each year a salary of 50 *tuman*s has to be deducted from the said endowments. The maximum income of the viziers of endowments, as has become repeatedly clear, was from 700 up to 1,000 *tuman*s.

PLACE
His place of seating. In the royal council he is seated on the right of His Majesty and higher than the vizier of Isfahan.

FUNCTION
His function is each year to record and manage all lands, real estate, shops, caravanserais and districts of the endowments of the Fourteen Infallible Ones p.b.u.t. [Further] to increase cultivation and prosperity of all [of those] he will do his utmost to make it happen. All endowments revenues and pensions of those who are entitled to them are turned into cash, in the manner as has been recorded above under the name of the chief religious authority of the crown domains (*sadr-e khāsseh*) and brought to His Majesty who himself gave that revenue to the pension holders. [48]

The said post was very esteemed and important, in particular during the reign of His Majesty the world conqueror the late Shah 'Abbās when it had extreme independence, to such an extent that it was the equal to that of the grand vizier. It is known that one day the endowments minister of the Fourteen Infallible Ones was in discussion with the grand vizier in the presence of His Majesty and said to him that "you may be the vizier of one Infallible One, I am the vizier of Fourteen Infallible Ones."

---

77 See further Willem Floor, "The sadr or head of the Safavid religious administration, judiciary and endowments and other members of the religious institution," *ZDMG* 150 (2000), pp. 471-72.

STEWARD OF THE ROYAL SECRETARIAT
nāzer-e daftar-khāneh-ye homāyun-e a'lā[78]

USUAL TITLES

Asylum of exaltedness and excellence, glory and loftiness of the administration, Companion of HM, he who adorns exaltedness and excellence, Mirza So-and-so.

EMOLUMENTS

From a regular salary and fees of regular salaries an amount of 400 *tuman*s and in the time of Your Majesty it was fixed at 125 *tuman*s.

Fees: on account of the original assessment of the revenue assignments of the emirs, the royal companions and yeoman on the basis of seven *dinar*s per *tuman*. On account of the regular salaries of the aforementioned group on the basis of 14 *dinar*s and four *dāng* per *tuman*. On account of cash payments to the great emirs, companions and yeomen on the basis of two *dinar*s and two *dāng* per *tuman*. On account of the stipends of the emirs and some who are not retainers of the *divān* and companions and yeomen and wages, user fee of the tax officials and tax exempt land grants, tax exemption and fiefs on the basis of 14 *dinar*s per *tuman*. On account of leases on account of 14 *dinar*s and three and a half *dang* per *tuman*.

All his income is estimated to be 1,000 *tuman*s per year and if the total is calculated according to reality it comes to 2,000 *tuman*s.

PLACE

His place of seating. In the council he is seated on the left of His Majesty and [below] the seal bearer of the great royal seal. If it happens that he seated to the right of His Majesty is he is seated below the vizier of Isfahan.

FUNCTION

His function is to come every day to the secretariat and to seal and register all royal orders and commands that are to be obeyed and are issued by the royal secretariat. The royal orders concerning offices and retainers or other royal orders that have an impact on the *divān* revenues he submits either to the secretary of the royal council or to the four viziers [**49**] by which is meant the viziers of the royal household troops, royal slaves, gunners and musketeers, who, for each of these aforementioned groups, make the appropriate entries after which they are brought to the secretariat for the sealing by the sun-like seal, which in accordance with regulations are recorded and in case of some of them it is written on the back and some [others] are sealed.

Some of the clerks are his subordinates and he has a separate office.

If the chief accountant of the state domains and clerks of the royal secretariat have made an error or mistake in the accounts and the government documents he has to be aware of it and to investigate it.

He is a steward of all heads of the royal department, so that without his cognizance and knowledge none of the heads of the secretariat can make transactions with *divān* revenues and all matters concerning the royal secretariat, or commit any fraud in the accounts. Just like in other offices a steward takes care that no waste and dissipation occurs in the royal secretariat, which is the most

---

78 For more details on this official and his staff, see Floor-Faghfoory, *Dastur al-Moluk*, p. 80 and Floor, *Fiscal History*, p. 74.

important of all offices. He also has to see to it that nothing untoward takes place and nothing of the revenues gets lost.

In the time of His Majesty Shah Soltān Hoseyn, when it was submitted that many of the revenues had been lost and had been given to undeserving persons, the supervision of the secretariat, in addition to that of the royal workshops, was bestowed and conferred on Safiqoli Khān who was a mature man. When all royal orders as command and *divān* documents were submitted for his view and seal no endorsement without his knowledge was written and left the secretariat and on the back of the royal orders and commands he put his seal on the right side higher than the chief accountant of the state domains.

The holder of this office is said to be the ear and confidante of the king who has appointed him to the secretariat. He has to have a secret way to inform His Majesty and to inform and make His Majesty aware of the income and expenditure dossiers, and the frauds of the heads of the secretariat and the chiefs of the groups of the victorious government staff so that His Majesty may institute the necessary investigation.

CHIEF OF THE ROYAL CORRESPONDENCE
monshi al-mamālek[79]

USUAL TITLES

Learning, nobility, glory and perfection of the administration, Companion of the Khaqan, the meritorious and hereditary royal secretary, he who adorns learning, nobility, glory and perfection, Mirza So-and-so. **[50]**

EMOLUMENTS

From a revenue assignment, *dārugheh* payment and fees. A revenue assignment has been assigned to him from Shiraz at 50 *tumans* and its estimate comes to an amount of 250 *tumans*. The *dārugheh* payment is from the town of Ordubad, which is the birth place of the Nasiri family. Since olden times he has a tax exemption and *dārugheh* payment, an annual fixed amount, of 18 *tumans*. The fees on account of the original amount of the assessment of the revenue assignment of the emirs, royal companions and yeomen on the basis of 25 Tabrizi *dinars* per *tuman*. On account of the regular salaries of the emirs, royal companions and yeomen on the basis of 16 *dinars* and four *dang* per *tuman*. On account of cash payment to the aforementioned group [he receives] 8 *dinars* and two *dāng* per *tuman*. On account of the stipends of the great emirs and some who were not retainers of the *divān* and royal companions, yeomen and salaries, user fee of tax officials, tax exempt land grants, fiefs and tax exemptions on the basis of 50 *dinars* per *tuman*. On account of leases on a basis of 18 *dinars* and one *dāng* per *tuman*.

PLACE

He sits on the right of His Majesty in the Eden-like council below the vizier of Isfahan. Previously he sat below the chief accountant of the royal domains, but gradually the holders of [other] offices sought precedence, and now the said place has become his rightful one.

---

79 For more information on this official as well as the changes in bureaucratic practices, see Floor, *Safavid Government*, p. 50ff.

FUNCTION

In the days of *abu'l-baqā* Shah Esmā'il, may God illuminate his proof, which was at the very beginning of the Safavid dynasty, the office of the secretary of the royal council had not yet been created and his work was [therefore] much and the writing of all letters, royal diplomas, commands, revenue assignment diplomas, orders for tax exempt land grants, tax exemptions, cash payments, diplomas for Sufis, were all his responsibility. Some he wrote himself and some were written by the royal secretariat and submitted for his endorsement (*toghrā*).

After the offices of secretary of the royal council and chief accountant of the state domains had been created the rule became such that the secretary of the royal council wrote all the appointment [diplomas for] the great emirs, governors-general, governors, viziers, provincial and tribal *kalāntar*s, and *divān* agents, while the letters, royal diplomas, appointment diplomas for Sufis and royal administrative commands that were issued by the royal secretariat and that have a relation with the secretary of the royal council and with the royal commands that are issued by the Lord Justice [51] were part of the chief of the royal correspondence's (*monshi al-mamālek*'s) responsibility. Royal orders and notes that are issued by the royal secretariat, after the chief accountant of the state domains and other department heads of the royal secretariat have each put their seal on the back, are submitted to the *monshi al-mamālek* to draw his endorsement (*toghrā*), either in gold or blue or red, each one up to his choosing, after which they are submitted for the grand vizier's seal. Ultimately, because the grand viziers are completely [entitled to] interfere with the documents, whenever he wants that the secretariat writes a royal order he wrote an apostil [instructing] that the secretariat write it. After it had been written, just like the other orders, his endorsement (*toghrā*) is drawn. In short, whatever commands and notes pass through the secretariat, except for orders from the royal household, which are the secretary of the royal council's charge, they all have to be submitted for the *monshi al-mamālek*'s endorsement (*toghrā*).

The said office has always been with the Nasiri clan and has been from father to son of this royal slave's [clan] and it has remained this clan's [charge] from the days of His Majesty Shah Esma'il until to-day.

In the early days of the reign of that king when the Safavid dynasty had not as yet grown and increased as much the endorsements on royal commands were drawn in red color.[80]

The title *bi'l-erth va'l-estehqāq* (by virtue of heredity and merit) therefore was bestowed on the chief of the royal correspondence (*monshi al-mamālek*) from that day onwards until to-day and this office has not gone to another [clan] and each one of this clan has committed himself to promote the worthiness and merit of this service.

The holder of this office has to be a clerk without peer and total competence in the art of style, knowledge of the language of kings and of the rules and behavior of the kings of this world and to know each language such as Arabic, Persian and Turkish so that when he is ordered to write a letter to each of these kings of the [quarters of] the world, he knows in what way to do it and in which manner and this highest office is his. He has to know the art of short-hand accounting, correspondence and royal chancellery regulations. He also has to have total trust, piety and truthfulness in writing so that later, when the document reaches him for his endorsement, he can testify to its correctness or inaccuracy.

Before this the holders of this office had selected a place to work in their own house, which place was called Epistolary House (*dār al-enshā*). Every day, the scribes and clerks of the *dār al-*

---

80 The term used, *gel-e sorkh*, refers to bole armoniac.

enshā had to be at that place to work on writing the commands and notes. Of late, this rule has been abandoned and the scribes went to the secretariat where they wrote the orders. [**52**]

SUBORDINATES

Sometimes 30 persons and sometimes less and each one was held in total respect and they had sensible regular salaries and salaries. All royal commands and notes were written by this group.

HEAD CLERK OF THE ROYAL SECRETARIAT
dārugheh-ye daftar-khāneh-ye homāyun-e aʿlā[81]

USUAL TITLES

Asylum of government, exaltedness and excellence, glory and loftiness of the administration, he who adorns government, exaltedness and excellence, So-and-so Beyg.

EMOLUMENTS

From a regular salary and fees. Regular salary: an amount of 400 Tabrizi *tuman*s. Fees: on account of the original assessment of the revenue assignments of the emirs, royal companions and yeomen eight and a half *dinar*s per *tuman*. On account of regular salaries of the aforementioned groups on the basis of five *dinar*s per *tuman*. On account of cash payment of companions and yeomen on the basis of two and a half *dinar*s per *tuman*. On account of stipends of emirs and some who are not retainers of the *divān* on the basis of 15 *dinar*s per *tuman*. On account of [of leases] on the basis of five and half *dinar*s per *tuman*. His total income per year is 1,000 *tuman*s.

PLACE

He sits in the royal council on the left of H.M and below the steward of the royal secretariat. If it happens that he sits on the right he sits lower than the *monshi al-mamālek*.

FUNCTION

His function is that he came every day to the royal secretariat, when the appointed tax collectors, receivers, lease-holders, and administrators of government taxes came to the royal secretariat. He instructs the senior accountants to audit the accounts of that group. Whenever there is something to observe with regards to the government taxes of that group he investigates each one of them and reports it to the *divān*. Whenever any of the department heads of the *divān* and the scribes of the royal secretariat do not come to the secretariat or they are delayed in coming he urges them to come. When between the staff of the secretariat or of the victorious government and the scribes of the royal secretariat a conflict, dispute or fight occurs he is charged to deal with that, because [maintaining] control over and order in the secretariat is his responsibility. All royal orders and commands, whether issued from the royal secretariat or whether from [**53**] outside, once they have reached the secretariat all have to be submitted to his seal and he has total authority with regards the management of the secretariat and the punishment and correction of scribes of the secretariat.

---

81 For more details on this official, see Floor-Faghfoory, *Dastur al-Moluk*, p. 81 and Floor, *Fiscal History*, pp. 74-75.

VIZIER OF THE ROYAL HOUSEHOLD TROOPS
vazir-e qurchiyān-e ʿozzām[82]

USUAL TITLES

Asylum of the vizierate, exaltedness and excellence, glory and loftiness of the administration, he who adorns exaltedness and excellence, Mirza So-and-so.

Now [these] are written for the vizier of the royal household troops as follows:

Asylum of sovereignty, nobility, vizierate, exaltedness and excellence, nobility, glory and loftiness of the administration, progeny of the great sayyeds, he who illuminates sovereignty, nobility, vizierate, exaltedness and excellence, Mirza Mohammad Sadeq, vizier of the royal household troops.

EMOLUMENTS

From a regular salary and fees. Regular salary: an amount of 100 Tabrizi *tuman*s. Fees: on account of the original assessment of the revenue assignments, the fixing and assigning of the wages and stipends of the royal household troops 200 *dinar*s per *tuman*, meaning that a person who has entered the ranks of the royal household troops has a salary of five *tuman*s of which he gets 200 *dinar*s per *tuman*, [or] an amount of 1,000 *dinar*s, from that royal household trooper as a chancery fee. On account of regular salaries and cash payments of 45 *dinar*s per *tuman*. The total income of the vizier of the royal household troops is estimated to 1,000 *tuman*s per year.

PLACE

His seating place in the royal council is on the right side if His Majesty and lower than the *monshi al-mamālek*. If it happens that he sits of the left he sits lower than the head clerk of the royal secretariat.

FUNCTION

His function is to give revenue assignments and regular salaries, cash payments to the royal household troops and the transactions of the group; the record keeping of departure and death of each person of that group was his responsibility. Without his seal and his mark not one *dinar* could be transacted.

If the chiefs of the department want to commit fraud in the department, this is impossible, because of the knowledge of the vizier of the royal household troops, unless he participates with the chiefs in the fraud.

The writing of all royal orders of employing royal household troops was the said vizier's task. The royal orders and commands of revenue assignments and regular salaries and [**54**] cash payments of this group that were issued by the royal secretariat have all to be sealed on the back by him.

---

82 For more details on this official and his colleague of the royal slaves, royal musketeers and royal gunners, see Floor-Faghfoory, *Dastur al-Moluk*, p. 70, see also Floor, *Safavid Government*, pp. 41, 50, 56, 153, 174, 187.

VIZIER OF THE DEPARTMENT OF ROYAL SLAVES
vazir-e sarkār-e gholāmān

USUAL TITLES

Asylum of the vizierate, exaltedness and excellence, glory and loftiness of the administration, he who adorns exaltedness and excellence, Mirza So-and-so.

EMOLUMENTS

Fom a revenue assignment and fees. The revenue assignment and its estimate 400 Tabrizi *tuman*s, which now has been fixed at 153 odd *tuman*s. Fees: on account of the original assessment of revenue assignments and the fixing of salaries and stipends of royal slaves 200 *dinar*s per *tuman*. On account of regular salaries and cash wages of that group [he receives] 45 *dinar*s per *tuman*. His total income is also estimated at 1,000 [*tuman*s] per year.

PLACE

Place of seating is on the right side of His Majesty and below the vizier of the royal household troops.

FUNCTION

His function is just like that of the vizier of the royal household troops without any difference as becomes quite clear, whenever a group of royal slaves has been placed among the workers of the workshops or among the royal household troops. The record keeping of the royal slaves is likewise the same and it is [the task of] the vizier of the royal slaves.

VIZIER OF THE ROYAL MUSKETEERS AND THE VIZIER OF THE ROYAL GUNNERS
vazir-e tofangchiyān va vazir-e tupchiyān

TITLES AND EMOLUMENTS

Titles and Emoluments and fees of these two viziers are also the same as for the vizier of the royal slaves as was known, except that the salary of the vizier of the royal slaves [sic; must be gunners] is 50 *tuman*s and the salary of the vizier of the musketeers 30 *tuman*s and the total income of each one is also 1,000 *tuman*s per year.

PLACE

The vizier of the musketeers sits lower than the vizier of the royal slaves and the vizier of the gunners lower than the vizier of the musketeers in the council.

These four viziers aforementioned are called the four viziers. [55]

CHIEF ACCOUNTANT OF THE GOVERNMENT STAFF
khalifeh-ye lashkar-nevis[83]

USUAL TITLES

Asylum of the lieutenancy, exaltedness and excellence, glory and loftiness of the administration, he who adorns exaltedness and excellence, Mirza So-and-so.

EMOLUMENTS

From revenue assignment and fees. Fees: (sic; must be revenue assignment) almost 30 *tuman*s. Fees: the same, more or less, they are like the fees of the *monshi al-mamālek* and there is no difference. His total income is 1,000 *tuman*s per year.

PLACE

Sitting place in the royal council. To the right of His Majesty and below the vizier of the royal slaves.

[FUNCTION]

The record keeping of the entire government staff is in his hands, whether of royal retainers and whether of the retainers of the emirs. If a general, commander-in-chief or commander is appointed to a place and an army is sent with them then the rule is that the chief accountant of the army appoints a deputy on his behalf, who will march with them so that he can register the absence and attendance [of members] of that army [as well as] confirm the services [rendered] by that army, i.e. who performed an act of daring or of courage. He records and takes all this to the royal secretariat where it is registered in the files so that a group that has well performed [its] service received a reward and those who have shirked their duty were reprimanded. The royal orders concerning the employment of the yeomen and the retainers of the royal household, who are called the shah's subordinates (*shāh-tābin*), as well as of the group who are the subordinates of the chief royal mace-bearer of the *divān* and the high steward from among workers of the workshops all of these he records and the transactions concerning these subordinates of these two departments are his [responsibility].

Like the vizier of the royal household troops is the vizier of the department of the royal household troops the chief accountant of the army likewise is the vizier of the department of the yeomen.

All royal appointment orders and commands for the great emirs, governors-general, governors, viziers, provincial accountants etc. are either written by the secretary of the royal council, after which they are taken to the secretariat for registration and the sealing with the sun-like seal, or they are written by the royal secretariat and submitted for the seal and mark of the chief accountant of the army.

---

83 For more details on this official, see Floor, *Safavid Government*, pp. 47-50, 62, 76.

ACCOUNTANTS OF THE DEPARTMENTS OF THE ROYAL HOUSEHOLD TROOPS, ROYAL SLAVES, ROYAL MUSKETEERS AND ROYAL GUNNERS
mostowfiyān-e sarkār-e qurchiyān va gholāmān va tofangchiyān va tupchiyān[84]

USUAL TITLES
Asylum of the nobility, exaltedness and excellence, glory and loftiness of the administration, he who adorns nobility, exaltedness and excellence, Mirza So-and-so. [56]

PLACE
These four accountants are seated to the right of His Majesty in the royal council and below the four viziers next to one another and in this order: first, the accountant of the royal household troops, then [of] the royal slaves, and then of the royal musketeers and then of the royal gunners.

Sometimes some of them are seated on the left.

EMOLUMENTS
The salary of the accountant of the royal troops is 50 *tuman*s and of the three other accountants it is 30 *tuman*s for each.

FUNCTION
The function of these four accountants is the same for each one of them and the transactions of each department is the responsibility of the accountant of that department.

If the vizier of the royal troops wants to transact one *dinar* without the knowledge of the accountant of the royal troops department it cannot be done.

All royal employment orders and commands, revenue assignments, regular salaries, and cash payments of that group take place with their administrative documents, the accountant of that department has to seal them, to ensure that the vizier of each department does not commit fraud, which the accountant has to prevent.

The income of each of the four persons with their salary is estimated at 500 *tuman*s per year.

CHIEF OF DISBURSEMENTS
sāheb-e towjih[85]

USUAL TITLES
Asylum of the nobility, exaltedness and excellence, glory and loftiness of the administration, he who adorns nobility, exaltedness and excellence, Mirza So-and-so.

EMOLUMENTS
From salaries and fees. Salaries: 30 *tuman*s and now 15 *tuman*s. Fees: on account of the original assessment of the revenue assignments of the emirs, royal companions and yeomen one *dinar* and one and a half *dāng* per *tuman*. On account of the regular salaries of the said group of seven and a half *dinar*s per *tuman*. On account of the cash payments of the aforementioned group three *dinar*s

---

[84] For more details on this official, see Floor-Faghfoory, *Dastur al-Moluk*, pp. 76-77.

[85] For more details on this official see Floor, *Fiscal History*, pp. 77-78; and Floor-Faghfoory, *Dastur al-Moluk*, pp. 99, 132.

and four and a half *dāng* per *tuman*. On account of the stipends of the emirs, some of whom are not retainers of the *divān*, of the companions, yeomen and the salaries, user fee (*haqq al-sa'y*) of the provincial tax officials, tax exempt land grants, fiefs, tax exemptions and leases 22½ *dinar*s per *tuman*. On account of salaries and revenue assignments, stipends, cash payments and regular salaries of the government staff of the royal troops, royal slaves, musketeers and gunners 20 *dinar*s per *tuman*.

His total income with authorized fees is estimated at 1,000 *tuman*s per year and he is of the category [57] of those that are standing [in the royal council].

FUNCTION

His function is demanding and he has to go every day to the royal secretariat and every royal order, after it has been sealed with the sun-like seal, has to be registered in the revenue registers or the commands and notes that have been issued by the royal secretariat have all to be submitted with the documents and administrative papers for his seal and initials. Some have to be sealed first, others are sealed at the end. No document leaves the secretariat that has not been submitted for his seal and mark. Even the government documents, concerning properties that have been bought by the royal household all have to be registered in his own book by the holder of this office and he has to keep a record of all of them.

The payment office has been likened to literary anthologies in which a person may find whatever he desires and what comes to his mind in that miscellany.

In the royal secretariat there is not a busier job than the aforementioned one and he is the equal of all the chiefs of the books of the secretariat. He has many clerks and a separate book.

CLERK OF RECEIPTS ACCOUNTABLE
sarkhatt-nevis[86]

USUAL TITLES

Asylum of the nobility, exaltedness and excellence, glory and loftiness of the administration, he who adorns nobility, exaltedness and excellence, Mirza So-and-so.

[PLACE]

He is of the number of those who stand in the royal council.

EMOLUMENTS

From a salary and fees. Salary: 30 *tuman*s. Fees: on account of the original assessment of the revenue assignments of the emirs, companions, and yeomen eight *dinar*s per *tuman*. On account of the regular salaries of the emirs five *dinar*s and two *dang* per *tuman*. On account of the cash payment of the emirs two *dinar*s and one and half *dāng* [per *tuman*]. On account of the cash payment to the royal companions and yeomen and their regular salaries 20 *dinar*s per *tuman*. [On account of] stipends of the emirs, royal companions and yeomen, salaries, user fees of the tax officials, tax exempt land grants, fiefs and tax exemptions 16 *dinar*s per *tuman*. On account of leases five *dinar*s and four *dang* per *tuman*.

His total income is estimated at 500 *tuman*s per year.

---

86 For more details on this official, see Floor-Faghfoory, *Dastur al-Moluk*, p. 103.

FUNCTION

His function is that each day he had to go to the secretariat and put his initials on the right side on the back of all royal orders and commands that reach the secretariat. [**58**] On the place where he put his initials on that same place the chief accountant of the army had put his seal. He himself is not the holder of a seal.

He has several clerks who were his subordinates; in the book that is his responsibility they are busy writing.

All royal employment orders have to be submitted for his registration and he is the counterpart of the chief accountant of the army. Just like the chief accountant of the army has the authority of the vizier of the department of the royal companions and yeomen he likewise is at the same level as the accountant of that department.

CLERKS OF THE ASSETS
āvārajeh-nevisān[87]

They are five persons. Of that number there is the *āvārajeh-nevis* of Iraq, after him the *āvārajeh-nevis* of Fars, the next one is the *āvārajeh-nevis* of Azerbaijan and yet another is the *āvārajeh-nevis* of Khorasan and one is the *āvārajeh-nevis* of the mines.

USUAL TITLES

They are the same for all and as follows:

Asylum of the nobility, exaltedness and excellence, glory and loftiness of the administration, he who illuminates nobility, exaltedness and excellence, Mirza So-and-so.

[PLACE]

They do not sit in the council.

EMOLUMENTS

From salary and fees. The salary of the *āvārajeh-nevis* of Iraq is 14 *tuman*s; of Azerbaijan 15 *tuman*s and there is no difference with the others. Fees: on account of the revenue assignments of the emirs, companions and yeomen 11 *dinar*s and one and a half *dāng* per *tuman*. On account of the regular salaries of the aforementioned group seven and a half *dinar*s [per *tuman*]. On account of the stipends of the emirs and of some who are not retainers of the *divān*, companions, and yeomen, and salaries, *haqq al-sa'y* of tax officials, tax exempt land grants, fiefs, and tax exemptions 22½ *dinar*s per *tuman*. On account of leases eight *dinar*s and two *dāng* [per *tuman*].

The total income of each one is estimated at 500 *tuman*s per year and the fees of each one are from the province that they are in charge of, meaning that, for example, each revenue that is charged to the districts of Iraq in the form of revenue assignments, salaries, etc. that are bestowed on each person, the *āvārajeh-nevis* of Iraq takes his fees from that person. The other *āvārajeh-nevisān* have no claim on this, on the contrary.

[FUNCTION]

The work of these five persons is that having gone each day to the secretariat they record truthfully the amounts of the total revenue of each province of which they are in charge in their registers

---

87 For more details on this official, see Floor, *Fiscal History*, pp. 75-76 and Floor-Faghfoory, *Dastur al-Moluk*, pp. 104-05.

so that each year [one may see] the amount of the revenues of that [**59**] province and to what end it will be used, what part of the government revenues of the provinces aforementioned will be transferred and collected from the tax payers. They are the clerks of the total amount of revenues, i.e. they register the *divān*'s finances every year in their own files; [to wit] what amount and what quantity is there and on the basis of their confirmation the grand vizier collects from the tax payers.

This group has to be completely pious and truthfull, because other than these four regions the country of Iran has no more [resources]. Whenever the records of the transactions of these regions are in the hands of these five persons they may add to the transfers as they like and they also can close their eyes when an amount from the finances of the *divān* is neglected. Therefore, in this situation, the men in authority have to have complete trust in the activities of this group.

As the development of mines mostly happened during the time of Mohammad Beyg who was the grand vizier of His Majesty Shah 'Abbās II, may God illuminate his resting place, the *āvārajeh-nevis* of the mines also developed a large establishment and his office became very important.[88]

They do not have seals and their office is of great importance.

ACCOUNTANT OF THE RECEIVERS OF THE SPECIAL PAYMENTS
mostowfi-ye arbāb al-tahāvil[89]

USUAL TITLES
Asylum of the nobility, exaltedness and excellence, glory and loftiness of the administration, he who adorns nobility, exaltedness and excellence, Mirza So-and-so.

[PLACE]
He is not a member of the council.

EMOLUMENTS
From salary and fees. Salary: 30 *tumans*. Fees: they receive from the group of district heads, equerries, and from the revenues that go to the royal treasury; per year it is estimated at 500 *tumans*.

FUNCTION
His function is to record the cash and in kind [items] that are received and collected by the royal treasury and the department heads of the workshops as well as the herds of horses, cows, sheep, and foals each one of which represent the total revenues of the district heads, herders, equerries, and the like, and to really look after them and to enter them into his own book. Also, the records of presents and confiscated property, [**60**] whatever it may be, that is transferred and entrusted to each person, are recorded in accordance with the regulations. The individual files of the daily ledgers of the workshops of whatever department it may be are checked and reviewed daily so that whenever there is a need it is enacted upon.

He has a large establishment and his office is very important.

---

88 On mining during this period see Floor, *Economy*, pp. 303-04.
89 For more details on this official, see Floor, *Fiscal History*, p. 99 and Floor-Faghfoory, *Dastur al-Moluk*, p. 122.

ADMINISTRATOR OF THE REGENT'S PERQUISITES
zābet-e dushallok-e divān-e aʿlā[90]

USUAL TITLES

Asylum of the nobility, exaltedness and excellence, glory and loftiness of the administration, he who adorns exaltedness and excellence, Mirza So-and-so.

EMOLUMENTS

From salary and fees. Salary: 100 *tuman*s. His fees with his salary are estimated to be 500 *tuman*s per year.

PLACE

Seating place on the left of His Majesty and of all the sitting council members the one sitting lowest.

FUNCTION

His function is that after the office of regent was abolished His Majesty the world conqueror the late Shah ʿAbbas confiscated the endowments, chancery fees, and fees of the regent and appointed for the registration of the said chancery fees an administrator who throughout the year received these revenues on behalf of the royal household.

CLERK OF CONFISCATED PROPERTIES AND DESIGNATED REVENUES
zābeteh-nevis-e divān-e aʿlā[91]

USUAL TITLES

Asylum of the nobility, exaltedness and excellence, glory and loftiness of the administration, he who adorns exaltedness and excellence, Mirza So-and-so.

[PLACE]

He is not a member of the royal council.

EMOLUMENTS

From salary and fees. Salary: 30 *tuman*s. His fees with salary and all his emoluments are estimated at 1,000 *tuman*s per year.

FUNCTION

His function is to record the presents and that which is received from outside and all the confiscated property, and to ensure that the registration of government property was done with total dedication.

The revenues that he receives from the subjects are of various kinds. One is the land tax, which amounts to 10 per cent. Another consists of other taxes such as the herd tax, the road tax, the tobacco excise, and fees [61] for the *dārugheh* and the like.

---

90 For more details on this official, see Floor-Faghfoory, *Dastur al-Moluk*, p. 77. For the term *doshallok* (perquisites, chancery fee) see Floor, *Fiscal History*, pp. 208-12.

91 For more details on this official, see Floor, *Fiscal History*, pp. 76-77 and Floor-Faghfoory, *Dastur al-Moluk*, p. 101.

Apart from the land tax, the transactions and the management of the recording of all the other revenues are all the responsibility of the *zābeteh-nevis* and based on his confirmation and records these were transferred and received.

This work is also one of the most important tasks and the holder of this office has to be truthful in writing, pious and knowledgeable.

ACCOUNTANT OF THE FISCAL ARREARS
mostowfi-ye baqāyā[92]

He was very important in the past and the accounting of the fiscal arrears in previous times was bestowed on some [officials] and an amount was established for salary and fees for each of them.

FUNCTION

His function had to do with those *divān* revenues that had remained with the subjects and tax payers, district managers, and tenants from previous years. It was the responsibility of the accountant of fiscal arrears and to identify and receive [them]. He had a separate office and clerks.

The minds of the department heads of the royal secretariat were at ease [knowing] that if an amount had not been transferred and had remained with the tax payers the accountant of the fiscal arrears would make out a draft. Some out of regard of the taxpayers and the administrators, some due to negligence did not transfer the *divān* revenues. This is the reason that some amounts of the *divān*'s revenues remained every year with the subjects and taxpayers. His Majesty the late Shah 'Abbas abolished the said office to take away the excuse of the chiefs of the secretariat and laid down the rule that whenever each year *divān* revenues had remained with the subjects and were not transferred he would demand compensation and its replacement from the office holders of the secretariat.

In the time of His Majesty Shah Soltān Hoseyn an accountant of fiscal arrears was appointed for some time and then again abolished.

ARCHIVIST
daftardār[93]

USUAL TITLES
Asylum of exaltedness and excellence.

EMOLUMENTS

From the salary and fees. Salary: it varies; it was 12 *tuman*s more or less. Fees: on account of the revenue assignments of the emirs, companions, and yeomen three *dinar*s and four and a half *dāng*. On account of regular salaries of the aforementioned group two and a half *dinar*s. On account of cash payment to the said group one *dinar*s and one and a half *dāng*. On account of the stipends of the emirs and some that are not retainers of the *divān* [**62**], companions, yeomen, salaries, user fees of the tax officials, tax exempt land grants, fiefs, and tax exemptions seven and a half *dinar*s. On account of leases two *dinar*s and four and a half *dāng*.

---

92 For more details on this official, see Floor, *Fiscal History*, p. 78 and Ibid., *Safavid Government*, pp. 46-47.
93 See also Floor-Faghfoory, *Dastur al-Moluk*, p. 133.

FUNCTION

His function is to protect the royal books that are in the secretariat from being eaten by mice and from dirt and dust as required. Each one of them is kept at a fixed place and he does not allow an outsider [to the administration] to see [them]. After the year has come to an end the book of that year is taken to the storage space, where they are kept. In the morning, before the department heads are present in the secretariat he arranges the books in their places and when the clerks are finished with the books and go outside of the secretariat he closed the books and kept them so that nothing would happen to them.

SCRIBES OF THE ROYAL SECRETARIAT
'azabān-e daftar-khāneh-ye homāyun[94]

USUAL TITLES
Asylum of exaltedness and excellence.

EMOLUMENTS

From salary and fees. Salary: it varies. Fees: on account of the revenue assignments of the emirs, companions, and yeomen three *dinar*s per *tuman*. On account of the regular salaries of the aforementioned group two *dinar*s. On account of cash payments of the said group one *dinar*s. On account of the stipends of the emirs and some who are not retainers of the *divān*, companions, yeomen, salaries, user fee (*haqq al-sa'y*) [of the tax officials], tax exempt land grants, fiefs, tax exemptions six *dinar*s. On account of leases two *dinar*s and two *dāng*.

FUNCTION

The function of this group is to perform secretarial duties and assist the chiefs of the secretariat. They are charged to handle every matter that is peculiar to the secretariat.

***

From the appelation of the chief accountant of the state domains up to here what has been written all are department heads and chiefs of the royal secretariat. Everyone of this group has to be present in the secretariat and to work on his responsibilities except for the vizier of trusts of the Fourteen Infallible Ones, p.b.o.t., the vizier of Isfahan, the *monshi al-mamālek*, although they are also men of the pen, but they are not working in the secretariat and have to do their tasks in their own house.

In the time of His Majesty the late Shah Tahmasp [I], may [God's] grace and forgiveness be upon him, [**63**] the [royal] secretariat was perfectly organized. It is well-known that he [i.e. the shah] had sat for 30 years in the secretariat, and had seen to the order, excellence and management of the affairs of the secretariat. What is clear is that whenever they were caused to take a humble person or a low person, first his book and account notebook are confiscated, in which the management of the properties of each one are all registered. Once the Crown had achieved stability the kingdom was extended. All the sources of income of the king were recorded in his books and

---

94 See also Floor-Faghfoory, *Dastur al-Moluk*, pp. 81, 134, 185, 281.

from there transfers and claims are made. The secretariat will have the order of the royal treasury. When some trusted, knowledgeable and esteemed persons are overseeing the management of that treasury it will, of course, thrive and it will not be the cause of the wasting of the *divān*'s finances. When the treasurers have emptied the treasury and have made it lusterless, the army and subjects are both neglected and kingship which exists due to the army and subjects will fall.

Each morning His Majesty came in person to the secretariat and was there until noon and he ate his food there, which they now call 'office fare', with the department heads and afterwards he walked gracefully to the harem.

For each of the office holders there a special place had been assigned and a large felt floor covering had been spread out on which they sat. Every time that His Majesty came to the place of each of them he took his seat on the felt [floor covering] of that [particular] department head.

This group always has to be dignified and honorable, and because of their dignity and the proximity of the king nobody could add more [importance] to that group. But when that group does not enjoy the esteem of kings, and because this group were not themselves an army and apart from the pen and the pen sharpener they did not have war and fighting tools, the military would dispute with them about the collection of revenues and every day they would be beaten and whipped by each tribe and having become without respect and discouraged by their own occupation was the cause of the disorder of the [royal] secretariat.

If some of this group commits a crime, if it is a group of subordinates, first its chief investigated it, if it is the chief, then the king himself will investigate and punish him.

This group should be given adequate revenues that are sufficient for the expenditures of each one [**64**] so that except for secretarial work they have nothing else on their mind. When they are hungry, then the only means available to them is to defraud the *divān*'s revenues which are in their hands. If they are greedy and crooked, whenever they do not abandon their actions due to admonition and reprimand, then there are no other means than to interfere with him. It is well-known that His Majesty Shah Tahmasp [I] gave instructions not to give the management of the [royal] secretariat to the Tafaroshi and Farahani clan.

The fees of the department heads of the royal secretariat that are collected from the original assessment of the revenue assignments of the emirs, companions, and the like is such that these have been listed under each one's name. That what is taken from the estimated part of the revenue assignments of each group as fees is done in the following way:

The grand vizier, 220 *dinar*s, the chief accountant of the state domains 30 *dinar*s, the chief of the royal correspondence (*monshi al-mamālek*) 25 *dinar*s, the chief accountant of the army likewise; the steward of the [royal] secretariat four *dinar*s and four *dāng*, the head clerk of the [royal] secretariat five *dinar*s, the chief of disbursements (*sāheb-towjih*) seven and a half *dinar*s, the clerk of receipts accountable (*sarkhatt-nevis*) five *dinar*s and two *dang*, the clerks of the assets (*āvārajeh-nevis*) seven and a half *dinar*s, the archivist two and a half *dinar*s.

***

VIZIER OF THE ROYAL WORKSHOPS
vazir-e boyutāt[95]

USUAL TITLES
Asylum of the vizierate, exaltedness and excellence, glory and loftiness of the administration, he who adorns exaltedness and excellence, Mirza So-and-so.

[PLACE]
He is not a member of the [royal] council.

EMOLUMENTS
From a salary, rations and fees. Salary: 80 *tuman*s. Rations: each day one plate; its value is 1,000 *dinar*s and per year it comes to 36 *tuman*s. Fees: recently it has become customary that from the revenues that are given for the expenditures of the workshops he receives 30 *dinar*s per *tuman*s.

FUNCTION
His function is that on a daily basis he inspects the individual files of the daily ledgers and put his mark on them; thereafter they are submitted to the high steward for his seal. The management of all department heads and the workers of the workshops and manufactories as well as of the use and expenditure of the royal manufactories is his responsibility. [**65**]

VIZIER OF THE TRIBES OF ISFAHAN
vazir-e qarā alus[96]

USUAL TITLES
Asylum of exaltedness and excellence, he who adorns exaltedness and excellence, Mirza So-and-so.

[PLACE]
He is not a member of the [royal] council.

EMOLUMENTS
It is estimated that with his salary and other [sources] he has 50 *tuman*s per year.

FUNCTION
His function is to supervise the revenues of the nomadic tribes and some of the clans and pastoralists of the black tents that are living in the environs of Isfahan and the transactions of that group are with him and drafts made out on this group are confirmed and recorded by him.

---

95 For more details on this official, see Floor-Faghfoory, *Dastur al-Moluk*, pp. 214-15.
96 See also Floor-Faghfoory, *Dastur al-Moluk*, pp. 108.

VIZIER OF THE MARCHES OF ISFAHAN
vazir-e sarhadd[97]

USUAL TITLES
The same as of the vizier of the tribes of Isfahan.

[PLACE]
He is not a member of the [royal] council.

EMOLUMENTS
It is estimated at 200 *tuman*s per year.

[FUNCTION]
The management of the revenues of a group that is at the borders of Isfahan is kept separate from the original assessment of Isfahan and is his responsibility.

VIZIER OF THE LAWFULLY ACQUIRED PROPERTIES
vazir-e halāl[98]

[An office] created in the time of Shah Soltān Hoseyn, because His Majesty wanted the expenditures of his department to be from a religiously lawful source. He [therefore] allotted some districts with some wealth and appointed a vizier of the lawfully acquired properties for the management of the transactions of the said districts.

ACCOUNTANT OF [THE ENDOWMENTS OF] THE FOURTEEN INFALLIBLE ONES P.B.U.T.
mostowfi-ye chahārdeh ma'sum salavāt 'aleyhom ajma'eyn

USUAL TITLES
Asylum of nobility, exaltedness and excellence, he who adorns nobility, exaltedness and excellence, Mirza So-and-so.

[PLACE]
He is not a member of the [royal] council.

EMOLUMENTS
From salary and fees. Salary 100 *tuman*s. His usual fees [yield] 100 *tuman*s per year. His total income and benefits are 250 *tuman*s per year.

FUNCTION
The transaction of all endowments of the Fourteen Infallible Ones p.b.u.t. were all his responsibility and all [their revenues] were collected from the subjects and tax payers [authorized by] his seal, writing and draft. He wrote the royal orders of these [**66**] inhabitants of the Abode of the Lote tree in the [same] manner as has been shown under the entry of the chief religious authority (*sadr*). His position was a very important one.

---

97 See also Floor-Faghfoory, *Dastur al-Moluk*, p. 110.
98 See also Floor-Faghfoory, *Dastur al-Moluk*, p. 68.

ACCOUNTANT OF THE STATE [ENDOWMENTS]
mostowfi-ye [mowqufāt-e] mamālek-e mahruseh[99]

USUAL TITLES
Asylum of nobility, exaltedness and excellence, he who adorns exaltedness and excellence, Mirza So-and-so.

[PLACE]
He sits in the [royal] council and on the left side of His Majesty and lower than [blank]

EMOLUMENTS
From a salary and fees. Salary: [blank]. Fees: [blank]

FUNCTION
His function was very important and the management of all transactions of the endowments in the God-protected kingdom, be it whether the king or others had deeded them, all were under his responsibility. Royal orders and commands of the department heads, the agents and the like who have a fixed pension from these aforementioned endowments or a fixed payment all have to be written by him.

This office holder is very important and the record-keeping of the *sadr*s was with him.

CLERK OF THE GUARDS
keshik-nevis-e divān-e aʿlā[100]

USUAL TITLES
The same as of the *vazir-e mowqufat*.

EMOLUMENTS
From a salary, 30 *tuman*s.

FUNCTION
His function is as follows. Each night there are emirs, royal companions and retainers of the royal household of every department present to guard His Majesty. Their names, which the crier of the guard reads out loud, are written in individual files. In the morning of that same day these aforementioned files are submitted to H.M and entrusted to each department as appropriate. When any of the retainers who are on permanent duty and the like were not present for their guard duty, he records the period of the absent days of that group and makes out a withdrawal transfer under their name so that no one can shirk his duty.

He is not a member of the [royal] council. **[67]**

---

99 See also Floor-Faghfoory, *Dastur al-Moluk*, p. 70.
100 See also Floor-Faghfoory, *Dastur al-Moluk*, pp. 98, 106, 141, 147, 155

RECORDER OF PRESENTS
pishkesh-nevis-e divān- a'lā[101]

USUAL TITLES

Asylum of exaltedness and excellence, he who adorns exaltedness and excellence, Mirza So-and-so.

EMOLUMENTS

From a salary and fees. Salary: 20 *tuman*s. Fees: from the regular and irregular presents that are brought for the royal household throughout the year his fees are 100 *dinar*s per *tuman*.

The senior accountants call the regular presents New Year's presents, because it is customary that each year the emirs, provincial governors and the like send these [at that time]. Per year seven thousand and six hundred *tuman*s and irregular [presents] twelve thousand *tuman*s are stipulated. On this basis his fees from these two revenues of presents are 250 *tuman*s per year and his total income is 300 *tuman*s per year.

FUNCTION

His function is to maintain the records of the presents that come from all parts [of the kingdom] to the royal household and he records all of them in his book. If there is a shortfall in the regular presents then based on his confirmation under the name of each person that has not sent [it] a draft is sent [to make up for the shortfall].

[PLACE]

He is not a member of the [royal] council.

INSPECTOR OF THE ROYAL TREASURY
moshref-e khazāneh-ye 'āmereh[102]

USUAL TITLES

Asylum of exaltedness and excellence, he who adorns exaltedness and excellence, Mirza So-and-so.

[PLACE]

He is not a member of the [royal] council.

EMOLUMENTS

From a salary, rations and fees. Salary: 50 *tuman*s. Rations: per day one plate, value 1,000 *dinar*s, and per year 36 Tabrizi *tuman*s. Fees: [blank] **[68]**

FUNCTION

His function is to maintain the records of the transactions of the royal treasury, i.e. what has entered into the royal treasury in cash and kind. All of these had to be recorded by him and to be entered into his own book. The holder of this office has always been esteemed and honored by the king.

---

101   For more details on this official, see Floor-Faghfoory, *Dastur al-Moluk*, pp. 157-59 and Floor, *Fiscal History*, pp. 84-85.

102   For this and the other inspectors mentioned hereafter, see also Floor-Faghfoory, *Dastur al-Moluk*, Index and TM, pp. 93-94.

INSPECTOR OF THE AVIARY
moshref-e qush-khāneh

USUAL TITLES

The same as of the *moshref* of the treasury.

[PLACE]

He is not a member of the [royal] council.

EMOLUMENTS

From a revenue assignment and fees. revenue assignment, 30 *tuman*s and its estimate based on four *dinar*s per *dinar*s. Fees, also from the salary of the falconers, the emirs, and the border governors who send falcons as a present to the royal household. His total income is 300 *tuman*s per year.

FUNCTION

His function is to register the pay, wages and cash payments of the falconers, which were all recorded in his book.

INSPECTOR OF THE TAILORING WORKSHOP
moshref-e qeychāchi-khāneh

USUAL TITLES

Asylum of exaltedness and excellence, he who adorns exaltedness and excellence, Mirza So-and-so.

EMOLUMENTS:

From a salary and rations. Salary 34 *tuman*s. Rations per day one plate and its annual value is nine *tuman*s.

All his benefits together with his fees come to 100 *tuman*s per year.

FUNCTION

His function is to keep the records of the tailoring department. The holder of this office had to be very good in the art of short-hand accounting and writing.

INSPECTOR OF THE STABLE
moshref-e establ

USUAL TITLES

The same as of the inspector of the tailoring department. **[69]**

EMOLUMENTS

Salary and rations. Salary: 40 *tuman*s, before it was 60 *tuman*s that had been settled on him from the revenues of Lahejan, what is now collected is 56 *tuman*s. Rations: per day half a plate, [a value of] 18 *tuman*s [per year].

All his emoluments with fees and minor benefits amount to 150 *tuman*s per year.

FUNCTION

His function is to keep the records of the royal stable with horses, camels and their fodder and it was totally his responsibility. He had to make daily entries into his book.

INSPECTOR OF THE ARSENAL
moshref-e qur-khāneh

USUAL TITLES

The same as of the *moshref* of the stable.

EMOLUMENTS

From salary and rations. Salary: 40 *tuman*s. Rations: one plate whose daily value is 1,000 *dinar*s and per year 36 *tuman*s.

His total emoluments, together with minor benefits from fees and the like, amount to 100 *tuman*s per year.

FUNCTION

His function is to keep the records of the equipment of the royal arsenal and in the arsenals and forts wherever they may be and he records them into his book and acts upon it.

INSPECTORS OF THE CAMEL STABLES, THE PANTRY, AND BEVERAGE DEPARTMENT
moshrefān-e shotor-khān va havich-khāneh va sharbat-khāneh

USUAL TITLES

These three persons' titles are like those of the stable inspector.

EMOLUMENTS

The emoluments of the inspector of the camel stables are 20 *tuman*s and his rations are half a plate. The salary of the inspector of the pantry is 15 *tuman*s and his rations are one plate. The salary of the inspector of the beverage department is 30 *tuman*s and his rations are one and quarter plate.

The emoluments of each one with the usual fees and occasional fees (*havā'i*) is estimated at 100 *tuman*s per year.

INSPECTOR OF THE MINT
moshref-e zarrāb-khāneh

USUAL TITLES

The same as the inspector of the stable.

EMOLUMENTS

From salary, rations and fees. Salary: previously it was 12 *tuman*s and now 15 *tuman*s. Rations per day one plate and its daily value is 1,000 *dinar*s and per year 36 *tuman*s [**70**] Fees. On account of those that are not official, but have become customary; from gold, from which *ashrafi* coins are struck in the Mint, per *methqāl* 10 *dinar*s and from copper, of which copper coins are made, per *mann* of shah weight likewise 10 *dinar*s. On account of what the inspectors have invented now, i.e. to strike 'white money' from silver, per *methqāl* half a *dinar*.

His total emoluments with minor benefits are 200 *tuman*s per year.

*

The intention of the kings in assigning fees concerning h [the rest is missing]

***

[CATEGORY TEN]

[The missing text[103] is followed by a few sentences introducing the governor-general of the Qandahar and his subordinate emirs, as is clear from the pattern in what follows. I have kept remarks on this list of governors as short as possible, because detailed additional information is given in the Commentary section for each individual entry.]

[THE TITLES OF THE] GEORGIAN [VICE-ROY] IN THE TIME OF SHAH SOLTĀN HOSEYN WERE WRITTEN AS FOLLOWS:

Asylum of the kingdom, province and authority, pomp, majesty of the administration, awakener of courage and valor, his excellency, emir of emirs, scion of kings, loyal and devoted royal slave of the threshold of the Imamate, he who adorns kingdom, province, authority, pomp, majesty, courage, valor and felicity Shahnavaz Khan, viceroy of Georgian Kartli and commander-in-chief of Iran, governor-general of the Abode of Rest Qandahar and the Abode of Faith Kerman and governor of Gereshk. (The viceroy of Georgian Kartli and commander-in-chief of Iran and governor-general of Qandahar and Kerman and governor of Gereshk).[104]

Qandahar is a border province belonging to the Qezelbāsh[105] and is situated between the provinces of the Qezelbāsh [kingdom] and India. Its citadel is totally fortified and strong so that there is no other impregnable citadel like it in the kingdom of Iran and taking it is very difficult by way of war and fighting and kings have always taken this citadel without a fight.

---

103   It is not known with which geographical location this list of administrative jurisdictions should have started. The TM starts with the region of Azerbaijan, which was governed by four governor-generals (Tabriz, Chokhur-e Sa'd, Qarabagh and Shirvan) and their subordinate governors. Then follows the region of Khorasan that was governed by five governor-generals (Herat, Mashhad, Qandahar, Merv, and Seystan) and their subordinate governors. Although with additions and variations this information is also found in this text. Then follow six governates-general (Astarabad, Gilan, Kerman, [Persian] Iraq, Kurdestan and Fars), which are entirely missing from this text. I do not know where the missing information originally was placed within the original text, which, as I note, currently is not properly organized. This is probably due to its incomplete nature so that whoever preserved this manuscript for posterity tried to put it in the order that he thought best.
104   On the viceroy of Georgia and of other parts, see Floor, *Safavid Government*, pp. 81-90.
105   The use of the term *Qezelbāsh* hails back to the early origins of the Safavid state when its troops mainly consisted of the tribes that adhered to the organization of the Safavid Sufi order and because they wore red Sufi hats they were called *Qezelbāsh* (red heads) by the Ottomans. By the end of the Safavid era and even thereafter the term is used to refer to Persian military might in general.

EMOLUMENTS

It comes to an amount of 16,799 *tuman*s and some, which shows a deficit of 1,936 *tuman*s and 1,000 *dinar*s. Another amount, on account of Chinese asafetida etc. and irregular fees, has not been fixed and is unspecified. He has an income estimated at 22,000 *tuman*s. [**71**] In the time of 'Ali Mardān Khān,[106] who had been rejected by this clan and went to India, its annual income was 30,000 *tuman*s and equal to that he also had an income from irregular fees.

RETAINERS

1,123 persons and the rule is that each year a group of members of Qezelbāsh tribes are appointed to take turn at garrison duty, which is to guard the aforementioned castle and to repulse enemies and have to go on mission there to do so.

CHIEF OF THE KARI VA YAKI TRIBE [107]

TITLES
Asylum of the province, So-and-so Soltan.

EMOLUMENTS
An amount of 141 Tabrizi *tuman*s.

RETAINERS
25 men.

GOVERNOR OF BOST AND GERESHK[108]

TITLES
Asylum of the province and authority, he who adorns, So-and-so Soltan.

EMOLUMENTS
An amount of 2,472 *tuman*s and 3,000 Tabrizi *dinar*s.

RETAINERS
314 persons.

---

106 'Ali Mardān Khān Zik felt threatened by his enemies at court and in 1637 handed Qandahar to the Moghuls and entered into their service.

107 The TM, pp. 103, 169 has K.ri and Lukeh instead of Yaki. I have not been able to identify these two groups. They were grouped together with some other tribes and districts, viz. Badghis, Timuri, 'Ali-Khvajeh [and?] Mir 'Arif Baluch. On the Timuri tribe see Ludwig W. Adamec, *Historical and Politcal Gazetteer of Afghanistan* 5 vols. (Graz, 1973), vol. 3, pp. 416-19.

108 Bost is not mentioned in the TM.

GOVERNOR OF ZAMINDAVAR[109]
TITLES
Asylum of the emirate and government, So-and-so Soltān.

Although the word *eyālat* is written for those who have the title of *khān*, [in this case] it is because the governance of that group has been given to [the chief of] the Baluch tribes such as 'Āref Soltān.

EMOLUMENTS
An amount of 2,258 *tuman*s and 9,000 odd *dinar*s. He also has an irregular income that is called 'unquantified'.

GOVERNOR OF THE ABDALI TRIBE[110]
TITLES
Asylum of the emirate and government, So-and-so Soltān. [**72**]

EMOLUMENTS
An amount of 1,324 *tuman*s and 9,000 *dinar*s and some regular and irregular [fees], which is called 'unquantified', due to revenues of the Kāferi, Kushi etc. tribe[111] that he also has.

The number of his retainers is not known.

CHIEF OF THE HUD JABALI, GHILZAY AND NASERI TRIBES WHO LIVE IN QANDAHAR AND THE TORMAK MOUNTAINS[112]
TITLES
Asylum of the emirate and government, he who adorns, So-and-so Soltān.

The chieftainship formerly was with Mir Weys who was the instigator of all the strife and ruin [in Iran].[113]

---

109 Its governor had 2,015 *tuman*s and 306 *dinar*s as emoluments as well as an unquantified amount on account of trees (*ashjar*?). He had to have 463 men. In TM, p. 103, 'Āref Soltān is not mentioned under Zamindavar, but under K.ri va Lukeh (see above).

110 See for this tribe the Commentary section.

111 Kushis or Kuchis, meaning 'nomads' in Persian, are a nomadic Pashtun tribe, who moved between Afghanistan and Pakistan to graze their herds. The Kaferis probably are those living in Kafiristan (now Nuristan) in N. E. Afghanistan.

112 I have neither been able to identify the Hud Jabali and Naseri tribes of Qandahar nor the Tormak Mountains. The Ghilzi (sing. Ghilzay) tribal confederation groups the Pashtun clans of the east, whose territory extended from Ghazni and Kalat-e Ghilzay eastward into the Indus valley. They had a special relationship with Qandahar, where the chiefs of the Ghilzi held the function of *kalāntar* at the end of the Safavid period. Lockhart, *Fall*, pp. 80-81. On the Ghilzi in the 20th century see Klaus Ferdinand, "Ost-Afghanische Nomadismus - ein Beitrag zur Anpassungsfahigkeit der Nomaden," in Willy Kraus ed., *Nomadismus als Entwicklungsproblem* (Bielefeld: Bertelsman Universitatsverlag, Reinhard Mohn, 1969) and Richard Tapper, "Nomadism in Modern Afghanistan: Asset or Anachronism?" in Louis Dupree and Linette Albert eds., *Afghanistan in the 1970s* (New York: Praeger Publishers, 1974), pp. 126-131.

113 On Mir Weys see Floor, *Afghan Occupation*, p. 39; Lockhart, *Fall*, pp. 85-92.

EMOLUMENTS
An amount of 255 odd *tuman*s.

RETAINERS
70 men.

GOVERNOR OF THE DISTRICT OF SEYSTAN
TITLES
Asylum of the province and authority, pomp of the administration, he who adorns the province and authority, So-and-so Soltan.

EMOLUMENTS
An amount of 1,886 *tuman*s and 2,000 odd *dinar*s.

RETAINERS
783 persons.

In the time of Shah Shah Soltān Hoseyn when Kerman was the seat of [government of] a governor-general, some of the time Shāhnavāz Khān and Khosrow Khān and ʿAliqoli Khān, *vāli* and sons of *vāli*s of Georgia, and Mohammad Zamān Khān Beygdeli Shāmlu, commander of the royal household troops,[114] were governors-general there. The governor of Seystan was the sub-governor[115] of that group and came forth from the family of subordinate emirs of the governor-general of Qandahar. If not, when there was not a governor appointed at Kerman, the governor of Seystan was the sub-governor of the governor-general of Qandahar.

GOVERNOR-GENERAL OF KUHGILUYEH AND THE SUBORDINATE EMIRS[116]
The number of his subordinate emirs is seven persons and the total emoluments of the said governor-general together with his subordinate emirs is an amount of 22,852 Tabrizi *tuman*s and the regular retainers in total number 2,896 persons.

---

114 Mohammad Zamān Khān Beygdeli Shāmlu was commander of the royal household troops during 1711-1714. He was governor-general of Kerman in 1123/1711; the Georgian officials mentioned served as governor-general of Kerman before him (see the Commentary).

115 The Safavid state was divided into various jurisdictions. The largest ones were under a *beygler-beygi* or governor-general. Because he had several governors of lower rank in his jurisdiction the governor-general also had the title of *amir al-omarā*, because he was the chief of all the emirs in his jurisdiction. Below the governor-general were governors who had the rank of *hākem*, often with the title of *khān*. Lower-ranked governors had the title of *soltān*, and the lowest-ranked governor was the *qol-beygi*. For more information see Floor, *Safavid Government*, pp. 90-105.

116 According to TM, p. 104 he had nine subordinate governors, who together had 12,000 *tuman*s as emoluments and had to have 2,000 men. This means that six have not been mentioned by this text, or, what is more likely, that one or more pages are missing.

GOVERNOR-GENERAL ABOVE-MENTIONED[117]
USUAL TITLES

Asylum of the province and authority, pomp and majesty of the administration, his excellency, emir of emirs, he who adorns the province, authority, pomp, majesty and felicity, So-and-so Khan.

Shah Soltān Hoseyn bestowed on Aslān Khān, the governor-general of the said province, the title of *gholām-zādeh-ye dirin va* [**73**] *mokhles-e 'aqidat-ā'in*, in addition to the abovementioned titles.

Towards the end of the reign of His Majesty the office of vizier of Shiraz with all the *divān* revenues of the province of Fars, which amounted to 100,000 *tuman*s, was bestowed on Mohammad Bāqer Beyg, son of Dāyeh Khātun. Thereafter the governor-generalship of Kuhgiluyeh and the whole province of Fars, with the regulations as for the governor-generalship of Khorasan, was given to Lotf 'Ali Khān, the confidante of His Majesty [the rest is missing]

GOVERNOR OF THE DISTRICT OF MANJAVAN [?] [118]
TITLES
Asylum of the emirate, So-and-so Soltan.

EMOLUMENTS
An amount of 251 *tuman*s and 9,000 odd *dinar*s.

RETAINERS
51 persons.

[Probably some text is missing here as the following district does not belong to Fars, but to Azerbaijan.]

GOVERNOR OF THE DISTRICT OF QEZEL AGHAJ[119]
TITLES
The same.

EMOLUMENTS
An amount of 313 odd *tuman*s.

RETAINERS
88 persons.

---

117 According to TM, p. 104, the governor-general of Kuhgiluyeh had 6,747 *tuman*s and 7,562 2/3 *dinar*s as emoluments and had to have 500 men.

118 Manjavān is a district unknown to me that is probably situated in Chokhur-e Sa'd. It is not mentioned in the TM.

119 This coastal district is situated in the northern part of the Talesh region, now part of the Republic of Azerbaijan.

GOVERNOR OF THE DISTRICT OF P.S.K [120]

TITLES
The same.

EMOLUMENTS
An amount of 62 odd *tuman*s.

RETAINERS
Their number it is not known and since olden times it has not been specified.

[Probably some text is missing missing here. According to the TM, the district of P.s.k is part of Azerbaijan, however, given its location, it may also have been part of Chokhur-e Saʿd.]

[GOVERNOR-GENERAL OF CHOKHUR-E SAʿD AND THE SUBORDINATE EMIRS] [121]

The governor-general of Chokhur-e Saʿd, which they also call Erevan, and his subordinate emirs. The total emoluments of that governor-general with that of his subordinate emirs is an amount of [blank] and the number of his subordinate emirs is nine persons. [74]

GOVERNOR-GENERAL ABOVEMENTIONED [122]

TITLES
Asylum of the province and authority, pomp and majesty of the administration, his excellency, emir of emirs, he who adorns the province, authority, pomp, majesty and felicity, So-and-so Khan.

EMOLUMENTS
An amount of 20,530 Tabrizi *tuman*s.

RETAINERS
2,640 persons.

Chokhur-e Saʿd is the border of the territory belonging to the Qezelbāsh, this side of the Ārpah Chāpi River, which passes through Erevan, is inside the protective cover and the border of Qezelbāsh and the other side of the said river is the border of the Rumi (i.e. Ottoman) kingdom.

---

120 The orthography of this district is uncertain, both P.s.k and B.s.k occur. Monshi, *Tarikh*, pp. 687-88 and Vahid, *Tarikh*, p. 162 list a Qalʿeh-ye P.s.k, which is situated near Maku. Monajjem, *Tarikh*, pp. 283, 342 has Qalʿeh-ye B.s.k. According to TM, p. 101, the name was Qalʿeh-ye P.sh.k, whose governor had 57 *tuman*s and 5,090 *dinar*s as emoluments and had to have 15 men.

121 According to TM, p. 101 the governor-general had eight sub-governors, who together had 25,910 *tuman*s and 6,326 *dinar*s as emoluments.

122 According to the TM, p. 101, its governor-general had 20,539 *tuman*s as emoluments and had to have 2,860 men.

GOVERNOR OF NAKHJEVAN DISTRICT[123]
TITLES
Asylum of the province and authority, pomp and majesty of the administration, his excellency, he who adorns the province, authority, pomp, majesty and felicity, So-and-so Khan.

EMOLUMENTS
an amount of 3,138 *tuman*s and 2,000 odd *dinar*s.

RETAINERS
832 persons.

GOVERNOR OF DARVALAKIS AND OF THE HARAMILU TRIBE[124]
TITLES
Asylum of the emirate, So-and-so Soltan.

EMOLUMENTS
256 *tuman*s and 4,000 odd *dinar*s.

RETAINERS
109 persons.

GOVERNOR OF ZARUZBIL AND KILANI[125]
TITLES
Asylum of the emirate and government, he who adorns, So-and-so Soltan.

EMOLUMENTS
an amount of 311 odd *tuman*s.

RETAINERS
205 persons. [75]

---

123 According to the TM, p. 101 its governor had 3,461 *tuman*s and 4,346 *dinar*s as emoluments and had to have 799 men. The term *tumān* used to denote certain districts in Iran came in vogue after the Mongol conquest. Normally the term would refer to an army group of 10,000, but it is unlikely that Nakhjevan could have supplied that many soldiers. It is more likely that the term indicates that the district was able to support 10,000 soldiers with the necessary pasture, fodder and other supplies.

124 I have not been able to identify the name and location of Darvalakes and the same holds for the Haramilu tribe. The latter perhaps is a copyist's error for Jaramilu, see Commentary.

125 Its governor had 438 *tuman*s and 4,675 *dinar*s as emoluments and had to have 200 men.

GOVERNOR OF THE BAYAZID FORT[126]

TITLES
Asylum of the emirate and government, he who adorns, So-and-so Soltan.

EMOLUMENTS
343 Tabrizi *tuman*s.

RETAINERS
100 persons.

GOVERNOR OF THE SA'DLU OF FORT AGHCHEH[127]

TITLES
Asylum of the emirate, So-and-so Soltan.

EMOLUMENTS
an amount of 165 *tuman*s and 6,000 odd *dinar*s.

RETAINERS
54 persons.

GOVERNOR OF MAKU WHOM THEY ALSO CALL THE GOVERNOR OF BAYAT[128]

TITLES
The same.

EMOLUMENTS
An amount of 1,043 *tuman*s and 5,000 odd *dinar*s.

RETAINERS
150 persons.

GOVERNOR OF SHADILU[129]

TITLES
The same.

EMOLUMENTS
An amount of 20 Tabrizi *tuman*s.

---

126 According to TM, p. 101 the Bayazid fort held 100 men and its governor's emoluments were 306 *tuman*s and 3,487 *dinar*s.

127 The Sa'dlu were a Kurdish tribe of whom various members served as governor in the Safavid administration, see, e.g., Molla Jalal, *Ruznameh*, p. 269 (Nafas Soltan Sa'dlu). Qal'eh-ye Aghcheh or Aghcheh Qal'eh is a border fort in north-western Azerbaijan, see, e.g., Monshi, *Tarikh*, vol. 2, pp. 667, 688, 742, 1025.

128 According to the TM, p. 101, the governor of Maku had 580 *tuman*s and 4,346 *dinar*s as emoluments and had to maintain 150 men.

129 This refers to the Kurdish Shadidlu tribe. According to the TM, p. 101 its chief had 20 *tuman*s as emoluments and had to have 30 men.

GOVERNOR OF THE DONBOLI KURDS[130]

TITLES

The same.

EMOLUMENTS

An amount of 10 Tabrizi *tuman*s.

RETAINERS

40 persons. [**76**]

GOVERNOR OF KURLUK [131]

TITLES

The same.

EMOLUMENTS

An amount of 73 *tuman*s and 1,000 odd *dinar*s.

RETAINERS

50 persons.

Governor-general of the province of Shirvan and his subordinate emirs

The total income of the said governor-general and his subordinate emirs an amount [blank] and his subordinate emirs number six persons.[132]

GOVERNOR-GENERAL ABOVE-MENTIONED[133]

TITLES

Out of respect for the fact that the custodianship of the tomb of Joneyd, who is the father of Heydar, the father of the Solomon-like Shah Esmāʿil,[134] may God have mercy on him, is in the charge of the governor-generals of Shirvan they are written as follows:

Asylum of custodianship, province and authority, pomp and majesty of the administration, his excellency, emir of the emirs, he who adorns custodianship, province, authority, pomp, majesty,

---

130 Moli-ye Akrad probably is a copyist's error, because the TM, pp. 101, 165 has Donboli-ye Akrad, which makes more sense. The Donboli district was a separate tribal district in Azerbaijan, near Khoy, on the border with Ottoman Turkey.

131 I have not been able to identify Kurluk.

132 According to the TM, p. 102 the governor-general of Shirvan had six subordinate governors.

133 According to the TM, p. 102 the governor-general of Shirvan had 21,983 *tuman*s and 9,033 *dinar*s as emoluments and had to have 2,581 men.

134 On Soltān Joneyd, Soltān Heydar and Shah Esmāʿil see e.g. Michel Mazzaoui, *The Origins of the Safawids* (Wiesbaden, 1972).

and felicity So-and-so Khan, custodian of the many splendored tomb of the Lord of the Sufis and Pole of the mystics Soltan Joneyd.

EMOLUMENTS
An amount of 21,986 and odd *tuman*s.

RETAINERS
2,581 persons.

GOVERNOR OF THE DISTRICT OF DARBAND[135]

TITLES
Asylum of the emirate and government, he who adorns the emirate and government, So-and-so Soltan.

EMOLUMENTS
An amount of 7,790 *tuman*s and 5,000 and odd *dinar*s.

RETAINERS
1,200 persons.

Darband is at the border of Qezelbāsh territory. Darband until Niyāzābād,[136] which is on the coast of the Caspian Sea which they also call the Green Sea, is a distance of four *farsakh*s and from there one goes in a space of eight days with a ship from the coast of Niyāzābād [77] to the coast of Astrakhan, which they also call Hājji Tarkhān and which is in the kingdom of the Russians. The said sea is contiguous with the Sea of Mazandaran. The provinces of Dār al-Marz and the [two] Gilans, which are Qezelbāsh territory, are situated on the coast of the abovementioned sea until [it reaches] Astarabad and Mini Qeshlāq, whose inhabitants are Turkmen. From the other side it is adjoined with the steppe, which is the abode of the Qalmāq. The river Atil [Volga] is also called Adil and runs into the said sea and is the winter-quarters of the Qalmāq tribe.

It is well-known that the above-mentioned river in winter is sometimes frozen so that the Qalmāq tribe lives on it and uses it as winter-quarters. In the spring season that ice reverbates loudly three times. The first time, the said group, which has made its winter grounds there, makes ready to migrate. The second time, they move and the third time the ice breaks and floats away.

It is quite well-known that when they suspect that the ice will break, they make a dog race on it; if the ice makes a noise it will break. So that now, when saying the famous proverb: "*mara sang ruye yakh kardeh'i*"[137], it is [actually] that same 'dog [*sag*] on the ice', where [instead] they say 'stone [*sang*] on ice.'

Two corners of the Darband citadel are situated in the sea. A dike had been built by Anushirvan from its side until Astarabad of which at present some signs are [still] to be seen, because of that the Russians and the Qalmāq, who are called the green tribe, and Sayyed al-Sājedin Imām Zeyn

---

135 According to the TM, p. 102 the governor of Darband had 6,487 *tuman*s and 3,955 *dinar*s as emoluments and had to have 1,600 men.

136 Niyazabad (Nizovoi in Russian), port south of Darband. One of the few ports on the West Coast of the Caspian Sea and not a very ideal one. For a description of this port see G. F. Müller, *Sammlung russischer Geschichte* 9 vols. (St. Petersburg, 1732-1764), vol. 4, pp. 103-07.

137 Literally: have you put us like a stone on ice? Meaning: have you shamed us by making us look like a stone on ice?

al-'Ābedin p.b.u.h. mentions in the complete book in 'the prayer of the border people' this tribe, cannot come to the provinces of Azerbaijan and Gilan.

GOVERNOR OF AGHDASH AND CHAMESHGEZEK[138]

TITLES

Asylum of the emirate.

EMOLUMENTS

180 Tabrizi *tuman*s without the 'unquantified' amount.

RETAINERS

30 persons.

GOVERNOR OF ALAPA'UT[139]

TITLES

Asylum of the emirate and government, he who adorns, So-and-so Soltan. [78]

EMOLUMENTS

1,134 Tabrizi *tuman*s

RETAINERS

230 persons.

GOVERNOR OF ARASH AND SHEKI[140]

TITLES

Asylum of the emirate and government, he who adorns emirate and government, So-and-so Soltan.

EMOLUMENTS

An amount of 2,121 *tuman*s and 4,450 *dinar*s. The estimate of the original assessment, if it is on the basis of four *dinar*s per *dinar*s, is estimated at 8,500 Tabrizi [*tuman*s].

RETAINERS

355 persons

---

138 According to the TM, p. 102 he had 1,002 *tuman*s and 6,195 *dinar*s as emoluments and had to have 30 men.
139 The Alapa'ut chief had 8,084 *tuman*s and 4,727 *dinar*s as emoluments and had to have 230 men. TM, p. 102.
140 According to TM, p. 102 the governor had 8,476 tumans and 2,465 dinars as emoluments and had to have 355 men.

GOVERNOR OF QOBEH, QOLHAN AND SALIYAN[141]

TITLES

Asylum of the province and authority, pomp and justice of the administration, he who adorns the province and authority, So-and-so Khan.

EMOLUMENTS

An amount of 6,330 *tuman*s and 1,179 Tabrizi *dinar*s without the 'unquantified' amount.

RETAINERS

274 persons.

GOVERNOR OF THE DISTRICT OF BAKU[142]

TITLES

Asylum of the emirate and government.

EMOLUMENTS

500 Tabrizi *tuman*s.

RETAINERS

100 persons.

Baku is a district in which much petroleum occurs and where wells have been dug to reach the petroleum. In the time of the 'Abbasid caliphs it was a major city and had substantial revenues.

GOVERNOR-GENERAL OF THE PROVINCE OF QARABAGH AND HIS SUBORDINATE EMIRS

His total income and that of his subordinate emirs is an amount of [blank] and his subordinate emirs number 10 persons.[143] [79]

---

141   According to the TM, p. 102, the governor of Qobbeh had 7,700 *tuman*s as emoluments and the one of Saliyan 3,342 *tuman*s and 3,845 *dinar*s. Together they had to have 860 men.

142   The governor of Baku had 500 *tuman*s as emoluments and had to have 100 men. TM, p. 102.

143   According to TM, pp. 101-02 there were 10 subordinate governors, with total emoluments of 16,472 *tuman*s and 553 *dinar*s, who had to have 6,084 men.

GOVERNOR-GENERAL ABOVEMENTIONED[144]
TITLES

Asylum of the province and authority, pomp and majesty of the administration, his excellency emir of emirs, he who embellishes the province, authority, pomp, majesty and felicity So-and-so Khan Ziyad-oghlu Qajar, the Associate.

As the governor-general of this province is always with the tribe of the Qājārs and with the clan of Ziyād-ughlu the title of associate (*mosāheb*) was given to this clan on account of their good services, it therefore was always written in one manner and [only] the name was changed.[145]

EMOLUMENTS
An amount of 1,619 *tuman*s and 9,000 and odd [*dinar*s].

RETAINERS
1,382 persons.

GOVERNOR OF LURI AND PANBAK AND OF THE BUZCHELU TRIBE[146]
HIS TITLES

Asylum of the province and authority, pomp of the administration, he who illuminates the province and authority, So-and-so Khan.

EMOLUMENTS
An amount of 6,504 *tuman*s and 4,000 and odd *dinar*s.

RETAINERS
434 persons.

GOVERNOR OF THE DISTRICT OF BARDAʿ[147]
TITLES
The same.

On Kalb ʿAli Khān Qājār, who was governor of the said district, His Majesty Shah Soltān Hoseyn bestowed the title of *khān-zādeh-ye qadimi*.

EMOLUMENTS
An amount of 3,002 *tuman*s and 3,000 and odd [*dinar*s].

RETAINERS
490 men.

---

144 According to TM, p. 102 his emoluments were 28,614 *tuman*s and 9,435 *dinar*s and he had to have 1,420 men.

145 Floor, *Safavid Goverrnment*, p. 92.

146 According to the TM, p. 102 its governor had 1,545 *tuman*s and 8,434 *dinar*s as emoluments and had to have 550 men.

147 According to the TM, p. 101 its governor had 3,792 *tuman*s and 2,735 *dinar*s as emoluments and had to have 515 men.

GOVERNOR OF THE DISTRICT BARGOSHAT, WHICH IS ALSO CALLED SHIRVANLU SHAHLU[148]

TITLES

Asylum of the emirate and government, he who adorns the emirate and government, So-and-so Soltan.

EMOLUMENTS

An amount of 584 *tuman*s and 6,000 and odd *dinar*s. [80]

RETAINERS

300 persons.

GOVERNOR OF QARA AGHAJ WHOM THEY ALSO CALL GOVERNOR OF THE BAYAT[149]

TITLES

The same.

EMOLUMENTS

666 *tuman*s and 5,000 and odd *dinar*s.

RETAINERS

212 persons.

GOVERNOR OF THE DISTRICT OF ARASBAR[150]

TITLES

Asylum of the emirate and government, he who adorns the emirate and government, So-and-so Soltan.

EMOLUMENTS

An amount of 1,806 *tuman*s and 3,000 and odd *dinar*s and some due to a shortfall has been collected under the heading 'deficit.'

RETAINERS

298 persons.

---

148 According to the TM, p. 102 its governor had 341 *tuman*s and 2,750 *dinar*s as emoluments and had to have 300 men.

149 According to TM, p. 102 its governor had 636 *tuman*s and 5,434 *dinar*s as emoluments and had to have 210 men.

150 According to TM, p. 102 its governor had 601 *tuman*s and 8,345 dinars as emoluments and had to have 300 men.

GOVERNOR OF PAYDAR[151]

TITLES

Asylum of the emirate, So-and-so Soltan.

EMOLUMENTS

An amount of 100 Tabrizi *tuman*s not including the 'unquantified' amount.

RETAINERS

238 persons.

GOVERNOR OF THE DISTRICT OF JAVANSHIR[152]

TITLES

Asylum of the emirate and government, he who adorns the emirate and government, So-and-so Soltan.

EMOLUMENTS

an amount of 2,543 *tuman*s and 6,003 Tabrizi *dinar*s.

RETAINERS

732 persons.

GOVERNOR OF ZAGAM AND THE SHAMS AL-DINLU TRIBE[153]

TITLES

Asylum of the emirate and authority, pomp of the administration, he who adorns the emirate and authority, So-and-so Khan.

EMOLUMENTS

5,998 *tuman*s and 5,000 and odd *dinar*s. [81]

RETAINERS

1,200 persons.

---

151 I have not been able to identify Paydar, unless a tribal district is meant. Otherwise, perhaps it is a copyist's error for Pay Hesar, see, e.g., Monshi, *Tarikh*, p. 541; Vahid, *Iran*, p. 132.

152 According to TM, p. 102 its governor had 2,102 *tuman*s and 8,000 *dinar*s as emoluments and had to have 832 men.

153 According to TM, p. 101 its governor had 5,998 *tuman*s and 5,980 *dinar*s as emoluments and had to have 1,200 men.

GOVERNOR OF AKHSANATABAD AND THE QAZAQLAR TRIBE[154]

TITLES

Asylum of the emirate and autority, pomp of the administration, he who adorns, So-and-so Khan.

EMOLUMENTS

An amount of 2,852 *tuman*s and 5,000 Tabrizi *dinar*s.

RETAINERS

700 persons.

GOVERNOR OF GEORGIA
hākem-e vālād-e Gorjestān[155]

[TEXT MISSING]

TITLES

Asylum of the emirate, So-and-so Soltan.

EMOLUMENTS

two *tuman*s and 2,000 Tabrizi *dinar*s.

RETAINERS

100 persons.

[TEXT MISSING]

The governor-general of the whole of Khorasan who is in Herat and his subordinate emirs: an amount of [blank] [missing text].[156]

Royal order from Shah Tahmāsp to Mohammad Khān Sharaf al-Din-ughlu with regards to the reception of [king] Homayun.[157]

This royal order has been issued so that the Asylum of Government, workshop of Majesty and sun of power and prestige, Mohammad Khān Sharaf al-Din-ughlu Tekkelu, tutor of [our] dear

---

154 Its governor had 852 *tuman*s and 5,930 *dinar*s as emoluments and had to have 700 men, according to TM, p. 102.

155 The term *vālād*, meaning a plastered or brick wall, an edifice or cupola, and in this case perhaps referring to the fact that the area functioned as a wall or buffer as it was a border area, also may be a copyist's error of *vālāt* or the *vāli*s, i.e. in this case the vice-roys of Georgia. However, the combination of *hākem-e vālāt* does not make sense. On the function of the *vāli*s see Floor, *Safavid Government*, pp. 81-89.

156 The introductory part concerning the governor-general of Herat is missing. This province, which was part of Khorasan, is situated in northwestern Afghanistan. According to TM, p. 102 the governor-general of Herat had 11 subordinate governors, who together had 15,611 *tuman*s and 5,066 *dinar*s as emoluments and had to have 2,780 men.

157 For a discussion of this order and its many copies and variants see Riazul Islam, *Indo-Persian Relations* (Tehran, 1970), pp. 27-28. For another version of this royal order see Shamlu, *Qesas al-Khaqani*, vol. 1, pp. 54-67. For a description about Homayun's entry into and reception in Herat, see, e.g., Qomi, *Kholasat*, vol. 1, pp. 304f. Mohammad Sharaf al-Din-oghlu Tekkelu was governor of Herat from 943-963/1536-1555 and *Laleh* or guardian/tutor of Soltan Mohammad Mirza, the eldest son of Shah Tahmasp I.

eldest son and governor of the royal city of Herat and emir of the *divān*, who has been honored with various royal bounties and favors, may know that the contents of his report, [**82**] which had been sent with His Excellency Kamāl al-Din Shahqoli Beyg, brother of the Asylum of Dignity, Qarā Soltān Shāmlu, to the royal court, the asylum of felicity, arrived on the date of the twelfth of the month Dhi'l-Hijjeh and its auspicious subject has become known and understood from beginning to end.

As to what has been written concerning the approach of the fortunate vice regent (i.e. Homayun), sphere-rider, sun-cupola, pearl of success and sovereignty's ocean, goodly tree ornamenting the garden of government and world-sway, world-illuminating light of the portico of sovereignty and glory, soaring cypress of the stream of auspiciousness and fortune, aromatic tree of glory and majesty's rose-garden, fruit of the tree of the caliphate and world-rule, altar and exemplar of just princes, greatest and best of the Khaqans, the lord of majesty, high-born sovereign of supremacy's throne, exalted king of the kingdom of dispensation of justice, khaqan of Alexander-like glorious potentate, an enthroned Solomon, lord of guidance amd assurance, world-guardian, lord of diadem and throne, lord of conjunction of the world of fortune and prestige, crowning diadem of famous Khaqans, the aided by God, Defender of the Faith King Mohammad Homayun. May the Almighty grant him greatness in accordance with desire until the last day! How may it be told what joy and delight have been caused by this.

VERSE

Good news, O courier of the morn, you bring of the friend's advent
May your tidings be true, O you ever the friend's confidante
May that day come when, in the feast of meeting,
I shall sit, having my heart's desire, breathing in unison with the friend.

The untroubled progress and advance of this angel-respecting king is considered to be a great boon, therefore know that for bringing that outstanding news we have bestowed as a reward the district of Sabzavar on that Asylum of Government from the beginning of [the month of] March-April (Aries) of *Taveshqān yil* (the Year of the Hare). He has to send his *dārugheh* and vizier to that place to collect there the government revenues and receipts due [**83**] from the beginning of the current year and to use these for the requirements of the victorious army and his own needs and, to act in accordance with the instruction detailed in this order, point by point, day by day, and not to deviate from its mandated contents.

Choose five hundred men from among prudent and experienced people, who each must have one led horse and one attendant mule, with the necessary accouterments, who have to go as the welcoming party of that king, the Lord of Fortune, with 100 fast horses that have been sent from the sublime court for the use of H.M, together with golden saddles. That Asylum of Government will choose from his own stables six fleet horses, quiet, nicely colored and strong of body that are fit to be ridden by that royal cavalier of the field of glory and success; he has to equip them with cobalt-blue saddles with covers of gold-brocade and gold-wrought silks such as befits the riding horses of that imperial King. Each horse has to be assigned to two of his retainers, whom he has to send on their way.

The royal household side-dagger, adorned with precious and beautiful jewels, which came to our royal person from the fortunate viceregent, the late pardoned prince of the sublime seat, the king our father [Shah Esmāʿil I], may God illuminate his proof, together with a gilt sword, and a jewel-studded belt, have been sent to this Alexander-like king, for victory, conquest, and as an auspicious omen.

Also, a quantity of 400 rolls of velvet, and European and Yazdi *atlas* have been sent, so that 120 dresses may be made for the use of that king and the rest for the retainers in attendance to that fortunate prince.

[In addition], two-pile gold-threaded velvet carpets and atlas-covered cushions made of goat-hair and three pairs of carpets 12 ells in size, from Qushqān[158] and of good quality and 12 red, green and white tents have been sent. May they arrive in excellent condition. [**84**]

Every day, at the start of the journey, sweet and pleasant drinks have to be sent to His Majesty as well as for each of the members of his high council and his other retainers together with white bread that has been prepared with clarified butter and [creamy] milk and which has to be sprinkled with fennel and poppy seeds.

Let is also be the rule that at tomorrow's halting stations and resting places where His Majesty will dismount, to-day clean, beautiful, white, and adorned tents with awnings of *atlas* and velvet, as well as the saddle-room, the kitchen and all his workshops have been properly erected, so that the necessary implements of each workshop are ready for use.

When he, in his glory and fortune, orders a halt, rose-water, sherbet and plesant-tasting lemonade has to be prepared and served after having been cooled with snow and ice. After the sherbet, apple preserves from Mashkān-e Mashhad,[159] water melon, grapes, and the like with white bread in the manner as has been ordered have to served and care has to be taken that all these drinks are examined by that Refuge of Sovereignty [i.e. Mohammad Sharaf al-Din[160]] and that rosewater and green ambergris are mixed with it.

Every day 500 plates of various foods with drinks have to be ready for consumption.

That Asylum of Government has to send Qazāq Soltan and the Repository of Authority Jaʿfar Soltan with his [i.e. Mohammad Sharaf al-Din's] sons and clansmen, up to 1,000 people, as a welcoming party after three days, when these 500 persons have gone. During these three days the said emirs and the various soldiers will parade on review. They have to give their retainers *Tupchāq*[161] and Arab horses, for there is no better military adornment than a good horse. The dress of these 1,000 people also has to be colorful and clean.

It is further mandated that when these emirs come to wait on His Majesty they will kiss the ground of service and glory with lips of respect and perform their service one by one. Care has to be

---

158 A village between Kashan and Isfahan and known for its high quality carpets.
159 A village near the Nishapur district, situated on the road between Kuchan and Sabzavar.
160 The term Asylum of Sovereignty is used in this royal order to denote Homayun, but that does not make sense in this context
161 I have not been able to identify this type of horse. The term is spelled differently in the various copies of the royal order. May be Qipchaq is meant, referring to a breed of Turkmen horses.

taken that in case of riding and [85] the like no sudden altercation occurs between the attendants of the emirs and those of the king; in no way or manner may the king's servants be offended.

When riding and marching the emirs perform their services from a distance, while staying with their own troops. However, each of the said emirs, whoever it may be, shall not shrink from taking turns at doing guard duty near the quarters which have been fixed [for the king] where they will serve, with the staff of service taken into their hands, in the same manner as when serving their own king and this must be observed and carried out with the utmost attentiveness.

In each district that he [Homayun] reaches this same royal edict has to be shown to the governor of that district and it is ordered that this emir does his duty and provides hospitality in such a manner that all the foods, sweetmeats, and drinks will not be less than 1,500 plates.

The service of, and attendance on that Asylum of Sovereignty [i.e. Homayun], is the responsibility of that Asylum of Government until Holy Mashhad. When the said emirs come to perform their service, each day 1,200 plates of various foods that are fit for a royal table have to be served in the high council of that esteemed king.

Each of the abovementioned emirs on the day when he is host has to give nine head of horses as a present of which three horses are for the king's use; one is to be given to the great emir Mohammad Beyrām Khān Bahādor, while the other five are for particular emirs, as deemed appropriate. The total of nine horses have to mustered for his eminent inspection and mention must be made which horse is for His Majesty and which one for such or such an emir, which [choice] has been agreed upon beforehand, so that this observation as improper as it may look will be appropriate and not unseemly.

By whatever possible means, keep the retainers in attendance on His Majesty pleased and show [86] them the utmost sympathy and care. Soothe the spirits of that group of people, which have become somewhat cloudy due to the turn of unequal fate, with affection and sympathy that in these kinds of times [of life] is appropriate and pleasing. This rule has to be observed all the time until they have reached our presence. Thereafter, whatever is appropriate will be done by us.

After the consumption of food, bring sweetmeats and comfits (*pāludeh*), which is made from sugar and rock-candy, various preserves and special Chinese sweetmeats that have to be perfumed with cool rosewater, musk, and grey ambergris, to the banquet.

The governor of the district, after having provided this aforementioned hospitality and service, may put his mind at ease about his district, and escort [His Majesty] until the royal city of Herat, making sure that not one single iota of service and attendance is neglected.

When he [Homayun] has arrived at 12 *farsakh*s from the province [i.e. Herat] that Asylum of Government [Mohammad Sharaf al-Din] will put one of his experienced clansmen in charge of our dearest eldest son, who knows how to take care of the city and that son. That Asylum of Government will take along as welcoming party the remainder of the victorious army from the city, province and its border areas, from Hazarehs to Nakodaris and the like, up to 30,000 men, which number must be exact. Tents, awnings and necessary furniture have to be taken along on camels and mules, so that the well laid-out camp is viewed by favorably by the king.

When [that Asylum of Government] is honored by attendance on His Majesty, before saying anything, convey to him many prayers for his welfare on our behalf. On that same day that he is distinguished to serve him, he halts in accordance with army rules and regulations. When he stands at attendance, this Asylum of Government will ask permission to give a banquet and will remain for three days at that halting place.

On the first day he will give all His Majesty's soldiers robes of honor made of mixed silk-cotton fabric and gold brocade from Yazd [**87**], of simple silk fabrics[162] from Mashhad and Khvāf and all are to be given an overcoat. Also, to each soldier and retainer two Tabrizi *tuman*s should be given for daily expenses. [Furthermore], various foods have to be prepared and served in the royal assembly, in accordance with the instructions, so that tongues may speak praise of it and shouts of approval may reach mankind's ears. Once a list of his [Homayun's] army has been made let it proceed to the sublime court.

An amount of 2,500 Tabrizi *tuman*s may be taken from the goods sent for the royal household that are sent the abovementioned royal city, which have to be used for the necessary purposes and the utmost zeal in perfoming this service has to be shown.

March from the aforesaid halting place until the city in four days; each day food servings should be as on the first day. During each serving it is required that the honored sons of that Asylum of Government bind, like valets and servants, girdles of service on their loins and perform [according to] the rules of service, and, out of gratitude that such a king, who is a gift from the gifts of God, has become our guest. While being in attendance and serving, the utmost loving care has to be shown and no shortcoming must occur, for, the more zeal and devotion are displayed towards His Majesty the more pleasing it will be [to us].

If he [Homayun] were to reach the city tomorrow it is commanded that to-day tents be erected in the *'Eyd-gāh* garden at the beginning of the avenue that on the inside are lined with red silk-cotton fabric, in the middle with coarse cotton fabric from Tabas and on top with fine cotton fabric from Isfahan which, during these days, were reported as having been readied.

Take care that wherever His Majesty's spirits are uplifted and in every flowered field that is known for its streams, air, amenities, and delights where he seeks his pleasure, while attending on His Majesty you approach with the hand servant-like, politely on the breast, and state that this camp, this army, these equipments are all gifts to His Majesty. While traveling, you yourself have to continuously lift His Majesty's spirits [**88**] with conversation that is of a reassuring nature.

You yourself will go [the day before] from the said halting station whence he will arrive at the city on the following day, after having obtained your dismissal, to attend on [our] son. On the [next] morning take that dearest eldest son from his residence in order to give welcome [to His Majesty]. You will dress him in the suit that we have sent to that son last year on the occasion of New Year, and leaving one of the chiefs of the Tekkelu tribe, who is approved of and trusted by that Asylum of Government, in the above mentioned royal city, have the said son mount up.

During the time that he has gone to the city, the Asylum of Government will put Qazāq Soltān in attendance on His Majesty. Let the tents, camels, and horses proceed, so that when the next day H.M will mount up, the army camp may also march, and the Asylum of Government will be his escort.

When the said son leaves the city, see to it that all the troops are mounted and have drawn up in standard review formation and proceed to the welcoming.

When they come near to this majestic king, i.e. there is [the distance of] a bow-shot between them, that Asylum of Government goes forward and begs that the king does not

---

162 For a discussion of these and other textile terms that are later mentioned in the same edict see Willem Floor, *The Persian Textile Industry in historical perspective 1500-1925* (Paris, 1989).

dismount from his horse. If he agrees, he has to return immediately and dismount the happy son from his horse to hurry forward and kiss the thigh and stirrup of that Solomon-like king and behave to the extent possible in accordance with the rules of service, respect and honor. If His Majesty does not agree and dismounts the said son has to dismount first and render service.

When His Majesty has mounted first, our son after having kissed his hand [also] mounts up and then rides, in accordance with etiquette, to his camp and halting place.

That Asylum of Government himself has to stay close to the abovementioned son who is in attendance on the king, [**89**] so that, if the king asks [our] son some questions, and that son, out of shyness, is unable to reply as required, that Asylum of the Government will give an appropriate answer.

In a good[163] halting station that son will host the king in such a manner that when they dismount for breakfast (*chāshtgāh*)[164] immediately 300 plates of various foods are brought to the assembly (such as is the rule in the paradisiacal council when they bring food, and between the two prayers [at mid-day] 1,200 plates of various kinds of food) on *langari* plates, which are known as *Mohammad Khāni*, and other plates of porcelain, gold, and silver, placing gold- and silver-wrought covers over them. Afterwards, [sweet] preserves, such as are available, sweetmeats, and comfits have to be served. Thereafter, seven excellent and beautiful horses have to be taken from the beloved son's stables, bedecked with horse covers [**90**] of velvet and silk-cotton fabric; the straps made of cotton-silk fabric have to be [on] the figured velvet patterned horse cover and the white straps have to be on the red velvet horse cover and the black straps on the green velvet horse cover.

It is proper that (Hāfez Sāber Barqāq, Mowlānā Qāsem Qānuni, Ostād Shāh Sornā'i, Hāfez Dust Mohammad Khvāfi, Ostād Yusof Mowdud and other) famous singers and players who may be in the city, are always present, and, whenever the king desires it, please him with music and singing without delay.

Everybody from nearby and afar, who is worthy of that assembly be in attendance so that they are present when called upon, and that they may make his hours pleasant ones by every possible means. [**91**]

Furthermore, give as presents falcons, hawks, white falcons, sparrow-hawks, royal falcons, peregrines and the like that may be in the son's establishment, or that of the Asylum of Government's or his sons.

His retainers have all to be dressed in silk robes of honor, of every kind, and of different colors suitable to each, such as various kinds of velvet, cotton-silk, and gold-work.

When (they arrive at their halting station all his retainers) have to be brought before the son's auspicious inspection, who will entertain them in the munificent manner that is hereditary with him, from father to son, and to each one of them he shall give an overcoat and a horse, according to his station. The gift should not exceed three *tuman*s. [**92**]

[Also], he has to give twelve times nine pieces of silken fabrics, such as velvet, silk-cotton fabric, European and Yazd gold brocade, royal taffeta and the like that have to be very elegant as well as 300 *tuman*s in cash in thirty purses together with the said fabrics and to each soldier and to each servant three Tabrizi *tuman*s which are equal to 600 *shahi*s.

(They have to tarry for three days at the head of the Avenue and at the laundry site and during those three days) the various guilds have to make triumphal arches and nice adornments from the

---

163 An alternative reading is "aforementioned."
164 This word also can refer to lunch.

gate of the *Chahār Bāgh* of the city, which is the royal halting station, until the head of the Avenue, which is in the *'Eyd-gāh* Garden. Assign to each craft guild one of the aforementioned emirs so that through their mutual rivalry every craft and mastery that they know will be realized.

It is befitting that as the king has honored this country with [his] auspicious arrival, [93] he should first come to a city, which is the light of mankind's eyes. Bring therefore before his alchemic eye genial and well-spoken people, such as are in the city, so that he may be cheered up.

On the third day, when your mind will be at ease concerning the triumphal arches, the Avenue, the city, the adornment of the *Chahār Bāgh*, public criers have to be ordered to make known in the city, its quarters, environs, and nearby villages that all men and women of the city shall gather on the morning of the fourth day in the Avenue, and that in every shop and bazaar, according to custom, carpets, covers, and rugs have to be spread (on the ground of passageways) where women and maidens[165] will be seated, as is the custom in that city; the women have to act and speak pleasantly to passers-by, and from every quarter and street, musicians have to come forward, so that the like of it will not be seen in any other city of the world. And bid all these people to come to the welcoming.

After all this, they have to ask this king in a respectful and polite manner to put the foot of state in the stirrup of felicity, and to mount up. The son will ride next to His Majesty, but so that the neck and head of his [the king's] horse is ahead. That Asylum of Government himself will follow close behind them, so that if he [the king] would ask any questions about palaces, mansions, and gardens he knows how to give a suitable reply.

When he auspiciously enters the city he should visit the *Chahār Bāgh*, and dismount in a small garden, which was built at the time of our residence in that good city, to be used as a place for residing and sleeping as well as for reading and writing and which at present is known as *Bāgh-e Shāhi*. [94] The bath-house of the *Chahār Bāgh* and the other bath-houses have to be whitewashed and cleaned and be made pleasant smelling with rosewater and musk, so that whenever he desires it, he may have an abode for bodily relaxation.

On the first day, the son will be host with an abundance of food and when he has gone to sleep that Asylum of Government himself will take care of the hosting in the manner as will be mentioned.

When he [Homayun] enters the city, on that same day you make a report and send it to the sublime court. It is commanded that Mo'ezz al-Din, the *kalāntar* of the royal city of Herat, appoints a good writer and an informed man, who has to write a complete Journal, from the day that these 500 men are welcomed until the day that he enters the city, which he has to submit for that Asylum of Government's registration and seal [for approval], and all the stories and remarks, (good and bad), that pass in the assembly, have to be written down and [then] is to be given into the hands of trusted persons to be forwarded to the sublime court so that our royal person is informed of all that occurs.

The banquet [given by] that Asylum of Government has to be as follows: 3,000 plates with food, sweetmeats, sweet drinks and fruits have to be served. The necessary accouterments have to be ready at the beginning of the journey as follows:

---

165 The text employs the word *peykhā* for which the editor has suggested the meaning of 'couriers.' However, the word probably was improperly copied, for it is more likely that this word, as suggested by Beveridge, should be read as *beykahā* or maidens, which makes perfect sense in this context.

First, 50 tents (and 20) awnings, and the large *ālātiyeh* [?] tent, which reportedly (had been prepared and readied for the royal household), with 12 pairs of carpets of 12 ells (*dharʿi*), of 10 ells, [96] of seven ells and (seven pairs of carpets of five ells), nine strings of female camels and 250 large and small porcelain plates; further plates and pots [complete] with white tin lids that have to be clean and a string of camels of eighteen have to be given as a gift (*pishkesh*) by the Asylum of Government during his banquet.

The above mentioned emirs have been ordered to give a banquet in the following manner: they have to serve food, sweetmeats, and comfits (*pāludeh*) to the extent of 1,500 plates as well as give as a present three horses, a string of camels and a string of mules, after that Asylum of Government has seen them and has approved of them.

The governors of Ghuriyān, Fushanj and Karshu will offer a banquet in their own district. (The governor of Bākharz will offer a banquet in Jām) and the governors of Khvāf, Torshiz, Zāveh, and Mahvalāt will offer a banquet in Mahvalāt in the Saray Farhādjerd, which is five *farsakh*s from Holy Mashhad. [96]

The names of those that have been commanded to provide sublime assistance during this journey are as follows: the dear prince Morād Mirzā, Budāq Khān Qājar (the tutor of the prince), Shāhqoli Soltān Afshār, governor of Kerman, Yār ʿAli Soltān Tekkelu, Soltān ʿAli Afshār, Soltān ʿAli Qurchi, Yaʿqub Khān, Mirzā Minā, Soltān Mohammad Mirzā Khudābandeh, Hasanqoli Soltān Shāmlu, brother of Ahmad Soltān governor of Seystan, Adham Beyg son of Div Soltān, Heydar Soltān Sheybāni, ʿAliqoli Bahādor [and] his sons, Maqsud Mirzā [97] Akhteh Beygi son of Zeyn al-Din Soltān Shāmlu, Mohammad Mirzā grandson of Jahānshāh, Shāhverdi Beyg Ostājalu, ʿAli Soltān Chalāq, sister's son of Mohammad Khān, Abuʾl-Fath Soltān Afshār, Hoseyn Soltān Shāmlu, Yādgār Soltān (Mowsellu), Ahmad Soltān Alāsh-oghlu, [?] Soltān Ostājalu, Sufi Soltān son of Sufiyān Khalifeh of the Rumlu (Oromlu), ʿAli Beyg, Dhuʾl-Feqār Beyg the Qājār librarian, and 300 outstanding royal household troops have been appointed. They have been instructed not to fail to do their duty.

[TEXT MISSING][166]

EMOLUMENTS

15,412 and odd *tuman*s.

RETAINERS

2,696 persons. [98]

---

166 The missing text is about the governor-general of Herat, who, according to TM, p. 102, had 15, 277 *tumans* and 6,034 *dinars* as emoluments and had to have 2,682 men.

GOVERNOR OF THE DISTRICT OF KHVAF[167]

TITLES

Asylum of the emirate and government, he who adorns the emirate and government, So-and-so Soltan.

EMOLUMENTS

An amount of 1,000 *tuman*s and 4,000 and odd *dinar*s.

RETAINERS

200 persons.

GOVERNOR OF THE DISTRICT OF MARUCHAQ[168]

TITLES

Asylum of the emirate and authority, pomp of the administration, his excellency he who adorns the emirate and authority, So-and-so Soltan.

Most of the time the district of Māruchāq was bestowed on the kinsmen of the governor-general of Herat.

EMOLUMENTS

An amount of 3,419 *tuman*s and 8,000 and odd *dinar*s.

RETAINERS

737 persons.

GOVERNOR OF NAHABABAD [?][169]

TITLES

Asylum of the emirate, So-and-so Soltan.

EMOLUMENTS

An amount of 109 *tuman*s and 6,000 and odd *dinar*s.

RETAINERS

30 persons.

---

167 According to TM, p. 102 its governor had 1,434 *tuman*s and 2,624 *dinar*s as emoluments and had to have 271 men.

168 According to TM, p. 102 its governor had 3,267 *tuman*s and 5,531 *dinar*s as emoluments and had to have 97 men.

169 I have not been able to identify this location.

GOVERNOR OF THE DISTRICT OF FARAH[170]

TITLES

Asylum of the emirate and authority, pomp and majesty of the administration, he who adorns the emirate and authority, So-and-so Soltan.

EMOLUMENTS

An amount of 4,645 *tuman*s and 2,000 and odd *dinar*s.

RETAINERS

603 persons.

GOVERNOR OF QEBCHAQ[171]

TITLES

Asylum of the emirate, So-and-so Soltan.

EMOLUMENTS

49 *tuman*s and 3,000 and odd [*dinar*s].

RETAINERS

unknown. [99]

GOVERNOR OF GHURI[172]

TITLES

The same.

EMOLUMENTS

An amount of 103 *tuman*s and 1,000 and odd *dinar*s.

RETAINERS

48 persons.

---

170 According to the TM, p. 102 its governor had 4,989 *tuman*s and 6,873 *dinar*s as emoluments and had to have 603 men.

171 The Qebchaq or Qepchaq steppe is located in Khvarezm, but some its Turkmen tribes became vassals under Shah ʿAbbas I and had their summer quarters next to that of the Gereyli and Hajjilar in the province of Astarabad. It was perhaps to collect taxes that a Safavid governor was appointed. Nasiri, *Dastur*, p. 242 (see also 'Astarabad' in the Commentary).

172 According to the TM, p. 102 its governor had 103 *tuman*s and 1,600 *dinar*s as emoluments and had to have 30 men.

GOVERNOR OF PANJDEH[173]

TITLES

Asylum of the emirate and government, So-and-so Soltan.

EMOLUMENTS

An amount of 958 *tuman*s and 4,000 and odd *dinar*s.

RETAINERS

161 persons.

GOVERNOR OF BALA MORGHAB[174]

TITLES

Asylum of the emirate, So-and-so Soltan.

EMOLUMENTS

An amount of 868 *tuman*s and 3,000 and odd *dinar*s.

RETAINERS

160 men.

GOVERNOR OF THE DISTRICT OF ZURI[175]

TITLES

The same.

EMOLUMENTS

He has an amount of 177 *tuman*s and 6,000 *dinar*s and 642 *dinar*s on account of herd tax of 30,000 sheep; he [also] has an unquantified amount.

RETAINERS

500 persons.

GOVERNOR OF KAROKH AND THE JAMSHIDI TRIBE[176]

TITLES

The same.

EMOLUMENTS

An amount of 442 *tuman*s and 6,000 and odd *dinar*s.

---

173 According to the TM, p. 102 its governor had 958 *tuman*s and 4,673 *dinar*s as emoluments and had to have 150 men.

174 According to the TM, p. 102 its governor had 883 *tuman*s and 3,466 *dinar*s as emoluments and had to have 100 men.

175 According to the TM, p. 102 its governor had 450 *tuman*s and 7,091 *dinar*s as emoluments and had to have 500 men.

176 According to the TM, p. 102 its governor had 442 *tuman*s and 3,737 *dinar*s as emoluments and had to have 199 men.

RETAINERS

194 persons. [**100**]

GOVERNOR OF BADGHIS[177]

TITLES

The same.

EMOLUMENTS

An amount of 30 *tuman*s and 3,000 and odd *dinar*s.

RETAINERS

30 persons.

GOVERNOR OF HERATRUD AND SHAFLAN[178]

TITLES

Were written in various ways; sometimes it was bestowed on Chengizid soltans and other times to another group and the titles were written as appropriate.

EMOLUMENTS

An amount of 1,405 *tuman*s and 4,000 and odd *dinar*s.

RETAINERS

440 persons.

GOVERNOR-GENERAL OF HOLY MASHHAD AND HIS SUBORDINATE EMIRS

The total income of the said governor-general and his subordinate emirs was an amount of [blank] and the number of all their retainers was [blank] and the number of subordinate emirs is 12.[179]

---

177 According to the TM, p. 102 its governor had 109 *tuman*s and 6,151 *dinar*s as emoluments and had to have 30 men.

178 The TM does not mention this district or that of Shaflan. For further information see the Commentary section.

179 According to the TM, pp. 102-03 its governor-general had 12 subordinate governors. Together they had 25,106 *tuman*s and 218 *dinar*s as emoluments and had to have 5,440 men, according to the TM, p. 103.

THE ABOVEMENTIONED GOVERNOR-GENERAL[180]
Beygler-beygi-ye mazbur

TITLES

Asylum of the province and authority, pomp and majesty of the administration, his excellency, emir of the emirs, he who adorns the province, authority, pomp, majesty and felicity So-and-so Khan.

EMOLUMENTS

An amount of 6,041 *tuman*s and 4,000 and odd *dinar*s.

RETAINERS

600 persons.

GOVERNOR OF THE DISTRICT OF JAM[181]

TITLES

Asylum of the emirate and government, he who adorns the emirate and government, So-and-so Soltan.

Sometimes the said governor was the sub-governor of the governor-general of Herat, sometimes he was the sub-governor of the governor-general of Holy Mashhad. [**101**]

EMOLUMENTS

An amount of 1,547 *tuman*s and 2,000 and odd *dinar*s.

RETAINERS

570 men.

GOVERNOR OF THE DISTRICT OF TORBAT-E HEYDARIYEH[182]

USUAL TITLES

Asylum of the emirate and government, he who adorns, So-and-so Soltan.

Mohammad 'Ali Soltān was bestowed with the additional titles of le'l-emārat va'l-hokumat in the reign of Your Majesty before this slave was secretary of the royal council. Now is also written in the same manner.

EMOLUMENTS

An amount of 362 *tuman*s and 2,000 and odd *dinar*s.

RETAINERS

67 persons.

---

180 According to the TM, p. 102 its governor-general had 7,443 *tuman*s and 9,195 *dinar*s as emoluments and had to have 670 men.

181 According to the TM, p. 102, Jam was part of the province of Herat. Its governor had 1,682 *tuman*s and 220 *dinar*s as emoluments and had to have 500 men.

182 According to the TM, p. 103 its governor had 379 *tuman*s and 4,701 *dinar*s as emoluments and had to have 55 men.

GOVERNOR OF THE DISTRICT OF ABIVARD[183]
TITLES
Asylum of the province and authority, pomp of the administration, he who adorns the province, authority and felicity, So-and-so Khan.

EMOLUMENTS:
An amount of 3,805 *tuman*s and 5,000 and odd *dinar*s.

RETAINERS
613 persons.

GOVERNOR OF THE DISTRICT OF BAZAVANDAQAN[184]
TITLES
Asylum of the emirate and government, So-and-so Soltan.

EMOLUMENTS
An amount of 117 *tuman*s and 2,000 and odd *dinar*s.

RETAINERS
55 persons.

GOVERNOR OF THE DISTRICT OF ESFARA'IN[185]
TITLES
Asylum of the province and government, he who adorns the province and government, So-and-so Soltan.

EMOLUMENTS
An amount of 858 *tuman*s and 8,048 *dinar*s and half a *dang*.

RETAINERS
131 persons. [**102**]

---

183 According to the TM, p. 103 its governor had 3,588 *tuman*s and 7,828 *dinar*s as emoluments and had to have 550 men.

184 According to the TM, p. 103 its governor had 117 *tuman*s and 1,287 *dinar*s as emoluments and had to have 50 men.

185 According to the TM, p. 103 its governor had 918 *tuman*s and 7,208 *dinar*s as emoluments and had to have 130 men.

GOVERNOR OF THE DISTRICT OF FARUMAD AND ARADVAR[186]

USUAL TITLES

Asylum of the emirate and government, So-and-so Soltan.

Before this royal slave became secretary of the royal secretariat in the time of Your Majesty in addition [the title] *nezāman le'l-emārat va le'l-hokumat* was written for the said governor and now it also written that way.

EMOLUMENTS

An amount of 176 *tuman*s and 5,000 Tabrizi *dinar*s.

RETAINERS

21 persons.

GOVERNOR OF THE DISTRICT OF PASAKUH[187]

TITLES

Asylum of the [emirate and] government, he who adorns, So-and-so Soltan.

EMOLUMENTS

216 *tuman*s and 7,353 *dinar*s and two *dāng*.

RETAINERS

45 persons.

GOVERNOR OF THE DISTRICT OF NISHABUR[188]

USUAL TITLES

Asylum of the province and authority, pomp of the administration, he who adorns the province and authority, So-and-so Khan.

For Fath 'Ali Khān Torkman in the time of His Majesty Shah Soltān Hoseyn when he became the governor of Nishapur in addition the title of *jalālat* and *'ālijāh* was written, which also was written in the same manner for Fath 'Ali Khān Bayāt, but this was not submitted for this royal slave's review.

EMOLUMENTS

Consists of an amount of 2,213 *tuman*s and 1,000 and odd *dinar*s and an amount of 514 *tuman*s and 8,000 and odd *dinar*s is its deficit.

RETAINERS

500 persons.

---

186 According to the TM, p. 103 its governor had 139 *tuman*s and 3,533 *dinar*s as emoluments and had to have 21 men.

187 According to the TM, p. 103 its governor had 216 *tuman*s and 7,353 *dinar*s as emoluments and had to have 45 men.

188 According to the TM, p. 102 its governor had 2,170 *tuman*s and 8,300 *dinar*s as emoluments and had to have 719 men.

GOVERNOR OF SABZAVAR[189]
TITLES
Asylum of the province and authority, pomp of the administration, he who adorns the province and authority, So-and-so Khan.

EMOLUMENTS
An amount of 1,843 *tuman*s and 3,000 and odd *dinar*s.

RETAINERS
277 persons. **[103]**

GOVERNOR OF THE DISTRICT OF SARAKHS AND ZURABAD[190]
TITLES
Asylum of the emirate, So-and-so Soltan.

EMOLUMENTS
An amount of 1,795 *tuman*s and 4,000 and odd *dinar*s.

RETAINERS
561 persons.

HIS EXCELLENCY THE GOVERNOR OF THE DISTRICT OF DORUN, WHICH IS ALSO CALLED KHABUSHAN[191]
USUAL TITLES
Asylum of the province and authority, pomp and majesty of the administration, his excellency, he who adorns the province and authority, So-and-so Khan.

Before this royal slave was secretary of the royal council, in the time of Your Majesty, for the said governor additionally was written *va'l-heshmat va'l-jalālat va'l-eqbāl* and it is now still written as such.

EMOLUMENTS
An amount of 3,738 *tuman*s and 9,000 Tabrizi *dinar*s. On the basis of the ledger of the vizier and accountant there in the time of Manuchehr Khān, the previous governor of the said district, the income consisted of an amount of 1,100 and odd *tuman*s and there was a deficit of 1,000 *tuman*s.

RETAINERS
844 persons.

---

189 According to the TM, p. 103 its governor had 1,302 *tuman*s and 1,151 *dinar*s as emoluments and had to have 272 men.

190 According to the TM, p. 102 its governor had 2,099 *tuman*s and 3,024 *dinar*s as emoluments and had to have 437 men.

191 According to the TM, p. 103 its governor had 2,923 *tuman*s and 3,329 *dinar*s as emoluments and had to have 1,320 men.

GOVERNOR OF THE DISTRICT OF NESA[192]

TITLES

Asylum of the province and government, he who adorns the province and government, So-and-so Soltan.

EMOLUMENTS

An amount of 3,228 *tuman*s and 7,000 and odd *dinar*s.

RETAINERS

555 persons.

GOVERNOR OF THE DISTRICT OF TUN AND TABAS[193]

TITLES

The same.

EMOLUMENTS

An amount of 290 *tuman*s and 6,000 and odd *dinar*s.

RETAINERS

300 persons.

GOVERNOR-GENERAL OF MERV-E SHAHIJAN[194]

He has one sub-governor and the total income of the said governor-general and his sub-governor is an amount of 147 *tuman*s and 9,053 [**104**] Tabrizi *dinar*s. His regular retainers number 3,044 persons.

[Here text is missing as both the entries of the sub-governors of Merv and of his sub-governor as well as the introductory entry of the governor-general of Azerbaijan are missing.]

GOVERNOR-GENERAL ABOVE MENTIONED

[TEXT MISSING]

USUAL TITLES:

Asylum of the province and authority.

[text is missing]

The province of Azerbaijan: the total income of its governor-general together with the income of his subordinate emirs and sub-governors is a total amount of 37,049 *tuman*s and 849 Tabrizi *dinar*s. The number of his subordinate emirs and sub-governor is 30 persons.[195]

---

192 According to the TM, p. 103 its governor had 2,812 *tuman*s and 337 *dinar*s as emoluments and had to have 555 men.

193 According to the TM, p. 102 its governor had 1,290 *tuman*s and 3,100 *dinar*s as emoluments and had to have 300 men.

194 According to the TM, p. 103 its governor-general had 7,193 *tuman*s and 6,140 *dinar*s as emoluments and had to have 2,352 men.

195 According to the TM, pp. 100-01, which correctly does not call this official the governor-general of Azerbaijan, but of Tabriz, its governor-general had 27 subordinate governors, who together had 34,234 *tuman*s

The titles of the said governor-general:

Asylum of the province and authority, pomp and majesty of the administration, his excellency, emir of emirs, he who adorns the province, authority, pomp, majesty and felicity, So-and-so Khan.

When a commander-in-chief or an army commander is appointed in Azerbaijan this [office] is usually given to the governor-general of Azerbaijan in addition to the revenue assignment and perquisites.

EMOLUMENTS

An amount of 10,966 *tuman*s and 5,000 Tabrizi *dinar*s.

RETAINERS

755 persons.

GOVERNOR OF THE DISTRICT OF ORUMI AND THE AFSHAR TRIBE[196]

TITLES

Asylum of the province and authority, pomp and majesty of the administration, he who adorns the province, authority and felicity, So-and-so Khan.

Before this royal slave was secretary of the royal council Your Majesty had bestowed titles on Mohammad Qāsem Khān Afshār governor of Orumi that were given and written as follows in his royal appointment order:

Asylum of the province and authority, pomp and majesty of the administration, he who adorns the province, authority, majesty and felicity, So-and-so Khan.

EMOLUMENTS:

An amount of 7,690 *tuman*s and 6,746 Tabrizi *dinar*s.

The vizier of Azerbaijan in the time of His Majesty Shah Soltān Hoseyn observed an amount of 2,040 *tuman*s of discrepancy in the abovementioned income, but no decision has been taken concerning this.

RETAINERS

1,980 persons. [**105**]

---

and 4,906 ½ *dinar*s as emoluments. The governor-general himself had 2,337 *tuman*s and 8,317 *dinar*s as emoluments and had to have 900 men.

196 According to the TM, p. 100 the chief of the Afshar tribe had 7,390 *tuman*s and 3,747 *dinar*s as emoluments and had to have 2,200 men.

GOVERNOR OF THE DISTRICT OF MARAGHEH AND OF THE MOQADDAM TRIBE[197]

TITLES

Asylum of the province and authority, pomp of the administration, he who adorns the province, authority and felicity, So-and-so Khan.

EMOLUMENTS

An amount of 3,999 *tuman*s and 3,922 Tabrizi *dinar*s except for the herd tax, which is an amount that has been assigned as a tax exemption for this governor.

RETAINERS

3,000 persons.

GOVERNOR OF ARDABIL[198]

TITLE

Asylum of the province and authority, pomp of the administration, he who adorns the province and authority, So-and-so Khan.

Before this royal slave was secretary of the royal council in addition the titles *va'l-heshmat va'l-jalālat va'l-eqbāl* were written in the royal appointment orders and now they are also written in the same way.

EMOLUMENTS

An amount of 2,009 *tuman*s and 3,819 Tabrizi *dinar*s.

RETAINERS

200 men.

GOVERNOR OF THE DISTRICT OF ASTARA[199]

TITLES

The same as for the governor of Ardabil.

EMOLUMENTS

An amount of 5,460 *tuman*s and 9,051 Tabrizi *dinar*s.

RETAINERS

607 persons.

---

197 According to the TM, p. 100 its governor had 3,729 *tuman*s and 7,450 *dinar*s as emoluments and had to have 2,700 men.

198 This governorship is not mentioned in the TM, for further information see the Commentary section.

199 According to the TM, p. 100 its governor had 5,052 *tuman*s and 5,357 *dinar*s as emoluments and had to have 300 men.

GOVERNOR OF THE DISTRICT OF THE MOGHANAT AND OF THE SHAHSEVAN, OF DASHTVAND AND UJARUD AND THEIR RIVERS AND ADJACENT STEPPES[200]

TITLES

The same as for the governor of Ardabil.

EMOLUMENTS

An amount of 3,192 *tuman*s and 2,000 Tabrizi *dinar*s.

Most of the time the said district is given in addition to the governors of the Moghānāt, sometimes to others. For Langkonān[201] and the Dashtvand a separate governor [is appointed] and for Ujarud a separate governor is [also] appointed. [**106**]

RETAINERS

607 persons.

GOVERNOR OF THE DISTRICT OF CHURS AND THE DONBOLI TRIBE[202]

TITLES

Asylum of the province and authority, majesty of the administration, he who adorns the province and authority, So-and-so Khan.

EMOLUMENTS

An amount of 2,456 *tuman*s and 361 *dinar*s.

RETAINERS

700 persons.

GOVERNOR OF THE DISTRICT OF THE SHAQAQI[203]

TITLES

Asylum of the emirate and government, he who adorns, So-and-so Soltan.

EMOLUMENTS

An amount of 705 *tuman*s and 4,850 Tabrizi *dinar*s.

RETAINERS

311 persons.

---

200 According to the TM, p. 101 these were separate governates, to wit: Moghanat, Inanlu Shahi-sevans, and Ujarud. The governor of the irrigated part of the arable land of the Moghanat had 2,202 *tuman*s and 2,222 *dinar*s as emoluments and had to have 50 men. The governor of the Shahsevans had 1,130 *tuman*s and 980 *dinar*s as emoluments and had to have 80 men. The governor of the Ujarud tribe had 510 *tuman*s and 2,095 *dinar*s as emoluments and had to have 70 men.

201 This is a copyist's error for Langarkonan or Lankoran.

202 According to the TM, p. 101, there were two separate governates for Chors and the Donboli tribe. The governor of the Chors had 1,168 *tuman*s and 9,640 *dinar*s as emoluments and had to have 700 men. The chief of the Donboli tribe had 319 *tuman*s and 9,096 *dinar*s as emoluments and had to have 141 men.

203 According to the TM, p. 101 its chief had 326 *tuman*s and 2,022 *dinar*s as emoluments and had to have 319 men.

GOVERNOR OF THE DISTRICT MESHKIN
WHOM THEY ALSO CALL THE GOVERNOR OF THE KALHOR[204]

TITLES
Asylum of the emirate, So-and-so Soltan.

EMOLUMENTS
An amount of 158 *tuman*s and 1,000 and odd *dinar*s.

RETAINERS
25 persons.

GOVERNOR OF THE DISTRICT OF SARAB[205]

TITLES
Asylum of the emirate and government, he who adorns the emirate and government, So-and-so Soltan.

EMOLUMENTS
An amount of 764 *tuman*s and 2,000 and odd *dinar*s.

RETAINERS
99 persons.

GOVERNOR OF THE DISTRICT OF VARGAHAN[206]

TITLES
The same.

EMOLUMENTS
An amount of 467 *tuman*s and 5,000 and odd *dinar*s.

RETAINERS
100 men. [**107**]

GOVERNOR OF THE NELQAS WHO IS ALSO CALLED
THE GOVERNOR OF THE DISTRICT OF HASHTRUD-E TABTAB[207]

TITLES
The same.

---

204 According to the TM, p. 101 its governor had 136 *tuman*s and 9,856 *dinar*s as emoluments and had to have 60 men.

205 According to the TM, p. 101 its governor had 845 *tuman*s and 1,706 *dinar*s as emoluments and had to have 319 men.

206 According to the TM, p. 101 its governor had 195 *tuman*s and 9,500 *dinar*s as emoluments and had to have 85 men.

207 According to the TM, p. 101, its governor had 119 *tuman*s and 6,532 *dinar*s as emoluments and had to have 115 men.

EMOLUMENTS

He has an amount of 840 *tuman*s and 3,000 and odd *dinar*s as a fixed income. He also has additional unquantified income of which it has not been fixed what amount it is.

RETAINERS

115 men.

GOVERNOR OF THE DISTRICT OF KAVERUD[208]

TITLES

The same.

EMOLUMENTS

An amount of 690 *tuman*s and 1,000 and odd *dinar*s.

RETAINERS

150 persons.

GOVERNOR OF THE DISTRICT OF QAPANAT[209]

TITLES

The same.

EMOLUMENTS

An amount of 935 *tuman*s and 5,000 and odd *dinar*s.

RETAINERS

188 persons.

GOVERNOR OF THE LAK OF SALMAS[210]

TITLES

Asylum of the emirate and government, he who adorns the emirate, So-and-so Soltan.

EMOLUMENTS

An amount of 352 and odd *tuman*s.

RETAINERS:

100 persons.

---

208 According to the TM, p. 257 its governor had 7,050 *tuman*s and 6,873 *dinar*s as emoluments and had to have 100 men.
209 According to the TM, p. 101 its governor had 822 *tuman*s and 5,560 *dinar*s as emoluments and had to have 188 men.
210 According to the TM, p. 101 its governor had 349 *tuman*s and 3,748 *dinar*s as emoluments and had to have 100 men.

GOVERNOR OF LAJAN, WHICH IS KURDESTAN[211]

TITLES

Asylum of the emirate and government, he who adorns the emirate and government, So-and-so Soltan.

EMOLUMENTS

An amount of 679 *tuman*s and 2,000 and odd [*dinar*s] except for the 'unquantified' amount.

RETAINERS

606 persons. [**108**]

GOVERNOR OF THE DISTRICT OF KALEHGIR[212]

TITLES

Asylum of the emirate and government, he who adorns the emirate, So-and-so Soltan.

EMOLUMENTS

An amount of 257 *tuman*s and 7,000 and odd [*dinar*s].

RETAINERS

100 persons.

GOVERNOR OF THE DISTRICT OF ZONUR[213]

TITLES

The same.

EMOLUMENTS

An amount of 394 *tuman*s and 6,000 and odd [*dinar*s].

RETAINERS

150 persons.

GOVERNOR OF THE DISTRICT OF QARAJEHDAGH[214]

The custodianship of the Sheikh Shehāb al-Din tomb, which is located in Ahar, is the responsibility of the governors of Qarājehdāgh. Sheikh Shehāb al-Din is the teacher and instructor of Soltān al-Awliyā Sheikh Safi al-Din Eshāq, may God bless his grave. The custodianship and governorship aforementioned have always been with the Nasiri clan, who are the kinsmen of this royal slave. Sometimes, the office of *khalifeh al-kholafā* in addition was also bestowed upon

---

211 The qualification that "it is Kurdestan," perhaps refers to the fact that the district was populated by successive Kurdish tribes, and by the end of the Safavid period by unnamed Kurds and therefore was considered to be part of Kurdestan. According to the TM, p. 101 its governor had 874 *tuman*s and 5,390 *dinar*s as emoluments and had to have 590 men.

212 Kalehgir was a fort one about 6 km distance from Erevan. See also the Commentary section.

213 According to the TM, p. 101 the governor of Zonuz had 455 *tuman*s and 5,280 *dinar*s as emoluments and had to have 150 men.

214 According to the TM, p. 101 its governor had 828 *tuman*s and 4,200 *dinar*s as emoluments and had to have 200 men.

them, and sometimes without the said office they were charged with the said custodianship and governorship.

TITLES

Asylum of the custodianship, emirate, government and excellence, he who adorns custodianship, emirate, government and excellence, custodian of the many splendored tomb of Sheikh Shehab al-Din Ahari, may God hallow his secret, and governor of the district of Qarachehdagh.

EMOLUMENTS

He has an amount of 659 *tuman*s and 6,000 and odd [*dinar*s] and an amount of 24 Tabrizi *tuman*s as a tax exempt land grant, which annually comes to an estimated 100 Tabrizi *tuman*s.

RETAINERS

100 men.

CAMPAIGN DUTY

In lieu of the granting of the said tax exempt land grant 24 persons.

Yasāq-kashi means campaigning. The rule is this that whenever the king grants an amount in the form of a tax exempt land grant or a tax exemption to his royal slave and servant instead of [the duty of] campaigning, then a few skilled young men who accept to do so have to prepare those who are going the said campaigns instead. Whenever they cannot prepare them it is the *divān*'s rule that it receives and charges [an amount] three *tuman*s and 3,000 Tabrizi *dinar*s per person to the name of that person who [**109**] is the entitlement holder of the tax exempt land grant and the tax exemption and has accepted to join the campaign. They accept three *tuman*s of the original amount and 3,000 *dinar*s on balance as supplementary revenue of 10 per cent.

Campaigning is of several kinds. Sometimes it is campaigning in a particular province. In that case, when a campaign takes place in that province he has to be present and does not go to another province. For example, some are obliged to campaign duty in Azerbaijan. Whenever travel or war occurs in Azerbaijan he has to campaign in Azerbaijan, for the time that he is obliged to be present in the army camp of the generals, which is in Azerbaijan. If there is travel or war in Khorasan then this group does not have to go to Khorasan and another group is obliged to do so and this is not peculiar to any province. They have to be present for each campaign that they are obliged to do and that occurs.

GOVERNOR OF THE DISTRICT OF GARMERUD[215]

TITLES

Asylum of the emirate, So-and-so Soltan.

EMOLUMENTS

An amount of 139 *tuman*s and 3,000 and odd [*dinar*s].

RETAINERS

27 persons.

---

215 According to the TM, p. 101 its governor had 136 *tuman*s and 890 *dinar*s as emoluments and had to have 25 men.

GOVERNOR OF THE DISTRICT OF MOKRI[216]

TITLES

Asylum of the emirate and government, he who adorns the emirate and government, So-and-so Soltan.

EMOLUMENTS

729 *tuman*s and 3,000 and odd [*dinar*s].

RETAINERS

1,136 persons.

GOVERNOR OF HASAN ABDĀLLU[217]

TITLES

Asylum of the emirate, So-and-so Soltan.

Previously, the governors of Hasan Abdāllu were not *soltān*s. The governorship and title of *soltān* [110] was granted by His Majesty the world conqueror the late Shah 'Abbās, because the governor of Hasan Abdāllu[218] with two or three other governors had fled from the war. His Majesty the world conqueror then ordered that they all had to be to be put on donkeys and taken around the royal army camp dressed like women in a square female mantel and female head cover on their head. When the turn came for the governor of Hasan Abdāllu, the said governor, who always had a Sufi hat on his head, after having seen the female mantle he went down on his two knees before the person who had been charged with this matter [i.e. to take him around the army camp], took off his Sufi hat and said loudly in the Turkish language in the dialect of the Hasan Abdāllu tribe: "I want to read the Fāteheh. Until now the glorious hat, the apparel of the Commander of the Believers, p.b.u.h., the King of Men, the Sainted 'Ali was on our head, now the apparel of the Sainted Fatemeh, may God's prayers be on her, is on our head."[219] At that very moment his saying and speech came to the notice of His Majesty the world conqueror who forgave him and saved him from that sorrow and made him a governor of that group and gave him the title of *soltān*.

EMOLUMENTS

An amount of 71 *tuman*s and 8,000 Tabrizi *dinar*s which are fixed. On account of the group of the Dhākerlu and Kamāllu[220] [he has] an 'unquantified' amount.

RETAINERS

100 persons.

---

216 According to the TM, p. 101 its governor had 729 *tuman*s and 3,709 *dinar*s as emoluments and had to have 1,179 men.

217 According to the TM, p. 101 its governor had 88 *tuman*s and 5,723 *dinar*s as emoluments and had to have 100 men.

218 See Monshi, *Tarikh*, vol. 2, p. 1084.

219 *Fāteheh ukhuylim! Ta imdiyeh dinj tāj-vahhāj keh hezrat Amir al-Mo'minin 'aleyhu al-salām Shāh Mardānenek kesvati [eydi] ba shamizdeh eydi; eydi Hezrat-e Fatemeh-ye Zahrā salāvāt allah 'aleyhha kesvatini be shamizeh bāghliruq.*

220 I have been unable to identify the Dhākerlu and Kamāllu.

GOVERNOR OF THE DISTRICT OF SOLTANIYEH[221]

USUAL TITLES

Asylum of the emirate and government, he who adorns the emirate and government, So-and-so Soltan.

His Majesty bestowed the following titles on Mostafāqoli Khān Beygdeli:

Asylum of the province and authority, pomp and majesty of the administration, his excellency loyal and devoted scion of devoted Sufis, he who adorns the province, authority, pomp, majesty and felicity Mostafa Khan Beygdeli Shamlu, governor of Soltaniyeh, Zanjan, and Abhar.

EMOLUMENTS

An amount of 1,735 *tuman*s and 9,000 Tabrizi *dinar*s that are fixed. [111] He also has an unquantified amount.

RETAINERS

173 persons.

GOVERNOR OF BARADUST, SUMAY AND TORGUR[222]

TITLES

Asylum of the emirate, So-and-so Soltan.

EMOLUMENTS

An amount of 16 *tuman*s and 1,000 and odd *dinar*s that are fixed. On account of the district of Bayāt etc. He also has an unquantified amount.

RETAINERS

47 persons.

GOVERNOR OF THE BANEH DISTRICT[223]

TITLES

Asylum of the emirate and government, he who adorns the emirate, So-and-so Soltan.

EMOLUMENTS

An amount of 1,500 Tabrizi *tuman*s.

RETAINERS

50 persons.

[The text ends here; the rest is missing.]

---

221 According to the TM, p. 101 Soltaniyeh and Zanjan formed one jurisdiction; its governor had 1,160 *tuman*s and 2,059 *dinar*s as emoluments and had to have 873 men.

222 According to the TM, p. 102, the governor of the district of Samavi (Somay) and Tergavar had 300 *tuman*s and 2,945 *dinar*s as emoluments and had to have 47 men.

223 The TM, p. 104 mentions that the governor had to have 50 men, but lists no emoluments.

COMMENTARY

In this section I only provide comments or rather a clarification concerning one aspect of the provincial administrative organization of the Safavid kingdom, viz. that of the governorships. This aspect of Safavid history has hardly been dealt with by historians so far, while Nasiri's *Alqab* almost urges me to do so as its last and longest section consists of a list of governors and their districts. There are only two lists of governorships for the Safavid period, which both are incomplete. The list in the TM is the most complete, while that in Nasiri's *Alqab* in not only incomplete, but also sometimes wrong (probably due to the wrong sequencing of the pages of the manuscript caused by missing pages). I therefore decided to try and make an inventory of all known governorships during the Safavid period. The result shows that even for some of the larger provinces the list of governors still remains incomplete. As many of the governorships may be unfamiliar to the reader I have identified the geographical position of each one and, in case of the larger administrative units, in particular of the ones that were allowed some measure of autonomy, I sketch the main developments in their administration. The governorships are listed alphabetically, and each entry provides the name of the governor, where available the years of his term of office, his title and the name of his jurisdiction and variants thereof, followed by the sources. In case of the name I give the name of the person as it was when he was appointed, which name often changed, because either on his appointment or later the *beyg* or *soltan* would repectively be promoted to the rank of *soltan* or *khan*. In these cases the name contains the title [*khan*] or [*soltan*] between brackets to indicate that the person concerned did not have that title at the time of his appointment.

The Safavid kingdom or the *mamalek-e mahruseh* as contemporary Persian chroniclers refer to it consisted of four large fiscal administrative regions, which are a holdover of Sasanian administrative organization. These regions were Iraq (both Arab and Persian), Khorasan, Azerbaijan, and Fars, to which sometimes Kerman and Shirvan were added.[1] Each large administrative region contained a number of provinces, which were governed by a governor-general, usually refered to as *amir al-omara* or in Turkish *beygler-beygi*. To each province a number of emirs were attached, who were appointed as governor of one or more districts that

---

[1] In 1566, the number of the regions was still small in bureaucratic usage: Fars, Kerman, Khorasan, Iraq, Azerbaijan, and Shirvan. Qomi, *Kholasat*, vol. 1, p. 461.

made up the province, hence the governor-general's appellation as *amir al-omara*. Over time the number of provinces that were governed by governor-generals or vice-roys (*vali*) grew and by the end of the 16th century included: Persian Iraq, Khorasan (Mashhad, Herat), Qandahar, Merv-e Shahejan, Azerbaijan, Shirvan, Qarabagh, Georgia, Fars, Kerman, Khuzestan, Dar al-Marz (Gilan-Mazandaran), Baghdad, 'Arabestan, Kurdestan, and Lorestan.[2] This is also clear from the contemporary description of the extent of the Safavid kingdom or from the regions where victory letters (*fathnameh*s) were sent to.[3] The number of these governors-general therefore also grew from about six to fourteen. For a detailed discussion of this administrative organization and changes therein over time as well as of the various titles to indicate a governor (*hakem*, *vali*, *beygler-beygi*) I refer the reader to my book *Safavid Government Institutions*, also as to all other related questions such as the difference between a *hakem* and a vizier in governing a jurisdiction. In the following I focus on the occurrence of governorships.

As Minorsky has pointed out the ancient administrative region of Azerbaijan by the time of the Safavids was divided into four governor-generalships, to wit: Tabriz (or Azerbaijan), Chokhur-e Sa'd, Qarabagh and Shirvan. I present both the data from the lists given by the TM and Nasiri's *Alqab* to see whether there are any differences and then compare these two lists with the governorships as found in contemporary Safavid chronicles and documents. According to Nasiri's *Alqab*, the governor-general of Azerbaijan had 30 subordinate emirs, while the list has a larger number. This may be explained by the fact that some of the governorships did not exist anymore at the end of the Safavid period (e.g. Van) and that in some cases two or more governorships were held jointly by one governor. The Donboli tribe was in possession of Khoy, according to Minorsky, but Nasiri's *Alqab* disagrees and states that it was in possession of Chors. Maku is not listed either, but it is listed under Chokhur-e Sa'd. Orumiyeh is not mentioned by the TM, which only lists the Afshar tribe who were in possession of Orumiyeh. Talesh is not listed by the TM, but perhaps the entry of Qara Aghach is a pars pro toto, although this is odd, as Talesh is much bigger and perhaps Qezel Aghach is meant.[4]

Tabriz (Azerbaijan)

Name jurisdiction	TM	Nasiri	Other
Abdallu	X	Hasan Abdallu	-
Afshar	X	X + Orumiyeh	Orumiyeh
Ardabil	X	Ardabil	Ardabil
Arasbar[an]	-	X	X
Arjish	-	X	X
Astara	X	X	X

---

2 Mohammad Yusof. *Dheyl-e Tarikh-e 'Alamara-ye 'Abbasi,* ed. Soheyl Khvansari (Tehran, 1317/1938), p. 15; see also next note.

3 Qomi, *Kholasat*, vol. 1, p. 282 (Azerbaijan, Iraq, Kerman, Fars, Khorasan, Khuzestan and the Persian Gulf littoral [savahel-e 'Oman]); Molla Jalal al-Din Monajjem. *Ruznameh-ye 'Abbasi ya Ruznameh-ye Molla Jalal,* ed. Seyfollah Vahidniya (Tehran, 1366/1967), p. 300. For an even longer list see Riazul Islam, *A Calendar of Documents on Indo-Persian Relations.* 2 vols. (Tehran/Karachi, 1979), vol. 1, p. 431.

4 For a much longer list of 46 districts and towns and 11 forts, which does not necessarily reflect administrative and jurisdictional reality, see Yazdi, *Mokhtasar*, vol. 1, pp. 163-78.

COMMENTARY

Baradust-Sowmey-Tergavar	-	Anzal-Sowmey and Baradust separately	as Nasiri
Bayat	-	X	X
Bedlis	-	-	X
Chors	X	X + Donboli	-
Donboli	X	-	-
Garmerud	X	X	X
Gavarud	X	X	X
Hashtrud-e TabTab	X	X + Nelqas	-
Jaramilu (see also Chokhur-e Saʻd table)	-	X	X Haramilu
Kalehgir	-	X	X
Khalkhal	-	-	X
Khoy	-	-	X
Kurluk	-	X	-
Lahijan	X	X Lajan	X Laja'an
Lankar-konan	-	X	X
Lak of Salmas	X	X	X
Maragheh	X + Moqaddam	X + Moqaddam	X
Marand	-	X	X
Meshkin	X	X + Kalhor	-
Moghanat	X	X	X
Mokri	X	X	X
Orumiyeh	-	X + Afshar	X
Pasak	X	X	X
Qapanat	X	X	X
Qara Aghaj – Talesh	X	-	-
Qarajehdagh	X	X	X
Qezel Aghaj	-	X	X
Sarab	X	X	X
Saru-qargan	-	-	X
Shahsevan	X	-	-
Shahqaqi	X	X	?
Sojas	-	-	X
Soltaniyeh-Zanjan	X	X	X
Surluq	-	-	X

Talesh	-	-	X
Tarom	-	-	X
Ujarud	X	X	X
Van	-	-	X
Vargahan	X	X	-
Zunuz; Qarni-yaraq	X	X	X

The province of Chokhur-e Sa'd had nine subordinate emirs, according to Nasiri's *Alqab*, but the table shows that although the number might be the same the composition of the these nine subordinate governorships was different and therefore the number also could be higher or lower as the case may be.[5] The differences may be explained by discounting forts, jointly held governorships and the fact that Maku sometimes was part of Azerbaijan.

Chokhur-e Sa'd

Name	TM	Nasiri	Other
'Adeljavaz Qal'eh	-	-	X
Aqcheh Qal'eh	-	X	X +Buri + Nabik
Bayazid	X	X	X
Darvalakis + Haramilu	-	X	Jaramilu
Donbolis	X	X	-
Kalehgir	-	X	X
Kurluk	-	X	-
Maghazberd	X	-	X
Maku	X	X + Bayat	X
Nakhjevan	X	X + Kangarlu	X
Ordubad	-	-	X
Sadarak	X	-	-
Shadidlu	X	X	-
Zaruzbil	X	X + Kalani	-

The governor-general of Qarabagh had 10 subordinate emirs, according to Nasiri's *Alqab*. The difference between the three lists can, as usual be explained, by a combination of factors such as joint governorships, ignoring forts and the like.[6]

---

5 For a much shorter list of three districts (Erevan, Olka-ye Sarur, Qars) and 6 forts (Sa'adat, Bakuyeh, Bayazid, Shurehgel, Aqcheh Qal'eh and Tajanker [?]), which does not necessarily reflect administrative and jurisdictional reality, see Yazdi, *Mokhtasar*, vol. 1, pp. 192-96.

6 Georgian sources also mention the following districts that were part of Qarabagh: Mowakan and Kazach (Qazaq?). Marie-Félicité Brosset, *Histoire de la Géorgie*, 2 vols in 4 parts (St. Petersburg, 1856-57), vol. 2/1, pp. 30, 348; vol. 2/2, p. 513.

Qarabagh

Name	TM	Nasiri	Other
Akhtabad	X	X + Qazaqlar	X
Aleshkert	-	-	X
Arasbar	-	X	X
Barda'	X	X	X
Bargushat	X	X	X
Javanshir	X	X	X
Lori and Pambak	X	X + Buzchelu	X
Paydar	-	X	X
Qara Aghaj	X	X + Bayat	-
Qazeqman	-	-	X
Shamakhi	-	-	X
Shurehgel	-	-	X
Somay – Tergavar	X	-	X
Tiflis	X	-	X
Zagam	X	X + Shams al-Dinlu	X

The governor-general of Shirvan had six subordinate emirs.[7] The differences are due to the usual suspects. Mahmudabad usually was joined with Saliyan or Baku, while Shaberan was in total ruins when both the TM and Nasiri's *Alqab* were written. It is also likely that it was usually jointly held with Darband, athough it occurs as a stand-alone governorship.

Shirvan

Name	TM	Nasiri	Other
Alpa'ut	X	X	X
Arash	-	-	X
Arash – Sheki	X	X	X
Baku	X	X	X
Chameshgezek –Aghdash	X	X	X
Darband	X	X	X
Fakhran	-	-	X
Mahmudabad	-	-	X

---

7   For a list of 17 districts and towns and 7 forts in Shirvan, which does not necessarily reflect administrative and jurisdictional reality, see Yazdi, *Mokhtasar*, vol. 1, pp. 325-46.

Qobeh, Qolhan, Saliyan	X	X	X
Shabaran	-	-	X
Zakhur	-	-	X

The Khorasan administrative region[8] was divided into four governor-generalships, to wit: Herat, Mashhad, Qandahar and Merv as well as the governorship of Seystan. The governor-general of Herat had 11 subordinate emirs, according to the TM, but Nasiri's *Alqab* has more. This may be due to the usual reasons of joint governorships (Abdali + Herat, e.g.) and changes in jurisdictions. For example, whereas the TM lists Jam as belonging to Herat, Nasiri's *Alqab* lists it as part of Mashhad. It is possible that depending on the political situation it belonged at certain moment to the one and at other times to the other governor-generalship.

Herat

Name	TM	Nasiri	Other
Abdali	-	X	X
Badghis	X	X	X
Bala Morghab	X	X	X
Durmi	X = Zuri?	-	-
Farah	X	X	X
Esfezar	-	-	X
Fusanj	-	-	X
Ghur	X	X Ghuri	X Ghuri
Heratrud + Shaflan	-	X	X
Torbat [-e Sheikh Jam]	X	-	X
Karokh	X	X + Jamshidis	X
Khvaf +Bakharz	X	X	X
Kushk	-	-	X
Maruchaq	X	X	X
Nahababad (?)	-	X	-
Panjdeh	X	X	X
Qebchaq	-	X	-
Tun	X	X	X
Ubeh	-	-	X
Zuri	= Durmi?	X	-

---

8 Yazdi, *Mokhtasar*, vol. 1, pp. 196-261 presents Khorasan as a combination of the provinces of Herat and Mashhad, which together had 84 towns and districts and 120 forts.

The governor-general of Mashhad had 12 subordinate emirs, according to Nasiri's *Alqab*. At times, there seems to have been a larger number of governorships, however, even when allowing for combined governorships. Also, when Merv was held for some time by an Uzbeg Safavid vassal the districts of Abivard and Nesa were subordinate to it and not to Mashhad.

Mashhad

Name	TM	Nasiri	Other
Abivard	X	X	X
Azadvar	X	Aradvar + Farumad	-
Bastam	-	-	X + Biyarjomand
Bazavandaq	X	X	-
Darun	X	X + Khabushan	X + Khabushan
Esfara'in	X	X	X
Gonabad	-	-	X
Jahan-Arghiyan	-	-	X
Jam	-	X	X
Kelidar	-	-	X
Mahvelat	-	-	X
Maneh	-	-	X
Nesa	-	X	X
Nishapur	X	X	X
Pasakuh	X = Y.saku	X	X
Qa'en	-	-	X
Sabzavar	X	X	X
Sarakhs-Zurabad	-	X	X
Torbat-e Heydari	X	X	X
Torshiz	X	X	X
Tun va Tabas	-	X	X
Zaveh	-	-	X

The number of subordinate emirs for Qandahar has not been reported, but it was probably five. Bost-Gereshk was also jointly held with Zamindavar thus partially explaining the difference between the lists. Nasiri's *Alqab* lists the Abdali as subordinates of Qandahar, which cannot be right as they were based around Herat, where I have inserted them. K.ri and Y.ki perhaps are copyist's errors for the districts of Duki and Chutiyali (q.v.), which are mentioned as being part of Qandahar during the reign of 'Abbas II. In addition to Zamindavar, the Garmsir-e Qandahar also was included as was Ghuriyan, and the tribal district of the Hazaras, which included Qalat, an area north-east of Qandahar.⁹ According to the *Haft Eqlim*, Badghis was also part of Qandahar, but that seems unlikely, as Minorsky has rightly argued.¹⁰

Qandahar

Name	TM	Nasiri	Other
Davar	-	-	X
Bost-Gereshk	-	X	X
Chutiyali + Duki	-	-	X
Ghilzay + Hud Jebali, Nasiri	-	X	-
Ghuriyan	X	X	X + Fusanj + Kusuyeh
Kushk	X	-	X
K.ri , Y.ki	X	X	-
Shal va Mostang	-	-	X
Zamindavar	X	X	X

Merv like Kerman was a single emir governor-generalship, although when the Safavids held Gharjestan for a short while its governor may have been his subordinate. The position of the governor of Balkh, which the Safavids held for a short while, is not clear. He may have been an independent governor.

Seystan was one governorship, and although some districts were separated from this jurisdiction such as Gah (Kah), Garmsirat, Neh va Bandan and Uq (q.v.) it is not always clear to which governor-general these governors were subordinate to.

Of the Caspian provinces only Astarabad and Gilan are mentioned by both the TM and the *Alqab*. Minorsky has suggested that the reason that Mazandaran was not mentioned had to do with the fact that it had been turned into crown domain, but so was Gilan and thus that cannot have been the reason. I therefore have added an overview of the districts of Mazandaran such as is to be found in the chronicles and official documents.

Astarabad

Name	TM	Nasiri	Other
Gera'i or Gereyli	X	-	X
Goklan	X	-	X
Hajjilar	X		X
Jalayer	X	-	-
Jorjan	-	-	X

---

9 Monshi, *Tarikh*, pp. 478, 672.
10 Amin Ahmad Razi, *Haft Eqlim*, ed. Javad Fazel 3 vols. (Tehran, n.d.), vol. 2, pp. 128-29; TM, pp. 102, 168; Röhrborn, *Provinzen*, p. 14 disagrees with Minorsky, but see below.

Kabud-Jameh	Hajjilar	-	X
K.ra-chupi (Gera-chopi?)	X	-	-
Mobarakabad	-	-	X
Yamut	X		?

Gilan or Dar al-Marz

Name	TM	Nasiri	Other
Deylaman	-	-	X
Fumen	-	-	X
Gaskar	X	-	X
Kuchesfahan	-	-	X
Kuhdom	X	-	X
Lahejan	-	-	X
Leshteh-nesha	-	-	X
Ranekuh	X	-	X
Rasht	-	-	X
Tonekabon	X	-	X

Mazandaran

Name	TM	Nasiri	Other
Amol	-	-	X
Kojur	-	-	X
Kolbar	-	-	X
Larijan	-	-	X
Mashhad-e Sar	-	-	X
Nur	-	-	X
Rostamdar	-	-	X
Savadkuh	-	-	X

Kerman was a governor-generalship which had no other subordinate emirs. Sometimes it was held together with Qandahar.

The term Iraq represented the central and western part of the kingdom. Iraq was divided into two parts, Arab Iraq and Persian Iraq. Arab Iraq roughly corresponds to much of modern-day Iraq, while Persian Iraq included the central regions of Hamadan, Tehran and Isfahan. The mountainous western region between these two Iraqs, comprising of Kurdestan, Lorestan and Bakhtiyari, belonged in part to either of these two regions, depending on the military situation, although usually they maintained a high degree of autonomy.

Safavid Arab Iraq consisted of two provinces, viz. Baghdad and Diyarbekr. Because the Safavids had already lost Diyarbekr in 1517, while they lost Baghdad permanently with the peace of Zohab of 1639, these do not figure either in the TM or Nasiri's *Alqab*. There were also a number of subordinate governorships, which I have listed in the table below. It is not clear whether the short-lived governorships of Kirkuk and Mosul were independent ones, although that seems likely.

Arab Iraq[11]

Name	Other
Diyarbekr*	X
Orfah [ye-Diyarbekr]	X
Kirkuk – Daquq	X
Mosul	X
Baghdad	X
Hillah	X
Jastan	X
Javazer	X
Najaf	X
Romahiyeh	X
Vaset	X

The term Persian Iraq includes the jurisdictions in Central and Western Persia between Isfahan, Yazd, Aberquh, Qom, Kashan, Hamadan, Qazvin, Tehran/Rey, Saveh, and Semnan/Khvar. Isfahan was a major province, but it was neither included in the TM nor in Nasiri's *Alqab*, because it was crown domain. However, not all of its dependent governorships were crown domain or if they were they had become so at a later date. Minorsky has reconstructed the likely list of governorships of Isfahan based on the list of judges that the *sadr-e khasseh* appointed in this jurisdiction. This list of governorships is not entirely borne out, however, by data from other sources.

Isfahan

Name	Minorsky	Other
Aberquh	X	X
Ardestan	X	X
Burburud	X	-
Delijan	X	-
Farahan	X	X
Fereydun	X	X

11 According to Lord Stanley ed., *Travels to Tana and Persia by J. Barbaro and A. Contarini*, 2 vols. in one, (London, 1873), pp. 145-46. Esma'il I, in addition to Diyarbekr and Orfah, also controlled Kharput, Mardin, Jazireh, Hisn Kaifa and Sert, which were all held by Kurdish governors.

Golpeygan	X	X
Japalaq	X	-
Kamara	X	-
Kashan	X	X
Khvansar	X	X
Kiyar	X	-
Mahallat	X	-
Mezdaj	X	-
Na'in	X	-
Natanz	X	X
Pudeh-Someyram	X - Someyram only	X
Qom	X	X
Qomisheh	X	-
Rar	X	-

Hamadan

Name	TM	Nasiri	Other
Farahan	-	-	X
Garrus or Zarrin-kamar	X	-	X
Harsin	X	-	X
Hashtajoft	X	-	-
Kalhor	X	-	X
Sa'dabad	-	-	X

The 'central region' did not have a governor-general, for the TM explicitly states that the governors in that area were independent emirs, and it included the following governorships:

'Central Province'

Name	Minorsky	Other
'Arab-e 'Amereh	-	X
Aveh	X	X
Damavand	-	X
Damghan	-	X
Firuzkuh	X	X
Hablerud – Hazar Jarib	-	X
Jorpardeqan	-	X

Khvar-Semnan	X	X
Qazvin	-	X
Rey-Tehran	X	X
Saveh	X	X
Savokh-Bulagh	-	X
Varamin	-	X

The Western region included three *vali*doms, to wit: Kurdestan-e Ardalan, Lurestan-e Feyli and Bakhtiyari. Minorsky also mentions Maba, for which he suggests the reading of Baneh. However, Baneh (q.v.) was a jurisdiction not at the same level as the other three and therefore its inclusion seems unlikely, also because, according to Eskander Beyg Monshi, it was part of Azerbayjan. Kurdestan also had a number of subordinate governorships, some of which were held by the governor of Kurdestan, while some others were held jointly with others.

Kurdestan-Ardalan

Name	TM	Nasiri	Other
Avroman	X	-	X
Baneh	X	X	X ?
Borujerd	-	-	X
Chamchal	-	-	X
Dinavar	-	-	X
Hasanabad	-	-	X
Javabrud	X	-	
Jazireh	-	-	X
Kermanshahan	-	X	X
Khorkhoreh	-	-	X
Mandali	-	-	X
Palangan	-	-	X
Shahr-e zur	-	-	X
Sonqor	-	-	X
Zohab	-	-	X

Lorestan-e Feyli had only the following subordinate governorships: Khaveh, Sadmareh and Khorramabad, of which the latter also was held by the *vali* of Lorestan. The Bakhtiyaris, who are related to the Lors, hence they are also known as Bakhtiyari-ye Lor, lived in the highlands between Lorestan, Isfahan and 'Arabestan.

The southern region included Fars, Kuhgiluyeh, and 'Arabestan. Fars, apart as a header, is not mentioned in the TM list, because it had been a crown domain since 1632. However, even after that time there continued to be governorships of districts that had been previously subordinate to the governor-general of Fars. Also, as of 1717 Fars was governed once again by a governor-general. After it had become crown domain, the governors of many of these districts seem to have become independent emirs, who depended directly from the royal court. Based on the data collected I therefore have made the following, undoubtedly incomplete, list of governorships of Fars.[12]

Fars

Name	TM	Other
Bahrain	X	X – not *khasseh*
Bandar 'Abbas (aka Hormuz, Jarun)	X	X
Bavanat	-	X
Birunat	-	X
Darabjerd		X
Dashtestan	X	X – not *khasseh*
Fasa		X
Ich		X
Karbal		X
Kazerun	X	X
Lar		X – *khasseh* since 1639
Manjavan		X
Neyriz		X
Parsi-Badan		X
Sajavand		X
Sarvestan	X	X – not *khasseh*
Shabankareh		X
Shiraz		X – *khasseh*
Shulestan		X

According to the TM, Kuhgiluyeh was part of Fars, which may have been correct from a fiscal organizational point of view, but not from an administrative one. In the past Kuhgiluyeh only seems to have been subordinate to Fars, when its governor-general was also governor of Kuhgilyeh. The latter province included the following districts: Dowraq and Zeydan.

'Arabestan or Khuzestan was held for the greater part by the *vali* of Hoveyzeh or 'Arabestan. Only the jurisdictions of Dezful and Shushtar were held directly by court appointed governors, while in the second half of the seventeenth century Ahvaz seems to have been held by independent governors, although these probably were family members of the *vali* who challenged his rule.

---

12 For a much longer list of 57 districts and towns and 24 forts, which does not necessarily reflect administrative and jurisdictional reality, see Yazdi, *Mokhtasar*, vol. 1, pp. 325-46.

ALPHABETICAL LIST OF GOVERNORSHIPS

So far I have offered information on the distribution of the various governorships among the different large provinces. In the remainder of this commentary I provide information on each known administrative jurisdiction in alphabetical order. For easy reference I have organized all the names of the governors in one table per jurisdiction if I found more than one name. I have not included the governors of Georgia and Daghestan, because the names of the governors or *vali*s of Georgia can be easily found in monographs dealing with the Georgian kingdom, while the situation of Daghestan is quite complicated, which I intend to addres later in a separate article. The tables look as in the sample table below. In the third column of this sample table I explain how to understand the dates in these tables. As to the dates themselves I have expressed them in *hijri-qamari* years just like they occur in the texts and have added thereafter the approximate Common Era (CE) year. For easy conversion to determine the exact beginning and end of the *hijri* year, I refer the reader to the following website [http://www.oriold.unizh.ch/static/hegira.html]. When dates occur in the text without the add-on of a conversion year this means that it is a CE year. Finally, the dates, as mentioned in Persian chronicles and documents, are not always reliable. There usually is a difference of one year, or sometimes even more, between two or more contemporary Persian histories and thus I selected the years that seemed to be most appropriate in view of other data and the sequence of governors. Sometimes, dates for a number of governors from different texts do not agree at all (see, e.g. Shushstar), or different persons are listed for the same year and jurisdiction, in which cases I mention this explicitly in the table.

Sample table with explanation of the meaning of the symbols concerning the years

Name	Year	Observations	
	?-999	means that the end date is known, but not begin date	
	999-?	means that the begin date is known, but not the end date	
	995-999-?	means that the begin date is known and another later year, which is not necessarily the end date	
	999	only a single date is known, which, may indicate both the begin and end date or it indicates just a single known year	
	998-999	indicates begin and end date	

? after a name means uncertain if he is the correct person	?-999-?	only one date is known, but also that the office holder governed both before and after that date	
	990s?	exact date unknown, but not the decade	
[?] after a name means its orthography is uncertain	[?]	means date or decade unknown	
n.a. = not available			
	IAB = *ishik aghasi-bashi*	H = *hakem*; BB = *beygler-beygi*	

Abdali is not only a tribal district, but also refers to the Abdali tribal confederation, which groups the Pashtun clans of the west. They are better known by the name of Dorrani since the reign of Ahmad Shah Dorrani (or Ahmad Shah Abdali: r. 1747-1772). Originally from the Qandahar area they were moved to Herat in the 1590s due to pressure from the Ghilzays. The Abdali chiefs, who were appointed by the Safavid shahs, from whom they also received the title of *soltan*, came from the Sadozai clan. The Abdalis rebelled in 1716 and took control of Herat.[13] The Abdali district was a dependency of the province of Herat (q.v.).

Name	Year	Observations	Source
Shamshir 'Ali	1057/1647	Emir *il-e* Abdali	Shamlu 1, 424
Hayat Soltan Sadozay	ca. 1101/1690	*Sardar il-e* Abdali	Safavi 19
'Abdollah Khan b. Hayat Soltan	ca. 1117/1705	*Sardar il-e* Abdali	Safavi 19
Asadollah Khan b. 'Abdollah Khan	ca. 1127/1715	*Sardar il-e* Abdali	Safavi 19

Aberquh is the name of a town and its surrounding district situated on the road between Isfahan and Shiraz, at the junction where another road splits off towards Yazd. This district was part of Persian Iraq and between 972/1564 and 980/1572 and probably beyond was *khasseh* or crown domain. As of 985/1577, Aberquh seems to have been under governors again. The high frequency of appointments during the year 998/1590 is an indication of the conflict that existed at that time between the central government and the Afshar governors of Yazd, Kerman and Shiraz. According to Nasiri's *Alqab*, towards the end of the Safavid period the Aberquh district was assigned to the *tofangchi aghasi*.

Name	Year	Observations	Source
Ra'is Mohammad Kera'i [Karreh]	909-911/1503-1505	H Aberquh; Lor chief	Hoseyni 29; Shamlu 1, 38; Monshi 31; Rumlu 116; Mozaffar 212

---

13 Safavi, *Majma'*, p. 19; Laurence Lockhart, *The Fall of the Safavi Dynasty* (Cambridge, 1956), pp. 95-102.

Hoseyn Beyg Shamlu*	910/1504	H Aberquh	Bidlisi II 511
	From 972/1564 until at least 980/1572	crown domain + Biyabanak	Haft Eqlim 3, 67
Qoli Soltan Afshar	985-?/1577-?	*Teyuldar* Aberquh-Bavanat - *qurchi-bashi*	Qomi 2, 665
Yusof Beyg Afshar b. Qoli Khan Beyg	994-998/1586-1590	H Aberquh - *qurchi-bashi*	Natanzi 361; Valeh 1372, 814; Qomi 2, 848; Monshi 354, 422; Molla Jalal 82
Mohammad Beyg	998/1590	illegal H Aberquh; appointed by Bektash Khan of Kerman	Molla Jalal 73
Morshedqoli Beyg	998/1590	*Darugheh* Aberquh	Molla Jalal 74-75
Heydar Beyg Hajjilar	998/1590	*Darugheh* Aberquh	Molla Jalal 82
Nadr Khan Dhu'l-Qadr or Afshar	998-?/1590-?	H Aberquh; nephew of Yusof Khan of Kerman	Monshi 425; Molla Jalal 85; Vahid 111 (Badr Khan)
'Aliqoli Khan	1006/1597	*Vali* Aberquh	Molla Jalal 161
'Ali Qobad Beyg Chuleh-ye Chaghatay	1053-1055/1643-1645	H Aberquh; IAB harem	Vahid 394, 412
Qalandar Soltan Chuleh-ye Chaghatay	1055-1072/1645-1661	H Aberquh - *tofangchi-aghasi*	Vahid 412, 731
Budaq Soltan	1072-?/1662-?	H Aberquh - *tofangchi-aghasi*	Vahid 731

* The governor was Mobarez al-Din 'Abdi Beyg, according to Jean Aubin, "Révolution chiite et conservatisme. Les soufis de Lahejan, 1500-1514 (Etudes safavides II)," *Moyen Orient & Océan Indien* 1 (1984), p. 5, n. 39.

Abhar, see Soltaniyeh.

Abivard is a town and district situated on the northwest frontier of Khorasan, midway between Darrehgaz and Kalat-e Naderi, at about 53 km from each place. This district is situated in northern Khorasan, in the northern foothills of the Hazar Masjed range and ws part of the province of Mashhad. The whole of this district, including Nesa (q.v.) and Sarakhs (q.v.), is known by the Turkish name of Ätäk, "the foothills." Abivard was already a border fortification in Sasanian times and also served as such in Safavid times as a defense against the Uzbegs, who, it seems, held the place until 1006/1598.[14] It was only as of 1009/1600 that the Safavids were able to occupy Abivard permanently. Prior to that time it was held by Uzbeg governors, be it since 1001/1592 by Uzbegs who were vassals of 'Abbas I.

---

14 For its history see C. E. Bosworth, "Abivard," *Encyclopedia Iranica*. For the Uzbeg occupation see, e.g., Sharaf al-Din Khan Bidlisi, *Sharafnameh*. Translated from the Persian by Francois Bernard Charmoy as *Cheref-Nameh ou Fastes de la Nation Kurde*. 2 vols. (St. Petersburg, 1868), vol. 2, p. 607; Mahmud b. Hedayatollah Afushteh-ye Natanzi. *Naqavat al-athar fi dhekr al-akhyar*, ed. Ehsan Eshraqi. (Tehran, 1350/1971), p. 568.

Name	Year	Observations	Source
'Ali Soltan Khvarezmi	934/1538	H. Abivard	Abrahams 137
n.a.	?-962-1006/?-1555-1597	Uzbeg occupation	Bidlisi 2, 607; Tatavi 626, 711
Abu'l-Khan	973/1565	*Vali* Abivard; declared his allegiance	Abrahams 145
Nur Mohammad Khan; Merv ruler's cousin	1006-1009/1597-1600	H Abivard-Nesa; Safavid Uzbeg vassal	Siyaqi 479; Monshi 590-91
Melkish Soltan b. Bektash Khan Ostajalu	1009-?/1600-?	H Abivard, Nesa, Baghbad	Monshi 605
Arz Beyg	1019/1610	H Nesa – Abivard	Molla Jalal 383
Jamshid Soltan Gorji	1038/1628	H Abivard -Georgian *gholam*	Yusof 21-22; Monshi 1088
Alzobar [?] Beyg (Soltan)	1044-?/1634-?	H Abivard - *bildar-bashi*	Yusof 199; Valeh 1380, 612; Vahid 694, 747
Badadeh Soltan	?-1069/?-1659	H Abivard	Valeh 1380, 612; Vahid 644
Najafqoli Soltan b. Alzobar [?] Soltan	1069-?/1659-?	H Abivard	Valeh 1380, 612; Vahid 644
Fath 'Ali Khan	1122-24/1710-1713	H Nishapur-Darun-Abivard	Khatunabadi 560, 565
Habil Khan	1124-?/1713-?	H Abivard	Khatunabadi 565
Hasan 'Ali Khan	1129-?/1717-?	H Abivard	Mervi 1, 22, 34, 36
Qorban 'Ali Beyg	1134/1722	H Abivard	Mervi 1, 35-36

'Adeljavaz was one of the frontier forts that often changed hands and usually was held by the Ottomans. In 961/1554, for example, Esma'il Mirza plundered Van, Soltan, Arjish and 'Azeljavaz.[15] The district was part of Chokhur-e Sa'd province.

Name	Year	Observations	Source
Mostafa Beyg	951/1553	H 'Adeljavaz	Fekete 409-11
Oveys Beyg Pazuki	?; under Tahmasp I	H 'Adeljavaz	Bidlisi 2, 193

Aghcheh Qal'eh see Aqcheh Qal'eh.

Aghdash is a district situated north of the Aras river and is a dependency of Shirvan (see also Chameshgezek).

---

15 Qomi, *Kholasat*, vol. 1, p. 368; Monshi, *Tarikh*, vol. 1, p. 76.

Akhesqeh[16] or Akheshkeh[17] was a fort in the Akhesqeh district of Meshkhia province of Georgia on the border with the Ottoman Empire (which held the remainder of Masq or Meshkhia). Of the first governor mentioned, who was a Georgian, it is reported that the fort and its surrounding area were his hereditary lands. According to Bedlisi, he surrendered his lands to the Ottomans in 987/1579 and thus Ottoman rule may have started at least two years later than Vakhusti indicates.[18]

Name	Year	Observations	Source
Manuchehr b. Grigori	987/1597	H Akheshkeh	Bidlisi 2, 648
	from 985/1577 until 1032/1622	under Ottoman rule	
Salim Khan Shams al-Dinlu	1032-1036/1623-1627	H *qal'eh-ye* Akhesqeh + Lori	Monshi 1007, 1031; Vahid 207 (Gori)
Shamshi Khan Qazaqlar aka Shams al-Din Qazaqlar	1036-1041/1627-1631	H *qal'eh-ye* Akhesqeh-ye Gorjestan+ *il-e* Qazaqlar	Monshi 1061; Yusof 81; Vahid 186, 218
Salim Khan Shams al-Dinluy-e Dhu'l-Qadr	1041-1043/1631-1633	H *qal'eh-ye* Akhesqeh	Yusof 82; Monshi 1060, 1085
Emamqoli Beyg	1043-1049?/1633-1639?	H Akhesqeh – IAB	Yusof 153
	as of 1049/1039	remained permanently in Ottoman hands	Vakhusti 66; Vahid 650; Esfahani 274, 277

Akhlat is a border district, situated on the western side of Lake Van, north-east of Bitlis, which usually was in Ottoman hands. In 932/1526 its Safavid governor was Delu Mantasha Ostajalu.[19]

Akhtabad,[20] Akhsabad,[21] Akhastabad,[22] and even Hasanabad[23] are probably copyist's errors of the name of the same district or its fort located near Erevan, which, presumably, is the Armenian

---

16 Monshi, *Tarikh*, vol. 2, pp. 1007, 1060, 1082; Yusof, *Dheyl*, pp. 81, 153, 235; Yazdi, *Mokhtasar*, pp. 365, 367.

17 Bedlisi, *Cheref-Nameh*, vol. 2, p. 648.

18 According to Vakhusti, (in Brosset, *Histoire*, vol. 1/ 2, p. 219), Tahmasp I had already formally ceded Meshkhia to the Ottomans in 1574. The treaty of 1022/1613 confirmed Ottoman possession of Akheshqeh. Monshi, *Tarikh*, vol. 2, p. 864.

19 Bacqué-Gramont, "Liste," pp. 98, 102.

20 TM, p. 77; Mohammad Mofid Mostoufi-ye Yazdi, *Mokhtasar-e Mofid* 2 vols. (Wiesbaden, 1989), vol. 1, p. 365-66 only reports that it is an extremely cold place.

21 al-Hoseyni, *Tarikh*, p. 9.

22 Monshi, *Tarikh*, vol. 2, pp. 719, 785, 901-02; Yusof, *Dheyl*, p. 171; Mohammad Yusof Valeh Qazvini, *Iran dar Zaman-e Shah Safi va Shah 'Abbas Dovvom*. ed. Mohammad Reza Nasiri (Tehran, 1380/2001), p. 222 (henceforth quoted as Valeh, *Iran*); Vahid, *Tarikh*, p. 272 (Beysanqor Soltan Buzchalu, governor of the fort); A.D. Papaziyan, *Persidskie Dokumenty Matenadarana I, Ukazy, vypusk vtoroi (1601-1650)* (Erevan 1959), doc. 12.

23 Khvandamir. *Habib al-Seyar*, 4 vols. ed. Mohammad Dabir-Siyaqi. (Tehran, 1362/1983 [3rd. ed.]), vol. 4, p. 454.

district of Akhpat in the Borchalu gorge, downstream from Pambak.[24] According to Nasiri's *Alqab*, the governorship was held jointly with that of the chieftainship of the Qazaqlar tribe.

Name	Year	Observations	Source
Khalil Soltan Qaramanlu	?-1044/?-1634	H Akhastabad	Yusof 171
'Isa Khan Soltan Buzchelu	1045-?/1635-?	H Akhastabad	Vahid 272

Alamut is an isolated mountain district, with its famous fort as its center, situated at some 35 km north-west of Qazvin. During the first two decades of Safavid rule Kargiya [sic] Hadi Kiya was governor of Alamut.[25]

Alba'ut or Alpa'ut is the name of the district situated south-west of Shamakhi. Minorsky noted in the TM that there are several villages with the name Alpa'ut south-west of Shamakhi and east of the Gök-chay. He rightly believed it to be tribal name, and more in particular that of the ruling family. The name is of Mongol origin meaning "the chief's subjects, estate owners."[26]

Name	Year	Observations	Source
Mohammad Khan Soltan	1105/1693	H Alba'ut	Nasiri 58
Ahmad Khan Soltan	1106/1694	H Alba'ut	Nasiri 81

Alashkert or Alashgerd is situated north of Lake Van and is bounded on the north by Qazeqman. It was a frontier district of the province of Qarabagh, which explains why, like in many other frontier districts, Kurdish chiefs with their retainers were appointed there (see also Qazeqman). It later had to be ceded to Ottomans in whose hands it remained.

Name	Year	Observations	Source
Yadgar Beyg b. Zeynal Pazuki	966/1559	H Alashgerd	Bidlisi 2, 195; Shirazi 114
Qara Khan Bayat	984/1576	H Shurehgel and Alashkert	Monshi 1, 141
Niyaz Beyg b. Yadgar Beyg Pazuki	985-?/1577-?	H half of Alashgerd	Bidlisi 2, 196
Qalich Beyg b. Oveys Beyg Pazuki	985-993/1577-1585	H half of Alashgerd	Bidlisi 2, 194, 197
Ebrahim Beyg Oqchu-oghlu	993-995?/1585-1587?	H part of Alashgerd	Bidlisi 2, 198

---

24 TM, p. 167. Röhrborn, *Provinzen*, p. 5, n. 14 argues that the correct name probably is Akstafa; see Papaziyan (1956), *Persidskie*, doc. 13 and pp. 209-11.
25 Laheji, *Tarikh*, pp. 111, 149, 205, 334-45, 347. For its history and situation see B. Hourcade, "Alamut," *Encyclopedia Iranica*.
26 TM, p. 167.

Amol a district named after its main center, the town of Amol, which is situated in Mazandaran on the banks of the river Haraz, between the Caspian Sea and the Elburz mountains. In Safavid times it was the main center of Mazandaran and a thriving commercial community.[27] It was held by governors, who were members of the local ruling dynasty of Mazandaran (q.v.) and when the latter province became crown domain Amol was henceforth managed by the vizier of Mazandaran.

Name	Year	Observations	Source
Sayyed Nasir al-Din	932/1526	*Vali* Amol	Tahmasp 7
Sayyed Mir Shahi	951/1544	H Amol	Hoseyni 152
Alvand Div	1005/1597	H Amol	Shamlu 1, 167; Monshi 519-20
Malek Bahman b. Malek Kayumarth b. Ka'us	1005-06/1597-1598	H Amol	Monshi 519-22

Anzal-Sowmey are two dependencies of Orumiyeh district. In 1017/1607, Owliya Beyg son of Kur Seyf al-Din was governor of Anzal and Sowmey (q.v.).[28]

Aqcheh Qal'eh is a fort on the border with the Ottoman Empire, near Shurehgel, and a dependency of Chokhur-e Sa'd.[29]

Name	Year	Observations	Source
'Isa Khan Soltan Buzchelu	1049/1640	H Buri, Nabik, Aqcheh Qal'eh	Yusof 239-40
Mehdi Khan Soltan Sa'dlu	?-1111/?-1700	H Aqcheh Qal'eh; succeeded by his son	Puturidze 1962, doc. 34
Mostafa Soltan Sa'dlu	1111-1133/1700-1721	BB Aqcheh Qal'eh	Puturidze 1962, doc. 34; Ibid., 1965, doc. 37

'Arab-e 'Ameri is the name of a district near Semnan. This governorship does neither occur in the TM nor in Nasiri's *Alqab*, but it is mentioned on two occasions, as far as I know. In 991/1583, Mortezaqoli Khan Pornak Torkman, the governor of Astarabad, Damghan, Bastam, Biyarjomand, and Hazar Jarib also was in charge of the [*olusat-e*] A'rab-e 'Ameri, who probably were an Arab tribe settled within the borders of this governor's district.[30]

'Arabestan or Khuzestan is a province in south-western Iran. Prior to the imposition of Safavid overlordship over the Mosha'sha' dynasty its rulers held sway over the whole of 'Arabestan,

---

27 For its history see C.E. Bosworth, "Amol," *Encyclopedia Iranica*.
28 Monshi, *Tarikh*, vol. 2, p. 795.
29 Yazdi, *Mokhtasar*, pp. 194-95.
30 Monshi, *Tarikh*, vol. 1, p. 290; Valeh, *Khold*, p. 678. One family of the 'Arab-e 'Ameri tribe played a leading role in Safavid administration and its members became notables of the town of Ardestan, see Abu'l-Qasem Rafi' Mehrabadi, *Tarikh-e Ardestan* 3 vols. (Tehran, 1367/1988), vol. 2, pp. 241-60.

as Khuzestan then was usually referred to, as well as part of S. Iraq.³¹ This meant that, in addition to Hoveyzeh, the Mosha'sha' capital, the dynasty also held Dezful and Shushtar.³² After their defeat against Shah Esma'il I in 914/1508 Sayyed Fayyaz fled and a Qezelbash emir was appointed as governor of 'Arabestan.³³ However, shortly thereafter the Mosha'sha's were allowed to remain in control over 'Arabestan west of the Karun, with their main center at Hoveyzeh. They had, of course, to pay tribute and give hostages as a guarantee for their good behavior. These hostages were brought up either at the Safavid court or in the provinces, and in one case (Sayyed Nasr) even became governor of Rey and an intimate of the grand vizier, Mirza Hatem Ordubadi.³⁴

It is only in the second half of the seventeenth century that we learn that there allegedly were Safavid governors of Ahvaz, indicating that this part of 'Arabestan was not under the direct control of the Mosha'sha's any more.³⁵ By that time, the governor of Hoveyzeh was increasingly referred to as *vali-ye* 'Arabestan, because throughout the sixteenth century and the early seventeenth century the normal appellation was *hakem* or *vali-ye* Hoveyzeh. The term Khuzestan in contrast was used more to denote eastern part of 'Arabestan, which included the regions of Dezful and Shushtar.³⁶ For some time, 'Arabestan was administratively part of Fars as was Kuhgiluyeh. When Fars was broken up and made into *khasseh* domain in 1632, 'Arabestan, Shushtar and Dezful were subordinated to the governor of Kuhgiluyeh for militarily purposes.

The *vali*s of Hoveyzeh behaved quite independently and, in fact, were more involved with politics in 'Arabestan and southern Iraq than with Safavid Iran during most of the 16th century. Apart from the fact that part of the Mosha'sha' political base was located there (they also held the town of Zakiyeh on the Euphrates river), the province was separated from the rest of Iran by a linguistic barrier and bad roads. The Mosha'sha' governor of Zakiyeh even pledged allegiance to the Ottoman government in 1534. Their active political role in S. Iraq brought the *vali*s of Hoveyzeh into conflict with the Ottomans, who in the 1570s invaded 'Arabestan and for a time occupied it. However, they soon had to withdraw their troops, which resulted in increased anti-Ottoman activites by Sayyed Mobarak, who also tried to take a more independent stance *vis à vis* the Safavids during the confused period of the so-called second 'Qezelbash civil war'. This attitude was not tolerated by Shah 'Abbas I who twice militarily intervened to call Sayyed Mobarak to order. In

---

31 For the history of this dynasty see Werner Caskel. "Ein Mehdi des 15. Jahrhunderts. Saijid Muhammad ibn Falah und seine Nachkommen," *Islamica* 4 (1929), pp. 48-93; Ibid., "Die Wali's von Huwezeh," *Islamica* 6 (1934), pp. 415-34; M.M. Mazzaoui. "Musha'sha'yan. A XVth Century Shi'i Mouvement in Khuzistan and Southern 'Iraq," *Folia Orientalia* (Krakow) XXII (1981-84), pp. 139-62; G.C. Scarcia. "Annotazioni Musha'sha'," in *La Persia nel medioevo* (Rome, 1971), pp. 633-37; Ahmad Kasravi. *Tarikh-e Panjsad-sad saleh-ye Khuzestan* (Tehran, 1333/1954); Ibid., *Mosha'sha'iyan* (Tehran, 2536/1977); Halil Muhammad al-Jabri. *Imarat al-Musha'sha'iyin* (Baghdad, 1965); Jasim Hasan Shubbar. *Tarikh al-Musha'sha'iyin wa tarajum i'lamihim* (Najaf, 1965); Muhammad Husayn Zubaydi. *Imarat al-Musha'sha'iyin, aqdam imarah 'arabiyah fi 'Arabistan* (Baghdad, 1982).
32 'Abdi Beyg Shirazi, *Takmelat al-Akhbar* ed. 'Abdol-Hoseyn Nava'i (Tehran, 1369/1990), p. 141. The residence of the *vali*s was Kamalabad. Yazdi, *Mokhtasar*, p. 276; Monshi, *Tarikh*, vol. 2, p. 524.
33 Hoseyn Beyg Rumlu, *Ahsan al-Tavarikh*. ed. 'Abdol-Hoseyn Nava'i (Tehran 1357/1978), p. 138; Heravi, *Fotuhat*, p. 310.
34 Monshi, *Tarikh*, vol. 2, p. 758.
35 Röhrborn, *Provinzen*, p. 78. It seems more likely that members of the *vali*'s family held sway there. In 1081/1670, according to Yazdi, *Mokhtasar*, p. 268, the place was in total ruins and thus it seems unlikely that there were any governors. Yazdi also relates the statement of wise men, according to whom, anyone who would live longer than one year in Ahvaz would completely loose his mind.
36 W. Barthold, *An Historical Geography of Iran* translated by Svat Soucek (Princeton, 1984), p. 184.

1034/1624, a scion of the Mosha'sha' family also governed Dowraq for a while. The last time that a *vali* of Hoveyzeh seriously challenged Savafid rule was in 1620 when Sayyed Mansur refused to obey direct orders from 'Abbas I, who then ousted him. In 1060/1650 Sayyed 'Ali Khan b. Mowla Khalaf b. 'Abdol-Motalleb became the new *vali*, but he was unable to control the Arab tribes. This resulted in an uprising, which was put down by Manuchehr Khan, the governor of Lorestan. The latter sent Sayyed 'Ali Khan and his children to Isfahan, and assumed control over Hoveyzeh. It is not clear who thereafter governed 'Arabestan; Manuchehr Khan remained in charge for two years, while in the years thereafter the citadel of Hoveyzeh was held by Persian troops, who were commanded until 1076/1665 by Mohammad Mo'men Beyg and thereafter by Safiqoli Beyg aka Taniya Beyg.[37] Around 1075, Sayyed 'Ali Khan was again reinstated as *vali* of Hoveyzeh due to the good offices of Zaman Khan, the governor of Kuhgiluyeh. In 1082/1671 the Ottomans occupied part of the lands of the *vali* of 'Arabestan, including Hoveyzeh, as part of their reconquest of Basra in 1669.[38] When Sayyed 'Ali Khan died in 1092/1681 (or 1098/1687) his brother ('Abdollah) and sons (of whom Heydar initially won) contested each other the succession and peace only returned when his son Sayyed Farajollah was appointed as *vali* in 1098/1687. He was the last *vali* who played a significant role. He got the Safavids involved in the invasion and occupation of Basra (1694-1701), but this adventure also led to his temporary dismissal as *vali*. After his fall in 1114/1702 disorder broke out again and the remainder of the Safavid period, like the preceding period, was characterized by family infighting. This meant that at times Safavid governors were appointed to govern Hoveyzeh awaiting the royal decision who was to become the new *vali*. The infighting among members of the Mosha'sha' family became more intense and the political situation more unstable as of about 1710, which required the stationing of a Safavid military garrison in Hoveyzeh.[39] In April 1713 'Evaz Khan, brother of the *divan-beygi* therefore came to Hoveyzeh to put the the local affairs in order.[40] He also became governor of Hoveyzeh and Dowraq. One year later he was dismissed and replaced by Hoseyn Beyg.[41] Despite these family squabbles and some Persian interlopers the governorship of Hoveyzeh remained in the hands of the Mosha'sha' family until the end of the nineteenth century.

---

37 Shamlu, *Qesas*, vol. 2, p. 18; Minorsky, "Musha'sha'," *Encyclopedia of Islam*¹. Formally the cost for this garrison had to be borne by the *vali* of Hoveyzeh, although towards the end of the Safavid dynasty these were borne by the central government, see Willem Floor & Mohammad Faghfoory, *Dastur al-Moluk, A Safavid State Manual* (Costa Mesa, 2007), pp. 11-12.

38 For the Ottoman takeover of Basra in 1669 see Floor, *Persian Gulf*, pp. 566-70. The simultaneous Ottoman occupation of Hoveyzeh is not mentioned in contemporary Safavid sources. For an interesting description of the religious ritual of the Mosha'sha' at that time (in 1082/1671) see Yazdi, *Mokhtasar*, vol. 1, pp. 270-71 (walking over and rolling in burning coals, playing with fire, etc., which ritual may explain their appellation of Mosha'sha'). For a description of other types of their ritual see Monshi, *Tarikh*, vol. 1, p. 35.

39 KA 1726, Gamron to XVII (23/04/1714), f. 2463; Caskel, "Wali," pp. 428-30; Sayyed 'Abdollah b. Sayyed Nur al-Din b. Sayyed Ne'matollah al-Hoseyni al-Shushtari, *Ketab-e Shushtari-ye Shushtar*. ed. Khan Bahadur Maula Bakhsh (Calcutta, 1924), pp. 67-69.

40 KA 1710, Isfahan to Gamron (27/04/1713), f. 244; KA 1735 II, Isfahan to Gamron, (11/05/1713), f. 154.

41 KA 1740, Gamron to XVII (05/05/1715), f. 2266vs.

Name	Year	H Hoveyzeh	Source
Soltan Mohsen b. Mohammad	915-920/1509-1514	H Hoveyzeh	Caskel, Mehdi 73; Shirazi 143; Khvandamir 497
Soltan 'Ali b. Mohammad	915-920/1509-1514	H Hoveyzeh	Caskel, Mehdi 73; Shirazi 143; Khvandamir 497
Sayyed Fallah b. Sayyed Mohsen	920-930/1514-1524	H Hoveyzeh	Shirazi 143; Kasravi 32-34
Sayyed Badran Shoja' al-Din b. Sayyed Fallah	930-948/1524-1542	H Hoveyzeh	Shirazi 143; Caskel, Mehdi 77; Monshi 85; Rumlu 380; Kasravi 33
Mowla Sajjad b. Sayyed Badran	948-995/1541-1587	H Hoveyzeh +Dezful or H 'Arabestan	Shirazi 143; Caskel, Mehdi 80; Qomi 1, 295; 2, 630 [984]; Natanzi 33; Monshi 206 (Sayyed Sahhar); Kasravi 33-35 (d. 992)
Sayyed 'Ali b. Mowla Sajjad	995/1587	H Hoveyzeh	Caskel, Mehdi 84; Kasravi 39
Sayyed Elyas b. Mowla Sajjad	995-998/1587-1591	H 'Arabestan	Caskel, Mehdi 84; Kasravi 39 (Sayyed Zanbur; 992-98)
Sayyed Mobarak b. 'Abdol-Motalleb b. Heydar b. Soltan Mohsen b. Mohammad b. Falah	998-1025/1591-1616	H 'Arabestan	Caskel, Mehdi 85; Caskel, Wali 425; Monshi 914; Valeh 1380, 191, 210, 357, 706; Yusof 157; Vahid 260; Kasravi 39-46
Sayyed Naser b. Sayyed Mobarak	1025-1026/1616-1617	H 'Arabestan	Caskel, Wali, 425; Monshi 915;
Sayyed Rashed b. Salem b. 'Abdol-Motalleb	1026-1029/1617-1620	H 'Arabestan - nephew of Sayyed Mobarak	Caskel, Wali 425; Monshi 915; Vahid 193, 196, 200, 202; Kasravi 46-47
Sayyed Mansur b. Mowla 'Abdol-Motalleb aka Mansur Khan	1030-1033/1621-1624	H 'Arabestan - brother of Sayyed Mobarak	Caskel, Wali 425; Monshi 959; Yusof, 157, 291-92; Kasravi 47-48
Sayyed Mohammad Khan b. Sayyed Mobarak	1033-1044/1624-1635	H 'Arabestan; grandson of Emamqoli Khan through his mother; or son-in-law Emamqoli Khan	Caskel, Wali 426; Monshi 1013; Yusof 152, 157, 291; Vahid 260, 329; Valeh 1380, 105, 107, 191, 197, 204, 210, 357
Sayyed Mansur b. Mowla 'Abdol-Motalleb aka Mansur Khan	1044-1054/1635-1644	H 'Arabestan; 2nd time	Vahid 260, 264-5, 329; Floor, "Mirza Taqi" 259; Valeh 1380, 191, 197, 210, 357, 411
Sayyed Barakah b. Sayyed Mansur	1054-1060/1644-1650	H 'Arabestan	Caskel, Wali 426; Valeh 1380, 87, 411; Vahid 404; Kasravi 51

Sayyed 'Ali Khan b. Mowla Khalaf b. 'Abdol-Motalleb	1060-1061/1650-1651	H 'Arabestan – nephew of Sayyed Mobarak and Sayyed Mansur	Caskel, Wali 426-27; Riyaz 231-32; Kasravi 51-53, 63
Manuchehr Khan	1061-?/1651-?	H Hoveyzeh + Lorestan	Luft 673
Qara Mostafa Pasha	1082/1671	H Hoveyzeh – Ottoman	Yazdi 1, 270
Sayyed 'Ali Khan b. Mowla Khalaf b. 'Abdol-Motalleb	1074-1088/1663-1677	H 'Arabestan – nephew of Sayyed Mobarak and Sayyed Mansur	Caskel, Wali 426-27 (1098); Kasravi 63 (1088)
Sayyed Heydar Khan b. Sayyed 'Ali Khan	1088-1094/1677-1683	H 'Arabestan; acted also as *vakil* for his father	Caskel, Wali 427-28
	1094-1097/1683-1686	interregnum due to many claimants for the position	Kasravi 65
Sayyed 'Abdollah	1097/1686	H 'Arabestan; brother of Sayyed 'Ali Khan; few months only	Kasravi 65
Sayyed Farajollah Khan b. Sayyed 'Ali Khan	1098-1111/1687-1700	H 'Arabestan	Caskel, Wali 428; Nasiri 142-50; Kasravi 65
Sayyed Heybatollah b. Mowla Khalaf	1111/1700	H 'Arabestan – brother of Sayyed 'Ali Khan	Caskel, Wali 428; Shushtari 66; Nasiri 250; Kasravi 67
Sayyed Farajollah Khan b. Sayyed 'Ali Khan	1112/1701	H 'Arabestan - reappointed	Caskel, Wali 428; Nasiri 419
Sayyed 'Ali b. Sayyed 'Abdollah	1112-1120/1701-1708	H 'Arabestan	Kasravi 67-68
Sayyed 'Abdollah b. Sayyed Farajollah	1119-1124/1707-1712	H 'Arabestan	Caskel, Wali 428; Shushtari 67-68
Sayyed Mohammad Khan b. Sayyed Farajollah	1124-1125/1712-1713	H 'Arabestan	Caskel, Wali 428
Sayyed 'Ali b. Sayyed 'Abdollah	1125/1713	H 'Arabestan - 2nd time	Kasravi 70
'Evaz Khan	1125-1126/1713-1714	H 'Arabestan	KA 1740, f. 2266vs; Shushtari 67; Kasravi 70
Hoseyn Beyg	1126-1127/1714-1715	H 'Arabestan	KA 1740, f. 2266vs
Sayyed 'Ali b. Sayyed 'Abdollah	1127-?/1715-?	H 'Arabestan – 3rd time	Mostowfi 129; Kasravi 70
Sayyed Mohammad Khan b. Sayyed Farajollah	1132-1136/1720-1724	H 'Arabestan – 2nd time	Caskel, Wali 430; Shushtari 69; Balfour 156

Aradvar, see Farumad.

COMMENTARY

Arasbar or Arasbaran, nowadays called Ahar, is situated some 75 km north-east of Tabriz in the Qaradagh region.[42] It was a district in the province of Qarabagh.

Name	Year	Observations	Source
Bayazid Soltan Shamlu	942/1535	H Moghan and Arasbar	Bakikhanof 94; Fumeni 25-26
Kur Sayyedi Soltan	1009/1600	H Arasbar + Anhar	Molla Jalal 202
Morad Khan Soltan Beybordlu	1038/1628	H Arasbar	Monshi 1086

Arash is a district situated in Sheki (q.v.).

Name	Year	Observations	Source
Ordughdi Khalifeh	985-?/1577-?	H Arash	Qomi 2, 664
'Ali Soltan	1013/1604	H Arash	Molla Jalal 276
Mohammad Hoseyn Soltan Dhu'l-Qadr *mohrdar*	?-1024/?-1615	H Arash – grandson of 'Emad al-Din Beyg Shirvani and nephew of Shahqoli Khalifeh	Monshi 886
N.N.	1110/1698	Soltan of Arash	de Maze 73, 75

Ardabil is situated on the left bank of the Qara-su, some 160 km east of Tabriz and some 60 km west of the Caspian Sea.[43] This governorship, which was the historical center of the Safavid family and its dervish order, is not mentioned in the TM, probably because as of 1066/1656 Ardabil was transformed into crown domain, when the management of the endowment of Ardabil was also separated from the governorship. Its manager became Mortezaqoli Khan, *qurchi-bashi* and *motavalli* of Ardabil, while for the district of Ardabil instead of a governor (*hakem*) a vizier was appointed.[44] It is not known how long this situation lasted, but probably until sometime before the end of Safavid rule, reason why Nasiri's *Alqab* mentions Ardabil as a governorship.

Name	Year	Observations	Source
Badenjan Soltan Ostajalu or Rumlu	?-933/?-1527	H Ardabil	Rumlu: Shirazi 63; Bidlisi 2, 55; Tahmasp 9; Tatavi 441; Qazvini 283; Ostajalu: Qomi 1, 170; Monshi 48
Soleyman Beyg Rumlu	933-?/1527-?	H Ardabil + Rey	Bidlisi 2, 552
Sam Mirza	956/1549	H and *motavalli* Ardabil	Abrahams 139
Abu'l-Fath Soltan Ebrahim Mirza	970/1563	H Ardabil – did not go there; see Qa'en	Qomi 1, 439-40

---

42 For the history of Arasbar see Hoseyn Beyburdi, *Tarikh-e Arasbaran* (Tehran, 1346/1968).
43 On the history of Ardabil see Baba Safari, *Ardabil dar godhargāh-e tārikh* 3 vols. (Tehran, 1350/1971).
44 Vahid, *Tarikh*, p. 612 (Mohammad Hoseyn Beyg b. Mir Jamal Soltan was the first vizier and *darugheh*).

Heydar al-Din Khan	972/1564	H and *motavalli* Ardabil	Abrahams 144-45
Sadr al-Din Khan Safavi	972-?/1565-?	H Ardabil	Afshar 385
Bayandor Khan	975/1567	H Ardabil	Qomi 1, 471
Soltan Ma'sum	?-982/?-1574	H Ardabil	Qomi 2, 828
Pireh Mohammad Khan Ostajalu	985-?/1577-?	H Ardabil, Tarom, Khalkhal	Qomi 2, 664
Mosib Khan	994-?/1586-?	H Ardabil + *motavalli*	Qomi 2, 828
Farhad Beyg b. Hosam Soltan Qaramanlu	996/1588	Amir Ardabil + Qezel Aqaj + dependencies	Shamlu 1, 135
Mehdiqoli Khan Chavoslu Ostajalu b. Simeon Khan	997-999/1589-1591	H Ardabil	Monshi 409; Bidlisi 2, 690; Vahid 113
Farhad Khan Qaramanlu	1001/1593	H Ardabil + *Amir al-omara* Azerbaijan	Monshi 455
Dhu'l-Feqar Khan Qaramanlu	1001-1020/1593-1611	*Vali* or H Ardabil	Yusof 261; Mofakhkham doc. 2; Monshi 492, 565, 588, 638; Molla Jalal 240, 280, 234; Papaziyan 1959, doc 1;
Shekari Soltan Esparlu	?-1038/?-1629	H Ardabil + Sarab	Monshi 1311
Kalb 'Ali Beyg [Khan] *davatdar* Qajar	1038-1048/1629-1638	H Ardabil, Kankarkonan + *darugheh* of Moghan	Yusof 191, 228; Valeh 1380, 282; Vahid 330
Nazar 'Ali Beyg [Khan] Suklan Dhu'l-Qadr	1048-1066/1638-1656	H + *motavalli* of Ardabil	Shamlu 1, 334, 343, 354, 416, 466, 473; Yusof 215; Vahid 330, 466, 504, 612; Valeh 1380, 288
	1066-? /1656-?	crown domain	Vahid 612

Ardestan is situated south-east of Natanz, north-east of Isfahan, north-west of Na'in, on the road between Kashan and Yazd.[45]

Name	Year	Observations	Source
Vali Khalifeh Shamlu	?-977/?-1569	H Qom + Ardestan	Qomi 1, 563
Heydar Beyg [Soltan] Chabuq Tarkhan Torkman	977-984/1570-1576	H Qom + Ardestan	Qomi 1, 563, 977, 2, 627; Monshi 140; Valeh 1372, 410
Vali Beyg Tekkelu b. 'Ali Soltan	984/1576	H Ardestan + Natanz	Qomi 2, 627
Qurkhmas Soltan Shamlu	985/1577	H Ardestan	Qomi 2, 665

45 For the history of Ardestan see Abu'l-Qasem Rafi' Mehrabadi, *Tarikh-e Ardestan* 3 vols. (Tehran, 1367/1988).

| Aslamas Khan b. Shahrokh Khalifeh | 996/1588 | *Teyuldar* of Ardestan; *mohrdar* | Qomi 2, 874 |
| Owtar Khan | 1052-?/1642-? | H Ardestan – *gholam* | Vahid 347 |

Arghiyan, see Jahan-Arghiyan.

Arjish was a border fort situated on the north side of Lake Van. This was one of the many border forts, which often changed hands. It is not known how long it was in the hands of the Safavids, but it was mostly in Ottomans hands where it also remained.

Name	Year	Observations	Source
Kurd Beyg Ostajalu	932/1526	H Arjish	Bacqué-Gramont 97
Ahmad Soltan Sufi-oghlu Ostajalu	941/1534	H *Qal'eh-ye* Arjish + Van; former governor of Kerman	Monshi 69; Shirazi 84; Qazvini 291 (*kutval*); Qomi 1, 245(*kutval*)

Arzenjan or Erzincan is situated in north-eastern Anatolia, on the north bank of the Qarasu, one of the headwaters of the Euphrates. This district was only held by the Safavids in the very beginning of their reign (in 913/1508) and became a permanent part of the Ottoman Empire after 921/1515. Around 1511 Nur 'Ali Khalifeh-ye Rumlu is mentioned as governor of Arzenjan.[46]

Astara or Astareh[47] is situated north of Ardabil, on the Caspian Sea, on the border with what now is the Republic of Azerbaijan; in Safavid times it was part of the province of Azerbaijan.[48] Its governor was also referred to as *hakem* of Talesh, suggesting that Astara was its capital.[49] Talesh or Tavalesh is a district is bounded in the east by the Caspian Sea, in the south by Gilan, in the west by Khalkhal and Ardabil, and in the north by Saliyan. This district with few exceptions was always held by Taleshi chiefs and as of 946/1539 the governorship was hereditary in the family of Bayandor Khan Talesh. In 1014/1605 Astara and Gaskar (q.v.) were turned into crown domain and brought under the jurisdiction of the vizier of Gilan, while the latter appointed a governor for both areas.[50] In 1021/1621 Astara and Gaskar were separated from Gilan again and it would seem that governors and not viziers were in charge of these districts (see Table).[51] Within the district of Talesh (and of the Moghanat district) there were several dependencies that might be given to emirs other than the governor of Talesh; in fact there were four soltans in total. For example, in 994/1586, Mohammad Khan Torkman was given a jurisdiction of several dependencies in Talesh and the Moghanat.[52] In 1684, the person in charge in Lenkoran was called Safiqoli Khan, while

---

46 Monshi, *Tarikh*, vol. 1, p. 41; Allah Deta Mozaffar ed. *Jahangosha-ye Khaqan* (Islamabad, 1986), p. 519. For its history see E.C. Bosworth, "Arzenjan," *Encyclopedia Iranica*.
47 Qomi, *Kholasat*, vol. 1, p. 288.
48 Fumeni, *Tarikh*, p. 190.
49 Monshi, *Tarikh*, vol. 2, p. 1086; Hazin, *Life*, p. 170.
50 Fumeni, *Tarikh*, p. 181.
51 Monshi, *Tarikh*, vol. 2, p. 853.
52 Qomi, *Kholasat*, vol. 2, pp. 828, 848.

one of the others was called Hoseyn. The khan, i.e. the governor, lived in Ardabil in 1684, but his name has not been reported.[53]

Name	Year	Observations	Source
Mohammad Beyg Talesh	945/1538	Possibly governor	Qomi 1, 278-79
Amireh Qobad Talesh	946/1539	H Astara; H Talesh	Rumlu 379; Qomi 1, 288-89
Bayandor Khan Talesh	946-989/1539-1581	H Astara - At least until 1630 his descendants held this post (Monshi)	Rumlu 380; Qomi 1, 289, 468; Monshi 112, 141, 267, 441; Valeh 1372, 411 (Tekkelu); Fumeni 35-37
Hamzeh [Beyg] khalifeh-ye Talesh aka Emir Hamzeh Khan b. Bayandor Khan Talesh	989-1000/1581-1592	H Astara; H Talesh	Qomi 1, 353-54, 471; Monshi 380, 442-43; Fumeni 116-17, 120-24, 140-41, 237-39; Bidlisi 2, 692
Qalich Khan b. Bayandor Khan	1000-?/1592-?	H Astara	Valeh 1372, 482-5, 488
Dhu'l-Feqr Khan	1014-1016/1605-1607	*Teyuldar* Astara + Gaskar	Fumeni 181
Jamshid Beyg Amireh	1016-?/1607-?	H Astara + Gaskar	Fumeni 181
Saru Khan b. Qalich Khan	1038-1058/1628-1648	H Astara + Talesh	Vahid 290, 330, 566; Monshi 1086; Yusof 215; Fumeni 275
Qalich Khan [b. Saru Khan]	1058-1070/1648-1659	H Talesh + Astara	Vahid 594, 706, 571
Amir Hamzeh Khan (Emir Naamsachan)	1095-1109/1684-1697	H Astara + Talesh	Kaempfer 62; Nasiri 218
'Abbasqoli Khan	1109-?/1697-?	H Astara + Talesh	Nasiri 218
Sobhanverdi Khan	1138/1726	H Astara + Talesh	Fragner, doc. 7
Yahya Khan Taleshi	1138/1726	H Astara; appointed by the Russians	Hazin 170

Astarabad, Gorgan or Jorjan (q.v.) province is bounded on the north by the Atrek river, south by the Elburz Mountains and Shahrud district, west by the Caspian and Mazandaran, and east by the district of Jajarm, although Monshi considered Astarabad to be a part of Mazandaran.[54] The province came and remained permanently in Safavid hands as of 906/1510 and it included the following administrative jurisdictions at the end of the Safavid period: Gira'i, Goklan, Hajjilar[55], Jalayer, K.ra-chupi, and Yamut. These were also the names of Turkoman tribes, to whom these districts had been assigned. Some elements of these tribes resided north of the Gorgan, but paid the Safavids nominal allegiance (q.v. Qepchaq). At the end of the sixteenth century, the Sa'en-khanis of the Yakka Turkoman tribe, who had settled in the area a few decades earlier, for a period (from

---

53 Engelbert Kaempfer, *Die Reisetagebücher* ed. K. Meier-Lemgo (Wiesbaden, 1968), p. 60.
54 Monshi, *Tarikh*, vol. 1, p. 580.
55 Hajjilar is now called Minudasht or Dasht-e minu.

997/1589 until 1006/1598) acted as caretaker governors for Astarabad in the absence of effective Safavid control of the province. 'Abbas I thereafter initiated a pacification campaign among the Torkmen tribes.[56] The Safavids continued to attract Torkman tribes to the province with a view to develop it and levy taxes.[57] The governor of Astarabad also sometimes held districts outside his province such as Damghan (q.v.) and Bastam (q.v.).

Name	Year	Observations	Source
Khalaf Beyg Talesh	?-920/?-1514	H Astarabad + Jorjan	Aubin 40, n. 260
Pir Gheyb Talesh	920-?/1514-?	H Astarabad	Rumlu 196; Qomi 1, 132
Zeyn al-Din Soltan Shamlu	?-928/?-1522	H Astarabad	Khvandamir 591 (Jorjan); Rumlu 229
Zeynal Khan Shamlu	928-934/ 1522-1528	H Astarabad	Rumlu 229; Hoseyni, 75, 87, 93; Monshi 1, 51; Qomi 1, 150, 171-2, 175; Ben Khvandamir 214, 255; Shirazi 64; Bidlisi 2, 553; Qazvini 284; Tahmasp 10
Shahverdi Beyg Ziyad-oghlu Qajar	934/1527	H Astarabad and Jorjan-zamin	Abrahams 187
	934/1528	Uzbeg governor	Qomi 1, 177
Badr Khan Ostajalu	938/1531	H Astarabad	Abrahams 135
Mohammad Khan Dhu'l-Qadr[-oghlu] b. Kur Shahrokh b. 'Ala al-Dowleh	?-939/?-1532	H Astarabad	Qomi 1, 222; Bidlisi 2, 560; Qazvini 286
Badr Khan Ostajalu	939/1532	*Laleh* of Elqas Mirza b. Esma'il	Qomi 1, 222; Qazvini 287; Vahid 66, 107 (Afshar)
Sadr al-Din Khan Ostajalu	939-944/ 1532-1537	H Astarabad	Qomi 1, 283-85; Hoseyni 145-46
	Interrupted in 944/1537 by	Uzbeg occupation	Rumlu 368; Dickson 373-83
Sadr al-Din Khan Ostajalu b. Saru Pireh	944-950/ 1537-1543	*Vali* Astarabad - *Laleh* of Esma'il Mirza b. Tahmasp as of 946	Rumlu 368, 395; Budaq 103; Hoseyni 146; Qomi 1, 300; Monshi 105; Khvandamir 368; Shirazi 90; Bidlisi 2, 572; Vahid 65; Tatavi 493
Shah 'Ali Soltan Ostajalu	955-957/ 1548-1550	BB Astarabad	Dhabehi-Setudeh 6, doc. 10; Monshi 107; Qomi 1, 335, 346; Shirazi 100; Qazvini 298
Shahqoli Soltan Ostajalu	?-957/1550	H Astarabad	Abrahams 139
Shahverdi Beyg [Soltan] Kachal Chavoshlu Ostajalu	957-?/1550-?	H Astarabad	Hoseyni 189; Monshi 107; Rumlu 447 ; Shirazi 112; Vahid 65, 72

---

56 Monshi, *Tarikh*, vol. 1, p. 580; Yazdi, *Mokhtasar*, vol. 1, pp. 302-03; Mohammad Taher Bastami, *Fotuhat-e Fereyduniyeh*. Sa'id Mir Mohammad Sadeq and Mohammad Nader Nasiri Moqaddam eds (Tehran, 1380/2001).
57 See Nasiri, *Dastur*, pp. 91, 138, 188, 242, 244, 273.

Soltan Amir Gheyb Beyg Ostajalu	957-962-?/ 1550-55-?	H Astarabad	Abrahams 139, 141
Ebrahim Khan Dhu'l-Qadr	965-?/1558-?	H Astarabad	Qomi 1, 393; Monshi 108; Shirazi 112; Bidlisi 2, 594; Qazvini 303; Vahid 73
Khalil Soltan b. Shahverdi Soltan Ziyad-oghlu Qajar	971-?/1563-?	H Astarabad	Shirazi 122
Panah Mohammad Khan Dhu'l-Qadr	970s?/1565?	BB Astarabad	Qomi 2, 686
Sayyed Beyg b. Sayyed Ma'sum Beyg	976-?/1569-?	H Astarabad	Tatavi 693
Soleyman Khalifeh-ye Shamlu	? before 981/1574	H Astarabad	Monshi 138; Valeh 1372, 408
Mohammad Khan Asayesh-oghli	? before 981/1574	H Astarabad	Dhabehi-Setudeh 6, doc. 6
Mohammad Khalifeh Dhu'l-Qadr, cousin of Ebrahim Khan Hajjilar*	? before 981/1574	H Astarabad	Monshi 140, 239; Valeh 1372, 410; Qomi 2, 686
Sayyed Beyg b. Ma'sum Beyg Safavi Sheykhavand	?-981/?-1574	H Astarabad	Qomi 1, 581; Monshi 141
Shahqoli Soltan Tati-oghlu Dhu'l-Qadr	981-983/ 1574-1576	Shahvali Soltan - H Astarabad	Qomi 1, 581, 591
Mohammad Soltan Dhu'l-Qadr	983-?/1576-?	H Astarabad	Qomi 1, 591
Mirza 'Ali Soltan Qajar	985-?/1577-?	H Astarabad	Qomi 2, 665
Mortezaqoli Khan Pornak Torkman	989-996/ 1581-1588	H Astarabad, Jorjan Damghan, Bastam, Biyarjomand, 'Arab-e 'Ameri and Hazar arib	Qomi 2, 751; Valeh 1372, 678, 831; Dhabehi-Setudeh 6, doc. 1; Natanzi 149, 152; Monshi 290; Bidlisi 2, 686
Badr Khan Afshar	997/1589	BB Astarabad + Bastam	Vahid 107; Monshi 402; Qomi 2, 884
	997-1007/ 1589-1598	Absence of direct Safavid control of some 10 years	
'Elyar Khan Imur	998-1005/ 1589-1597	chief of the Sa'en-khanis of the Yakka Turkmen	Monshi 530, 580-81; Molla Jalal 188; Vahid 138
Mohammad Yar Khan Imur	1005-1006/ 1587-1588	His son; idem	Monshi 530, 545, 581, 587; Vahid 138
Qalij Beyg Imur	1006/1588	His brother; idem	Monshi 545, 588
Farhad Khan Qaramanlu	1007/1589	H Astarabad- also governor of Mazandaran	Monshi 564
Hoseyn Khan Ziyad-oghlu Qajar	?-1012/?-1604	H Astarabad – he may have been appointed in 999 given the date on a royal order addressed to him	Monshi 581; Dhabehi-Setudeh 6, doc. 12 (dated 999); Vahid 149; Molla Jalal 189, 221
Yusof Khan *mir shekar-bash*i	1012/1604	H Astarabad; *qushchi-bashi*	Molla Jalal 240

Faridun Khan Cherkes	1013-1029/ 1605-1620	BB Astarabad-H Semnan Damghan; succeeded by his son	Monshi 835, 966; Molla Jalal 294, 327, 438 [1020]; Vahid 202
Behbud Khan Cherkes	1029-1038/ 1620-1629	BB Astarabad; succeeded by his son	Shamlu 1, 203
Khosrow Khan Cherkes	1038-1048/ 1629-1639	BB Astarabad	Monshi 1088; Shamlu 1, 203; Yusof 22, 289; Vahid 280
Qazaq Khan Cherkes	1048-1049/ 1639-1640	BB Astarabad	Vahid 280, 296, 329; Astarabadi 255
Hoseyn Khan b. Zaman Beyg Mazandarani	1049-1051/ 1640-1642	BB Astarabad + *nazer-e boyutat*	Vahid 297, 305, 329; Shamlu 1, 257, 253
Mehrab Beyg [Khan]	1051-1058/ 1642-1648	BB Astarabad - *gholam*; kinsman of Safiqoli Beyg BB Baghdad; for some time this post was not filled	Shamlu 1, 257, 343, 429; Vahid 305, 466; Yusof 251
Allahverdi Beyg [Khan]	1060/1650	BB Astarabad – *amir shekar-bashi*	Valeh 1372, 141, 151, etc.; Vahid 514, 745
Mohammadqoli Khan b. Siyavosh Khan	1060-1064/ 1650-1654	BB Astarabad	Vahid 525, 539
Hajji Manuchehr Khan	1064-1066/ 1654-1656	BB Astarabad - Succeeded by his son	Vahid 539, 541, 593-94, 612; Riazul Islam 1, 404
Jamshid Khan	1066-1074-? /1656-1664-?	BB Astarabad + Semnan-Damavand + *il-e* Pazuki	Valeh 1372, 461, 591; Vahid 612, 706, 751
Ja'farqoli Beyg [Khan]	1077/1666	BB Astarabad - Grandson Emamqoli Khan	Dhabehi-Setudeh 6, docs. 20, 21, 23.
Mohammad Khan	1083/1672	BB Astarabad	Bardisiri 402
Pesand Khan	?-1103/?-1692	BB Astarabad	Khatunabadi 548
Oghurlu Beyg	1105-06/ 1694-1695	BB Astarabad	Nasiri 70, 72, 80
'Ali Khan	1106-1109/ 1695-1697	BB Astarabad	Nasiri 91, 242-44, 246, 247
Mirza Ahmad	1116/1705	H Astarabad	Floor, "Lost files," 49
Kalb 'Ali Beyg	?-1120/?-1708	H Astarabad	Khatunabadi 558
Aslan Khan	1120-1121-?/ 1708-1709-?	H Astarabad	Khatunabadi 558; Shushtari 66
Rostam Mohammad Khan Sa'dlu	1123/1711	BB Astarabad	Dhabehi-Setudeh 6, doc. 38
Fath 'Ali Khan Qajar	1129-?/1717-?	BB Astarabad	Mervi 1, 27, 37, 54, 1171

* Monshi mentions that Mohammad Khalifeh was appointed by Shah Mohammad Khodabandeh as governor of Astarabad, but he also mentions that in that same year he was appointed as governor of Shirvan and in that connection he relates that Mohammad Khalifeh had been governor of Astarabad at the end of the reign of Shah Tahmasp I. This implies that he probably was not appointed for a second time as governor of Astarabad or for a short time only. Monshi, *Tarikh*, vol. 1, pp. 227, 239.

Aveh is a small district situated south-east of Saveh and it was sometimes held together with the districts of Saveh (q.v.) and Jorbadeqan (q.v.).

Name	Year	Observations	Source
Soltan Ma'sum Soltan Torkman	985-?	H Saveh, Jorbadeqan, and Aveh	Qomi 2, 665
Shah Budaq	996-?	H Aveh	Qomi 2, 874

Avroman is a mountainous border district in Kurdestan bounded on the west by Sanandaj and Shahr-Zur, on the north-east by Senneh and on the south by Javanrud. As of 1045/1635 'Abbasqoli Soltan was its governor.[58]

Azadvar, see Farumad.

Azerbaijan was one of the main administrative regions of Persia situated in the north-west of the country. Its governor-general was also referred to as governor of Tabriz, its capital city. It was here that Esma'il I was crowned in 907/1501 and Tabriz remained the capital city of the Safavid kingdom until 962/1555. From 996/1588 to 1012/1603 Tabriz and much of the rest of Azerbaijan was under Ottoman occupation, so that the jurisdiction of the governor-general of Azerbaijan effectively was limited to that of Ardabil

(q.v.), where he resided.

Name	Year	Observations	Source
Elyas Beyg Eyghut-oghlu Khonoslu	907-909/1501-1503	H Tabriz	Mozaffar 181-82, 193-95; Aubin 5, n. 49; Haneda 78
Hoseyn Beyg Laleh	909-915/1503-1509	H Tabriz	Aubin 4, n. 23, 12; Fekete 275-77; Rumlu 146
Mohammad Beyg Sofrechi Ostajalu aka Chayan Soltan	915-920/1509-1514	H Tabriz	Rumlu 146; Qomi 1, 100; Qazvini 272; Lobb 250
Durmish Khan Shamlu?	920/1514	H Tabriz	Aubin 31, n. 128 (Afzal)
Montasha Soltan Ostajalu	920/1514	H Azerbaijan	Mozaffar 471; Aubin 32
Mohammad Khan Tekkelu	930-?/1524-?	H Tabriz	Afshar 22
Musa Soltan	937/1530	H Azerbaijan	Abrahams 134
Ulameh Soltan Tekkelu	937/1531	*Vali* Azerbaijan, *amir al-omara*	Hoseyni 112; Qomi 1,215; Monshi 49; Rumlu 311

---

58 Vahid, *Tarikh*, p. 278; Astarabadi, *Az Sheykh Safi*, p. 254 ('Abbasqoli Beyg).

Musa Beyg [Soltan] Mowsellu b. 'Isa Beyg	938-941/1532-1534	H Azerbaijan, H or *vali* Tabriz	Qomi 1, 223, 231, 946; Shirazi 74; Bidlisi 2, 193, 561; Qazvini 287
	from 941/1534 until 981/1573 intermittently	crown domain	
Amir Gheyb Beyg Ostajalu	?-966-?/ ?-1559-?	H Tabriz	Qomi 1, 403; Afshar 157, 188, 190
Khvajeh Qasem 'Ali	970s?/1562s	Vizier Azerbaijan; remained at court	Monshi 164
Yusof Beyg Ostajalu	981/1573	H Azerbaijan	Abrahams 146
Allahqoli Beyg b. Shahqoli Soltan	981-?/1573-?	H Tabriz	Rumlu 587
Amir Khan Mowsellu Torkman	985-992/1577-1584	H or BB Tabriz- *vali* or BB Azerbaijan	Valeh 1372, 610, 683, 689-90; Monshi 225; Qomi 1, 610, [2], 664, 700, 706, 761, 764-70, 767; Natanzi 102; Bidlisi 2, 647
'Aliqoli Beyg [Khan] Fath-oglu Ostajalu	992/1584	H Tabriz– BB Azerbaijan	Monshi 301; Qomi 2, 771; Bidlisi 2, 666; Valeh 1372, 789
Hoseynqoli Khan brother of 'Aliqoli Khan Ostajalu	993/1585	H Tabriz and Soltan, H and *darugheh* Tabriz	Valeh 1372, 716; Qomi 2, 778
Mohammadi Khan Tokhmaq Ostajalu	994/1586	H Tabriz; BB Azerbaijan	Valeh 1372, 768; Qomi 2, 813; Monshi 333
	From 996/1588 to 1012/1603	under Ottoman occupation	
Mehdiqoli Khan Chavoslu Ostajalu b. Simeon Khan	997-999/1589-1591	H Ardabil	Monshi 409; Bidlisi 2, 690
Haqqverdi Soltan	998-?/1590-?	H *olka-ye* Tabriz	Molla Jalal 79
Farhad Khan Qaramanlu	1001/1593	*Amir al-omara* Azerbaijan	Monshi 455
Dhu'l-Feqar Khan Qaramanlu	1001-1014/1593-1605	*Amir al-omara* Azerbaijan	Monshi 492, 565, 588, 643, 681, 683; Molla Jalal 240
Pir Budaq Khan Pornak Torkman	1014-1025/1605-1616	H Tabriz; *amir al-omara* of that frontier zone	Monshi 686, 737, 773, 783, 901-02; Molla Jalal 258, 270, 322, 361, 413; Vahid 147 (1028), 329
Shahbandeh b. Pir Budaq Khan Pornak Torkman	1025-1027/1616-1618	*Amir al-omara* Azerbaijan – H Tabriz.	Monshi 902
Qarachqay Khan	1027-1029/1618-1620	BB Azerbaijan; H Tabriz + *amir al-omara*	Monshi 936; Shamlu 1, 202; Vahid 199
Shahbandeh Khan Torkman b. Pir Budaq Khan Pornak Torkman,	1029-1034/1620-1625	BB Azerbaijan – 2nd time	Monshi 1017, 1030; Shamlu 2, 135; Vahid 212; Yusof 166, 287

Name	Dates	Position	Sources
Pir Budaq Khan b. Shahbandeh Khan	1034-1045/1625-1635	H Tabriz + *amir al-omara* Azerbaijan, *eqta'dar* of Tabriz - he was 3 years old	Vahid 199 [1032], 266, 329; Yusof 166, 287
Rostam Khan	1045-1053/1635-1643	H Tabriz- BB Azerbaijan- *eqta'dar* Tabriz; *sepahsalar*	Yusof 166, 182, 215, 287, 289-91; Vahid 266, 329; Shamlu 1, 283; Agulis 38
Pir Budaq Khan Pornak Torkman b. Shahbandeh Khan	1053-1060/1643-1650	H Tabriz; BB Azerbaijan -2nd time – *sepahsalar*	Shamlu 1, 283, 351; Vahid 384, 476, 508, 511
'Aliqoli Khan Davalu	1062-1064/1652-1654	H Tabriz	Agulis 48, 162; Vahid 541; Chardin 9, 561-62; Riazul Islam 1, 404
Mortezaqoli Khan Qajar	1065-1074/1655-1664	BB Azerbaijan, *qurchi-bashi*	Vahid 586, 636
Hajji 'Ali Khan	1091/1680	BB Tabriz	Agulis 154
Rostam Khan	1106/1694	BB Azerbaijan + *sepahsalar*, *tofangchi-aghasi*	Qarakhani doc. 5; Khatunabadi 550
Anusheh Khan	1107/1695	*Vali* Tabriz	Nasiri 96
Mohammad Taleb Khan	1108/1696	BB Tabriz	Nasiri 215, 218
Lotf 'Ali Beyg	1109/1697	BB Tabriz	Nasiri 240
Musa Beyg	1114/1702	H Tabriz; *qollar-aghasi*	Khatunabadi 551
Mohammad Zaman Khan	1123-?/1711-?	H Tabriz-Kerman; *sepahsalar*	Khatunabadi 564
Mansur Khan Shahseven Moghani	?-1127/?-1715	*Sepahsalar*- Possibly BB Tabriz	Floor, *Afghan*, 26
Safiqoli Khan Ziyad-oghlu Qajar aka 'Aliqoli Khan	1127-1130/1715-1718	*Sepahsalar* – BB Tabriz	Floor, *Afghan*, 26, 29
Mohammad 'Ali Khan	1131-1132/1719-1720	BB Azerbaijan	Floor, *Afghan*, 35
Mikhri [Mehdi?] Khan	1132-1133/1720-1721	H Tabriz	Beneveni 52-53
Mohammad Beyg [Khan] Beygdelu Shamlu	1133/1721	BB Azerbaijan	Musavi 1965, doc. 19; Floor, *Afghan*, 36

Badghis is situated in the northeast of Herat province, between the Hari Rud in the west and the Kushk River in the east and Siyah Bubak in the south and forms a border area with Iran. The only reference to a governor for this area that I have come across is when it fell under the jurisdiction of the governor of Khvaf (q.v.). In 989/1581, Shahqoli Soltan son of Morshedqoli Khan was governor of the market town (*qasabeh*) of Khvaf as well as of Bakharz, the *velayat-e* Torbat, Badghis, and Mahvelat.[59]

---

59 Shamlu, *Qesas*, vol. 1, p. 123.

Bafrud is a district that I have not been able to identify, which, moreover is mentioned by only one source. In 998/1590, Beyram Soltan, nephew of Ya'qub Khan Dhu'l-Qadr became governor of Bafrud.[60]

Baghbad, a district adjacent to Nesa (q.v.) and Abivard (q.v.), which, together with Merv, were the hereditary lands of Nur Mohammad Khan's family and the Nayman Uzbeg tribe. Nur Mohammad Khan, the lukewarm Uzbeg vassal of 'Abbas I was, among other things, governor of Baghbad, although by 1002/1593 this and the other districts he governed had been overrun by the troops of 'Abdollah Khan, the ruler of Bokhara.[61] After the defeat of the Bokhara Uzbegs and the conquest of Merv and other districts by Shah 'Abbas I, in 1099/1600 Melkish Soltan son of Bektash Khan was appointed governor of Nesa, Abivard, and Baghbad.[62]

Baghdad is the capital of the province of Arabian Iraq and became part of the Safavid kingdom in 914/1508 until 941/1534, when the Ottomans conquered it. The latter kept it until 1033/1623 when Shah 'Abbas I was able to retake the city and much of Iraq, but these conquests were all lost by the Safavids in 1048/1638, a situation that was made permanent by the treaty of Zohab of 1049/1639. The subordinate districts of Baghdad included Hillah, Romahiyeh, Waset/Javazer, Kirkuk/Daquq, Kalhor/Mandali and Zohab (q.v.), as well as other districts. In 914/1508, for example, Khadem Beyg was governor of Baghdad and of Najaf, Karbala, Kazemeyn and Samarah.[63]

Name	Year	Observations	Source
Khadem Beyg Talesh Khalifeh aka Kholafā Beyg	914-?/1508-?	*Vali* Baghdad	Budaq 27; Shamlu 1, 40; Rumlu 137; Shirazi 47; Bidlisi 2, 521; Heravi 308
Sayyed Soleyman aka Sayyed Beyg	before 924/1518	H Baghdad – son of Sayyed Mohammad Kamuneh	Vahid 74
Shah 'Ali aka 'Evaz Soltan	924-?/1519	H Baghdad	Khvandamir 564
Zeyn al-Din Soltan Shamlu	925?/1519?	H Baghdad	Qomi 1, 160, 218
Ebrahim Soltan [Khan] Mowsellu grandson of Sufi Khalil Torkman	926?-934/1520?-1528	H Baghdad	Hoseyni 97, 103; Rumlu 273; Monshi 95; Qomi 1, 176; Shirazi 64; Bidlisi 2, 553; Tahmasp 11
Marjumak Soltan b. Amir Khan	934/1528	His brother – *vali* Arab Iraq	Qomi 1, 176; Qazvini 284; Tahmasp 11

---

60 Molla Jalal, *Ruznameh*, p. 94.
61 Monshi, *Tarikh*, vol. 1, pp. 415, 444, 452, 464, 549, 567, 581. See also Aubin, "Les soufis," p. 35, n. 174 for the same situation in 1511.
62 Monshi, *Tarikh*, vol. 1, p. 605.
63 Vahid, *Tarikh*, p. 31.

Dhu'l-Feqar	934-935/1528-1529	His cousin – usurper; H Kalhor	Rumlu 273; Qomi 1, 189; Monshi 95; Qazvini 284-85; Tahmasp 11
'Ali Beyg Mowsellu	935-936/1528-1529	H Baghdad	Afshar 165
Mohammad Soltan [Khan] Tekkelu Sharaf al-Dinoghlu aka Mohammad Khan	936-940/1529-1534	*Amir al-omara* of Arab Iraq; H Baghdad *khalifeh-al-kholafā*	Rumlu 334; Qomi 1, 190, 235, 236; Bidlisi 2, 556; Shirazi 66; Bidlisi 2, 564; Qazvini 284, 289; Abrahams, p. 208 (935)
	940/1534 until 1033/ January 1623	Ottoman Governors	Monshi 1004-05
Safiqoli Khan b. Qurkhoms Samkhuti b. Malek Mirman	1033-1042/1623-1633	BB Iraq; in 1035 he was named Shir 'Ali; also remained governor of Hamadan; was ex-Christian *gholam*	Monshi 1004, 1057; Shamlu 1, 204; Yusof 64, 80, 126, 292; Vahid 236-37; Khatunabadi 511
Bektash Beyg [Khan]	1042 -end 1048/1633-1639	His kinsman – BB Baghdad – *motavalli*; *gholam*	Shamlu 1, 255, Yusof 126, 156, 204, 216, 292; Vahid 237, 253
	As of 1048/1639	Ottoman governors	

Bahrain was part of the kingdom of Hormuz until 1602 when the Safavids seized it and it then became a part of the province of Fars (Shiraz). They remained in control of the island until 1717 when the Omanis took it, who returned the island in 1722 to Safavid control.[64]

Name	Year	Observations	Source
Behzad Soltan	1011/1602	H Bahrain	Molla Jalal 235
Sevenduk Soltan	1042-?/1633-?	H Bahrain	Vahid 250
Baba Beyg [Soltan, Khan]	?-1050/?-1641	H Bahrain	Valeh 1380, 311, 253; Astarabadi 260
Badr Khan	?-1071/?-1660	H Bahrain	Vahid 731
Zaman Soltan	1071-?/1660-?	H Bahrain + Dashtestan	Vahid 731
Baqer Soltan	Before 1108/1696	H Bahrain	Nasiri 177
Mehdiqoli Soltan b. Baqer Soltan	1108/1696	H Bahrain	Nasiri 177
Mehrab Khan	1126-1129/1714-1717	H Bahrain	Safavi 37-39
	From 1129/1717 to 1135/1722	in Omani hands	

Bakharz, see Khvaf.

---

64 For its history during the Safavid period see Willem Floor, *Persian Gulf*.

Bakhtiyari is the term that refers to the Bakhtiyari tribe, also known as Bakhtiyari-Lors, as well as to the district that was assigned to them for their sustenance. The Bakhtiyari tribal district roughly was equal to the area known as the Bakhtiyari Mountains, which was delineated by its natural boundaries, to wit: "the Sezar River, the northwestern tributary to the Dez River, forms the boundary against Lorestan; the Karun Vanak, Kersan, and Marun delineate the boundary between the Bakhtiyari Mountains and the Kuhgiluyeh part of the Zagros."[65]

Name	Year	Observations	Source
Emir Tajmir Bakhtiyari	1005-?/1597-?	H Bakhtiyari –Lors	Monshi 529; Molla Jalal 206
Amir Shah Hoseyn Bakhtiyari	?-1010/?-1602	H Bakhtiyari	Molla Jalal 205
Jahangir Khan	1029-?/1620-?	H Bakhtiyari	Monshi 950, 959
Khalil Khan Bakhtiyari brother of Jahangir Khan	1038-1066-?/ 1629-1656-?	H [Lor-e] Bakhtiyari; as of 1066 also *teyuldar* of Khvansar	Monshi 1086; Shamli 1, 283; Yusof 251; Vahid 228, 231, 304, 602
Yusof Khan	1108-1109/ 1697-1698	H Bakhtiyari	Nasiri 218
'Isa Khan	1109/1698	H Bakhtiyari	Nasiri 252
Qasem Khan	1109/1698	H Bakhtiyari	Nasiri 257
Mohammad 'Ali Khan b. Yusof Khan	?-1124/?-1712	H Bakhtiyari	Shustari 57
Sa'id Khan b. Haqqnazar Khan	1124-?/1712-?	H Bakhtiyari	Shustari 57-58
Yahya Khan b. Yusof Khan	1129/1717	H Bakhtiyari	Shustari 69
Mohammad Hoseyn Khan	ca. 1141/1728	H Bakhtiyari [Lor-e Bozorg]	Balfour 155

Baku or Badkubeh is a town situated on the southern shore of the Apsheron peninsula in Azerbaijan.[66] It and its surrounding area was part of the province of Shirvan. Apart from a short-term early Safavid governor, until 947/1540, Baku remained under the Shirvanshahs. During that period, like Shaberan and Darband, it had no governor, but a castellan (*kutval* or *mostahfez*).[67] Thereafter Safavid governors were in charge of Darband, who usually had the rank of Soltan.[68]

---

65 See E. Ehlers, "Bakhtiyari Mountains, *Encyclopaedia Iranica*. For the Bakhtiyaris see Gene R. Garthwaite, *Khans and shahs: a documentary analysis of the Bakhtiyari in Iran* (Cambridge, 1983).

66 On the history of Baku see Sara Ashurbeyli. *Ocherk istorii sredne vekovogo Baku, viii-nachala xix vv.* (Baku, 1964).

67 Shirazi, *Takmelat*, p. 48; Mozaffar, *Jahangosha*, pp. 306-07.

68 Anonymous, "Mémoire de la province du Sirvan, en forme de Lettre addressée au Pere Fleuriau", *Lettres Edifiantes et Curieuses* (Paris, 1780), vol. 4, p. 17.

Name	Year	Observations	Source
Laleh Beyg Shamlu	915/1509	H Baku + Shabaran	Bidlisi 2, 521
Mansur Beyg	916?/1510?	H Baku	Heravi 321
Ghazi Khan Tekkelu	947-950/1540-1543	H Baku + Saliyan, Mahmudabad	Bidlisi 2, 574, 577; Qazvini 294-95
	From 986/1578 to 1016/1607	under Ottoman occupation	
Dhu'l-Feqar Khan Qaramanlu	1015-1019/1606-1610	*Vali* Shirvan, Shamakhi, Darband, Baku	Monshi 2, 733; Shamlu 1, 187
Son of Rostam Soltan Soklan	1019-?/1610-?	*Vali* Baku	Molla Jalal 378
N.N.	1044/1635	H Baku	Astarabadi 251
Mohammad Reza Soltan	1107-?/1696-?	H Baku	Nasiri 96

Bala Morghab is situated on the banks of the river Morghab, about 200 km northeast of Herat and 80 km from Panjdeh. It was also known as Mervrud[69] and served as a frontier fort. This district apparently only became part of the Safavid kingdom under 'Abbas I, who in 1008/1600 gave orders to develop the deserted area.[70] In 1030/1621 only a *kutval* or castellan was in charge.[71] However, soon thereafter, this official was called a *hakem* or governor. This may reflect a change in administrative practice, or, what is more likely, sloppy appellation, as it not infrequently happens that authors indiscriminately use the terms *hakim* and *kutval* to refer to the commander of an important fort. In 1038/1629, Fazl 'Ali Soltan Shamlu, was governor of Bala Morghab.[72]

Balkh was taken by the Safavids in 916/1510 from the Uzbegs, who retook it in 922/1516. Balkh and its dependencies remained in their hands until 1051/1641 when the Moghuls conquered the city; they held it until 1057/1647, when the Uzbegs retook it. Around 1000/1592 the Uzbeg ruler of Balkh was a Safavid vassal, but Safavid influence on the Balkh region disappeared when the Uzbegs took firm control over it in 1010/1601.

Name	Year	Observations	Source
Beyram Beyg Qaramanlu	916-919/1510-1514	H Balkh,* Shoborghan, Andkhud, Chichketu, Gharjestan, Meymaneh, Faryab, Morghab	Qomi 1, 115, 120; Shirazi 50; Bidlisi 2, 525; Qazvini 274; Budaq 32; Monshi 1, 40; Rumlu 164; Ben Khvandamir 139, 148
Div Soltan Rumlu	919-922/1514-1516	H Balkh*4	Hoseyni 62; Shamlu 1, 43; Rumlu 181, 211; Mozaffar 454

---

69 Guy Le Strange, *The Lands of the Eastern Caliphate* (London, 1960); Riazul Islam, *Calendar*, vol. 1, p. 268.
70 Monshi, *Tarikh*, vol. 1, p. 576.
71 Monshi, *Tarikh*, vol. 2, p. 961.
72 Monshi, *Tarikh*, vol. 2, p. 1084.

	922/1516	End of Safavid rule	
Kaskan Qara Soltan Chingizi	934/1536	H Balkh	Abrahams 136
Mohammad Ebrahim Khan	?-1009/?-1600	H Balkh; vassal of Shah 'Abbas I	Monshi 612; Molla Jalal 202

* Mozaffar, *Jahangosha*, p. 454 mentions that Div Soltan's jurisdiction also would include Kheyjun and Tokharestan, once he had conquered those areas.

Bandar 'Abbas district included the islands of Hormuz, Qeshm and Larek as well as Bandar 'Abbas and its surrounding area (Minab, Shamil). It had been part of the kingdom of Hormuz until 1614 (Bandar 'Abbas), 1621 (Qeshm) and 1622 (Hormuz). Thereafter the governorship of the district intitially was also referred to as that of Hormuz or Jarun (the orginal name of the island), but gradually the name of Bandar 'Abbas became the usual appellation for this governorship, the more so since Hormuz after 1622 played neither a commercial nor a militarily role any more.[73]

List of governors of Bandar 'Abbas between 1622-1732

Soltan of Bandar 'Abbas	Year	Observations	Source
Sevenduk Beyg Zanganeh	1031-1040/1622-1631	H Bandar 'Abbas	Floor, *Persian Gulf*, 301
Barkhordar Soltan Qolkhanchi Ughli Dhu'l-Qadr.	1040-1041/1631-1632	H Bandar 'Abbas	Valeh 1372, 150; Esfahani 147-48; Yusof 293
Fulad Khan	1041-1042/1632-1633	H Bandar 'Abbas	Floor, *Persian Gulf*, 302; Esfahani 141
Barkhordar Soltan Qolkhanchi Ughli Dhu'l-Qadr.	1042-1047/1633-1638	H Bandar 'Abbas	Floor, *Persian Gulf*, 301
Safiqoli Khan Qolkhanchi-oghlu	1048-1055/1638-1645	H Bandar 'Abbas	Esfahani 276; Floor, *Persian Gulf*, 301
Qara Khan Soltan; then Mir Jamal Soltan	1055-1056/1645-1646	H Bandar 'Abbas	KA 1057, f. 94; KA 1059, f. 822v; Vahid 404 (Qara Khan)
'Evaz Beyg	1056-1057/1646-1647	H Bandar 'Abbas	Floor, *Persian Gulf*, 301
Saru Khan Soltan (Sarrew Ckawny Sultan his jannezene, then Zarthen sent by the Asaf of Shiraz, Sultan Vizeere)	1057-1058/1647-1648	H Bandar 'Abbas	Floor, *Persian Gulf*, 301

---

73 For the history of Bandar 'Abbas (or rather Bandar 'Abbasi, which was its official name) during the Safavid period see Floor, *Persian Gulf*, chapter five. According to Shoshtari, *Tadhkereh*, p. 56, Mohammad Soltan b. Hatem Aqa (the latter was a close collaborator of the in 1668 ousted Hoseyn Pasha of Basra), was governor of Bandar 'Abbas, but this is not borne out by other sources and he does not fit in the sequence of table of governors of that port.

Tahmaspqoli [Beyg] Khan arrived 10/01/49	1058-1063/1648-1653	H Bandar 'Abbas; he died end of September 1653	KA 1069 bis, f. 762; Floor, *Persian Gulf*, 301
Jowhar Aqa	1063-1064/1652-1653	H Bandar 'Abbas	Floor, *Persian Gulf*, 301; Coolhaas 2, 734 per April 1653
Jowhar Aqa; then Aqa Hasan Changrudi	1064-1065/1653-1654	H Bandar 'Abbas	VOC 3988, f. 578; Floor, *Persian Gulf*, 301; Vahid 393
N.N. arrived on September 27; he died after 30 days and was succeeded by Pir Budaq Khan Pornak Torkman	1065-1066/1654-1655	H Bandar 'Abbas; he was relieved from his post at his own request.	VOC 1215, f. 786 vs.; Vahid Qazvini, p. 216; Valeh, *Iran*, p. 576; Coolhaas 2, 766-67
Taleb Beyg *gholam-e khasseh qurchi-ye zereh*	1066-1071/1656-1661	H Bandar 'Abbas; successor came in December 1655	Vahid Qazvini, p. 216; VOC 1215, f. 786 vs.; Valeh, *Iran*, p. 576
Mirza Homayun	1072-1073/1661-1662	H Bandar 'Abbas	Bafqi 3/1, 263; VOC 1239, f. 1211 v
Taleb Khan	1073-1074-1663-1664	H Bandar 'Abbas	VOC 1241, f. 638 v; VOC 1242, f. 1056 v
Fereydun Beyg, his son	1074-1075/1664-1665	H Bandar 'Abbas	VOC 1252, f. 708; Shamlu 2, 18
Allahverdi Beyg?	1076-1078/1665-1667	H Bandar 'Abbas	VOC 1253, f.1555; VOC 1253, f. 1696; VOC 1245, f. 515r-v; VOC 1255, f. 901-02
Zeynal Khan	1078/1667	H Bandar 'Abbas	Coolhaas 3, 703, 717; VOC 126, f. 925v-926; KA 1160, f. 970
Mehrab Khan till 01/1669; then the Georgian Shahqoli Khan	1078-1079/1668-1669	H Bandar 'Abbas	VOC 1285, f. 386; Coolhaas 3, 704; KA 1160, f. 906
Mortezaqoli Khan	1079-1083/1669-1673	H Bandar 'Abbas	VOC 1266, f. 952v
Safiqoli Soltan	1083-1084/1673-1674	H Bandar 'Abbas	Bardsiri 93, 400, 406, 410, 413, 415; Coolhaas 4, 17
Naser 'Ali Khan	1084-1088/1674-1677	H Bandar 'Abbas	KA 1221, f. 211; Coolhaas 4, 17; VOC 1250, f. 213; VOC 1507, f. 466v
Mohammad 'Ali Beyg ex-*shahbandar* (substituted in 1677-78?)	1088-1089/1677-1678	H Bandar 'Abbas	VOC 1250, f. 213; VOC 1507, f. 466v; VOC 1355, f. 394v.
Naser 'Ali Khan	1089-1092/1678-1681	H Bandar 'Abbas	KA 1222, f. 692v; VOC 1355, f. 394v.
Mortezaqoli Beyg	1092-1098/1681-1687	H Bandar 'Abbas	Bardsiri 341; VOC 1355, f. 399v.
Mohammad 'Ali Khan	1098-1105/1687-1694	H Bandar 'Abbas	Bardsiri 675; VOC 1430, f. 1512

'Abbasqoli Beyg	1105-1106/1694-1695	H Bandar 'Abbas; grandson of 'Evaz Beyg	VOC 1549, f. 588r; Nasiri, 81; Safavi 36
Mohammad 'Ali Khan	1106-1108/1695-1697		VOC 1611, f. 37; Nasiri 177; VOC 1549, f. 588r; Aubin, *L'Ambassade*, 22, 33, 76-77.
'Evaz Beyg (Khan), brother of Safiqoli Beyg *nazer-e boyutat*	1108-1110/1697-1699	H Bandar 'Abbas	Coolhaas 5, 860; Valentyn 5, 284
'Abbasqoli Khan	1110-1111/1699-1700	H Bandar 'Abbas	Coolhaas 6, 136; VOC 1652, f. 750 v; Aubin, *L'Ambassade*, 32-33
'Evaz Beyg (Khan), brother of Safiqoli Beyg *nazer-e boyutat*	1111-1113/1700-1702	H Bandar 'Abbas	KA 1559, f. 231; VOC 1652, f. 752v, 770r; Safavi 36-37.
Mohammad Mo'men Khan Jahromi	1115-1116/1704-1705	H Bandar 'Abbas	Coolhaas 6, 380, 409
Mohammad 'Ali Khan	1117-1120/1705-1708	H Bandar 'Abbas	Le Bruyn 2, 69, 72; Coolhaas, 6, 380
Mohammad Mo'men Beyg Jahromi	1120-1121/1708-1709	H Bandar 'Abbas	Safavi 36-37.
'Ali Reza Khan till 02/06/1709; then 'Evaz Khan	1121-1122/1709-1710	H Bandar 'Abbas	VOC 1768, f. 1872; VOC 1790, f. 501
'Ali Reza Khan	1122-1127/1710-1715	H Bandar 'Abbas	KA 1721, f. 55
Zakariya Khan	1127-1128/1715-1716	H Bandar 'Abbas	KA 1740, f. 2266, f. 2383v
Safiqoli Khan	1128-1129/1716-1717	H Bandar 'Abbas; until October 1717	KA 1789, f. 18, 23, 272; VOC 2168, f. 193; KA 1805, f. 210; Safavi 31,38
Ya'qub Soltan	1129-1131/October 1717-1719	H Bandar 'Abbas	KA 1805, f. 315; KA 1796, f. 2363; Safavi 31; VOC 1913, 499
Mohammad Zahed Soltan	1131-1133/1719-21	H Bandar 'Abbas	Coolhaas 7, 439; KA 1805, f. 85; KA 1796, f. 2297, 2357vs, 2363; VOC 1983, f. 143
Nurollah Khan	1133-1134/1721-1722	H Bandar 'Abbas	Floor, *Aghan*, 72, 205
Mirza 'Abdol-Qasem (acting)	1134-1136/1722-1724	H Bandar 'Abbas	Floor, *Afghan*, 210, 213-15
Idem/Hasan 'Ali Beyg	1136-1137/1724-1725	H Bandar 'Abbas	Floor, *Afghan*, 216-17
	From 1725 until the end of 1729	Afghan appointed officials	

Baneh is the name of a Kurdish tribe as well as the name of the frontier district where they lived, which was situated south of Lake Orumiyeh, halfway to Marivan, on the banks of a tributary of the river Kalvi. It was an independent Kurdish principipality, before it was incorporated into Safavid Iran.[74] Sekandar Beyg Baneh'i, a chief of the Baneh tribe, declared his love for Shah 'Abbas (*shahsevan*) after the Ottoman occupation in 1590. The latter gave him the district of Baneh, which was part of Maragheh, after the capture of Erevan in 1606.[75] Vahid Qazvini also lists it as a seperate governate, but, according to Minorsky, it "often stood in a vassal relationship to the valis of Ardalan," although he does not provide any evidence for this.[76] However, Baneh was considered to be an administrative part of Azerbaijan, in particular of the Maragheh jurisdiction.[77] This probably had been done for military reasons to have better control over the Ardalans, reason why Nasiri's *Alqab* still lists Baneh as a district of Azerbaijan.

Name	Year	Observations	Source
Mirza Beyg	ca. 930-940?/1524-1533?	*Vali* Baneh	Bidlisi 2, 183
Qatenamish Beyg	ca. 940?/1533?	Temporary usurper	Bidlisi 2, 183
Budaq Beyg b. Mirza Beyg	ca. 950?/1543?	*Vali* Baneh	Bidlisi 2, 183
Soleyman Beyg b. Mirza Beyg	ca. 950-970?/1543-1562	*Vali* Baneh	Bidlisi 2, 184
Sekandar Soltan Baneh'i	1013-?/1604-?	H Baneh	Monshi 814
Amir Eskandar Kord	1019/1610	H Baneh	Molla Jalal 389
Esma'il	1045-?/1635-?	H Baneh	Vahid 278
Mohammad Soltan	1109/1698	H Baneh	Nasiri 234

Baradust is the name of a Kurdish tribe as well as of the district assigned to them. One of its members, Qara Taj, declared his 'love for Shah Tahmasp I (*shahsevan*) and as a result the shah allocated the districts of Targavar and Margavar (just south of Lake Orumiyeh) to the Baradust tribe.[78] Sumāy (or Sowmay, Samavi), Baradust and Targavar (also Torgur) are districts of the Tabriz jurisdiction, and are situated south and west of Salmas and Orumiyeh.[79] According to the TM, the districts of Samavi (Sumāy) and Targavar are said to be part of Qarabagh. Minorsky therefore rightly remarked that this "looked entirely out of place".[80]

Barda', the chief town of Arran, was situated on the Terter river, north of Shusheh and east of Ganjeh. After 1038/1628, if not earlier it was held by members of the Igirmi-dört Qajar clan. It was part of Qarabagh province (q.v.).

---

74 Bidlisi, *Cheref-Nameh*, vol. 1, p. 320.
75 Monshi, *Tarikh*, pp. 814, 856-57.
76 Vahid, *Tarikh*, p. 278; TM, p. 172.
77 Monshi, *Tarikh*, vol. 2, p. 814.
78 Monshi, *Tarikh*, vol. 2, p. 792.
79 A.K.S. Lambton, *Landlord and Peasant in Iran* (Oxford, 1953), p. 109f.
80 TM, p. 102

Name	Year	Observations	Source
Sardar Beyg	932/1526	Beyg of Ganjeh + Barda'	Bacqué-Gramont 97
Khanuli Soltan Baharlu	957/1550	H Barda'	Abrahams 140
'Abdollah Beyg Ostajalu	973/1566	H Barda'+ Ganjeh + *Laleh* of Soltan 'Ali Mirza; succeeded by his son	Shirazi 125
Amir Hamzeh Beyg Ostajalu b. 'Abdollah Beyg	973-974?/1566-1567?	H Barda'+ Ganjeh + *Laleh* of Soltan 'Ali Mirza	Shirazi 125, 127 prince returned to court
Yusof Beyg Ziyad-oghlu Qajar	977/1571	H Barda'+ Ganjeh + *Laleh* of Soltan 'Ali Mirza	Tatavi 700
Emamqoli Khan Qajar	987/1579	H Barda'+ Ganjeh	Bidlisi 2 648
Peykar Khan Igirmi-dört Qajar*	1038-1043/1628-1633	H Barda'	Monshi 1085
Ebrahim Igirmi-dört Qajar	?-1050/?-1640	H Barda'	Yusof 435; Vahid 301
Safiqoli Beyg	1069/1659	H Barda'	Vahid 690
Soleymanqoli Beyg	1105-07/1694-1696	H Barda'	Nasiri 58, 96
Kalb 'Ali Khan	1110/1699	Emir Barda'	Nasiri 273

* In 1043 Peykar Khan (*hakem*-e Kakht) died and was succeeded by his brother Ebrahim Khan as governor of the Igremi-dort. Vahid, *Tarikh*, pp. 201, 210-11, 258.

Bargushat or Bargoshad is situated near the Bargoshat River, on the right bank of the Akera River and is a district of the province of Qarabagh.

Name	Year	Observations	Source
Domri Beyg	932/1526	H Bargoshat	Bacqué-Gramont 97
Tahmaspqoli Soltan Dhu'l-Qadr	994/1586	H Bargoshat	Qomi 832
Farrokhrow Soltan	1013/1604	H Bargoshad	Molla Jalal 276
Maqsud Soltan Donboli	1038/1628	H Bargoshat	Monshi 1086
Fazl 'Ali Sharvan Shaluy	1069/1659	H Bargoshat	Vahid 690

Basra was at the time of the establishment of the Safavid kingdom a quasi-independent emirate, but nominally owed allegiance to the Aq-Qoyunlu governor of Baghdad. As Esma'il I acquired Aq-Qoyunlu territory in Iraq, in particular Baghdad, Vaset and Jazayer, the latter two districts being adjacent to Basra, the ruler of Basra considered it politic to offer his submission to the new overlord. In 909/1504, Sheikh Afrasiyab, the *vali* of Basra, came to Shiraz to pledge his allegiance to Shah Esma'il I, who confirmed him in his position and possessions. In the years thereafter, despite Safavid control of adjacent territories ('Arabestan, Jazayer, etc.), the rulers of Basra pretty much ignored the Safavids and vice versa.[81]

Bastam is a town and its district eight km north-east of Shahrud (Khorasan), in the southern foothills of the Elborz Mountains. It would seem that this was always a combined governorship with the district of Damghan and sometimes, in addition, with some other adjacent districts such as Biyarjomand, Firuzkuh and Hazar Jarib. There is also conflicting information as to who was governor during the years 932 and 933 as the sources do not agree with one another. I have listed all governors found as it is not clear which source is at fault, if any.

Name	Year	Observations	Source
Yar-Ahmad Khuzani aka Najm al-Din Mas'ud II	916-918/1510-1512	*teyuldar* Damghan	Aubin 12 (Afzal)
Damri Soltan Shamlu	?-933/1528	H Damghan/ Bastam	Tahmasp 10; Dickson 66, 102 n. 1 Abrahams, p. 172
Mohammad Beyg Rumlu	933/1528	H Damghan	Tahmasp 10
Alash Soltan	933/1528	*teyuldar* Damghan, Bastam	Hoseyni 92
	934-?/1529-?	Uzbeg occupation Damghan-Bastam	Hoseyni 98
Emir Gheyb Soltan Ostajalu	ca. 960/1553	H Damghan-Bastam	Monshi 108; Vahid 65
Shahverdi Soltan Afshar	971/1564	H Damghan, Bastam, Firuzkuh, Hazarjarib, Biyarjomand	Budaq 141
'Ali Khalifeh Aghcheh-Qoyunlu Qajar	?-984/?-1576	H Damghan-Bastam	Valeh 1372, 411; Monshi 140, 203
Mortezaqoli Khan Pornak Torkman	989-996/1581-1588	H Astarabad, Jorjan Damghan, Bastam, Biyarjomand, A'rab-e 'Amereh and Hazar arib	Qomi 2, 751; Valeh 1372, 678, 831; Dhabehi-Setudeh 6, doc. 1; Natanzi 149, 152; Monshi 402
Farrokh Khan Pornak	997-1004/1589-1596	H Damghan – Bastam	Qomi 2, 884, 889, 906, 932; Monshi 507
Hasan 'Ali Khan Chapni	1006/1597	H Bastam –Damghan	Vahid 138 (Chakni)
Beyram 'Ali Soltan Chapni	1006-?/1598-?	H Bastam	Vahid 139 (Chakni)

Bavanat is a district that in the past was part of Fars, but by the end of the sixteenth century, if not earlier, had been transferred to Persian Iraq.[82]

---

81 Mozaffar, *Jahangosha*, p. 187. For a discussion of the situation of Basra during the early Safavid period see Floor, *Persian Gulf*, pp. 139-62.
82 Yazdi, *Mokhtasar*, vol. 1, p. 108.

Name	Year	Observations	Source
Qoli Soltan Afshar	985-?/1577-?	*Teyuldar* Aberquh-Bavanat; *qurchi-bash*i	Qomi 2, 665
Sayyed Beyg Kamuneh	994-?/1586-?	H Bavanat + *olka-ye* Kabir va Tassuj	Qomi 2, 828
N. N.	998/1590	*Kalantar* and *darugheh* Bavanat	Molla Jalal 75

Bayat is the name of a Kurdish tribe as well as of the district assigned to it for its sustenance, which formed part of Azerbaijan.

Name	Year	Observations	Source
Oghurlu Soltan Bayat	?-1002/?-1594	H *il-e* Bayat - replaced by his brother	Monshi 471-712
Shahqoli Soltan	1002-?/1594-?	H *il-e* Bayat	Monshi 713

Bayazid a strategic border fort situated approximately twenty-five kilometers south-west of Mt. Ararat, on the road between Erzerum and Tabriz, which usually was in Ottoman hands. In 1629, Yar 'Ali Soltan Bayat was the Safavid governor of *Qal'eh-ye* Bayazid.[83]

Bazavandaqan is a district in Mashhad province, which is only mentioned by Nasiri's *Alqab* as being a governorship. See Naravandaqan.

Bedlis or Betlis was one of the Kurdish pricipalities on the border between the Ottoman Empire and the Safavid kingdom. It was strategically situated south-west of Lake Van in the narrow valley of Bedlis Chay, a tributary of the Tigris, where it commanded the only route between the Van basin and Iraq. Like other Kurdish chiefs the lords of Bedlis sometimes supported the Safavids and sometimes the Ottomans, if they had no choice. Although initially part of the Safavid kingdom, Sharaf Khan, the Lord of Bedlis after 1514 gave allegiance to the Ottomans until 1532, when he turned back into the Safavid fold. He was killed the next year by Olameh Tekkelu, the Safavid renegade and thereafter Bedlis was governed by others than members of its hereditary rulers. In 1578, Sharaf al-Din Khan, the author of the *Sharafnameh* and grandson of Sharaf Khan, defected from Safavid rule and accepted investiture by the Ottomans. Thereafter, the Lords of Bedlis maintained an autonomous position between the two powers, a situation that lasted until 1847, when Ottoman rule became uncontested.

Name	Year	Observations	Source
Sharaf al-Din Beyg	912/1506	H Betlis	Valeh 1372, 161; Bidlisi 2, 276f; Heravi 281; Mozaffar 260
Kord Beyg Charqlu? Ostajali	913/1507	H Betlis	Bidlisi 2, 285

---

83 Monshi, *Tarikh*, vol. 2, p. 1086.

'Evaz Beyg Ostajalu brother of Mohammad Khan	920/1514	H Betlis	Bidlisi 2, 296
Sharaf Khan [Rudaki Kurdi]	923-939/1517-1533	*Vali* Bedlis + 'Emadiyeh	Budaq 77; Rumlu 314; Bidlisi 2, 285f, 297-98, 311, 562; Qazvini 286, 287; Monshi 66
	As of 939/1533	Ottoman territory	Rumlu 380

Birunat or Birunat-e Hormuz, because it had been part of the kingdom of Hormuz until 1602, was the term to indicate the district situated north-east of Bandar 'Abbas extending to Jask, which included the districts of Shamil, Minab and Manujan. Another term used to denote this area was Moghestan. In 1011/1602, Qanbar Soltan Zanganeh was its governor.[84]

Biyarjomand is a district south-east of Shahrud and Bastam, situated on the border of the Great Salt Desert or the Kavir. It was also known as Birjumand or Biyar.

Name	Year	Observations	Source
Shahverdi Soltan Afshar	971/1564	H Damghan, Bastam, Firuzkuh, Hazarjarib, Biyarjomand	Budaq 141
Mortezaqoli Khan Pornak Torkman	989-996/1581-1588	H Astarabad, Jorjan Damghan, Bestam, Biyarjomand, A'rab-e 'Amereh and Hazarjarib	Qomi 2, 751; Valeh 1372, 678, 831; Dhabehi-Setudeh 6, doc. 1; Natanzi 149, 152; Monshi 290

Bon Fahl, also Fahl (now Bampur), some 500 km south-east of Kerman, is a district in northern Kij-Makran, where the Safavids acquired some measure of control, as of 1610 or thereabouts, although it had to be enforced at times. After non-locals under 'Abbas I (r. 1588-1629) local Baluch chiefs were appointed as governor. Elsewhere in Kij-Makran (q.v.) Safavid rule was nominal at best.[85]

Name	Year	Observations	Source
Shahverdi Khan Kord Mahmudi	?-1021/?-1612	H Bon Fahl; replaced by his brother	Monshi 852; Vahid 180
Shirazi Soltan	1021-?/1612-?	H Bonfahl	Monshi 852; Vahid 180
Malek Shams al-Din	?-1043/?-1634	H Bonfahl	Khatunabadi 512
Malek Ekhtiyar al-Din	1043-?/1634-?	H Bonfahl	Yusof 132; Khatunabadi 512

---

84 Yazdi, *Mokhtasar*, vol. 1, p. 331; Molla Jalal, *Ruznameh*, p. 236.
85 Molla Jalal, *Ruznameh*, p. 372; Monshi, *Tarikh*, vol. 2, p. 852.

Borujerd is a town with its surrounding district that borders on Lorestan and is situated in the extreme north-east corner of Bakhtiyari country.

Name	Year	Observations	Source
Mehdiqoli Khan Shamlu	999/1591	H Vorujerd + Khorramabad	Natanzi 494
Oghurlu Soltan Bayat	1000/1592	*Vakil* of Mohammad Baqer Mirza, H Borujerd	Vahid 114, 120-21, 140

Bost or *Qal'eh-ye* Bost is situated near the junction of the Helmand and the Arghandab, about 55 km south of Gereshk. The latter town is situated on the right bank of the Helmand, about 120 km from Qandahar. According to the editor of Vahid Qazvini, it was a separate governate as of the days of Shah Soltan Hoseyn, but it appears that this was the case much earlier.[86] Part of Qandahar province was the district of Zamindavar, in which fort Bost was situated. Usually both the district and the fort had a separate governor, but (initially?) the two were also held by one person. It also happened that the governor of Bost also held sway over other areas such as Gereskh (q.v.), which may have well been the norm rather than an exception, as suggested by Nasiri's *Alqab*.

Name	Year	Observations	Source
Hamzeh Beyg Dhu'l-Qadr aka Qur Hamzeh	966-984/1559-1576	*Laleh* Soltan Hoseyn Mirza b. Bahram Mirza; H Zamindavar + the districts of the Garmsirat	Hoseyni 177; Shamlu 1, 79; Monshi 136, 307; Qomi 1, 397, 448, 575, [2], 629, 651
Hamzeh Beyg Dhu'l-Qadr aka Qur Hamzeh	985-997/1576-1589	*Laleh* Rostam Mirza b. Soltan Hoseyn Mirza; H Bost + Zamindavar	Monshi 408
Rostam Mirza b. Soltan Hoseyn Mirza	997-999/1589-1591	H Bost + Zamindavar	Monshi 477-85
Mohammad Zaman Soltan Shamlu	999-1000/1591-1592	H Bost	Monshi 673
	From 1000/1592 until 1012/1603	Moghul governors	Monshi 674
Rezaqoli Soltan Siyah-Mansur	1038/1628	H Bost	Monshi 1086
Mehrab Soltan [Khan]	1048-1051/1638-1641	H Bost + Gereshk	Yusof 213, 253; Valeh 1380, 126-7, 265, 355;Yusof 289
Dust 'Ali Khan Zanganeh	1058/1648	H Mohall-e Bost	Vahid 495
Kalb 'Ali Khan nephew of Mohammad Zaman Soltan	1058/1648	H Bost	Shamlu 1, 369
Pordel Khan	1059/1649	H Bost	Shamlu 1, 416

---

86 Vahid, *Tarikh*, p. 288.

Mehdiqoli Soltan Siyah-Mansur	?-1064/?-1654	H + qal'ehdar Bost	Vahid 467, 542-43; Valeh 1380, 515
Emamqoli Soltan Siyah-Mansur	1064-?/1654-?	H + qal'ehdar Bost	Valeh 1380, 515-16; Vahid 542

Buri is a border district that I have not been able to identify, but, like the two other locations mentioned, it was a dependency of Chokhur-e Sa'd. In 1049/1640, 'Isa Khan Soltan Buzchelu was governor of Buri, Nabik, and Aqcheh Qal'eh.[87]

Buzchelu, see Lori.

Chahar Mahall, see Farideyn.

Chamchal or Chamkhal (also Jamjama or Chamchamal) a district situated in Kurdestan on the road connecting Kermanshah with Tabriz, at four leages distance from Sahneh and six leagues from Kermanshah.[88]

Name	Year	Observations	Source
Vali Khan Tekkelu	988/1580	H Chamchal+Lorestan	Valeh 1372, 680
Sulaq Hoseyn	994/1586	H Chamkhal	Natanzi 178
Shahverdi Khalifeh Shamlu	998/1590	H Chamkhal	Natanzi 337

Chemeshgezek is the name of a Kurdish Shi'a tribe of Dersim (Erzinjan), of which some 1,000 families had entered into Safavid service[89] as well as of the district occupied by this tribe in the province of Shirvan. Part of the tribe was later settled in Khorasan, where they formed a major part of the Safavid military force at the end of the dynasty's reign.[90]

Name	Year	Observations	Source
Yusof Soltan *gholam*	1047/1638	H Chemeshgezek	Vahid 283; Astarabadi 255
Owtar Khan	1058/1648	H Chemeshgezek	Vahid 476; Riazul Islam 1, 349
NN	1720s	H Chemeshgezek + Aghdash	*Alqab*

Chokhur-e Sa'd province was thus named since the fourteenth century after the name of the then governor Emir Sa'd. The governor of Chokhur Sa'd was initially just referred to as *hakem*

---

87 Yusof, *Dheyl*, pp. 239-40; Valeh, *Iran*, p. 296.
88 Le Strange, *The Lands*, p. 193.
89 Bedlisi, *Cheref-Nameh*, vol. 1, p. 163, vol. 2, pp. 1-9; Monshi, *Tarikh*, pp. 533, 569, 631, 927, 1088; Esfahani, *Kholasat*, p. 248.
90 Safavi, *Majma'*, p. 28; TM, p. 167.

either of Chokhur-e Sa'd or of Erevan, which was the capital of the province and the seat of residence of the governor.[91] Occasionally the governor was also referred to as *hakem-e sarhadd* or governor of the frontier, due to the fact that it was a frontline province that regularly was attacked by Ottoman forces.[92] Safavid control of this province dates from the very beginning of the dynasty's rule as is clear from royal edicts from 911/1505 and 912/1506.[93] Like other provinces in the Caucasus, Chokhur-e Sa'd also suffered from Ottoman encroachment, who occupied the province from 991/1583 until 1013/1614. At the end of the Safavid period this province consisted of the following jurisdictions: Bayazid, Maghazberd, Maku, Nakhjevan, Sadarak, Shadidlu, Zaruzbil and the tribal district of the Donbolis.

Name	Year	Observations	Source
Qaracheh-Elyas Beybordlu	908-?/1502-?	H Chokhur-e Sa'd	Aubin 8 (Afzal)
Amir Beyg Mowsellu Torkman	915?/1509?	H Chokhur-e Sa'd; 2 months only	Aubin 15, n. 172
Hamzeh Beyg b. Hoseyn Beyg *Laleh* Ostajalu [sic]*	920-?/1514-?	H Chokhur-e Sa'd	Aubin 29, n. 90 (Afzal)
Div Soltan Rumlu	922-933/1516-1527	H Chokhur-e Sa'd	Rumlu 218
Soleyman Beyg Rumlu	933/1527	H Chokhur-e Sa'd + Rey	Bidlisi 2, 552
Hoseyn Khan Soltan Rumlu	956-957/1549-1550	H Chokhur-e Sa'd	Rumlu 441; Qomi 1, 342
Shahqoli Soltan Ostajalu b. Hamzeh Soltan Qazaq	958-975/1551-1568	H Chokhur-e Sa'd; H Erevan, Nakhjevan and Chokhur-e Sa'd (Tatavi 680); succeeded by his son	Rumlu 524; Qomi 1, 403, 418, 477, 584; Shirazi 104, 128, 130; Bidlisi 2, 586, 597, 627; Qazvini 300; Monshi 1, 76
Mohammad or Mohammadi Khan Tokhmaq Ostajalu	975-983/1568-1575	BB Chokhur-e Sa'd – Erevan	Shirazi 131; Valeh 1372, 408, 683; Monshi 121, 139, 204; Bidlisi 2, 647, 648
Abu Torab Soltan	983-984/1575-1576	BB Chokhur-e Sa'd - his cousin	Monshi 204, 216
Khalil Khan Afshar	985-986/1576-1577	H Chokhur-e Sa'd	Qomi 2, 664
Mohammad or Mohammadi Khan Tokhmaq Ostajalu	986-991/1578-83	BB Chokhur-e Sa'd – Erevan – 2nd time	Monshi 225, 233, 293; Bidlisi 2, 663; Qomi 2, 677, 717, 757; Kanaker 330
	991-1013/1583-1604	Ottoman pashas	

---

91 TM, p. 165; A. D. Papaziyan *Persidskie Dokumenty Matenadarana I, Ukazy, vypusk vtoroi (XV-XVI vv.)* (Erevan, 1956), doc. 9 (dated 911/1505).
92 Qubad, *Tarikh*, pp. 177-78, 192.
93 Papaziyan, *Persidskie*, docs. 9 and 10.

Name	Dates	Position	Sources
Amir Guneh Khan Aghcheh-Qoyunlu Qajar aka Saru Aslan	1013-1034/1604-1625	BB Chokhur-e Sa'd	Papaziyan 1959, docs 10, 11; Akulis 43-44etc, 68; Kanaker 330; Yusof 293; Monshi 782, 864, 1007, 1041; Vahid 159, 215; Shamlu 1, 184; Molla Jalal 257-58, 381
Tahmasp 'Ali Khan Aghcheh-Qoyunlu Qajar aka *Shir-bachcheh*	1034-1045/1625-1635	His son - H and *qal'ehdar* Erevan or BB Chokur-e Sa'd + *amir al-omara* Erevan	Monshi 1041; Yusof 70, 138, 144, 153, 155; 163, 293; Vahid 215, 255 (Tahmaspqoli); Kanaker 330
Morteza Pasha	1045-1046/1635-1636	Ottoman governor	Kanaker 330
Kalb 'Ali Khan Afshar	1046-1050/1636-39	H or BB Erevan	Akulis 119, 141; Valeh 1380, 222, 225, 303, 600, 609; Yusof 246; Kanaker 330; Vahid 284, 301; Shamlu 1, 256; Bafqi 3/1, 212-14
Mohammadqoli [Beyg] Khan Chaghatay aka Chagatay Kotuk Mohammad Khan	1050-1058/1639-1648	BB Chokur-e Sa'd	Vahid 301; Shamlu 1, 256, 327; Agulis 141; Kanaker 330; Papazian 1959, doc. 28; Puturidze 1962, doc. 7
Key Khosrow Khan Cherkes	1058-1063/1648-1653	BB Chokur-e Sa'd	Papazian 1959, doc. 39; Agulis 151, 163; Vahid 436; Kanaker 330; Agulis 163
Mohammadqoli Khan b. Laleh Beyg	1064-1066/1654-1656	BB Chokur-e Sa'd	Shamlu 1, 294; Vahid 597; Kanaker 330; Agulis 48
Najafqoli Khan**	1066-1073/1656-1663	BB Chokur-e Sa'd; also H of Shamakhi	Vahid 597, 738; Kanaker 330; Agulis 64, 66-69, 77, 128
'Abbasqoli Khan Qajar b. Amir Guneh Khan	1074-1077/1663-1666	H Chokur-e Sa'd	Vahid 753; Agulis 75, 77-78, 128
Alghas Mirza aka Safi Khan Lezgi	1077-1085/1666-1674	H Chokur-e Sa'd	Kanaker 330; Agulis 75, 104, 128; Khatunabadi 541
Saru Khan Beyg	1085/1674	interim governor	Kanaker 330; Agulis 75
Safiqoli Khan b. Rostam Khan	1085-1089/1674-1679	H Chokur-e Sa'd	Kanaker 330; Agulis 128-29, 131, 139-40
Zal Khan	1089-1099/1679-1688	H Chokur-e Sa'd	Kanaker 330; Agulis 129, 140-41, 146-50, 153-8
Mortezaqoli Khan	1099-1101/1688-1690	H Chokur-e Sa'd	Kanaker 330
Mohammadqoli Khan	1101-1104/1690-1693	H Chokur-e Sa'd	Kanaker 330; Agulis 48, 51, 53, 163
Farz 'Ali Khan	1104/1693	H Chokur-e Sa'd	Kanaker 330

Allahqoli Khan	1107-1109/1695-1698	*Vali* Erevan and Chokhur-e Sa'd	Nasiri 96, 214
Farz 'Ali Khan	1111/1700	H Chokur-e Sa'd	Kanaker 330
Mohammad Khan	1116/1704	H Erevan	Floor, "Lost files," 61
'Abd al-Mas'ud Khan	1117/1705	H Erevan	Floor, "Lost files," 87
Mohammad 'Ali Khan	?-1128/?-1716	H Erevan - *sepahsalar*	VOC 1879, Isfahan-Gamron (22/08/1716), f 281
NN his 2-year old son	1128-?/1716-?	H Erevan	VOC 1879, Isfahan-Gamron (22/08/1716), f 281
Kostandil Mirza	1137/1723	BB Erevan; *vali* Kartli + Kakhetia; H Shams al-Dinlu + Qazakh	Brosset 2/2, 513

* Aubin has pointed out that it was very odd to appoint a Shamlu in Chokhur-e Sa'd. Therefore, he probably was not the son of Hoseyn Beyg Shamlu, but indeed of an Ostajalu. This also seems to be indicated by the fact that later Shahqoli Soltan, who perhaps is his son, also becomes governor of Chokhur-e Sa'd (see Table). If not, and Aubin is right, this must have been a temporary appointment due to a shortage of qualified persons as this occurred just after the defeat at Chalderan.

** Klaus-Michael Röhrborn, *Provinzen und Zentralgewalt Persiens im 16. und 17. Jahrhundert* (Berlin 1966), p. 34 has a certain Qazaq Khan Cherkes or Zanganeh follow Najafqoli Khan as governor, but neither the printed versions of Shamlu, *Qesas* nor Vahid Qazvini, *Tarikh*, which he cites as his sources, mention such a fact.

Chors or Churs is a district situated on the left affluent of the Qotur River, north of Khoy.[94] Under Shah 'Abbas I there was a governor of Chors and Salmas.[95]

Name	Year	Observations	Source
Khan Mohammad Khan	920/1514	H Churs	Astarabadi 48
Zeynal Beyg [Khan] Mahmudi	1015-1017/1607-1609	H Chors – *nazer-e boyutat*	Monshi 721; Vahid 166, 213-17
Salman Soltan [Khan] Donboli Su-bashi	1017-1034/1609-1625	H Chors + Salmas	Monshi 783, 1031, 1086
Ayub Khan	1107/1696	H Chors	Nasiri 96

Chutiyali (now Chotiali in Pakistan) and Duki, situated on the border with Moghul India, were both dependencies of Qandahar and, although one may question the extent of Safavid control over these two districts, it is explicitly stated that they were within the confines of the *mamalek-e mahruseh*. In 1064/1654, Dowlatkhan Afghan had been its Safavid governor for a long period.[96]

---

94 TM, p. 164. Monshi, *Tarikh*, 669, 695, 721, 783, 1031; Valeh, *Iran*, pp. 163, 166 (Churs); Molla Jalal, *Ruznameh*, p. 350 (Jurs).
95 Monshi, *Tarikh*, vol. 2, p. 1086.
96 Vahid, *Tarikh*, pp. 540, 658. In the British magazine *The Graphic* (1883), there is a double page woodblock six-panel illustration of "Life at Thul-Chotiali in Southern Afghanistan," showing British officers at polo and engaged in other activities with onlooking Afghans.

Damavand is a district situated south of the Damavand Mountain, some 60 km north of Tehran. It was apparently often held together with other jurisdictions such as Firuzkuh (q.v.), Khvar (q.v.), Hablerud (q.v.) and Semnan (q.v.).

Name	Year	Observations	Source
Amir Hasan Kiya	909/1504	H Firuzkuh-Damavand	Hoseyni 23
Hoseyn Kiya Cholavi	910?/1505?	H Firuzkuh, Damavand, Khvar, Semnan	Valeh 1372, 133
	from 985/1578 until 987/1579	crown domain of the queen Kheyr al-Nesa Beygom	Qomi 2, 665
Shahqoli Beyg b. Ras Khan	986-?/1578-?	*Teyuldar* Damavand + Hablehrud	Qomi 2, 668
Mohammad Khan Torkman	?-996/?-1588	H Hablehrud + Hazar Jarib	Qomi 2, 869
Shahqoli Soltan Kholafā Rumlu	996-997/1588-1589	*Teyuldar* and H Damavand + Hablehrud	Qomi 2, 745, 847, 874
Mir Shah Mir	997/1589	H Damavand	Shamlu 1, 167
Jamshid Khan	1066/1656	H Damavand see Astarabad	Vahid 612, 706, 751
	From 1067/1657 until 1072/1661	it was crown domain	see Semnan

Damghan a town and district of the same name situated some 95 km south of Astarabad and 65 km from Shahrud (see Bastam).

Daquq, a town situated 45 km south of Kirkuk (q.v.).

Darabjerd is the easternmost district of Fars and almost exactly corresponded with the old province of Shabankareh. It is bounded in the north by Neyriz and Ich, in the east by Sa'adatabad, in the south by Lar, in the west by Jahrom and Fasa.[97]

Name	Year	Observations	Source
Badr Khan Ostajalu	932/1526	H Darabjerd	Qomi 1, 162
Charandab Soltan Shamlu	950/1543	H Darabjerd	Budaq 105
Allahqoli Beyg Ichik-oghlu Gerampa Ostajalu	955/1548	H Darabjerd	Hoseyni 170; Shirazi 98; Tahmasp 53
Shahqoli Khalifeh Mohrdar Dhu'l-Qadr	ca. 960/1553	H Darabjerd	Valeh 1372, 410, 416; Monshi 225, 361

---

97 Le Strange, *The Lands*, p. 289; Massoud Kheirabadi, "Darab," *Encyclopedia Iranica*.

Shah 'Ali Khalifeh-ye Dhu'l-Qadr	985-994/1577-1586	H Darabjerd	Qomi 2, 664; Monshi 1, 499
Tahmaspqoli Soltan b. 'Aliqoli Khan	994/1586	Probably did not assume function	Monshi 361
Mohammad Soltan Dhu'l-Qadr	994-?/1586-?	H Darabjerd	Qomi 2, 828
Mantasha Khan Ostajalu	997/1588-89	H Darabjerd	Qomi 2, 888
Mohammadqoli Khan Pornak b. Mortezaqoli	997/1589	H Darabjerd	Qomi 2, 888
Hasan Soltan Qaracheh-oghlu	998/1590	H and *vakil* Darabjerd; became *khasseh*	Molla Jalal 79, 85
Tahmaspqoli Soltan b. 'Ali Khan	999-?/1591-?	H Darabjerd	Valeh 1372, 816
Shamshi Khan Qazaqlar	?-1038/?-1629	H Darabjerd	Monshi 1086

* He was seal bearer from 939 to 965/1532-1559, but his time in office as governor of Darabjerd is unknown.

Darband or Darband-e Shirvan or Derbend is situated on the western shore of the Caspian Sea, south of the Rubas River, on the slopes of the Tabarsaran Mountains. It occupied a strategic location controlling a three km wide strip between the sea and the Caucasus Mountains. After an early and short-term Safavid governor the town was governed by the Shirvanshahs (see Shirvan), usually through castellans.[98] When this local dynasty was done away with by Tahmasp I in 935/1538, Darband probably was governed by a Safavid governor again, but data are lacking on Safavid governors until 1015/1606. Thereafter Safavid governors were in charge of Darband, who usually held the rank of Soltan.[99]

Name	Year	Observations	Source
Mansur Beyg	915/1509	H Darband; (*kutval* Mozaffar)	Shirazi 48; Qazvini 273; Qomi, 1, 98; Mozaffar 308-09
Mozaffar Soltan	942/1536	H Darband	Bakikhanuf 94; Fumeni 24-25
	From 996/1588 to 1015/1606	Ottoman governors	
Usmi Khan Qeytaq	1015/1606	H Darband	Molla Jalal 309, 315, 319; Monshi 734–35
Qanbar Beyg	1016/1607	H Darband; *selahdar-bashi*	Lavrov 160
Cheragh Soltan Gerampa Ostajalu	1016-1019/1607-1610	H or *vali* Darband + Shaberan	Monshi 752; Molla Jalal 320, Lavrov 160
Cheragh Soltan	?-1019/?-1610	*Vali* Darband	Molla Jalal 377
Jamshid Beyg	1019/1610	H Darband pro-tem	Molla Jalal 377

---

98 Mozaffar, *Jahangosha*, pp. 307, 309.
99 Anonymous, "Mémoire", p. 17.

Mohammad Hoseyn Soltan brother of Shahqoli Soltan Kholafā-ye Rumlu	1019-1024-?/1610-1614-?	*Vali* Darband	Molla Jalal 378; Lavrov 160
Barkhordar Soltan	1027-1031/1618-1621	H Darband	Lavrov 160
Yutam Soltan Gorji	?-1023-1035/?-1623-1626	H Darband, Shaberan-e Shirvan	Monshi 1070; Valeh 1380, 360; Lavrov 160
Qara Khan Beyg Suvazlu b. Pulad Beyg	1036/1626-1627	H Darband	Lavrov 160
Farrokh Soltan [Khan]	1036-1042/1627-1632	H Darband + Shaberan-e Shirvan; a *gholam*	Monshi 1070; Vahid 328; Yusof 100, 293; Valeh 1380, 120, 360
Siyavosh Beyg [Soltan]	1042-1045/1632-1635	H Darband	Vahid 266, 299; Yusof 100, 165; Astarabadi 251
Shahverdi Beyg [Soltan] Ostajalu	1045-1048/1635-1638	H Darband	Vahid 247, 266, 288; Yusof 166, 228; Valeh 1380, 375
Bahram Beyg [Soltan] Ostajalu	1048-?/1638-?	H Darband - *keshikchi-bashi*	Yusof 228; Vahid 288; Astarabadi 256
'Arab Beyg [Khan] Aghzivar-oglu Shamlu	?-1053/?-1643	H Darband + BB Shirvan	Vahid 280, 328, 406
Bayazid Soltan b. Bahram Soltan	1053/1653-1654	H Darband	Lavrov 160
Urah [?] Khan	?-1083/?-1672/73	H Darband	Lavrov 160
Eshaq Soltan	1098/1687	H Darband	Lavrov 160
Ahmad Khan Soltan	?-1133/?-1721	H Darband	Lavrov 160
Emamqoli Beyg	1134-1139/1722-1728	Deputy H Darband	Lavrov 160
Mohammad Hoseyn b. Emamqoli Khan	1139-1147/1728-1735	H Darband; as deputy until 1730	Lavrov 160

Dargazin or Darhazin and also Darjazin is a district located in Hamadan province (between Hamadan and Zanjan) and remained a Sunni stronghold throughout the Safavid period. Its inhabitants enthusiastically collaborated with the Sunni Afghans conquerers of Safavid Iran after 1722.[100] Perhaps because its inhabitants were Sunnis, the Safavids, starting with Shah 'Abbas I, usually, if not always, appointed a refugee Uzbeg prince as governor of Dargazin, according to Yazdi.[101]

Name	Year	Observations	Source
Mohammad Khan Uzbek	979?/1572?	H Darhazin	Valeh 1372, 124
Rostam Mohammad Khan	1031-?/1622-?	H Dargazin	Monshi 997-98

---

100 See Floor, *Afghan*, p. 198; Lockhart, *Fall*, pp. 202, 288.
101 Yazdi, *Mokhtasar*, vol. 1, p. 112.

Darun or Dorun is situated in Khorasan between 'Ashqabad and Qezel-Arvat, and borders on the north-east on Borjnord and on the south-east on Esfara'in. It was a border fort and a dependency of Khabushan.[102] It had been abandoned by the Safavids after the death of Esma'il I (930/1524) and was only retaken in 1008/1599.

Name	Year	Observations	Source
Qarachqay Soltan	?-1011/?-1603	H Darun	Molla Jalal 232
Shahqoli Soltan Chemesgezek	1011-?/1603-?	H Darun	Monshi 631; Molla Jalal 239
Oghurlu Soltan aka Dastkesh	1039/1628	H Darun; a *gholam*	Bastami 112, 129; Monshi 1088; Valeh 1380, 26, 29; Yusof 18, 24
Yusof Soltan	1044/1635	H Darun	Yusof 206
Owtar Khan	1059, 1063/1650, 1653	H Darun	Riazul Islam 1, 399, 422
Dhu'l-Feqar Khan	1066-1073/1656-1663	BB Qandahar ; his son Safiqoli Beyg was the *mohafez-e* Darun	Vahid 596, 742; Valeh 1380, 572
Safiqoli Khan b. Karjasi Beyg or Manuchehr Khan	1073/1663	H Darun	Vahid 742
Najafqoli Khan	Before 1103/1691	H Darun	Khatunabadi 548
Manuchehr Khan	1109-1110/1698-1699	H Darun	Nasiri 246, 273
Fath 'Ali Khan	1122-?/1710-?	H Nishapur-Darun-Abivard	Khatunabadi 560

Darvalakis is the name of a district located in the province of Qarabagh. Its governor was at the same time (at least at the end of the Safavid era) chief of the Jaramilu tribe, according to Nasiri's *Alqab*. I have not been able to find any other reference to this governorship.

Dashtestan is a district that was part of Fars province and one which included Bushire. It was bounded on the south by Dashti and on the west by Tangestan and Ganaveh.[103]

Name	Year	Observations	Source
Qara Shahverdi Soltan Dhu'l-Qadr	998/1580	H Dashtestan + *vakil* of the Dhu'l-Qadr	Molla Jalal 94
Pir Budaq Soltan b. Shahbandeh Khan Pornak	1050/1640	H Dashtestan	Yusof 247
Da'ud Beyg	1053-?/1643-?	H Dashtestan - *uzangu qurchi*	Shamlu 1, 283; Vahid 384

---

102 Monshi, *Tarikh*, pp. 141, 227, 257, 1088 (fort Khabushan), 631 (fort Darun); Molla Jalal, *Ruznameh*, pp. 186 (Khabushan), 230, 238 (fort Darun).
103 For its history see, e.g., Mohammad Javad Fakhra'i, *Dashtestan dar godhar-e tarikh* (Shiraz, 1383/2004).

Zaman Soltan	1069-1071-?/ 1659-1661-?	H Dashtestan (+ Bahrain per 1071)	Valeh 1380, 375, 591, 641; Vahid 697, 731
Safiqoli Khan Soltan	Before 1082/1671	H Dashtestan	Bardsiri 396
Safiqoli Beyg	?-1129/1717	H Dashtestan	Floor, *Afghan*, 30
Hoseynqoli Khan	1129/1717-?	H Dashtestan - *tofangchi-aghasi*	Floor, *Afghan*, 30
Nurollah Khan Farahani	1135/1723	H Dashtestan	Floor, *Afghan*, 197

Daver is a district in the valley of Daver, near Qandahar.

Name	Year	Observations	Source
Budaq Khan Qajar	944/1537-38	H Daver	Bidlisi 2, 571
Khan Afghan	1069/1659	H Daver	Valeh 1380, 618; Vahid 659

Deylaman is a mountainous district in Gilan, which, well into the seventeenth century, was governed by the Ghaziyan-e Sufi family, a local dynasty that also held sway over Ranekuh (q.v.).[104] It would seem that in 1660 or thereabouts it had been incorporated into the crown domain administration.

Name	Year	Observations	Source
Kiya Jalal al-Din Mohammad	1001/1593	H Deylaman	Vahid 116
Ne'matollah Sufi	1015?/1606-?	H Deylaman	Fumeni 170
Bahramqoli Soltan Sufi or Beyramqoli Soltan Mir Sufi	1038/1629	H Deylaman	Fumeni 267, 274-75, 284-85; Yusof 16; Vahid 223-25
Ahmad Beyg Esfahani	1071-?/1661-?	Vizier Deylaman	Vahid 731

Dezful is a town situated on the banks of the Ab-e Diz (Khuzestan) and a district bounded by Lorestan and the Bakhtiyari mountains in the north, by Shushtar in the east, by Ahvaz in the south and by Iraq in the west. Like Hoveyzeh, after the conquest of 'Arabestan in 914/1508, Dezful was left in the hands of a local dynasty, this one known as the Ra'nashis. However, when the last ruling scion of that family rebelled in 947/1541 Shah Tahmasp I intervened militarily and as of 948/1542-42 Dezful came under direct Safavid administrative control.

Name	Year	Observations	Source
Khalilollah b. Sheikh Mohammad Ra'nashi	914-?/1508-?	H Dezful	Rumlu 138; Shirazi 143

---

104 H.L. Rabino, "Les dynasties locales du Gilan et du Daylam," *Journal Asiatique* 237 (1949), pp. 301-350; 445, 455, 463; Monshi, *Tarikh*, vol. 1, p. 451; Yusof, *Dheyl*, p. 16; Vahid, *Tarikh*, pp. 223-25.

'Ala al-Dowleh Ra'nashi aka 'Abbasi [Budaq] b. Khalilollah Ra'nashi	?-948/?-1541	H Dezful; fled to Baghdad	Rumlu 388; Monshi 95; Budaq 105; Qomi 1, 295; Shirazi 92, 143
Abu'l-Fath Beyg [Soltan] Afshar	948/1541	H Dezful	Shirazi 92; Bidlisi 2, 576; Qazvini 295; Tatavi 510 (949)
Heydarqoli Soltan Afshar	949-?/1542-?	H Dezful	Rumlu, 389; Qomi 1, 295
Eyqut Soltan Chavoshlu Ostajalu	980-982/1572-1574	H Dezful-Shushtar	Valeh 1372, 409; Shushtari 43
Sayyed Zonbur b. Mowla Sajjad	996-?/1588-?	H Dezful	Caskel, Mehdi, 84.
Tahmaspqoli Beyg	1035-1037/1626-1628	H Dezful + Shushtar	Vahid 342
Abu'l-Fath Khan	ca. 1141/1728	H Dezful - *gholam*	Balfour 155

Dinavar is a district in Kurdestan, north of Bisitun, near Kermanshah. It was often held in conjuction with other districts. It is of interest to note that Kurdish governors only appear as of the late 1620s, despite the fact that in other border areas Kurdish governors already prevailed at an earlier date.

Name	Year	Observations	Source
Cheragh Soltan Gerampa Ostajalu	955-?/1548-?	H Sonqor + Dinavar	Shirazi 98
Hoseyn Beyg Fath-oghlu or Hasan Soltan Feyj-oghlu Ostajalu	965-?/1558-?	*Teyuldar* Sonqor + Dinavar	Qomi 1, 394; Bidlisi 2, 595
Ahmad Khalifeh-ye Vafadar-e Rumlu	975-?/1568-?	H Sonqor	Qomi 1, 471
Sulaq Hoseyn Tekkelu	985-?/1577-?	H Dinavar + Kurdestan	Qomi 2, 665; Rumlu 643
Shahverdi Khalifeh brother of Esma'il Khan	994-?/1586-?	H Dinavar-Sa'dabad + some parts from the *olka-ye* Sulagh	Qomi 2, 828
Mostafa Pasha	1017-?/1609-?	*Teyuldar* Sonqor; *amir al-omara* of the Jalalis	Monshi 781
'Ali Beyg Zanganeh aka 'Ali Baba	1038-1043/1629-1633	H Dinavar + Kermanshahan, Kolhar+ Sonqor	Yusof 273
Shahrokh Soltan Zanganeh	1043-1050/1633-1640	H Dinavar + Kermanshahan; H *il-e* Kolhar-Zanganeh + Dinavar- succeeded by his brother	Yusof 246; Vahid 294 [1048], 301 [1049], 317. 331

| Sheikh 'Ali Beyg [Khan] Zanganeh | 1049-1067/1639-1657 | H Dinavar + Kermanshahan; H *il-e* Kolhar-Zanganeh + Dinavar- succeeded by his brother | Vahid 301, 317, 331, 569, 577, 626 |

Diyarbekr is a province situated in south-east Anatolia and was held by the Safavids as of 910/1504 until 920/1514, as of which time it permanently remained in Ottoman hands. Its main city was Diyarbekr aka Qara Amid or Hamid. In addition, the Safavids held sway over six other districts in that province, to wit: Orfeh (q.v.), Jazireh (q.v.), Kharput, Mardin, Sert and Hesn Keyfeh, which were all governed by their traditional Kurdish rulers.[105]

Name	Year	Observations	Source
Qaracheh Soltan aka Qara Khan	910/1504	H Diyarbekr	Shamlu 1, 37; Vahid 37
Amir Khan b. Golabi Beyg b. Amir Beyg Mowselu	910-912/1504-1506	H Diyarbekr	Qomi 1, 90; Mozaffar 258
Khan Mohammad Ostajalu b. Mirza Beyg aka Mohammad Beyg	912-920/1506-1514	H Diyarbekr —succeeded by his brother	Rumlu 125; Monshi 28; Budaq 39; Shamlu 1, 40; Bidlisi 2, 186 287; Heravi 282
Qara Beyg [Khan] brother of Khan Mohammad	920/1514	H Diyarbekr died fighting-Safavids lost the city	Rumlu, 197; Qomi 1, 132, 135 ; Monshi 1, 43; Shamlu 1, 45; Bidlisi 2, 296; Mozaffar 529
	As of 920/1514	Ottoman governors	

Donboli is a name of a Kurdish tribe and of a tribal district in Azerbaijan, in Chors (q.v.), near Khoy, on the border with Ottoman Turkey, which is only mentioned by the TM.

Dowraq is a district in southern 'Arabestan, bounded in the west by Mohammarah, in the north by Ahvaz, in the east by Jarrahi and Ma'shur and in the south by the Persian Gulf. This district was part of Kuhgiluyeh province. The Afshar tribe that held Kuhgiluyeh province by the end of the reign of Tahmasp I also held Dowraq, which then was temporarily taken from them by the *vali* of Hoveyzeh.[106] As of 1022/1613 Emamqoli Khan held it, as part of his governorship of Kuhgiluyeh, but it is not known whom he appointed as governor of Dowraq. After the latter's death three consecutive Arab governors were appointed,[107] after which mostly Qezelbash governors were appointed.

---

105 Stanley, *Travels*, part 2, pp. 146-56.
106 Monshi, *Tarikh*, vol. 2, p. 951.
107 Yazdi, *Mokhtasar*, vol. 1, p. 272 writes that Mehdi Beyg 'Arab built a fort there and put a stop to the marauding of the nomadic Arabs in the area.

Name	Year	Observations	Source
Sayyed Salameh	1034-?/1625-?	H Dowraq	Vahid 200
Mehdi Khan 'Arab	1042-1048/1633-1638	H Dowraq	Yusof 117; Vahid 250
Morad Khan Beyg b. Mehdi Khan Soltan 'Arab	1048/1638	H Dowraq	Yusof 215; Vahid 290
Mehdiqoli Soltan	1048-1054/1638-1644	H Dowraq	Vahid 403, 559
Khandanqoli Soltan	1054-?/1644-?	H Dowraq	Vahid 403
Imani Beyg	?-1060/?-1650	H Dowraq	Shamlu 2, 14
Nowruz Beyg Inanlu	1060-?/1650-?	H Dowraq	Shamlu 2, 19
Shahverdi Soltan	?-1066/?-1656	H Dowraq	Vahid 612; Valeh 1380, 572
Geda 'Ali Beyg Qajar b. Mehrab Khan	1074-?/1564-?	H Dowraq	Vahid 754; Shamlu 2, 14
Da'ud Khan	1109/1698	H Dowraq	Nasiri 249, 253, 257, 262

Duki, see Chutiyali.

Erevan, see Chokhur-e Sa'd.

Esfara'in district is situated in northern Khorasan. It is bounded on the north by Bojnord and Khabushan (Kuchan), on the south by Sabzavar and on the southeast by Nishapur.

Name	Year	Observations	Source
Borun Soltan Tekkelu	920-928/1514-1522	H Esfara'in	Rumlu 196; Qomi 1, 132; Khvandamir 591
Zeyn al-Din Soltan Shamlu	928-933/1522-1526	H Esfara'in (+ Nishapur; Mozaffar 595)	Rumlu 229, 257; Qomi 1, 150, 169; Ben Khvandamir 214, 591
Pirqoli Soltan Kangarlu	933/1526	H Esfara'in	Hoseyni 92
Timur Kord	939/1533	H Esfara'in; *amir akhur-bashi*	Tahmasp 25
Majnun Soltan Shamlu	?-959/?-1551	H Esfara'in	Rumlu 475; Qomi 1, 361
Qanbar Soltan Asayesh-oghlu Ostajalu	?-967/?-1560	H Esfara'in	Qomi 1, 412
Mostafa Soltan Varsaq	?-972/?-1565	H Esfara'in	Budaq 141
Ighud [Ighuth] Beyg Chavoshlu Ostajalu	972-?/1565-?	H *qal'eh* Kelidar and Esfara'in; H *qal'eh-ye* Khabushan + Nishapur	Shirazi 123; Qazvini 309; Qomi 1, 447, but somebody else was its *teyuldar*.

Name	Year	Observations	Source
Ebrahim Soltan brother of Morshedqoli Soltan Chavoshlu Ostajalu	985/1577	H Esfara'in	Qomi 2, 665; Monshi 227, 304-06; Molla Jalal 43; Valeh 1372, 701
Mostafa Soltan Chavoshlu	986/1578	Rival H Esfara'in	Molla Jalal 47
Morshedqoli Soltan	990/1582	H Esfara'in	Qomi 2, 727
Abu Moslem Soltan [Khan] Chavoshlu Ostajalu	994-999/1586-1591	H Esfara'in	Qomi 2, 1074; Monshi 364, 408, 444; Valeh 1372, 836; Molla Jalal 111
	999-1000/1591-1592	Uzbeg governor	Bidlisi 2, 689 [999]
Mohammad Soltan b. Baba Elyas Bayat	1001-?/1593-?	H Esfara'in	Monshi 453 [see also Nishapur]
Daghkhan Chenagi	1003/1595	H Esfara'in	Molla Jalal 137
Mirza Mohammad Soltan Bayat	1003-1004/1595-1596	H Esfara'in	Monshi 507; Natanzi 567; Vahid 131
Budaq Khan Chegani	1004/1596	H Esfara'in	Monshi 510
Emamqoli Soltan Siyah-Mansur	?-1038/?-1629	H Esfara'in	Valeh 1380, 461, 515-16; Monshi 1086
Mohammad Soltan Chagani	1058/1648	H Esfara'in + Sabzavar	Vahid 473
Emamqoli Soltan Siyah-Mansur	?-1064/?-1654	H Esfara'in	Valeh 1380, 461, 515-16; Vahid 542
Mohammad Soltan	1108/1697	H Esfara'in	Nasiri 201
Habil Khan Siyah-Mansur	1137/1724	H Esfara'in	Mostowfi 181

Esfezar is the obsolete name of the district aka Sabzavar (nowadays also as Shindand) situated at 70 miles south of Herat, between the Taymani Hills and the Persian border. It was a dependency of the province of Herat.[108]

Name	Year	Observations	Source
Ahmad Beyg [Soltan] Afshar	928-?/1522-?	H Farah + Esfezar	Rumlu 29; Qomi 1, 150; Ben Khvandamir 214, 274; Khvandamir 591 (Sabzavar)
Yakan Beyg [Soltan, Khan] Afshar	985-987/1577-1579	H Farah + Esfezar	Qomi 2, 665; Monshi 140, 254-55; Valeh 1372, 601; Valeh 1380, 125
Morad Beyg Afshar	987-?/1579-?	H Esfezar	Monshi 254; Valeh 1372, 601
Ordughdi Khan Alplu Afshar	1030-1046/1629-1637	H Farah + Ezfezar	Yusof 192; Monshi 1085; Vahid 278

---

108 Qomi, *Kholasat*, vol. 1, p. 245.

COMMENTARY 183

Fakhran is a district of the province of Shirvan.

Name	Year	Observations	Source
Masal Beyg	Before 1114/1703	H Fakhran	Musavi 1965, doc. 12
Amir Goli Beyg	1114/1703	H Fakhran	Musavi 1965, doc. 12

Fars, see Shiraz.

Farah is a town and district situated in southwestern Afghanistan. In the west it borders on Seystan, on Herat and Ghor in the north, in the east on Qandahar, and Chakhansur in the south.

Name	Year	Observations	Source
Ahmad Beyg [Soltan] Afshar	928-936-?/ 1522-1530-?	H Farah + Esfezar + Ukh + Kah	Rumlu 29; Qomi 1, 150, 196; Ben Khvandamir 214, 274; Valeh 1372, 294; Khvandamir 591
Ahmad Soltan Afshar	935/1539	H Farah; ex-H Kerman	Abrahams 206
Khalifeh Soltan	941/1534	H Farah	Abrahams 136
Morad Soltan Timurlu	941/1535	H Farah	Qomi 1, 251; Seystani 156
Sanjab Soltan Afshar	947/1541	H Farah	Shamlu 1, 71
Esma'ilqoli Afshar	Before 971/1564	H Farah	Valeh 1372, 411
Hoseyn Soltan Afshar	971-984/1564-1576	H Farah, Kah, Uq, and parts	Budaq 141 [972]; Monshi 1, [302]
Yakan Beyg Afshar	985-987/1577-1579	H Farah + Esfezar	Qomi 2, 665; Monshi 140, 254; Valeh 1372, 601
Hoseyn Soltan Afshar	988-990/1580-1583	H Farah 2nd time	Monshi 275; Molla Jalal 36
'Ali Khan Soltan Afshar	990/1583	H Farah - his brother	Monshi 275
Yakan Soltan Afshar	991-999/1584-1591	H Farah	Monshi 275; Bidlisi 2, 690; Vahid 125
	From 999/1591 to 1006/1597	Uzbeg governors	
Esma'ilqoli Soltan [Khan] Alplu Afshar	1006-1012-?/ 1597-1604-?	H Farah and dependencies	Siyaqi 479; Molla Jalal 184; Monshi 620, 674
Ordughdi Khan Alplu Afshar	1038-1044/ 1629-1637	H Farah + Ezfezar	Yusof 192; Monshi 1085; Vahid 278
Khandanqoli Khan Afshar	1044-?/1635-?	H Farah	Yusof 192
Qoli Khan Afshar	?-1055/?-1645	H Farah	Shamlu 1, 292
Kalb 'Ali Khan Afshar	1055-?/1645-?	H Farah + Kuhdom	Shamlu 1, 292, 334; Vahid 476, 497

Mohammadqoli Khan	?-1064/?-1654	H Farah	Vahid 570
Aslan Khan	1064-1068/1654-1658	H Farah	Vahid 570, 642; Valeh 1380, 609, 642
'Abbasqoli Khan	1068-1070/1058-1660	H Farah	Vahid 642; Valeh 1380, 609
Qoli Khan Dhu'l-Qadr	1070-?/1660-?	H Farah	Vahid 731
Khandanqoli Khan	?-1074/?-1664	H Farah	Vahid 753
Mohammad 'Ali Khan Afshar b. Qasem Khan	1074-?/1664-?	H Farah	Vahid 753
Hoseynqoli Khan	?-1123/?-1711	H Farah	Khatunabadi 564
Mohammad Zaman Khan	1123/1711	H Farah; *charkhchi-bashi*	Khatunabadi 564
	As of 1716	Under Abdali control	Safavi 25, 28

Farahan is a district of Hamadan, situated west of Qom. It was usually governed jointly with Garmerud, a district situated on the Qarangu River, bounded in the west by Hashtrud, in the north by Saveh, in the east by Miyaneh, and in the south by the Qezel Uzun River.[109]

Name	Year	Observations	Source
Sharaf al-Din Khan Bedlisi	968-?/1561-?	H Garmerud	Bidlisi 2, 337
Adham Soltan	991-994/1583-1586	H Farahan + Garmerud + *ba'zi az mahall-e* Qom	Qomi 2, 755, 828
Shahverdi Khalifeh-ye Enanlu	994/1586	H Farahan, Gamrerud + *ba'zi az mahall-e* Qom	Qomi 2, 828
Morshedqoli Soltan brother of Esma'ilqoli Khan	994/1586	H Farahan	Valeh 1372, 789

Farideyn, Lanjan, and Chahar Mahall are districts to the south of Isfahan. A royal decree from 1097/1669 is addressed to its governors.[110]

Farumad is situated at about 25 km from Mazinan in the Shahrud-Bastam region of Khorasan. Aradvar (or Azadvar) is about 24 km east of Jajarm. Nasiri's *Alqab* is the only source that mentions this governorship, while the TM only mentions Azadvar.

Fasa is a district in Fars, which is bounded in the north by Estanabat and Shiraz, in the east by Darabjerd, to the south by Jahrom and the west by Shiraz. From at least 955/1548 until his death in 957/1550, Charandab Soltan Shamlu was governor of Ichi, Neyriz, and Fasa.[111]

---

109 Monshi, *Tarikh*, pp. 235, 812, 814, 938, 1021; Molla Jalal, *Ruznameh*, pp. 386, 389 (Garmerud).

110 Esmail Ra'in, *Iraniyan-e Armani* (Tehran 1349/1970), doc. 11; L. Minasiyan, *Honar va Mardom* 84 (1348/1969), doc. 10.

111 Khurshah b. Qubad al-Hoseyni, *Tarikh-e Ilchi-ye Nezam Shah*. ed. Mohammad Reza Nasiri and Koichi Haneda (Tehran, 1379/2000), p. 170; Qomi, *Kholasat*, vol. 1, 327, 349.

Firuzkuh is a town and district situated on the road to Semnan, at some 150 km east from Tehran. It was initially under the control of the Kiya clan of Cholav[112], whose members also held the governorship of some of the adjacent districts such as Damavand and even Khvar and Semnan. This practice to award the governor of Firuzkuh also the governorship of other districts seems to have been continued when the post was held by Safavid governors, although more examples than one are needed to confirm this.

Name	Year	Observations	Source
Amir Hasan Kiya*	909/1503	H Firuzkuh-Damavand	Hoseyni 23
Hoseyn Kiya Cholavi	909/1503	H Firuzkuh, Damavand, Khvar, Semnan	Valeh 1372, 133**
Elyas Beyg Eyghud-oghlu Ostajalu	909-?/1503-?	H Firuzkuh, Damavand, Khvar, Semnan	Valeh 1372, 133
Domri Soltan	933/1526	H Firuzkuh, Semnan	Hoseyni 86;
Mostafa Soltan Shamlu	933/1527	H Firuzkuh + Saveh	Tahmasp 10
Shahverdi Soltan Afshar	972/1565	H Damghan, Bestam, Firuzkuh, Hazarjarib, Biyarjomand	Budaq 141

* Perhaps an error for Mir Sin Kiya, the castellan (*kutval*) of the Fort of Firuzkuh. Laheji, *Tarikh*, pp. 41, 45-49, 111, 156, 158-59, but Vahid, *Tarikh*, pp. 28-29 has Hasan Kiya Firuzkuhi as governor of Rostamdar and Firuzkuh suggesting that Amir Hasan and Hoseyn Kiya are the same person.

Fumen, a town and its district in western Gilan, situated on the north side of the Masuleh pass into Azerbaijan.[113]

Name	Year	Observations	Source
'Ali Beyg Soltan aka 'Ali Khan	1001-?/1593	H Fumen	Fumeni 136-39
Oghurlu Soltan Chapni	1004/1596	H Fumen	Monshi 514 (Chini); Fumeni 165, 170-71 (Chagini; Chini); Vahid 132 (Chapni)
Soltan Mohammad Beyg	1006/1598	H Fumen	Fumeni 175, 181, 207, 211

Fusanj or Fushanj, also Pushanj and even Pushang or Poshang,[114] was situated some 60 km from Herat south of the Hari Rud and was an important station on the commercial route to

---

112 For more information see Rabino, *Astarabad*, pp. 141-42.
113 For more information see M. Bazin, "Fumen," *Encyclopedia Iranica*.
114 Yazdi, *Mokhtasar*, vol. 1, p. 295 (Poshang); Monshi, *Tarikh*, vol. 2, pp. 1074 (Pushang), 1087 (Poshang).

and from India. Although the town was destroyed early in the 16th century,[115] it continues to be mentioned (as of 1540) as a jurisdiction that together with Ghuriyan and Sabzavar (i.e. Esfezar) was (regularly?) jointly governed by a Safavid governor. When the governor of Poshanj, Shir Khan Afghan came to court in 1037/1627-28 he received many favors and 'Abbas I asked him to see to it that the trade routes to India were safe for merchants and travelers.[116] Fusanj was still a way station in 1108/1696, where caravans and other travelers, such as troops, stopped.[117] It has been argued that Ghuriyan is built on the site of Fusanj, but both districts are mentioned as separate entities. The town and district of Sabzavar mentioned here should not be mistaken for Sabzavar in western (Iranian) Khorasan, for this Sabzavar aka Esfezar (q.v.) is situated in Afghanistan at 120 km from Herat.

Name	Year	Observations	Source
Piri Soltan Rumlu	919/1513	H Fushanj; *Darugheh* (Hari Soltan; Tatavi)	Qomi 1, 126; Mozaffar 448; Tatavi 359
Sufi Vali Rumlu	972/1565	H Ghuriyan, Fusanj, Sabzavar	Budaq 141
Khoshkhabar Khan Shamlu b. Aghazivar Khan	988/1580	H Ghuriyan + Fusanj	Monshi 254; Valeh 1372, 90 (Pushanj)
Shir Khan Afghan	?-1038-?/?-1629-?	H Poshanj	Monshi 1074, 1087; Yusof 120
Shir Khan's son	1040/1631	H Qushang	Yusof 73, 75

Gah or *Qal'eh-ye* Gah, see Kah.

Ganjeh, see Barda' and Qarabagh.

Garmerud, see Farahan.

Garmsir is a district in southern Seystan.

Name	Year	Observations	Source
Pordel Khan	?-1056-1058/?-1646-1648	H Garmsir	Shamlu 1, 340, 417
Dust 'Ali Khan	1058-?/1648-?	H Garmsir – H *il-e* Zanganeh – *teyuldar* Khvaf + Bakharz	Shamlu 1, 423

Garmsirat is a generic term to denote the "Hot Countreys" as the contemporary English translated this term, meaning the coastal areas adjacent to the Persian Gulf. In this case, for there

---

115 C.E. Bosworth, "Fusanj," *Encyclopaedia Iranica*.
116 Monshi, *Tarikh*, vol. 2, p. 1074.
117 Nasiri, *Dastur*, p. 121.

is also a Garmsirat district in Seystan (see previous entry), probably a district north of the Birunat (q.v.) is meant that belonged to Kerman.[118] In 1011/1602, Keyvan Soltan was governor of the Garmsirat and commander of the Safavid forces that were attacking Shamil and other localities in the Birunat.[119]

Garrus, also Karrus, is the name of a Kurdish tribe as well as of a district situated between Khamseh and Kurdestan and was part of the province of Hamadan. It was also refered to as Zarrin-kamar.

Name	Year	Observations	Source
Emirqoli Garrusi	?-1028/?-1619	H Garrus; succeeded by his son	Monshi 946
Nafsqoli Soltan	1028-?/1619-?	H Garrus	Monshi 946
Lotf 'Ali Soltan	1107-1109/1696-1698	H Karrus	Nasiri 128, 224; Qarakhani doc. 6

Gaskar is a town and district in Gilan (although in Safavid times it was part of Azerbaijan[120]), situated at some 32 km west of Rasht. In 1002/1594, as part of the unification of Gilan and its incorporation into the Safavid state, Gaskar was united with Tavalesh and Astara. Mir Siyavosh of Gaskar was arrested.[121] However, that decision was revoked shortly thereafter. In 1014/1606, Gaskar was turned into crown domain and brought under the jurisdiction of the vizier of Gilan, although the latter appointed a *darugheh* and tax receiver for the district. In 1021/1621 Astara and Gaskar were separated from Gilan again and it would seem that governors and not viziers were in charge of these districts as of 1024/1615, although as of ca. 1060/1650 viziers are occasionally mentioned (see Table).[122]

Name	Year	Observations	Source
Amireh Sasan aka Amir[eh] Soltan	971-979/1565-1572	H Gaskar	Rumlu 561, 579; Qomi 1, 471-72, 474; Monshi 111, 113; Fumeni 41-43, 59
Amir Siyavosh b. Amireh Sasan	?-984/?-1576	H Gaskar	Rumlu 621; Valeh 1372, 629; Fumeni 93-06, 119-22, 132-37, 152, 155, 248
Amir[eh] Sasan b. Amireh Siyavosh	984-985/1576-78	H Gaskar	Shamlu 1, 85; Qomi 2, 997
Fulad khalifeh-ye Rumlu	985-?/1578-?	H Gaskar	Qomi 2, 617

---

118 Yazdi, *Mokhtasar*, pp. 287 (Garmsirat-e kenar-e ab-e Hirmand), 355 (Garmsirat-e Kerman).
119 Molla Jalal, *Ruznameh*, p. 235.
120 Fumeni, *Tarikh*, p. 190.
121 Monshi, *Tarikh*, vol. 2, p. 460.
122 Fumeni, *Tarikh*, p. 181; Monshi, *Tarikh*, vol. 2, p. 853.

Amireh Siyavosh Gaskari	988-1002/1580-1593	H Gaskar + Khalkhal - in 1002 temporarily replaced by his brother	Monshi 267, 449-51, 460; Molla Jalal 114; 1118, 134; Vahid 115-16, 119, 128, 201
Amireh Mozaffar	1002-1003/1593-1594	H Gaskar	Monshi 492, 495-96
Abdal Soltan Qajar	1003-?/1594-?	H Gaskar	Monshi 497
Sa'id Beyg Fumeni	1014-?/1606-?	*Darugheh* Gaskar	Fumeni 181
Mortezaqoli Khan Gaskari b. Amireh Siyavosh	1024-1029/1615-1620	H Gaskar	Monshi 893, 955; Fumeni 190-93, 206
Behbud Khan Cherkes	1029/1620	H Gaskar	Monshi 955
Yusof Soltan*	1029-1036/1620-1627	H Gaskar – *gholam*	Monshi 955, 1036, 1074, 1081; Vahid 201, 214
Gorgin Soltan	1036-?/1627-?	H Gaskar	Monshi 1081; Yusof 16; Fumeni 264, 267, 275, 277, 282; Vahid 224-25
Manuchehr Khan	?-1042/?-1633	H Gaskar	Valeh 1380, 120; Vahid 247
Amir Beyg [Khan]	1042-1053/1633-1643	H Gaskar; *shirehchi-bashi*, first aka Amir Beyg Armani	Vahid 247; Shamlu 1, 283; Yusof 177, 279; Vahid 321
Barbideh Beyg	1053-?/1643-?	H Kaskar	Shamlu 1, 283
'Abbasqoli Khan	1058-?/1648-?	H Kaskar	Shamlu 1, 334, 343; Valeh 1380, 461; Vahid 467
Allahverdi Beyg	?-1066/?-1656	Vizier Kaskar; replaced by his father's sister's nephew	Vahid 613
Allahqoli Beyg	1066-?/1656-?	Vizier Kaskar	Vahid 613
Mirza Sadeq Kermani	1072-?/1662-?	Vizier Kasgar	Vahid 731
Mohammadqoli	1095/1684	deputy; H had died	Kaempfer 64
N.N.	1698	Khan of Kaskar	de Maze 76

* The governorship had first been given to Behnud Khan, but then Yusof Soltan was appointed. Vahid, *Tarikh*, p. 201.

Gaverud or Gavehrud[123] perhaps is a district named after the river of the same name, which is situated at some 45 km from Senneh (Sanandaj). An Afshar chief was already governor of Gaverud

---

123 Molla Jalal, *Ruznameh*, p. 72.

under Shah 'Abbas I.[124] However, Minorsky believed that this Gaverud cannot have been meant.[125] There is another Gaverud that is situated in Azerbayjan, near Maragheh, which probably is the district in question.[126]

Name	Year	Observations	Source
Qapan Soltan Beygdeli Shamlu	1017/1609	H Gaverud + Saru-qargan	Monshi 782, 856; Vahid 172 (Qaban)
Emamqoli Soltan Usallu [Afshar]	1628	H Gaverud	Monshi 1085

Gereshk a town and district situated at 115 km west of Qandahar. This district was subject to the authority of the governor-general of Qandahar. It may therefore be assumed that Safavid control over this district came to an end at the same time as over Qandahar (q.v.).

Name	Year	Observations	Source
Mirza Qoli Soltan Siyah-Mansur	1031/1622	H Gereshk	Monshi 972
Durmish Khan Soltan	1105/1694	H Gereshk + BB Qandahar	Nasiri 59
Mohammad 'Ali Soltan	1106/1695	H Gereshk	Nasiri 54, 64, 65
Bahram Soltan	1108/1697	H Gereshk	Nasiri 177

Gereyli is a Turkic tribe that had come with the Mongol invasion to Iran and had settled in Khorasan in the Khabushan-Bojnord area. They were driven out by Kurdish tribes around 1600 and moved to the Astarabad area, including in parts north of the Gorgan.

Name	Year	Observations	Source
'Ali Khan Gereyli	?-1004/?-1596	H Gereyli	Monshi 510-11; Molla Jalal 137, 158
Mansur Khan Gereyli and Tavakkol Khan	1004-1006/1596-1598	each had half of the tribe; they later also received Jajarm and some other districts	Monshi 511, 541; Molla Jalal 138, 158; Vahid 132, 262, 289
Dervish 'Ali Khalifeh Gereyli b. Mirza 'Ali Khalifeh	1006-?/1598-?	He replaced Mirza 'Ali who had rebelled and received the Forts Pa-ye Hesar, Rugad and some other places	Monshi 533, 541
Tavakkol Khan	1011/1603	H Gereyli	Molla Jalal 233
Mansur Khan Gereyli	?	H Gereyli	Yusof 148

---

124 Monshi, *Tarikh*, vol. 2, p. 1085.
125 TM, p. 164.
126 Molla Jalal, *Ruznameh*, pp. 72, 110-11; Monshi, *Tarikh*, pp. 782, 811, 856, 1085.

'Olyar Khan brother of Mansur Khan	?-1043/?-1634		Valeh 1380, 28-9, 205, 266, 282; Yusof 148; Vahid 262, 289, 293
Mansur Khan Gereyli	1043-?/1634-?	H Gereyli 2nd time	Yusof 148
'Ayyar Khan or 'Ali Yar Beyg	1047-?/1638-?	H Gereyli	Yusof 215; Astarabadi 256
Abdal Khan Gereyli	1066-1073/1656-1663	Succeeded by his paternal uncle's son	Vahid 594, 742; Valeh 1380, 570
Tavakkol Khan	1073-?/1663-?	H Gereyli	Vahid 742
Allahverdi Khan	1106-1109/1695-1698	H Gereyli and *vali* Shirvan	Nasiri 81, 96, 117, 177
Rostam Khan	1109-1110/1698-1699	H Gereyli	Nasiri 346, 273
Shahverdi Beyg	1110/1699	H Gereyli	Nasiri 273
NN	1136/1724	H Gereyli + Hajjilar	Dhabehi-Setudeh 7, doc. 1

Gharjestan is an area in the northern foothills of the Hindu Kush, which was contolled by the Uzbegs of Balkh.[127] Although the Safavids undertook a number of campaigns to subdue Gharjestan they only were able to hold on to the district for two very short periods of only a few months in 927/1521 and 955/1548 and otherwise had to abandon hope to incorporate it into their kingdom.

Name	Year	Observations	Source
Mahmud Beyg Tupchi	927/1521	H Gharjestan	Ben Khvandamir 188
Pir Mohammad Khan	955/1548	H Gharjestan	Ben Khvandamir 410

Ghur is situated in Central Afghanistan, between Herat and Kabul. I have come across only one reference to a governor of this district. Mohammad Zaman Soltan, who was governor of Ghur and of some parts of Khorasan.[128]

Ghuri is the name of one of the tribes and their tribal district in the neighborhood of Herat. In 1629 or prior to that date Mir Mohammad Soltan Ghuri was its chief.[129]

Ghuriyan district was situated on the south bank of the Hari Rud, 65 km from Herat. Fort Kusuyeh was the residence of the governor.[130]

---

127 Originally the district was attached to Heart, but in 1511 Najm II attached it to Balkh. Aubin, "Les soufis," p. 15.
128 Monshi, *Tarikh*, vol. 2, p. 1084.
129 Monshi, *Tarikh*, vol. 2, p. 1087.
130 Shirazi, *Takmelat*, p. 124.

Name	Year	Observations	Source
Vali Khalifeh Rumlu or Safi Vali Khalifeh b. Sufiyan Rumlu	972/1565	H Ghuriyan, Fusanj, Sabzavar	Budaq 141[Sufi Vali Rumlu]; Qomi 1, 448; Shirazi 123; Qazvini 310 [Vali Soltan Rumlu]; Tatavi 635
Mozaffar Soltan Asayesh-oghlu Ostajalu	Before 985/1577	H Kusuyeh-Ghuriyan	Valeh 1372, 409
Abu'l-Fath Khan Shamlu b. Aghzivar Khan	985-?/1577-?	H Ghuriyan	Monshi 227
Khoshkhabar Khan Shamlu b. Aghazivar Khan	1006/1598	H Ghuriyan + Fusanj	Monshi 254-55; Molla Jalal 41
Qanbar Soltan [Khan] Shamlu	1007-?/1599-?	H Ghuriyan	Vahid 149; Monshi 603; Molla Jalal 184
Hasan Khan	1038/1629	BB Ghuriyan	Yusof 27

Gilan traditionally was divided into two parts; the part west of the Safid-rud was known as Gilan-e biyeh-pish, with Lahejan as its capital. The part east of the Safid-rud known as Gilan-e biyeh-pas and had Fumen and later Resht as its capital was ruled by the Dobbaji or Esqavand clan, who were Sunnites. They claimed to be descendents of the Sasanians and even beyond from the prophet Isaac, being in power for more than 4,000 years.[131] The independent local dynasts of Gilan-e biyeh-pas gave the Safavids headaches. Amireh Hosam al-Din had to be called to order by Safavid military intervention 911/1505. Thereafter he continued to make trouble, but only locally. He was succeeded by his son Amir Dobbaj, who made overtures to the Ottomans, but when faced with the invasion of a Safavid army in 925/1519 gave presents to court. To appease him Esma'il I gave him one of his daughter's in marriage and the new title of Mozaffar Soltan. He then bet on the wrong horse in the Qezelbash civil war and fearing for his position initiated contacts with the Ottomans, whom he joined during their invasion of Azerbaijan in 940/1534. As a result, Mozaffar Soltan later was arrested and executed.

In Gilan-e biyeh-pish Khan Ahmad Khan had actively supported the Safavids and when he died in in 940/1534 he had ruled for more than 32 years. He was succeeded by his son Kar Kiya Hasan, who died after one year. His successor was his one-year old son Khan Ahmad Khan. Shah Tashmasp I therefore sent his brother Bahram Mirza in 944/1537 to care of the Biyeh-pish affairs, but he had to flee after a few months having greatly upset the notables. Tahmasp I therefore in 945/1538 made Khan Ahmad Khan the infant ruler of all of Gilan. The new arrangement was not liked by people of Biyeh-pas, who invited Amireh Shahrokh, a relative of Mozaffar Soltan to become their ruler in 950/1543. He ruled for seven years when he was murdered; his murder was followed by a period of anarchy. Tahmasp therefore appointed Soltan Mahmud son of Mozaffar Soltan in 965/1558, but Khan Ahmad Khan was able to engineer his imprisonment where he was killed. Khan Ahmad Khan now ruled uncontested over both Gilans. Because he was mistrusted Tahmasp I appointed Jamshid Khan, grandson of Mozaffar Soltan as governor of Gilan Biyeh-pas and also ordered Khan Ahmad Khan to return Gaskar to its governor. Khan Ahmad Khan complied, but refused to return Kuchesfahan, claiming it was part of Biyeh-pish. In 974/1567

---

131 Qomi, *Kholasat*, vol. 1, pp. 254-55.

Tahmasp sent troops to arrest Khan Ahmad Khan, who was defeated and finally captured and imprisoned. Biyeh-pas now had peace under Jamshid Khan. Biyeh-pish was divided among the emirs of the invading army, while Lahejan was given to Allahqoli Beyg as tutor (*Laleh*) of Mahmud Mirza, Tahmasp I's son. This was a period of oppressive rule in Biyeh-pish resulting in a revolt that was suppressed harshly. Khan Ahmad Khan was released in 985/1578 by Shah Mohammad Khodabandeh, who reinstated him as governor of Biyeh-pish. This led to new fights between the two parts of Gilan, for Khan Ahmad Khan had not given up his desire to control all of it. Matters did not improve when Jamshid Khan was removed in 988/1590 by a coup of his own military and the weak shah gave his government to the leader of the coup Mirza Kamran, governor of Kuhdom. Later he regretted this decision and sent an army with orders to divide Biyeh-pas among the Ostajalu emirs, who led this army. They installed Mohammad Amin son of Jamshid Khan in Resht, who then was kidnapped by Khan Ahmad Khan, resulting in more confusion. The new shah 'Abbas I therefore wanted to straighten out the affairs of Gilan and in particular Khan Ahmad Khan, but the latter rebuffed all the shah's overtures. When he made common cause with the Ottomans 'Abbas I sent an army to Gilan in 1000/1592; Khan Ahmad Khan was defeated and fled to Istanbul where he died. Shah 'Abbas I then completed the unification of Gilan under his control and put it under central government rule, with Kiya Jalal al-Din as supervisor (*rish safid*) of the whole of Gilan.[132] Initially he still appointed local notables as governors with *darugheh*s for Resht and Fumen, but when these notables rebelled in 1002 he suppressed the revolt and appointed a Qezelbash governor. In 1008/1599 the province was turned into crown domain (*khasseh*) and henceforth was governed by viziers. Within the province there seem to have been nevertheless some districts that were governed by governors, for in 1035/1626 Adam Soltan is reported to be governor of some districts in Gilan (*ba'zi az mahall-e Gilan*).[133] In 1035/1626, the vizierate of Gilan-e biyeh-pas was temporarily added to that of Mazandaran.[134] By the end of the Safavid period Gilan included the following administrative jurisdictions: Gaskar, Kuhdom, Ranekuh, and Tonakebun.[135]

Governors of Gilan-e biyeh-pish

Name	Year	Observations	Source
Karkiya Mirza 'Ali	883- 910/1478-1504	*Vali* Gilan	Hoseyni 32-33; Qomi, I, 88; Rumlu 110, 120; Shirazi 136; Khatunabadi 443, 445
Karkiya Soltan Hasan	910-911/1504-1505	*Vali* Gilan	Khatunabadi 445

---

132 Vahid, *Tarikh*, p. 116.
133 Shamlu, *Qesas*, vol. 1, p. 294.
134 Fumeni, *Tarikh*, p. 223.
135 For more details see Manouchehr Kasheff, "Gilan – History under the Safavids," *Encyclopedia Iranica*.

Karkiya Soltan Ahmad b. Soltan Hasan	911-940/1505-1534	*Vali* Gilan biyeh-pish; H Lahejan [Rumlu]	Hoseyni 73, 141; Qomi 1, 141; Rumlu 120, 258, 361; Shirazi 57, 86, 136; Qazvini 279; Budaq 95, 98; Monshi 111; Khatunabadi 445
Karkiya Sayyed 'Ali Kiya b. Soltan Ahmad	940-941/1534-1535	H Gilan-e Lahejan	Shirazi 136
Karkiya Soltan Hasan b. Soltan Ahmad	941-943/1535-1537	H Gilan-e Lahejan	Shirazi 136-37; Bidlisi 2, 569; Qazvini 292
Kar Kiya Khan Ahmad Khan brother of Kar Kiya Soltan Hasan	943/1537	*Vali* Gilan-e biyeh-pish – H Lahejan; replaced by	Rumlu 363, 558; Shamlu 1, 85; Qomi 1, 262, 462, 468, 469, 470, 477; Monshi 110-11; Budaq 145; Shirazi 128 137; Bidlisi 2, 627
Bahram Mirza	943-944/1537-1538	*Vali* Gilan-e biyeh-pish	Budaq 98; Qomi 1, 262; Monshi 110; Rumlu 361-62; Shirazi 86, 137; Bidlisi 2, 569, 571; Qazvini 292
Kar Kiya Khan Ahmad Khan brother of Kar Kiya Soltan Hasan	944-975/1538-1568	*Vali* Gilan-e biyeh-pish – H Lahejan	Rumlu 363, 558; Qomi 262; Shamlu 1, 85; Qomi 1, 462, 468, 469, 470, 477; Monshi 110-11; Budaq 145; Shirazi 128 137; Bidlisi 2, 627; Fumeni 46, 93, 131 (Lahejan), 245
Allahqoli Beyg Ijik-ogh-lu aka Allahqoli Soltan Gerampa Ostajalu	976-984/1568-1576	H Gilan-e Lahejan; *Laleh* of Soltan Mahmud Mirza [or Mohammad Mirza-Bidlisi]; rest of Gilan among the emirs	Bidlisi 2, 628, 630 [Mahmud]; Shirazi 132; Rumlu 578; Monshi 112, 114, 117-19, 139; Abrahams 145
Emamqoli Mirza	978/1570	H Gilan	Abrahams 146
Pireh Mohammad Khan Chavoslu Ostajalu	984-985/1576-1577	*Laleh* of Emamqoli Mirza	Qomi 2, 627; Valeh 1372, 408; Monshi 134, 139; Bidlisi 2, 632
Khan Ahmad Khan	985-1001/1577-1593	H Gilan-e biyeh-pish	Monshi 223, 227, 450-51; Bidlisi 2, 690; Molla Jalal 43
Qara Beyg Qajar	1001/1593	*Darugheh* Gilan-e biyeh pish	Molla Jalal 118
Mehdiqoli Khan Shamlu	1001-1002/1593-1594	H and *amir al-omara* Gilan-e biyeh-pish	Monshi 451
Ahmad Beyg Beygdelu	1002/1594	*Darugheh* of Lahejan	Monshi 460
Farhad Khan Qaramanlu	1002-1003/1594-1595	*Amir al-omara* of Gilan-e biyeh-pish	Monshi 464, 492

Dervish Mohammad Khan Rumlu	1003/1595	H Lahejan and BB Gilan	Monshi 500; Molla Jalal 139; Fumeni 164, 167-78, 171
Oghurlu Soltan Chegini	1003-?/1595-?	H Lahejan	Fumeni 171
Mirza Taqi Esfahani	1003-?/1595-?	*Vazir-e Gilanat*	Fumeni 172, 196, 209, 215, 223, 261
Khvajeh Mohammad Shafi' aka Mirza-ye 'Alamiyan	1013-1016/1605-1608	*Vazir-e koll* Gilan	Monshi 674, 708; Molla Jalal 260; Fumeni 171, 173, 188
Behzad Beyg	1016-1018?/1608-1610?	*Vazir-e Gilanat*	Fumeni 200; Vahid 181
Aslan Beyg Qurchi-ye Shamlu	1018-1032/1610-1623	Vizier Gilan-e biyeh-pish	Fumeni 209-222
Mirza 'Abdollah Esfahani	1032-1038/1623-1629	Vizier Gilan-e biyeh pish	Vahid 333; Yusof 297; Valeh 1380, 18
Mirza Taqi	1038-1044/1629-1634	*Vazir-e koll*	Vahid 333; Yusof 18, 297; Esfahani 70; Fumeni 165
Mirza Taqi Dowlatabadi	1044-1046/1634-1637	Vizier Lahejan + Gilan-e biyeh pish	Vahid 333; Yusof 148, 208
Mirza Saleh b. Eskander Beyg Monshi	1046-?/1637-?	Vizier Gilan-e biyeh pish	Vahid 333; Yusof 208, 297
Mirza Ja'far Qazvini	?-1064/?-1654	Vizier Gilan-e biyeh pish	Vahid 570
Mirza Hashem	1064-?/1654-?	Vizier Gilan-e biyeh pish	Vahid 570

Governors of Gilan-e biyeh-pas

Name	Year	Observations	Source
Amireh Hosam al-Din	?-915/1509-10	*Vali* Gilan-e biyeh-pas	Budaq 94; Qomi 1, 87; Monshi 1, 31; Hoseyni 221-2; Qomi 1, 141; Shirazi 44; Heravi 264
Amireh Dobbaj b. Amireh Hosam al-Din aka Mozaffar Soltan	915-943/1510-1537	*Vali* Resht	Budaq 94; Valeh 1372, 336; Monshi 1, 47; Monshi 110; Hoseyni 207, 222; Qomi 254-55; Rumlu 355; Shirazi 57; Bidlisi 2, 539, 563, 568; Qazvini 279; Fumeni 11
Khan Ahmad Khan b. Soltan Hasan	943-?/1537-?	*Vali* of both Gilans	Qomi 1, 262
Amireh Shahrokh	950-957/1544-1550	H Gilan-e biyeh-pas	Fumeni 28-31; Rabino 432

Khan Ahmad Khan	958-975/1551-1568	*Vali* Gilan-e biyeh-pish and biyeh-pas	Hoseyni 224 ; Monshi 110; Shirazi 137; Bidlisi 2, 623, 627
Soltan Mahmud b Mozaffar Soltan	975/1568	H Gilan-e biyeh-pas	Fumeni 32-38; Rabino 432-33
Jamshid Khan b. Soltan Mahmud b. Amireh Dobbaj	975-986/1568-1578	H Gilan-e biyeh-pas or *vali* Resht-e Gilan	Natanzi 33; Shamlu 1, 86; Qomi 2, 630; Rumlu 560; Bidlisi 2, 631
Mirza Kamran, governor of Kudom	986-989/1578-1581	H Gilan-e biyeh-pas –usurper	Monshi 265; Fumeni 69-90
Salman Khan	989/1582	H Resht	Monshi 267
Mostafa Soltan Qajar	1001/1592	*Darugheh* and H Gilan-e biyeh-pas	Fumeni 137
'Ali Beyg [Khan] Fumeni	1001-1002/1593-1594	H Gilan-e biyeh-pas?; H Resht+Fumen [see Fumen]	Monshi 449, 460, 462-63, 492; Molla Jalal 133-34; Natanzi 475, 476, 483; Fumeni 157
Emir Shah Malek	1002/1594	*Darugheh*s in Resht and Fumen	Monshi 460-61
Farhad Khan Qaramanlu	1004/1596	H Gilan-e biyeh-pas	Monshi 515
Khosrow Beyg Chaharyar	1004/1596	*Darugheh* Resht - *gholam*	Monshi 514
Khvajeh Mohammad Shafi' aka Mirza-ye 'Alamiyan	1012-1016/1604-1608	*Vazir-e koll* Gilan	Monshi 675, 760; Molla Jalal 260
Esma'il Beyg b. Aslan Beyg	1032-1038/1624-1629	Vizier Gilan-e biyeh-pas (3 yrs as vizier Fumeni)	Vahid 333; Yusof 297; Fumeni 222, 259, 261
Mirza Taqi	1038-1044/1629-1634	*Vazir-e koll*	Vahid 333; Yusof 297
Aqa Zaman Esfahani	1044-?/1635-?	Vizier Gilan-e biyeh-pas + Resht	Vahid 333; Yusof 148, 297
Lachin Aqa-ye Gholam Yusof Aqa	?-1052-?/?-1643-?	Vizier biyeh-pas	Yusof 297; Vahid 333
Nezam al-Molk	1059/1649	Vizier Gilan	Riazul Islam 1, 336
Morad Beyg [Khan]	1064-?/1654-?	*Teyuldar* Gilan-e biyeh-pas	Vahid 546
Mirza Sadr al-Din Mohammad Jaberi	?-1070/?-1660	Vizier Gilan-e biyeh-pas	Vahid 720
'Evaz Beyg	1070-1074/1660-1664	Vizier Gilan-e biyeh-pas; *gholam*	Vahid 720, 759
Mirza Mohammad Karim b. Adam Soltan	1107/1695	Vizier Gilan-e biyeh-pas	Qa'em-maqam, doc. 24
Mirza Mohammad Hoseyn	1122/1710?	Vizier Gilan	Floor, *Afghan*, 25
Kalb 'Ali Khan	Before 1124/1712	Vizier Gilan	Khatunabadi 566

Goklan is the name of the district occupied by the Goklan Torkmans, east of Astarabad until Bojnord. It also included the territory of the Ukhli, another Torkman tribe. Given the uncertain allegiance of these tribes the governors of this territory seem to have been drawn from the pool of *gholam*s under Shah 'Abbas I, as is indicated by these two known examples. In the period of Shah Mohammad Khodabandeh another Torkman tribe was used to keep control the area outside Astarabad (q.v.). By the end of the Safavid period the Goklan district was an administrative part of Astarabad.

Name	Year	Observations	Source
Ommat Soltan	1014/1606	H Goklan	Molla Jalal 260
Behbud Khan Cherkes	?-1030/?-1621	H Goklan and Ukhli territory	Monshi 967
NN	1030-?/1621-?	H Goklan and Ukhli territory	Monshi 967

Gonabad, Jonabad, or Jonahabad is a dependency of Tun (q.v.). In 999/1590 it was occupied by the Uzbegs.[136]

Gukeh va Kiseh is a district in Mazandaran of which Amir Kiya Gugi was its governor in the two first decades of the sixteenth century.[137]

Guri va Baratili were two districts in Georgia. Guri or Gori was the capital of Kartli and Barateli was one of its districts. In 985/1577, Simun Khan son of Luarsab is mentioned as being the governor of Gori and Barateli.[138]

Hablerud or Harirud is a district situated some 150 km east of Tehran, on the road from Tehran to Mazandaran via the Gaduk pass. The governor of Hablerud sometimes also was governor of another district such as Damavand (q.v.). Initially this district seems to have been held by the ruler of Gilan, later Qezelbash emirs took over.

Name	Year	Observations	Source
Shahqoli Beyg b. Ras Khan	986-?/1578-?	*Teyuldar* Damavand + Hablehrud	Qomi 2, 668
Shahqoli Beyg [Soltan] b. Aras Khan	996-?/1588-?	H Damavand + Hablehrud	Qomi 2, 668; Shamlu 1, 167

Hajjilar, see Gereyli.

Hamadan province, situated in western Iran, was part of Persian Iraq (Iraq-e 'Ajam). It was also known as Qalamru-ye 'Ali Shükr. Esma'il I took control over Hamadan as of 908/1503. The province became crown domain as of 1064-65/1653-54 until the end of the reign of Shah

---

136 Bidlisi, *Cheref-Nameh*, vol. 2, p. 689.
137 Laheji, *Tarikh*, pp. 29, 84-85, 88, 202, 284, 287, 326, 336, 345-49, 354.
138 Molla Jalal, *Ruznameh*, p. 43; Yazdi, *Mokhtasar*, pp. 367, 372.

Soleyman in 1105/1694. Hamadan included the following administrative jurisdictions: Garrus, Harsin, Hastajoft, Kalhor, Khvar-Semnan, Rey, and Saveh-Haveh (q.v.).[139]

Name	Year	Observations	Source
Dedeh Beyg	909-?/1503-?	H *qalamru-ye* 'Ali Shükr aka Qara Olus	Aubin 4 (Afzal)
Amir Beyg Mowsellu	914/1508	H Hamadan; uncertain	Aubin 33, n. 148 (Afzal)
Yegan Beyg Ostajalu	915/1509	H Hamadan; *qurchi-bashi*	Bidlisi 1, 125; Aubin 33, n. 148
Qarajeh Soltan Tekkelu	921-931-?/1515-1524-?	*Teyuldar* or H Hamadan	Rumlu 245; Qomi 1, 159; Shirazi 61; Qazvini 282; Tatavi 403 (Qaracheh)
Bahram Mirza	943/1537	H Hamadan	Tatavi 532
'Abdollah Khan Ostajalu	950/1543	*Vali* Hamadan	Bidlisi 2, 577; Budaq 105
Mohammad Soltan Alayinoghli	950/1544	H Hamadan	Budaq 105
Cheragh Soltan Gerampa Ostajalu	951-962/1545-1555	H Hamadan [+ Khuzestan/Qazvini] *Laleh* of Bahram Mirza b. Esma'il	Hoseyni 155; Qomi 1, 379; Qazvini 296; Budaq 117
	963/1556	H Hamadan; Esma'il Mirza, but never came; as of 959	Qomi 2, 976; Abrahams 140
Beyram Khan b. Seyf 'Ali Beyg Baharlu	?-968/?-1561	H Dinavar, Hamadan, Kurdestan + Qalamru-ye 'Ali Shükr	Rumlu 534
Mohammadi Khan b. Amir Khan Mowselu	968-975/1561-1568	H Hamadan	Qomi 2, 765; Bidlisi 2, 337
Amir Khan Mowselu Torkman b. Mohammadi Khan	975-980/1568-1573	H Hamadan or Qalamru-ye 'Ali Shükr	Budaq 141; Qomi 1, 448, 471, 579, 765; Tatavi 725, 739
Fulad Khalifeh-ye Rumlu or Shamlu	980-984/1573-1576	H Hamadan	Shamlu: Monshi 138; Qomi 1, 579, 2, 617, 630, [2], 644; Molla Jalal 35; Vahid 72; Rumlu: Rumlu 621; Budaq 163; Valeh 1372, 408; Tatavi 739
Amir Khan Mowselu Torkman	985/1577	H Hamadan + Khvar	Molla Jalal 41; Tatavi 768
Vali Beyg [Soltan] Tekkelu b. 'Ali Soltan Sharaf al-Din-oghlu	985-992/1577-1584	H Hamadan	Monshi 227; Qomi 2, 664, 727, 755, 769

---

139 Under 'Abbas I the districts of Tuy va Sarkan, Nehavand and Borujerd also were part of the province of Hamadan, although they are not mentioned in Safavid state manuals. Monshi, *Tarikh*, vol. 1, p. 471; Qomi, *Kholasat*, vol. 1, p. 884.

Pir Gheyb Khan Ostajalu	?-994/?-1586	H 'Ali Shükr	Monshi 341-42; Qomi 2, 828, 853; Valeh 1372, 658; Natanzi 217, 338; Vahid 91, 105
Shahverdi Khalifeh-ye Shamlu	994/1586	H Hamadan	Qomi 2, 848; Monshi 357; Valeh 1372, 820-1; Natanzi 338
Vali Khan Tekkelu	994/1586	H Hamadan	Valeh 1372, 681, 699, 745; Qomi 2, 828; Bidlisi 2, 673
Qurkhoms Khan Rumlu	996/1588	H Hamadan	Qomi 2, 874; Vahid 108 [997]
Budaq Khan Chegani	997/1589	H Hamadan - *Laleh* Hasan Mirza b. 'Abbas —never went there	Qomi 2, 885-87, 1081
Qurkhoms Khan Shamlu	997/1589	H Hamadan	Monshi 407-07
Tahmaspqoli Soltan Arashlu Afshar	998/1590	H Hamadan – succeeded by his brother	Monshi 410; Molla Jalal 86-7
Hoseynqoli Khan Arashlu Afshar	998/1590	H Hamadan	Molla Jalal 87
Hasan 'Ali b. Budaq Khan Cheghani	999/1591	H Hamadan	Monshi 434; Qomi 2, 921
Oghurlu Soltan Bayat	1000-?/1592-?	*Vakil* of Mohammad Baqer Mirza b. 'Abbas	Monshi 440; Vahid 114
Hoseyn 'Ali Khan Cheghani	?-1004/?-1596	H Hamadan	Monshi 515
[Qara] Hasan Khan Ostajalu	1004-1020/1596-1611	BB 'Ali Shükr or BB Hamadan	Monshi 649, 863, 760, 764, 781, 823, 1041; Molla Jalal 203, 245, 258, 400, 414; Yusof 126; Vahid 154, 169
Safiqoli Khan	1020-1032/1611-1623	BB 'Ali Shükr - H Hamadan; as of 1022 with Baghdad	Yusof 126 [*gholam*]; Shamlu 1, 204; Monshi 958, 997
Hoseyn Khan Chavoshlu Ostajalu	1033-1035/1623-1626	BB *qalamru-ye* 'Ali Shükr	Vahid 215
Pir Gheyb Ostajalu	1046/1637	H Hamadan, + *qalamru-ye* 'Ali Shükr; later BB of that region	Shamlu 1, 254; Valeh 1380, 820-1; Yusof 286
Bektash Khan	Before 1052/1643	BB *qalamru-ye* 'Ali Shükr + BB Baghdad	Yusof 292 [*gholam*]; Vahid 327
Mortezaqoli Khan	1058-1059/1648-1649	H 'Ali Shükr; *khane-hzad qadimi, sepahsalar*	Shamlu 1, 429; Vahid 464, 476; Valeh 1380, 439, 468
	Khasseh as of 1065/1653-?		Vahid 567
'Abdol-Qasem Khan	ca. 1085-1094/1675-1683	H Hamadan	Sanson 78

Saru Khan Sahandlu	?-1103/?-1691	H Hamadan + Semnan + Kazerun	Sanson 80
'Abbas Khan Ziyad-oghlu Qajar	1105/1694	BB *qalamru-ye* 'Ali Shükr	Mervi 18, 1310
Safiqoli Khan	1126/1714	H Hamadan	Floor, *Afghan*, 27
Abu'l-Qasem Khan	1136?/1723?	H Hamadan	Balfour 164
	As of 1137/1724	end of Safavid rule	

Harsin district is situated some 50 km east of Kermanshah, but it was part of the province of Hamadan (q.v.). In 1012/1603, Shah 'Ali Soltan Khodabandehlu was governor of Harsin.[140]

Hasanabad like Palangan (q.v.), was a fort on the Persian border with the Ottoman Empire, situated some 60 km north-west of Kermanshah. Given its strategic importance the Ardalan governor of Kurdestan was sometimes even refered to as the governor of Palangan. However, as is clear from the case Timur Khan Ardalan, who was governor of both Hasanabad and Palangan, the fort usually was held by a member of his family.[141] (q.v. Kurdestan).

Hasan Abdallu is a tribal district, which is not mentioned in any source, except for Nasiri's *Alqab*, which states that it was created by Shah 'Abbas I, probably in the first decade of the seventeenth century. The Hasan Abdallu tribal district perhaps is the same as that of the 'Abdallu mentioned by the TM, which perhaps refers to the 'Abdallu tribal group, as Minorsky has suggested.[142] If correct, which is not certain at all, the Hasan Abdallu would then be a sub-division of the Shamlu tribe.[143]

Hashtrud-e TabTab, see Nelqas.

Hazar Jarib is a mountain district situated in the Elburz mountains some 40 km south of Ashraf (see also Damavand). This district was part of Gilan and therefore initially it was held by a local chief, a scion of the clan of Morteza'i sayyeds. A Safavid army subdued its chief in 924/1518 because of his disloyal behavior.[144] After the crushing of the rebellion in Gilan in 1592, Hazar Jarib like its adjacent districts such as Damavand, Firuzkuh and Hablehrud were henceforth held by Qezelbash emirs. Sometimes it was even held by the governor of Astarabad together with a number of other adjacent districts.

Name	Year	Observations	Source
Mir Harun	?-916/?-1510	H HazarJarib	Hoseyni 252
Emir Mo'ezz al-Din	916/1510	H HazarJarib	Hoseyni 252

---

140 Monshi, *Tarikh*, vol. 2, p. 661.
141 Monshi, *Tarikh*, vol. 1, p. 141.
142 TM, p. 165.
143 Monshi, *Tarikh*, p. 1084.
144 Shirazi, *Takmelat*, pp. 56-58; Qazvini, *Tarikh*, p. 278; Rabino, *Astarabad*, p. 144.

Emir Soltan Hashem	916-?/1510-?	H HazarJarib	Hoseyni 252
Sayyed Hasan Hazar Jaribi	924/1518	H HazarJarib	Qomi 1, 140
Emir Soltan Hoseyn	?-929/1523	H HazarJarib	Hoseyni 252
Eskandar Khan Afshar	Before 985/1577	H HazarJarib	Valeh 1372, 411
	from 985/1577 until 987/1579	crown domain of the queen Kheyr al-Nesa Beygom	Qomi 2, 874
Mortezaqoli Khan Pornak Torkman	991-996/1583-1587	H Astarabad, Damghan, Bestam, Biyarjomand, A'rab 'Ameri, HazarJarib	Monshsi 290, 362; Valeh 1372, 678, 831
Mohammad Khan Torkman + son Vali Jan Khan Torkman	996/December 1587	H Hablehrud + HazarJarib	Qomi 2, 869
Amir Shahrokh	997/1588	H HazarJarib	Shamlu 1, 167

Herat province was the other half that, together with Mashhad, constituted the administrative region of Khorasan. Nevertheless, when texts refer to Khorasan they usually mean Herat rather than Mashhad. Like Mashhad, Herat bore the brunt of Uzbeg attacks and incursions, while it also was a province that often was ruled by Safavid princes. Tahmasp Mirza ruled Khorasan from the border of Semnan until the Oxus.[145] To mobilize all its resources for battle with the Uzbeg, Shah Esmail in 917/1511 gave his chief-executive, the *vakil* Najm II, total control over the tribes of Khorasan and their government donations.[146] Due to the revolts that had broken out in many of the outlying provinces of Safavid Persia after 1710, the Abdali tribe of Herat also rebelled and took effective control over the province in 1717. The central government still appointed governors for Herat, but these were generals charged to suppress the rebellion and take their governorship by force, in which endeavor they all failed. At the end of the Safavid period Herat included the following administrative jurisdictions: Badghis, Bala Morghab, Durmi, Farah, Ghur, Jam, Karokh, Khvaf, Maruchaq, Panjdeh and Tun (see also Abdali).

Name	Year	Observations	Source
Hoseyn Beyg Laleh Shamlu	916-918/1510-1512	H Herat	Monshi 1, 40; Budaq 32; Rumlu 170; Shirazi 50; Bidlisi 2, 524, 534; Qazvini 274; Heravi 368, 375
Ahmad Beyg Sufi-oghlu Ostajalu	918/1512	H Herat	Heravi 375; Khvandamir 526; Aubin 21

---

145 Qomi, *Kholasat*, vol. 1, p. 134.
146 Aubin, "Les soufis," p. 20.

Zeynal Khan Shamlu	919-921/1513-1515	H Herat	Shamlu 1, 43; Monshi 1, 41; Hoseyni 70; Qomi 1, 126; Rumlu 196; Bidlisi 2, 534; Qazvini 276, 284;
Amir Khan Mowsellu Torkman	921-927/1515-1521	*Laleh* of Tahmasp Mirza; *saltanat* over the whole of Khorasan	Hoseyni 64, 70, 75, 87; Qomi 1, 134, 148; Shamlu 1, 46-7; Monshi 44; Ben Khvandamir 205; Bidlisi 2, 536, 543; Qazvini 278; Shirazi 56; Mozaffar 450
Ebrahim Soltan [Khan] Mowsellu Torkman	927/1521	H Herat - his brother	Shirazi 58
Durmish Khan Shamlu	927-932/1521-1526	BB Khorasan - *Laleh* of Sam Mirza	Monshi 1, 44, 50-52; Budaq 42; Shamlu 1, 47; Hoseyni 87, 90; Vahid 60; Qomi 148, 163; Ben Khvandamir 234; Shirazi 62; Bidlisi 2, 543; Qazvini 283
Hoseyn Khan Shamlu b. 'Abdi Beyg	932-936/1526-1529	H Herat - his brother; *Laleh* of Sam Mirza	Qomi 1, 163; Monshi 52, 56-7; Qomi 1, 188, 213; Shamlu 1, 43; Ben Khvandamir 237, 269; Shirazi 62
NN	936/1529-1530	'Aliqoli Mirza b. Tahmasp; died and never came to Herat	Röhrborn 42, quoting Qomi; however Tahmasp I had no son called 'Aliqoli Mirza and Emamqoli Mirza never was in Herat
Ghazi or Qazi Beyg [Khan] Tekkelu [or Shamlu]	936-939/1530-1533	*Laleh* of Bahram Mirza	Shamlu 1, 51; Budaq 69; Monshi 58; Qomi 2, 212; Khvandamir 275 [Qazi Khan]; Tahmasp 14 [Qazi Beyg]
Aghzivar Khan Shamlu b. Damri Soltan Shamlu*	939-942/1533-1536	*Laleh* of Sam Mirza – h Herat + *amir al-omara* Khorasan; Qazvini has Oghorlu Arjan b. Dehri Soltan Shamlu	Monshi 61, 62; Qomi 1, 226; Khvandamir 285; Bidlisi 2, 562; Qazvini 287; Tahmasp 24; Abrahams 135
Khalifeh Soltan Shamlu aka Sufiyan Khalifeh Shamlu [Rumlu]	942/1536	H Herat pro-tem	Rumlu 344; Hoseyni 135; Khvandamir 293 [Rumlu], 301; Qomi 1, 256; Shirazi 86; Qazvini 292

Mohammad Sharaf al-Dinoghlu Tekkelu	943-963/1537-1556	*Amir al-omara* Khorasan - *Laleh* of Soltan Mohammad Mirza b. Tahmasp	Rumlu 346; Shamlu 1, 52, 54; Qomi 1, 266, 270-71, 292, 304, 344; Monshi 125; Hoseyni 141, 148, 155, 189; Shamlu 1, 78; Khvandamir 327, 331; Shirazi 87, 95, 112; Bidlisi 2, 571, 591; Qazvini 292
'Ali Soltan Tekkelu	963/1556	*Laleh* of Esma'il Mirza, he only remained June-December 1556/963 in Herat; 'Ali Soltan returned and was killed by the shah, see Bidlisi	Rumlu 508; Hoseyni 189; Shamlu 1, 78; Qomi 1, 385; Monshi 214; Shirazi 110; Bidlisi 2, 591; Tatavi 563
Mohammad Sharaf al-Dinoghlu Tekkelu	963-969/1556-1562	H Herat – *Laleh* of Esma'il Mirza b. Tahmasp until 964	Bidlisi 2, 591-93; Qazvini 302, 303; Tatavi 576-77
Qazaq Khan Tekkelu b. Mohammad Khan	969-972/1562-1565	H Herat - *Laleh* of Soltan Mohammad Mirza; BB Khorasan as of 964	Qomi 1, 435, 448; Monshi 126; Shamlu 1, 83; Bidlisi 2, 611; Qazvini 309-10; Abrahams 142
Emir Gheyb Beyg Ostajalu	972-974/1565-1567	H Herat- *Laleh* of Soltan Mohammad Mirza	Shirazi 125; Bidlisi 2, 611
Shahqoli Soltan Yekan Ostajalu	974-985/1567-1576	H Herat – BB Khorasan - *Laleh* of Soltan Mohammad Mirza; then of the latter's son Soltan 'Abbas Mirza as of 981/1573	Shirazi 129; Rumlu 650; Shamlu 1, 84, 119; Natanzi 37; Monshi 93, 126, 139; Qomi 1, 457, 576 [2], 631; Valeh 1372, 408; Molla Jalal 36; Abrahams 146
Aras Soltan Rumlu	985/1576	H Herat - *Laleh* of 'Abbas Mirza; does not seem to have gone there	Qomi 2, 631; Natanzi 37
'Aliqoli Beyg [Khan] Shamlu [Gurgan] grandson Durmish Khan Shamlu	985-996/1576-1588	*Laleh* of 'Abbas Mirza *Amir al-omara* Herat; BB Khorasan	Rumlu 643; Shamlu 1, 100, 107, 119-21; Vahid 87; Qomi 2, 650; Valeh 1372, 403, 687, 830; Bidlisi 2, 651; Monshi 203, 213, 387-88; Qomi 2, 794-96, 875-79; Shamlu 1, 100-01, 107, 121
Vali Khalifeh Shamlu	990/1582	H Herat – was appointed but 'Aliqoli Khan had him killed	Shamlu 1, 107, 121
	From 996/1588 to 1007/1598	Uzbeg governors	

Farhad Khan Qaramanlu	1004-1007/1595-1598	H Herat + *amir al-omara* Khorasan - H Khvar, Semnan, Damghan, Bestam, Firuzkuh, Boyarjomand, Hazarjarib."	Monshi 515, 571, 574; Shamlu 1, 183
Hoseyn Khan 'Abdallu Shamlu	1007-1027/1598-1618	H Herat + *amir al-omara* Khorasan	Shamlu 1, 183, 202; Vahid 149, 199 Monshi 574, 598, 745, 847, 893, 947; Siyaqi 479; Molla Jalal 184, 201, 307, 328
[Mir Sayyed] Hasan Khan 'Abdallu Shamlu b. Hoseyn Khan	1027-1051/1618-1641	H Herat + *amir al-omara* Khorasan; BB	Monshi 947; Shamlu 1, 202; Yusof 26, 103; Shamlu 1, 257, 406; Valeh 1380, 34, 125, etc 349, 418; Vahid 237, 260; Yusof 144, 158, 163; Vahid 305; Yusof 253, 287; Riazul Islam 1, 260-75, 278-79.
'Abbasqoli Khan Shamlu aka 'Abbasqoli Beyg [Khan] b. Akbar Hasan Khan *qurchi-ye shamshir*	1051-1055/1641-1645	H Herat - His oldest son - BB *be'estaqlal-e belad-e Khorasan - gholamzadeh-ye qadim*	Shamlu 1, 257, 332, 434, 449, 512; Valeh 1380, 410, 510; Vahid 305, 566; Yusof 253; Riazul Islam 1, 280, 285, 316
Safiqoli Khan	?-1103/?-1692	H Herat	Khatunabadi 549
Jani Khan	1107/1696	BB Herat	Nasiri 157, 280, 281
Mohammad Zaman Khan Shamlu	1110/1699	BB Herat	Nasiri 281
Safiqoli Khan	1120/1708	H Herat -2nd time	Khatunabadi 558
Abu'l-Ma'sum Beyg	?-1122/?-1710	H Herat	Khatunabadi 560
Heydarqoli Khan	1122-1123/1710-1713	H Herat - *divan-beygi*	Khatunabadi 560
Mohammadqoli Beyg b. Mohammad Mo'men Khan E'temad al-Dowleh	1123/1713	H Herat – *tupchi-bashi*	Khatunabadi 564
Mohammad 'Ali Khan	?-1126/1714	H Herat	Floor, *Afghan*, 27
'Abbasqoli Khan Shamlu	1126/1714-?	BB Herat	Safavi 20; Floor, *Afghan*, 27;
Ja'far Qoli Khan Ostajalu aka Hatami	?-1129/1717	BB Herat	Mostowfi 117; Safavi 20; Floor, *Afghan*, 29; Mervi 1, 20-22
Safiqoli Khan Torkestan-oghlu	1129/1717-1719	H Herat	Floor, *Afghan*, 40; Safavi 26-8
'Aliqoli Khan	1129-1134/1717-1722	H Herat – Mashhad	Mervi 1, 22, 38-39
	As of 1128/1716	under Abdali control	
Asadollah Khan Abdali	1128/1716		Safavi 29

Zaman Khan Abdali	1129/1717		Safavi 29
Mohammad Khan Abdali	1131/1719		Safavi 29
Dhu'l-Feqar Khan b. Zaman Khan Abdali	1139/1726	Followed by civil war	Safavi 30

* Fekete, *Einführung*, pp. 371-73 reproduces a royal edict dated 940, appointing Shams al-Din Khan as governor of Herat succeeding his deceased father Hajji Sharaf al-Din Aqa. I have been unable to identify these two persons.

** Although Farhad Khan had been appointed governor over these various districts he had not as yet re-taken them from the Uzbegs, which occurred during 1006/1597 and 1007/1598.

Heratrud, a district situated south-east of Herat, is a governorship that seems to have been jointly held with that of Shaflan or Shaqlan, as well as that of Ubeh (q.v.). Nomads living in the area also paid taxes to Esma'il I and Tahmasp I, thus implying that there were governors during that period, although their names are as yet unknown.[147]

Name	Year	Observations	Source
Ahmad Beyg Afshar	928/1522	H Heratrud	Khvandamir 591
Soleyman Beyg Khonoslu [?]	1018/1610	H Heratrud	Molla Jalal 370
Rostam Beyg	1042/1633	H Ubeh, Shaqlan	Yusof 103
Mohammad Amin Khan	?-1070/?-1660	H Ubeh, Shaqlan, Heratrud - succeeded by his brother	Vahid 720; Valeh 1380, 601, 655
Mohammad Rahim Khan	1070-?/1660-?	H Ubeh, Shaqlan, Heratrud	Vahid 720

Hillah is a district in central Iraq and a *sanjaq* of Baghdad, which was held by the Safavids during two different time periods, when they also held Baghdad and some other towns in Iraq. The first period was between 1508 and 1534 and the second period was between 1623 and 1639. The dates for these two time periods probably are the same for Safavid rule at Hillah.

Name	Year	Observations	Source
Sayyed Beyg aka Sayyed Mohammad Kamuneh	935-?/1529	H Hillah	Budaq 68; Shamlu 1, 40; Qomi 1, 190
	From 1534 to 1623	Ottoman governors	
Saru Soltan Beygdelu	1033-?/1624-?	H + *motavalli* of Hillah	Monshi 1011; Vahid 208, 213, 217, 403

---

147 Heratrud is a district situated like the neighboring district of Shaflan or Shaqlan on the southbank of the Hari Rud. Molla Jalal, *Ruznameh*, pp. 370 (Heratrud), 36, 174, 347 (Shaqlan), TM, p. 102; Gonabadi, *Rowzat*, pp. 883-84 (Shaflanat).

| Abu'l-Qasem Soltan b. Pir Gheyb Khan Sharaflu Ostajalu | ?-1038/1629 | H Hillah | Monshi 1085 |

Hormuz, see Bandar 'Abbas.

Hoveyzeh, see 'Arabestan.

Ich, Ichi, Ij or Ig is a town and district situated in the province of Fars near Darabjerd. To the north-east is Neyriz and in the west it borders on Fasa. The town was known for its production of bows and glass.[148] It would seem that its governorship was usually held together with that of one or more neighboring district, in particular those of Neyriz and Fasa (q.v.).[149]

Name	Year	Observations	Source
Charandab Soltan Shamlu	955-957/1548-1550	H Ichi, Neyriz, Fasa (+ Shabankareh; Tahmasp)	Hoseyni 170; Qomi 1, 327, 349; Shirazi 98; Tahmasp 53
Shahverdi Khalifeh Shamlu b. Vali Khalifeh Shamlu	994-996/1586-1588	H Ij, Neyriz	Natanzi 338 (Ig); Monshi 420

Isfahan province was part of the administrative region of Persian Iraq. Initially Isfahan was governed by governors, but when it was changed into *khasseh* or crown domain in 940/1534, it was governed by viziers and *darugheh*s, a situation that lasted until 985/1577. During the second Qezelbash 'civil war' (1577-1588) instead of viziers, once again governors were in charge of Isfahan, and even a few years later, i.e. until 1590, still some officeholders are referred as governor. Thereafter, Isfahan continued to be governed by a vizier and thus had become crown domain again.

Name	Year	Observations	Source
Yar-Ahmad Khuzani	909/1503	*Darugheh-Hakem*	Aubin 11, n. 110 (Afzal)
'Abdi Beyg Shamlu	910/1504	*Hakem*	Tatavi 323
Durmish Khan Shamlu b. 'Abdi Beyg Shamlu	911-927/1505-1521	H Isfahan	Rohrborn 21; Qomi 1, 151 [929; vizier-*darugheh*]; Mozaffar 148, 224
Jukheh or Juheh Soltan Tekkelu	931-938/1524-1531	H Isfahan (Jowhar Soltan; Tatavi) H Golhar*	Monshi 46; Shirazi 61; Qazvini 282; Tahmasp 15; Tatavi 304; Abrahams 150
Mohammad Khan Dhu'l-Qadr	935/1528	*Hakem* (possibly)	Dickson 134

---

148 Yazdi, *Mokhtasar*, p. 330.
149 Le Strange, *The Lands*, pp. 289-90.

Name	Date	Role	Source
Shah Qobad Beyg [Soltan] Tekkelu b. Juheh Soltan	938/1531	*Hakem*	Tahmasp 15
'Ali Beyg [Soltan] Tekkelu b. Juheh Soltan	939/1531	*Hakem*	Tahmasp 15
N.N.	939-941/1532-1534?	*Darugheh*	Aubin, Archives 16
Mohammad Khan Sharaf al-Dinoghlu Tekkelu	941-942/1534-1535	*Teyuldar*	Quiring-Zoche 120
Khvajeh Mir Ne'matollah Malamiri	942-955/1535-1548	*Vizier*	Bafqi 3/1, 255
Amir Aslan Soltan Arshlu	955/1548	H Isfahan	Afshar 109
Mohammad Beyg b. Mir Ja'far Savaji	972-/1564-	*Vizier* Isfahan	Tatavi 739
Khvajeh Mir Ne'matollah Malamiri	?-973/?-1565	*Vizier*	Bafqi 3/1, 255
Khvajeh Mohammad Sharif Tehrani	973/1565	*Vizier*	Monshi 165; Bafqi 3/1, 167
Mir Fazlollah Shahrestani Esfahani	973-?/1565-?	*Vizier*	Monshi 164
Farhad Beyg Gholam	985-995/1577-1586	*Vizier, motasaddi-ye khaleseh va hakem be'esteqlal*	Natanzi, 238, 274; Monshi 356, 381, 493; Valeh 1372, 817, 824
Sayyed Beyg Kamuneh	995-996/1586-1587	*Hakem* and *darugheh*	Natanzi, 221-22; Monshi 1, 359; Valeh 1372, 825
Ahmad Kofrani Esfahani	995-996/1586-1587	*Vizier* and *motasaddi*	Natanzi, 222; Monshi 359; Valeh 1372, 824
Morshedqoli Khan	996/1587	H Isfahan	Qomi 2, 874
Mir Hoseyn Khan Mazandarani	997/1588	*Vali* Isfahan	Molla Jalal 73
Ebrahim Khan Torkman	997/1588	*Hakem* and *darugheh*	Natanzi, 286, 270; Qomi 2, 865; Monshi 362; Valeh 1372, 832
Amir Esma'il Savaji	998/1589	*Vizier*	Qomi 2, 1066, 1070
Morshedqoli Khan	998/1589	*Teyuldar*	Idem
Mohammad Beyg Saruqchi	998/1589	*Darugheh*	Monshi 401; Shamlu 1, 134 [Mohammadi; 3 yrs]
Yoli Beyg Gholam**	998/1590	*Hakem* and *darugheh*	Monshi 417, 426, 433, 437; Natanzi 332; Qomi 2, 891, 903-04, 919; Molla Jalal 87
'Ali Beyg Ostajalu	999/1590	*Hakem* and *darugheh*	Natanzi, 374; Qomi
Aqa Kamal Dowlatabadi	1002/1593	*Saheb-e ekhteyar*	Natanzi, 537
Qadi Soltan Torbati	999/1589 & 1007/1598	*Hakem* and *darugheh*	Monshi 568; Natanzi, 603

	Viziers		
N.N.	1000/1590	Vizier and *darugheh*	Aubin, "Archives" 17
Mirza Mohammad	1014/1605 & 1017/1608	Vizier Isfahan	Minasiyan doc. 3; Qa'em-Maqami p. 22
Mir Fazlollah Shahrestani	1019/1610	Vizier Isfahan	Monshi 950
Mir Shams	1020-?/1611-?	Vizier Isfahan	Molla Jalal 411
Shah Taher Khorasani	?-1039/1629	Vizier Isfahan	Yusof 296; Vahid 228, 332
Mohammad Mo'men Beyg	1039/1629	Vizier Isfahan	Yusof 296; Shamlu 1, 294; Vahid 228, 333
Mir Shah Taher Torshizi or Khorasani	1040-1045/1631-1636	Vizier Isfahan	Yusof 166, 296 [not long]; Vahid 266 [1045 again], 332; Astarabadi 251 [as of 1044]
Mohammad Mo'men Beyg	1045-1047/1636-1638	Vizier Isfahan	Vahid 266, 333; Astarabadi 256, 258
Mohammad 'Ali Beyg Garagyaraq Esfahani	1047-1049/1638-1640	Vizier Isfahan – later *nazer*	Yusof 199-200, 235, 296; Vahid 297, 333
Mirza Taqi Dowlatabadi	1049-?/1640-?	Vizier Isfahan	Yusof 235, 296; Vahid 297, 333
Mirza Razi Savaji aka Mirza Razi al-Din Mohammad	1053-1068-?/1643-1658	Vizier Isfahan	Shamlu 1, 284, 524; Valeh 1380, 604; Vahid 636
Mirza Ja'far	?-1103/?-1692	Vizier Isfahan	Khatunabadi 548
Mirza 'Isa Khan	1103-1111/1692-1700	Vizier Isfahan	Khatunabadi 549
Sayyed 'Ali Khan b. Mirza 'Isa Khan	1111-1114/1700-1703	Vizier Isfahan	Khatunabadi 549
Mirza Asadollah grdsn Khalifeh Soltan	1114-?/1703-?	Vizier Isfahan	Khatunabadi 549

* Golhar, properly Golbar, is a suburb of Isfahan. Dhu'l-Feqar b. 'Ali Bey Torkman is also mentioned as governor of Golhar in 934/1528. Abrahams, p. 180.

** According to Vahid, *Tarikh*, p. 110 Yoli Beyg was *darugheh*, but Farhad Aqa was governor of Isfahan in 998.

Ishkerduqa [?] is a district, probably attached to Chokhur-e Sa'd, that I have not been able to identify. Moreover, it is mentioned only by one source. In 966/1558 Yadgar Beyg Pazuki was its governor.[150]

Jahan-Arghiyan or Jahan in Arghiyan district is situated in Khorasan, east of Jajarm and south-west of Khabushan.[151]

---

150 Qazvini, *Tarikh*, p. 304.
151 Monshi, *Tarikh*, vol. 1, p. 454 (Jahan Az'iyan), 604 (Jahan Araghban); Valeh, *Khold*, p. 660 (Jahan Arghanan), while Yazdi, *Mokhtasar*, p. 212 also has Jahan Arghanan, but only mentions that it is in the Fourth

Name	Year	Observations	Source
Shahqoli Soltan Qomari	ca. 1038/1629	H Jahan-Arghiyan	Monshi 1087
Rowshan Soltan Legzi	?-1059-?/?-1649-?	H Jahan-Arghiyan	Valeh 1380, 464, 485; Vahid 473

Jam is a small district in northeastern Khorasan, situated north and east of Bakharz and in the east bounded by the Hari Rud, which forms the border with Afghanistan. Its main town was Torbat-e Sheikh Jam and it was part of the governor-generalship of Herat.[152] See also Zaveh.

Name	Year	Observations	Source
Mir Hoseyn Khan Tavakkoli	935/1529	H Jam; see also Sarakhs	Abrahams 200
Ebrahim Khan Dhu'l-Qadr	967/1560	H Jam	Monshi 95
Emamqoli Soltan Chenagi	972/1565	H Jam	Budaq 141
Zeynal Beyg [Soltan] b. Ebrahim Khan Dhu'l-Qadr	?-976/?-1569	H Jam	Rumlu 573; Qomi 1, 562; Vahid 62
Heybat Aqa Dhu'l-Qadr	976-?/1569-?	H Jam	Qomi 1, 563; Vahid 73 (Tebat Aqa)
son [?] of Hoseyn Khan	977/1569	H Jam	Abrahams 146
Tabat Aqa Dhu'l-Qadr	before 984/1576	H Jam	Valeh 1372, 410; Monshi 140
Shahqoli Soltan Afshar	988-?/1580-?	H Jam	Valeh 1372, 606; Monshi 257
Shahqoli Soltan Qarenjeh-oghlu Ostajalu	991-?/1583-?	H Jam - *Laleh* of Salman Khan; *tabin* of H of Mashhad (Valeh)	Valeh 1372, 678, 685; Monshi 290
Eyguth Soltan Chavoshlu	994-?1586-?	H Jam	Monshi 364
Mohammad Khan Chavoslu	?-998/?-1590	H Jam	Valeh 1372, 836
Amin Hoseyn Firuz-jang	1007/1598	H Jam, Sarakhs, Zirabad	Molla Jalal 184
Ebrahim Beyg brother of Hafezak Soltan	1009-?/1600-?	H Jam	Monshi 603
Shahnazar Soltan Tükeli Chaghatay	?-1017-?/?-1609-?	H Jam; see Mashhad	Monshi 802, 942; Vahid 199
Qalandar Soltan Tavakkoli	1027-1041-?/1618-1632-?	H Jam + *il-e* Tavakolli; nephew of Shahnazar	Vahid 199, 237; Monshi 1086

Clime. Brian Spooner, "Arghiyan: The Area of Jajarm in Western Khurasan," *IRAN* 3 (1963), pp. 97-107 following LeStrange, *The Lands*, p. 392 says it is the same as Jajarm, while Dorothea Krawulsky, *Iran, das Reich der Ilkhane* (Wiesbaden, 1978), p. 66, following Jean Aubin, "Le réseau pastoral," pp. 109-16, argues that it is east of Jajarm, and south and west of Khabushan and bordering Joveyn.

152 Monshi, *Tarikh*, vol. 2, p. 603.

Hasan Soltan Tavakkoli	?-1064/?-1654	H Jam	Valeh 1380, 464, 536; Vahid 570
Abdal Soltan b. Qalandar Soltan	1064-?/1654-?	H Jam; *tofangchi-aghasi*	Vahid 570

Jaramilu is the name of a tribal district, probably in Azerbaijan. In 1107/1695, Shahnavaz Khan Soltan was the governor of Jaramilu.[153] This may be the same tribe as the Haramilu mentioned by Nasiri's *Alqab*, although it is not clear which of the two is the correct orthography.

Jastan district was a dependency of the province of Baghdad. Jastan was probably held by the Safavids during two different time periods, when they also held Baghdad and some other towns in Iraq. The first period was between 1508 and 1534 and the second period was between 1623 and 1639. The dates for these two time periods probably are the same for Safavid rule at Jastan. Only one governor is known for this district Mostafa Soltan Jastani aka Abdal 'Ali, who held office in or before 1038/1629.[154]

Javanshir is a district situated on the upper Terter River in the eastern part of the province of Qarabagh. It is also the name of a Turkic tribe living in that area.

Name	Year	Observations	Source
Khosrow Soltan Armani Jadid al-Eslam	?-1042/?-1633	H *il-e* Javanshir	Yusof 272; Vahid 235, 247
Soleyman Soltan	1042-?/1633-?	H Javanshir	Vahid 247, 277
Nowruz Soltan	1050/1640	Mir *il-e* Javanshir + Otuzayeki-ye Qarabagh	Yusof 241
Budaq Soltan	1059/1649	H *il-e* Javanshir	Valeh 1380, 461

Javazer is a district situated between Mada'en, Vaset and Basra on both sides of the Tigris.[155] It was held by the Safavids during period, when they also held Baghdad and some other towns in Iraq. As of 1032/1623, Abu'l-Qasem Soltan son of Pir Gheyb Soltan Ostajalu was governor of Javazer and its dependencies.[156]

Jazireh is a Kurdish principality, north of Baghdad. It was conquered by the Safavids around 918/1512. In 1514 Owlash Beyg became its governor. He was the brother of Mohammad Khan Ostajalu, governor of Diyarbekr (q.v.), who until that time also had governed this district. Safavid control over this district came to end when the Ottomans took Diyarbekr in 923/1517.[157]

---

153 Mohammad Ebrahim b. Zeyn al-'Abedin Nasiri, *Dastur-e Shahriyan*. ed. Mohammad Nader Nasiri Moqaddam (Tehran 1373/1995), p. 96.
154 Monshi, *Tarikh*, vol. 2, p. 1313.
155 Yazdi, *Mokhtasar*, p. 40.
156 Monshi, *Tarikh*, vol. 2, p. 1007; Vahid, *Tarikh*, p. 207, 213 (1035 hijri).
157 Bidlisi, *Chereh-Nameh*, vol. 1, p. 296.

Jeyjan va Rahmatabad is a rural district on the right side of the Safid Rud, opposite Rudbar and Rostamabad; it was a dependency of Gilan.

Name	Year	Observations	Source
Amireh Rostam Kohdomi	887-?/1482-?	H Jeyjan va Rahmatabad	Laheji 20-21, 382
Amireh Siyavshah b. Amireh Rostam	920/1514	H Jeyjan va Rahmatabad	Laheji 382

Jonabad, see Gonabad and Tun.

Jorbadeqan or Jorpardeqan[158] district, or Golpeygan, is situated 145 km north-west of Isfahan.[159] It seems that it was often held together with the governorship of Saveh and Aveh (q.v.) and was part of Persian Iraq.

Name	Year	Observations	Source
Heydar Soltan Tarkhan	972/1565	H Saveh, Jorbadeqan	Budaq 141
Soltan Ma'sum Soltan Torkman	985-?/1577-?	H Saveh, Jorbadeqan, Aveh	Qomi 2, 665
Allahverdi Beyg *zargar-bashi*	997-?/1589-?	H Jorpadeqan and dependencies	Monshi 401

Jorjan is either used as a synonym of Astarabad, or as the name of the province that, according to Yazdi, included the following districts: Astarabad (q.v.), Dehestan, Ro'ad (?)[160], Shahrabad, Kabud-Jameh (q.v.), Mowredestan (?), the island of Ham Mardan, and *Qal'eh-ye* Mobarakabad (q.v.).[161] In 994/1586, Mortezaqoli Khan Torkman was dismissed as governor of Astarabad and Jorjan,[162] thus implying that they were not always viewed as identical jurisdictions, as is also clear from Yazdi's description. In 1650 or somewhat later the district of Jorjan was destroyed.[163]

Kabud-Jameh is a district in Astarabad or Jorjan province, adjacent to the districts of Nesa, Abivard, Darun, and Baghbad (q.v.).[164] The Kurdish Chegani tribe had been moved there from Hamadan.[165] In 1038/1628 or earlier Mostadam Soltan Hajjilar Ostajalu was governor of Kabud-

---

158 Yazdi, *Mokhtasar*, p. 110.

159 For its history see Firuz 'Eshraqi, *Golpeygan dar A'ineh-ye Tarikh* (Isfahan, 1383/2004).

160 I have not been able to identify Ro'ad. It may be a copyist's error for Rowghad, which probably was part of Kabud-Jameh, see Masih Dhabehi ed. *Gorgannameh* (Tehran, 1363/1984), pp. 47, 59.

161 Yazdi, *Mokhtasar*, vol. 1, pp. 300-05. The inhabited island of Ham Mardan was situated at a distance of 3 *farsakh* from Astarabad. Boats from Gilan and Mazandaran came to anchor there. Ibid., p. 305.

162 Natanzi, *Naqavat*, pp. 149, 152.

163 Yazdi, *Mokhtasar*, p. 305.

164 Monshi, *Tarikh*, vol. 1, p. 581.

165 Molla Jalal, *Ruznameh*, p. 420; Masih Dhabehi and Manuchehr Setudeh, *Az Astara ta Astarabad*, 10 vols. (Tehran 1354/1975), vol. 6, doc. 17.

Jameh.¹⁶⁶ In 1650 or somewhat later the district was destroyed.¹⁶⁷ However, the district was developed again, for in 1106/1694, and most likely much earlier, it had a governor again.¹⁶⁸

Kah or Qal'eh-ye Kah, Gah, Qal'eh-ye Gah was situated in Seystan and in the early period of the Safavid rule held by the governor of Seystan (q.v.). However, it would appear that under Shah 'Abbas I, and may be earlier, this fort as as well as that of Uq and some other parts of Seystan, was held by Qezelbash emirs, presumably to bolster the defense of Farah against the Uzbegs who then held much of Khorasan (q.v. Herat and Mashhad). This conclusion is suggested by the political situation at the time when Hoseyn Soltan Afshar was governor of Farah, Kah, Uq, and parts.¹⁶⁹

Kalehgir is the name of a Kurdish or Lor tribe as well as of a fort situated at some 6 km from Erevan. It is likely that the district in which the fort was situated was the area allotted to the Kalehgir for their sustenance.

Name	Year	Observations	Source
Qalandar Soltan Kalehgir	1038 or before/1629	H Kalehgir	Monshi 1087
Mehrab Soltan	1109/1698	H Kalehgir	Nasiri 229

Kalhor is the name of a large Kurdish tribe, of which there three branches (Palangan, Dartang and Mahi-dasht) in the 16th century.¹⁷⁰ It was also the name of the tribal district that they inhabited, situated in the province of Hamadan.¹⁷¹ The Kalhors were also to be found elsewhere such as at Meshkin (q.v.). In this case reference is made to the tribe's original lands that were situated between Mahi-dasht and Mandali. See also Dinavar and Sonqor.

Name	Year	Observations	Source
Juheh [or Chuheh] Soltan Tekkelu	931-?/1524-?	H Kalhor	Rumlu 245; Qomi 1, 159; Mozaffar 569
Dhu'l-Feqar b. 'Ali Beyg aka Nakhud Soltan Torkman b. Golabi Beyg Mowselu Torkman	934/1528	H Kalhor; Khtran (Tahmasp)	Rumlu 272; Qomi 1, 174; Monshi 94-95; Shirazi 64; Tahmasp 10-11; Vahid 42
Ghazi Khan Tekkelu	935-?/1529-?	H Kalhor and Mandali	Budaq 68; Qomi 1, 190
Sheikh 'Ali Khan Zanganeh	1077/1667	H Kalhor-Sonqor	Shamlu 2, 20

---

166 Monshi, *Tarikh*, vol. 2, p. 1085.
167 Yazdi, *Mokhtasar*, vol. 1, p. 305.
168 Nasiri, *Dastur*, p. 54.
169 Budaq, *Javaher*, p. 141; Monshi, *Tarikh*, vol. 1, pp. 204, 275.
170 Bidlisi, *Cheref-Nameh*, vol. 2/1, pp. 177-78.
171 See e.g. Monshi, *Tarikh*, vol. 2, p. 651.

Kangarlu is the name of a sub-section of the Ostajalu tribe and possisbly of the district assigned to them for their sustenance in Nakhjevan, which also was governed by the chief of the Kangarlu.

Name	Year	Observations	Source
Maqsud Soltan Kangarlu	1038 or before/1629	H Nakhchevan	Monshi 1085
Mortezaqoli Khan	1107-1111/1667-1700	H Nakhchevan and Kangarlu	Nasiri 96, 281

Kankarkonan is a district of Ardabil, which is a copyist's error for Langarkonan (q.v.). In 1044/1635, Kalb 'Ali Beyg Qajar *davatdar* was governor of Ardabil, Kankarkonan as well as *darugheh* of the Moghan.[172]

Karbal or Karbar is a district in Fars, of which there was a lower and higher one.[173] In 998/1590, Haqqverdi Soltan son of Vali Soltan was governor of Karbal.[174]

Karend is a district situated at some 93 km east of Kermanshah; it had already a Safavid governor in 935/1529, if not earlier. In 942/1535 it was held by Morad Beyg Keroghlu as *teyul*.[175]

Karokh is a district situated at about 40 km from Herat of which it was a dependency. It would seem that this governorship was hereditary since ca. 1600 and held by the chief of the Jamshidi tribe (q.v. Seystan).[176]

Name	Year	Observations	Source
Mir Heydar Soltan Jamshidi	?-1038/1629	H Karokh	Monshi 1087
Nur 'Ali Soltan Jamshidi	1110/1699	H Karokh	Nasiri 281

Karshu is a district situated in Herat province, which, according to a royal edict of 1540, was a governorship.

Kashan is a town and district situated on the road connecting Tehran and Isfahan. It was bounded by Qom in the north and west and by Jushqan and Mahallat in the south. Initially

---

172 Yusof, *Dheyl*, pp. 191, 228 (he died in 1048).
173 It was famous for the cultivation of rice, which was exported to the provinces of Persian Iraq, Fars and Kerman. Yazdi, *Mokhtasar*, pp. 345-46.
174 Molla Jalal, *Ruznameh*, p. 78.
175 Fekete, *Einführung*, pp. 349-51, 379-81.
176 See, e.g., Molla Jalal, *Ruznameh*, pp. 52 ('Abdol-Samad Jamshidi), 347 (Hasan Khors Jamshidi). The Jamshidi tribe originated in Seystan and it chiefs claim to be descended from the Kayani kings of Seystan. For more information see Ludwig W. Adamec, *Historical and Politcal Gazetteer of Afghanistan* 5 vols. (Graz, 1973), vol. 3, pp. 184-86.

governed by governors it was turned into crown domain as of 930/1523 until 985/1576. It became once again crown domain for a short while in 987/1579, probably after the governor had been dismissed.[177] However, soon thereafter governor were in charge of Kashan once again indicating that it was crown domain no longer. In 994/1586 it was once again crown domain, which year was followed by strife and unrest in and around Kashan with two opposing governor. When order had been restored, in 999/1591, Kashan was once again turned into crown domain and as of that time it was governed by viziers until the end of the Safavid period.[178]

Name	Year	Observations	Source
Jalal al-Din Mas'udi Bidgoli	905-910/1500-1505	H Kashan	Aubin 10, n. 100 (Afzal)
Qadi Mohammad Kashi Sadr	910-915/1505-1510	H Kashan + some *mahall* of Persian Iraq	Qomi 1, 98; Rumlu 146; Qazvini 272
Ma'sum Beyg Safavi	957-976?/1550-1568	*Teyuldar* Kashan	Qomi 1, 344
Ebrahim Mirza	984/1576	*Teyuldar* Kashan	Qomi 2, 630, 642
Mohammad Soltan [Khan] Torkman or Mowsellu	985-994/1577-1586	H Kashan; also *mosaheb* Kashan	Qomi 2, 664, 772; Monshi 223, 242, 304, 353; Valeh 1372, 699, 745; Bidlisi 2, 673; Molla Jalal 48
Kashan was made *khasseh* in 994	994/1586	divided among three *mir*s as *teyul*; a *darugheh* was appointed	Qomi 2, 828; Monshi 353
Vali Khan Torkman b. Mohammad Soltan	995/1587	H Kashan – self-appointed. Had been its governor in the past	Valeh 1372, 810; Monshi 353 [Valijan Khan]
'Aliqoli Khan Sharaf	995/1587	H Kashan held by Valijan Khan	Monshi 354; Valeh 1372, 812
Shahverdi Khalifeh	995-?/1587-?	H Kashan	Natanzi 218, 220, 444
	In 996/1588	made into crown domain	Qomi 2, 874
Vali Jan Khan Torkman	997-998/1589-1590	H Kashan ?	Valeh 1372, 810, 812, 824, 826, 823, 836, 840
Morshedqoli Soltan Shamlu brother Esma'ilqoliKhan	998/1580	H Kashan	Valeh 1372, 824,
	In 999/1591	turned into crown domain	Qomi 2, 828
Mohammad Zaman Beyg	1013-?/1605-?	vizier Yazd + Kashan – Ghazi Beyg's brother	Bafqi 3/1, 182-84
Mohammad Sa'id Qomi	1072-?/1662-?	Vizier Kashan	Vahid 731
NN	1115/1703	Vizier	Le Brun 1, 178

---

177 Molla Jalal, *Ruznameh*, p. 48; Monshi, *Tarikh*, vol. 1, p. 242.
178 According to Röhrborn, *Provinzen*, p. 120, Kashan became crown domain as of the beginning of 996/1588, but that is contradicted by the occurrence of a governor in 998/1590 (see Table) as well as the date given by Qomi.

Kaverud, see Gaverud.

Kazerun is a district situated between Shiraz and Bushire.

Name	Year	Observations	Source
Elyas Beyg Dhu'l-Qadr aka Kachal Beyg	909/1504	H Kazerun	Bidlisi 2, 510; Qazvini 268
NN	From 909/1504 until 955/1548	H Kazerun; governed by Kachal Beyg's descendents	Bidlisi 2, 510
Kepek Soltan Afshar	955-?/1548-?	H Kazerun	Shirazi 98; Tahmasp 53
Morad Soltan	998/1590	H Kazerun	Molla Jalal 97
Amir Khan Afshar	999-1003/1591-1595	H Kazerun	Vahid 130
Esma'il Khan Alplu Afshar	1003-?/1595-?	H Kazerun (+Kerman)	Vahid 112, 130
Saru Khan Sahandlu	?-1103/?-1691	H Hamadan + Semnan + Kazerun (Cazran)	Sanson 80

Kelidar or Kelideh was a fort that was part of Esfara'in and the governor of the latter district usually also was governor of the fort.[179]

Name	Year	Observations	Source
Pahlavan Qomari	972/1565	H Kelidar. Qazvini has Klbdd [?]	Bidlisi 2, 607; Qazvini 309
Ighud Beyg Chavoshlu	972-973/1565-1566	H *qal'eh* Kelidar and Esfara'in	Qomi 1, 447

Kerman was one of the major administrative regions of Safavid Persia situated in the south-central part of the country.[180] Its borders are not very well known for the Safavid period and its jurisdiction certainly was larger than just the city and its environs, as Röhrborn submits.[181] It did not include the littoral as that was part of the kingdom of Hormuz. Although the governor of Kerman occasionally encroached on that area, when it was incorporated into the Safavid kingdom it became part of Shiraz (q.v.).[182] The eastern border with Kij-Makran (q.v.) was formed by Khabis, Narmashir and Rudbar.[183] After two early Ostajalu governors, emirs from the Afshar tribe held the office of governor of Kerman for the remainder of the 16th century. This pattern was broken

---

179 Siyaqi, *Fotutat*, p. 464.
180 For its history see Ahmad 'Ali Khan Vaziri Kermani, *Tarikh-e Kerman (Salariyeh)* ed. Ebrahim Bastani-Parizi (Tehran, 1352/1973).
181 Röhrborn, *Provinzen*, p. 12; see e.g. Yazdi, *Mokhtasar*, pp. 351-56, according to whom Kerman included Anar va Piyaz, Bam, Barakuh, Jiroft, Khabis, Sirjan, Shahr-e Babak, Kubnan, Mahan, Nowqat and some forts. See also Moshiri, *Tadhkereh* (Index), which provides additional information.
182 Floor, *Persian Gulf*, p. 195.
183 Nasiri, *Dastur*, p. 68; Safavi, *Majma'*, p. 53.

by ʿAbbas I in 1598, as part of his general policy to break the power of the Qezelbash tribes, when he and his successors thereafter appointed representatives from other tribes to this function. From 1068/1658 to 1105/1694 Kerman was turned into crown domain and was governed by viziers,[184] but from 1694 until the end of the Safavid period governors were in charge of the province again.

Name	Year	Observations	Source
Khan Mohammad Khan Ostajalu	909-920/1503-1514	H Kerman	Bidlisi 2, 511; Qazvini 268; Vaziri 665; Mozaffar 184
Ahmad Soltan Sufi-oghlan [ogli] Ostajalu	920-933/1514-1526	*Vali* or H Kerman	Budaq 62; Qomi 1, 163; Shirazi 63; Qazvini 283
Ahmad Khan	933-935/1526-1529	H Kerman	Abrahams 134
Aqa Kamali Kermani	935/1529	H Kerman	Abrahams 134
Shahqoli Beyg Afshar	935/1529	H Kerman	Abrahams 205
Ahmad Khan Afshar	Shaʿban 936/April 1530	H Kerman	Abrahams 276
Ahmad Soltan Afshar	937-?/1531-?	H Kerman	Qomi 1, 213
Shahqoli Soltan Afshar	945-972/1539-1565	*Vali* Kerman; Vaziri 665 has the year 933, which is not borne out by other sources	Khvandamir 276, 396; Rumlu 428; Budaq 141; Hoseyni 152, 168, 170; Qomi 1, 275, 309, 328, 353, 448; Monshi 99; Shirazi 123; Tahmasp 53
Yaʿqub Beyg [Soltan]*	977/1570	*Vali* or *Mir* Kerman	Rumlu 571; Shamlu 1, 89; Qomi 2, 665
Qoli Beyg Afshar	983/1576	*Vali* Kerman	Budaq 155, 165; Monshi 193-95
Aslan Khan Afshar aka Aslan Soltan Arashlu Afshar	983/1576	H Kerman - was appointed but stayed at court	Valeh 1372, 411; Monshi 218
Mahmud Beyg [Soltan] Afshar	983/1576	H Kerman	Qomi 2, 622; Monshi 213
Vali Soltan [Khan] Afshar	986-997/1578-1589	H Kerman	Valeh 1372, 617, 658, 813; Qomi 2, 665, 729, 753; Monshi 227, 261, 384, 402
Yusof Soltan b. Qoli Soltan Afshar *qurchi-bashi*	994/1586	H Kerman –Yazd self-appointed	Qomi 2, 848
Bektash Khan *qurchi-bashi* b. Vali Khan Afshar	997-998/1587-1589	*Vali* Kerman	Qomi 2, 903-04, 1055; Natanzi 325; Vahid 107; Monshi 418-26; Molla Jalal 73
ʿAbbas Soltan, uncle of Beyktash Khan	998/1589	*Vali* Kerman - killed by Bektash Khan	Monshi 419; Vahid 110

---

184 As of 990/1590, the town itself, as well as some parts of the province of Kerman (such as Khabis), were turned into crown domain for about two years. Qomi, *Kholasat*, vol. 2, p. 913.

Yusof Khan Afshar b. *qurchi-bashi*-ye Afshar	998/begin 1590	*Vali* Kerman	Qomi 2, 904, 912-13; Monshi 425; Molla Jalal 95; Bidlisi 2, 688
Vali Khan Afshar**	Until 1004/1595	H Kerman -2nd time part of Kerman	Monshi 433; Qomi 2, 913, 1078
Esma'il Khan Alplu Afshar	999-1003-?/1591-1595-?	H Kerman - the other part (e.g. Khabis)*** + Kazerun (Vahid)	Monshi 433; Qomi 2, 913, 1079; Vahid 112, 130
Hasan Khan Chavoshlu Ostajalu	1001/1593	shah changed his mind (Monshi); he left to Kerman (Qomi)	Monshi 458; Qomi 2, 1087 [as of 1000/Jan 1592]; Vahid 119, 262
Esma'ilqoli Khan Afshar	1001-?/1593-?	H Kerman	Vahid 118; Röhrborn 37
Ganj 'Ali Khan Zik****	1007-1034/1598-1624	H Kerman; later together with Qandahar	Vahid 215; Monshi 562, 620, 897; Molla Jalal 183
Tahmaspqoli Khan Tarkhan Torkoman	1034-1035/1625-1626	H Kerman	Bardsiri 189; Monshi 1058; Vahid 217
Amir Khan Morabbi Söklen Dhu'l-Qadr b. Rostam Soltan Söklan Dhu'l-Qadr	1035-1042/1625-1636	H Kerman; *mohrdar*, as of 1042 *qurchi-bashi*	Bardsiri 187, 189, 207; Yusof 99; Esfahani 142, 145, 246; Vahid 231
Qara Khan brother of Amir Khan	ca. 1042/1632	H Kerman; more likely that he was his brother's agent	Vaziri 665; Bardsiri 187
Jani Khan Shamlu	1047-1055/1638-1645	H Kerman - *qurchi-bashi*	Bardsiri 207
Ologh [or Abu] Khan brother of Jani Khan	1055/1645-46	H Kerman	Bardsiri 212
Mortezaqoli Khan Bijerlu	1055/1059-1645	H Kerman - *qurchi-bashi*	Bardsiri 209, 215-6; Vahid 475, 504
'Abbasqoli Khan	1062-1068/ 1652-1658	H Kerman	Bardsiri 224, 279; Vahid 642
	From 1068/1652 to 1105/1694	*khasseh* governed by a vizier	Vahid 642
Safiqoli Beyg	1068-1070-?/ 1652-1660-?	Vizier - *shirehchi-bashi*	Bardsiri 287; Vahid 642
Mirza Hatem Beyg	1080/1670	Vizier	Bardsiri 359, 362, 642-3
Mohammadqoli Khan	1105/1694	H Kerman - *qurchi-bashi*	?
Shahverdi Khan	1106/1695	H Kerman	Nasiri 68, 76, 82
Rezaqoli Khan	1107/1696	H Kerman	Nasiri 80
Shahnavaz Khan III aka Gorgin Khan	1111-1121/1700-1709	BB Kerman-Qandahar-Kushk -*sepahsalar*	Khatunabadi 552, 558; Lockhart 46
Khosrow Mirza his nephew	1121-1123/1709-1711	Idem	Khatunabadi 559, 564
'Aliqoli Khan	1123/1711	H Kerman	Khatunabadi 564; Savafi 8

Mohammad Zaman Khan	1123-?/1711-?	H Kerman-Tabriz -sepahsalar	Khatunabadi 564; Savafi 17
Safiqoli Khan	?-/1126/1714	H Kerman	Floor, *Afghan*, 25
Ya'qub Soltan	1126/1714-?	H Kerman	Floor, *Afghan*, 25
Ebrahim Khan	1128/1716	H Kerman	Floor, *Commercial*, 39
Rostam Mirza	1129/1717	H Kerman - *qollar-aghasi*	Floor, *Commercial*, 43
Mohammadqoli Mirza his brother	1131/1719	H Kerman	Floor, *Afghan*, 43
Sobhanverdi Khan	1132/1720	H Kerman	Floor, *Afghan*, 51
Mohammadqoli Khan	1133/1721 appointed	H Kerman	Floor, *Afghan*, 53
Hoseyn Khan Seystani	1133/1721 appointed	H Kerman	Safavi 53; did not come
Shahrokh Khan	1133/1721 replaced by	H Kerman	Floor, *Afghan*, 53 did not come
Rostam Mohammad Khan Sa'dlu	1133/1721	H Kerman	Floor, *Afghan*, 55; Mervi I, 25-26
Hajji Geda 'Ali Khan	1134/1722 later imprisoned	H Kerman	Floor, *Afghan*, 224
Madmudqoli Khan	1135/1723	H Kerman; unknown whether he came	Floor, *Afghan*, 226
Vali Mohammad Khan	1138/1725	H Kerman	Floor, *Afghan*, 228
Bahador Khan	1138 ca./1725	Afghan H Kerman	Vaziri 666
Sayyed Ahmad Khan	1138-1140/1725-August 1728	H Kerman	Floor, *Afghan*, 268, 288-89; Vaziri 666
'Abdollah Khan	1141-1142/1728-1729	[Afghan governor]	Floor, *Afghan*, 289

* Ahmad 'Ali Khan Vaziri, *Tarikh-e Kerman (Salariyeh)* ed. Ebrahim Bastani-Parizi (Tehran, 1352/1973), p. 665, mentions hereabouts the governorship of Sadr al-Din Khan, son of Ma'sum Beyg. Such an appointment in an Afshar fiefdom seems, however, unlikely.

** According to Vaziri, *Tarikh*, p. 665 he was preceded by Farhad Khan, which is not borne out by other sources.

*** A third part of Kerman was transformed into crown land in 999/1590-91. Qomi, *Kholasat*, vol. 2, p. 913.

**** According to Vaziri, *Tarikh*, p. 665 he was succeded by his son 'Ali Morad Khan Zik in 1031/1621, which is not borne out by other sources.

Kermanshahan is a province in Western Persia with the town of the same name at its center. However, it does not seem to have constituted a separate administrative jurisdiction before the reign of Safi I (r. 1629-1642) as I have not been able to find any mention of such a fact prior to that date.[185] Even after that date the occurrence of a governor of Kermanshah is rare and then it seems that it was a kind of dependency of Dinavar, for the same governor who held Dinavar (q.v.) and Kermanshahan in another text is not mentioned as also being in charge of Kermanshahan,

---

185 The town of Kermanshah existed, of course, prior to that period. See, e.g., Bidlisi, *Cherehnameh*, vol. 1, pp. 218-19.

but only of Dinavar.[186] It is only towards the end of Safavid rule that its name is also regularly mentioned[187] and that there is a *beygler-beygi* of Kermanshah (see Table),[188] which in post-Safavid Persia was the norm.

Name	Year	Observations	Source
Shahrokh Soltan	1050/1641	H Dinavar+ Kermanshahan	Yusof 246; Vahid 331
Sheikh 'Ali Khan Zanganeh	1064/1654	H Kermanshahan; see also Dinavar	Vahid 569
Shahverdi Khan Zanganeh b. Sheikh 'Ali Khan	?-1097-1103-?/? -1686-1692-?	BB Kermanshahan	Khatunabadi 547; Sanson 80; Hedges 1, 216
Mortezaqoli Beyg; later Mehr 'Ali Beyg	1107/1696	deputy H Kolhar, Sonqor + Kermanshahan	Nasiri 124, 129, 133
N.N.	1108/1697	H Kermanshahan	Qarakhani doc. 6

Khabushan nowadays called Quchan, although it was also referred to as such occasionally in Safavid times, such as in the case of Budaq Soltan Chegani, who was reported to be governor of Quchan on one occasion, but more often as governor of Khabushan.[189] It is situated between the Turkestan border in the north, Dargaz and Mashhad in the east, Nishapur and Esfara'in in the south and by Bojnord in the west.

Name	Year	Observations	Source
Pahlavan Qomari [?]	972/1564	H Khabushan – Uzbeg governor	Rumlu 550; Bidlisi 2, 607
Ighuth Beyg Chavoshlu Ostajalu	972/1565	H *qal'eh-ye* Khabushan + Nishapur	Shirazi 123; Qazvini 309
Oghlan Budaghi Chegani	985-995/1577-1578	H Khabushan+ some districts of Khorasan	Monshi 141, 227, 257, 364
Budaq Khan Chegani	996-997/1579-1580	H Khabushan	Valeh 1372, 606, 836, Monshi 402; Bidlisi 2, 190-91, 686; Qomi 2, 674
Hasan 'Ali Soltan and Hoseyn 'Ali Soltan, sons of Budaq Khan	997-?/1580-?	H Khabushan	Vahid 107; Monshi 2, [579]
Gorgin Soltan	1039/1628	H Chamesh-gezek tribe + Khabushan	Monshi 1088

---

186 Vahid, *Tarikh*, p. 331 (governor of the *il-e* Kalhor-Zanganeh and of Dinavar).

187 Nasiri, *Dastur*, pp. 124, 129, 132-34, 163.

188 But in a document dated 1108/1697 only the governor (*hakem*) of Kermanshahan is referred to. Hasan Qarakhani, "Boq'eh-ye Ayyub Ansari dar takab- faramin-e shahan-e Safavi dar bareh mowqufat-e an," *Barrasiha-ye Tarikhi* 9 (1353/1974), doc. 6.

189 Qomi, *Kholasat*, vol. 2, p. 674.

Owtar Khan	?-1059/?-1650	H Khabushan	Shamlu 1, 351, 498-99, 504-523
Safiqoli Khan b. Dhu'l-Feqar Khan	1059-1060/1650-1651	H Khabushan	Shamlu 2, 16
Zaman Beyg *jabbehdar-bashi* b. Kalb 'Ali Khan	1060-?/1651-?	H Khabushan	Shamlu 2, 16

Khalkhal district, situated between the Aras and the Qezel Uzun, was part of the Azerbaijan region, although sometimes its governorship was combined with that of Gaskar, which was part of Gilan. More often the combination with other governorships in Azerbaijan is found.

Name	Year	Observations	Source
Nazar Soltan Ostajalu	972/1565	H Soltaniyeh, Tarom and Khalkhal	Budaq 141
Amir Gheyb Beyg Ostajalu	974/1567	H Soltaniyeh + Khalkhal	Tatavi 663
Pireh Mohammad Khan Ostajalu	985-?/1577-?	H Ardabil, Tarom, Khalkhal	Qomi 2, 664
Amireh Siyavosh Gaskari	988-1002/1580-1593	H Gaskar + Khalkhal - in 1002 temporarily replaced by his brother	Monshi 267, 449-51, 460; Molla Jalal 114; 1118, 134; Vahid 115-16, 119, 128, 201

Kharzavil is a dependency of the district of Kuhdom.[190] In 995/1587, Pir Gheyb Khan Ostajalu was governor of Tarom and Kharzavil.[191]

Khaveh is a small district in Lorestan, near Khorramabad, of which, in 984/1576, Shah Rostam 'Abbasi was the governor.[192]

Khorkhoreh or Khurkhureh is situated north-west of Sanandaj. It is not known when Khorkhoreh was created as a separate jurisdiction, but by the end of the 17th century it seems to have been in existence for some time already. Nowadays it is known as Gol Tappeh.

Name	Year	Observations	Source
'Ali Soltan	1106/1695	H Khorkhoreh	Nasiri 81
Jahangir Soltan	1109/1698	H Khorkhoreh	Nasiri 234

Khoy is a town, from which its district takes its name, situated between Turkey in the west, Maku in the north, Marand and Tabriz in the east, and Salmas in the south. Its governor often also held the governorship of Salmas.

---

190 Vahid, *Tarikh*, p. 128.
191 Qomi, *Kholasat*, vol. 2, p. 817; Monshi, *Tarikh*, vol. 1, p. 332.
192 Valeh, *Khold*, p. 411.

Name	Year	Observations	Source
Malek Beyg Khoy'i	934-941/1528-1535	H Khoy	Dickson 134, 140; Astarabadi 64; Abrahams 202
Hajji Beyg Donboli	955/1548	H Khoy	Qomi 1, 336; Rumlu 438
Emamqoli Beyg b. Badr Khan Ostajalu	?-981/?-1574	H Khoy + Salmas	Qomi 1, 581
Mostafa Soltan Ostajalu, his brother	981-?/1574-?	H Khoy + Salmas	Qomi 1, 581
Deli Budaq Rumlu	Before 985?/1577	H Khoy	Monshi 140
Hoseyn Khan Soltan Shamlu Khanuslu	985-986/1577-1578	H Khoy + Salmas	Qomi 2, 664, 680; Monshi 231
Mahmud Beyg Rumlu	986/1578	H Khoy + Salmas	Bidlisi 2, 647
Ghazi Beyg	1012-?/1604-?	H Khoy and Salmas	Monshi 642
Shahnazar Soltan	1019/1610	H Khoy	Molla Jalal 382

Khushab, which also occurs in the bastardized form of Khushat, is a district situated in Kurdestan. In 1005/1596, 'Abdollah Beyg Mahmudi was its governor.[193]

Khvaf is situated 110 km east of Torbat-e Heydari (Khorasan). It is bounded on the north by Bakharz, on the south by Qa'en, on the east by Afghanistan, and on the west by Tabas. Its main fortification was the Fort of Bakharz, which was built on top of a mountain 2 to 3,000 ells high and only accessible via a footpath.[194] It would seem that the governor of Khvaf usually also held jurisdiction over another district or districts, for generally Khvaf and Bakharz were held by the same governor. Also, at times Khvaf did not belong to the province of Herat, but rather to that of Mashhad, the other part of Khorasan, in which case it was often jointly held by the governor of Damghan (q.v.). For much of the first four decades of the sixteenth century Khvaf was held by Uzbeg governors until 944/1538.

Name	Year	Observations	Source
Qazaq Soltan	955/1548	H Bakharz	Khvandamir 415
Nazar Soltan Asayesh-oghlu	972/1565	H Khvaf and Bakharz	Budaq 141
Vali Khan Sharaflu Ostajalu	985/1577	H Khvaf only	Monshi 139, 227; Valeh 1372, 409
Morshedqoli Khan Yakan Ostajalu b. Shahqoli	985-989/1577-1581	H Khvaf – Bakharz (or Makharz) Zaveh, Mahvelat	Monshi 227, 293-95; Bidlisi 2, 651; Molla Jalal 43; Qomi 2, 665
Hamzeh Khan b. 'Abdollah Khan Ostajalu	986/1578	H Khvaf + Bakharz; rival governor	Molla Jalal 47

---

193 Vahid, *Tarikh*, p. 166; Monshi, *Tarikh*, vol. 2, p. 721 (Khushat).
194 Bidlisi, *Cheref-Nameh*, vol. 2, p. 570.

Shahqoli Soltan Qarenjeh-oghlu	989/1581	H *qasabeh* Khvaf, Bakharz, *velayat-e* Torbat, Badghis, Mahvelat	Shamlu 1, 123
Ganj 'Ali Khan	?-999/?-1591	H Khvaf and Bakharz	Qomi 2, 1069
Mehrab Khan Qajar	?-1007/?-1599	H Khvaf-Bakharz, Tun-Junabad	Monshi 576, 620-21; Siyaqi 479; Molla Jalal 184
Shahrokh Soltan Zanganeh	1039-?/1630-?	H Khvaf	Vahid 231
Zaman Khan	1052-1055/1643-1645	H Khvaf	Vahid 347
Dust 'Ali Khan Zanganeh	1055-?/1645-?	H Khvaf-e Khorasan as *eqta'*; Khvaf + Bakharz	Shamlu 1, 292, 423
	from 1067/1657 until 1072/1662	crown domain	see Semnan
Afrasiyab Soltan	1107/1696	H Khvaf	Nasiri 158
Rostam Khan Zanganeh	1109-1110/1698-1700	H Khvaf + Jam	Nasiri 213, 269

Khvansar is a town and district situated to the north-west of Isfahan and to the east of Golpeygan. In 1066/1655, Khalil Khan Bakhtiyari was its governor.[195]

Khvar, see Semnan.

Kij-Makran, a large province situated in the south-east of the country bounded in the south by the Gulf of Oman, in the west by Biyaban district, in the north by Seystan and in the east by Kalat. During the period of 984-985/1576-1577 and from 1017-1031/1608-1621 Safavid hold over the province was transitory, while from 1030-1031/1621-1622 until 1077-1105/1667-1694 the rulers of Makran were tributary to the Safavids. To ensure that taxes would be paid the Safavids installed a *darugheh* at Bon Fahl (q.v.) in 1018/1609.[196] However, the province remained a difficult place to control and the failed military campaign of the 1670s is emblematic of the nature of Safavid control, or rather the lack thereof, over that area.[197] Under Shah Soltan Hoseyn (r. 1694-1722) the province was no longer under Safavid control and constituted a permanent source of Baluch incursions into Safavid territory, in particular Kerman and the littoral.[198]

Name	Year	Observations	Source
Malek Dinar	935/1528	*Vali* Kich va Makran	Qomi 1, 192; Monshi 862

---

195 Vahid, *Tarikh*, pp. 602-03.
196 Molla Jalal, *Ruznameh*, p. 375. For the information that the Safavids had about the region see Ibid., pp. 371-72; Yazdi, *Mokhtasar*, pp. 373-75 and for the ignorance of the Makranis about the Safavids, see Monshi, *Tarikh*, vol. 2, p. 862.
197 See Floor, *Persian Gulf*, pp. 275-76; see for the situation two decades later Nasiri, *Dastur*, pp. 277-78.
198 See Floor, *Commercial*, pp. 39f; Ibid., *Afghan*, pp. 22, 25, 27, 30, 37.

| Malek Shams al-Din b. Malek Dinar | ?-1018-1022/?-1609-1613 | H Kij-Makran | Monshi 861; Molla Jalal 372 |
| Malek Mirza | 1022-1043-?/1613-1634-? | *Vali* Makran | Valeh 1380, 161-63; Monshi 957; Yusof 132; Khatunabadi 512 |

Kirkuk is a town and district in Iraq, which was held by the Safavids during two different time periods, when they also held Baghdad and some other parts of Iraq. The first period was between 1508 and 1534 and the second period was between 1623 and 1639. The dates for these two time periods probably are the same for Safavid rule at Kirkuk.

Name	Year	Observations	Source
Sufiyan Khalifeh	936/1529	H Daquq and Kirkuk	Budaq 68
Qasem Soltan Inanlu Afshar	1033/1624	H Kirkuk-Shahr-e zur	Vahid 207

Kojur, a district in Mazandaran consisting of the valley of Pul and Kojur adjoining the district of Kalarustaq to the east (see Rostamdar).

Malek Ashraf b. Taj al-Dowleh	?-911/?-1506	H Rostamdar-Kojur	Shirazi 138
Malek Ka'us b. Malek Ashraf	911-947/1506-1541	H Rostamdar-Kojur	Qomi 1, 140; Hoseyni, 246; Shirazi 138
Malek Jahangir b. Malek Ka'us	947-950/1541-1544	H Rostamdar - Kojur	Shirazi 138-39; Rumlu 386
Malek Kayumarth b. Malek Ka'us	950-963/1544-1556	H Rostamdar-Kojur	Shirazi 139
Malek Jahangir b. Malek Ka'us	963-975/1556-1568	H Rostamdar-Kojur	Shirazi 139
Malek Soltan Mohammad b. Jahangir; aka Malek-e divaneh	975-997 [?]/1568-1589	H Rostamdar + Kojur	Monshi 503, 521; Bidlisi 2, 632-33
Malek Jahangir b. Malek Soltan Mohammad	997-1006/1589-1598	H Rostamdar + Kojur; here ended the line of this dynasty	Monshi 399, 503
Allahqoli Beyg Qapana-oghlu Qajar	1006-?/1598-?	H Kojur - *qurchi-bashi*	Monshi 535

Kolbar is a district in Mazandaran near Ashraf, of which Mir Morad Kolbari was governor in 1004/1595.[199]

Kuchesfahan, a district in Gilan, between Resht and the Safidrud, whose ownership was a bone of contention between the governors of West and East Gilan (q.v.) throughout the sixteenth century.

---

199 Molla Jalal, *Ruznameh*, p. 143.

Name	Year	Observations	Source
Shahqoli Qarancheh Ostajalu	989/1582	H Kuchesfehan	Monshi 267
'Ali Soltan Chepelu	1006/1598	H Kuchesfehan	Fumeni 170

Kuhdom, also Kuhtom or Kohdom, is a district in Gilan, situated on the road between Qazvin and Resht at 25 km south of the latter. It was one of the four major administrative subdivisions of Gilan (q.v.). It would seem that until 1640 the governorship was held by local notables and thereafter the first Qezelbash governor was appointed. This seems to have been an exception rather than the beginning of a trend as in 1684 a hereditary governor is mentioned.

Name	Year	Observations	Source
Hoseyn Khan Shamlu	932-36	H Kohdom + Herat	Fumeni 139-45
Amireh Hatem	941-949-?/1535-1543-?	H Kutom; Kohdom	Hoseyni 131, 223; Fumeni 19-20, 22-23, 26-27
Mirza Kamran	975-988/1568-1580	H Kutom; Kohdom	Monshi 111, 264; Qomi 1, 471, 474; Rumlu 561
Hoseyn Khan Gilani	1003-1024/1595-1615	H Kuhdom	Monshi 492, 892; Fumeni 145; Vahid 128, 189
Mohammadi Khan Gowhari	1024-1042/1615-1633	H Kuhdom; replaced by his brother	Yusof 16, 119; Valeh 1380, 19, 155; Fumeni 269, 275, 277, 282
Mohammad Mo'men Khan	1042-?/1633-?	H Kuhdom	Yusof 119; Valeh 1380, 19, 155
Kalb 'Ali Khan Afshar	1055/1645	H Farah + Kuhdom	Shamlu 1, 292
Mohammadi Khan	1095/1684	Hereditary governor of Rudbar and Chotüm	Kaempfer 67

Kuhgiluyeh province was held by governors of the Afshar tribe, during much of the sixteenth century, who also sometimes held governorships in Dezful (q.v.) and Shushtar (q.v.), two districts which militarily were subordinate to the governor of Kuhgiluyeh. The Afshars also held Dowraq (q.v.) in 'Arabestan for some time, until the *vali* of Hoveyzeh took control over that area.[200] From 1005-1042/1596-1632 Kuhgiluyeh was held by Allahverdi Khan and his son Emamqoli Khan (together with Fars, Lar, Bahrain, and the Persian Gulf littoral), but when the latter was executed in 1042/1632, Kuhgiluyeh was once again held as a separate jurisdiction. At the end of the Safavid period the province allegedly included the districts of Bahrain, Bandar 'Abbas, Dashtestan, Dowraq, Sarvestan, Sumeyram, Zeybadat, and 'Arabestan. However, this is probably due to a fluke, when 'Ali Mardan Beyg was governor, who, in 1696, had been charged with the invasion of Oman and as such had been given authority to raise troops and provisions in those jurisdictions.[201] The same holds for the additional districts mentioned by Röhrborn in 'Arabestan, for, as is clear

---

200 Monshi, *Tarikh*, vol. 2, p. 951.
201 Floor, *Persian Gulf*, pp. 42-43.

from the situation in Dezful and Shushtar, the governor of Kuhgiluyeh held no position there. Only after 1694, when the political situation in Hoveyzeh was fluid and uncertain, the governor of Kuhgiluyeh had some measure of influence there due to his armed support for the occupation of Basra (1694-1700).[202]

Name	Year	Observations	Source
Alvand Soltan [Khan] Afshar	935-942/1529-1536	H Kuhgiluyeh	Qomi 1, 200, 235; Monshi 671; Shirazi 78, 84; Qazvini 289
Mohammadi Beyg b. Hasan Soltan grandson of Mansur Beyg Afshar	942-?/1536-?	H Kuhgiluyeh	Shirazi 84
Mahmud Khan Afshar	955/1548	H Kuhgiluyeh	Hoseyni 168; Qomi 1, 328; Monshi 73; Shirazi 98; Tahmasp 53
Rostam Khan Afshar	?-965/?-1558	H Kuhgiluyeh	Qomi 1, 394; Bidlisi 2, 594; Qazvini 303
Khalil Khan Afshar	984-988/1576-1580	*Vali* Kuhgiluyeh	Rumlu 634; Monshi 140, 227, 261, 273; Valeh 1372, 411, 416; Qomi 1, 475, 2, 660, 695, 701, 714
Eskander Khan	988-991-?/1580-1583-?	*Vali* Kuhgiluyeh – nephew of Khalil Khan	Valeh 1372, 643; Shamlu 1, 110; Monshi 140, 274; Molla Jalal 60; Vahid 95
Shahqoli Khan b. Khalil Khan Afshar	997-998/1589-1590	H Kuhgiluyeh	Monshi 409
Hasan Beyg [Khan] b. 'Abdol-Latif Afshar	998-1002/1590-1594	H Kuhgiluyeh	Monshi 409, 432, 502; Molla Jalal 78, 129, 129-30; Vahid 130
Amir Khan Afshar	1003-1005/1595-1597	H Kuhgiluyeh	Monshi 503, 524; Vahid 130
Allahverdi Khan	1005/1597	H Kuhgiluyeh	Monshi 525
Lachin Beyg	1006/1598	H Kuhgiluyeh	Siyaqii 441; Molla Jalal 165
Hamdan Beyg	1006-1012/1598-1604	H Kuhgiluyeh	Siyaqii 442; Molla Jalal 165, 244
Emamqoli Khan	?-1041/?-1632	H Kuhgiluyeh -with Fars	Yusof 267
Oghurlu Khan b. Mehdiqoli Khan Shamlu	1041/1632	BB Kuhgiluyeh	Yusof 267; Vahid 250
Naqdi Khan Shamlu	1041-1048/1632-1639	BB Kuhgiluyeh	Yusof 117, 215, 227; Vahid 250, 274, 290, 321
Zeynal Beyg [Khan] b. Naqdi Khan	1048-1055/1639-1645	BB Kuhgiluyeh	Shamlu 1, 285; Vahid 410

202 On the occupation of Basra and the role of the Kuhgiluyeh governor see Floor, *Persian Gulf*, pp. 578-84.

Siyavush Khan	1055-1059/1645-1649	H and BB Kuhgiluyeh - *qollar-aghasi*	Vahid 411, 475, 504, 745; Shamlu 1, 288
Allahverdi Khan	1066-1073/1656-1663	BB Kuhgiluyeh - *qollar-aghasi*; *shekar-bashi*	Vahid 611, 636, 744-75
Pir Budaq Khan Pornak Torkoman	?-1074/?-1664	BB Kuhgiluyeh	Röhrborn 36
[Mohammad] Zaman Khan b. Qazaq Khan	1074-?/1664-?	BB Kuhgiluyeh	Shamlu 2, 14; Röhrborn 36
Hoseyn 'Ali Khan Zanganeh b. Sheikh 'Ali Khan	1101-?/1690-?	BB Kuhgiluyeh	Khatunabadi 547
Safiqoli Beyg	1103-?/1692-?	H Kuhgiluyeh; former *nazer-e boyutat*	Khatunabadi 549
'Ali Mardan Khan	1106-1108/1695-1697	*Vali* Kuhgiluyeh	Nasiri 95, 152-54, 181, 183
Mohammad 'Ali Khan	1109-?/1698-?	*Vali* Kuhgiluyeh	Nasiri 257
Aslan Khan Daghestani	1114-1120/1702-1708	BB Kuhgiluyeh	Shushtari 66
Safiqoli Beyg	1122-1129/1710-1717	H Kuhgiluyeh; see also Shiraz - *qollar-aghasi*	Khatunabadi 560; Floor, *Afghan*, 30
Geda 'Ali Beyg	1129/1717	H Kuhgiluyeh	VOC 1879, Isfahan-Gamron (22/07/1717), f 271; Floor, *Afghan*, 30 (Geyth 'Ali)
Lotf 'Ali Khan	1130/October 1717-December 1720	H Kuhgiluyeh	VOC 1913 (31/03/18), f. 499; Floor, *Afghan*, 31; Safavi 31
Bijan Khan	1135-1137/1723-1724	H Kuhgiluyeh	Floor, *Afghan*, 201; Shushtari 70
Qalich Qurchi-ye Safi Mirza	1141-1142/1729-1730	H Kuhgiluyeh	Shushtari 87
Mohammad 'Ali Khan b. Aslan Khan	1142-1143/1730-1731	H Kuhgiluyeh	Shushtari 87

Kurdestan or **Ardalan**, a region that stretches from Anatolia in the north to Lorestan and the plains of the Tigris in the south, and, as its name implies, referred to the region that was inhabited mostly by Kurds. Then as now the region was divided among more than one state. The Ardalan family, who held sway over part of Kurdestan when the Safavids rose to power, had ruled that area since 1168 CE and constituted one of several Kurdish principalities that controlled an area stretching from the Caucasus to S. Iraq, from Kermanshah to Diyarbekr. The Ardalans at the height of their power held sway over Zalm, Gol 'Anbar, Shamiran, Hawar, Siman, Dawdan, Nafsud, Hashli, Palangan, Hasanabad, Esfandabad, Marivan, Saqqez, Tanura, Avraman, Kolos, Neshkash, Javanrud, Sarutchek, Qaradagh, Shahr-e Bazar, Alan, Arbil, Harir, 'Emadiyeh and Ravanduz, although the extent of this territory fluctuated and changed as a result of political and military developments. Sorkhab Beyg, for example, controlled at the end of his rule Sanandaj, Hashli, Soleymaniyeh, and parts of Shahrizur, while he moved his capital to Marivan.[203] However, in one Safavid chronicle he is simply referred to as the governor of Hasanabad and Palangan,

---

203 Bidlisi, *Cheref-Nameh*, vol. 1, p. 84.

which was probably due to the author's focus of attention on the control of his two main forts, which were disputed at that time by his brother. The rulership of the Ardalan chiefs did not always go unchallenged, for the governing of Ardalan territory was shared among family members, who sometimes chafed at the control over the Ardalan chief. The Soltan Mahmud mentioned by Hoseyn b. 'Abd al-Samad al-'Ameli as governor of the 'Kurdish kingdom' in 1548 must have been such a family member, probably in charge of Fort Palangan or some other border fort.[204] This family-based system of government provided an entry for Safavid influence and eventually for more control. Under Begeh Beyg (1494-1535), the Ardalans did not acknowledge Safavid overlordship, while they also remained aloof of the Ottomans, while his brother Sorkhab even gave refuge to the rebel Elqas Mirza for a while.[205] Things changed towards the end of the rule of Sorkhab, whose position was threatened and he therefore twice appealed to the Safavids to asssist him against his brother and once against encroachment of the Ottomans on his territory.[206] As a result Hoseyn Beyg Fath-ohglu was appointed *teyuldar* of Sonqor and Dinavar in 965/1558.[207] Gheyb Soltan Rumlu was even appointed governor of Kurdestan and Lorestan in 975/1567 by Shah Tahmasp I, while Ahmad Khalifeh-ye Vafadar-e Rumlu became governor of Sonqor in that year, thus indicating that Sonqor and Dinavar had been separated from Kurdestan.[208] It is therefore no surprise that at the end of Tahmasp I's reign in 984/1576 unnamed parts of Lorestan and Kurdestan were considered to part of the Safavid kingdom (*ba'zi az Lorestan va Kurdestan [...] mamalek-e mahruseh*). Some of these lands must have been Sonqor and Dinavar.

Sorkhab also considered it politic to have his son Soltan 'Ali Beyg marry the daughter of Mantasha Soltan Ostajalu, a powerful Qezelbash emir (perhaps also because the Ostajalus are believed to have been of Kurdish origin), who became the mother of Timur Khan and Halow Khan. His son Besat Beyg also appealed to the Safavids for help against his brother Eskander, and Esma'il II sent troops to assist him. After the capture of Palangan, Solaq Hoseyn Tekkelu, a Safavid governor, as of 985/1577 held the province of Sonqor and Dinavar and he is even referred to as the governor of Dinavar and Kurdestan.[209] It would seem that henceforth the Safavids indeed kept control over this area for as of 994/1586 Shahverdi Khalifeh was the governor of Dinavar and Sa'dabad as well as of some parts of the Solagh district.[210] In 1017/1609, 'Abbas I even appointed Mostafa Pasha (an Ottoman governor who had defected and whom he had appointed *amir al-omara* of the rebellious Jalalis) as *teyuldar* of Sonqor, thus providing him with a basis for carrying out attacks on the Ottomans.[211] Sonqor and Dinavar remained under direct Safavid control although as of 1048/1639 its governorship became hereditary in the Kurdish Zanganeh family.

Although reduced in size, Ardalan Kurdestan proper thus remained relatively independent of the Safavids, until in 1611 Shah 'Abbas I marched with an army against the Ardalans. At the

---

204 Devin J. Stewart, "An episode in the 'Amili migration to Safavid Iran: Husayn b. 'Abd al-Samad al-'Amili's travel account," *Iranian Studies* 39, p. 489. Similarly, other persons who are sometimes reported to be governor of Kurdestan in effect were not and only were governor of some part of Kurdestan other than that held by the Ardalans. See, e.g. the case of Dowlatyar Pazuki and that of Juji Soltan. Shamlu, *Qesas*, vol. 1, p. 131 (q.v. Sojas); Valeh, *Khold*, p. 275.
205 Shirazi, *Takmelat*, p. 102; Bidlisi, *Cheref-Nameh*, vol. 2, p. 584 (in 956); Qazvini, *Tarikh*, p. 299 (in 955).
206 Rumlu, *Ahsan*, pp. 445 (in 957/1550), 484 (in 961/1554).
207 Qomi, *Kholasat*, vol. 1, p. 394.
208 Qomi, *Kholasat*, vol. 1, p. 471.
209 Qomi, *Kholasat*, vol. 2, p. 665; Rumlu, *Ahsan*, p. 643.
210 Qomi, *Kholasat*, vol. 2, p. 828.
211 Monshi, *Tarikh*, vol. 2, p. 781.

last moment an invasion of Kurdestan was avoided, but Halow Khan had to send his oldest son Khan Ahmad to court as a hostage. The latter, when he returned to Kurdestan usurped his father's position and was confirmed by 'Abbas I. By joining the Safavid cause Khan Ahmad was able to extend his territory to include Ravanduz, 'Emadiyeh, Mosul and Kirkuk. He made Hasanabad his capital. When Shah Safi I blinded his only son Khan Ahmad rebelled and declared himself to be king and moved his residence to Mosul and Kirkuk, which at that time had a Safavid governor, whom he expelled.[212] Khan Ahmad struck money and appointed governors for Kermanshah, Hamadan, Sonqor, Nehavand, Lorestan, Garrus and Orumiyeh. Khan Ahmad was defeated in 1636 and he died in that same year. At the eve of the battle, Shah Safi I had appointed his cousin Soleyman Khan, who had been at court, as governor of Kurdestan, but on condition of the destruction of the impregnable forts of Hasanabad, Zalm, Marivan and Palangan. The new governor chose Senneh or Sanandaj as his new capital. The 1639 treaty of Zohab meant that Western Kurdestan became Ottoman territory, which signified for the Ardalans the loss of the western part of Avraman, Shahrezur, Qaradagh, Qezelja, Sarutchek, Kirkuk, Rawandez, 'Emadiyeh, Koy and Harir. Henceforth Kurdestan was limited to the area of Senneh, Marivan, Avraman, Baneh, Saqqeh and Javanrud as well as part of the Jaf confederacy. Thus the treaty also meant the end of the old Kurdish principalities of Shahrezur and Dinavar. Thereafter the independence of the Ardalan *vali*s also decreased, who were appointed and dismissed at the shah's pleasure, one of them even was beheaded (Khosrow Khan in 1682). Also, Kurdish problems were henceforth not resolved in Kurdestan, but by appealing to Isfahan. Shah Soleyman and Shah Soltan Hoseyn even appointed non-Kurdish governors, whose administration was a total failure, one even being chased from Kurdestan. As of 1715 members of the Ardalan family therefore were henceforce appointed to the post of governor of Kurdestan until the mid-19th century. By the end of the Safavid period the province of Kurdestan included the following administrative jurisdictions: Avraman, Baneh, Bakhtiyari, Javanrud, Khorkhoreh, and Lorestan-e Feyli.[213]

Name	Year	Observations	Source
Begeh Beyg Ardalan	900-942/1495-1536	*Vali* of Kurdestan	Hoseyni 174; Bidlisi 1, 108
Ma'mun Beyg b. Begeh Beyg	942-945/1536-1539	H Kurdestan	Bidlisi 1, 108
Soltan 'Ali Betlich	946/1540	H Kurdestan	Rumlu 380
Sorkhab Beyg b. Ma'mun Beyg Ardalan	946-975/1540-1568	H Kurdestan	Rumlu 445, 484; Bidlisi 1, 109
Gheyb Soltan Ostajalu	975/1568	H Kurdestan + Lorestan	Qomi 1, 471
Soltan 'Ali Beyg b. Sorkhab Beyg Ardalan	975-978/1568-1571	H Kurdestah; succeeded by his brother	Bidlisi 1, 111; Ardalan. *Les Kurdes*, 20
Besat Beyg b. Sorkhab Beyg Ardalan	978-986/1571-1578	H Kurdestan	Bidlisi 1, 112; Ardalan. *Les Kurdes*, 20
Sulagh Hoseyn Tekkelu	984 or 985/1576 or 1577	H tribes of Kurdestan and some areas in Hamadan	Monshi 213
Eskandar Ardalan	986/1578	*Vali qal'eh-ye* Palangan	Rumlu 640

---

212 Qasem Soltan Enanlu Afshar, governor of Kerkuk-Shahr-e zur in 1033/1624. Vahid, *Tarikh*, p. 207.
213 Sherin Ardalan. *Les Kurdes Ardalan entre la Perse et l'Empire ottoman* (Paris, 2004).

228 OFFICIALS IN SAFAVID IRAN, A THIRD MANUAL: COMMENTARY

Timur Khan Soltan 'Ali Beyg Ardalan	986-998/1578-1590	H Hasanabad + Palangan	Bidlisi 1, 112; Monshi 141; Valeh 1372, 411 (Talankan)
Halow Khan b. Soltan 'Ali Beyg Ardalan	998-1026/1590-1617	Succeeded by his son	Bidlisi 1, 113; Monshi 867, 927, 1070
Khan Ahmad Khan b. Halow Khan Ardalan	1026-1046/1617-1637	*Amir al-omara* Kurdestan, BB Shahezur; BB Kurdestan; h Ardalan succeeded by his son	Monshi 927, 1019, 1047, 1070, 1086; Yusof 156, 189, 288; Vahid 328; Astarabadi 254 [1045]
Soleyman Khan Ardalan	1046-1067/1637-1657	H Ardalan and/or BB Kurdestan, succeeded by his oldest son	Yusof 289; Vahid 328, 625-26; Astarabadi 254 (Amir Soltan; 1045)
Kalb 'Ali Khan Ardalan	1067-1089/1657-1678	BB Kurdestan	Vahid 626
Khosrow Khan Ardalan	1091-1093/1680-1682	BB Kurdestan	Ardalan, *Les Kurdes*, 21
Timur Khan Ajarlu Shamlu	1093-1099/1682-1688	*Zabet* Kurdestan	Ardalan, *Les Kurdes*, 21
Khan Ahmad Khan II Ardalan	1099-1105/1688-1694	BB Kurdestan	Nasiri 128; Ardalan, *Les Kurdes*, 21
Mohammad Khan Ardalan	1105-1113/1694-1702	BB Kurdestan	Nasiri 20, 128, 133, 225; Ardalan, *Les Kurdes*, 21
Mohammad Khan Gorji	1113-1116/1702-1705	BB Kurdestan	Ardalan, *Les Kurdes*, 21
Hasan 'Ali Khan b. Mohammad Mo'men Khan the grand vizier	1116-1118/1705-1707	BB Kurdestan	Ardalan, *Les Kurdes*, 21
Hoseyn 'Ali Khan b. Mohammad Mo'men Khan the grand vizier	1118-1120/1707-1709	BB Kurdestan	Ardalan, *Les Kurdes*, 21
Key Khosrow Beyg	1120-1123/1709-1711	BB Kurdestan	Ardalan, *Les Kurdes*, 21
'Abbasqoli Khan Ardalan	1122-1136/1710-1724	BB Kurdestan	Ardalan, *Les Kurdes*, 21
'Aliqoli Khan Ardalan	1129-1132/1717-1720	BB Kurdestan	Ardalan, *Les Kurdes*, 21
Sobhanverdi Beyg Ardalan	1142-1162/1730-1749	BB Kurdestan	Ardalan, *Les Kurdes*, 21

Kuri, see Guri.

Kurluk is a governorship only mentioned by Nasiri's *Alqab*. It was probably situated in Azerbaijan.

Kushk probably is the district now known as Kushk-e Nakhud, located at some 40 miles west of Qandahar. Gorgin Khan was governor between 1114/1703 and 1120/1708 and he was succeeded there by Khosrow Mirza in 1121/1709. Together with Qandahar it was governed by the governor of Kerman during that period.[214]

---

214 Khatunabadi, *Vaqaye'*, pp. 552, 558-59.

Kusuyeh or Fort Kusuyeh was the residence of the governor of Ghuriyan (q.v.).[215]

Name	Year	Observations	Source
[Sufi] Vali Khalifeh Rumlu	972/1565	H Kusuyeh + Ghuriyan	Shirazi 123-24; Bidlisi 2, 608
Mozaffar Soltan Asayesh-oghlu Ostajalu	?-985/?-1577	H Kusuyeh + Ghuriyan	Valeh 1372, 409
Khosh-khabar Khan Shamlu b. Aghzivar	985/1577	H Kusuyeh	Monshi 227
Hajji Kutval Chaghatay	?-989/?-1581	H Kusuyeh	Shamlu 1, 122
Ganj 'Ali Khan	989/1581	H Kusuyeh	Shamlu 1, 122

Lahejan a district in Gilan, bounded in the west by Resht, in the south and south-west by Rudbar, in the south-east by Rudsar and in the north-east by Langerud. The name *Lahejan* was often used as a synonym for Gilan-e biyeh-pish (q.v.).

Name	Year	Observations	Source
Kar Kiya Mirza 'Ali	?-911/?-1506	*H Lahejan*	Mozaffar 239
Kiya Soltan Ahmad	925/1519	*Vali* Lahejan	Valeh 1372, 273
Soltan Hasan	943/1537	*Vali* Lahejan	Hoseyni 131, 207, 214-15, 223-24
Khan Ahmad Karkiya	?-965/?-1558	H Lahejan	Shirazi 128; Fumeni 35
N.N.	?-975/?-1568	H Lahejan – Safavid governor	Fumeni 58
Amireh Dobbaj	975-977/1568-1570	H Lahejan + Leshteh-nesha	Fumeni 58-59
Allahqoli Soltan Ichek-oghlu Ostajalu (or Ijik-oghlu)	975-979/1568-1572	H Gilan-e Lahejan; *Laleh* of Soltan Mahmud Mirza b. Tahmasp	Qomi 1, 563; Budaq 146 (*Laleh* of Emamqoli Mirza)
Pireh Mohammad Khan Ostajalu	979-984/1572-1576	H Lahejan, *Laleh* of Emamqoli Mirza	Valeh 1372, 402, 408, 514-16, 548
Ahmad Beyg Ostajalu	1001/1593	H Lahejan	Molla Jalal 119
Mehdiqoli Khan	1001-?/1593-?	H Lahejan	Vahid 116
Dervish Mohammad Khan Orumlu	1003/1595	H Lahejan (Rumlu)	Fumeni 164, 167-68, 171; Vahid 129
Mirza Taqi Dowlatabadi Esfahani	1044-1047/1635-1637	Vizier Lahejan	Vahid 262, 284

Laja'an or Lajan is a fertile district of Azerbaijan, situated at the sources of the Lesser Zab river on the border between Iran and Iraq, south of Oshnu, and in the west is bounded by the Zagros

---

215 Shirazi, *Takmelat*, p. 124.

mountains. In 1106/1695, Ahmad Khan Soltan was governor of Laja'an.[216] Nasiri mentions that the district was also called "Kurdestan," which implies that it was peopled by Kurds and/or situated in the Kurdish region. Laja'an was also called Layejan.[217]

Lak, see Salmas.

Langarkonan or Lenkoran is a district of Gilan, according to Yazdi.[218] However, its location makes this unlikely, for Lenkoran is an open roadstead on the Caspian Sea, situated in northern Talesh.

Name	Year	Observations	Source
Mir Qubad Ostajalu	932/1526	H Langarkonan	Bacqué-Gramont 97
Alvand Soltan brother of Farhad Khan Qaramanlu	1000/1592	H Langarkonan	Monshi 442
Kukeh Ta Khan	1107-1109/1696-1698	H Langarkonan	Nasiri 96, 228

Lanjan, see Farideyn.

Lar is situated between Shiraz and Bandar 'Abbas and was an independent principality prior to the advent of the Safavid rule.[219] After its ruler had pledged allegiance to the Safavids, it remained an autonomous principality, which even had its own coinage (the *lari*), although it did not mention the name of the ruler of Lar. The *vali* of Lar considered himself the equal of the governor-general of Fars. To show that Lar was no longer an autonomous jurisdiction after its incorporation into the Safavid kingdom in 1602, its new governor received a robe of honor from his superior, the governor-general of Fars. Molla Jalal noted that "it had never been the rule that the governor of Lar would don a robe of honor from the governor of Fars."[220] In 1042/1633, when Emamqoli Khan was executed and his functions divided over a number of officials, Lar was separated from Fars and once again became an independent jurisdiction. As of 1046/1637, Lar was governed by a vizier, because it had been changed into crown domain. The title of the governor of Lar was vizier and *darugheh* of Lar, which also included Bandar-e Kong. As of 1694 the government of Lar included that of Bandar 'Abbas, where a deputy was appointed by the vizier of Lar. As of 1640, when 'Evaz Beyg, a royal *gholam*, was appointed as vizier of Lar, the government of Lar (and later also of Bandar 'Abbas) was held by his descendants until 1725.[221]

---

216 Nasiri, *Dastur*, p. 81.
217 Fort Lahejan mentioned by Monshi, *Tarikh*, vol. 1, pp. 449, 514 refers to another district in Azerbaijan.
218 Yazdi, *Mokhtasar*, p. 358.
219 For a list of the forts of Lar see Jean Aubin, "Quelques notices du Mukhtasar-i Mufid," *Farhang-e Iran Zamin* 6 (1337/1958), p. 177; see also Yazdi, *Mokhtasar*, vol. 1, pp. 346-49 for the towns and strongholds of the principality of Lar.
220 Molla Jalal, *Ruznameh*, p. 81.
221 Floor, *The Persian Gulf*, pp. 282-84, 290-92, 296-98, 493.

Vizier of Lar	Year	Observations	Source
Amir Harun b. 'Ala al-Molk	?-909/?-1504	*Soltan* or *Vali* Lar	Shirazi 144; Mozaffar 187
Mohammadi Beyg b. 'Ala al-Molk	909-930/1504-1524	*Vali* Lar	Qomi 1, 94; Shirazi 47, 144; Qazvini 272 [Mir 'Ala al-Molk]
Amir Nushirvan b 'Ala al-Molk aka 'Adel Shah	930-948/1524-1542	*Soltan* Lar	Shirazi 144
Amir Ebrahim b. Mohammadi aka Ebrahim Khan	948-?/1542-?	*Vali* Lar	Shirazi 144; Valeh 1372, 359, 536; Yusof 293; Monshi 206
Nur al-Din b. Ebrahim Khan aka Shah 'Adel	?-ca. 988/1580	*Vali* Lar	Monshi 616
Mirza 'Ala al-Molk aka Ebrahim Khan II	?-1010/1602	*Vali* Lar	Monshi 616; Molla Jalal 213ff
Keyvan Beyg	1010-?/1602-?	H + *darugheh* Lar; *gholam*	Molla Jalal 215
Beyram Beyg	1012/1604	*Darugheh* Lar	Molla Jalal 242
Emamqoli Khan	?-1012/?-1604	H Lar	Molla Jalal 243
Amir Khorshid	1012/1604	H Lar - usurper	Molla Jalal 242-43
Nazar 'Ali Beyg Sarem Beyg Lor	1012/1604	*Darugheh* Lar	Molla Jalal 244
Emamqoli Khan b. Nur al-Din	1018-?/1609-?	H Lar	Monshi 807; Molla Jalal 404
Tahmaspqoli Beyg or Mohammadqoli Beyg	1032-1038/1622-1628	H Lar	Esfahani 148; Floor, *Persian Gulf*, 301.
Khvajeh 'Abdol-Reza (Codgea Obdruzzy)	1038/1629	H Lar	Herbert 62; Dunlop 299-300, 425
Safiqoli Khan b. Emamqoli Khan	1039-1040/1629-1630	H Lar	Floor, *Persian Gulf*, 301; Monshi 2, 1088; Yusof 293
Ebrahim Khan	1040-1041/1630-1631	H Lar	Floor, *Persian Gulf*, 301
Safiqoli Khan	1042/1632	H Lar	Valeh 1380, 150; Esfahani 147-48; Yusof 293; Vahid 250
Kalb 'Ali Beyg [Khan]	1042-1046/1632-1637	*Vali* or H Lar	Esfahani 141, 211; Valeh 1380, 224, 228, 234; Yusof 174, 177; Dunlop 420, 616 until April 1636; Bafqi 3/1, 212; Vahid 250
Fulad Beyg	1047-1049/1637-1639	Vizier Lar	Esfahani, 276-77; Dunlop 616; Yusof 295; Vahid 297, 332

'Evaz Beyg	1049-1069/1639-1658	Vizier Lar	VOC 1135, f. 730; Esfahani 276-77; Coolhaas 3, 41; Valeh 1380, 290; VOC 1224, f.282; VOC 1224, f. 800; Yusof 239, 295; Vahid 613
Allahverdi Beyg	1069-1080/1658-1669	Vizier Lar	VOC 1226, f. 802; Vahid 613; VOC 1285, f. 386; Coolhaas 3, 704; KA 1160, f. 906
Allahverdi Beyg's uncle Ala Houraga	1080-1081/1669-1670	Vizier Lar	VOC 1266, f. 952vs (Mortezaqoli Khan); VOC 1284; Bardsiri, 93, 400, 406, 410, 413, 415; Coolhaas 4, 17; Floor, *Persian Gulf*, 302
N.N.	1086-1105/1675-1693	Vizier Lar	Floor, *Persian Gulf*, 302
'Abbasqoli Beyg	1105-1109/1693-1697	Vizier Lar	VOC 1549, f. 588r; Nasiri 81, 177; VOC 1790, f. 410; Coolhaas 5, 860; Aubin, *L'ambassade*, 22, 33, 76-77; VOC 1582, f. 24;
'Evaz Beyg	1109-1110/1697-1698	Vizier Lar	Coolhaas 5, 860; Floor, *Persian Gulf*, 302
Mohammad Mo'men Beyg	1110-1111/1698-99	Vizier Jahrom + Lar	Nasiri 273 (*vali*); Coolhaas 6, 43
'Abbasqoli Beyg [Khan]	1111-1112/1699-1700	H Lar	Coolhaas 6, 136; VOC 1652, f. 750 v; Aubin, *L'ambassade*, 32-33
Mohammad Mo'men Beyg Jahromi	1112-1113/1700-1701	H Lar	KA 1559, f. 231; VOC 1652, f. 752v, 770r; Safavi 36-37.
Mohammad Mo'men Beyg Jahromi – 'Evaz Khan replaced him	1113-1114/1701-1702	H Lar	KA 1559 (06/12/01), f. 230; KA 1559 (21/08/01), f. 284, 288; KA 1559, (17/04/01), f. 45; Nasiri 273
'Evaz Khan	1114-1115/1702-1703	H Lar	Floor, *Persian Gulf*, 302
'Abdol-Qasem Beyg	1116-1117/1704-1705	H Lar	Coolhaas 6, 380, 409
'Abbasqoli Khan	1120-1121/1708-1709	H Lar	Safavi 36.
'Ali Reza Khan	1121-1128/1709-1716	H Lar - till 02/06/1709; then 'Evaz Khan for a while, and then until 1716	VOC 1768, f. 1872; VOC 1790, f. 501; KA 1740, f. 2266; KA 1740, f. 2383vs;
Mirza Nurallah/ Safiqoli Khan	1129/1716	H Lar - Until January 1717	Floor, *Afghan*, 30; KA 1789, f. 18, 23; VOC 2168, f. 193

Safiqoli Khan *qapuchi-bashi*	1129-1130/1717-1718	H Lar - As of January 1717	KA 1789, f. 272; KA 1805, f. 210; Safavi, 38 (*gholam*)
Mirza 'Abdol-Rahim; then Lotf 'Ali Khan Daghestani	1130-1131/1718-1719	H Lar -As of October 1717	Floor, *Afghan*, 31; KA 1805, f. 315; KA 1796, f. 2363; Safavi 31
Safiqoli Khan*	1131-1132/-1719-1720	H Lar	Coolhaas 7, 439; KA 1805, f. 85; KA 1796, f. 2297, 2357v, 2363
Nurollah Khan	1134-35/1721-1722	H Lar	Floor, *Aghan*, 72, 205
Mirza 'Abdol-Qasem	1135-1136/1722-1723	Deputy governor	Floor, *Afghan*, 206, 210
Ebrahim Beyg Shamakhi	1136/1723	Appointed but never came	Floor, *Afghan*, 202, 213-15
	As of 1723	under Afghan control	
	As of December 1729	Under Safavid control	
Hajjiqoli Khan	1142-1144/1730-1732	H Lar	Floor, *Persian Gulf*, 304
Mir Mehr 'Ali	1144-1145/1732-1733	H Lar; per August 1732	VOC 2254, f. 1052; VOC 2269, f. 6604.

* According to Touzard, *Le Dragoman*, p. 154 the governor of Lar was a certain 'Ali Mardan Khan who was dismissed from office in December 1719.

Larijan is a district of Mazandaran, which comprises the entire area watered by the Lar River. Like Kojur it was a very inaccessible area, reason why its chiefs tended to be rebellious. Larijan had been a dependency of Kojur and was ruled by members of a local dynasty. Members of this dynasty also ruled in Kojur and Nur, both parts of Rostamdar (q.v.). After the suppression of their rebellion in 1005/1596 and 1006/1598 this dynasty was annihilated and Larijan was incorporated into the Safavid kingdom.[222]

Name	Year	Observations	Source
Malek Bahman Larijani	946-1005/1540-1597	H Larijan, but also *vali* of Rostamdar	Qomi 1, 140; Natanzi 395; Monshi 399, 521-22; Rumlu 386; Molla Jalal 123
Key Khosrow b. Malek Bahman	1005-1006/1597-1598	H Larijan	Monshi 534

Lashgerd or rather Aleshgerd (q.v.). See also Qazeqman.

Leshteh-nesha, a district is situated in Gilan, adjacent to the Caspian Sea, bounded on the east by Lahejan and on the south by Mavazi. Originally it was part of Kuchesfahan.[223]

---

222 Molla Jalal, *Ruznameh*, p. 153ff.
223 H.L. Rabino, *Les Provinces Caspiennes de la Perse – Le Guilan* (Paris, 1917), pp. 249-53.

Name	Year	Observations	Source
Shahsovar Beyg	977/1570	*Vali* Leshteh-nesha	Bidlisi 2, 629
Mir 'Abbas	1001-1003/1592-1595	H Leshteh-nesha	Monshi 492; Vahid 116
Oghurlu Soltan Chapni	1004-?/1596-?	H Leshteh-nesha	Monshi 372, (Chini) 514; Fumeni 171
Morad Khan Chapni	1020/1611	H Leshteh-nesha	Fumeni 206 (Chini)

Lorestan, also Lor-e Kuchek and Lor-e Feyli, "is bounded on one side by the province of Hamadan and on the other by that of Khuzestan, according to Eskandar Beyg Monshi. East-west it stretches from the town of Borujerd to the environs of Baghdad - a distance of some one hundered farsakhs." He further remarked that most Lor tribes lived "in the districts of Khorramabad, Khaveh, Aleshtar, Sadmara, and Khazameyn."[224] The 'Abbasi dynasty had ruled over Lorestan-e Feyli since the end of the 12th century. Esma'il I ensured that Lorestan pledged allegiance to the Safavid cause and became tributary in 914/1508 as it was surrounded by his lands after the conquest of Bagdad. On his return from Baghdad he confirmed the hereditary ruler Shah Rostam 'Abbasi as governor of Lur-e kuchek or of the districts of Sadmara, Harunabad, and Silakhur. Already in the 1540s the Safavids took direct control of part of Lorestan, such as Khorramabad. The governor of Lorestan was also referred to as governor of Khorammabad and Lorestan, because Khorammabad was his seat of residence. Later the rulers of Lorestan also added Jassan, Badreh and Mandali to their jurisdiction, which normally were part of Baghdad, when in 985-995/1578-1587 they made common cause with the Ottomans during the period of Qezelbash 'civil war' as well as during the period when the Safavids once again had taken possession of Baghdad. Like the Ardalan Kurds, the 'Abbasi Lors also tried to keep both Safavids and Ottomans at arms' length, although this proved to be more difficult where the Safavids were concerned. Internal conflict between family members gave the Safavids the opening they needed and when asked to intervene militarily to help one party against the other they gladly did. To bring matters under control Gheyb Soltan Ostajalu even was appointed governor of Kurdestan and Lorestan in 975/1567. He stayed only for a few months when Shah Tahmasp I decided to divide Lorestan-e kuchek between the 'Abbasi brothers Mohammadi Lori and Shah Rostam. Shah Rostam received Khaveh and Lashtar plus the title khan and the appointment as *Laleh* of Shahbanu Khanom. His brother Mohammadi received Khorammabad and the rest of Lorestan.[225] When Shah 'Abbas I acceded to the throne Mohammadi's son Shahverdi Khan became governor of Lorestan.[226] When Shahverdi became rebellious, 'Abbas I marched against him. Shahverdi fled and in 1002/1593 was succeeded by his nephew Soltan Hoseyn b. Shah Rostam, as governor of Lorestan, minus Khorramabad, because Shah 'Abbas I had made Mehdiqoli Khan Shamlu governor of Khorramabad.[227] This arrangement did not last long for Soltan Hoseyn was killed in 1002/1594 by Shahverdi 'Abbasi who had returned from exile. He wanted to gain control over the whole of Lorestan and the Safavids even gave him control over Khorammabad again in 1003/1595.[228] However, when he rebelled again, Shah 'Abbas I marched against him and had him executed. Furthermore, he also had all

---

224 Monshi, *Tarikh*, vol. 1, p. 469; see also Mozaffar, *Jahangosha*, p. 300.
225 Monshi, *Tarikh*, vol. 1, p. 141; Shirazi, *Takmelat*, pp. 143-44.
226 Monshi, *Tarikh*, vol. 1, 407, 443, 470.
227 Monshi, *Tarikh*, vol. 2, 472.
228 Monshi, *Tarikh*, vol. 2, 501.

male members of the 'Abbasi family blinded or incarcerated. This was the end of the 'Abbasi dynasty. Shahverdi was replaced by a cousin from his mother's side Hoseyn Khan b. Mansur Beyg Solvizi.[229] However, he was governor of a reduced Lorestan, for as of 1006/1597, he held Lorestan except for Sadmara, Hendamin and other districts adjacent to Baghdad, which were allotted to Tahmaspqoli Soltan Inanlu.[230] As of 1011/1603 the governorship of Lorestan-e kuchek became hereditary in the Solvizi family, although in the 1670s, Shah Soleyman once appointed a non-Lori governor to Lorestan, who was expelled by the population, however.

Name	Year	Observations	Source
Shah Rostam 'Abbasi aka Malek Rostam	909/1504	H Khorramabad + Lorestan or H Lor-e Kuchek or Sadmara, Harunabad and Silakhur	Rumlu 138; Qomi 1, 94; Monshi 35, 141, 206, 469; Shirazi 143; Vahid 32; Mozaffar 297, 300
Mir Ughur b. Shah Rostam	?-947/?-1540	H Lorestan	Shirazi 143
Mir Jahangir b. Shah Rostam aka Kuchek Jahangir	948-949/1541-1542	H Khorramabad Lorestan	Rumlu 388; Qomi 1, 295; Monshi 469; Shirazi 143
Bahram Mirza	?-956/?-1549	H Khorramabad + Mankara [=Sadmara?]	Fekete 397-99
Rostam Khan	956-?/1549-?	H Khorramabad + Mankara?	Fekete 397-99
Gheyb Soltan Ostajalu	975/1568	H Kurdestan + Lorestan	Qomi 1, 471
Mohammadi Lori aka Mohammad Tarka	975-993/1568-1585	H of half of Lorestan-e Feyli or h Lorestan-e Kuchek = Khorammabad + the rest	Monshi 141, 143, 469; Valeh 1372, 500; Shirazi 143
Shah Rostam II	975-984-?/1568-1576-?	H of other half of Lorestan = Khaveh and Lashtar	Monshi 141, 469; Shirazi 143; Rumlu 628; Qomi 2, 629
Soltan Mohammad Shah or Shahverdi Khan b. Mohammadi Khan	997-1002/1589-1594	H Lorestan	Monshi 407, 443, 470-71; Bidlisi 2, 693 [Shahverdi]
Soltan Hoseyn b. Shah Rostam	1002/1594	H Lorestan except for Khorramabad	Natanzi 494; Monshi 471; Vahid 129
Mehdiqoli Khan Shamlu	1002-1003/1594-1595	H Khorramabad	Monshi 472; Bidlisi 2, 694; Vahid 121
Shahverdi 'Abbasi	1002-1006/1594-1598	As of 1003 H of whole of Lorestan	Monshi 500-11; Molla Jalal 158
Tahmaspqoli Khan Inanlu	1006-?/1598-?	H Sadmareh, Hendamin, areas close to Baghdad	Vahid 140

---

229 Monshi, *Tarikh*, vol. 2, p. 539.
230 Monshi, *Tarikh*, vol. 2, p. 541.

Hoseyn Khan b. Mansur Beyg Solvizi	1006-1040/1598-1631	H of part, later whole of Lorestan; BB Lorestan - *Mir* of the Bakhtiyaris; succeeded by his son	Monshi 539, 649; 661, 925, 950, 959, 1001, 1019, 1086; Vahid 200; Molla Jalal 159, 414; Yusof 77
Shahverdi Khan	1040-1050/1631-1641	BB Lorestan - Succeeded by his minor son	Shamlu 1, 283; Yusof 66 77, 156, 172, 190, 251; Valeh 1380, 80-1, 189 etc; Vahid 140, 304, 328
'Aliqoli Khan	1050-1058-?/ 1641-1648-?	BB Lorestan; Lor-e kuchek; *vali* Lorestan;	Yusof 252, 288; Vahid 305, 328, 471, 575
Manuchehr Khan	1061-?/1651-?	H Lorestan [uncle of the previous one]	Vahid 568-69 [1064], 575-77
N.N.	1095/1684	Qezelbash governor	Kaempfer 129
Shahverdi Khan	1105-1106/1694-1695	H Lurestan Feyli	Nasiri 60
'Ali Mardan Khan b. Hoseyn Khan	1134/1722	H Lorestan [Khorramabad]	Floor, *Afghan*, index; Balfour 126; Mervi 1, 34, 246, 700

Lori or Luri or Luri-Pambak is situated near Shurehgel, south of the Somkhetian Mountains in Qarabagh.[231] It seems to have been separated from Georgia (Kartlia) after 1014/1606, when Shah 'Abbas I forced the king of Kartlia to cede Lori and Barduj to him.[232] Initially the Qazaqlar were settled in the district, but when they proved to be unreliable they were resettled in Fars.[233] Shah 'Abbas I then brought the Buzchalu tribe (who roamed in Borchalu) from Central Persia,[234] who seem to have held the governorship of Lori, according to Nasiri's *Alqab*.

Name	Year	Observations	Source
Mohammad Khan Qazaqlar	?-1021/?-1612	H Lori –succeeded by his brother	Monshi 856; Vahid 181
Mostafa Beyg [Khan]	1021-1023/1612-1614	H Lori	Monshi 856, 882
Salim Khan Shams al-Dinlu	1032/1623	H Lori	Monshi 1007
'Isa Khan Soltan Buzchelu	1049-1066/1640-1656	H Luri va Panbak; (H Luri va Palank-Astarabadi)	Vahid 299, 613; Esfahani 279; Astarabadi 258
Tahmaspqoli Beyg	?-1122/?-1710	H Luri	Puturidze 1965, doc. 20
Bahador Khan	1122-?/1710-?	H Luri	Puturidze 1965, doc. 20

231 TM, p. 167; al-Hoseyni, *Tarikh*, p. 158 has Peynak, which must be a copyist's error. V.S. Puturidze, *Persidskie istoricheskie dokumenty v knigoxraniloshchax Gruzii* (Tiflis, 1965), doc 18 (Luri).
232 Brosset, *Histoire*, vol. 2/1, pp. 43, 66 (Vakhusti); Monshi, *Tarikh*, vol. 2, p. 716.
233 Monshi, *Tarikh*, vol. 2, p. 883 (in 1023/1614).
234 'Abbasqoli Aqa Bakihanuf, *Golestan-e Eram* ed. A.A. Alizade (Baku, 1970), pp. 92, 173; see also Monshi, *Tarikh*, pp. 38 (Bozchelu), 785-56, 717, 882, 1007 (Luri); Molla Jalal, *Tarikh*, p. 381 (Luri); Khvajeh Esfahani, p. 279; Valeh, *Iran*, pp. 222, 296, 577-78; Vahid, *Tarikh*, pp. 299, 613.

Madhar is a district attached to the province of Balkh. In 919/1513 Tukret Beyg was appointed as its governor.[235]

Maghazberd or Qal'eh-ye Maghazberd is situated in Shurehgel, at the Ottoman border, facing Qars. It was held by a governor.[236]

Mahmudabad, see Saliyan.

Mahvelat is a dependency of Torbat-e Heydari (q.v.) and adjacent to the sub-districts of Zaveh and Dughabad.[237]

Name	Year	Observations	Source
Hajji Mohammad Soltan Kutval Chagatay	?-985/?-1577	H Zaveh + Mahvelat	Monshi 141
Morshedqoli Khan Yakan Ostajalu b. Shahqoli	985-989/1577-1581	H Khvaf – Bakharz, Torbat-e Zaveh, Mahvelat	Monshi 227, 293-95; Bidlisi 2, 651; Molla Jalal 43; Qomi 2, 665
Shahqoli Soltan b. Morshedqoli Khan	989/1581	H *qasabeh-ye* Khvaf, Bakharz, *velayat-e* Torbat, Badghis, Mahvelat	Shamlu 1, 123
	999/1590	Uzbeg occupation	Bidlisi 2, 689

Maku is situated in North-West Azerbaijan; the district takes it name from the mountain stronghold of Maku. It is bounded in the west by Turkey, in the north-east by the Republic of Azerbaijan, in the east by Marand and in the south-east by Tabriz.[238]

Name	Year	Observations	Source
Mostafa Beyg Mahmudi [Kurdi]	?-1005-1015/?-1597-1607	H Maku	Monshi 663, 687, 721; Vahid 166
Geda 'Ali Soltan Bayat	1038/1629	H Maku	Monshi 1086

Mandali is a stronghold on the Ottoman-Safavid border, west of Kermanshah. It usually was in Ottoman hands, but in 935/1528, Ghazi Khan Tekkelu was governor of Kalhor and Mandali.[239]

---

235 Fekete, *Einführung*, pp. 255-58.
236 Vahid, *Tarikh*, p. 265 (in 1044/1635).
237 Yazdi, *Mokhtasar*, vol. 1, pp. 217-18.
238 For the history of Maku see Mir Asadollah Musavi Maku'i. *Tarikh-e Maku* (Tehran: Bisetun, 1376/1997).
239 Budaq, *Javaher*, p. 68; Qomi, *Kholasat*, vol. 1, p. 190.

Maneh is a dependency of Bojnord, nowadays known as Maneh va Samalqan. In 1044, Esmaʿil Soltan was governor of Maneh.[240]

Manjil is a dependency of the district of Kuhdom.[241]

Manjavan [?] is a district probably situated in Qarabagh, which, according to Nasiri's *Alqab* also was a governorship. I have found no other references to it.

Maragheh is situated at some 120 km from Tabriz, on the Safi-chay, bounded in the west by Lake Van, in the north by Tabriz, in the east by Hashtrud and in the south by Miyandoab.[242] The Kurdish Mokri tribe inhabited the Gavdul district of Maragheh, Solduz and Miyandoab. In the time of Shah Tahmasp I, Amireh Beyg was the chief of the tribe, but he rebelled under Shah Mohammad Khodabandeh. When Amireh Beyg died his son Sheikh Heydar became chief, who then became governor of Maragheh.[243] The latter's son was replaced after yet another Mokri rebellion, after which the position of the Mokri tribe at Maragheh was taken over by the Moqaddam clan of the Otuzayeki tribe of Qarabagh, who held this position until the end of the Qajar period.[244]

Name	Year	Observations	Source
Chayan Soltan Ostajalu	932/1526	H Maragheh	Bacqué-Gramont 97
Hasan Beyg Dhu'l-Qadr	940/1534	H Marageh	Fumeni 23, 26
Yolqoli Beyg b. Aydin Aqa Dhu'l-Qadr	?	*Vali* Maragheh	Bidlisi 2, 184
Amireh Beyg	?-986/?-1578	H Maragheh	Monshi 812
Sheykh Heydar Mokri	99?-1017/158?-1608	Was succeeded by his minor son	Monshi 643, 812
Qobad Khan Mokri	1017-1018/1608-1609	H Maragheh	Monshi 781, 812; Vahid 172, 177, 212
Aqa Khan Moqaddam	1018-1034/1609-1625	H Maragheh (*eqtaʿ*) + H *il-e* Moqaddam	Yusof 286; Monshi 814, 888, 1031; Vahid 330; Molla Jalal 419
Ghazi Soltan aka Aqa Khan II Moqaddam	1034-1058/1625-1648	H *il-e* Moqaddam	Yusof 286; Vahid 330, 476
Hoseynqoli Khan b. Aqa Khan	1088-1089/1677-1678	H Maragheh	Agulis 37, 142
ʿAbdol-Ghaffar Khan	1105-1106/1694-1695	H *il-e* Moqaddam	Nasiri 81, 225

---

240 Yusof, *Dheyl*, p. 192.
241 Vahid, *Tarikh*, p. 128.
242 On its history and of the Moqaddam see Yunes Morvarid, *Maragheh az nazar-e owzaʿ-ye tabiʿi, ejtemaʿi, eqtesadi va tarikhi* (Tehran, 1360/1981).
243 Monshi, *Tarikh*, vol. 2, pp. 811-13.
244 Yusof, *Dheyl*, p. 286; Monshi, *Tarikh*, vol. 2, p. 814.

Marand, a town and district, in East Azerbaijan, bounded in the west by Khoy, in the northwest by Maku, in the east by Arasbaran, and in the south by Tabriz.

Name	Year	Observations	Source
Mehdi Khan Soltan 'Arab	1011/1603	H Marand	Shamlu 1, 192 [as *teyul*]
Jamshid Soltan Donboli	1012-1014/1604-1606	H Marand	Monshi 643, 678; Molla Jalal 279
Amir Shahnazar Soltan Beyburdi	1020/1611	H Marand	Puturidze 1961, doc. 4
Lajin Beyg aka Lachin Soltan Kord Mahmudi	1043-?/1634-?	H Marand	Yusof 140; Vahid 257

Maruchaq, Fort Maruchaq, or Merv-e kuchek is situated on the banks of the river Morghab, about 35 km northwest of Bala Morghab in northern Afghanistan. This district was sometimes also held in conjunction with another jurisdiction such as the fort of Morghab.[245] This district apparently only became part of the Safavid kingdom under 'Abbas I, who in 1008/1600 gave orders to develop the deserted area.[246]

Name	Year	Observations	Source
Bektash Soltan Ostajalu	1007-1009/1599-1601	H Maruchaq + the Morghab area generally	Vahid 176, 245, (Takash) 149; Monshi 576, 603
Nazar 'Ali Soltan Shamlu	1009-1011/1601-1603	H Maruchaq	Monshi 630
Yusof 'Ali Khan	1011/1603	H Maruchaq	Monshi 630
'Ezzat 'Ali Khan	1011/1603	H Maruchaq	Vahid 152
Qazaq Khan b. Hoseyn Khan Shamlu	1016-1024/1607-1615	H Maruchaq	Monshi 894; Vahid 190; Molla Jalal 328
Khosrow Beyg [Soltan]	1024-1040/1615-1631	H Maruchaq + Morghab	Monshi 893, 914, 1088; Yusof 26; Vahid 190
Hasan Khan	1041-?/1631-?	H Maruchaq	Vahid 245
Dust 'Ali Soltan Zanganeh	1050-?/1640-?	H Maruchaq	Vahid 305; Astarabadi 259
'Abdollah Soltan	1100/1689	H Morghab	Sanson 81
	As of 1129/1716	under Abdali control	Lockhart 101

Mashhad, also Mashhad-e Tus, is the name of the city and province in northeastern Khorasan. It was under Safavid control as of 916/1510, although the Uzbegs continued to challenge this during the next two decades. From 996/1588 to 1007/1598 the Uzbegs first occupied part of the province and later the whole of Khorasan (incl. Herat). In the west the province bordered on Semnan

---

245 Le Strange, *The Lands*, p. 405.
246 Monshi, *Tarikh*, vol. 1, p. 576.

(q.v.), Damghan (q.v.) and Bastam (q.v.) and in the north the border was formed by Khabushan (q.v.), Sarakhs (q.v.) and Zurabad (q.v.), while in the east Jam (q.v.), Khvaf (q.v.) and Tun (q.v.), districts all belonging to Herat, had that function. Mashhad was one of the provinces where often one of the royal princes was appointed as pro-forma governor under the supervision of a tutor (*Laleh*). The jurisdiction of the provincial vizier might be extended, such as in 1540s, when he held the entire province of Khorasan from the border at Semnan until Herat and Seystan. On another occasion, Monshi referred to the prince's jurisdiction as that of "half of Khorasan."[247] The province of Mashhad included the following administrative jurisdictions: Abivard, Azadvar, B.zavandaq [?], Darun, Esfara'in, Nesa, Nishapur, Pasakuh, Sabzavar, Torbat (-e Heydari), and Torshiz.

Name	Year	Observations	Source
Sayyed Zeyn al-'Abedin*	917/1511	H Mashhad; Shah Esma'il I's uncle	Heravi 375
Ahmad Beyg Afshar	927-928/1521-1522	H Mashhad	Khvandamir 585
Burun Soltan Tekkelu	928-931 or ?-933/1522-1524 or 1527	H Mashhad	Monshi 51; Shirazi 61; Qazvini 282; Qomi 1, 169; Khvandamir 591
Durmish Khan	933-?/1527-?	H Mashhad	Qomi 1, 169
Aghzivar Soltan Shamlu	935/1529	H Mashhad	Dickson 146
Delu Mantasha Soltan Ostajalu	937/1531	H Mashhad	Rumlu 312; Monshi 59
Mosib Soltan Ostajalu	938?/1532?	H Mashhad	Vahid 47
Shahqoli Soltan Ostajalu	939/1532	H Mashhad	Abrahams 135
Sufiyan Khalifeh Shamlu [or Rumlu]	941-942/1535-1536	H Mashhad	Rumlu 322, 346, 355 [Rumlu]; Monshi 103; Afshar 27 (Sufi Khalifeh Rumlu); Abrahams 136
Shahqoli Soltan Ostajalu b. Hamzeh Soltan Qazaq	942-958/1536-1551	H Mashhad	Hoseyni 149; Qomi 1, 306, 313, 347, 349; Shirazi 104; Bidlisi 2, 586; Qazvini 300
'Ali Soltan Tati-oghlu Damurchilu Dhu'l-Qadr	958-963 or 965/1551-1556 or 1558	H Mashhad	Qomi 1, 349; Shirazi 104; Bidlisi 2, 586; Qazvini 300
Abu'l-Fath Soltan Ebrahim Mirza	963- or 965-970/1558-1563	H Mashhad – no *Laleh*	Qomi 1, 415, 551-52, 434, 440; Shirazi 110, 123; Bidlisi 2, 592; Qazvini 302; Abrahams 142 (as of 964)
Amir Gheyb Soltan Ostajalu	970-973/1563-1566	H Mashhad	Qomi 1, 349-50, 452; Budaq 141; Shirazi 125
Abu'l-Fath Mirza Soltan Ebrahim	973-974/1566-1567	No *Laleh* -2nd time	Qomi 1, 452, 460; Tatavi 635 (972)

---

247 Röhrborn, *Provinzen*, p. 101; Monshi, *Tarikh*, vol. 1, p. 140.

COMMENTARY 241

Shah Vali Soltan Tati-oghlu	974-981/1567-1573	*Laleh* Soltan Soleyman Mirza	Qomi 1, 460, 581; Abrahams 146 (also *Motavalli*)
Vali Khalifeh Rumlu	981-?/1574	H Mashhad	Qomi 1, 581
Vali Khalifeh Evji Shamlu	981?/1574	H Mashhad; probably the same as above	Valeh 1372, 407; Monshi 138
Shahqoli Khan Pornak	984/1576	H Mashhad	Monshi 138
Mortezaqoli Soltan [Khan] Pornak Torkman	985-989/1577-1581	BB of half of Khorasan	Monshsi 213, 229, 290, 364; Qomi 2, 651, 665, 673; Natanzi 36-7, 149; Valeh 1372, 602, 647; Shamlu 1, 109, 122; Bidlisi 2, 652 [Mostafaqoli]
Shahqoli Beyg Qarencheh-oghlu	989/1581	H Mashhad *Laleh* of Salman Khan grandson of 'Abdollah Khan Ostajalu	Valeh 1372, 677-78, 684-88; Monshi 290; Shamlu 1, 109; Bidlisi 2, 662; Vahid 97-98
'Aliqoli Khan Shamlu	990-991/1582-1583	H Mashhad	Molla Jalal 69
Morshedqoli Khan Chavoshlu Ostajalu	991-?/1583-?	H Mashhad; replaced by	Monshi 293, 295; Bidlisi 2, 662; Valeh 1372, 677
Ebrahim Beyg [Khan] Ostajalu	?-997/?-1589	*Laleh* of Safi Mirza b. 'Abbas	Valeh 1372, 836; Vahid 107; Monshi 401; Qomi 401, 860, 865
Ommat Beyg [Khan] Qarasarlu Köshek-oglu Ostajalu	997/1589	H Mashhad	Vahid 107; Monshi 401; Bidlisi 2, 686, 687
Budaq Khan Chegani	997/1589	H Mashhad - *Laleh* of Soltan Hasan Mirza	Vahid 107; 149; Monshi 402
	997-1007/1589-1598	Uzbeg governors	Monshi 561
Budaq Khan Chegani	1007-1009/1598-1600	Succeeded by his son; H Mashhad	Monshi 599; Siyaqi 479; Vahid 148-49
Yusof 'Ali Khan or Yusof Khan b. Oghlan Bedagh Chegani	1009-1011/1600-1603	H + *motavalli* Mashhad	Monshi 630; Molla Jalal 185
Mehrab Khan Qajar	1011-1018/1603-1610	H Mashhad	Monshi 630, 760; Vahid 207; Molla Jalal 328, 366
Shahnazar Soltan [Khan] Tükeli Chaghatay	1018-1020-?/1610-1611	H Mashhad	Monshi 735, 802; Molla Jalal 366 [Tekkelu], 415, 419
Nazar Khan Tavakolli	?-1027/?-1618	BB Mashhad	Vahid 199 [d.1028]
Qarchaqay Khan	1027-1034/1618-1625	H Mashhad and most of Khorasan	Monshi 989, 1039; Vahid 199 [in 1029]

Manuchehr Khan	1034-1052/1625-1643	BB Mashhad – succeeded by his son	Monshi 1039; Shamlu 1, 211; Valeh 1380, 27, 34 etc; Vahid 226, 264, 328, 383; Yusof 22, 104, 150, 294
Qarchaqay Khan b. Manuchehr Khan	1052-1054/1643-1644	BB Mashhad	Shamlu 1, 272, 282, 283, 296; Vahid 328, 403; Valeh 1380, 410, 439
Mortezaqoli Khan Qajar b. Mehrab Khan	1054-1056/1644-1646	BB Mashhad	Vahid 403; Shamlu 1, 283, 296; Valeh 1380, 410, 439
Manuchehr Khan b. Qarchaqay Khan	1056-1074/1646-1664	BB Mashhad	Vahid 754; Valeh 1380, 439
Safiqoli Beyg [Khan] b. Rostam Khan	1074-1076/1664-1666	BB Mashhad; *divan-beygi*	Shamlu 2, 20; Vahid 754; Khatunabadi 525;
Elyas Khan	1105/1694		Nasiri 80
Heydarqoli Khan	1106-1108/1695-1697		Nasiri 80, 117, 201
Hoseyn Khan	1114-?/1703-?	H Mashhad; *tupchi-bashi*	Khatunabadi 551
Safiqoli Khan	Before 1120/1708	H Mashhad	Khatunabadi 558
Mohammad Khan b. Aslan Khan	Before 1120/1708	H Mashhad	Khatunabadi 558
'Ali Mardan Khan	?-1122/?-1710	H Mashhad	Khatunabadi 561
Mansur Khan Shahseven	?-1126/?-1714	H Mashhad	Mostowfi 118; Safavi 20
Fathollah Khan Torkman	1128/1716	H Mashhad	Lockhart 97
Safiqoli Khan Torkestan-oghlu	1129/1717	H Mashhad	Lockhart 98
Rostam Khan	1131/1719	BB Mashad	Floor, *Afghan*, 40
'Aliqoli Khan	?-1136/?-1723	H Mashhad	Mostowfi 175-76; Mervi 1, 22, 38-39
Esma'il Khan	1136/1723-?	H Mashhad	Mostowfi 176

* According to the *Afzal al-Tavarikh* (quoted by Aubin, "Les soufis," p. 19), the governor at that time was Ahmad Beyg Sufi-oghlu Ostajalu, which is erroneous, because in that year the latter became governor of Herat. Heravi, *Fotuhat*, p. 375.

Mashhad-e Sar, a small port on the Caspian Sea, some 22 km north of Barforush at the mouth of the Babol river. Nowadays it is called Babolsar. In 997/1589, Yusof Ra'is was governor of Mashhad-e Sar.[248]

Mazandaran province, also called Tabarestan, was ruled by the descendants of Mir 'Abdollah Khan, the maternal grandfather of Shah 'Abbas I.[249] Under Mir Sayyed Sharif, Mazandaran

---

248 Shamlu, *Qesas*, vol. 1, p. 167.
249 Monshi, *Tarikh*, vol. 2, p. 518.

became tributuary to the Safavids as of 909/1504, although its rulers kept much autonomy. They were attacked by a Safavid army in 924/1518 to put an end to disloyal behavior, after which they submitted.[250] The province was divided into two parts after Mir Sayyed Sharif's death. Mir 'Abdol-Karim b. Mir 'Abdollah together with Shams al-Din brother of Sayyed Zeyn al-'Abedin henceforth ruled Mazandaran. He died in 933/1527 and was succedeed by Mir 'Abdol-Karim, who was expelled by Aqa Mohammad Ruzafzun, who was killed in 939/1533. Thereafter, Mir 'Abdollah Khan together with Aqa Mohammad ruled Mazandaran and after the latter's death in 954/1547 or 955/1548 Mir 'Abdollah Khan became sole ruler and he assumed control over the whole of Mazandaran.[251] His rule was challenged by his cousin Mir Soltan Morad. To avoid turmoil Shah Tahmasp I decided to divide the province into two parts again. Mir 'Abdollah Khan was deposed by the shah for misbehavior and was succeded by Mir Soltan Morad b. Mir Shah b. Mir 'Abdol-Karim, and Mir 'Abdollah sought refuge at court in 969/1561. This did not stop the family quarrel, where enmity ran so high that Mir Morad strangled Mir 'Abdollah and then ruled over the whole of Mazandaran, but soon thereafter he died. Soltan Morad then became ruler of whole of Mazandaran, although Mir 'Abdol-Karim b. Mir 'Abdollah was co-ruler with Soltan Morad for 2 years, but he was dismissed and died in 972/1565 en route to Qazvin.[252] Shah Tahmasp I then gave one part of the province to Soltan Hoseyn Mirza, one of his sons.[253] The other half was given to Morad's son, Soltan Mohammad Khan b. Morad Khan, *vali* of Mazandaran.[254] This meant that between 977-984/1569-1576 there was a Safavid governor in part of Mazandaran. After the withdrawal of Soltan Hoseyn Mirza from Mazandaran, Mirza Khan controlled the whole province. He was confirmed in his post by Shah Mohammad Khodabandeh. When he rebelled he was replaced by Mir 'Ali Khan as governor of Mazandaran, who was killed in 986/1578.[255] Because there was no male descendants in the family the province fell into anarchy and only one half was under nominal Safavid control through emir Sayyed Mozaffar Morteza'i, in the other half anarchy prevailed.[256] This situation resulted in three local chiefs grabbing power, who as of 1004/1595, if not earlier, ruled Mazandaran. They were Sayyed Mozaffar Morteza'i in Sari, Malek Bahman Larijani in Amol, and Alvand Div in Savadkuh. After they behaved in a disloyal manner and then rebelled, Shah 'Abbas I appointed Mirza 'Alameyn in 1003/1594 as vizier of Mazandaran and ordered Farhad Khan to crush their opposion. The latter was appointed governor of Mazandaran for one year, while the province was incorporated into the kingdom during the years 1005-1006/1596-1598,[257] and turned in crown domain and henceforth it was governed by viziers.[258] In 1035/1626, the vizierate of Gilan-e Biyeh-pas was temporarily added to that of Mazandaran.[259]

---

250 Shirazi, *Takmelat*, pp. 56-58; Bidlisi, *Cheref-Nameh*, vol. 2, p. 534; Qazvini, *Tarikh*, p. 278.

251 Shirazi, *Takmelat*, p. 139; Monshi, *Tarikh*, vol. 1, p. 240. Prior to that time members of ruling family served as governors of Amol and Sari. Tahmasp, *Tadhkereh*, p. 7.

252 Shirazi, *Takmelat*, p. 140; Monshi, *Tarikh*, vol. 1, p. 241.

253 Qomi, *Kholasat*, vol. 2, p. 650. Or is it Soltan Hasan Mirza, see Monshi, *Tarikh*, 1, p. 126.

254 Natanzi, *Naqavat*, p. 33; Qomi, *Kholasat*, vol. 2, p. 630 (984 aka Mirza Khan); see further Qomi, *Kholasat*, vol. 2, p. 690 for details; Monshi, *Tarikh*, vol. 1, p. 241 (has Soltan Mahmud).

255 Monshi, *Tarikh*, vol. 1, pp. 210, 241-43; Qomi, *Kholasat*, vol. 2, p. 665.

256 Monshi, *Tarikh*, vol. 1, p. 242.

257 Monshi, *Tarikh*, vol. 2, pp. 518-21.

258 Fumeni, *Tarikh*, pp. 181, 188; Gonabadi, *Rowzat*, p.743.

259 Fumeni, *Tarikh*, p. 223.

Name	year	Observations	Source
Mir Sayyed Sharif	?-915/?-1510	*Vali* Mazandaran	Qomi 1, 100-01 [915]; Shirazi 48
Aqa Rostam Ruzafzun	916-?/1511-?	H Mazandran; *vali* of Sari and some other places of Mazandaran (Mozaffar)	Hoseyni 229-30, 240; Qomi 1, 114; Rumlu 163; Shirazi 51; Heravi 369; Mozaffar 402
Aqa Mohammad Ruzafzun	917-927/1512-1521	*Vali* of half of Mazandaran (Amol +)	Rumlu 218, 226; Qomi 1, 148; Monshi 1, 39; Shirazi 51; Bidlisi 2, 525; Qazvini 274
Amir 'Abdol-Karim	917-927?/1512-1521?	*Vali* of the rest of Mazandaran; H Sari (Mozaffar 558; Tatavi 385)	Rumlu 226; Hoseyni 250; Qomi 1, 148; Monshi 1, 39; Bidlisi 2, 525; Mozaffar 403, 557-58
Sayyed Qavam al-Din	?	*Vali* Mazandaran	Hoseyni 227
Mir 'Abdollah Khan	971/1564		Monshi 240; Fumeni 65
Mir Morad Khan	971?/1564	*Vali* Mazandaran	Qomi 1, 41; Qazvini 309
Mir 'Abdol-Karim b. Mir 'Abdollah Khan	?	*Vali* Mazandaran	Monshi 241
Soltan Hoseyn Mirza	?-984/?-1576	Half of Mazandaran; no *Laleh* given	Qomi 2, 650 or is it Soltan Hasan Mirza see Monshi 126; Vahid 86
Soltan Mohammad Khan b. Soltan Morad Khan aka Mirza Khan	984/1576	*Vali* of half of Mazandaran	Rumlu 630; Natanzi 33; Qomi 2, 630 [aka Mirza Khan], 690; Monshi 241 has Soltan Mahmud
Mirza Khan or Mir 'Abd or Mir 'Ali Khan	984-985/1576-1577	*Vali* or H of the whole of Mazandaran; brother of queen	Monshi 241, 206; Bidlisi 2, 652; Qomi 2, 665
Sayyed Mozaffar Morteza'i	986?/1578?	Controlled half of the province for the Safavids; the remainder in anarchy	Monshi 242
Mir Morad	?-988/?-1580	*Vali* Mazandaran	Bidlisi 2, 652
	1004-1005/1595-1596	Several chiefs controlled parts of Mazandaran*	
Farhad Khan Qaramanlu	1005-?/1596-?	H Mazandaran	Monshi 519
Mirzay 'Alameyn	1003-1015/1594-1607	H Mazandaran	Fumeni 181, 188
Mir Abo'l-Qasem**	?-1008/?-1600	Vizier Mazandaran	Vahid 176
Aqa Mohammad Abhari	1008-?/1600-?	*Vazir koll* Mazandaran	Molla Jalal 191

Khvajeh Mohammad Shafi' aka Mirza-ye 'Alamiyan	1016-1018/1607-1609	Vizier of Dar al-Marz, Qazvin, Rey and all of Khorasan	Molla Jalal 328; Fumeni 181
Mirza Abu'l-Qasem Torshizi [or Khorasani]	1018-?/1609-?	*Vazir-e koll* Mazandaran	Molla Jalal 365; Fumeni 181
Mirza [Mohammad] Taqi	1020-1043/1611-1634	Vizier of Dar al-Marz, comprising Mazandaran and Rostamdar; succeeded by his brother	Monshi 850; Vahid 333; Yusof 94-95, 296; Shamlu 1, 201
Mohammad Saleh Beyg	1044-1052/1634-1642	Vizier Mazandaran; succeeded by his son	Vahid 262, 333; Yusof 148, 296; Astarabadi 250
Mirza Qasem	1052-1063/1642-1653	Vizier Mazandaran	Yusof 296-97; Vahid 333, 539
Mirza Sadeq	1063-?/1653-?	Vizier Mazandaran	Vahid 539
Mirza Hashem	1086/1675	Vizier Mazandaran	Rabino 139
Ma'sum Beyg	1110-?/1699-?	Vizier Mazandaran; IAB	Nasiri 273

* Despite the absence of Safavid control over Mazandaran, Mirzay 'Alameyn was appointed vizier of Qazvin, Khorasan and Mazandaran in 1003/1594. He remained vizier of Mazandaran and Gilan for 12 years. Fumeni, *Tarikh*, pp. 181, 188.

** Mirza Abu'l-Qasem and Aqa Mohammad Abhari presumably were acting for Mirzay 'Alameyn, who also was vizier of Qazvin and Khorasan at the same time.

Mazinan is a dependency of Sabzavar (Khorasan), which on the west and south is bounded by the Kavir, on the north by Saviz and Jaghatay mountains and on the east by Sabzavar. In 990/1582 and 991/1583, Hoseyn Khan Soltan Dehdehlu[y] Torkman, was governor of Mazinan.[260]

Merv or Merv-e Shahejan came into Safavid hands in 916/1510 after the defeat of Sheyban Khan, the Uzbeg leader. Safavid rule did not last long, because due to Uzbeg pressure on Khorasan they had to abandon the city in 932/1526 and, according to Eskandar Beyg Monshi, it would take 76 years before the Shi'ite *khotbeh* was again read in Merv, ignoring the few weeks in 943/1536 that the Safavids had regained control over Merv.[261] 'Abbas I during his campaign against the Uzbegs in the 1590s, supported Nur Mohammad Khan, an Uzbeg prince and vassal ruler, and the Safavids considered Merv, Nesha, Abivard and Marv to be his hereditary domains.[262] Shah 'Abbas I even helped him to regain his possessions, but when the two sides fell out he took possession of Merv and appointed a Qezelbash governor and incorporated the city and its lands into his kingdom in 1009/1600.[263]

---

260 Qomi, *Kholasat*, vol. 2, pp. 732, 755.
261 Monshi, *Tarikh*, vol. 2, p. 604.
262 Monshi, *Tarikh*, vol. 2, p. 568.
263 Nur Mohammad Khan, hereditary governor of Merv. Monshi, *Tarikh*, vol. 2, pp. 577 (reinstalled in 1007), 598 (in 1009 replaced by Bektash Khan Danalu Ostajalu).

Name	Year	Observations	Source
Dedeh Beyg aka Abdal Beyg Dedeh	916-919/1510-1513	H Merv	Budaq 32; Qomi 1, 113, 126; Shamlu 1, 43; Hoseyni 62; Shirazi 48; Bidlisi 2, 524, 534; Qazvini 274
Div Soltan Rumlu	919-?/1513-?	H Merv	Monshi 41; Bidlisi 2, 534; Qazvini 276
	From 932/1526 to 1007/1598	Uzbeg governors	
Budaq Khan Qajar	943/1536	H Merv + dependencies- for a short while – either this is the wrong person or the next one is	Qomi 1, 266
Shahqoli Soltan Afshar b. Mostafa Soltan	943/1536	H Merv – for a short while; see above	Shirazi 87
Nur Mohammad Khan	1007-1009/1598-1600	hereditary H Merv, Nesa, Abivard, Baghbad – Uzbeg vassal of the Safavids	Monshi 515, 577, 598; Molla Jalal 184, 195ff, 205
Bektash Khan Danalu Ostajalu	1009-1018/1600-1610	H Merv	Monshi 603, 620, 745, 804; Shamlu 1, 197; Molla Jalal 199, 312, 366; Vahid 168-69
Mehrab Khan Qajar	1018-1032/1610-1623	H *il-e* Qajar, H Merv	Monshi 830, 884, 1008; Shamlu 1, 197, 204; Vahid 244; Vahid 207; Molla Jalal 366
'Ashur Khan Chapni or Chekani	1033-1042/1623-1632	H Merv	Monshi 1086; Yusof 28; Vahid 226, 244 (Chakni)
Mortezaqoli Khan b. Mehrab Khan Qajar	1042/1632	H Merv	Shamlu 1, 271, 283; Yusof 103, 249; Vahid 244, 328; Yusof 249; Vahid 303; Valeh 1380, 155
Naqdi Beyg Shamlu [Khan]	1042-?/1633-?	H Merv	Yusof 107; Vahid 321
Mortezaqoli Khan b. Mehrab Khan Qajar	1051-1053/1641-1643	H Merv	Shamlu 1, 271, 283; Yusof 103, 249; Vahid 244, 328, 303
'Aliqoli Khan	1053-1058/1643-1648	H Merv	Shamlu 1, 283, 513; Vahid 403
Qurkhoms Khan	1058-1068/1648-1658	H Merv	Shamlu 1, 514; Valeh 1380, 609; Vahid 641-42
Aslan Khan	1068-?/1658-?	H Merv	Vahid 642
Heydar Khan	1087/1676	H Merv	Bardsiri 456
Yahya Khan	1134/1722	H Merv	Mervi I 38, 56
Esma'ilqoli Khan	1137/1724	H Merv	Mostowfi 145

Meshkin, a district of Azerbaijan, is situated on the northern slopes of the Savalan Mountain, between Ahar and Ardabil.[264] It seems to have become the tribal area of the Kurdish Kalhor, because Nasiri writes that the governor of Meshkin was also called the governor of the Kalhor.

Mobarakabad was a border fort, which the govenors of Gorgan took as their residence. It was built under Shah 'Abbas I.[265]

Moghan or Moghanat district (see also Ardabil) was a steppe, which extends from an area north of Ardabil to the mouths of the Kur River.[266] It was a favorite camping ground for pastoralists and as of ca. 1600 it was the winter quarters of the Shahsevan tribe, whose chiefs usually also were governor of Moghan.

Name	Year	Observations	Source
Nowshir Beyg Talesh	907/1501	H Moghanat	Valeh 1372, 86
Hamzeh Beyg Ostajalu	932/1526	H Moghan	Bacqué-Gramont 97, 106
Bayazid Soltan Shamlu	942/1536	H Moghan	Bakikhanuf 94
Vali Khalifeh Shamlu	976-981/1568-1573	H Moghanat	Qomi 1, 563, 581
Kalb 'Ali Beyg Qajar *davatdar*	1044-1048/1635-1639	H Ardabil, Kankarkonan + *darugheh* Moghan	Yusof 191, 228
NN	1095/1684	*Kalantar*; no khan	Kaempfer 58
'Abbasqoli Khan	1115/1703	H Moghanat	Puturidze 1965, doc. 3

Mokri is the name of a Kurdish tribe as well as the name of the district in Azerbaijan assigned to it for the substance of its tribesmen.

Name	Year	Observations	Source
Budaq Soltan	1107/1695	H Mokri	Nasiri 124
'Aziz Soltan	1107/1696	H Mokri	Nasiri 127, 129
Musa Soltan	1109/1698	H Mokri	Nasiri 234

Moqaddam was the name of a Turkic tribe as well as of the district assigned to it for its sustenance, which since 1018/1609 was situated in Maragheh (q.v.). In 1019/1610, Eskandar Soltan was governor of the Moqaddam tribe.[267] This suggests that the chief of this tribe was not always

---

264 Monshi, *Tarikh*, pp. 23, 682, 1021 (Meshkin); 94, 472 (Kolhar); Molla Jalal, *Ruznameh*, p. 280 (Meshkin).
265 Monshi, *Tarikh*, vol. 2, pp. 579-80; Yazdi, *Mokhtasar*, vol. 1, p. 305. There existed already a fort called Mobarakeh in Asterabad in 932/1526. Abrahams, p. 174.
266 On the history of the Shahsevan see Richard Tapper, *Frontier nomads of Iran. A political and social history of the Shahsevan* (Cambridge, 1997).
267 Molla Jalal, *Ruznameh*, p. 389.

also governor of Maragheh (q.v.) at the same time, although this tended be the case in the years thereafter.

Mostang, see Shal.

Mosul, a town and district in Iraq, which for a short while was in Safavid hands, when they held Baghdad and other parts of Iraq. For example, in 1031/1622, Qasem Khan Afshar was governor of Mosul.[268]

Nabik, see Buri.

Nahababad (?) is a district of the province of Herat and was held by a governor, according to Nasiri's *Alqab*.

Najaf, a town and district in Iraq, which for a short while was in Safavid hands, when they held Baghdad and other parts of Iraq. For example, in 924/1518, Sayyed Mohammad Kamuneh was custodian (*motavalli*) of the shrine of Najaf and governor of some places in Iraq.[269]

Nakhjevan borders on the Aras River in the south and the Zangezur mountains (Armenia) in the west. It would seem that the chief of the Kangarlu also held the governorship of Nakhjevan.

Name	Year	Observations	Source
Shahqoli Soltan Ostajalu	975/1568	H Nakhjevan + Chokhur-e Sa'd	Tatavi 680
Sharaf Khan Bedlisi	985-986/1577-1578	H Nakhjevan	Bidlisi 2, 341
Cheragh Soltan Ostajalu	1012/1604	H Nakhjevan	Monshi 644
Maqsud Soltan Kangarlu Ostajalu	1013-1039/1605-1630	*Teyuldar* Nakhjevan	Monshi 656, 670, 901, 1085; Yusof 32; Molla Jalal 258, 272, 322; Vahid 155, 192
Morad Khan Kangarlu	?-1066/?-1656	Replaced by his brother	Vahid 613
'Aliqoli Soltan [Khan] Kangarlu	1066-1077/1656-1667	H Nakhjevan + H *do dang* of Georgia as of 1070	Vahid 613, 707-08; Puturidze 1961, doc. 31; Ibid., 1962, doc. 4; Valeh 1380, 577
Mohammad Reza Khan	1088/1677	H Nakhjevan	Agulis 139, 147, 150
Mortezaqoli Khan	1107-1110/1696-1699	H Kangarlu + Nakhjevan	Nasiri 96, 281; Anon, "Asnad" 1351, 61

---

268 Shamlu, *Qesas*, vol. 1, p. 204.
269 Valeh, *Khold*, 171; Rumlu, *Ahsan*, p. 137.

Mortezaqoli Khan	1117/1705	H Nakhjevan and ambassador en route to the Porte	Floor, "Lost files," 88

Naravandaqan probably is the same as Bazavandaq, which is listed by the TM as one of the districts in the Mashhad jurisdiction,[270] and as Bazavandaqan listed by Nasiri's *Alqab*. It is unknown which orthography is the correct one. In 1108/1697, Najm al-Din Soltan was governor of Naravandaqan.[271]

Natanz is district, with a town of the same name as its center, situated between Kashan and Isfahan. It is possible that the combination of the governorship of Natanz with that of Ardestan (q.v.) was a regular one.

Name	Year	Observations	Source
Nazar Soltan	983/1575	H Natanz + *Laleh* of Soltan Mostafa Mirza	Valeh 1372, 389
Amir Hamzeh Beyg Ostajalu	984-?/1576-?	H Ardestan + Natanz	Qomi 2, 627
Shahverdi Khalifeh-ye Shamlu	993/1585	H Natanz	Monshi 304; Valeh 1372, 700
Hasan Soltan b. Shahverdi Khalifeh brother's son of Morshedqoli Soltan	994-?/1586-?	H Natanz	Valeh 1372, 389

Neh va Bandan district was a dependency of Seystan, but it was turned into a separate governorship at an unknown date, probably already in the 16th century (q.v. Seystan). In 1108/1696, Kalb 'Ali Beyg was governor of Neh va Bandan.[272]

Nelqas is the name of a tribe, which is a sub-section of the Shamlu confederacy. Its chief appears to have been at the same time also governor of Hashtrud-e TabTab, which presumably was the district assigned to this tribe for its sustenance.[273] Hashtrud, which is listed by the TM, is a very fertile and water-rich district in Azerbaijan, situated on the slopes of the Sahand mountain, west of Miyaneh. TabTab, nowadays TapTap, is a district in Azerbaijan south of Kaleh Zuhak. Only Nasiri's *Alqab* mentions the governorship of Nelqas, for I have not been able to find other references to it.

Nesa is situated near Bagir, west of 'Ashqabad. Its governor appears to have been also simultaneously governor of Abivard (q.v.).

---

270 TM, pp. 103, 168.
271 Nasiri, *Dastur*, p. 201.
272 Nasiri, *Dastur*, pp. 203-04, 206.
273 The Nelqas or Nelwaz (TM, p. 16) are a sub-division of the Shamlu. Monshi, *Tarikh*, vol. 2, p. 1084.

Name	Year	Observations	Source
Din Mohammad Soltan	934/1528	H Nesa [the same as next one?]	Abrahams 136-137
Din Mohammad b. Olush Khan	945/1539	H Nesa va Barud [?] [=Abivard?]	Qomi 1, 287; Monshi 104
	962-1006/1555-1597	Uzbeg occupation	Bidlisi 2, 607; Tatavi 626, 711
Nur Mohammad Khan	1006-?/1597-?	H Nesa-Abivard-Baghbad	Siyaqi 479; Monshi 415
Arz Beyg ?	1019/11610	H Nesa – Abivard	Molla Jalal 383
Mohebb 'Ali Soltan b. Bektash Khan	1039/1630	H Nesa	Valeh 1380, 26, 29; Monshi 1085; Yusof 24

Neyriz a town and district in Fars, south of Shiraz, situated near Lake Neyriz, now Lake Bakhtegan.

Name	Year	Observations	Source
Sayyed Mohammad b. Sayyed Naser Ostajalu	932/1526	H Neyriz	Bacqué-Gramont 112
Charandab Soltan Shamlu	955-957/1548-1550	H Ich, Neyriz, Fasa	Hoseyni 170; Qomi 1, 327, 349
Shahverdi Khalifeh Shamlu b. Vali Khalifeh Shamlu	997-998/1589-1599	H Ij, Neyriz	Natanzi 338; Monshi 420

Nimruz, see Seystan.

Nishapur is a town and district in northern Khorasan. It is bounded in the west by Sabzavar, in the north by Khabushan, in the east by Mashhad and in the south by Torbat-e Heydariyeh and Kashmar. It became Safavid territory in 916/1510 when Shah Esma'il took Khorasan defeating Sheybani Khan of the Uzbegs.

Name	Year	Observations	Source
Shahrokh Beyg Afshar	917/1511	H Nishapur + Sabzavar	Aubin 19 (Afzal)
Zeyn al-Din Soltan Shamlu	927-?/1521-?	H Nishapur (+ Esfara'in)	Valeh 1372, 294; Khvandamir 591; Mozaffar 595
Baba Elyas Bayat	933/1526	H Nishapur	Dickson 102, n.1 (Afzal al-Tavarikh)
Jabrgeh Soltan	933/1527	H Nishapur	Hoseyni 92
Dhu'l-Qadr Khan	935-?/1529-?	H Nishapur	Afshar 166-68
Aghzivar Khan Shamlu	937-?/1531-?	H Nishapur	Monshi 59; Vahid 47
Heydar Soltan	951/1544	H Nishapur	Qomi 1, 309; Khvandamir 392

Soleyman Soltan Dhu'l-Qadr	972/1564	H Nishapur	Budaq 141
Ighuth Beyg Chavoshlu Ostajalu	972/1565	H *qal'eh-ye* Khabushan + Nishapur +Esfara'in	Shirazi 123; Qazvini 309
Mahmud Soltan Sufi-oghlu	985-987/1577-1579	H Nishapur	Qomi 2, 665, 674.
Dervish Mohammad Khan b. Aras Khan Rumlu	987-?/1579-?	H Nishapur	Qomi 2, 712; Monshi 257; Bidlisi 2, 654; Molla Jalal 43
Mirza Ahmad, vizier Morshedqoli Khan	987-991/1579-1583	Rival *vali* Nishapur	Molla Jalal 53-54, 62
Vali Khalifeh Shamlu	?-990/?-1582	H Nishapur	Shamlu 1, 107
Shahnazar Soltan Köshek-oghlu Ostajalu	?-997/?-1589	H Nishapur	Monshi 407-08
Mahmud Soltan Sufi-oghlu	997-998/1589-1590	rebel	Monshi 407, 411
	999-1001/1591-1593	Uzbeg occupation	Bidlisi 2, 689
Dervish Mohammad Khan Rumlu	1001-?/1593-?	2nd time H Nishapur	Valeh 1372, 606; Monshi 453-54; Vahid 117
	For some time in 1007/1598	Uzbeg occupation	
Mirza Mohammad Soltan Qara-Bayat Chaghatay	1007-1019/1598-1610	H Nishapur	Vahid 149; Monshi 566, 827; Molla Jalal 328
Beyram 'Ali Soltan [Khan] Qara-Bayat	1019-1064/1610-1654	Kinsman-H Nishapur	Monshi 828; Yusof 22; Shamlu 1, 282, 351; Valeh 1380, 27; Vahid 383, 476, 570
Ebrahim Khan Qara-Bayat	1064-?/1654-?	His son H Nishapur	Vahid 570
Fath 'Ali Khan	1122-1124/1710-1712	H Nishapur-Darun-Abivard	Khatunabadi 560, 565
Qasem Khan	1124-?/1712-?	H Nishapur	Khatunabadi 565

Nur, a district in Mazandaran situated between Kojur in the west and Amol in the east (see also Rostamdar).

Name	Year	Observations	Source
Malek 'Aziz	ca. 978/1570	H Nur and Kojur	Monshi 534
Malek Jahangir	ca. 996/1588	H Nur and Kojur	Monshi 534
Malek Soltan Hoseyn	997/1589	H Nur and Kojur	Shamlu 1, 167

Ordubad is a town and district in Nakhjevan situated near the river of the same name, which is tributary of the Aras River.

Name	Year	Observations	Source
'Abdol-Ghani Beyg	986-?/1578-?	*Teyuldar* Ordubad	Qomi 2, 676
Heydarqoli Soltan Ostajalu	994-?/1586-?	H Ordubad	Qomi 2, 832

Orfah, Orufah or Orufah-ye Diyarbekr was a town and district situated in Kurdestan, in the Diyarbekr province. The Safavids held it for a short time, from at least 920/1514 (or quite likely earlier) until 923/1517, when Diyarbekr was permanently lost to the Ottomans. In 920/1514, Acheh Soltan Qajar was named governor of Orfah, while he also was renamed Qadurmish Khan, because he killed Morad Mirza, the Aq-Qoyunlu rival of Shah Esma'il I.[274]

Orumi or Orumiyeh is situated on a plain, west of Lake Orumiyeh, some 165 km south-west of Tabriz and borders on Turkey. After initially having been governed by representatives of various tribes as of 1039/1630 Orumi would remain in the hands of the Afshar tribe well into the twentieth century.[275]

Name	Year	Observations	Source
Vali Soltan Dhu'l-Qadr	954/1547	H Orumi	Rumlu 418; Qomi 1, 522
Soleyman Chelebi Chini [rather Chapni]	955-?/1548-?	H Orumi	Qomi 1, 337; Rumlu 438
Hoseyn Jan Beyg Khonusi	?-986/?-1578	H Orumi	Bidlisi 2, 647
Amir Khan Chulaq Baradust	1017-1018/1608-1609	As of 1017 he received the districts of Targavar, Margavar, Orumiyeh and Ushniyeh, which under Tashmasp had been a Qezelbash governorship	Monshi 782, 791-97, 810
Qapan Khan Beygdelu	1018-1024/1610-1615	H Oromi + BB from Soltaniyeh till Van. From 1024 also of Domdom	Monshi 811, 889-890; Molla Jalal 389, 432
Pir Budaq Khan	1024/1615	H Orumiyeh +DomDom	Monshi 890
Aqa Khan Moqaddam	1024-1039/1615-1630	H Orumiyeh +DomDom	Monshi 890
Kalb 'Ali Soltan [Khan] Afshar b. Qasem Khan Inanlu	1039-1058/1630-1648	H Orumi (+ Farah)	Valeh 1380, 467, 477; Yusof 138; Vahid 476; Monshi 1085

274 Qomi, *Kholasat*, vol. 1, 133.
275 On the Afshar tribe, which is spread out all over Iran, and in particular its role in the Orumiyeh area see Mirza Rashid Adib al-Sho'ara, *Tarikh-e Afshar* eds. Mahmud Ramiyan and Parviz Shahriyar Afshar (Tabriz, 1345/1966).

Ganj 'Ali Khan	?-1064/?-1654	H Orumi	Vahid 570
Mohammad 'Ali Khan	1064-?/1654-?	H Orumi	Vahid 570, 581
Jani Khan	1105/1694	H Orumi va Afshar	Nasiri 54,
Aghzivar Khan	1106/1695	H Orumi va Afshar	Nasiri 80
Fazl 'Ali Khan Afshar	1107/1696	H Orumi va Afshar	Nasiri 96
Jani Khan	1108/1697	H Orumi va Afshar and *sardar* of Khorasan	Nasiri 54, 119, 128, 133, 158-60, 202, 203, 206

Palangan was a Kurdish principality, although a part of Ardalan Kurdestan (q.v.). It was usually governed by a member of the Ardalan family, although in 1576 a Qezelbash emir was appointed as its governor. Palangan was the main center of the district and boasted of a very strong fort, which was destroyed by Safi I.[276]

Name	Year	Observations	Source
Gheybollah Beyg	ca. 920-40s?/1514-1530s	H Palangan; succeeded by his son	Bidlisi 2, 179
Mohammad Beyg	ca. 940-60s?/1530s-1550s	H Palangan; succeeded by his son	Bidlisi 2, 179
Emir Eskandar	?-984/?-1576	H Palangan	Bidlisi 2, 179
Sulaq Hoseyn Tekkelu	984-?/1576-?	H Palangan + Dinavar	Bidlisi 2, 179

Panbak, see Lori.

Panjdeh is situated southeast of Herat province, between Sabzavar (Farah) in the west and Hazarajat in the east.

Name	Year	Observations	Source
Fazl 'Ali Soltan	?-1044/?-1635	H Panjdeh	Yusof 166; Astarabadi 251
His son	1044-?/1635-?	H Panjdeh	Yusof 166; Astarabadi 251
Naqdi Soltan	1059/1649	H Panjdeh	Shamlu 1, 513

Parsi-Badan is a district that I have not been able to identify, but from internal evidence it seems it is situated in the province of Fars. Until 1590, Abu'l-Qasem Beyg was governor of Parsi-Badan.[277]

---

276 Bidlisi, *Cheref-Nameh*, vol. 2, p. 179f.
277 Qomi, *Kholasat*, vol. 2, p. 919.

Pasakuh or Basaku was a fort situated in Khorasan in the Darrehgaz area.[278] Monshi even states that Pasakuh was in the district of Mamshad, which I have not been able to identify.[279] The *Tadhkirat al-Moluk* has Hwrz-va y.saku, where Nasiri's *Alqab* mentions Pasakuh.[280]

Name	Year	Observations	Source
Morsheqoli Soltan Jalayer b. Khodaverdi Khan	1007/1599	H Ft Pasakuh	Monshi 602-03
Shahvali Soltan Jala'er	?-1038/1629	H Ft. Pasakuh	Monshi 1087

Pasak is a district under a governor, according to Nasiri's *Alqab*. It probably is situated in Qarabagh or Chokhur-e Sa'd.[281]

Paydar possibly is a tribal district in Shirvan or Chokhur-e Sa'd. In 1038/1629 or prior to that time Nur al-Din Soltan Paydar was a surbordinate to the governor of Tiflis,[282] while Nasiri's *Alqab* lists it as a governorship at the end of the Safavid era.

Pudeh is the main village of the district of Someyram (q.v.) in the Isfahan jurisdiction. In 1110/1698, Namdar Soltan was governor of Pudeh.[283]

Qabaleh is a town and district in the province of Shirvan. In 1043/1633, Soleyman Beyg Qushchi *gholam* was governor of Qabaleh and Qolhan.[284]

Qa'en is a mountainous district in the south-east corner of Khorasan, extending from south of Khvaf to Seystan and from the crest of the Tun range to the Afghan border.

Name	Year	Observations	Source
Amir Soltan Mowselu	919-921/1513-1515	H Qa'en (+ Qohestan [Mozaffar 450, 517])	Hoseyni 62; Valeh 1372, 246; Qomi 1, 134; Bidlisi 2, 534; Qazvini 276; Ben Khvandamir 166
Amir Khan Rumlu*	921-?/1515-?	H Qa'en	Shirazi 56
Ebrahim Mirza	970-971/1563-1564	H Qa'en -without *Laleh*	Qomi 1, 440
Vali Beyg Ostajalu	981/1574	H Qa'en	Rumlu 586

278 Monshi, *Tarikh*, 602-03, 605, 884, 1087.
279 Monshi, *Tarikh*, vol. 2, p. 1087.
280 TM, p. 102; for a possible other identification see Ibid., p. 168.
281 Monshi, *Tarikh*, vol. 2, pp. 687-88.
282 Monshi, *Tarikh*, vol. 2, p. 1087.
283 Nasiri, *Dastur*, p. 272.
284 Yusof, *Dheyl*, p. 153; Valeh, *Iran*, p. 211.

Vali Khalifeh Shamlu	?-986/1578	Rival H Qa'en of next one	Qomi 2, 688, 705; Molla Jalal 47
Fulad Khalifeh-ye Shamlu	987-991/1579-1583	H or *Mir* Qa'en [or Soltan 'Ali Khalifeh who was his nephew]	Qomi 2, 711, 732 , 739; Monshi 303; Molla Jalal 43
Soltan 'Ali Soltan Shamlu	991-994/1583-1585	H Qa'en	Qomi 2, 794; Natanzi 258
Salman Khalifeh Torkman, son-in-law of Morshedqoli Khan	?-996/?-1588	H Qa'en	Vahid 107
Soltan 'Ali Khalifeh Shamlu b. Fulad Khalifeh	997-?/1589-?	H Qa'en	Valeh 1372, 703, 709; Vahid 107
	999/1591	Uzbeg occupation	Bidlisi 2, 689
'Aliqoli Khan Ostajalu	?-1001/?-1593	H Qa'en –but besieged in Ft. Jur by Uzbegs	Monshi 456
Soltan 'Ali Khalifeh Soltan b. Fulad Khalifeh Shamlu	1001-?/1593-?	H Qa'en - usurper	Monshi 456
Mehrab Soltan [Khan]	1009/1600	H Qa'en	Molla Jalal 201
Najafqoli Soltan	1011/1602	H Qa'en	Monshi 620

* According to Tatavi, *Tarikh*, p. 372, Delu Soltan Rumlu was governor of Qa'en in 921.

Qolhan, see Qobeh and Qabaleh.

Qandahar province was initially left in the hands of the former Timurid governors, who had pledged allegiance to the Safavids. Because this loyalty was very nominal in 919/1511 a Qezelbash army marched on Qandahar to take it, but peace was made with its governor as the citadel was considered too strong to take.[285] Following the disaster in Ghujduvan (1512) and Chalderan (1514) Shah Esma'il I did not have strength to do something about Qandahar. Babur Mirza, who had wanted to take Qandahar for a long time finally took possession of it in 1522, while Sam Mirza and Amir Khan made an unauthorized and failed attempt to take the city in 1534/35. In 1537 Shah Tahmasp I marched to take the city and its dependencies and appointed one of his sons as governor, but the Moghul prince Kamran Mirza retook it in 1537/38. Tahmasp I helped Homayun take the city in 1545, who handed it over to the Safavids. However, shortly thereafter he retook the city promising to return it. Because neither Homayun nor his son Akbar returned Qandahar as had been promised Shah Tahmasp I therefore seized the city in 1558. It remained in Safavid hands until 1595, when Akbar in agreement with the Uzbegs and taking advantage of the unsettled situation during the early part of Abbas I's reign occupied Qandahar. 'Abbas I asked for the return of the city and following a refusal launched unsuccessful attacks in 1604/05 and in 1607. 'Abbas I was finally able to retake the city in 1622, but his successor (Safi I) lost the city when its governor, 'Ali Mardan Khan defected to the Moghuls and handed over the city in 1047/1638. 'Abbas II retook the city in 1059/1649 and despite three Moghul attempts (1649, 1652, and 1653) to capture Qandahar it remained in Safavid hands until 1709, when Mir Weys, the leader of the Ghilzay

---

285 Shirazi, *Takmelat*, p. 54; Qazvini, *Tarikh*, p. 276.

tribe permanently expelled the Safavids. Shah Soltan Hoseyn tried to put a pretty face on an ugly reality when in 1716 he appointed Mahmud Khan, son of Mir Weys as governor of Qandahar and bestowing the new name of Hoseynqoli Khan upon him. This was a reward for having defeated the Abdalis, who had clobbered the Safavid army on two consecutive occasions, but it failed to make the harsh reality go away that Safavid influence had come to an end.[286]

Shah Tahmasp I appointed first one of his sons and later Soltan Hoseyn Mirza, his nephew, as governor of Qandahar, of course, under the supervision of a tutor (*Laleh*). His nephew's son succeeded his father just when Tahmasp I died and during the following years of Qezelbash civil war, according to Molla Jalal, Soltan Hoseyn Mirza struck coins in his name in 986/1578.[287] 'Abbas I put an end to the governorships of princes in general and henceforth Qandahar was governed by Qezelbash and *gholam* governors (see Table). By the end of the Safavid period, according to Nasiri's *Alqab*, Qandahar province included the following administrative jurisdictions: Kushk, K.ri.-Y.ki, Ghuriyan, and Zamindavar. According to another source, Qandahar included Qalat-e Ghilzai, Fushanj (q.v.), Shal va Mostang (q.v.), and Qalat-e banchareh-ye Baluch (probably Kalat), although these only nominally acknowledged Safavid rule, if at all towards the end.[288] Yazdi calls this province Nimruz and states that it had six districts and two forts: Bost, Zamindavar, Farah, Qandahar, Keresk, Garmsirat-e kenar-e ab-e Hirmand, Qal'eh-ye Qalat and Qal'eh-ye Band-e Timur.[289]

Name	Year	Observations	Source
Budaq Khan Qajar	943-944/1537-1538	H Qandahar – *Laleh* Soltan Morad Mirza b. Tahmasp	Monshi 66; Qazvini 292; Abrahams, p. 136
	From 944 to 952/1538-1545	Moghul governors	Monshi 91-92
Budaq Khan Qajar	952/1545 [a few months]	H Qandahar - *Laleh* Soltan Morad Mirza b. Tahmasp	Monshi 69; Qazvini 292
	From 952-965/1545-1558	Moghul governors	Monshi 92
Hamzeh Beyg Dhu'l-Qadr aka Qur Hamzeh	965-984/1558-1576	H Qandahar - *Laleh* Soltan Hoseyn Mirza b. Bahram Mirza + Zamindavar + the districts of Garmsirat	Hoseyni 177; Shamlu 1, 79; Monshi 136, 207; Qomi 1, 397, 448, 575, 2, 629; Riazul Islam I, 93-94
Fulad Khalifeh-ye Shamlu	984/1576	H Qandahar – *Laleh* of Mozaffar Hoseyn Mirza in Qandahar and of Rostam Mirza in Zamindavar + Garmsirat	Shamlu 1, 98; Qomi 2, 630; Monshi 138, 477

---

286 Lockhart, *Fall*, pp. 100-01; Floor, *Afghan*, pp. 40-41.
287 Molla Jalal, *Ruznameh*, p. 35. This must have been his son Mozaffar Hoseyn Mirza, because his father had died in 984 already.
288 Safavi, *Majma'*, p. 4.
289 Yazdi, *Mokhtasar*, vol. 1, pp. 285-88.

Hamzeh Beyg Dhu'l-Qadr aka Qur Hamzeh	985-?/1577-?	H Qandahar – *Laleh* for the children of Soltan Hoseyn Mirza b. Bahram Mirza	Qomi 2, 666
Mozaffar Hoseyn Mirza b. Bahram Mirza	995/1587	H Qandahar	Monshi 408
Qur Hamzeh	996/1588	H Qandahar	Monshi 408
Rostam Mirza b. Bahram Mirza	996/1588	H Qandahar -	Monshi 408
Mozaffar Hoseyn Mirza b. Bahram Mirza	997-1000/1589-1592	H Qandahar – his *vakil* was Mohammad Beyg Bayat	Monshi 484- 881
	From 1000/1592 to 1031/1622	Moghul governors	Monshi 973-74
Ganj 'Ali Khan Zik	1031-1035/1622-1626	Initially with Kerman; succeeded by his son	Monshi 977, 1041; Yusof 73; Vahid 215
'Ali Mardan Khan Zik	1035-1047/1626-1638	H Qandahar	Monshi 1041; Shamlu 1, 242; Yusof 73, 120, 149, 293; Vahid 215, 285-88
Nazar Beyg Zik or 'Ali Morad Khan*	1047/1638	A retainer of 'Ali Mardan Khan, but he never came there	Astarabadi 256
	From 1047/1638 to 1059/1649	Moghul governors	
Mehrab Khan	1059/1649	H Qandahar + Astarabad	Shamlu 1, 429, 498; Vahid 510; Riazul Islam 1, 343
Owtar Khan aka Dhu'l-Feqar Khan	1059-1073/1649-1663	H Darun; BB Qandahar	Vahid 596, 658, 697, 742; Riazul Islam I, 349, 399, 422, 439; Valeh 1380, 601
Karjasi [Garjasi] Beyg aka Mansur Khan	1073-?/1663-?	BB Qandahar; brother of previous governor	Vahid 742; Shamlu 2, 19; Valeh 1380, 461 (Garjasb)
Dervish Khan Soltan	1105-1106/1694-1695	BB Qandahar	Nasiri 59, 177
Mohammad 'Ali Khan	1107/1696		Nasiri 119, 123
Aslamas Beyg aka Aslan Khan	1107, 1108/1696, 1697	BB Qandahar	Nasiri 107, 177, 260; Shushtari 65
Kalb 'Ali Khan	1110/1698	BB Qandahar + *vali* Astarabad	Nasiri 273
'Abdollah Khan	1110/1698-1699	BB Qandahar	Lockhart 83; Durri 94
Shahnavaz Khan III = Gorgin Khan	1114-1121/1704-1709	BB Qandahar + Kerman + Kushk + *sepahsalar*	Mostowfi 116; Lockhart 84, 88; Savafi 3-7; Khatunabadi 552, 558; Mervi 1, 17, 19
Khosrow Mirza	1121-1123/1709-1711	H Qandahar; nephew of Gorgin Khan	Khatunabadi 559, 564; Safavi 8
	As of 1121/1709	end of Safavid rule	Lockhart 90

* 'Ali Morad Khan surrendered the citadel of Qandahar to the governor of Kabul and then Nazar Beyg Zik was appointed as the new governor with orders to retake Qandahar, which he was unable to do.

Qapan, Qapanat or Qabanat (in Armenian Syunik) is a district of Azerbaijan, north of Ordubad, on the northern banks of the Aras River. In 1628-1629 or thereabouts Hasan Soltan Ordaklu Torkman was the governor of Qapanat.[290]

Qara Aghach is situated on the road between Shah Takht and Khoy, about 19 km north of Qareh Ziya al-Din.[291] However, according to Minorsky, this district is situated in eastern Kakhetia, southeast of Signakh.[292] From the available sources it is not clear which of the two districts is meant. The fact that, according to Nasiri's *Alqab*, its governor was also called governor of the Bayat is not helpful either, because the Bayat resided both in Azerbaijan and in Shirvan and adjacent territories.

Qarabagh is a province situated between the rivers Kur and Aras, with Ganjeh as its main urban center. As of 961/1554 Qarabagh and Ganjeh were both governed by members of the Ziyad-oghlu Qajar family (see Table); other dependent districts are listed in the Table concerning Qarabagh in the introduction. From 996/1588 until 1014/1605 Qarabagh was occupied by the Ottomans.

Name	Year	Observations	Source
Piri Beyg Qajar	907-918?/1501-1512?	H Qarabagh	Aubin 8 (Afzal)
Hoseyn Beyg Ostajalu	932/1526	H Qarabagh	Bacqué-Gramont 97
Ya'qub Soltan Qajar	934/1528	H Qarabagh	Dickson 134, 140; Abrahams 200
Shahverdi Soltan Qajar	958-975/1551-1566	BB Qarabagh	Abrahams 140
Shahverdi Khan Soltan Ziyad-oghlu	961-971/1554-1564	H Qarabagh	Qomi 1, 392, 420; Monshi 76, 385; Shirazi 118, 122
Ebrahim Beyg [Soltan] Ziyad-oghlu Qajar	971-975-?/1564-1568-?	BB Ganjeh + Qarabagh - *Laleh* Soltan 'Ali Mirza b. Shah Tahmasp,	Qomi 1, 609; Monshi 134, Shirazi 122, 125; Vahid 67; Abrahams 145
Yusof Khalifeh Ziyadoghlu b. Shahverdi Soltan	983/1575	*Laleh* of Soltan 'Ali Mirza [who remained at court]	Valeh 1372, 411; Monshi 140, 213
Peykar Soltan	984/1576	H Ganjeh + *amir al-omara* of Qarabagh	Monshi 212

---

290 Valeh, *Khold*, p. 57 (Qabanat); Yusof, *Dheyl*, p. 43; Monshi, *Tarikh*, vol. 2, p. 1085. In 1727, Da'vud Beyg, an Armenian chief, was appointed by Tahmasp II as its governor. Brosset, *Collection*, vol. 2, pp. 248-49.
291 Molla Jalal, *Ruznameh*, pp. 369, 377.
292 TM, p. 167.

Emamqoli Beyg [Soltan] [Khan] Qajar	985-996/1576-1588	H Qarabagh – Ganjeh [- Barda'] he was a *qurchi*	Qomi 2, 665; Monshi 213, 227, 233, 270, 326, 346, 385; Qomi 2, 645, 686, 803; Valeh 1372, 624, 638, 756, 797, 808; Vahid 106; Bidlisi II 648
Mohammad Khan Ziyadoghlu Qajar b. Khalil Khan Qajar b. Shahverdi Soltan	996-998/1588-1590	BB Qarabagh	Monshi 385, 407, 417; Yusof 261; Vahid 106
	From 997-1014/1589-1605	Ottoman rule	
Hoseyn Khan Ziyad-oghlu Qajar	1014-1015/1605-1606	BB Qarabagh	Monshi 716; Vahid 155, 157
Mohammad Khan Ziyadoghlu Qajar b. Khalil Khan Qajar b. Shahverdi Soltan	1015-1025/1606-1616	BB Qarabagh - in 1024; ordered to move his residence from Ganjeh to Tiflis	Monhsi 716, 788, 818, 887, 892; Molla Jalal 381; Yusof 262
Mohammadqoli Khan Ziyadoghlu b. Mohammad Khan	1025-1036/1616-1637	BB Qarabagh	Shamlu 1, 205; Monshi 1024, 1065; Yusof 109, 262; Vahid 210, 219, 329
Da'ud Khan b. Allahverdi Khan	1036-1042/1627-1633	BB Qarabagh	Monshi 1069; Shamlu 1, 205; Yusof 81, 107 n, 289; Vahid 218-19, 329
Mohammadqoli Khan Ziyadoghlu	1042- ?/1633-?	BB Qarabagh - 2nd time	Yusof 169, 177, 289; Vahid 329; Astarabadi 252
Mortezaqoli Khan Ziyadoghli	1061-1074/1651-1664	BB Qarabagh +some Kakheti forts; as of 1070 H *chahar dang* of Georgia	Musavi 1965, doc. 10; Puturidze 1961, doc. 31; Vahid 707, 757, 759
Oghurlu Khan	1074-?/1664-?	BB Qarabagh	Vahid 759
'Abbasqoli Khan	1105/1694	BB Qarabagh + H Kakhetia	Nasiri 56; Brosset 2/2, 13
Kalb 'Ali Khan Ziyad-oghlu	1107/1695	BB Qarabagh + H Kakhetia	Puturidze 1962, doc. 21
Kostandil Mirza	?-1135-?/?-1723-?	BB Qarabagh; *vali* Kartlia + Kakhetia; h Shams al-Dinlu + Qazaqlar	Brosset 2/2, 513, 515-17

Qara Alus probably is a tribal district in Qarabagh or Azerbaijan. In 1024/1634 mention is made of the governors of Qara Alus and Nakhjevan in a royal decree without indicating their names.[293]

Qarach is a district situated in Khorasan. In 1016/1607, Esma'ilqoli Khan was governor of Qarach.[294]

---

293 Puturidze 1961, doc. 12. On the Qara Alus see Floor-Faghfoory, *Dastur*, pp. 108-09.
294 Molla Jalal, *Ruznameh*, p. 328.

Qara Hesar is a fort situated on the border near Maku. In 1005/1596, Zeynal Khan was its governor.[295]

Qarajehdagh or Qaradagh is a hilly district of Azerbaijan, situated north of Tabriz between Sahand and Jolfa, bordering in the west on the Aras River. Ahar is its largest town. As is clear from the table, Nasiri is misleading when he writes that this governorship was usually held by one of his family members.

Name	Year	Observations	Source
Khalifeh-ye Ansar	975-997/1568-1589	H Qarajehdagh	Rumlu 561; Qomi 471; Bidlisi 2, 632
Shahverdi Khan b. Khalifeh-ye Ansar	997-1001/1589-1593	H Qarajehdagh	Monshi 407, 447; Vahid 115
N.N.	1001-?/1593-?	H Qarajehdagh	Monshi 447
Elyas Khalifeh Qaradaghlu	1014-1018/1605-1609	H Qarajehdagh Replaced by a kinsman	Monshi 756, 810
Maqsud Soltan Donboli	1018-1023/1610-1614	H Qarajehdagh	Monshi 820, 882
Borhan al-Din Khalifeh b. Elyas Khalifeh	1038/1629	H Qarajehdagh	Monshi 1085
Bayandor Soltan	before 1052/1642	H Qarajehdagh	Yusof 278; Vahid 321
Pir Budaq Khan b. Shahbandeh Khan	before 1052/1642	H Qarajehdagh + *kholafa* of that district	Yusof 286
Bayandor Soltan	1105-1113/1694-1702	H Qarajehdagh	Nasiri 81, 229; Petrushevskij doc 3

Qazeqman, also Qazeghman (now Kazicman in Turkey), is a district in the province of Qarabagh and is situated between Qars and Pasin. Uch-Kalisa or Etsmiadzin is located nearby.[296]

Name	Year	Observations	Source
Yadgar Beyg Pazuki	966/1559	*Teyuldar* Lashgerd + Qazeghman	Shirazi 114
'Aliqoli Soltan Sa'dlu	997/1589	H Qaqezman	Monshi 743
Nafas Soltan Sa'dlu b. 'Aliqoli Soltan	1012-?/1603-?	*Teyuldar* Qazeqman	Monshi 656; Vahid 155

Qazvin, the second capital of the Safavids (1540-1590), and the center of a district of the same name, situated some 145 km north-west of Tehran. It was part of Persian Iraq.[297] The governor and later the vizier of Qazvin was usually governed the district together with that of Savokh-Bolagh. Between 946/1539 and 983/1575 and as of 1043/1634 the district was transformed into crown domain, which situation seems to have lasted until 1133/1721, when once again a governor of Qazvin was appointed.

---

295 Vahid, *Tarikh*, p. 166.
296 Bidlisi, *Cherefnameh*, vol. 1, p. 238.
297 For its history see Parviz Varjavand, *Simay-e Tarikh va Farhang-e Qazvin* 3 vols. (Tehran, 1377/1998).

Name	Year	Observations	Source
Abdal Beyg Dedeh Dhu'l-Qadr*	?-915/?-1509	H Qazvin, Savokh-Bolagh, Rey	Qomi 1, 100; Shirazi 48; Bidlisi 2, 51 (+Khvar); Qazvini 272
Zeynal Khan Shamlu	915-918?/1509-1512?	H Qazvin	Hoseyni 70, 75; Qomi 1, 100; Shirazi 48; Bidlisi 2, 521; Qazvini 272, 284
Khames Beyg aka 'Abdollah Khan Ostajalu?	932/1526	H Qazvin	Bacqué-Gramont 97
Mantasha Soltan Ostajalu	932/1527	H Qazvin	Qomi 1, 162
Akhi Soltan Tekkelu	933/1527	H Qazvin + Bastam	Budaq 61; Qomi 1, 172; Shirazi 64; Qazvini 284; Dickson 68; Tahmasp 8, 10; Bidlisi 2, 552
Mohammad Beyg [Khan] Sharaf al-Dinoghlu Tekkelu aka Mohammad Soltan	933-?/1527-?	H Qazvin + Bastam	Qomi 1, 172; Shirazi 64; Budaq 68; Qazvini 284; Dickson 68, 102, n. 1; Tahmasp 10; Bidlisi 2, 552
Amir Beyg [Soltan] Rumlu	940-946/1534-1540	H Qazvin + Savokh-Bolakh	Rumlu 382; Qomi 1, 293; Shirazi 75
	from 946/1540 until 983/1575	crown domain	
Mir Sayyed 'Ali Razavi Qomi	950 and 960s?/1540s-1550s	Vizier Qazvin; succeeded by the next one	Monshi 166
Jarandab Soltan Shamlu [?]	964/1554	*Darugheh* Qazvin	Abrahams 141
Mirza 'Abdol-Baqi aka Zadeh-ye Makhdum	?-983/?-1575	Vizier Qazvin	Monshi 166
Ebrahim Soltan Ostajalu b. Shahqoli Yakan	983-985/1576	H Qazvin	Monshi 205
Soltan Hoseyn Khan Shamlu father of 'Aliqoli Khan	985-988/1576-1579	H Qazvin	Qomi 2, 664, 691, 707; Monshi 227
Esma'ilqoli Khan Shamlu	988-995/1579-1587	H Qazvin – was *tovachi-bashi* and it was his *teyul* (q.v. Abhar)	Monshi 259; Valeh 1372, 767; Qomi 2, 763, 808; Bidlisi 2, 676, 681

	In 996/1588	One part of Qazvin + Savokh-Bulagh turned into crown domain; the other part divided among the *qurchi*s	Qomi 2, 874
Mohammad Sharif Beyg Chavoshlu Ostajalu grandson Hasan Beyg	997-998/1589-1590	H Qazvin	Vahid 107; Monshi 399, 418
Qurkhmas Khan Shamlu	998/1590	H Qazvin	Valeh 1372, 838
Qara Hasan Khan Chavoshlu Ostajalu	999/1591	*Darugheh* + H Qazvin	Molla Jalal 103; Qomi 2, 1087
Jamshid Beyg [*gholam*]	1001/1593	H Qazvin	Monshi 449
Sheikh Ahmad Aqa	1002/1594	H + *darugheh* Qazvin	Natanzi 544
Mirzay 'Alameyn	1003-1008/1594-1600	Vizier Qazvin	Fumeni 181, 188
Salman Khan Ostajalu b. Shah 'Ali Mirza	1021/1612	H Qazvin; dismissed that same year;	Monshi 853; Vahid 181 (Soleyman - 1022)
Aslan Beyg	?-1028/?-1619	Vizier Qazvin	Vahid 176
Mirza Mohammad Abhari	?-1039/?-1629	Vizier Qazvin	Vahid 228
Mirza Musa	1039-?/1629-?	Vizier Qazvin	Vahid 228
Mortezaqoli Soltan b. Mehrab Khan	1042/1633	H + *darugheh* Qazvin	Yusof 103
'Emada Mohammad aka Mirza 'Emad	1043/1634	Vizier Qazvin	Yusof 148; Astarabadi 250
Mirza Mohammad	1073/1662	Vizier Qazvin	Vahid 742
N.N.	1095/1684	Vizier Qazvin	Kaempfer 71
Mohammad 'Ali	1106/1695	Vizier Qazvin	Nasiri 81
Tahmasp Khan Gholam	1133/1721	H Qazvin	DM 503

* Another source mentions Saru Pireh, the *qurchi-bashi* as governor. Aubin, "Les soufis," p. 13, n. 147.

Qezel Aqaj is a coastal district situated in northern Talesh (now in the Republic of Azerbaijan) bounded in the south by Ardabil, in the west by Lenkoran, in the north by the Caspian Sea and in the east by Gilan.[298]

Name	Year	Observations	Source
Mohammad Mirza b. Bahram Beyg Qaramanlu	932/1526	Beyg of Qezel-Aghaj	Bacqué-Gramont 97, 110
Farhad Beyg b. Hosam Soltan Qaramanlu	9971589	Amir of Ardabil-Qezel Aqaj and dependencies	Shamlu 1, 135

298 It also occurs as Qezel 'Ajaj, see Yusof, *Dheyl*, p. 192; Vahid, *Tarikh*, pp. 185, 278, 729; Fragner, "Ardabil", docs. 2, 3.

COMMENTARY 263

Dhu'l-Feqar Khan Qaramanlu	?-1004/?-1596	H Qezel-Aghaj; replaced by his son	Yusof 192; Vahid 278
Hosam Soltan	1004-?/1596-?	H Qezel-Aghaj	Yusof 192
Hosam Beyg b. Dhu'l-Feqar Khan	1045-?/1635-?	H Ghez-Agjaj	Astarabadi 254

Qepchaq or Qebchaq steppe is located in Khvarezm, but some its Turkmen tribes became vassals under Shah 'Abbas I and had their summer quarters next to that of the Gereyli and Hajjilar tribes in the province of Astarabad. In 945/1538, Din Mohammad Khan was appointed as governor of Hazd-Asp Qebchaq, but it would appear that this was but a temporary submission of the local ruler, for in 952/1545 Din Mohammad Khan invaded Safavid territory.[299] Towards the end of the Safavid period, at least according to Nasiri's *Alqab*, it had a Safavid governor. This is not corroborated by any other source. Perhaps it was to collect taxes that a Safavid governor was appointed.[300]

Qobeh is situated on the north-eastern slopes of the Shahdagh range (part of the Greater Caucasus) at a height of 600 m above sea level, on the right bank of the Kudyal river. Qolhan was part of the same district and was situated adjacent to Qobeh. According to the TM and Nasiri's *Alqab*, Qobeh, Qolhan and Saliyan (q.v.) formed one governate, although the latter also occurs as a separate governorship.[301] All three towns and districts were dependencies of the province of Shirvan.

Name	Year	Observations	Source
Soleyman [Beyg] Soltan Qushchi	1044-1046/1635-1637	H Qobeh and Qolhan	Yusof 192; Vahid 265, 280
'Ashur Soltan b. Seydom Soltan	1046-?/1637-?	H Qobeh-Qolhan	Vahid 280

Qom is part of Persian Iraq and is bounded on the north by Tehran, on the east by the Kavir, on the south by Kashan and on the west by Hamadan, Farahan and Saveh. Its governor sometimes also held sway over other jurisdictions, such as Jasb, a district 50 km south of Qom, while sometimes the district was divided between two governors. By 1006/1597 Qom had become crown domain and henceforth a vizier governed the district.

Name	Year	Observations	Source
Aqa Fathollah	?-910-?/?-1504	H Qom; Qomi's maternal uncle	Qomi 1, 99
Durmish Khan Shamlu	?-924/?-1519	H Qom	Qomi 1, 140
Amir Soltan	?-938/?-1532	H Qom	Qomi 1, 225

---

300 Abrahams, pp. 137-38.
300 Nasiri, *Dastur*, p. 242 (see also 'Astarabad' in the Commentary).
301 TM, p. 102; Qomi, *Kholasat*, vol. 2, p. 928; Vahid, *Tarikh*, p. 280 has Qalban.

Shahqoli Khalifeh Dhu'l-Qadr *Mohrdar*	938-969/1532-1562	H Qom	Qomi 1, 394, 436
Vali Khalifeh Shamlu	969-979/1562-1572	H Qom	Budaq 141; Rumlu 561; Bidlisi 2, 632; Qazvini 310
Heydar Soltan [Chabuq Tarkhan] Torkman	979-987/1572-1579	H Qom + Ardestan	Qomi 1, 563, 2, 627, 648, 659, 665, 688, 710; also Monshi 140, 227, 265; Valeh 1372, 410
Ebrahim Beyg [Soltan] [Chabuq Tarkhan] Torkman	987-?/1579-?	H Qom *va navahi va tavabe' ba mahallat*	Monshi 256; Qomi 2, 710
Adham Khan Torkman	?-994/?-1586	H Qom (or H Farahan + Garmrud - Qomi)	Monshi 340-41; Qomi 2, 755
'Abbasqoli Soltan Dhu'l-Qadr	994/1586	H Qom + *ba'zi bolukat*	Qomi 2, 828
Morshedqoli Soltan Shamlu brother of Esma'ilqoli Khan and son of Vali Khalifeh	994/1586	H of *boluk-e* Vazvan?, Jasb, Vashnaveh-ye Qom; H *ba'zi az velayat-e* Qom	Qomi 2, 828, 735; Natanzi 200, 226; Qomi 2, 851
'Aliqoli Soltan Quroghlu Dhu'l-Qadr grandson of Shahqoli Khalifeh-ye *mohrdar*	994/1586	H *ba'zi az velayat-e* Qom [jointly held]	Natanzi 226; Qomi 2, 851; Monshi, 359; Valeh 1372, 789, 824, 828, 832
Soleyman Khalifeh-ye Torkman	996/As of Januarr 1588	H Qom+ Farahan	Qomi 2, 874, 882
Hoseyn Beyg [Khan] Shamlu	999-1006/1591-1598	H Qom, Farahan, Natanz	Qomi 2, 889, 895, 1069, 1075, 1084, 1091; Monshi 433, 441, 533; Vahid 112
Mirza Hoseyn	1095/1684	Vizier	Kaempfer 75
N.N.	1110/1698	Soltan of Qom	de Maze 99

Ranekuh, a district in Gilan, forming its eastern boundary.

Name	Year	Observations	Source
Vali Soltan Sufi	1001-?/1593-?	H Ranekuh	Monshi 499; Vahid 116
Adam Soltan Gorji	before 1038/1629	H Ranekuh + Deylaman	Fumeni 285
Beyram 'Ali Beyg	1038/1629	H Ranekuh + Deylaman	Vahid 223-25
Lotf 'Ali Soltan	1105/1694	H Ranekuh	Nasiri 31

Rasht is a town in Gilan, situated near Enzeli (see Gilan). Usually the governor of Gilan-e biyeh-pas was also governor of Rasht, but once the province had been united and incorporated into the Safavid state non-local governors were appointed to govern Rasht.

Name	Year	Observations	Source
Emir Hosam al-Din	911/1506	H Rasht + Fumen	Monshi 1, 28; Vahid 29; Mozaffar 236
Amireh Dobbaj Rashti renamed Mozaffar Soltan	?-940/?-1534	*Vali* Rasht = Gilan-e biyeh-pas; H Jilan-e Rasht	Hoseyni 207, 221-2; Qomi 1, 141, 254-55; Monshi 111
Jamshid Khan	975-985/1568-1577	*Vali* Rasht-e Gilan	Natanzi 33; Shamlu 1, 86; Qomi 2, 630
'Ali Beyg	985/1577	H Rasht+Fumen [Gilan]	Natanzi 33; Shamlu 1, 86; Qomi 2, 630
Kiya Rostam	985/1577	H Rasht	Shamlu 1, 86
'Ali Beyg	1002/1594	H Rasht + Fumen	Natanzi 475, 476, 483
Khosrow Beyg Chaharyari	1004/1596	*Darugheh* Rasht – *gholam*	Monshi 515; Fumeni 170, 229
Jamshid Khan	1038/1629	H Rasht	Yusof 15
Aqa Zaman Esfahani	1044-?/1635-?	Vizier Rasht	Vahid 262
Lachin Aqa	1049-?/1639-?	Vizier Rasht	Vahid 298

Rey, also indiscriminately referred to as Tehran. For a certain period of time this district was considered to be the exclusive domain of the Tekkelu and Torkman tribe or in Persian, their 'mine' (*ma'dan*).[302] However, Monshi reports that Rey always belonged to the Shamlus.[303] From the list is clear that Monshi's statement seems to be more correct than the other one, although there was no exclusive hold on this function by the Shamlus. Also, that the governor of Rey often was also the governor of one or more other districts, notably Qazvin and Savokh-bulagh, and that sometimes a governor only held sway over part of the district of Rey. Finally as of 1043/1634, for the next 40 years and perhaps beyond, Rey became the fief of the *ishik aghasi-bashi* or the master of ceremonies of the royal court.

Name	Year	Observations	Source
Elyas Beyg Ighud [-oglu] b. Ya'qub Aqa	?-909/?-1504	H Rey	Hoseyni 23; Qomi 1, 81; Shirazi 42; Bidlisi 2, 510; Qazvini 268
Abdal Beyg Dedeh	?-915/?-1509	H Qazvin, Savokh-Bolagh, Rey	Qomi 1, 100; Rumlu 145; Qazvini 272
Zeynal Beyg [Khan] Shamlu	915-919/1509-1513	H Qazvin, Savokh-Bolagh-e Rey	Rumlu 145; Qazvini 272
Saru Pireh ?	919?/1513?	H Qazvin, Savokh-Bolagh-e Rey; *qurchi-bashi*	Aubin 13
Qalich Beyg b. Ostajalu Mohammad Khan	932/1526	H Tehran-e Rey	Bacqué-Gramont 97

---

302 Valeh, *Khold*, p. 623; Yusof, *Dheyl*, p. 147.
303 Monshi, *Tarikh*, vol. 2, p. 835.

Ahmad Soltan Kangarlu	933/1527	H Rey	Dickson 102, n. 1 (*Afzal al-Tavarikh*)
Soleyman Beyg Rumlu	933-?/1527-?	H Rey + Chokhur-e Sa'd	Bidlisi 2, 552
Hoseyn Khan Soltan	950/1544	H Rey	Budaq 105
Timur Khan b. Montasha Soltan Sheikhler Ostajalu	953/1546	H Rey	Shirazi 95
Aras Soltan Rumlu	972-973/1565-1566	*ba'zi az mahall-e* Rey – succeeded by	Qomi 1, 448, 454
Pireh Mohammad Beyg Chavoshlu	973-?/1567-?	*ba'zi az mahall-e* Rey	Qomi 1, 454
Piri Beyg Quchlu[y] or Pari Beyg Quchlu [Ostajalu]	983/1575	H Rey; *qurchi-ye tir va kaman*	Monshi 121, 138; Tatavi 768 [984]
Mosib Khan Sharaf al-Din-oghlu Tekkelu b. Mohammad Sharaf al-Dinoghlu	984-985/1576-1577	H Rey or H Tehran	Monshi 212, 227; Qomi 2, 874
Ordughdu Khalifeh-ye Tekkelu	985/1577	H Rey	Rumlu 643
'Ali Khalifeh-ye Qajar	985-?/1577-?	H Tehran	Qomi 2, 650
Mosib Khan Sharaf al-Din-oghlu	994/1586	H Rey; 2nd time	Bidlisi 2, 673; Monshi 322-23
Soltan Ma'sum Khan	994/1586	H Rey	Monshi 340-41
'Aliqoli Khan Fath-oghlu Ostajalu	994-1006?/1586-1598?	H Rey; his brother Hoseynqoli Fath-oghlu was his deputy	Valeh 1372, 789; Qomi 2, 878-79; Monshi 341, 365; Valeh 838; Vahid 104
Mosib Khan Tekkelu	996/1588	H Tehran-Rey	Qomi 2, 874; Monshi 227
Farrokh Khan Pornak	996/1588	H Rey – Tehran	Qomi 2, 889, 906, 923
Qobad Khan	999/1591	H Rey	Vahid 112
Hoseyn Khan Mosaheb Qajar	1006-?/1598-?	H Rey	Vahid 139
'Aliqoli Beyg Geramillu Shamlu	1012-1034/1604-1625	H Tehran-Varamin - IAB + *divan-beygi* + *eqta'* Tehran	Monshi 674, 1040; Vahid 215; Molla Jalal 437
Zeynal Beyg [Khan] Beygdelu Shamlu	1034-?/1625-?	H Rey; IAB	Monshi 1059; Yusof 291; Vahid 217
Emamqoli Beyg yuz-bashi-ye Enanlu Shamlu	1044-?/1635-?	H Rey; IAB	Yusof 147; Vahid 262
Mehdiqoli Khan Shamlu	1056-1074/1646-1664	H Rey; IAB–succeeded by his son	Vahid 421, 476, 636, 752
Oghurlu Khan Shamlu	1074-?/1664-?	H Rey; IAB	Vahid 742

Romahiyeh, a town and district in Iraq, in fact a *sanjaq* of Baghdad, which for a while was in Safavid hands, when they also held Baghdad and other parts of Iraq. As of 935/1528, Saleh Soltan was governor of Romahiyeh probably until 940/1534, when the Safavids yielded Baghdad to the Ottomans.[304]

Rostamdar is a district situated between Gilan and Mazandaran. "It consists of the plains and the mountains of Tavelesh from Amol and Mazandaran on the east, to Tonakabon in Gilan on the west; in width, Rostamdar consists of the strip between Mount Damavand and the Caspian Sea."[305] The district was ruled by a local dynasty that claimed descent from the Sasanians and allegedly had ruled the area since those days.[306] Rostamdar was split in two parts (Nur and Kojur) after Timur's death, and continued to be ruled by members of that same dynasty. Although nominally tributary to the Safavids the rulers of Rostamdar were quite independent,[307] but in 924/1518 they were subdued by a Safavid army and their emoluments were reduced.[308] In the mid 1530s, Shah Tahmasp I sent his brother Elqas Mirza to subdue the region, but due to heavy losses that he sustained the prince withdrew. Malek Ka'us fearing Safavid retaliation sent many presents to court and renewed his pledge of allegiance, which was accepted. Malek Ka'us's long reign came to an end when his son Jahangir murdered and succeeded him.[309] The dynasty thereafter split into three branches: Larijan (q.v.), formerly a dependency of Kojur, ruled by Malek Bahman; Kojur, ruled by Malek Soltan Mohammad, and Nur, ruled by Malek 'Aziz. Smaller districts were given to relatives to govern such as in 957/1550 when Malek Oveys b. Malek Gostaham b. Bisetun governed a subdistrict of Nur.[310] When 'Abbas I acceded to the throne the latter two rulers had died and their successors, both called Jahangir, submitted their services to the new shah. The ruler of Nur gave his lands to the Shah in exchange of which he received a few villages at Saveh. Malek Jahangir of Kojur was given a place among the confidents of Shah 'Abbas I. He returned later (about 1005) to his ancestral lands and rebelled. Shah 'Abbas sent an army to subdue him and as a result Malek Jahangir and his entire family was killed and Rostamdar was incorporated into the Safavid kingdom in 1006/1598. Allahqoli Beyg, *qurchi-bashi*, then became governor of Kojur.[311]

---

304 Qomi, *Kholasat*, vol. 1, p. 190; Budaq, *Javaher*, p. 68.
305 Qomi, *Kholasat*, vol. 1, p. 190; Budaq Qazvini, *Javaher*, p. 68..
306 For details see H. L. Rabino, *Mazandaran and Astarabad* (London, 1928), pp. 144-46; Yazdi, *Mokhtasar*, vol. 1 pp. 309-14.
307 Nevertheless in 910/1504, Shah Esma'il I had appointed Elyas Beyg Ya'qub Oghlon as governor of Rostamdar, but he was killed by Hoseyn Kiya Cholavi, ruler of Firuzkuh, Khvar and Damavand. Although the shah eliminated the rebellious ruler he did not appoint a new governor to Rostamdar, which was left in the hands of its traditional rulers. Tatavi, *Tarikh*, p. 322.
308 Shirazi, *Naqavat*, pp. 57-58; Bedlisi, *Cheref-Nameh*, vol. 2, p. 539; Qazvini, *Tarikh*, p. 278. During the first two decades of the sixteenth century some other governors for Rostamdar are also mentioned, although it is likely that they governed only parts of the district. Laheji, *Tarikh* (see index) mentions Malek Ashraf, Malek Ka'us b. Malek Ashraf, Malek Hoseyn and Malek Taj al-Dowleh as governors of Rostamdar.
309 al-Hoseyni, *Tarikh*, pp. 246-47.
310 Shirazi, *Takmelat*, p. 138.
311 Monshi, *Tarikh*, vol. 2, pp. 535f; Molla Jalal, *Ruznameh*, pp. 144f, 153f, 160-61.

Name	Years	Observations	Source
Malek Jahangir b. Ka'us	871-904/1466-1499	H Rostamdar	Shirazi 137; Rabino 146
Malek Ka'us b. Malek Jahangir - Malek Bahman	904/1499	H Rostamdar; killed by his brother Kayumarth	Shirazi 137; Laheji 48, 84, 87-88, 90-93
Malek Kayumarth b. Jahangir	904-910?/1499-1505?	H Rostamdar [Nur]; killed by his brother Kayumarth	Shirazi 137-38
Malek Bisetun b. Jahangir	904-913/1505-1508	H Rostamdar	Shirazi 138
Malek Bahman b. Malek Bisetun	913-957/1508-1550	H Rostamdar	Shirazi 138; Qomi 1, 140; Hoseyni, 246
Malek Kayumarth b. Bahman	957-?/1550-?	H Rostamdar [minus Nur]	Shirazi 138
Malek 'Aziz b. Kayumarth	?	H Rostamdar	Rabino 146
Malek Jahangir b. 'Aziz	?-997/?-1589	H Rostamdar	Rabino 146
Ebrahim Beyg	1003/1594	H Rostamdar	Rabino 139

Sabzavar is district in north-west Khorasan, bounded on the west by Shahrud, on the north by Bojnurd and Esfara'in, on the east by Nishapur and on the south by Kashmar. Its main town is also called Sabzavar.

Name	Years	Observations	Source
Shahrokh Beyg Afshar	917/1511	H Nishapur + Sabzavar	Aubin 19 (Afzal)
Jekur [or Chegur or] Chakergeh Soltan Shamlu	928-934/1522-1528	H Sabzavar or *Saheb* (Tahmasp)	Monshi 52; Shirazi 64; Qazvini 284; Tahmasp 10; Khvandamir 591; Abrahams 173 (Jagavna)
Mohammad 'Ali Khalifeh	950?/1543?	*Vali* Sabzavar	Afshar 357-58
Abu'l-Fath Mirza Soltan Ebrahim	974-980/1566-1572	H Sabzavar – No *Laleh*	Qomi 1, 460; 2, 642
Hoseynqoli Beyg Shamlu	984/1576	H Sabzavar	Qomi 633; Tatavi 758 (Soltanqoli Beyg Shamlu)
Qobad Soltan [Khan] Qajar b. Budaq Khan	985-987/1577-1579	H Sabzavar	Qomi 2, 664, 709, 739; Monshi 247; Molla Jalal 43, 47; Vahid 88
Ordughdi Khalifeh-ye Tekkelu	987/1579	driven away by Qobad Soltan [Khan] Qajar	Qomi 2, 709
Ahmad Soltan Yazar Tekkelu	987-?/1579-?	H Sabzavar	Qomi 2, 709
Hoseyn Beyg [Soltan] b. Sevenduk Afshar *qurchi-bashi*	990-991/1582-1583	H Sabzavar	Qomi 2, 732; Monshi 290; Bidlisi 2, 662

Ahmad Soltan Tekkelu	991-?/1583-?	H Sabzavar	Monshi 292
Hoseyn Beyg Afshar	994/1586	H Sabzavar	Valeh 1372, 678
Mehdiqoli	996/1588	H Sabzavar	Vahid 105
Emamqoli Khan Qajar b. Qobad Khan	997/1589	H Sabzavar	Qomi 2, 859; Monshi 408; Vahid 97
Mohammad Khan Chavoshlu Ostajalu b. Eyguth Soltan	997-?/1589-?	H Sabzavar	Monshi 408
	From 997/1589 until 1001/1593	Uzbeg governors	
Mohammad Soltan grandson Mir Shams al-Din 'Ali Soltan Mokhtar al-Hoseyni	1001-?/1593-?	H Sabzavar	Monshi 453
Mirza Mohammad Mo'men Soltan	?-1004/?-1595	H Sabzavar	Monshi 511; Vahid 132
Budaq Soltan Qajar	1004-?/1596-?	H Sabzavar	Monshi 512; Vahid 132 (1003)
'Ali Khan Soltan Sufilar	?-1007/?-1598	H Sabzavar	Molla Jalal 184
Mohammad Soltan Bayat	?-1007/?-1599	H Sabzavar [see also Nishapur]	Monshi 565
Yusof Khan Soltan	1020/1611	*Darugheh-motasaddi* Sabzavar	Molla Jalal 438
Ahmad Soltan Chekani b. Jami Soltan	1038/1629	H Sabzavar	Monshi 1086; Yusof 22, 104
Mir Sayyed Mohammad Soltan	1046/1637	H Sabzavar	Astarabadi 255
Mohammad Khan Ghekani	1047-?/1638-?	H Sabzavar	Vahid 283
Ebrahim Khan	1107/1695	H Sabzavar	Nasiri 177
Hajji Mohammad	1135/1722	H Sabzavar [refused]	Mostowfi 179

Sabzavar, see Esfezar.

Saddi, see Tianeti.

Sadmareh or Sadmard (perhaps also Samireh) is a district in Lorestan (q.v.) on the road to Baghdad.

Tahmaspqoli Soltan Enanlu	1006-?/1596-?	Sadmareh, Hendemin and other districts near Baghdad	Monshi 540
Qasem Soltan Inanlu Afshar	1020/1611	Sadmareh + Haltiyan	Molla Jalal 160, 414, 418

Sa'dabad, As'adabad or Asadabad is a town and district some 40 km west of Hamadan. The governor of Dinavar (q.v.) also was (occasionally?) governor of Sa'dabad and of parts of Sulagh, as was the case in 994/1586, when Shahverdi Khalifeh brother of Esma'il Khan, was governor of Dinavar, Sa'dabad and of some dependencies of Sulagh.[312]

Sa'dlu Aghcheh was a fort in Chokhur-e Sa'd and under a governor, according to Nasiri's *Alqab*. It may have been the center of the district assigned to the Sa'dlu tribe.

Sajavand is a district that I have not been able to locate. Prior to 984/1576, Khalil Khan Shah Mansur[313] was governor of Sajavand and its dependencies.[314]

Sakhar is situated in the province of Herat, adjacent to Farsi. In 928/1522 its governor was Ahmad Beyg Afshar.[315]

Saliyan is a district located in and around the estuary of the Kur River. It appears to have been combined with the governorship with that of Darband towards the end of the Safavid period, while the combination with Fort Mahmudabad that is situated near Baku also occurs. The districts of Saliyan and Mahmudabad plus those of 'Abdalabad and Fakhrabad were given as *teyul* (revenue assignment) to the Chakerlu in 1020, when Shah 'Abbas I forced them to move from the Talesh and the Moghan to that area.[316]

Name	Year	Observations	Source
Ghazi Khan Tekkelu	947	*Teyuldar* Saliyan + Mahmudabad	Qomi 1, 293; Shirazi 91; Abrahams 137
Sharaf al-Din Khan Bedlisi	961-964	H Saliyan + Mahmudabad	Bidlisi 2, 337

Salmas, a district of Azerbaijan bounded on the west by Iraq, on the north by Khoy, on the east by Tabriz and on the south by Orumiyeh. The Lak are a southern Kurdish tribe, who settled in the Salmas area at the end of the 16th century. It would seem that as of that time the government of Salmas and the Kurdish Lak tribe were interchangeable. There is still a Lakestan area in the district, possibly a last trace of the Lak tribe, which in the post-Safavid period lived dispersed over Iran.[317]

Name	Year	Observations	Source
Khan Emir b. Ghazi Beyg Kord	1017/1608	H Salmas	Monshi 795

---

312 Qomi, *Kholasat*, vol. 2, pp. 828, 853.
313 Shah Mansur probably should be Siyah Mansur.
314 Valeh, *Khold*, p. 412.
315 Khvandamir, *Habib*, vol. 4, p. 579.
316 Molla Jalal, *Ruznameh*, p. 429.
317 Monshi, *Tarikh*, vol. 2, pp. 1000, 1087.

Saru Khan Soltan Salmasi	1038/1629	H *Il-e* Lak of Salmas	Monshi 1087
Ayub Khan	1043-1044/1644-1645	H Salmas	Yusof 147, 157; Vahid 263
Rezaqoli Soltan	1106/1695	H *il-e* Salmasi	Nasiri 81

Sarab is a district in Azerbaijan bounded on the west by Tabriz, on the north by Meshkinshahr, on the east by Ardabil and on the south by Miyaneh. It was sometimes held together with the governorship of Ardabil, while it also seems to have been held by members of the Esparlu tribe during much of the 17th century.

Name	Years	Observations	Source
Shekari Soltan Esparlu	ca. 1038/1629	H Ardabil and Sarab	Monshi 1085
Mohammad Soltan Esparlu	1058/1648	H Sarab	Valeh 1380, 461; Vahid 467

Sarakhs or Fort Sarakhs is situated on the left bank of Hari Rud in north-eastern Khorasan. Its governor often (if not invariably) was also governor of Fort Zurabad (q.v.) at the same time. Despite the fact that Sarakhs apparently remained a desolate abandoned place for 25 years after 916/1510, there was a Safavid governor during that period.[318]

Name	Years	Observations	Source
Ahmad Beyg Afshar	917/1511	H Sarakhs	Heravi 367
Sevenduk Beyg	?-927/?-1521	H Sarakhs	Rumlu 222; Valeh 1372, 279; Khvandamir 579
Mir Hoseyn Khan Tavakkoli	935/1529	H Sarakhs + Zurabad	Abrahams 200
Mir Hoseyn Soltan Tobadkani?	?-976/?-1569	H Sarakhs + Zurabad	Qomi 1, 562
Sayyed Hoseyn Tobadkani	976-985/1569-1577	H Sarakhs + Zurabad	Qomi 1, 563
Ebrahim Soltan Qorughlu b. Shahqoli Soltan Yakan Ostajalu	984/1576	H Sarakhs	Valeh 1372, 409; Monshi 139, 204, 1085
Ebn Hoseyn Khan b. Mir Hoseyn Soltan Tobadkani	985-?/1577-?	H Sarakhs + Zurabad	Qomi 2, 665; Vahid 149, 194
Nabi Hoseyn Khan	996/1588	H Sarakhs	Shamlu 1, 139
Amir Hoseyn Firuz-jang aka Ebn Hoseyn Khan b. Hoseyn Soltan Firuz-jang Chaghatay	998-1025/1588-1616	H Jam, Sarakhs, Zurabad - Succeeded by his son	Vahid 109, 149; Molla Jalal 184, 329; Monshi 141, 389, 414, 537, 603, 914

---

318 Razi, *Haft Eqlim*, vol. 2, p. 36.

Mozaffar Hoseyn [Khan]	1025-?/1616-?	H Sarakhs	Monshi 914
Badi' al-Zaman Soltan	?-1050/?-1641	H Sarakhs	Astarabadi 259
'Abdollah Khan	1108/1697	H Sarakhs	Nasiri 201
Hoseynqoli Khan	1122-?/1710-?	H Sarakhs	Khatunabadi 560
Mowjudqoli Khan or Mowdudqoli Soltan Chaghatay	1134/1722	H Sarakhs	Mervi 1, 47, 152; Jahangosha 50
Yahya Khan	1135/1723	H Sarakhs	Mostowfi 176

Saruqargan, Saruqazqan, Saruqurqan, Saruqurghan or Sarufarqan[319] is situated near Orumiyeh.

Name	Year	Observations	Source
Heydar Soltan brother of Mohammad Beygdeli	1012/1604	H Saruqazqan	Molla Jalal 258
Qaban Soltan Beygdeli Shamlu	1017/1608	H Gaverud + Saru-qargan	Monshi 2, [978]
Qobad Khan	?-1019/?-1610	H Sarufarqan; succeeded by his brother	Molla Jalal 409
Saru Beyg aka Saru Khan Soltan Beygdelu	1019-1022-?/1610-1613	H Sarufarqan	Molla Jalal 409, 413, 431; Vahid 181

Sarvestan is a district situated east of Shiraz. Although situated in Fars it was not subject to Emamqoli Khan in 1621, but its governor was directly appointed by Abbas I, as was the case with some other districts.[320]

Name	Year	Observations	Source
Nader Khan	1031/1621	H Sarvestan	della Valle 3, 332
Khalil Soltan Dhu'l-Qadr Suseh-oghlu	1039-?/1630-?	H Sarvestan (appointed by Emamqolikhan)	Vahid 222
Naser 'Ali Khan	ca. 1081/1670	H Sarvestan	Floor, *Persian Gulf*, 309
'Aliqoli Soltan	1109/1698	H Sarvestan	Nasiri 250

Savadkuh is a mountainous district in Mazandaran. In 997/1589, Div Jamal al-Din was governor of Ft. Owlad and Savadkuh.[321]

Saveh, a town a district some 110 km south of Tehran was bounded in the west by Hamadan, in the north by Qazvin and Karaj, in the east by Rey and Qom, and in the south by Tafrash. It seems to have turned into crown domain by the 1680s, because Kaempfer observed that it was

---

319 Molla Jalal, *Ruznameh*, pp. 409, 413, 431; Vahid, *Tarikh*, pp. 172, 181.
320 Pietro della Valle, *Les fameux voyages* 4 vols. (Paris, 1663-84), vol. 3, p. 332.
321 Shamlu, *Qesas*, vol. 1, p. 167.

governed by a vizier in 1684. Sometimes its governors were also in charge of other jurisdictions such as Jorbadeqan, Aveh and Torshiz (q.v.).

Name	Year	Observations	Source
Domri Beyg Ostajalu	932/1526	H Saveh	Bacqué-Gramont 97
Mostafa Soltan Shamlu (or Afshar in Qazvini; Bidlisi)	934/1528	*Teyuldar* Saveh	Shirazi 64; Qazvini 284; Tahmasp 10; Dickson 102, n.1, Bidlisi 2, 533
'Ali Beyg	935/1529	H Saveh-Jorbadeqan	Qomi 1, 190
Shah Soltan b. Hamzeh Soltan Qazaq Ostajalu	950/1543	H Saveh + other district	Shirazi 92
Yadgar Mohammad Soltan Torkman	965/1558	H Saveh	Qomi 1, 394; Bidlisi 2, 595
Mohammad Beyg Mowsilu Tarkhan b. Marjumak Soltan b. Amir Khan Torkman	?-969/?-1562	H Saveh	Qomi 1, 435; Qazvini 307
Heydar Beyg [Soltan Tarkhan] Torkman	972-976/1565-1569	H Saveh, Jorbadeqan; see Qom	Rumlu 561; Qomi 1, 448, 471, 563; Budaq 141
Mahmud Beyg Afshar	?-984/?-1576	H Saveh	Qomi 2, 622
Soltan Ma'sum Soltan Torkman aka Abu'l-Ma'sum Soltan Tarkhan Torkman	985-?/1577-?	H Saveh, Jorbadeqan, Aveh	Qomi 2, 665; Monshi 227
Adham Khan [Torkman]	994-?/1586-?	H Saveh	Qomi 2, 828
Soltan Morad Khan Torkman b. Amir Khan	996/January 1588	H Saveh	Qomi 2, 874
Ebrahim Khan Torkman	998-999/1589-1590	H Saveh	Qomi 2, 835, 861, 889, 1069
Shahqoli Soltan Piyadeh Torkman	999/1591	H Saveh	Qomi 2, 906, 1083
Ganj 'Ali Khan	999-?/1591-?	H Saveh	Qomi 2, 1083
Mohammad Soltan Orumlu	1006-?/1598-?	H Saveh-Torshiz	Siyaqi 479
Sayyed Naser b. Sayyed Mobarak Mosha'sha'	1015/1607	H Saveh	Monshi 756
N.N.	1095/1684	Vizier Saveh	Kaempfer 73

Semnan, a town and district in central Iran, bounded in the west by Damavand, in the north by Amol, in the east by Damghan and in the south by Na'in. It seems that the governor of Semnan also held the same position for the districts of Firuzkuh, Damavand, Hablehrud, and Khvar. This was already the case before Safavid rule was imposed.[322] The first three were administratively

---

322 Qazvini, *Tarikh*, p. 268.

part of Gilan, while Khvar and Semnan fell within the jurisdiction of Iraq.[323] From 985 to 986 Semnan (plus Damavand, Hazar Jarib, Hilrud, Khvar) was turned into *khasseh* or crown domain (see Table). In 1066 Semnan (and Damavand plus Khvaf) was once again made crown domain, which as of then depended from the governor-general of Astarabad. Its first vizier was Geda 'Ali Beyg Qajar *davatdar*.[324] However, this situation does not appear to have lasted long, because already in 1073/1662 there was a governor rather than a vizier of Semnan. This may have to do with the fact that the Pazuki tribe for some time did not have a chief, because it had been campaigning. In 1073/1662, when Morteza Qoli Khan Sa'dlu was appointed as the new tribal chief, he also became governor of Semnan, Firuzkuh, Damavand and Hablerud. By the end of the Safavid period Semnan was part of the province of Mashhad.

Name	Year	Observations	Source
Amir Hasan Kiya	909/1503	H Firuzkuh-Damavand	Hoseyni 31
Hoseyn Kiya Cholavi	909/1504	H Firuzkuh, Damavand, Khvar, Semnan	Valeh 1372, 133; Shirazi, 42; Qazvini 268
Abdal Beyg Dedeh	?-915/?-1509	H Khvar + Qazvin, Rey, Savokh bolagh	Bidlisi 2, 521
Zeynal Khan Shamlu	915-?/1510-?	Idem	Bidlisi 2, 521
Demri Soltan	931/1525	H Semnan-Firuzkuh	Hoseyni 86
Pirqoli Soltan Kangarlu	932/1526	H Semnan + Khvar (see also Esfara'in)	Dickson 102, n.1 (*Afzal al-Tavarikh*); Abrahams 173
Manuchehr Beyg	948/1542	H Semnan	Valeh 1372 296
Khalil Beyg Mansur-Siyah	965?/1558?	H Khvar	Bidlisi 2, 186
Hasan Soltan Shamlu	980-?/1572-?	H Semnan and Khvar + Firuzkuh	Qomi 1, 579
Amir Khan Mowselu Torkman	984/1576	H Khvar + Hamadan	Tatavi 768
Shahqoli Soltan Tabat-oghlu Dhu'l-Qadr	985-?/1577-?	H Khvar + Semnan	Monshi 227
Navab Beygom	985/1577	*khasseh* of Semnan, Damavand, Hazarjarib, Hablehrud	Qomi 2, 665
Shahqoli Beyg b. Ras Khan	986/1578	*teyuldar* Damavand + Hablehrud	Qomi 2, 668
Sayyed Beyg Kamuneh	987-994/1579-1586	H Semnan + Taleqan	Qomi 2, 699, 725, 755, 828
Shahverdi Soltan Tati-oghlu Dhu'l-Qadr	994/1586	H Semnan	Qomi 2, 828, 834 (Pesarzadeh-ye Tabat-oghlu [Dhu'l-Qadr]); Valeh 837; Monshi 366

323 Monshi, *Tarikh*, vol. 2, p. 835; Ben Khvandamir, Amir Mahmud. *Iran dar Ruzgar-e Shah Esma'il va Shah Tahmasp*, ed. Gholam Reza Tabataba'i (Tehran 1370/1991), p. 204 (borders Khorasan); Bidlisi, *Cheref-Nameh*, vol. 2, 186; Shirazi, *Takmelat*, p. 56.
324 Vahid, *Tarikh*, pp. 612, 742.

Ahmad Soltan	994/1586	H Semnan – appointed as *pro-tem* governor by tribal elders	Valeh 1372, 838; Monshi 365
Ahmad Soltan Dhu'l-Qadr	995-?/1587-?	H Semnan + Khvar	Qomi 2, 861, 874
Ommat Soltan	1014/1606	*Teyuldar* Semnan and dependencies + H Goklen tribe	Molla Jalal 260
Amir Khan Mohrdar Soklan Dhu'l-Qadr	?-1035/?-1626	H Semnan	Vahid 289; Bardsiri 193, n.
Owtar Khan Dhu'l-Qadr	?-1048/?-1638	H Semnan - Khvar	Valeh 1380, 296; Vahid 299
Manuchehr Beyg	1048-?/1639-?	H Semnan - Khvar; *gholam*	Valeh 1380, 296; Vahid 299
Jamshid Khan	1056-1066/1646-1656	H Semnan - Damavand etc; see Astarabad – *qollar-aghasi*	Vahid 594, 612, 742; Shamlu 1, 343; Valeh 1380, 570, 577; Vahid 612, 706, 751
Geda 'Ali Beyg Qajar *Davatdar*	1066-?/1656-?	Vizier Semnan	Vahid 612, 742
Mortezaqoli Khan Sa'dlu	1073-1074/1663-1664	H *il-e* Pazuki + Semnan + Damavand	Vahid 742, 741
Saru Khan Sahandlu	?-1103/?-1691	H Hamadan + Semnan (Sambran) + Kazerun	Sanson 80
Mostafaqoli Khan Qajar	1110-?/1699-?	H Semnan + Khvar	Nasiri 273
Mortezaqoli Khan Sa'dlu	1133/1711	H Khvar + Semnan	Durri 82

Seystan is the border lowland region of south-west Afghanistan and eastern Iran, between Mashhad province in the north and Baluchistan in the south. Safavid rule had been recognized as of 1510.[325] Seystan, also referred to as Sejestan,[326] had been ruled by the so-called Kaianid or Mehrabanid dynasty that claimed descent from Ya'qub b. al-Leyth. When Esma'il I had conquered Khorasan and Merv by 916/1510 the then de-facto ruler of Seystan since about 890/1485, Malek Soltan Mahmud went to Merv to pledge his allegiance. At that time, the Kaianids held the following areas: Neh or Neh va Bandan, Kah/Gah or Qal'eh-ye Gah, Khass or Khass-e Sarhadd, Khoshk-rud and the Garmsirat, i.e. the area bordering the lower course of the Helmand river. Esma'il accepted Malek Mahmud's pledge of allegiance and confirmed him as governor of Seystan, but nevertheless sent him 1,000 Qezelbash troops under the command of Mir Pir Qoli, who acted as his *vakil* (agent) at the governor's side. On his return to Seystan Malek Soltan Mahmud added Uq to the province of Seystan. Two years after Shah Tahmasp I's accession to the throne Malek Soltan Mahmud ordered the Qezelbash *vakil* to leave Seystan proper and gave him the Garmsirat

---

325 On its history and administration see Da'udi, Hoseyn. "Asnad-e khvandan-e kalantari-ye Seystan", *Barrasiha-ye Tarikhi*, 4 (1348/1969), pp. 1-34; Bosworth, C.E. *The History of the Saffarids of Sistan and the Maliks of Nimruz (247/861 to 949/1542-3)* (Costa Mesa 1994).

326 Qomi, *Kholasat*, vol. 1, pp. 380 [962], 396 [965], 396, 448), Nimruz (263, 289, 334, 343, 355, 473) or Zabulistan (Shamlu, *Qesas*, vol. pp. 2, 124, 128; Hazin, *Life*, pp. 135, 173 (Nimroz, or Sistan). According to Yazdi, *Mokhtasar*, vol. 1, pp. 282, 284, the term Nimruz refers to an area that includes Qandahar province (q.v.), while Zabolestan is an area distinct from Seystan.

to govern, with an annual payment of 1,000 *tumans*. Malek Soltan Mahmud assisted Sam Mirza's rebellion in 943/1534 and expelled the Safavid governor from Farah. Sam Mirza then appointed Malek Soltan Mahmud governor of "Farah, Esfezar, Ghur, Dara, Askan [?], the fortress of Kah, Uq, Sakhir [?], and Tulak", i.e., the northern parts of Seystan plus the adjoining parts of Ghur. However, Malek Soltan Mahmud did not in person welcome Sam Mirza on his arrival in Seystan, but only sent his servants. The 'rebellion' was put down and to bolster Safavid rule Tahmasp I then appointed Ahmad Soltan Shamlu as his *vakil* over four (Garmsir, Khvash, Khoshkrud and Neh va Bandan) of Seystan's 14 *boluk*s or districts, while the remaining ten were bestowed on Malek Soltan Mahmud. The offer was not acceptable to Malek Mahmud who fled across the border to Moghul India. As a result Seystan was governed by Safavid princes or governors from 943/1537-1538 to 985/1578. After the death of Shah Esma'il II there was no effective Safavid control of the provice and a scion of the Mehrabanid dynasty, Malek Mahmud took de-facto control over Seystan. In 1578, Malek Mahmud was reinstated as governor of Seystan, because the central government was not able at that time to impose its rule from the center and thus allowed the local dynast to do the job for it. His son Malek Jalal al-Din succeeded him as governor of Seystan, which was only officially confirmed in 1002/1594. He fled to the Safavid court when the Uzbegs overran the province in the 1596 and he had been driven out by the Uzbegs. Thereafter the province had been allotted to Ganj 'Ali Khan, the governor of Kerman. When 'Abbas I retook Khorasan and Seystan in 1598 Malek Jalal al-Din pledged his allegiance and was confirmed as governor of Seystan in 1007/1598.[327] For the remainder of the period Mehrabanid governors were in charge of the province, except for 1042/1632, when the succession was held in abeyance due to inter-family squabbles.

As part of the Safavid drive to extend their control over Kij-Makran the governor of Seystan also played a role and for a time saw his territory enlarged such as under 'Abbas I when he was in charge of Dezak.[328] Also later in the century, Nosrat Khan, the grandson of Malek Jalal al-Din Khan, who, in addition to being governor of Seystan, also was given jurisdiction over some places in Kapach and Mekran in 1054/1644.[329] On the other hand there also were some parts of Seystan that no longer were part of the province, but were governed by separate Safavid governors such as in the case of Gah and Uq that were held by the governor of Farah in 962/1555,[330] or Neh va Bandad, where in 1109/1697 Kalb 'Ali Beyg ruled.[331]

Name	Year	Observations	Source
Malek Soltan Mahmud	916-943/1510-1537	*Vali* Seystan	Monshi 57

---

327 Siyaqi, *Fotuhat*, p. 479.
328 Seystani, *Ehya al-Molk*, pp. 406, 408, 412, 417, 472-3, 484-6, 506-7; Yusof, *Dheyl*, p. 133.
329 Shamlu, *Qesas*, vol. 1, pp. 289 (family tree), 334, 343, 355, 473.
330 Budaq, *Akhbar*, p. 141. For Neh see Monshi, *Tarikh*, vol. 1, p. 227 (985/1578), which in 963/1555 was part of Seystan
331 Nasiri, *Dastur*, pp. 203-04, 206.

COMMENTARY 277

Ahmad Soltan Shamlu	943-957-?/1536-1550-?	*Vali* Sejestan	Rumlu 401; Shamlu 1, 71; Qomi 1, 303, 309, Monshi 99; Vahid 63
Allahqoli Soltan Ijek-oghlu Ostajalu aka Hoseyn Beyg	962-965/1555-1558	H Sejestan and *Laleh* of Soltan Hoseyn Mirza b. Bahram Mirza	Qomi 1, 380, 396
Mohammad Jan Beyg Dhu'l-Qadr or Emamqoli Beyg b. Badr Khan [Dhu'l-Qadr or Ostajalu]	965-972/1558-1565	H Sejestan and *Laleh* of Badi' al-Zaman Mirza (Seystani: Emamqoli Beyg b. Nadr Khan)	Qomi 1, 396, 448; Seystani 165, 169
Mohammad Khan Mowsellu Torkman	972-984/1565-1576	H Seystan and *Laleh* of Badi' al-Zaman Mirza	Monshi 139; Shirazi 123
Teymur Soltan [Khan] Ostajalu b. Mantasha Soltan	984-985/1576-1577	H Seystan and *Laleh* of Badi' al-Zamani Mirza	Hoseyni 177; Monshi 139; Valeh 1372, 306; 409, 2, 644; Seystani 189; Tatavi 767
Morshedqoli Soltan Ostajalu b. Shahqoli Yakan	985/1577	H Seystan	Monshi 206
	For some time no	Safavid control	
Ja'far Soltan Arashlu Afshar	985-986/1577-1578	H Seystan	Vahid 123
Malek Mahmud	986-999/1578-1591	First independent then confirmed as H Seystan by Shah Mohammad Khodabandeh	Monshi 1, 478-84
	999/1591	Uzbeg occupation	Bidlisi 2, 690
Malek Jalal al-Din b. Malek Mahmud	999-1005/1591-1597	H Seystan	Monshi 487, 529; Vahid 126-27, 329
	1005-1006/1597-1598	Under Uzbeg control	
Malek Jalal al-Din b. Malek Mahmud aka Shoja' al-Din Hamzeh Beyg	1007-1042/1599-1633	H Zabolestan	Monshi 576; Molla Jalal 184, 238, 328; Riazul Islam 1, 161; Yusof 287
Bahram Beyg Gholam	1042/1633	H Seystan	Yusof 117
Malek Hamzeh Khan b. Malek Jalal al-Din	1043-1076/1634-1666	H Nimruz or Zabolestan	Yusof 132-3; Vahid 329-30; Shamlu 1, 263, 289; Khatunabadi 512
Nosrat Khan grandson Malek Jalal al-Din Khan	1076-?/1666-?	H Nimruz and some places in Kich-Makran	Shamlu 1, 289, 334, 343, 355, 473; Bardsiri 321, 383
Ja'far Khan	1108/1697	H Seystan	Nasiri 177
Malek Mahmud Kayani Seystani	1129/1717	H Seystan	Mervi 1, 24, 37, 43, 1184

Shabankareh is a district of Fars adjacent to Dashtestan. According to Yazdi, by the seventeenth century, Ich, Darabjerd and Estebanat, were not part of Shabankareh anymore.[332]

Name	Year	Observations	Source
Charandab Soltan Shamlu	955-957/1548-1550	H Shabankareh (+ Ich, Neyriz, Fasa q.v.)	Tahmasp 53
Shahqoli Khalifeh-ye Dhu'l-Qadr	984/1576	H Shabankareh	Rumlu 634

Shaberan is a town and district between Baku and Qobeh, which was completely destroyed in 1723. In 1016/1607, Budaq Soltan was governor of Shaberan.[333]

Shadilu was the name of a Kurdish tribe, which had a district assigned to it near Mount Ararat in Chokhur-e Sa'd.

Shaflan, also found as Shaqlan, is a district in the province of Herat,[334] which is nowadays known as Shahfilan. It is situated on the southern bank of the Hari Rud and stretches from about 12 km above Tunian up the river to the junction of the Kaoghan stream with the Hari Rud. In 986/1588, Khosrow Soltan Afshar was governor of Shaqlan.[335]

Shahr-e zur, a district in Kurdestan, situated between Zohab and Soleymaniyeh. The Ardalans once ruled it, but it usually was held by the Ottomans and permanently so after the 1639 peace of Zohab. In 1033/1624, it had a Qezelbash governor, Qasem Soltan Inanlu Afshar, who was governor of Kerkuk and Shahr-e zur.[336]

Shal, or Shal-e Mostan or Shal va Mostan, is situated at 20 *farsakh* from Qandahar (near Quetta) of which it was a dependency. It was situated on the border with Moghul India. In 980/1573 its governor had 500 retainers.[337]

Shamakhi a town and its district situated at 110 km west of Baku. It usually was the capital of Qarabagh province.

Name	Year	Observations	Source
Dhu'l-Feqar Khan	?-1018/?-1609	H Azerbayjan + Shamakhi	Monshi 806
Yusof Khan	1019-?/1610-?	H Shamakhi + Qabaleh	Molla Jalal 377

---

332 Yazdi, *Mokhtasar*, pp. 325f.
333 Molla Jalal, *Ruznameh*, p. 325.
334 Vahid, *Tarikh*, pp. 202, 295, 629, 720; Gonabadi, *Rowzat*, pp. 883-84 (Shaflanat).
335 Molla Jalal, *Ruznameh*, p. 36.
336 Vahid, *Khold*, p. 207.
337 Qomi, *Kholasat*, vol. 1, pp. 302, 575-76; Nasiri, *Dastur*, pp. 120-21

Allahverdi Khan	1116/1704	BB Shamakhi	Le Brun 1, 150
Hoseyn Khan	ca. 1127/1715	H Shamakhi	VOC 1886, f. 352
Esma'il Beyg	?-1132/March 1720	H Shamakhi	Bushev 55ff; Beneveni 48; Touzard 148
Hasan 'Ali Khan	1132-1133/ March 1720-1721?	H Shamakhi; nephew of Fath 'Ali Khan Daghestani	Beneveni 48; Touzard 149, 156

Shams al-Dinlu (q.v. Zagam) is a tribal district in Qarabagh inhabited by the Shams al-Dinlu tribe and governed by its tribal leader. Before 961/1554 it probably was part of Georgia, but thereafter it remained part of Qarabagh until the end of the Safavid period and beyond.[338] In 1039/1629, Esma'il Khan succeeded his father Salim Khan as governor of the district and tribe of Shams al-Dinlu, but because he was a minor Aslan Khan was his guardian.[339]

Shaqaqi is the name of the originally Kurdish Shaqaqi tribe that had become turkicized, which lived scattered in an area between Moghan and Sarab. It is also the name of the tribal district in Azerbaijan assigned to this tribe for its sustenance. Monshi mentions that 'Ali Jan Soltan Shaqaqi was an emir and chief of his tribe in 1038/1628 or before that time, while Nasiri's *Alqab* still mentions Shaqaqi district as a separate governorship at the end of the Safavid era.[340]

Shaqlan, see Shaflan.

Sheki or Arash-Sheki is a district situated in the northern part of the Republic of Azerbaijan on the southern part of the Greater Caucasus mountain range, adjoining Shirvan from the west. Arash, now Khanabad, is situated north of the Kur river, on the road from Nukhi to Barda'.[341] After the Safavid conquest of the region, Sheki continued to be governed by its hereditary rulers. As of 958/1551 Sheki was incorporated into the Safavid kingdom, i.e. ruled by a Qezelbash governor, after Dervish Mohammad Khan had rebelled, but now as part of the province of Shirvan. Arash (q.v.) was also (sometimes, usually?) under a seperate governor.

Name	Year	Observations	Source
Hasan Beyg	?-930/?-1524	H Sheki	Rumlu 225, 236; Qomi, 1, 147, 153
Dervish Mohammad Khan	930-958/1524-1551	H Sheki - His son	Rumlu 373, 387, 413, 449; Monshi 1, 80, 82-83; Musavi 1977, doc. 1; Budaq 120; Qomi 1, 279, 295, 318, 347; Bidlisi 2, 575, 586; Qazvini 300

---

338 Brosset, *Histoire*, vol. 2/2, p. 515; Nasiri, *Alqab*, supra.
339 Vahid, *Tarikh*, p. 228 (Salim Khan had been captured by the Ottomans and was governor of Kakht and Ta'us-Chay).
340 Monshi, *Tarikh*, vol. 2, p. 1086.
341 TM, p. 167.

Tuygun Soltan Qajar	958-?/1551-?	H Sheki	Qomi 1, 349; Rumlu 452; Abrahams 140 [957]
'Isa [Khan] Gorji	967-970/1560-1563	H Sheki	Bidlisi 2, 600, 604; Qazvini 308
'Ali Khan Beyg aka Qezel 'Ali Khan	970-?/1563-?	H Sheki	Bafqi 3/1, 211
Shamkhal Soltan Cherkes	985/1577	H Sheki [as of 1577; killed before his departure in February 1578]	Monshi 90, 223-24; Qomi 2, 627; Shirazi 132; Vahid 60
'Isa Khan Gorji	985-?/1577-?	H Sheki – 2nd time	Qomi 2, 664; Molla Jalal 43
Shahmir Khan or Shah Amir Khan	1012-1014/1604-1606	H Sheki - scion of the hereditary khans of Sheki	Monshi 671, 809; Molla Jalal 276; Vahid 158, 160, 163
Mohammad Soltan Jagirlu	1038/1629	H Sheki	Monshi 1086
Allahqoli Soltan	1102/1691	H Sheki	Musavi 1977, doc. 9
Mohammad Khan Beyg	1113/1701	H Sheki	Musavi 1977, Ibid., doc. 10; 1965, doc. 11
NN	1134/1722	H Sheki + Zakhur	Qa'em-maqami doc. 40

Shiraz was and is the capital city of the province of Fars. The governor (*hakem*, *vali*) of Shiraz was also called the *vali* of Fars and both appellations denoted the same function. The use of the name Shiraz was just a substitute for the province of Fars of which it was the capital and residence of the governor. Lar (q.v.) was a separate kingdom, while the littoral was mostly part of the kingdom of Hormuz, with the exception of the stretch from Bushire to the Shatt al-Arab.[342] In 909/1503, Esma'il I conquered Fars and immediately appointed a governor, who until 1590 always was from the Dhu'l-Qadr tribe, with two exceptions of short duration in 911/1505 and 915/1509. Mansur Beyg Afshar was governor of Shiraz for a few days only, while the relationship of Qadi Mohammad Kashi to the government of Shiraz is not very clear. Some sources report that he was appointed governor of Shiraz, while one reports that he was governor of a few dependencies of Shiraz only. Whatever, he was, he does not seem to have actually exercised this function, while his appointment also did not last very long. The jurisdiction of the governor-general of Fars was greatly enhanced under Emamverdi Khan, who conquered Lar and the kingdom of Hormuz. Moreover, parts of Persian Iraq were also added to Fars, while Emamverdi Khan also became governor of Kuhgiluyeh. His son Emamqoli Khan, who inherited his father's functions was described as being the governor of "all districts of Fars, Lar, Kuhgiluyeh, Shamil, Mina, Bahrain, Jarun (Bandar 'Abbas), some districts of 'Arabestan, such as Hoveyzeh and Dowraq, and of a part of Persian Iraq, such as Golpeygan, Tuysarkan and Mahallat."[343] After the murder of Emamqoli Khan in 1042/1633, Fars was turned into crown domain and henceforth governed by a vizier, who resided in Shiraz. The province of Fars was also reduced in size, because Lar (q.v.) was immediately separated from Fars. As of 1066/1656 the vizierate of Fars was divided into five parts for a number of years, one of these

---

342 See Floor, *Persian Gulf*, pp. 32-33.
343 Röhrborn, *Provinzen*, p. 10, n. 62; Yusof, *Dheyl*, pp. 81, 115, 285; Valeh, *Iran*, p. 350; Esfahani, *Kholasat*, pp. 41, 48; Valeh, *Iran*, p. 350. For Allahverdi Khan's jurisdiction see, e.g., Gonabadi, *Rowzat*, p. 736.

parts was the town of Shiraz and its environs.[344] Other parts included Jahrom and Darab.[345] Fars remained a crown domain until 1124/1712, when once again a governor was appointed. It was only in 1717 with the appointment of Lotf 'Ali Khan Daghestani as governor-general of Fars and Kuhgiluyeh that the reach of the latter's jurisdiction came close to that of Allahverdi Khan and Emamverdi Khan. This situation seems to have been reversed again in 1721 (see Table).[346]

Name	Year	observations	Source
Elyas Beyg aka Kachal Beyg Dhu'l-Qadr	909-911/1503-1505	H Shiraz or H Fars	Budaq 24; Qomi 1, 80; Shirazi 44; Mozaffar 188, 223
Mansur Beyg Afshar	911/1506	A few days *vali* of Shiraz	Qazvini 269
Ommat Beyg Sarusheykhlu Dhu'l-Qadr aka Khalil Soltan	911-926/1506-1520	H Shiraz	Qomi, 1, 88; Hoseyni 61, 83, 146; Ben Khvandamir 158; Shirazi 44, 53, 57; Rumlu 199; Bidlisi 2, 540; Qazvini 269, 279
Qadi Mohammad Kashi	?-915/?-1510	H Shiraz; *ba'zi owqat-e* Shiraz (Shirazi)	Rumlu 146; Shirazi 48; Qazvini 272; Khatunabadi 447
'Ali Beyg [Soltan] Dhu'l-Qadr Chichkelu; his original name was 'Ezz al-Din	926-931/1520-1524	H or *vali* Shiraz	Rumlu 199, 245, 248; Bidlisi 2, 540; Qazvini 279, 283; Monshi 47; Qomi 1, 146, 152, 161; Budaq 42, 56; Valeh 1372, 442; Shirazi 57, 61-62
Morad Soltan Dhu'l-Qadr	931/1525	H Shiraz; brother's son	Qomi 1, 161; Shirazi 62; Qazvini 283
Hamzeh Beyg Jameselu [Chameshlu] Dhu'l-Qadr or Hamzeh Soltan Khames 'Ali Dhu'l-Qadr	931-939/1525-1533	H Shiraz	Qomi 1, 161, 180; Monshi 54; Ben Khvandamir 262; Shirazi 75; Bidlisi 2, 562; Qazvini 283, 287
Ghazi Khan Dhu'l-Qadr brother of Soltan Khalil	939-946/1533-1540	H Shiraz; *vali* Shiraz	Rumlu 387 Budaq 87; Qomi 1, 275, 289; Khvandamir 362; Bidlisi 2, 562; Qazvini 287, 291, 294 Tahmasp 24, 27

---

344 Vahid, *Tarikh*, p. 610.

345 Vahid, *Tarikh*, p. 633 (Fars, Lar, Jahrom); Mostowfi, *Jame'*, vol. 3/1, p. 204; Nasiri, *Dastur*, p. 96, 273 (Darab, Jahrom); W. Ph. Coolhaas, *Generale Missieven van Gouverneurs-Generaal en Raden aan Heren XVII der Verenigde Oostindische Compagnie*, 6 vols. (The Hague, 1960-1980), vol. 6, p. 43 (Mohammad Mo'men Beyg, former vizier of Jahrom). The financial administration of Fars was also divided, in this case in two parts. Mostowfi, *Jame'*, vol. 3/1, p. 204.

346 For example, for the year 1722 a vizier of Fars is mentioned (see Table and Anne-Marie Touzard, *Le Drogman Padery* (Paris, 2005), p. 315, but p. 264 mentions a governor, be it in a generic way), while there also exists a document that mentions an unnamed *beygler-beygi* of Fars in April of that same year. Qa'em-Maqami, Jahangir. *Yaksadupanjah sanad-e tarikhi az Jala'iriyan ta Pahlavi* (Tehran, 1348/1969), doc. 41.

Ebrahim Beyg [Khan] b. Kachal Beyg Hajilar	946-962/1540-1555	H Shiraz -*Laleh* Soleyman Mirza b. Tahmasp 961-962	Hoseyni 155, 168, 189; Monshi 74, 95; Qomi 1, 289, 295, 328, 353, 377-8; Shirazi 90, 98, 109; Qazvini 294, 302; Tahmasp 53
'Ali Soltan Tati-oghlu Dhu'l-Qadr	962-965/1555-1558	H Shiraz; *Laleh* Soleyman Mirza b. Tahmasp 962-965	Qomi 1, 378, 396-7; Shirazi 109; Qazvini 302; Tatavi 559
Shahvali Soltan Tati-oghlu Dhu'l-Qadr	965-973/1558-1566	H Shiraz	Qomi 1, 455-6
Mohammad Khan Beyg Dhu'l-Qadr	973-?/1566-?	H Shiraz	Qomi 1, 456
Shahqoli Khalifeh Mohrdar Dhu'l-Qadr	before 978/1571	BB Fars	Valeh 1372, 416
Vali Soltan [Khan] Qalkhanji-oghlu Dhu'l-Qadr	978-985/1571-1576	BB Fars - H Shiraz- *Laleh* Soltan Mohammad Mirza b. Tahmasp, who remained there until he became shah in 1577; *Laleh* Shoja' al-Din Mohammad Mirza b. Esma'il II in 985/1577	Rumlu 644; Valeh 1372, 410; Monshi 126, 140 [Qalmanchi-oghlu], 213; Qomi 1, 567, [2], 622, 649, 658; Molla Jalal 34; Shamlu 1, 101; Tatavi 773
'Aliqoli Khan Du'l-Qadr	985-?/1577-?	BB Fars	Valeh 1372, 658; Monshi 223
Khalil Khan Dhu'l-Qadr	988/1580	BB Fars	Monshi 261; Valeh 1372, 417
Ommat Beyg [Khan] Dhu'l-Qadr	989-994/1581-1586	BB Fars – H Shiraz – H Fars; *tovachi-bashi*	Valeh 1372, 658, 747; Monshi 274, 322-25; Qomi 2, 749, 755, 801-02; Bidlisi 2, 673; Molla Jalal 60
'Ali Khan Shadi Beygluy Dhu'l-Qadr	994/1586	H Shiraz - BB Fars	Valeh 1372, 789; Monshi 342; Qomi 2, 808 [first H Shiraz then upped to bb Fars], 852; Bafqi 3/1, 174
Mehdiqoli Soltan Sheikh Dhu'l-Qadr	994-996/1586-1588	BB Fars –(Mehdiqoli Beyg [Khan] Sadi Tekkelu; Monshi 355)	Qomi 2, 848, 852; Monshi 342, 355, 381, 384; Natanzi 343; Bafqi 3/1, 174
Shahqoli Khalifeh Dhu'l-Qadr	995/1587	BB Fars – never took up his post	Monshi 361, 366
Ya'qub Beyg [Khan] Dhu'l-Qadr b. Ebrahim Khan	996-999/1588-1590	BB Fars or H Fars, but Mortezaqoli Soltan Ostajalu was H and *darugheh* of Shiraz (Molla Jalal 97)	Monshi 384, 418-26, 431; Qomi 2, 888, 904, 908, 910, 1081; Natanzi 339, 342; Shamlu 1, 134; Vahid 106; Bidlisi 2, 688
Bonyad Beyg [Khan] Dhu'l-Qadr	999/October 1590	H Shiraz	Qomi 2, 918; Monshi 432; Molla Jalal 95

Hoseyn Khan Mosaheb Qajar* or Hoseyn Khan Ziyad-oghlu Qajar	1000-1001/1592-1593	H and *darugheh* Shiraz	Monshi 456; Molla Jalal 94; Vahid 119
NN Dhu'l-Qadr emir	1002/1594	H Fars	Röhrborn 37
Farhad Khan Qaramanlu	1003-1004/1595-1596	H Fars; also Azerbaijan-Mazandaran-Astarabad	Monshi 500
Allahqoli Beyg	1003/1595	*Vali* Shiraz - *zargar-bashi*	Molla Jalal 140
Allahverdi Khan	1004-1022/1596-1613	H Fars + Kuhgiluyeh as of 1005 - *qollar-aghasi*	Monshi 515, 525, 871; Ra'na-Hoseyni 348; Molla Jalal 150
Emamqoli Khan	1022-1042/1613-1632	BB Fars + H Lar, Kuhgiluyeh, Bahrain, Jarun	Yusof 115, 117; Vahid 326; Monshi 1088
	As of 1042/1632	Governed by Viziers	
Mirza Mo'in	1042-?/1632-?	Vizier Shiraz	Vahid 250, 332
Mir Mohammad Ahmad	1052?/1642-?	Vizier Fars	Vahid 332
Badadeh Arestu Beyg	1054-?/1644-?	Vizier Fars	Vahid 412
Mirza Hadi b. Mirza Mo'in	?-1061-1066/?-1651-1656	Vizier Fars	Hotz 86; Vahid 609; VOC 1224, f. 316 vs (09/12/1656)
Babunah Beyg (Bubonabeecq)	1066-?/1656-?	Vizier Fars	VOC 1224, f. 316 vs (09/12/1656)
Shahverdi Khan Seyl-Sopor	1107/1696	Vizier Fars	Nasiri 96
Mohammad 'Ali Beyg	1109/1698	Vizier Fars	Nasiri 251
Mohammad Baqer Beyg	?-1124/?-1712	Vizier Fars	Khatunabadi 566
Kalb 'Ali Khan	?-1126/April 1714	H Fars	Floor, *Afghan*, 25; Khatunabadi 566
Mirza Mohammad Hoseyn	1126/April 1714-?	H Fars	Floor, *Afghan*, 25
Safiqoli Beyg	?- 1129/January 1717	H Fars + Kuhgiluyeh, Dashtestan, Lar, Bandar 'Abbas + *qollar-aghasi*	Floor, *Afghan*, 30
Mortezaqoli Khan	1129/January 1717	H Shiraz	Floor, *Afghan*, 30
Lotf 'Ali Khan Daghestani	1129-1134/22 October 1717-December 1720	BB Fars	Floor, *Afghan*, 31; Safavi 31
Mohammad 'Ali Jaberi Ansari	1134/1722	Vizier	Floor, *Afghan*, 175
Nurollah Khan Farahani	1135/1723	Vizier	Floor, *Afghan*, 197
	From 1724 to early 1730	under Afghan control	

* Molla Jalal, *Ruznameh*, p. 97 is the only source who has a different sequence for the three last-mentioned governors, to wit: Hoseyn Khan Qajar, Bonyad Beyg, and Ya'qub Beyg and hence his dates also differ. Hoseyn Khan Mosaheb Qajar probably is wrongly placed here by Monshi (see Rey).

Shirvan is a large region in the southeastern Caucasus with Shamakhi as its main city.[347] When the Safavids took possession of Shirvan in 1500 it was ruled by the dynasty of the Shirvanshahs, who had held the area since the 14th century CE. Despite the enmity that existed between the Shirvanshahs and the Safavids, Shah Esmaʿil I allowed the son of his slain foe to govern Shirvan again, after a brief period of direct control through a Qezelbash governor. Because of persistent disloyalty of Shahrokh, the last Shirvanshah governor, Shah Tahmasp I expelled him and put his own brother Elqas Mirza as independent governor in his place. Members of the Shirvanshah family (who have been indicated by an * in the table) tried several times to regain control of the province, but failed, even when assisted by Ottoman troops, who occupied the province from 1578 until 1607. By the end of the Safavid period the province of Shirvan included the following administrative jurisdictions: Alpaʾut, Arash-Sheki, Baku, Chemeshgazak-Aghdash, Darband, Qobeh-Qolhan and Saliyan. It is of interest to note that Shamakhi (q.v.) is not mentioned separately, although it had a separate governor.

Name	Year	Observations	Source
Farrokh Yassar Shirvanshah*	867-906/1462-1500	Shirvanshah	Shirazi 135; Khatunabadi 441
Bahram Beyg b. Farrokh Yassar*	906-907/1500-1501	Shirvanshah	Khatunabadi 441; Dorn 590
Ghazi Beyg brother of Bahram Beyg*	908-908/1501-02	Shirvanshah	Shirazi 135; Khatunabadi 441
Soltan Mahmud b. Ghazi Beyg*	908/1502	Shirvanshah	Dorn 590
Sheikhshah or Sheikh Ebrahim II brother of Soltan Mahmud*	908-915/1502-1509	Shirvanshah	Qomi 1, 139; Shirazi 58-59, 135; Khatunabadi 441
Hoseyn Beyg Laleh	916-926/1510-1519	H Shirvan etc., but without Darband	Qomi 1, 98; Monshi 36; Shamlu 1, 41; Shirazi 48; Qazvini 273; Mozaffar 309
Sheikhshah or Sheikh Ebrahim II brother of Soltan Mahmud*	926-930/1519-1524	Shirvanshah	Qomi 1, 153; Monshi 43; Shirazi 58-59, 135; Khatunabadi 441; Heravi 318; Mozaffar 306
Khalilollah b. Sheikhshah*	930-942/1523-1535	Shirvanshah	Qomi 1, 256; Hoseyni 142, 207; Rumlu 355; Shirazi 135
Shahrokh b. Farrokh Mirza* nephew of Khalilollah	942-945/1535-1538	Shirvanshah	Qomi 1, 256, 277, 278; Rumlu 355, 381-82; Shirazi 135; Bidlisi 2, 572; Qazvini 293
		End of Shirvanshah rule	

---

347 For its history see Sara Ashurbeyli, *Gosudarstvo Shirvanshakhov* (vi-xvi vv.) (Baku, 1983); Rahim Raʾis-Niya, *Tarikh-e ʿOmumi-ye Mantaqeh-ye Shirvan (dar ʿahd-e Shirvanshahan)* (Tehran, 1380/2001); and Bernhard Dorn, "Beiträge zur Geschichte der Kaukasischen Ländern und Völker, aus der Morgenländischen Quellen. I. Versuch einer Geschichte der Schirwanschahe," *Mémoires de l'Académie Impériale des Sciences de St. Petersburg* (St. Petersburg, 1845), pp. 523-602.

COMMENTARY 285

Badr Khan Ostajalu	945-947/1538-1541	H Shirvan - *Laleh* of Elqas Mirza b. Esma'il	Rumlu 376, 407f; Qomi 1, 282; Hoseyni 145; Monshi 81; Shirazi 90, 93; Bidlisi 2, 56, 572; Qazvini 293
Ghazi Khan Tekkelu	947-950/1538-1543	H Shirvan - *Laleh* of Elqas Mirza b. Esma'il, who fled in 950	Rumlu 376, 407f; Qomi 1, 282; Hoseyni 145; Monshi 81, 91, 93; Shirazi 90, 93; Bidlisi 2, 561, 572; Qazvini 293; Tatavi 501
Badr Khan Ostajalu	950-954/1543-1547	H Shirvan - *Laleh* of Elqas Mirza b. Esma'il	Qazvini 296-97; Rumlu 413; Shirazi 90, 93, 95; Bidlisi 2, 580
Gokcheh Soltan Qajar	954-956/1547-1549	H Shirvan –*Laleh* of Esma'il Mirza b. Tahmasp	Monshi 182; Shirazi 97; Tatavi 535
Borhan 'Ali Soltan b. Khalilollah *	955-957/1548-1550	usurping H Shirvan	Monshi 80; Rumlu 422, 440
Mehrab Mirza, a relative of Borhan 'Ali Soltan*	956/1549	usurping H Shirvan	Monshi 81; Rumlu 422, 440
Qorban 'Ali Mirza, kinsman of Mehrab Mirza*	956/1549-1550	usurping H Shirvan	Monshi 81; Rumlu 422, 440
Qasem, descendant of Farrokh Yassar*	961/1554	usurping H Shirvan	Monshi 82
'Abdollah Khan Ostajalu b. Qara Khan aka Damad†	956-972/1549-1565	H Shirvan - also governor of Sheki [as of 956/1549-50]	Musavi 1977, doc. 1, 2; Budaq 120, Shamlu 1, 76; Qomi 1, 372, 553; Monshi 81; Rumlu 440; Shirazi 101; Qazvini 298 [955]
Mostafa Beyg [Tekkelu?]	973/1566	H Shirvan	Qomi 1, 456
Shah 'Ali Beyg	974/1566	H Shirvan; son of previous	Abrahams 145
Farrokhzad Beyg Qaradaghlu IAB	974/1567	H Shirvan – *Laleh* of Soltan Mahmud Mirza b. Tahmasp	Qomi 2, 632, 1033
Bars or Aras Khan Rumlu	974-984/1567-1576	H Shirvan - *Laleh* of Soltan Mahmud Mirza b. Tashmasp [he never went to Shirvan; see Barda']	Monshi 49, 134; Qomi 2, 632, 665, 679, 681-84, 1020; Natanzi 37; Valeh 1372, 410 [Orus]; Shamlu 1, 76 [Orus], 95; Aras Soltan Rumlu, h Rey, Qomi 1, 454, [2], 631; Shirazi 127
Abu Torab Soltan Ostajalu	985/1577	H Shirvan – appointed by Esma'il II	Monshi 216

Tavus Mirza, sister's son of Borhan 'Ali Soltan*	985/1577	usurping H Shirvan	Qomi 2, 645
Aras Soltan [Khan] Rumlu	985/1577	H Shirvan - as *Laleh* of Soltan Mahmud Mirza, who never went there; appointed by Mohammad Khodabandeh	Rumlu 632; Qomi 2, 645, 665; Monshi 227, 236; Bidlisi 2, 648
Abu Bakr Mirza *	986/1578	usurping H Shirvan	Monshi 233
Panah Mohammad Khan Dhu'l-Qadr	986/1578	BB Shirvan	Qomi 2, 686
Mohammad Khan Khalifeh Hajjilar Dhu'l-Qadr	986-?/1578-?	H Shirvan	Monshi 239; Qomi 2, 688 [as of 986]
Salman or Soleyman Khan Ostajalu††	988/1579	BB Shirvan	Monshi 260-64; Valeh 1372, 616, 623; Fumeni 81-84, 103
Beygler or Peykar [Beyg] Khan Ziyadoghlu	989-990/1580-1583	BB Shirvan	Monshi 267; Valeh 1372, 624, 638 [+other Qajar]; Shamlu 1, 106; Vahid 92
Khalifeh Ansar Qaradajlu	990/1583	H Shirvan	Monshi 271[he died soon thereafter]
	From 986/1578 to 1016/1607	**Ottoman Governors**	
Kostandil Mirza b. Alexander Khan	1012-1014/1604-1606	*Vali* and *amir al-omara* Shirvan	Monshi 670-71, 681, 693
Dhu'l-Feqar Khan Qaramanlu brother of Farhad Khan	1015-1018/1606-1609	*Vali* Shirvan, Shamakhi, Darband, Baku – *amir al-omara* Shirvan	Monshi 732, 787, 806; Shamlu 1, 187; Vahid; Molla Jalal 314, 377
Yusof Khan	1018-1033/1610-1624	H Shirvan – *gholam-mir shekar-bashi*	Yusof 71, Vahid 210; Monshi 806, 898, 989, 1025, 1033, 1040; Khatunabadi 505
Qazaq Khan Cherkes	1033-1042/1624-1633	BB Shirvan –*gholam*	Shamlu 1, 204, 205; Yusof 100, 289, 294; Vahid 247, 329
Farrokh Khan	1042-1045/1633-1636	BB Shirvan -*gholam*	Shamlu 1, 221; Valeh 1380, 120, 155, 229, 342, 360; Yusof 100, 169, 178, 279, 294; Vahid 247, 274, 328; Astarabadi 252
'Arab Beyg [Khan] Aghzivar-oglu Shamlu	1046-1053/1636-1643	BB Shirvan	Shamlu 1, 221, 284; Yusof 196, 279, 294; Vahid 280, 328, 406

Khosrow Khan	1053-1063/1643-1653	BB Shirvan; *mir shekar-bashi*	Shamlu 1, 284; Puturidze 1961, doc 22, 25; Musavi 1965, doc. 9; Ibid., 1977, doc. 7; Vahid 553; Riazul Islam 1, 346
Najafqoli Khan b. Qazaq Khan Cherkes	1063/1653	BB Shirvan	Musavi 1977, doc. 8
Bakhtan Beyg aka Mehr 'Ali Khan	1064-1066/1654-1656	BB Shirvan; kinsman of Dhu'l-Feqar Khan	Vahid 553, 612
Hajji [Manuchehr] Khan	1066-1070/1656-1660	H - BB Shirvan 3 years	Vahid 662, 684-92, 720
Mohammad[i] Beyg [Khan] b. Siyavosh Beyg.	1070-1073/1660-1663	BB Shirvan – *gholam* -2 yrs	Vahid 720, 737-38
Najafqoli Khan b. Qazaq Khan Cherkes	1074-1080/1663-1667	BB Shirvan - 7 years	Bakikhanuf 86
Mehr 'Ali Khan	1081-1083/1667-1670	BB Shirvan – 3 yrs	Bakikhanuf 86
Mokri or Makri Qoli Khan	1084-1085/1670-1672	BB Shirvan – 2 years	Bakikhanuf 86
Sayyed Khan	1086-1092/1672-1679	BB Shirvan – 7 years	Bakikhanuf 86
'Aliqoli Khan	1092-1096/1679-1685	BB Shirvan – 6 years	Bakikhanuf 86
Mirza Hedayat Jaberi	1097/1685	BB Shirvan	Parham doc. 2
Musa Khan†††	before 1106/1694	BB Shirvan	Bakikhanuf 86
Allahverdi Khan	1106-1116/1694-1705	BB or *vali* Shirvan + *motavalli* Joneyd shrine; H Gereyli	Nasiri 81, 96, 117, 177; Puturidze 1965, doc. 11
Fath 'Ali Beyg	?-1121/?-1709	H Shirvan - *amir shekar-bashi*	Khatunabadi 559
Khosrow Khan	?-1130/?-1718	H Shamakhi -Shirvan	Bushev 39f, 206, 212, 224, 230, 233
Hasan 'Ali Khan	1130/1718	BB Shirvan	Bakikhanuf 86
Hoseyn Khan Beyg	1131-1133/1719-1721	BB Shirvan -2 years	Puturidze 1965, doc. 36; Bakikhanuf 86; Touzard 49

* Indicates that the person is a member of the Shirvanshah dynasty.

† According to the catalogue of Persian and Persian-Georgian Documents, preserved at the K. Kekelidze Institute of Manuscripts (Georgian Academy of Sciences), a certain "Abdol-Reza Mir Soltan" was appointed governor of Shirvan and Sheki in 957/1550 by Shah Tamaz, see the Institute's website at [http://www.persian-doc.org.ge/catalogue.html]

†† For a picture of this governor see one of the miniatures in Filiz Cagman, Zeren Tanindi, "Remarks on Some Manuscripts from the Topkapi Palace Treasury in the Context of Ottoman-Safavid Relations," *Muqarnas*, Vol. 13, 1996 (1996), pp. 132-148, which depicts Salman Khan, governor of Shirvan, praying at the tomb of the Bibi Haybat (fol. 128b).

††† The person deputizing for Hasan Beyg Laleh was Sho'eyb. *Tatavi*, Tarikh, p. 333.

Shaborghan was the first important town at seven *farsakh* (ca. 40 km) to the west of Balkh.

Name	Year	Observations	Source
Beyram Beyg Qaramanlu	916-919/1510-1513	H Balkh, Shaborghan, Andkhud, Chichketu, Gharjestan, Meymaneh, Faryab, Morghab	Qomi 1, 115, 120; Shirazi 50; Bidlisi 2, 525; Qazvini 274; Budaq 32; Monshi 1, 40; Rumlu 164; Ben Khvandamir 139, 148
Tukret Beyg	919/1513	H Shaborghan	Fekete 255-57

Shulestan is a district situated west of Shiraz and was known for its white fort.[348]

Name	Year	Observations	Source
Hamzeh Beyg	990/1582	*Teyuldar* Shulestan	Molla Jalal 66-67
Bahram Soltan	?-998/?-1590	*Vali* Shulestan	Molla Jalal 78
Beyram Soltan, nephew of Ya'qub Khan	998-?/1590-?	H Shulestan	Molla Jalal 94

Shurehgel was a border district situated in Chokhur-e Sa'd and was sometimes also held in combination with another neighboring district.

Name	Year	Observations	Source
Qara Khan Bayat	before 984/1576	H Shurehgel and Aleshkert	Monshi 140
Hamzeh Soltan Tekkelu	before 984/1576	H Shurehgel	Valeh 1372, 411

Shushtar is situated on the northern end of the Khuzestan plain just south of the location where the Karun bifurcates. It came probably under direct Safavid administrative control in 914/1508, although its first Safavid governor is only known as of 932/1525. This was followed by a period where no particular tribal affiliation made itself felt, but after 1630 *gholam* governors dominated. As of 1042/1633, Wakhushti, a *gholam*, and his descendents held the governorship of Shushtar until the end of the Safavid period. The *Tadhkereh-ye Shushtar* gives what probably is the most complete list of governors in any Persian history for any town, although it poses problems. For if we apply its chronology it does not always tally with the dates given by other texts for the same governor. I have therefore tried to make the fit between the two sets of data, although this must be wrong in certain instances. For example the first governor ended his term of office in 941 according to the *Tadhkereh-ye Shushtar*, but according to two other sources five years later in 946/1539. Also, Sayyed Mohammad 'Arab governed for eight years, but this does not not tally with the dates of other governers from other texts and therefore to make them all fit I had to reduce his term of office from eight to only one year. In a few cases I have given the conflicting dates between brackets in the 'source' column so that the reader may form of an opinion of the nature of the problem.

---

348 Molla Jalal, *Ruznameh*, p. 67.

Mehdiqoli Soltan b. Chuli Beyg Afshar aka Qanqara [Soltan]	932-941/1532-1534	H Shushtar; succeeded by his brother	Shushtari 42 [from 932 for 10 years]; Qazvini 294 [d 946]; Qomi 1, 289 [d 946]; Rumlu 380 [d946]
Sundar Beyg b. Qanqara Soltan	942/1535	H Shushtar	Shushtari 42 [1 year]
Kachal Afshar	943-944/1536-1538	H Shushtar	Shushtari 42 [2 years]
Heydarqoli Soltan Afshar	945-948/1538-1541	H Shushtar	Shushtari 42 [945; 3 years]; Abrahams 137 [from 946]; Rumlu, 389 [from 948]; Qomi 1, 295 [as of 949]
Sayyed Mohammad 'Arab	949/1542	H Shushtar	Shushtari 42 [governed for 8 years!]
Abu'l-Fath Beyg [Soltan] Afshar	950-952/1543-1545	H Shushtar	Shushtari 42 [3 years]; Shirazi 92; Bidlisi 2, 576 [950]; Qazvini 295 [949]
Hasan Beyg [Afshar?]	953-956/1546-1549	H Shushtar	Shushtari 42
'Abdollah Khan	955/1548	H Shushtar	Afshar 111
Sayyed Beyg	956-960/1549-1553	H Shushtar	Shushtari 42
Rostam Soltan Arashlu	961-963/1554-1556	H Shushtar	Shushtari 42
Seyf Beyg	964-966/1557-1559	H Shushtar	Shushtari 42
Amir Khan Torkman	967/1560	H Shushtar	Shushtari 42
Qasem 'Ali Soltan	968/1561	H Shushtar	Shushtari 43
Mansur Khan Dhu'l-Qadr	969/1562	H Shushtar	Shushtari 43
Mohammad Soltan	970-972/1563-1564	H Shushtar –brother of Khalil Khan Afshar	Shushtari 43
Quch Beyg Rumlu	973-974/1565-1566	H Shushtar	Shushtari 43
Mohammad Soltan Rumlu	975-976/1567-1568	H Shushtar	Shushtari 43
Hoseynqoli Khan Shamlu	977/1569	H Shushtar	Shushtari 43
Sayyed Jamaz 'Arab	978-979/1570-1571	H Shushtar	Shushtari 43
Qiyas Soltan Ostajalu	980/1572	H Shushtar	Shushtari 43
'Isa Khalifeh	981/1573	H Shushtar	Shushtari 43
Eyqut Soltan Chavoshlu Ostajalu	982-983/1574-1575	H Dezful-Shushtar	Valeh 1372, 409; Shushtari 43; Qomi 2, 665 [from 985]; Monshi 139 (Eyguth)
Mirza 'Ali Beyg	984/1576	H Shushtar	Shushtari 43

Mir Rashid al-Din b. Mir 'Abdol-Vahhab	985/1577	H Shushtar	Shushtari 43 [in 985]
Dehdar Soltan	986/1578	H Shushtar [a few days]	Shushtari 43
Shahverdi Soltan Kandazlu [?]	986/1578	H Shushtar	Shushtari 43
'Ali Soltan b. Khalil Khan Afshar	987-989/1579-1581	H Shushtar	Shushtari 43
Ahmad Soltan Afshar	990-991/1582-1583	H Shushtar	Shushtari 43
Khosrow Soltan Afshar	992-993/1584-1585	H Shushtar	Shushtari 43
Shahverdi Khan Kandazlu [?]	994-1001/1586-1593	H Shushtar -2nd time	Shushtari 43; Molla Jalal 127 [1002]; Monshi 500 [in 1003]
Morad Aqa *jelowdar-bash*i	1002/1594	H Shushtar – usurper for a few days	Shushtari 43
Ghayath Beyg	1002/1594	H Shushtar; a few days; deputy of Farhad Khan	Shushtari 43
Sayyed Mobarak Khan b. Sayyed Motalleb vali of Hoveyzeh	1002/1594	H Shushtar – usurper – few weeks	Shushtari 43; Molla Jalal 127-28
Mehdiqoli Khan Shamlu	1002-1008/1594-1599	H Shushtar - *ishik aghasi-bashi*	Shushtari 43; Molla Jalal 129, 159; Monshi 502, 524-25; Vahid 135
Mohammad Soltan Chaghatay	1008-1019/1600-1610	H Shushtar – succeeded by his brother	Shushtari 45; Molla Jalal 245, 357 [Bayat], 397 [Bayat]
'Ali Soltan Chaghatay	1019-1034/1610-1625	H Shushtar	Shushtari 45; Molla Jalal 397; Monshi 959; Vahid 227 [as of 1039!]
Tahmasp Soltan b. Mohammad Soltan Chaghatay	1035-1037/1625-1627	H Shushtar + Dezful (Tahmaspqoli Soltan b. Mohammad Soltan Qara-bayat)	Shushtari 45; Monshi 1087; Vahid 342
Shebli Soltan Cherkes	1038/1628	H Shushtar – 6 months	Shushtari 46; Yusof 43
Allahverdi Soltan b. Shebli Soltan	1038-1641/1629-1632	H Shushtar – he was a child; his uncle Behruz Beyg acted as his deputy for 3 years; then Baba Soltan as deputy for 6 months	Shushtari 46
Behruz Beyg Cherkes	1042/1632	H Shushtar- for a short while	Shushtari 46
Aqa Moharram *mehtar-e rekabkhane*h	1042/1632	H Shushtar	Vahid 247
Vakhushtu Beyg [Soltan] [Khan] *gholam*; brother of Mansur Khan Dhu'l-Feqar Khan	From Rabi I 1042-1080/September 1632-1669	H Shushtar - succeeded by his youngest son	Shushtari 46; Vahid 247

Fath 'Ali Khan	1080-1106 /1669-1694	H Shushtar – succeeded by his brother	Shushtari 56; Nasiri 59
Kalb 'Ali Khan	1106-1607/1694-1697	H Shushtar	Nasiri 59; Shushtari 65
'Isa Khan b. Dhu'l-Feqar Khan	1107-1108/1696-1697	H Shushtar	Shushtari 66; Nasiri 257
'Abdollah Khan b. Aslan Khan	1109-1124/1698-1712	H Shushtar	Shushtari 66-67; Nasiri 260
Bijan Beyg b. Fazl 'Ali Beyg	1124 -Ramazan 1126/1712-September 1714	H Shushtar – his deputy Hajji Shahnazar Beyg was in charge of the town	Shushtari 67
'Abdollah Khan b. Aslan Khan	Ramazan 1126-1129/ September 1714-1717	H Shushtar - 2nd time	Shushtari 68-69
Yahya Khan Bakhtiyari	Ramadan-Dhu'l-Qa'deh 1129/August-October 1717	H Shushtar	Shushtari 69
Mehr 'Ali Khan b. Kalb 'Ali Khan	Dhu'l-Qa'deh 1129-1132/October 1717-1720	H Shushtar	Shushtari 69
'Abdollah Khan b. Aslan Khan	1132/1720	H Shushtar - 3rd time	Shushtari 69
Mohammad Reza Khan b. Aslan Khan	1132/1720	H Shushtar – was dismissed before he even reached the town	Shushtari 69
Hachhamr? Khan b. Kalb 'Ali Khan	1132-1134/1720-1722	H Shushtar	Shushtari 69
Mehr 'Ali Khan	1134-1135/1722-1723	H Shushtar	Shushtari 69
Abu'l-Fath Khan b. Mohammad 'Ali Khan b. Aslan Khan	1135-1137/1723-1725	H Shushtar	Shushtari 70
Sheikh Fares	1138-1140/1726-1728	H Shushtar on behalf of pretender Safi Mirza; anarchy ruled in reality	Shushtari 71
Sheikh Fars + Mirza Esfandiyar Beyg	1141/1729	H Shushtar	Shushtari 86
Kalb 'Ali Beyg b. Mehr 'Ali Khan	1141-1142/1729-1730	H Shushtar	Shushtari 86
Abu'l-Fath Khan b. Mohammad 'Ali Khan b. Aslan Khan	1142/1730	H Shushtar	Shushtari 87

Sojas was a border fort situated in the Soltaniyeh district (q.v.). Dowlatyar Khan son of Khalil Beyg Mansur-Siyah had been appointed by Shah Mohammad Khodabandeh as governor of his ancestral Kurdish lands, but when the Ottomans conquered most of Azerbaijan he switched his allegience and undertook to hold and defend the border districts of Kereshp, Zarrin-kamar (=Garrus), Sojas, Zanjan, Surloq (q.v.), Qeydar, Shabestan, Anguran and high and low Quntchuqeh against the Safavids. He developed Kereshp as his residence.[349]

---

349 Bidlisi, *Cheref-Nameh*, vol. 2, p. 187.

Soltaniyeh is situated some 120 km from Qazvin on the road to Tabriz and some 42 km south-east of Zanjan. According to Minorsky, following Sanson, in Safavid times the district was part of Azerbaijan.[350] Zanjan or Zanjanrud was the chief town of the district, which is bounded in the west by Kurdestan, in the north by Azerbaijan, in the northeast by Gilan, in the east by Tehran, and in the south by Hamadan provinces. Only a few times reference is made to a governor of Zanjan[351] rather than of Soltaniyeh (see also Tarom). Abhar is some 90 km from Zanjan.

Name	Year	Observations	Source
Khalil Beyg Siyah-Mansur	960-?/1552-?	H Soltaniyeh, Zanjan, Abhar, Zarrin-kamar + other districts in Persian Iraq (Sojas + Surloq)	Bidlisi 2, 186; Monshi 141
Badr Khan Ostajalu	965/1558	*Teyuldar* Soltaniyeh + Tarom	Qomi 1, 394; Qazvini 303 [Taromeyn]
Nazar Beyg [Soltan] Ostajalu	972/1565	H Soltaniyeh, Tarom and Khalkhal	Budaq 141; Qomi 1, 448
Amir Gheyb Beyg Ostajalu	974/1567	H Soltaniyeh + Khalkhal	Tatavi 663
Soleyman Khalifeh-ye Shamlu	984/1576	H Soltaniyeh	Tatavi 762
Ahmadqoli Khalifeh *pesarzadeh* Shahqoli Khalifeh *mohrdar* Dhu'l-Qadr	985-987/1577-1579	H Soltaniyeh	Qomi 2, 655, 704
Badr Khan [Ostajalu?]	?-990/?-1583	H Soltaniyeh + Tarom	Qomi 2, 732
Pir Gheyb Khan Ostajalu	990/1583	H Soltaniyeh + Tarom	Qomi 2, 732
Ahmadqoli Khalifeh-ye Dhu'l-Qadr	994-?/1586-?	H Soltaniyeh -2nd time	Qomi 2, 817
Dowlatyar Khan Siyah-Mansur or Zanganeh	997-999/1589-1591	H Soltaniyeh, Sojas, Gavehrud - H Abhar, Soltaniyeh, Surlugh till Ft Sojas [Natanzi]	Monshi 440; Molla Jalal 72; Qomi 2, 894-95 [Zanganeh]; Natanzi 332
Geda'i Soltan Kulani	ca. 1038/1629	H Zanjan	Monshi 1086
Safiqoli Soltan Beygdeli	1039-?/1630-?	H Soltaniyeh-Zanjanrud; nephew of Zeynal Khan	Vahid 227
Khosrow Soltan Jadid al-Eslam	before 1052/1642	H Abhar – *mir shekar-bashi*	Vahid 316
Safiqoli Beyg b. Saru Soltan	1054-?/1644-?	H Soltaniyeh-Zanjan	Vahid 403

---

350 TM, p. 165; M. Sanson, *The Present State of Persia* (London, 1695), p. 32 ("Sultan One at Sultanie under the Buegler-Begui of Tauris").

351 For its history see Ramin Soltani, *Tarikh-e Zanjan* (Zanjan, 1379/200); Parvaneh Porchekani, *Hameh chiz dar bareh-ye Zanjan* (Tehran, 1383/2004); Hajj Sayyed Ebrahim Musavi Zanjani, *Olama va Daneshmandan-e Zanjan* (Tehran, 1352/1973).

Someyram is a district situated at 83 km from Shah Reza, on the central plateau north-east of Kuh-e Dina, between Fars and Isfahan.

Name	Year	Observations	Source
Qalandar Soltan Chuleh-ye Chaghatay	?-1053/?-1643	H Someyram – *tofang-chi aghasi*	Valeh 1380, 405; Vahid 598
Budaq Soltan Chuleh	1053-1072-?/ 1643-1662-?	H Someyram	Valeh 1380, 405, 645-46; Vahid 709, 730
Namdar Soltan	1108/1697	H Someyram	Nasiri 204

Sonqor, is situated in Kurdestan at 90 km from Kermanshah and consists of two valleys, that of Gavehrud and Shajurud. Kolhar was often held at the same time by the governor of Sonqor and/ or Dinavar. After 1048/1636, this post became hereditary in the Zanganeh family.[352]

Name	Year	Observations	Source
Hoseyn Beyg Fath-oghlu	965/1558	*Teyuldar* Sonqor + Dinavar	Qomi 1, 394
Ahmad Khalifeh-ye Vafadar-e Rumlu	975/1568	H Sonqor	Qomi 1, 471
Sulaq Hoseyn Tekkelu	985-?/1577-?	H Dinavar + Kurdestan	Qomi 2, 665; Rumlu 643
Shahverdi Khalifeh brother of Esma'il Khan	994-?/1586-?	H Dinavar-Sa'dabad + *ba'zi mahall* of olka-ye Sulagh	Qomi 2, 828
Mostafa Pasha	1017/1609	*Teyuldar* Sonqor – *amir al-omara* of the Jalalis	Monshi 781
Shahrokh Soltan b. Ali Beyg	1044-?/1634-?	H Kolhar, Dinavar, Sonqor	Vahid 263, 317
Shahrokh Beyg [Soltan] Zanganeh	1048-1050/1639-1641	H Dinavar+ Kermanshahan or H *il-e* Kolhar-Zanganeh + Dinavar- succeeded by his brother	Yusof 246, 273; Vahid 294, 331
Sheikh 'Ali Khan Zanganeh	1050-1067/1641-1657	H Kolhar-Dinavar-Sonqor	Vahid 331, 626
Mortezaqoli Beyg	1107/1696	H Kolhar, Sonqor + Kermanshahan	Nasiri 124

Sovagh-bulagh or Sovaj-bulagh, see Rey.

---

352 Yusof, *Dheyl*, pp. 227, 292.

Sufi, a district probably situated in Azerbaijan at some 30 km south-east of Maku.

Name	Year	Observations	Source
Adam Soltan	?-1052-1058/?-1642-1648-?	H Sufi – succeeded by his son	Vahid 377-79; Valeh 1380, 393
Manuchehr Soltan	1058-?/1648-?	H Sufi	Vahid 467

Sumay is a district situated west of Salmas. As of 1110/1698, Lachin Soltan was governor of Sumay and Targevar, succeeding his father Shir 'Ali Soltan Baradust.[353]

Surloq or Surlugh is a district situated in Azerbaijan, near Soltaniyeh.[354]

Name	Year	Observations	Source
Khalil Soltan Siyah-Mansur	before 984/1576	H Sojas + Surloq	Monshi 141
Hoseyn Beyg *qurchi-ye shamsi*	998/1590	H Abhar, Soltaniyeh Surlugh till Ft Sojas	Natanzi 332

Tabas or Tabas-e Gilaki is a district situated in southwestern Khorasan, except for the north it borders on the Lut desert; on the north it borders on the Turshiz and Torbat-e Heydari districts. Tun is one of the dependencies of the district, which was generally known as Tun and Tabas. The TM presents it as part of the jurisdiction of the governor-general of Herat.[355]

Name	Year	Observations	Source
Qara Soltan Shamlu	941/1535	*Vali* Tabas	Budaq 79; Qomi 1, 550
	999/1591	Uzbeg occupation	Bidlisi 2, 689
Mostafa Soltan Kangarlu	?-1002/?-1594	H Tabas-e Gilaki	Qomi 2, 913-15; Monshi 488
Timur Soltan	1002/1594	H Tabas; soon replaced by	Monshi 490; Vahid 128
Mehrab Soltan [Khan] Qajar	1002-1032/1594-1623	H Tabas [-e Gilaki]	Monshi 490, 525, 576, 1008; Molla Jalal 162; Vahid 207
'Ashur Khan Chegani	1032-1042/1623-1633	H Tabas-e Gilaki	Monshi 1008; Yusof 21, 28, 103

Tabriz, see Azerbaijan.

---

353 Lambton, *Landlord*, p. 109.
354 According to Qomi, *Kholasat*, vol. 1, pp. 84-85 and Mozaffar, *Jahangosha*, pp. 235, 243, Surloq was just a *yeylaq* or summer quarters in the early Safavid period.
355 TM, p. 102. For the origin of the add-on of Gilaki see Le Strange, *The Lands*, pp. 359-60.

TabTab, see Nelqas.

Talesh or Tavalesh, see Astara.

Tarom is situated on both banks of the Kezel Uzun, between the Elburz and Masuleh ranges. It is sometimes called Tarom-e 'Iraq-e 'Ajam,[356] indicating that it was part of Persian Iraq.[357] The term Taromeyn is also found referring to the fact that Tarom is divided into two districts, to wit: Tarom-e Khalkhal and Tarom-e Pa'in[358] (see also Soltaniyeh). It is perhaps for this reason that often its governor was referred to as being in charge of Tarom and Khalkhal. Kharzavil that is mentioned as a district that also was governed by the governor of Tarom is situated in Gilan.[359]

Name	Year	Observations	Source
Chalapan or Chalipa Beyg Khalkhali	?-911/?-1506	H Tarom + Khalkhal	Shirazi 44; Qazvini 270; Khatunabadi 445; Valeh 1372, 156; Mozaffar 235, 238
Mohammad Soltan Dhu'l-Qadr-oghlu	?-941/?-1535	H Tarom + Khalkhal	Bidlisi 2, 564
Pireh Mohammad Khan	985-?/1577-?	H Tarom and Khalkhal	Monshi 227
Pir Gheyb Khan Ostajalu	994/1586	H Tarom + Kharzavil	Qomi 2, 817; Monshi 332
Morshedqoli Soltan Quchilu	994/1586	H Taromeyn	Qomi 2, 832

Tehran, see Rey.

Tianeti is a district mentioned in Savory's translation of Eskander Monshi Beyg's *History*. However, in the Persian text this appellation is not used, but rather that of Sadi, which is a fort situated in Azerbaijan. This different appellation between the two texts may be due to the fact that Savory also used a manuscript that had not been used for the edition of the printed Persian text. In 984/1576, or prior to that date, Shahqoli Soltan Qarancheh-oghlu Mahi-Faqihlu Ostajalu was governor of Tianeti or Sadi, as the case may be.[360]

Tiflis was part of the kingdom of Kartli. Isma'il I and Tahmasp I had undertaken a number of campaigns against Kartli during which they had occupied Tiflis. However, this occupation was not lasting until 958/1551 when a Safavid garrison was permanently stationed in Tiflis. Thereafter Safavid governors were appointed, some of whom were members of the Kartlian royal family. From

---

356 Shirazi, *Takmelat*, p. 44.
357 However, according to Heravi, *Fotuhat*, p. 263, Tarom was a dependency of Gilan.
358 Qazvini, *Tarikh*, p. 303.
359 Fumeni, *Tarikh*, pp. 18-19, 42, 48, 145, 258. The Harzavil (properly Kharzavil) district (*olka*) is also mentioned in Shah Tahmasp's *Tadhkereh-ye Shah Tahmasp*, p. 7.
360 Monshi, *Tarikh*, vol. 1, p. 139 translated by Roger M. Savory as *History of Shah 'Abbas the Great*, 2 vols. (Boulder 1978), vol. 1, p. 224; Vahid, *Tarikh*, p. 72.

987/1579 until 1014/1606 Tiflis was occupied by the Ottomans. Thereafter, Safavid governors returned and held Tiflis and its dependencies.

Name	Year	Observations	Source
Sharif Beyg Rudhaki Kord	?-938/?-1532	H Tiflis	Hoseyni 112
	938-?/1532-?	Ottoman occupation	Hoseyni 112
Sharif Beyg Rudhaki Kord	944/1538	H Tiflis	Vahid 51, 74
Da'ud Pasha b. Luarsab	969/1562	H Tiflis	Qazvini 308
Qarenjehoghlu Ostajalu	before 984/1576	H Tiflis	Valeh 1372, 409
Da'ud Pasha b. Luarsab	987/1579	H Tiflis	Bidlisi II 648
	From 987/1579 to 1015/1606	under Ottoman control	
Ziya al-Din b. Sharaf Khan	?-1015/?-1606	H Tiflis	Monshi 721, 741, 923
Mohammad Soltan Shams al-Dinlu aka Deli Mohammad	1015-1018/1606-1609	H Tiflis	Monshi 719; Molla Jalal 321
Luarsab Khan grandson of Simon Khan, king of Kartli	1018-?/1609-?	H Tiflis	Monshi 816

Tonekabon, a district in Mazandaran situated between the Miyaneh-rud and the Namakrud-sar.

Name	Year	Observations	Source
Sharaf al-Din Bedlisi	974-981/1567-1574	H Tonakebun	Rabino 139; Valeh 1372, 411; Monshi 140
Sharaf Khan	1003/1595	H Tonakebun	Rabino 139; Fumeni 164-65
Heydar Soltan Quylu [or Qavi] Hesarlu	1004/1596	H Tonakebun	Rabino 139; Fumeni 167, 273-74
Farhad Khan Qaramanlu	1005/1597	H Tonakebun	Rabino 139
Mir b. Hoseyn Khan Firuzjang	?-1006/?-1598	H Tonakebun	Monshi 536
Heydar Soltan Quyleh Hesarlu Rumlu b. Bayazid Soltan	1038-1041/1629-1632	H Tonakebun	Monshi 1085; Yusof 17, 85; Valeh 1380, 18, 20, 141; Vahid 214, 223
Ebrahim Beyg sofrehchi [Soltan] b. Khalaf Beyg sofrehchi	1042-?/1632-?	H Tonakebun	Yusof 85; Vahid 247

Torbat-e Heydari or Torbat is the name of a district and its main town is situated in central Khorasan. In the southeast it borders on Afghanistan, in the south on Berjand and Gonabad, in the west on Kashmar and in the north on Mashhad and Nishapur. Its governor sometimes was also in charge of other adjacent districts and dependencies such as Badghis, Bakharz, Khvaf, Mahvelat and Zaveh (q.v.). Berjand and Zaveh were dependencies of Torbat-e Heydari.[361]

Name	Year	Observation	Source
Morshedqoli Soltan Chavoshlu b. Yakan Shahqoli	985-?/1577-?	H Torbat, Zaveh, Mahvelat, Bakharz	Qomi 2, 665
Farrokh Khan brother of Mortezaqoli Khan	?-988/?-1580	H Torbat	Monshi 257
Shahqoli Soltan b. Morshedqoli Khan	994/1586	H *qasabeh-ye* Khvaf, Bakharz, *velayat-e* Torbat, Badghis, Mahvelat	Shamlu 1, 123
Dervish Mohammad Khan Rumlu	998/1580	H Torbat	Monshi 256
Qadi Soltan Torbati	1005-1026/1597-1617	*teyuldar* of Torbat-e Heydari	Monshi 568, 928
Faridun Hoseyn Soltan grandson Ebn Hoseyn Khan Firuzjang	1038/1629	H Torbat	Monshi 1086

Torshiz is a district situated in Khorasan, east of the Kavir and bounded on the north by Kuh Azqand. Its main town is also known as Torshiz. Its governor sometimes simultaneously also held responsibility for other districts such as Mahvelat, Sabzavar, Saveh and Zudeh [?].

Name	Year	Observations	Source
Mahmud Khan Sufi-oghlu Ostajalu	985-?/1577-?	H Torshiz	Monshi 139, 227; Valeh 1372, 409; Molla Jalal 47
Vali Khan Ostajalu	986/1578	Rival H Torshiz	Molla Jalal 47
Shah 'Ali Soltan Afshar	985-986/1577-1578	H Torshiz	Qomi 2, 665, 674
Brothers of Pir Gheyb Soltan Ostajalu	990-?/1582-?	Mir of Torshiz	Qomi 2, 727
Mantasha Khan [Sheikhlar] Ostajalu	995-996/1586-1587	H Torshiz	Qomi 2, 859
Ebrahim Khan Torkman	996-?/1587-?	H Torshiz	Qomi 2, 874, 889
Pir Oveys	?-1006/?-1598	H Torshiz, succeeded by	Siyaqi 479
Mohammad Soltan Orumlu	1006/1598	H Torshiz + Saveh	Siyaqi 479
Dervish Mohammad Khan Rumlu	1007/1599	H Torshiz-Mahvelat-Zudeh	Molla Jalal 184

---

361 Yazdi, *Mokhtasar*, vol. 1, p. 218.

Yusof Soltan [Khan] Rumlu	1016/1607	H Torshiz; in 1020 also *darugheh-motasaddi* of Sabzavar	Molla Jalal 328-29, 438
Ahmad Soltan Mochaki	1031-?/1622-?	H Torshiz	Monshi 978

Tulak a district in the province of Herat, situated south of Ishlan, north of Ghorat and northeast of Farsi. In 1522 its governor was Ahmad Beyg Afshar, who was also in charge of Sakhar, Farah, Sabzavar (=Esfezar), Uk (or Uq), *Qal'eh-ye* Kah and Tus (q.v.).[362]

Tun va Tabas are two adjacent districts situated in south-western Khorasan and were invariably held by the same governor. Tun is now known as Ferdows. Tun and Tabas are bounded in the north by Shahrud, in the east by Berjand, in the south of Kerman and in the north by Bafq and Ardakan. This governorship was sometimes combined with that of Bakharz, Gonabad and Khvaf (see also Tabas).

Name	Year	Observations	Source
Qara Ishik	930/1525	*Teyuldar* Tabas	Abrahams 129
Shoja 'Beyg Varsaq	974/1566	H Tun va Tabas	Abrahams 145
Soleyman Khalifeh-ye Torkman b. Sohrab Khalifeh	985-996/1577-1587	H Tun va Tabas, Gonabad + dependencies	Molla Jalal 43; Valeh 606; Qomi 2, 729, 755, 759, 874, 913; Natanzi 139; Monshi 140, 256, 488; Natanzi 139
Salman Khan Ostajalu b. Shah 'Ali Mirza	996-997/January 1588-1589	H Tun va Tabas	Qomi 2, 759, 874; Monshi 403
Soleyman Khalifeh Torkman b. Sohrab Khalifeh	998, 1002/1589, 1594	Usurper -H Tun va Tabas, Gonabad + dependencies	Qomi 2, 913-15; Monshi 488
	999-1001/1591-1593	Uzbeg occupation	Bidlisi 2, 689
Mostafa Beyg Kangarlu [Ostajalu]	1001-?/1593-?	H Tun va Tabas	Monshi 455-56; Vahid 118
Mehrab Beyg Qajar	1006-?/1598-?	H Tun, Jonabad, Khvaf-Bakharz	Siyaqi 479; Molla Jalal 184
Fereydun Soltan	1108/1687	H Tuneyn	Nasiri 203, 206
Eftekhar Soltan	1110/1699	H Tun	Nasiri 273

Ubeh or Obeh is a dependency of Herat and is situated some 90 km above Herat on the right bank of the Hari Rud, between Karokh in the north-west, Badghis in the north, Tulak in the south and Chest in the east. The governor appears to have been generally appointed for the jurisdiction of Ubeh – Shaflan or Ubeh – Shaflan-Heratrud, while in the latter case one governor, Mohammad Amin Khan, was also referred to as the governor of Heratrud only. However, this seems to have been a shorthand appelation for the multi-district governorship, because not only is

---

362 Khvandamir, *Habib*, pp. 585, 591.

he also mentioned in another source with the full compliment of jurisdiction, so is his brother and immediate successor.

Name	Year	Observations	Source
Rostam Beyg	1042/1633	H Ubeh, Shaqlan	Yusof 103
Mohammad Amin Khan	?-1070/?-1660	H Ubeh, Shaqlan, Heratrud - succeeded by his brother	Vahid 720; Valeh 1380, 601, 655
Mohammad Rahim Khan	1070-?/1660-?	H Ubeh, Shaqlan, Heratrud	Vahid 720

Ujarud is a district of Azerbaijan, bounded in the north by the Moghan steppe and in the east by the Bala-Rud and is watered by the rivers Barzand and Balharu. Although mentioned as a governosrship by the TM and Nasiri's *Alqab* I have not been able to find the names any of its governors.[363]

Uq is situated north of Zarang. This district had always been part of Seystan and therefore it seems to have been separated from it and added to other jurisdictions, just as the fort of Kah (or Gah) (q.v.), either to have better control over the ruler of Seystan, or in this case, to bolster the defenses of Farah (q.v.) against the Uzbegs, who held most of Khorasan by that time. In 984/1576, Hoseyn Soltan Afshar was governor of Farah, Kah, Uq, and dependencies.[364]

Van was a border fort, which was usually held by the Ottomans. The Safavids had lost control over the fort early in their reign, but for a short while it was held again by the Safavids between 942/1535 and 955/1548, when the Ottomans retook it.[365] In 959, Tahmasp I destroyed Van and took Arjish,[366] but later it was lost again, permanently this time.

Name	Year	Observations	Source
Ahmad Khan Sufi-oghlu Ostajalu	942/1535	H Van + Arjesh	Shirazi 84; Bidlisi 2, 568
Soleyman Soltan b. Mohammad Hoseyn Soltan Tekkelu	955/1548	H Van	Afshar 96
Shah 'Ali Soltan Chegani	955/1548	H or *kutval* of Van	Hoseyni 165; Monshi 72 [*kutval*]; Qomi 1, 324, 336; Shirazi 100; Tahmasp 47

Varamin or Varamin-e Rey is a town and district situated at some 45 km south of Tehran (see also Rey).

---

363   TM, p. 165; Fragner, "Ardabil", doc 2.
364   Budaq, *Akhbar*, p. 141; Monshi, *Tarikh*, vol. 1, pp. 204, 275 (d. in 990).
365   Qomi, *Kholasat*, vol. 1, p. 336; Shirazi, *Takmelat*, p. 100
366   Bidlisi, *Cheref-Nameh*, vol. 2, p. 588.

Name	Year	Observations	Source
Ahmad Soltan Ostajalu	932/1526	H Shahryar-e Varamin	Bacqué-Gramont 97
Ahmad Soltan Yazar [?]	985-?/1577-?	H Varamin	Qomi 2, 664
Ordughdi Khalifeh-ye Tekkelu	987-990/1579-1583	H Varamin	Qomi 2, 709, 725, 729 [+ bio]
Ahmad Soltan b. Mohammad Khan Sharaf al-Din-oghlu Tekkelu	990-?/1583-?	H Varamin	Qomi 2, 729
Ebrahim Soltan Ostajalu	996-?/1588-?	H Varamin	Qomi 2, 874
Cheragh Soltan Gerampa Ostajalu	998-?/1590-?	H Varamin	Qomi 2, 923
'Aliqoli Khan Shamlu	1020/1611	*Vali* Tehran – Varamin; IAB	Molla Jalal 437

Vargahan is a district of Qarajedagh, situated north-east of Ahar (Azerbaijan). Only the TM and Nasiri's *Alqab* mention this governorship.[367]

Vaset and Javazer were two districts in south and central Iraq (in fact, Javazer was a *sanjaq* of Baghdad), which were in the hands of the Safavids during two different time periods, when they also held Baghdad and some other towns in Iraq. The first period was between 1508 and 1534 and the second period was between 1623 and 1639. The dates for these two time periods probably are the same for Safavid rule in Vaset and Javazer.[368]

Name	Year	Observations	Source
Qansu Beyg	935-?/1528-?	H Vaset + Javaz[er]	Qomi 1, 190 (Qanisa Beyg); Budaq 68
	As of 941/1534 until 1032/1622	Under Ottoman control	Bidlisi 2, 566
Abu'l-Qasem Soltan b. Pir Gheyb Soltan Ostajalu	1032-1033/1622-1624	H Javazer + dependencies	Monshi 1007; Vahid 207
	As of 1048/1639	Ottoman governors	

Yazd, a town and province situated in south-eastern Iran, some 320 km south-east of Isfahan. Although usually governed by governors it was turned into crown domain from 946/1539 until 992/1584 or thereabouts[369] and once again as of ca. 1010/1601 and was henceforth governed by viziers (see Table). It would seem that just before the fall of the Safavid dynasty governors once again were appointed to look after Yazd.

---

367 TM, pp. 101, 164.

368 According to Yazdi, *Mokhtasar*, vol. 1, p. 80, it was in ruins by the 1670s and only nomadic Arabs lived there who preyed on travelers.

369 Bafqi, *Jame'*, vol. 3/1, p. 167, Razi, *Haft Eqlim*, vol. 3, p. 67.

COMMENTARY 301

Name	Year	Observations	Source
Hasan Beyg Laleh[30]	909-910/1504-1505	H Yazd	Hoseyni 29; Rumlu 111; Qomi 1, 85; Shirazi 43; Bidlisi 2, 511; Qazvini 629
Qadi Mohammad Kashi	910-915/1505-1510	H Yazd, Kashan *va kheyli az mahall-e* Iraq, Fars	Rumlu 146; Qazvini 272
Amir Beyg Torkman	before 913/1507	H Yazd; offered but taken away shortly thereafter	Aubin 15, n. 172
Mirza Mohammad Talesh	945?/1538?	H Yazd	Afshar 210
	From ca. 946/1539 until 994/1586	crown domain	
Mohammad Sharif Tehrani	964-972/1539-1565	vizier Yazd	Bafqi 3/1, 167; Monshi 166
Jamal al-Din Mohammad	973-?/1566-?	vizier Yazd	Bafqi 3/1, 169
Mirza 'Abdollah Jaberi Ansari	985-987?/1577-1579?	vizier Yazd	Bafqi 3/1, 172-73
'Aliqoli Beyg	991/1583	*Darugheh* Yazd - *qurchi-ye tarkesh*	Molla Jalal 68
Bektash Khan Afshar	?-994/?-1586	H Yazd; reappointed [also a *darugheh* + *garakyaraq*]	Qomi 2, 848
Soheyl Beyg	995/1587	*Darugheh* Yazd	Molla Jalal 73, 75
'Ali Khan Beyg Sufilar	998/1590	*Darugheh* Yazd	Molla Jalal 74
Bektash Khan Afshar	998/1590	Usurped Yazd – Kerman	Molla Jalal 73
'Aliqoli Beyg [Khan] Shamlu	1005-1006/1596-1598	H Yazd + Aberquh - *qurchi-ye tarkesh*	Monshi 525; Siyaqii 444 ; Molla Jalal 161, 165 [*darugheh*]; Shamlu 1, 134; Bafqi 3/1, 190
Khosrow Bayat	1013/1604	*Darugheh* Yazd	Molla Jalal 295
Ghazi Beyg	?-1013/?-1604	vizier Yazd	Bafqi 3/1, 176-82
Mohammad Zaman Beyg	1013-1015-?/1604-1606	vizier Yazd + Kashan – Ghazi Beyg's brother	Bafqi 3/1, 182-84
Ebrahim Khalil	ca. 1020/1611	vizier Yazd	Bafqi 3/1, 184
Mohammad Amin Shurehbiz Khorasani	ca. 1020s/1610s	vizier Yazd	Bafqi 3/1, 185-86
Nura Mohammada	ca. 1020s/1610s	vizier Yazd	Bafqi 3/1, 186
Khvajeh Shehaba-ye Kermani	ca. 1020s/1610s	vizier Yazd	Bafqi 3/1, 186-87
Mirza Hasan 'Ali Esfahani	?-1031/?-1622	vizier Yazd	Bafqi 3/1, 188-89
Mirza 'Enayatollah Esfahani	1032/1623	vizier Yazd	Bafqi 3/1, 189-90; Vahid 208 [d. 1033]

Mirza Khalilollah	1032-1041/1623-1632	vizier Yazd	Bafqi 3/1, 190-92
Mirza Shah Taher	1042-?/1632-?	vizier Yazd	Bafqi 3/1, 192
Emamverdi Beyg	1054-?/1644-?	vizier Yazd	Vahid 412
Mirza Mo'in	?-1059/?-1649	vizier Yazd	Bafqi 3/1, 193
Mirza Mohammad Shafi'	1059-1064/1649-1654	vizier Yazd	Bafqi 3/1, 194
Safiqoli Beyg	1064-1066/1654-1656	vizier Yazd	Bafqi 3/1, 195-97
Mirza Ja'far	1066-1070/1656-1660	vizier Yazd	Bafqi 3/1, 198-203
Mirza Mohammad Shafi'	1070-1074/1660-1664	vizier Yazd – 2nd time	Bafqi 3/1, 204
Hajji Mohammad Baqer Beyg	1074-1078/1664-1668	vizier Yazd	Bafqi 3/1, 204-05; Bardsiri 662
Allahqoli Beyg	1078-1089/1668-1678	vizier Yazd	Bafqi 3/1, 206-10, 230
Mohammad Hoseyn Beyg	1092/1681	vizier Yazd	Bardsiri 483
Mirza Shafi' b. Mir Hashem	?-1101-1106-?/ 1690-1695	vizier Yazd	Nasiri 81; Bardsiri 584
Shamshir Khan	1134/ 18/07/1722-?	H Yazd	Floor, *Afghan Occupation*, 149
	As of 1723	under Afghan governors	Mostowfi 135

Zabulistan, see Seystan.

Zagam, Zagham or Zakam is situated in north Kakhetia, 25 km south of modern Zakataly and 170 km west of Tiflis.[370] This district was a dependency of Ganjeh-Qarabagh. Qalich Beyg, son of Oveys Beyg Pazuki assumed the governorship of Zagam and of the Pazuki principality in the 1550s and he ruled for nine years.[371] According to Nasiri's *Alqab*, by the end of the Safavid period the governor of Zagam also was the governor of the Shams al-Dinlu tribe, which was a subdivision of the Dhu'l-Qadr tribe.[372]

Zakhur is district situated in the province of Shirvan.

Name	Year	Observations	Source
'Ali Soltan	1116/1695	H Zakhur	Puturidze 1965, doc. 11
NN	1134/1721	H of Zakhur and Sheki	Puturidze 1965, doc. 38

Zalem is a mountain fort situated in Kurdestan on the border with Shahr-e Zur. As of 1045/1635, 'Ali Soltan Zalem was governor of *Qal'eh-ye* Zalem.[373]

---

370 TM, p. 166.
371 Bidlisi, *Cheref-Nameh*, vol. 2, p. 194.
372 Monshi, *Tarikh*, vol. 1, p. 417; vol. 2, pp. 839, 1080; Vahid, *Tarikh*, p. 228 (governor).
373 Vahid, *Tarikh*, p. 278; Bidlisi, *Chereh-Nameh*, vol. 1, p. 111.

Zamindavar is situated on the right bank of the Helmand, northeast of Gereshk. According to the TM, Zamindavar and Ghuriyan formed one jurisdiction.[374] Ghuriyan (q.v.), however, is situated at 65 km from Herat, of which it is a dependency. The district of Zamindavar, in which Fort Bost (q.v.) is situated, was part of Qandahar province. Usually both the district and the fort had a separate governor, but the two were also held by one person. It also happened that the governor of Bost held sway over other areas such as Gereskh, which may have well been the norm rather than an exception.

Name	Year	Observations	Source
	From 932/1526 until 963/1556	Moghul governors	
Heydar Soltan	963/1556	H Zamindavar	Shamlu 1, 77
Hamzeh Beyg Dhu'l-Qadr aka Qur Hamzeh	966-984/1559-1576	H Zamindavar + the districts of Garmsirat *Laleh* Soltan Hoseyn Mirza b. Bahram Mirza	Hoseyni 177; Shamlu 1, 79; Monshi 478-81; Qomi 1, 397, 448, 575, 2, 629, 651
Hamzeh Beyg Dhu'l-Qadr aka Qur Hamzeh	985-998/1577-1590	H Bost + Zamindavar *Laleh* Rostam Mirza b. Soltan Hoseyn Mirza	Monshi 477-85
Rostam Mirza b. Soltan Hoseyn Mirza	998-999/1590-1591	H Zamindavar	Monshi 487-88
	From 1000/1592 until 1006/1597	Moghul governors	Monshi 674
Ganj 'Ali Khan Zik	1006-?/1597-?	H Zamindavar	Siyaqi 479
Rezaqoli Soltan Siyah-Mansur	1038/1629	H Zamindavar	Monshi 1086
Mohammad Soltan Chekani	1058/1648	H Zamindavar	Vahid 495
Sayyed Asadollah Khan	1059/1649	H *Qal'eh* Zamindavar	Shamlu 1, 414

Zanjan, see Soltaniyeh.

Zaruzbil and the Kilani tribe seem to have been a joint governorship. Zaruzbil is a district situated in the southeast corner of Sevan or Gökchay Lake (Erevan),[375] which apparently was governed by the chief of the Kalani, who were among the strongest tribes of Kurdestan.

---

374 TM, p. 103.
375 TM, pp. 101, 166.

Zaveh or Torbat-e Zaveh is a district in north Khorasan adjacent to Mahvelat and was a dependency of Torbat-e Heydari.[376]

Name	Year	Observations	Source
Durmish Khan Shamlu	919-?/1513-?	H Zaveh	Aubin, Soufis, 40, n. 259
Hajji Mohammad Soltan Kutval Chagatay	?-984/?-1576	H Zaveh + Mahvelat	Monshi 141
Mohammad Khan Torkman	984/1576	H Torbat-e Zaveh	Seystani 189
Morshedqoli Khan Yakan Ostajalu b. Shahqoli	985-989/1577-1581	H Khvaf – Bakharz, Torbat-e Zaveh, Mahvelat	Monshi 227, 293-95; Bidlisi 2, 651; Molla Jalal 43; Qomi 2, 665

Zeydan or Zeybadat (Zeydanat), as the name occurs in the TM, is a district on the lower course of the Ab-e Shirin, which flows past Zeydan and Hindiyan, in south-west Kuhgiluyeh.

Name	Years	Observations	Source
Mohanna Khan 'Arab Khaza'i	1051/1641	H Zeydan	Yusof 252
Farajollah Beyg	1108/1697	H Zeydan	Nasiri 181-82

Zeytunat is a district in Fars, which, according to Yazdi, was always governed by an emir. However, neither he nor other sources mention any governor.[377]

Zohab is a border fort in Kurdestan, which was also known as *Qal'eh-ye* Lak, and served to protect Persia's western border and prevent incursions by the Ottomans. It is also the site where the famous and important treaty of Zohab was concluded in 1639. In 1034/1625, the Safavid governor of Zohab was Nafas Soltan Garrus.[378]

Zonuz is a mountainous district, situated on a northern branch of the river Marand and the fort of Qarniyaraq. The name Zonur is also mentioned in several histories, which seems to be an incorrect orthography.[379]

Name	Years	Observations	Source
Khalil Soltan Seylpur	1019/1610	*Vali-ye* Zonur + dependencies	Molla Jalal 389
Kalb Reza Soltan Zonuzi	before 1038/1629	H Zonuz	Monshi 1087

---

376 Yazdi, *Mokhtasar*, vol. 1, p. 218.
377 Yazdi, *Mokhtasar*, vol. 1, p. 335.
378 Monshi, *Tarikh*, vol. 2, p. 1036.
379 TM, p. 101; Monshi, *Tarikh*, vol. 1, p. 406 (Zonur), vol. 2, p.1087 (Zonuz); Molla Jalal, *Ruznameh*, pp. 273, 389 (Zonur).

| Hatem Soltan | 1107/1696 | H Zonur | Nasiri 96 |

Zurabad is situated some 60 km from Sarakhs. It was one of the frontier forts; its purpose was to prevent and stop Uzbegs from making incursions into Persia. It seems that both Sarakhs and Zurabad were (usually/always?) held by the same governor, presumably to better coordinate the patrolling and protection of the border area.

Name	Years	Observations	Source
Mir Hoseyn Soltan Tobadkani	?-976/?-1569	H Sarakhs + Zurabad succeeded by his brother	Qomi 1, 562
Sayyed Hoseyn Tobadkani	976-985/1569-1577	H Sarakhs + Zurabad	Qomi 1, 563
Ebn Hoseyn Khan b. Mir Hoseyn Soltan Tobadkani	985-?/1577-?	H Sarakhs+ Zurabad	Qomi 2, 665
Hoseyn Khan Firuz-jang	1016/1607	H Sarakhs + Zurabad	Molla Jalal 329

Zuri refers to a tribe in Herat province as well as the district assigned to them for their sustenance.[380]

---

380 TM, pp. 102, 168 has Durmi.

GLOSSARY

accountants, *mostowfi*s

administrative documents, *keyfiyāt-e daftari*.

administrative wages, *talab-e daftari*.

administrators, *zābetān*.

apostil, *ta'liqeh*.

archivist, *daftardār*

army accountants, *lashkar-nevisān*.

army commander, *sardār*.

assayers, *mo'ayyerān*.

authorized fees, *rosum-e hokmi*.

banquet, *mehmāni*.

blank royal orders, *arqām- e bayāzi*.

blank order and office memorandum, *parvancheh-ye bayāzi va daftari*.

cash [salaries or payment], *tankhvāh*.

chancery fee, *dushallok*.

chanter, *dhāker*.

chantry, *towhid-khāneh*.

cheetah keepers, *bārschiyān*.

chief of the royal huntsmen, *amir shekār-bāshi*.

chief accountant of the army, *khalifeh-ye lashkar-nevis*.

chief accountant of the royal domains, *mostowfi-ye khāsseh*.

chief accountant of the state domains, *mostowfi al-mamālek*.

chief army musterer, *tovāchi-bāshi*.

chief justice, *divān-beygi bāshi*.

chief royal mace-bearer of the royal harem, *ishik āghāsi-bāshi-ye haram-e 'oliyeh-ye 'āliyeh*.

chief royal mace-bearer [of the *divān*], *ishik āghāsi-bāshi*.

chief royal physician, *hakim-bāshi* or *hakim-bāshi-ye asl*.

chief-vizier, *sar-vazir-e a'zam*.

clerk of the seal, *vazir-e mohr*.

coarse cotton fabric, *karbās*.

coiners, *zarrābiyān*.

commander-in-chief, *sepahsālār*.

commander of the royal household troops, *qurchi-bāshi*.

commander of the royal musketeer corps *tofangchi-āghāsi*

commander of the royal slave corps, *qollar-āghāsi*.

commands, *farāmin*.

cotton-silk fabric, *qasab*.

cotton-silk, *khārā*.

counterpart, *ham-qalam*.

craft guilds, *mohtarafeh-ye asnāf*.

custodian, *motavalli*.

custodianship, *towliyat*.

diplomas for Sufis, *shajarāt*.

district heads, *boluk-bāshiyān*.

equerries, *amir ākhurān*.

estimate, *bar āvardi*.

eunuchs, *āqāyān*.

fees, *rosumāt*.

female head cover, *meqna'eh*.

fighters for the faith, *ghāzis*

fine cotton fabric, *metqāli*.

fiscal officials, *'ommāl*.

fixed [salary, pension, etc.], *moqarrari*.

four viziers, *vozarā-ye arba'eh*.

gold-thread, *golābtun*.

goods sent to the royal household, *tahvilāt*.

governor-general, *beygler-beygi*.

grand vizier, *vazir-e divān-e a'lā* and *E'temād al-Dowleh*

great royal seal, *mohr-e āthār-e ashraf*.

head clerk of the royal secretariat, *dārugheh-ye daftar-khāneh-ye homāyun-e a'lā*.

herders, *ilkhichiyān*

herders, *ilkhiyān*.

high steward [of the royal household] (*nāzer-e boyutāt*)

horsebreakers, *rāyezān*.

horse trainers, *dāychiyān*.

inspector, *moshref*.

junior chief royal physician, *hakim-bāshi-ye kuchek*.

landed fiefs, *eqtā'-ye tamliki*.

led horse, *asb-e kotal*.

Lord High Justice, *divān-beygi*.

Lord of the Seal, *amir-e mohr*.

mace-bearers, *ishik āghāsis*.

master of the royal herds, *mir ākhur-bāshi-ye sahrā* or *amir ākhur-bāshi-ye ilkhi*.

master of the royal stables, *amir ākhur-bāshi-ye jelow*.

mint-masters, *zarrāb-bāshiyān*.

occasional or irregular fees, *havā'i*.

official fees, *rosum-e hokmi*.

one-tenth thread, *dah-yek*.

perquisites, *madākhel*.

physician of the royal harem, *hakim-bāshi-ye haram*

processed [?] dust or ore, *khāk-e konh*.

regent, *vakil-e divān-e a'lā*.

registrar, *sarreshteh-nevis*.

regular salary [for the duration of the appointment], *hameh-sāleh*.

rent[s], *ejārat*.

resplendent headgear, *tāj-e vahhāj*.

revenue assignment, *teyul*.

royal administrative commands, *ahkām-e daftari*.

royal armorer [eunuch], *jabbehdār-bāshi*.

royal armorer [non-eunuch], *selahdār-bāshi*.
royal astrologer, *monajjem-bāshi*.
royal diplomas, *manāsher*.
royal bakery, *churak-khāneh*.
royal companions, *moraqqabān*.
royal domains *khāsseh*.
royal edicts, *ahkām*.
royal gunners, *tupchi*s.
royal household troops, *qurchi-ye khāsseh-ye sharifeh*.
royal notes, *parvānejāti*.
royal commands, *ahkām*.
royal orders, *arqām*.
royal slaves, *gholām*s.
royal sun-like seal, *mohr-e mehr-e āthār*.
royal workshops, *boyutāt*.
saddle-room, *rekāb-khāneh*
salaries, *mavājeb*
scribes of the royal secretariat, *'azabān-e daftar-khāneh-ye homāyun*
secretary of the royal council, *majles-nevis-e mahfal-e behesht-ā'in*.
senior squire, *yasāvol-e sohbat*.
Shah Soltan Hoseyn, *mālek-e reqāb*,
Shah Soleymān, *navvāb towbi-āshiyān*,
silk-cotton fabric *atlas*
silver thread, *naqdeh*.
shoulder [?] meat, *gusht-e par-shāneh*.
son, *farzand*.
square female mantel, *lāchak*.
squire, *yasāvol*.
steward, *nāzer*.
stipend, *an'ām*.
sub-governor, *qol-beygi*.

subordinates, *tābinān*.
Sufi hat, *tāj*.
supplementary revenue, *far'*.
surcoat, *arkhāliq*.
tax exempt land grant, *soyurghāl*.
tax exemption, *ma'āfi*.
the same, *beh dastur*.
triumphal arches, *chahār tāq-bandi*.
'unquantified', *bilā-mablagh*.
user fee, *haqq al-sa'y*.
usher, *rikā*s.
viceroy, *vāli*.
victorious government staff, *'asāker-e mansureh*.
vizier of the chancellery, *vazir-e divān*.
vizier of the endowments, *vazir-e mowqufāt*.
vizier's fee, *rasm al-vezārat*.
wooden stick, [*chub-e*] *tariq*.
workshop, *dastgāh*.
yeomen, *āqāyān*.
Your Majesty, *abad-e tow'amān*.

BIBLIOGRAPHY

Archives

National Archief (National Archives, The Hague, The Netherlands)

KA and VOC – Records of the Verenigde Oostindische Compagnie (Dutch East Indies Company)

Overgekomen brieven en papieren (Letters and documents received), vols. 1215-2322

Books and articles

Abrahams, Simin. *A Historiographical Study and Annotated Translation of Volume 2 of the Afzal al-Tavarikh by Fazl Khuzani al-Isfahani*, unpublished PhD dissertation, University of Edinburgh, 1999.

Afshar, Iraj ed. *'Alamara-ye Shah Tahmasp* (Tehran, 1370/1991).

Agulis, Zak'aria. *The Journal of Zak'aria of Agulis* translated by George A. Bournoutian (Mazda, 2003).

Anonymous, "Mémoire de la province du Sirvan, en forme de Lettre addressée au Pere Fleuriau", *Lettres Edifiantes et Curieuses* (Paris, 1780), vol. 4, pp. 13-53.

Anonymous, "Asnad va namehha-ye tarikhi," *Majalleh-e Hur* 1 (1351), pp. 60-64.

Ardalan, Sherin. *Les Kurdes Ardalan entre la Perse et l'Empire ottoman* (Paris, 2004).

Astarabadi, Mirza Mehdi Khan. *Tarikh-e Jahangosha-ye Naderi* (Tehran, 1368/1989).

Astarabadi, Sayyed b. Morteza Hoseyni *Az Sheikh Safi to Shah Safi*. ed. Ehsan Eshraqi (Tehran, 1364/1985).

Aubin, Jean. *L'Ambassade de Gregório Fidalgo à la cour du Châh Soltân-Hoseyn* (Lisbon, 1971).

———. "Révolution chiite et conservatisme. Les soufis de Lahejan, 150-1514 (Etudes safavides II)," *Moyen Orient & Océan Indien* 1 (1984), pp. 1-40.

Bacqué-Gramont, Jean-Louis. "Une liste d'émirs Ostajlu révoltéees en 1526," *Studia Iranica* 5/1 (1976), pp. 91-114.

Bafqi, Mohammad Mofid Mostowfi-ye. *Jame'-ye Mofidi*. 3 vols. ed. Iraj Afshar (Tehran, 1340/1961).

Bakikhanuf, 'Abbasqoli Aqa, *Golestan-e Eram* ed. A.A. Alizade (Baku, 1970).

Balfour, F.C. *The Life of Sheikh Mohammed Ali Hazin* (London, 1830).

Bardsiri, Mir Mohammad Sa'id Moshizi. *Tadhkereh-ye Safavi*, ed. Ebrahim Bastani Parizi (Tehran, 1369/1990).

Bastami, Mohammad Taher. *Fotuhat-e Fereyduniyeh* ed. Sa'id Mir Mohammad Sadeq and Mohammad Nader Nasiri Moqaddam (Tehran, 1380/2001).

Beneveni, Florio. *Poslannik Petra I na Vostoke. Posol'stvo Florio Beneveni v Persiyu u Bukharu v 1718-1725 godakh* ed. V.G. Volovnikova (Moscow, 1986).

Ben Khvandamir, Amir Mahmud. *Iran dar Ruzgar-e Shah Esma'il va Shah Tahmasp*, ed. Gholam Reza Tabataba'i (Tehran, 1370/1991).

Beyburdi, Hosein. *Tarikh-e Arasbaran* (Tehran, 1346/1968).

Bidlisi, Sharaf Khan. *Cherefnama ou Histoire des Kourdes*, publiée par V. Veliaminof-Zernof, 2 vols. (St. Petersburg 1860-62).

Budaq Qazvini. *Javaher al-Akhbar*. Mohammad Reza Nasiri and Koichi Haneda eds. (Tokyo, 1999).

Bushev, P.P. *Posol'stvo Artemiya Volinskogo v Iran v 1715-1718 gg.* (Moscow 1978).

Caskel, Werner. "Ein Mehdi des 15. Jahrhunderts. Saijid Muhammad ibn Falah und seine Nachkommen," *Islamica* 4 (1929), pp. 48-93.

———. "Die Wali's von Huwezeh," *Islamica* 6 (1934), pp. 415-34.

Chardin, Jean. *Voyages*, ed. L. Langlès, 10 vols. (Paris, 1811).

Coolhaas, W. Ph. ed. *Generale Missieven van Gouverneurs-Generaal en Raden aan Heren XVII der Verenigde Oostindische Compagnie*, 6 vols. (The Hague, 1960-1980).

De Maze, Père. "Journal du voyage du Pére de la Maze, de Chamakié à Ispahan, par la province du Guilan," *Lettres Edifiantes et Curieuses* (Paris, 1780), vol. 4, pp. 53-112.

Dhabihi, M. and Setudeh, M. *Az Astara ta Astarabad*, 10 vols. (Tehran 1354/1975).

Dorn, B. *Geschichte Shirwans unter den Statthaltern und Chanen von 1538-1820* (Beiträge zur Geschichte der Kaukasischen Länder und Volker, vol. 2, Mémoires de l'Academie etc. (St. Petersbourg 1840).

Dorri, Ahmad. "Sefaratnameh-ye Ahmad Dorri," in Mohammad Amin Riyahi ed. *Sefaratnamehha-ye Iran* (Tehran, 1368/1989), pp. 67-98.

Esfahani, Mohammad Ma'sum b. Khvajegi. *Kholasat al-Siyar*, ed. Iraj Afshar. (Tehran, 1368/1989).

Fekete, L. *Einführung in die persische Palaeographie*. ed. G. Hazai (Budapest, 1977).

Floor, Willem. "The rise and fall of Mirza Taqi, the eunuch grand vizier (1043-55/1634-45)," *Studia Iranica* 26 (1997), pp. 237-66.

———. *Commercial Conflict between Persia and the Netherlands 1712-1718*, University of Durham Occasional Paper Series no. 37 (1988).

———. *The Afghan Occupation of Persia, 1722-1730* (Paris 1999).

———. "The Lost Files of Jean Billon of Cancerilles and French-Persian Relations during the beginning of the eighteenth century," *Eurasian Studies* 2 (2003), pp. 43-94.

———. & Faghfoory, Mohammad. *The First Dutch-Persian Commercial Conflict* (Costa Mesa: Mazda, 2004).

———. *The Persian Gulf 1500-1730. The Political Economy of Five Port Cities* (Washington DC, 2006).

Foster, W. ed., *The English Factories in India 1618-1669.* 13 vols. (London 1906-27).

Fragner, Bert. "Ardabil zwischen Sultan und Schah. Zehn Urkunden Schah Tahmasps II." *Turcica* 6 (1975), pp. 177-225.

Fumeni, 'Abd al-Fattah. *Tarikh-e Gilan dar vaqaye'-ye salha 923-1038 hejri qamari*, ed. Manuchehr Setudeh (Tehran, 1349/1970).

Hedges, William. *The Diary of William hedges Esq. during his Agency in Bengal: as well as his Voyage out and Return Overland (1681-1687)*. ed. R. Barlow 3 vlols. (London. 1887-89).

al-Hoseyni, Khurshah b. Qubad. *Tarikh-e Hoseyni-ye Nezam Shah.* ed. Mohammad Reza Nasiri and Koichi Haneda (Tehran, 1379/2000).

Molla Jalal al-Din Monajjem, *Ruznameh-ye 'Abbasi ya Ruznameh-ye Molla Jalal*, ed. Seyfollah Vahidniya (Tehran 1366/1967).

Kaempfer, Engelbert. *Die Reisetagebücher* ed. K. Meier-Lemgo. (Wiesbaden, 1968).

Kanakert, Zak'aria. *The Chronicle of Zak'aria K'anaker* translated by George A. Bournoutian (Mazda, 2004).

Khatunabadi, Sayyed 'Abdol-Hoseyn al-Hoseyni. *Vaqaye' al-Sennin va A'vam.* ed. Mohammad Baqer Behbudi (Tehran, 1352/1973).

Khvandamir. *Habib al-Seyar*, 4 vols. ed. Mohammad Dabir-Siyaqii. (Tehran, 1362/1983).

Laheji, 'Ali b. Shams al-Din b. Hajji Hoseyn. *Tarikh-e Khani*, ed. Manuchehr Setudeh (Tehran, 1352/1973).

Lambton, A.K.S. *Landlord and Peasant in Persia* (London, 1953).

Le Bruyn, Cornelius. *Travels into Moscovy, Persia and part of the East-Indies*, 2 vols. (London, 1737).

Luft, Paul. "Mush'sha'," *Encylcopedia of Islam²*.

Mehrabadi, Abu'l-Qasem Rafi'. *Tarikh-e Ardestan* 3 vols. (Tehran, 1367/1988).

Mervi, Mohammad Kazem. *Tarikh-e 'Alamara-ye Naderi*, 3 vols. ed. Mohammad Amin Riyahi. (Tehran, 1369/1990).

Minassiyan, L. "Faramin-e mowjud dar muzeh-ye Jolfa," *Honar va Mardom* 84 (1348/1969), pp. 14-19.

Minorsky, Vladimir. *The Tadhkirat al-Muluk, A Manual of Safavid Administration* (Cambridge, 1980).

Mofakhkham, Mohsen. "Asnad va mokatebat-e tarikhi", *Barrasiha-ye Tarikhi* 2 (1346/1967), pp. 361-66.

Monshi, Eskander Beyg. *Tarikh-e 'Alamara-ye 'Abbasi*. Iraj Afshar ed. 2 vols. (Tehran, 1350/1971).

Mostowfi, Mohammad Mohsen. *Zobdat al-Tavarikh*. ed. Behruz Gudarzi (Tehran, 1375/1996).

Mozaffar, Allah Deta ed. *Jahangosha-ye Khaqan* (Islamabad, 1986).

Musavi, Mamad Taqi. *Orta asr Azarbaijan tarikhina dair fars dilinda jazymysh sanadlar* (Baku, 1965).

———. *Baky tarikhna dair orta asr sandalari* (Baku, 1967).

———. *Orta asr Azarbaijan tarikhina dair fars-dili sanadlar XVI-XVIII asrlar* (Baku, 1977).

Nasiri, Mirza 'Ali Naqi. *Alqab va mavajeb-e dowreh-ye salatin-e Safaviyeh* ed. Yusef Rahimlu (Mashhad, 1371/1992).

Nasiri, Mohammad Ebrahim b. Zeyn al-'Abedin, *Dastur-e Shahriyan*. ed. Mohammad Nader Nasiri Moqaddam (Tehran, 1373/1995).

Natanzi, Mahmud b. Hedayatollah Afushteh-ye. *Naqavat al-athar fi dhekr al-akhyar*, ed. Ehsan Eshraqi. (Tehran, 1350/1971).

Papaziyan, A.D. *Persidskie dokumenty Matenadarana* (Erivan, 1956).

———. *Persidskie Dokumenty Matenadarana I, Ukazy, vypusk vtoroi (1601-1650)* (Erevan, 1959).

Parham, Sirus. "Asnad-e sazman-e asnad-e melli-ye Iran," *Rahnama-ye Ketab* 17 (1353/1964), pp. 409-14.

Petruchevskij, I. P. *Ocherki po istorii feodal'nych otnoshenij v Azerbaidzane I Armenii v XVI-nachale XIX vv.* (Leningrad, 1949).

Puturidze, V.S. *Persidskie istoricheskie dokumenty v knigoxraniloshchax Gruzii*, 4 vols., (Tiflis, 1961; 1962; 1965; 1977).

Qa'em-Maqami, Jahangir. *Yaksadupanjah sanad-e tarikhi az Jala'iriyan ta Pahlavi* (Tehran 1348/1969).

Qarakhani, Hasan. "Buq'eh-ye Ayyub Ansari dar Takab - faramin-e shahan-e Safavi dar bareh-ye mowqufat-e an", *Barrasiha-ye Tarikhi* 9 (1353/1974), pp. 71-122.

Qazvini Ghaffari, Qadi Ahmad. *Tarikh-e Jahanara* (Tehran, 1343/1964).

al-Qomi, Qadi Ahmad b. Sharaf al-Din al-Hoseyn al-Hoseyni. *Kholasat al-Tavarikh*, 2 vols. ed. Ehsan Eshraqi. (Tehran, 1363/1984).

Quiring-Zoche, Rosemarie. *Isfahan im 15. und 16. Jahrhundert* (Freiburg, 1980).

Rabino, H. L. *Mazandaran and Astarabad* (London, 1928).

Ra'na-Hoseyni, Karamat. "Farmani az Shah 'Abbas," *Rahnama-ye Ketab* 9 (1345/1966), pp. 348-50.

Riazul Islam, *A Calendar of Documents on Indo-Persian Relations*. 2 vols. (Tehran/Karachi, 1979).

Röhrborn, Klaus-Michael. *Provinzen und Zentralgewalt Persiens im 16. und 17. Jahrhundert* (Berlin 1966).

Rumlu, Hoseyn Beg. *Ahsan al-Tavarikh*. ed. 'Abdol-Hoseyn Nava'i (Tehran, 1357/1978).

Sam Mirza, *Tadhkareh-ye Tohfat-e Sami*. ed. Rokn al-Din Homayunfarrokh (Tehran, n.d.).

Safavi, Mohammad Khalil Mar'ashi. *Majma' al-Tavarikh*. ed. 'Abbas Eqbal (Tehran, 1328/1949).

Savory, Roger M. translator. *History of Shah 'Abbas the Great*, 2 vols. (Boulder 1978).

Seystani, Malek Shah Hoseyn b. Malek Ghayath al-Din Mohammad b. Shah Mahmud. *Ehya al-Moluk*. ed. Manuchehr Setudeh (Tehran, 1344/1966).

Shamlu, Valiqoli b. Da'udqoli. *Qesas al-Khaqani*, 2 vols., ed. Hasan Sadat Naseri. (Tehran, 1371/1992).

Shirazi, 'Abdi Beg. *Takmelat al-Akhbar*. ed. 'Abdol-Hoseyn Nava'i (Tehran, 1369/1990).

Shushtari, Sayyed 'Abdollah b. S. Nur al-Din b. S. Ne'matollah al-Hoseyni. *Ketab-e Tadhkereh-ye Shushtar* ed. Khan Bahadur Maula Bakhsh (Calcutta, 1924).

Siyaqi-Nezam. *Fotuhat-e Homayun*. Persian text edited and translated into French by Chahryar Adle as *Les Victoires augustes, 1007/1598* (unpublished thesis Sorbonne – Paris 1976).

Stewart, Devin J. "An episode in the 'Amili migration to Safavid Iran: Husayn b. 'Abd al-Samad al-'Amili's travel account," *Iranian Studies* 39 (2006), pp. 481-508.

Touzard, Anne-Marie. *Le drogman Padery* (Paris, 2006).

Valeh Esfahani, Mohammad Yusof. *Khold-e Barin*. ed. Mir Hashem Mohaddeth (Tehran, 1372/1993).

———. *Iran dar Zaman Shah Safi va Shah 'Abbas Dovvom* ed. Mohammad Reza Nasiri (Tehran, 1380/2001).

Vahid Qazvini, Mirza Taher. *Tarikh-e Jahanara-ye 'Abbasi* ed. Sa'id Mir Mohammad Sadeq (Tehran, 1383/2004).

Yusof, Mohammad. *Dheyl-e Tarikh-e 'Alamara-ye 'Abbasi*. ed. Soheyli Khvansari (Tehran, 1317/1938).

INDEX

A

abad-e tow'aman 15, 35, 309
Abbasi [Budaq] b. Khalilollah Ranashi 179
Abbas Khan Ziyad-oghlu Qajar 199
Abbasqoli Beyg 154, 232
Abbasqoli Beyg [Khan] 203, 232
Abbasqoli Khan 150, 163, 184, 188, 216, 232, 247, 259
Abbasqoli Khan Ardalan 228
Abbasqoli Khan Qajar 172
Abbasqoli Khan Shamlu 203
Abbasqoli Soltan 154
Abbasqoli Soltan Dhul-Qadr 264
Abbas Soltan Afshar 215
Abdalabad 270
Abdal Ali 209
Abdal Beyg Dedeh 246, 261, 265, 274
Abdal Beyg Dedeh Dhul-Qadr 261
Abdali 128, 137
Abdal Khan Gereyli 190
Abdallu 124
Abd al-Masud Khan 173
Abdal Soltan b. Qalandar Soltan 209
Abdal Soltan Qajar 188
Abdi Beyg Shamlu 205
Abdol-Ghaffar Khan 238
Abdol-Ghani Beyg 252
'Abdol-Jamil Nasiri 10
Abdollah Beyg 165
Abdollah Beyg Mahmudi 220
Abdollah Beyg Ostajalu 165
Abdollah Beyg Zanganeh 50
Abdollah Khan 10, 137, 157, 217, 220, 257, 272, 289, 291
Abdollah Khan b. Aslan Khan 291
Abdollah Khan Ostajalu 197, 261
Abdollah Khan Ostajalu b. Qara Khan 285
Abdollah Soltan 239
Abdol-Qasem Beyg 232
Abdol-Qasem Khan 198
Aberquh 34, 132, 137
Abhar 138
Abivard 109, 129, 138, 157, 177, 245, 251
Abu Bakr Mirza 286
abul-baqa 17
Abul-Fath Beyg [Soltan] Afshar 179, 289
Abul-Fath Khan 179
Abul-Fath Khan b. Mohammad Ali Khan b. Aslan Khan 291
Abul-Fath Khan Shamlu b. Aghzivar Khan 191
Abul-Fath Mirza Soltan Ebrahim 268
Abul-Fath Soltan Afshar 103
Abul-Fath Soltan Ebrahim Mirza 147, 240
Abul-Masum Beyg 203
Abul-Masum Soltan Tarkhan Torkman 273
Abul-Qasem Beyg 253
Abul-Qasem Khan 199
Abul-Qasem Soltan b. Pir Gheyb Khan Sharaflu Ostajalu 205
Abul-Qasem Soltan b. Pir Gheyb Soltan Ostajalu 300
Abul-Qasem Soltan Ostajalu 209
Abu Moslem Soltan [Khan] Chavoshlu Ostajalu 182
Abu Taleb Beyg Nasiri 10
Abu Torab Beyg Nasiri 9
Abu Torab Soltan 171
Abu Torab Soltan Ostajalu 285
Acheh Soltan Qajar 252
Adam Soltan 294
Adam Soltan Gorji 264
Adeljavaz 126

Adham Beyg 103
Adham Beyg Nasiri 9
Adham Khan [Torkman] 273
Adham Khan Torkman 264
Adham Soltan 184
Afghans 7, 53, 176
Afshar 124, 125
Aghcheh Qaleh 139
Aghdash 127, 139
Aghzivar Khan 253
Aghzivar Khan Shamlu 250
Aghzivar Khan Shamlu b. Damri Soltan Shamlu 201
Aghzivar Soltan Shamlu 240
Ahar 47, 118
ahkam 309
ahkam-e daftari 308
Ahmad Beyg Afshar 204, 240, 270, 271, 298
Ahmad Beyg Beygdelu 193
Ahmad Beyg Esfahani 178
Ahmad Beyg Ostajalu 229
Ahmad Beyg [Soltan] Afshar 182, 183
Ahmad Beyg Sufi-oghlu Ostajalu 200, 242
Ahmad Khalifeh-ye Vafadar-e Rumlu 179, 293
Ahmad Khan Soltan 141, 230
Ahmad Khan Sufi-oghlu Ostajalu 299
Ahmad Kofrani Esfahani 206
Ahmadqoli Khalifeh Dhul-Qadr 292
Ahmad Soltan 103, 275
Ahmad Soltan Afshar 215, 290
Ahmad Soltan Alash-oghlu 103
Ahmad Soltan b. Mohammad Khan Sharaf al-Din-oghlu Tekkelu 300
Ahmad Soltan Chekani b. Jami Soltan 269
Ahmad Soltan Dhul-Qadr 275
Ahmad Soltan Kangarlu 266
Ahmad Soltan Ostajalu 300
Ahmad Soltan Shamlu 277
Ahmad Soltan Sufi-oghlan [ogli] Ostajalu 215
Ahmad Soltan Sufi-oghlu Ostajalu 149

Ahmad Soltan Tekkelu 269
Ahmad Soltan Yazar 300
Ahmad Soltan Yazar Tekkelu 268
Akhastabad 140
Akheshkeh 140
Akhesqeh 140
Akhi Soltan Tekkelu 261
Akhlat 140
Akhpat 141
Akhsabad 140
Akhtabad 127, 140
Akhteh Beygi 103
Ala al-Dowleh Ranashi 179
Ala Houraga 232
Alamut 141
Alashgerd 141
Alashkert 141
Alash Soltan 166
alatiyeh tent 103
Albaut 141
Aleshkert 127
Alghas Mirza 172
Ali Beyg 103, 265, 273
Ali Beyg [Khan] Fumeni 195
Ali Beyg Mowsellu 158
Ali Beyg Ostajalu 206
Ali Beyg Soltan 185
Ali Beyg [Soltan] Dhul-Qadr Chichkelu 281
Ali Beyg [Soltan] Tekkelu 206
Ali Beyg Zanganeh 179
Ali Jan Soltan Shaqaqi 279
Ali Khalifeh Aghcheh-Qoyunlu Qajar 166
Ali Khalifeh-ye Qajar 266
Ali Khan 153, 185
Ali Khan Beyg 280
Ali Khan Beyg Sufilar 301
Ali Khan Gereyli 189
Ali Khan Shadi Beygluy Dhul-Qadr 282
Ali Khan Soltan Afshar 183
Alikhan Soltan Sufilar 269
Ali Mardan Khan 82, 225, 242
Ali Mardan Khan b. Hoseyn Khan 236
Ali Mardan Khan Zik 257
Ali Morad Khan 257

Ali Qobad Beyg Chuleh-ye Chaghatay 138
Aliqoli Bahador 103
Aliqoli Beyg 301
Aliqoli Beyg Geramillu Shamlu 266
Aliqoli Beyg [Khan] Fath-oglu Ostajalu 155
Aliqoli Beyg [Khan] Shamlu 301
Aliqoli Khan 84, 138, 156, 203, 216, 236, 246
Ali Qoli Khan 287
Aliqoli Khan Ardalan 228
Ali Qoli Khan Davalu 156
Aliqoli Khan Dul-Qadr 282
Aliqoli Khan Fath-oghlu Ostajalu 266
Aliqoli Khan Ostajalu 255
'Aliqoli Khan Shamlu 10, 241, 300
Aliqoli Khan Shamlu 10, 241, 300
Aliqoli Khan Sharaf 213
Aliqoli Mirza b. Tahmasp 201
Aliqoli Soltan 272
Aliqoli Soltan [Khan] Kangarlu 248
Aliqoli Soltan Quroghlu Dhul-Qadr 264
Aliqoli Soltan Sadlu 260
Ali Reza Khan 163, 232
Ali Soltan 147, 219, 302
Ali Soltan b. Khalil Khan Afshar 290
Ali Soltan Chaghatay 290
Ali Soltan Chalaq 103
Ali Soltan Chepelu 223
Ali Soltan Tati-oghlu Damurchilu Dhul-Qadr 240
Ali Soltan Tati-oghlu Dhul-Qadr 282
Ali Soltan Tekkelu 202
Ali Soltan Zalem 302
Ali Yar Beyg 190
Allahqoli Beyg 188, 283, 302
Allahqoli Beyg b. Shahqoli Soltan 155
Allahqoli Beyg Ichik-oghlu Gerampa Ostajalu 174
Allahqoli Beyg Ijik-oghlu 193

INDEX 317

Allahqoli Beyg Qapana-oghlu Qajar 222
Allahqoli Khan 173
Allahqoli Soltan 280
Allahqoli Soltan Gerampa Ostajalu 193
Allahqoli Soltan Ichek-oghlu Ostajalu 229
Allahqoli Soltan Ijak-oghlu Ostajalu 277
Allahverdi Beyg 153, 162, 188, 232
Allahverdi Beyg zargar-bashi 210
Allahverdi Khan 224, 225, 279, 283, 287
Allahverdi Soltan b. Shebli Soltan 290
Alpaut 91, 127, 141
Alvand Div 142
Alvand Soltan [Khan] Afshar 224
Alvand Soltan Qaramanlu 230
Alzobar [?] Beyg 139
Amin Hoseyn Firuz-jang 208
Amir Abdol-Karim 244
amir akhuran 308
amir akhur-bashi 181
amir akhur-bashi-ye ilkhi 308
amir akhur-bashi-ye jelow 40, 308
amir akhur-bashi-ye sahra 50
Amir Aslan Soltan Arshlu 206
Amir Beyg [Khan] 188
Amir Beyg Mowsellu 197
Amir Beyg Mowsellu Torkman 171
Amir Beyg [Soltan] Rumlu 261
Amir Beyg Torkman 301
Amir Ebrahim b. Mohammadi 231
amir-e divan 46
Amireh Dobbaj 194, 195, 229
Amireh Dobbaj Rashti 265
Amireh Hatem 223
Amireh Hosam al-Din 194
Amireh Mozaffar 188
Amireh Qobad Talesh 150
Amireh Rostam Kohdomi 210
Amireh Sasan 187
Amir[eh] Sasan b. Amireh Siyavosh 187
Amireh Shahrokh 194

Amireh Siyavosh Gaskari 188, 219
Amireh Siyavshah b. Amireh Rostam 210
Amir[eh] Soltan 187
amir-e mohr 46, 308
Amir Eskandar Kord 164
Amir Esmail Savaji 206
Amir Gheyb Beyg Ostajalu 155, 219, 292
Amir Gheyb Soltan Ostajalu 240
Amir Goli Beyg 183
Amir Guneh Khan Aghcheh-Qoyunlu Qajar 172
Amir Hamzeh Beyg Ostajalu 165, 249
Amir Hamzeh Khan 150
Amir Harun b. Ala al-Molk 231
Amir Hasan Kiya 174, 185, 274
Amir Hoseyn Firuz-jang 271
Amir Khan Afshar 214, 224
Amir Khan b. Golabi Beyg b. Amir Beyg Mowselu 180
Amir Khan Chulaq Baradust 252
Amir Khan Mohrdar Soklan Dhul-Qadr 275
Amir Khan Morabbi Söklen Dhul-Qadr 216
Amir Khan Mowsellu Torkman 155, 201
Amir Khan Mowselu Torkman 197, 274
Amir Khan Mowselu Torkman b. Mohammadi Khan 197
Amir Khan Rumlu 254
Amir Khan Torkman 289
Amir Khorshid 231
Amir Kiya Gugi 196
Amir Nushirvan b Ala al-Molk 231
Amir Shah Hoseyn Bakhtiyari 159
Amir Shahnazar Soltan Beyburdi 239
Amir Shahrokh 200
amir shekar-bashi 39, 153, 307
Amir Siyavosh b. Amireh Sasan 187
Amir Soltan 263
Amir Soltan Mowselu 254
Amol 131, 142

an'am 309
anbar-e gholaman 19
Andkhud 160
Anhar 147
Anusheh Khan 156
Anushirvan 90
Anzal-Sowmey 125, 142
Aqa Fathollah 263
Aqa Hasan Changrudi 162
Aqa Kamal Dowlatabadi 206
Aqa Khan II Moqaddam 238
Aqa Khan Moqaddam 238, 252
Aqa Mohammad Abhari 244
Aqa Mohammad Ruzafzun 244
Aqa Moharram 290
Aqa Rostam Ruzafzun 244
aqayan 32, 33, 308, 309
Aqa Zaman Esfahani 195, 265
Aqcheh Qaleh 126
Aqcheh-Qaleh 142
Arab Ameri 152
Arab Beyg [Khan] Aghzivar-oglu Shamlu 176, 286
Arab-e Amereh 133
Arab-e Ameri 142
Arabestan 135, 142
Arab Iraq 132
Aradvar 129, 146
Arasbar 124, 127, 147
Arash 91, 127, 147
Arash-Sheki 279
Aras Khan Rumlu 285
Aras Soltan [Khan] Rumlu 286
Aras Soltan Rumlu 202, 266
Ardabil 9, 114, 115, 124, 147, 154, 155, 212, 247, 271, 299, 312
Ardalan 228
Ardestan 132, 148
Aref Soltan 83
Arghiyan 149, 207
Arjish 124, 149
arkhaliq 309
Arpah Chapi River 86
arqam 309
arqam-e bayazi 307
Arz Beyg 139, 250
Arzenjan 149
Asadabad 40, 270

Asadollah Khan 137
Asadollah Khan Abdali 203
asaker-e mansureh 309
asb-e kotal 308
Ashraf Khan 7
Ashur Khan Chapni or Chekani 246
Ashur Khan Chegani 294
Ashur Soltan b. Seydom Soltan 263
Aslamas Beyg 257
Aslamas Khan 30
Aslamas Khan b. Shahrokh Khalifeh 149
Aslan Beyg 262
Aslan Beyg Qurchi-ye Shamlu 194
Aslan Khan 85, 153, 184, 246, 257
Aslan Khan Afshar 215
Aslan Khan Daghestani 225
Aslan Soltan Areshlu Afshar 215
Astara 124, 149
Astarabad 10, 24, 45, 90, 130, 150
Astareh 149
Astrakhan 90
Atil 90
atlas 98, 309
avarajeh-nevisan 69
Aveh 133, 154
Avroman 134, 154
Ayub Khan 173, 271
Ayyar Khan 190
'azaban-e daftar-khaneh-ye homayun 73, 309
Azadvar 129, 154
Azeljavaz 139
Azerbaijan 10, 11, 23, 27, 29, 47, 48, 69, 85, 91, 112, 113, 119, 154
Aziz Soltan 247

B

Baba Beyg [Soltan, Khan] 158
Baba Elyas Bayat 250
Babolsar 242
Babunah Beyg 283
Badadeh Arestu Beyg 283
Badadeh Soltan 139
Badenjan Soltan Ostajalu 147
Badghis 128, 130, 156
Badi al-Zaman Mirza 277
Badi al-Zaman Soltan 272
Badkubeh 159
Badr Khan 158
Badr Khan Afshar 152
Badr Khan [Ostajalu?] 292
Badr Khan Ostajalu 151, 174, 285, 292
Bafrud 157
Baghbad 139
Baghdad 132, 157
Bagh-e Shahi 102
Bahador Khan 217, 236
Bahrain 135, 158
Bahram Beyg b. Farrokh Yassar 284
Bahram Beyg Gholam 277
Bahram Beyg [Soltan] Ostajalu 176
Bahram Mirza 193, 197, 201, 235
Bahram Mirza b. Esmail 197
Bahramqoli Soltan Sufi 178
Bahram Soltan 189, 288
Bakharz 103, 128, 158, 220
Bakhtan Beyg 287
Bakhtiyari 131, 134, 159
Baku 127, 159
Bala Morghab 128, 160
Balkh 130, 160
Baluch 83
Bampur 168
Bandar Abbas 135, 161
bandeh-zadeh-ye qadimi 57
Baneh 134, 164
banner 31, 33, 34, 38
Baqer Soltan 158
Baradust 121, 164
Baradust-Sowmey-Tergavar 125
Baratili 196
bar avardi 308
Barbideh Beyg 188
Barda 93, 127, 164
Bargoshad 165
Bargoshat 165
Bargushat 127
Barkhordar Soltan Qolkhanchi Ughli Dhul-Qadr 161
barschiyan 307
Basaku 254
Basra 165
Bastam 129, 152, 166
bath-house 102
Bavanat 135, 138, 166
Bayandor Khan 148
Bayandor Khan Talesh 150
Bayandor Soltan 260
Bayat 121, 125, 126, 127, 167, 258
Bayazid 126, 167
Bayazid Soltan Shamlu 147, 247
Bazavandaq 129, 249
Bazavandaqan 167
Bedlis 125, 167
Begeh Beyg Ardalan 227
Behbud Khan Cherkes 153, 188, 196
beh dastur 309
Behruz Beyg Cherkes 290
Behzad Beyg 194
Behzad Soltan 158
Bektash Beyg [Khan] 158
Bektash Khan 198
Bektash Khan Afshar 215, 301
Bektash Khan Danalu Ostajalu 246
Bektash Soltan Ostajalu 239
Besat Beyg b. Sorkhab Beyg Ardalan 227
Betlis 167
Beyg Bayat 257
beygler-beygi 12, 27, 45, 84, 308
Beyram Ali Beyg 264
Beyram Ali Soltan Chapni 166
Beyram Ali Soltan [Khan] Qara-Bayat 251
Beyram Beyg 231
Beyram Beyg Qaramanlu 160, 288
Beyram Khan b. Seyf Ali Beyg Baharlu 197
Beyramqoli Soltan Mir Sufi 178
Beyram Soltan 157
Beyram Soltan Dhul-Qadr 288
Bijan Beyg b. Fazl Ali Beyg 291

Bijan Khan 225
bila-mablagh 309
bildar-bashi 139
Birjumand 168
Birunat 135, 168
Biyabanak 138
Biyar 168
Biyarjomand 129, 152, 166, 168
black eunuchs 20
Bokhara 157
boluk-bashiyan 308
Bon Fahl 168
Bonyad Beyg [Khan] Dhul-Qadr 282
Borhan al-Din Khalifeh b. Elyas Khalifeh 260
Borhan Ali Soltan b. Khalilollah 285
Borujerd 134, 169
Borun Soltan Tekkelu 181
Bost 82, 129, 130, 169
boyutat 309
Bozavandeqan 170
brand 40
Budaq Beyg b. Mirza Beyg 164
Budaq Khan Chegani 182, 198, 218, 241
Budaq Khan Qajar 103, 178, 246, 256
Budaq Soltan 138, 209, 247, 278
Budaq Soltan Chuleh 293
Budaq Soltan Qajar 269
Burburud 132
Buri 126, 142, 170
Burun Soltan Tekkelu 240
Buzchelu 93, 127, 170

C

calendar 55
cameleers 40
carpets 98, 102, 103
Chagatay Kotuk Mohammad Khan 172
Chahar Bagh 18, 102
Chahar Mahall 170
chahar taq-bandi 309
Chakerlu 270
Chalapan or Chalipa Beyg Khalkhali 295
Chamchal 134, 170
Chamchamal 170
Chameshgezek 91, 127
Chamkhal 170
Charandab Soltan Shamlu 174, 184, 205, 250, 278
charkhchi-bashi 184
Chayan Soltan 154
Chayan Soltan Ostajalu 238
cheetah keepers 18, 40
Chemeshgezek 170
Cheragh Soltan Garampa Ostajalu 300
Cheragh Soltan Gerampa Ostajalu 175, 179, 197
Cheragh Soltan Ostajalu 248
Chichketu 160
Chokhur-e Sad 86, 126
Chokhur Sad 170
Chors 115, 125, 173
chub-e tariq 33, 309
churak-khaneh 309
Churs 115, 173
Chutiyali 129, 173
cotton fabric 100, 101, 309

D

daftardar 72, 307
Daghestan 136
Daghkhan Chenagi 182
dah-yek 308
Damavand 133, 153, 174
Damghan 133, 152, 153, 166, 174
Damri Soltan Shamlu 166
Daquq 132, 174
Darabjerd 135, 174
dar al-ensha 62
Dar al-Marz 131
Darazjin 40
Darband 90, 127, 160, 175, 284
Darband-e Shirvan 175
Dargazin 176
Darhazin 176
Darjazin 176
darugheh 61, 63, 71, 97, 138, 148, 155, 167, 186, 187, 188, 193, 195, 205, 206, 213, 231, 247, 262, 265, 269, 282, 298, 301, 308
darugheh-ye daftar-khaneh 63
darugheh-ye daftar-khaneh-ye homayun-e a'la 63, 308
Darun 129, 139, 177, 251, 257
Darvalakes 87, 177
Darvalakis 126
Dashtestan 135, 158, 177
Dasht-sar 41
dastgah 309
Daud Beyg 177
Daud Khan 181
Daud Khan b. Allahverdi Khan 259
Daud Pasha b. Luarsab 296
Davar 130
Daver 178
daychiyan 308
Dede Beyg 197
Dedeh Beyg 246
Dehdar Soltan 290
Dehestan 210
Delijan 132
Deli Mohammad 296
Delu Mantasha Soltan Ostajalu 240
Demri Soltan 274
deputy grand vizier 24
Derbend 175
Dervish Ali Khalifeh Gereyli 189
Dervish Khan Soltan 257
Dervish Mohammad Khan 279
Dervish Mohammad Khan b. Aras Khan Rumlu 251
Dervish Mohammad Khan Orumlu 229
Dervish Mohammad Khan Rumlu 194, 251, 297
Deylaman 131, 178
Dezful 135, 145, 178
dhaker 307
Dhakerlu 120
Dhul-Feqar 158
Dhul-Feqar b. Ali Beyg 211
Dhul-Feqar Beyg 103
Dhul-Feqar Khan 257, 278

Dhul-Feqar Khan b. Zaman Khan Abdali 204
Dhul-Feqar Khan Qaramanlu 148, 155, 160, 263, 286
Dhul-Feqr Khan 150
Dhul-Qadr Khan 250
Dinavar 134, 179
Din Mohammad b. Olush Khan 250
divan-beygi 203, 266, 308
divan-beygi bashi 46, 307
Div Jamal al-Din 272
Div Soltan Rumlu 160, 171, 246
Diyarbekr 180
dog-keepers 40
DomDom 252
Domri Beyg 165
Domri Beyg Ostajalu 273
Domri Soltan 185
Donboli 89, 115, 124, 125, 180
Donbolis 126
Donboli-ye Akrad 89
Dorrani 137
Dorun 177
Dowlatkhan Afghan 173
Dowlatyar Khan Mansur-Siyah 291
Dowlatyar Khan Siyah-Mansur 292
Dowraq 135, 180
Duki 129, 173, 181
Durmi 128
Durmish Khan 240
Durmish Khan Shamlu 154, 201, 205, 263, 304
Durmish Khan Soltan 189
dushallok 25, 71, 307
Dust Ali Khan 186
Dust Ali Khan Zanganeh 169, 221
Dust Ali Soltan Zanganeh 239

E

Ebn Hoseyn Khan b. Hoseyn Soltan Firuz-jang Chaghatay 271
Ebn Hoseyn Khan b. Mir Hoseyn Soltan Tobadkani 271, 305
Ebrahim Beyg 208, 268
Ebrahim Beyg [Khan] b. Kachal Beyg Hajilar 282
Ebrahim Beyg [Khan] Ostajalu 241
Ebrahim Beyg Oqchu-oghlu 141
Ebrahim Beyg Shamakhi 233
Ebrahim Beyg sofrehchi 296
Ebrahim Beyg [Soltan] [Chabuq Tarkhan] Torkman 264
Ebrahim Beyg [Soltan] Ziyad-oghlu Qajar 258
Ebrahim Igirmi-dört Qajar 165
Ebrahim Khalil 301
Ebrahim Khan 217, 231, 269
Ebrahim Khan Dhul-Qadr 152, 208
Ebrahim Khan II 231
Ebrahim Khan Qara-Bayat 251
Ebrahim Khan Torkman 206, 273, 297
Ebrahim Mirza 213, 254
Ebrahim Soltan Chavoshlu Ostajalu 182
Ebrahim Soltan [Khan] Mowsellu 157
Ebrahim Soltan [Khan] Mowsellu Torkman 201
Ebrahim Soltan Ostajalu 300
Ebrahim Soltan Ostajalu b. Shahqoli Yakan 261
Ebrahim Soltan Qorughlu b. Shahqoli Soltan Yakan Ostajalu 271
ejarat 308
Elqas Mirza b. Esmail 151, 285
Elyar Khan Imur 152
Elyas Beyg 281
Elyas Beyg Dhul-Qadr 214
Elyas Beyg Eyghud-oghlu Ostajalu 185
Elyas Beyg Eyghut-oghlu Khonoslu 154
Elyas Beyg Ighud [-oglu] b. Yaqub Aqa 265
Elyas Khalifeh Qaradaghlu 260
Elyas Khan 242
Emada Mohammad 262
Emadiyeh 168
Emamqoli Beyg 140
Emamqoli Beyg b. Badr Khan [Dhul-Qadr] 277
Emamqoli Beyg Ostajalu 220
Emamqoli Beyg [Soltan] [Khan] Qajar 259
Emamqoli Beyg Suklan 48
Emamqoli Beyg yuz-bashi-ye Enanlu Shamlu 266
Emamqoli Khan 145, 224, 231, 283
Emamqoli Khan b. Nur al-Din 231
Emamqoli Khan Qajar 165
Emamqoli Khan Qajar b. Qobad Khan 269
Emamqoli Mirza 193, 229
Emamqoli Soltan Chenagi 208
Emamqoli Soltan Siyah-Mansur 170, 182
Emamqoli Soltan Usallu [Afshar] 189
Emamverdi Beyg 302
emarat-panah 13
Emir Eskandar 253
Emir Gheyb Beyg Ostajalu 202
Emir Gheyb Soltan Ostajalu 166
Emir Hamzeh Khan b. Bayandor Khan Talesh 150
Emir Hosam al-Din 265
Emir Moezz al-Din 199
Emirqoli Garrusi 187
Emir Shah Malek 195
Emir Soltan Hashem 200
Emir Soltan Hoseyn 200
Emir Tajmir Bakhtiyari 159
eqta 13
eqtadar 156
eqta'-ye tamliki 308
Erevan 86, 171, 181
Esfaharan-e Lenjan 52
Esfarain 129, 181
Esfezar 128, 182, 183
Eskandar Ardalan 227
Eskandar Khan Afshar 200
Eskandar Soltan 247
Eskander Khan 224
Esmail 164
Esmail Beyg 279
Esmail Beyg b. Aslan Beyg 195

INDEX 321

Esmail I 9, 143, 154, 165, 177, 191, 267
Esmail Khan 242
Esmail Khan Alplu Afshar 214, 216
Esmail Khan Shams al-Dinlu 279
Esmail Mirza 197, 202
Esmail Mirza b Tahmasp 285
Esmail Mirza b. Tahmasp 151
Esmailqoli Afshar 183
Esmailqoli Khan 246, 259
Esmailqoli Khan Afshar 216
Esmailqoli Khan Shamlu 261
Esmailqoli Soltan [Khan] Alplu Afshar 183
Esmail Soltan 238
Esparlu tribe 271
E'temad al-Dowleh 308
eunuch 17, 44
Evaz Beyg 161, 163, 195, 232
Evaz Beyg Ostajalu 168
Evaz Khan 146
Eyd-gah garden 100
Eyguth Soltan Chavoshlu 208
Eyqut Soltan Chavoshlu Ostajalu 179, 289
Ezzat Ali Khan 239

F

Fahl 168
fahwa 17
Fakhrabad 270
Fakhran 127, 183
falconers 39, 79
falcons 79, 101
far' 309
Farah 128, 183
Farahan 132, 133, 184
Farahani clan 74
Farajallah Khan Abdallu 23
Farajollah Beyg 304
faramin 308
Farhad Aqa 207
Farhad Beyg b. Hosam Soltan Qaramanlu 148, 262
Farhad Beyg Gholam 206
Farhad Khan Qaramanlu 45, 148, 152, 155, 193, 195, 203, 244, 283, 296

Farideyn 184
Faridun Hoseyn Soltan 297
Faridun Khan Cherkes 153
Farrokh Khan 286, 297
Farrokh Khan Pornak 166, 266
Farrokhrow Soltan 165
Farrokh Soltan [Khan] 176
Farrokh Yassar Shirvanshah 284
Farrokhzad Beyg Qaradaghlu 285
Fars 54, 69, 85, 135, 280
Farumad 129, 184
Faryab 160
Farz Ali Khan 172
farzand 309
Fasa 135, 184, 205
Fateheh 33, 48, 120
Fath Ali Beyg 287
Fath Ali Khan 22, 24, 25, 30, 139, 177, 251, 291
Fath Ali Khan Bayat 110
Fath Ali Khan Daghestani 279
Fath Ali Khan Qajar 45, 153
Fath Ali Khan Turkman 110
Fathollah Khan Torkman 242
Fazl Ali Khan Afshar 253
Fazl Ali Sharvan Shaluy 165
Fazl Ali Soltan 253
Fazl Ali Soltan Shamlu 160
Fereydun 132
Fereydun Beyg 162
Firuzkuh 133, 166, 174, 185
foot-kiss 23, 28, 31
Friday prayers 21
Fulad Beyg 231
Fulad khalifeh-ye Rumlu 187, 197
Fulad Khalifeh-ye Shamlu 255, 256
Fulad Khan 161
Fumen 131, 185
Fusanj 128, 130, 185, 186
Fushanj 103, 185

G

Gah 130, 186, 211
Gamron 8, 144, 173
Gamsirat 169
Ganj Ali Khan 221, 229, 253, 273

Ganj Ali Khan Zik 216, 257, 303
Ganjeh 165, 186
garakyaraq 301
Garmerud 119, 125, 184, 186
Garmsir 186
Garmsirat 130, 186
Garmsir-e Qandahar 129
Garrus 133, 187
Gaskar 131, 150, 187
Gavarud 125
Gavehrud 188
Gaverud 189, 272
Geda Ali Beyg 225
Geda Ali Beyg Qajar 181
Geda Ali Beyg Qajar Davatdar 275
Geda Ali Soltan Bayat 237
Gedai Soltan Kulani 292
gel-e sorkh 62
Georgia 136
Georgian 81, 136, 140, 162
Gerai 130
Gereshk 81, 82, 129, 130, 169, 189
Gereyli 130, 189
Gharjestan 130, 160, 190
Ghayath Beyg 290
Ghazi Beyg 220, 284, 301
Ghazi Khan Dhul-Qadr 281
Ghazi Khan Tekkelu 160, 211, 237, 270, 285
ghazis 308
Ghazi Soltan Moqadddam 238
Gheybollah Beyg 253
Gheyb Soltan Ostajalu 227, 235
Ghilzay 7, 83, 130, 255
gholam 25, 30, 139, 149, 153, 158, 162, 176, 177, 179, 188, 195, 231, 233, 265, 275, 286, 287, 290, 309
gholaman-e anbar 19
gholam-zadeh-ye dirin 85
gholamzadeh-ye qadim 203
gholam-zadeh-ye qadimi gholam-e yek-rang-e ma 27
Ghur 128, 190
Ghuri 105, 128, 190
Ghuriyan 103, 130, 190, 229
Gilan 91, 131, 191

Gilan-e biyeh-pas 194
Gilan-e biyeh-pish 192, 229
Gilan-e Lahejan 193
giti-setan 14
Gokcheh Soltan Qajar 285
Goklan 130
Goklen 195
golabtun 308
Golpeygan 133, 210
Gol Tappeh 219
Gonabad 129, 196
Gorgan 150
Gorgin Khan 216, 228, 257
Gorgin Soltan 188, 218
Gori 196
Gorjestan 96
Gowharshad Beygom 19
Green Sea 90
guard-house 44
Gukeh va Kiseh 196
Guri 196
gusht-e par-shaneh 309

H

Habil Khan 139
Habil Khan Siyah-Mansur 182
Hablehrud 174
Hablerud 133, 196
Hachhamr? Khan b. Kalb Ali Khan 291
Hajji Ali Khan 156
Hajji Beyg Donboli 220
Hajji Geda Ali Khan 217
Hajji Kutval Chaghatay 229
Hajjilar 130, 196
Hajji [Manuchehr] Khan 287
Hajji Manuchehr Khan 153
Hajji Mohammad 269
Hajji Mohammad Baqer Beyg 302
Hajji Mohammad Soltan Kutval Chagatay 237, 304
Hajjiqoli Khan 233
Hajji Sharaf al-Din Aqa 204
Hajji Tarkhan 90
hakem-e sarhadd 171
hakim-bashi 53, 307
hakim-bashi-ye asl 307
hakim-bashi-ye haram 308

hakim-bashi-ye kuchek 308
hakim-e haram 54
Halow Khan b. Soltan Ali Beyg Ardalan 228
Haltiyan 269
Hamadan 40, 133, 196
Hamdan Beyg 224
hameh-saleh 13, 38, 39, 40, 43, 308
Ham Mardan island 210
ham-qalam 308
Hamzeh Beyg 171, 288
Hamzeh Beyg Dhul-Qadr 169, 256, 303
Hamzeh [Beyg] khalifeh-ye Talesh 150
Hamzeh Beyg Ostajalu 247
Hamzeh Soltan Khames Ali Dhul-Qadr 281
Hamzeh Soltan Tekkelu 288
haqq al-qarar 25
haqq al-say 68, 69, 73, 309
Haqqverdi Soltan 155, 212
Haramilu 125, 126, 209
harem 17, 20, 33, 43, 54, 74
Harirud 196
Harsin 133, 199
Harunabad 235
Hasanabad 134, 140, 199, 228
Hasan Abdallu 120, 199
Hasan Ali b. Budaq Khan Cheghani 198
Hasan Ali Beyg 163
Hasan Ali Khan 139, 279, 287
Hasan Ali Khan b. Mohammad Momen Khan 228
Hasan Ali Khan Chapni 166
Hasan Ali Soltan 218
Hasan Beyg 279
Hasan Beyg [Afshar?] 289
Hasan Beyg Dhul-Qadr 238
Hasan Beyg [Khan] b. Abdol-Latif Afshar 224
Hasan Beyg Laleh 301
Hasan Khan 191, 239
Hasan Khan Abdallu Shamlu 203
Hasan Khan Chavoshlu Ostajalu 216
Hasan Mirza b. Abbas 198
Hasanqoli Soltan Shamlu 103

Hasan Soltan b. Shahverdi Khalifeh 249
Hasan Soltan Feyj-oghlu Ostajalu 179
Hasan Soltan Ordaklu Torkman 258
Hasan Soltan Qaracheh-oghlu 175
Hasan Soltan Shamlu 274
Hasan Soltan Tavakkoli 209
Hashtajoft 133
Hashtrud-e TabTab 116, 125, 199, 249
Hatem Beyg Nasiri 9
Hatem Soltan 305
havā'i 80, 308
Hayat Soltan Sadozay 137
Hazarehs 99
Hazarjarib 152, 166
HazarJarib 133, 199
Hendamin 235
Herat 10, 46, 96, 99, 102, 104, 108, 124, 128, 129, 137, 200
Heratrud 128, 204
Heybat Aqa Dhul-Qadr 208
Heydar 89, 238
Heydar Beyg Hajilar 138
Heydar Beyg [Soltan] Chabuq Tarkhan Torkman 148
Heydar Beyg [Soltan Tarkhan] Torkman 273
Heydar Khan 246
Heydarqoli Khan 203, 242
Heydarqoli Soltan Afshar 179, 289
Heydarqoli Soltan Ostajalu 252
Heydar Soltan 250, 303
Heydar Soltan Beygdeli 272
Heydar Soltan [Chabuq Tarkhan] Torkman 264
Heydar Soltan Quyleh Hesarlu Rumlu b. Bayazid Soltan 296
Heydar Soltan Quylu [or Qavi] Hesarlu 296
Heydar Soltan Sheybani 103
Heydar Soltan Tarkhan 210
high steward 24, 35, 36, 37, 38, 53, 66, 75
Hillah 132, 204
Hisn Kaifa 132

Homayun 46, 96, 97, 98, 99, 100, 102, 162, 255, 314
Hormuz 205
horses 40, 70, 80, 97, 98, 100, 101, 103
Hosam Beyg b. Dhul-Feqar Khan 263
Hosam Soltan 263
Hoseyn Ali Khan b. Mohammad Momen Khan 228
Hoseyn Ali Khan Cheghani 198
Hoseyn Ali Khan Zanganeh 225
Hoseyn Ali Soltan 218
Hoseyn Beyg 146, 277
Hoseyn Beyg Afshar 269
Hoseyn Beyg Fath-oghlu 179, 293
Hoseyn Beyg [Khan] Shamlu 264
Hoseyn Beyg Laleh 154, 284
Hoseyn Beyg Laleh Shamlu 200
Hoseyn Beyg Ostajalu 258
Hoseyn Beyg qurchi-ye shamsi 294
Hoseyn Beyg Shamlu 138
Hoseyn Beyg [Soltan] b. Sevenduk Afshar 268
Hoseyn Jan Beyg 252
Hoseyn Khan 242, 279
Hoseyn Khan Abdallu Shamlu 203
Hoseyn Khan Beyg 287
Hoseyn Khan b. Mansur Beyg Solvizi 236
Hoseyn Khan b. Zaman Beyg Mazandarani 153
Hoseyn Khan Chavoshlu Ostajalu 198
Hoseyn Khan Firuz-jang 305
Hoseyn Khan Gilani 223
Hoseyn Khan Mosaheb Qajar 266, 283
Hoseyn Khan Seystani 217
Hoseyn Khan Shamlu 223
Hoseyn Khan Shamlu b. Abdi Beyg 201
Hoseyn Khan Soltan 266
Hoseyn Khan Soltan Dehdehlu[y] Torkman, 245
Hoseyn Khan Soltan Rumlu 171
Hoseyn Khan Soltan Shamlu Khanuslu 220

Hoseyn Khan Ziyad-oghlu Qajar 152, 259, 283
Hoseyn Kiya Cholavi 174, 185, 274
Hoseynqoli Beyg Shamlu 268
Hoseynqoli Fath-oghlu Ostajalu 266
Hoseynqoli Khan 155, 178, 184, 272
Hoseynqoli Khan Areshlu Afshar 198
Hoseynqoli Khan b. Aqa Khan 238
Hoseynqoli Khan Shamlu 289
Hoseyn Soltan Afshar 183, 211, 299
Hoseyn Soltan Shamlu 103
Hoveyzeh 135, 143
Hud 83, 130

I

Ich 135, 205
Ichi 205
Ig 205
Ighud Beyg Chavoshlu 214
Ighud [Ighuth] Beyg Chavoshlu Ostajalu 181
Ighuth Beyg Chavoshlu Ostajalu 218, 251
Ij 205
ilkhichiyan 308
ilkhiyan 308
Imani Beyg 181
Iraq 69
Iron Gate 17
Isa Khalifeh 289
Isa Khan 28, 159
Isa Khan b. Dhul-Feqar Khan 291
Isa [Khan] Gorji 280
Isa Khan Soltan Buzchelu 141, 142, 170, 236
Isfahan 54, 76, 132, 205
ishik aghasi-bashi 22, 34, 40, 307
ishik aghasi-bashi-ye divan 32
ishik aghasi-bashi-ye haram 43, 307
ishik aghasis 308
Ishkerduqa 207

J

Jabali 83
jabbehdar-bashi 308
Jabrgeh Soltan 250
Jafar Khan 277
Jafarqoli Aqa Khvajeh 39
Jafarqoli Beyg [Khan] 153
Jafar Qoli Khan Ostajalu 203
Jafar Soltan 98
Jafar Soltan Ereshlu Afshar 277
Jahan 207
Jahan-Arghiyan 129, 207
Jahangir Khan 159
Jahangir Soltan 219
Jahrom 232
Jalal al-Din Masudi Bidgoli 213
Jalalis 293
Jalayer 130
Jam 103, 129, 208
Jamal al-Din Mohammad 301
Jameselu [Chameshlu] Dhul-Qadr 281
Jamjama 170
Jamshid Beyg 175, 262
Jamshid Beyg Amireh 150
Jamshidi 106, 212
Jamshidis 128
Jamshid Khan 174, 265, 275
Jamshid Khan b. Soltan Mahmud 195
Jamshid Soltan Donboli 239
Jamshid Soltan Gorji 139
Jani Khan 203, 253
Jani Khan Shamlu 216
jannat-makan 17
Japalaq 133
Jaramilu 125, 126, 209
Jasb 264
Jastan 132, 209
Javabrud 134
Javanshir 127, 209
Javazer 132, 209, 300
jazayer 31
Jazireh 132, 134, 209
Jekur [or Chegur or] Chakergeh Soltan Shamlu 268
jelowdar-bashi 290
Jewish 50

Jeyjan 210
Jonabad 196
Jonahabad 196
Joneyd 89
Jorbadeqan 154, 210
Jorjan 130, 150, 151, 210
Jorpardeqan 133, 210
Jowhar Aqa 162
Jowhar Soltan 205
Juheh Soltan Tekkelu 211
Jukheh Soltan Tekkelu 205

K

Kabir va Tassuj 167
Kabud-Jameh 131, 210
Kachal Afshar 289
Kachal Beyg 214
Kachal Beyg Dhul-Qadr 281
Kaferi 83
Kah 130, 183, 186, 211
Kakhetia 259
Kalani 126, 303
kalantar 9, 25, 39, 43, 62, 83, 102, 167, 247
Kalb Ali Beyg 148, 153, 249
Kalb Ali Beyg b. Mehr Ali Khan 291
Kalb Ali Beyg [Khan] 231
Kalb Ali Beyg Qajar 212, 247
Kalb Ali Khan 165, 169, 195, 257, 283, 291
Kalb Ali Khan Afshar 172, 183, 223
Kalb Ali Khan Ardalan 228
Kalb Ali Khan Qajar 93
Kalb 'Ali Khan Ziyad-oghlu 259
Kalb Ali Soltan [Khan] Afshar 252
Kalb Reza Soltan Zonuzi 304
Kalehgir 125, 126, 211
Kalhor 133, 211, 247
Kamal al-Din Shahqoli Beyg 97
Kamallu 120
Kamara 133
Kamareh 48
Kangarlu 126, 212, 248
Kankarkonan 148, 212
Karbal 135, 212
Karbar 212

karbas 307
Karend 212
Kargiya Hadi Kiya 141
Karjasi [Garjasi] B 257
Kar Kiya Khan Ahmad Khan 193
Karkiya Mirza Ali 192
Kar Kiya Mirza Ali 229
Karkiya Sayyed Ali Kiya b. Soltan Ahmad 193
Karkiya Soltan Ahmad b. Soltan Hasan 193
Karkiya Soltan Hasan 192
Karkiya Soltan Hasan b. Soltan Ahmad 193
Karokh 106, 128, 212
Karrus 187
Karshu 103, 212
Kartli 81, 173, 196, 295
Kashan 133, 213
Kazerun 27, 135, 214, 216, 275
Kazicman 260
Kelidar 214
Keliddar 129
Kelideh 214
Kepek Soltan Afshar 214
Kerman 35, 131, 214
Kermanshahan 134, 179, 217
keshikchi-bashi 176
keshik-nevis 77
keyfiyat-e daftari 307
Key Khosrow Beyg 228
Key Khosrow b. Malek Bahman 233
Key Khosrow Khan Cherkes 172
Keyvan Beyg 231
Keyvan Soltan 187
Khabushan 129, 218
Khadem Beyg Talesh Khalifeh 157
khak-e konh 308
Khalaf Beyg Talesh 151
khalifeh al-kholafa 8, 11, 12, 24, 47, 48, 49, 53, 118
Khalifeh Ansar Qaradajlu 286
Khalifeh Soltan Shamlu 201
Khalifeh-ye Ansar 260
Khalil Beyg Mansur-Siyah 274, 291
Khalil Beyg Siyah-Mansur 292
Khalil Khan Afshar 171, 224

Khalil Khan Bakhtiyari 159, 221
Khalil Khan Dhul-Qadr 282
Khalil Khan Shah Mansur 270
Khalilollah b. Sheikh Mohammad Ranashi 178
Khalilollah b. Sheikhshah 284
Khalil Soltan b. Shahverdi Soltan Ziyad-oghlu Qajar 152
Khalil Soltan Dhul-Qadr Suseh-oghlu 272
Khalil Soltan Qaramanlu 141
Khalil Soltan Seylpur 304
Khalil Soltan Siyah-Mansur 294
Khalkhal 125, 148, 149, 188, 219, 292, 295
Khames Beyg 261
Khan Afghan 178
Khan Ahmad Karkiya 229
Khan Ahmad Khan 193, 195
Khan Ahmad Khan b. Halow Khan Ardalan 228
Khan Ahmad Khan b. Soltan Hasan 194
Khan Ahmad Khan II Ardalan 228
Khandanqoli Khan Afshar 183
Khandanqoli Soltan 181
khaneh-ye gav 19
Khan Emir b. Ghazi Beyg Kord 270
Khan Mohammad Khan 173
Khan Mohammad Khan Ostajalu 215
Khan Mohammad Ostajalu b. Mirza Beyg 180
khan-zadeh-ye qadimi 93
khara 308
Kharput 132
Kharzavil 219, 295
khasseh 309
Khaveh 134, 219
Khodaverdi Khan 254
Kholafa Beyg 157
Khorasan 69, 96, 128
Khorkhoreh 134, 219
Khorramabad 134, 169
Khosh-khabar Khan Shamlu 229
Khoshkhabar Khan Shamlu b. Aghazivar Khan 186, 191
Khosrow Bayat 301

Khosrow Beyg Chaharyar 195
Khosrow Beyg Chaharyari 265
Khosrow Beyg [Soltan] 239
Khosrow Khan 37, 84, 287
Khosrow Khan Ardalan 228
Khosrow Khan Cherkes 153
Khosrow Mirza 216, 228, 257
Khosrow Soltan Afshar 278, 290
Khosrow Soltan Armani Jadid al-Eslam 209
Khosrow Soltan Jadid al-Eslam 292
Khoy 9, 89, 124, 125, 219
Khurkhureh 219
Khushab 220
Khushat 220
Khuzestan 143
Khvaf 100, 103, 128, 220
Khvajeh Abdol-Reza 231
Khvajeh Atiq 9
Khvajeh Mohammad Shafi 194, 195, 245
Khvajeh Mohammad Sharif Tehrani 206
Khvajeh Qasem Ali 155
Khvajeh Shehaba-ye Kermani 301
Khvansar 133, 159, 221
Khvar 134, 197
Kich-Makran 277
Kij-Makran 221
Kirkuk 132, 222
Kiya Jalal al-Din Mohammad 178
Kiyar 133
Kiya Rostam 265
Kiya Soltan Ahmad 229
Kohdom 223
Kojur 131, 222
Kolbar 131, 222
Kolhar 179, 180, 293
Konstandil Mirza 259
Kord Beyg Charqlu? Ostajali 167
Kostandil Mirza 173
K.ra-chupi 131
K.ri 130
Kuchek Jahangir 235
Kuchesfahan 131, 222
Kuhdom 131, 183, 223
Kuhgiluyeh 84, 85, 134, 135, 143, 144, 159, 223

Kuhtom 223
Kukeh Ta Khan 230
Kunstandil Mirza b. Alexander Khan 286
Kurd Beyg Ostajalu 149
Kurdestan 118, 124, 131, 134, 179, 225, 226, 230, 293
Kurluk 89, 125, 126, 228
Kur Sayyedi Soltan 147
Kushi 83
Kushk 128, 130, 228
Kushk-e Nakhud 228
Kusuyeh 130, 191, 229
kutval 159, 175, 299

L

lachak 309
Lachin Aqa 265
Lachin Aqa-ye Gholam Yusef Aqa 195
Lachin Beyg 224
Lachin Soltan 294
Lachin Soltan Kord Mahmudi 239
Lahejan 79, 131, 229
Lahijan 125
Lajaan 125, 229
Lajan 118, 125, 229
Lajin Beyg 239
Lak 117
Lak of Salmas 125
Lak tribe 270
laleh 96, 151, 160, 165, 169, 192, 193, 197, 198, 201, 202, 208, 229, 234, 240, 241, 244, 249, 254, 256, 257, 258, 268, 277, 282, 285, 286, 287, 303
Laleh Beyg Shamlu 160
laleh-ye gholaman 19
langari plates 101
Langarkonan 115
Lanjan 184
Lankar-konan 125
Lar 8, 135, 230
Larijan 131, 233
lashkar-nevis 9, 66, 69, 307
lashkar-nevisan 307
Layejan 230
Lenkoran 230

Leshteh-nesha 131, 233
librarian 103
Lor-e Bozorg 159
Lor-e Feyli 234
Lor-e Kuchek 234
Lorestan 131, 134, 146, 234
Lori 127, 236
Lotf Ali Beyk 156
Lotf Ali Khan 85, 225
Lotf Ali Khan Daghestani 233, 283
Lotf Ali Soltan 187, 264
Luarsab Khan 296
Lurestan 134
Luri 93, 236
Luri-Pambak 236

M

ma'afi 13, 309
madakhel 308
Madhar 237
Madmudqoli Khan 217
Maghazberd 126, 237
Mahallat 133
Mahdiqoli Khan Chavoslu Ostajalu 148, 155
Mahdiqoli Khan Shamlu 235
Mahmudabad 127, 160, 270
Mahmud Aqa 53
Mahmud Beyg 36
Mahmud Beyg Afshar 273
Mahmud Beyg Rumlu 220
Mahmud Beyg [Soltan] Afshar 215
Mahmud Beyg Tupchi 190
Mahmud Khan 7, 256
Mahmud Khan Afshar 224
Mahmud Khan Sufi-oghlu Ostajalu 297
Mahmud Soltan Sufi-oghlu 251
Mahvelat 103, 129, 237
majles-nevis 8, 9, 10, 11, 22, 23, 41, 42, 43, 62, 66, 108, 111, 113, 114
majles-nevis-e mahfal-e behesht-a'in 41, 309
Majnun Soltan Shamlu 181
Maku 126, 237

Malek Ashraf b. Taj al-Dowleh 222
Malek Aziz 251
Malek Aziz b. Kayumarth 268
Malek Bahman b. Malek Bisetun 268
Malek Bahman b. Malek Kayumarth b. Kaus 142
Malek Bahman Larijani 233
Malek Bahram Ordubadi 9
Malek Beyg Khoyi 220
Malek Bisetun b. Jahangir 268
Malek Dinar 221
Malek Ekhtiyar al-Din 168
malek-e reqab 15, 309
Malek Hamzeh Khan b. Malek Jalal al-Din 277
Malek Jahangir 251
Malek Jahangir b. Aziz 268
Malek Jahangir b. Kaus 268
Malek Jahangir b. Malek Kaus 222
Malek Jahangir b. Malek Soltan Mohammad 222
Malek Jalal al-Din b. Malek Mahmud 277
Malek Kaus b. Malek Ashraf 222
Malek Kaus b. Malek Jahangir -Malek Bahman 268
Malek Kayumarth b. Bahman 268
Malek Kayumarth b. Jahangir 268
Malek Kayumarth b. Malek Kaus 222
Malek Mahmud 277
Malek Mahmud Kayani Seystani 277
Malek Mirza 222
Malek Rostam 235
Malek Shams al-Din 168
Malek Shams al-Din b. Malek Dinar 222
Malek Soltan Hoseyn 251
Malek Soltan Mahmud 276
Malek Soltan Mohammad b. Jahangir 222
Mamun Beyg b. Begeh Beyg 227
manasher 309
Mandali 134, 211, 237
Maneh 129, 238
Maneh va Samalqan 238

Manjavan [?] 238
Manjil 238
Mankara 235
Mansur Beyg 160, 175
Mansur Beyg Afshar 281
Mansur Khan 145, 257
Mansur Khan Dhul-Feqar Khan 290
Mansur Khan Dhul-Qadr 289
Mansur Khan Gereyli 189
Mansur Khan Shahseven 242
Mansur Khan Shahseven Moghani 156
Mantasha Khan Ostajalu 175
Mantasha Khan [Sheikhlar] Ostajalu 297
Mantasha Soltan Ostajalu 261
Manuchehr Beyg 274, 275
Manuchehr Beyg Gholam 33
Manuchehr b. Grigori 140
Manuchehr Khan 111, 146, 177, 188, 236, 242
Manuchehr Khan b. Qarchaqay Khan 242
Manuchehr Soltan 294
Maqsud Mirza 103
Maqsud Soltan Donboli 165, 260
Maqsud Soltan Kangarlu 212
Maqsud Soltan Kangarlu Ostajalu 248
Maragheh 114, 125, 238
Marand 125, 239
mara sang ruye yakh kardehi 90
Mardin 132
Margavar 252
Marjumak Soltan b. Amir Khan 157
Maruchaq 128, 239
Masal Beyg 183
Mashhad 10, 18, 24, 99, 100, 103, 128, 129, 239
Mashhad-e Sar 131, 242
Mashhad-e Tus 239
Mashkan-e Mashhad 98
Masum Beyg 245
Masum Beyg Safavi 213
mavajeb 13, 309
Mazandaran 18, 35, 38, 41, 58, 90, 131, 242
Mazinan 245

Mehdi Khan Arab 181
Mehdi Khan Soltan Arab 239
Mehdi Khan Soltan Sadlu 142
Mehdiqoli 269
Mehdiqoli Beyg [Khan] Sadi Tekkelu 282
Mehdiqoli Khan 229
Mehdiqoli Khan Shamlu 169, 193, 266, 290
Mehdiqoli Soltan 181
Mehdiqoli Soltan b. Baqer Soltan 158
Mehdiqoli Soltan Sheikh Dhul-Qadr 282
Mehdiqoli Soltan Siyah-Mansur 170
Mehdqoli Soltan b. Chuli Beyg Afshar 289
mehmani 307
Mehrab Beyg [Khan] 153
Mehrab Khan 158, 162, 257
Mehrab Khan Qajar 221, 241, 246
Mehrab Mirza 285
Mehrab Soltan 211
Mehrab Soltan [Khan] 169, 255
Mehrab Soltan [Khan] Qajar 294
Mehr Ali Beyg 218
Mehr Ali Khan 287, 291
Mehr Ali Khan b. Kalb Ali Khan 291
mehtar-e rekabkhaneh 290
Melkish Soltan 139, 157
meqna'eh 308
Merv 128, 130, 245
Merv-e kuchek 239
Merv-e Shahejan 245
Meshkhia 140
Meshkin 116, 125, 211, 247
metqali 308
Meymaneh 160
Mezdaj 133
Mikhri [Mehdi?] Khan 156
mines 69
Mini Qeshlaq 90
mint master 50
Mir Abbas 234
Mir Abdol-Karim b. Mir Abdollah Khan 244
Mir Abdollah Khan 244

INDEX

Mir Abol-Qasem 244
Mirak Beyg Nasiri 9
mir akhur-bashi-ye sahr 308
Mir Ali Khan 244
Mir b. Hoseyn Khan Firuzjang 296
Mir Fattah Beyg Esfahani 34
Mir Fazollah Shahrestani 207
Mir Fazollah Shahrestani Esfahani 206
Mir Harun 199
Mir Heydar Soltan Jamshidi 212
Mir Hoseyn Khan Mazandarani 206
Mir Hoseyn Soltan Tobadkani 271, 305
Mir Jahangir b. Shah Rostam 235
Mir Jamal Soltan 161
Mir Mehr Ali 233
Mir Mohammad Ahmad 283
Mir Mohammad Soltan Ghuri 190
Mir Morad 244
Mir Morad Khan 244
Mir Morad Kolbari 222
Mir Qubad Ostajalu 230
Mir Rashid al-Din b. Mir Abdol-Vahhab 290
Mir Sayyed Ali Razavi Qomi 261
Mir Sayyed Mohammad Soltan 269
Mir Sayyed Sharif 244
Mir Shah Mir 174
Mir Shah Taher Torshizi 207
Mir Shams 207
Mir Ughur b. Shah Rostam 235
Mir Weys 83, 255
Mirza Abdol-Baqi 261
Mirza Abdol-Hoseyn Nasiri 10
Mirza Abdol-Karim 23
Mirza Abdollah Esfahani 194
Mirza Abdollah Jaberi Ansari 301
Mirza Abdol-Qasem 163, 233
Mirza Abdol-Rahim 233
Mirzā Abu'l-Hasan 56
Mirza Abul-Qasem Torshizi 245
Mirza Abu Taleb Nasiri 10
Mirza Ahmad 41, 153, 251
Mirza Ala al-Molk 231
Mirza Ali Beyg 289
Mirza Ali Soltan Qajar 152
Mirza Asadollah 207
Mirza Beyg 164
Mirza Emad 262
Mirza Enayatollah Esfahani 301
Mirza Esfandiyar Beyg 291
Mirza Esma'il 54
Mirza Hadi b. Mirza Moin 283
Mirza Hasan Ali Esfahani 301
Mirza Hashem 194, 245
Mirza Hatem Beyg 216
Mirza Hedayat Jaberi 287
Mirza Homayun 162
Mirza Hoseyn 264
Mirza Isa Khan 207
Mirza Jafar 207, 302
Mirza Jafar Qazvini 194
Mirza Jalala 54
Mirza Kafi 9
Mirza Kamran 195, 223
Mirza Khalilollah 302
Mirza Khan 244
Mirza Mehdi b. Mirza Ahmad 41
Mirza Mina 103
Mirza Mo'ezz al-Din 54
Mirza Mohammad 207, 262
Mirza Mohammad Abhari 262
Mirza Mohammad Baqer 53
Mirza Mohammad Hoseyn 23, 56, 195, 283
Mirza Mohammad Kafi Nasiri 48
Mirza Mohammad Karim b. Adam Soltan 195
Mirza Mohammad Momen Soltan 269
Mirza Mohammad Rahim 9, 24, 56
Mirza Mohammad Shafi 302
Mirza Mohammad Soltan Bayat 182
Mirza Mohammad Soltan Qara-Bayat Chaghatay 251
Mirza Mohammad Taher 22
Mirza Mohammad Talesh 301
Mirza [Mohammad] Taqi 245
Mirza Mohammad Taqi 54
Mirza Mohammad Taqi Shirazi 8
Mirza Moin 283, 302
Mirza Momen Hoseyni 24
Mirza Musa 262
Mirza Naqi Nasiri 9, 11
Mirza Nurallah 232
Mirza Qasem 245
Mirza Qoli Soltan Siyah-Mansur 189
Mirza Rabi' 57
Mirza Razi al-Din Mohammad 207
Mirza Razi Savaji 207
Mirza Sadeq 41, 245
Mirza Sadeq Kermani 188
Mirza Sadr al-Din Mohammad Jaberi 195
Mirza Saleh b. Eskander Beyg Monshi 194
Mirza Shafi b. Mir Hashem 302
Mirza Shah Taher 302
Mirza Sharif b. Mirza Jalala 54
Mirza Taqi 194, 195
Mirza Taqi Dowlatabadi 194, 207
Mirza Taqi Dowlatabadi Esfahani 229
Mirza Taqi Esfahani 194
Mirzay Alameyn 244, 262
Mirza-ye Alamiyan 194, 195, 245
Mirza Zeyn al-Abedin Nasiri 10
moayyer al-mamalek 50, 52
mo'ayyeran 307
Mobarakabad 131, 247
Mobarez al-Din Abdi Beyg 138
Moghan 147, 247
Moghanat 115, 125, 247
mohafez 177
Mohammad Ali 262
Mohammad Ali Beyg 162, 283
Mohammad Ali Beyg Garagyaraq Esfahani 207
Mohammad Ali Jaberi Ansari 283
Mohammad Ali Khalifeh 268
Mohammad Ali Khan 24, 156, 162, 173, 203, 225, 253, 257
Mohammad Ali Khan Afshar b. Qasem Khan 184
Mohammad Ali Khan b. Yusof Khan 159
Mohammad Ali Khan Mokri 23
Mohammad Ali Soltan 108, 189
Mohammad Amin Khan 299

Mohammad Amin Khan Nasiri 48
Mohammad Amin Shurehbiz Khorasani 301
Mohammad Baqer Beyg 85, 283
Mohammad Beyg 70, 138, 253
Mohammad Beyg b. Mir Jafar Savaji 206
Mohammad Beyg [Khan] Beygdelu Shamlu 156
Mohammad Beyg [Khan] Sharaf al-Dinoghlu Tekkelu 261
Mohammad Beyg Mowsilu Tarkhan 273
Mohammad Beyg Rumlu 166
Mohammad Beyg Saruqchi 206
Mohammad Beyg Sofrechi Ostajalu 154
Mohammad Beyg Talesh 150
Mohammad Beyram Khan Bahador 99
Mohammad Ebrahim Khan 161
Mohammad Ebrahim Nasiri 10
Mohammad Hoseyn Beyg 147, 302
Mohammad Hoseyn Khan 159
Mohammad Hoseyn Soltan 176
Mohammad Hoseyn Soltan Dhul-Qadr 147
Mohammadi Beyg b. Hasan Soltan 224
Mohammad[i] Beyg [Khan] b. Siyavosh Beyg 287
Mohammadi Beyk b. Ala al-Molk 231
Mohammadi Khan 223
Mohammadi Khan b. Amir Khan Mowselu 197
Mohammadi Khan Gowhari 223
Mohammadi Khan Tokhmaq Ostajalu 155, 171
Mohammadi Lori 235
Mohammad Jan Beyg Dhul-Qadr 277
Mohammad Khalifeh Dhul-Qadr 152
Mohammad Khan 153, 158, 173
Mohammad Khan Abdali 204
Mohammad Khan Ardalan 228

Mohammad Khan Asayesh-oghli 152
Mohammad Khan b. Aslan Khan 242
Mohammad Khan Beyg 280
Mohammad Khan Beyg Dhul-Qadr 282
Mohammad Khan Chavoshlu Ostajalu b. Eyguth Soltan 269
Mohammad Khan Chavoslu 208
Mohammad Khan Dhul-Qadr 205
Mohammad Khan Dhul-Qadr[-oghlu] 151
Mohammad Khan Ghekani 269
Mohammad Khan Gorji 228
Mohammad Khani plates 101
Mohammad Khan Khalifeh Hajjilar Dhul-Qadr 286
Mohammad Khan Mowsellu Torkman 277
Mohammad Khan Qazaqlar 236
Mohammad Khan Sharaf al-Din-oghlu 46, 96
Mohammad Khan Sharaf al-Dinoghlu Tekkelu 206
Mohammad Khan Soltan 141
Mohammad Khan Tekkelu 154
Mohammad Khan Torkman 174, 200, 304
Mohammad Khan Uzbek 176
Mohammad Khan Ziyadoghlu Qajar 259
Mohammad Mirza 103, 193
Mohammad Mirza b. Bahram Beyg Qaramanlu 262
Mohammad Momen Beyg 144, 163, 207, 232, 281
Mohammad Momen Beyg Jahromi 163, 232
Mohammad Momen Khan 223
Mohammad Momen Khan Beygdeli Shamlu 22, 32
Mohammad Qasem Khan Afshar 113
Mohammad Qasem Soltan Nasiri 47
Mohammadqoli 188
Mohammadqoli Beyg 231

Mohammadqoli Beyg b. Mohammad Momen Khan 203
Mohammadqoli [Beyg] Khan Chaghatay 172
Mohammadqoli Khan 172, 184, 216
Mohammadqoli Khan Beygdeli Shamlu 23, 27
Mohammadqoli Khan b. Laleh Beyg 172
Mohammadqoli Khan b. Siyavosh Khan 153
Mohammadqoli Khan Pornak b. Mortezaqoli 175
Mohammadqoli Khan Ziyadoghlu 259
Mohammadqoli Khan Ziyadoghlu b. Mohammad Khan 259
Mohammadqoli Mirza 217
Mohammad Rabi Nasiri 10
Mohammad Rahim Khan 204, 299
Mohammad Reza Khan 248
Mohammad Reza Khan Abdallu 24, 27
Mohammad Reza Khan b. Aslan Khan 291
Mohammad Reza Nasiri 10
Mohammad Reza Soltan 160
Mohammad Said Qomi 213
Mohammad Saleh Beyg 245
Mohammad Sharaf al-Dinoghlu Tekkelu 202
Mohammad Sharif Beyg Chavoshlu Ostajalu 262
Mohammad Sharif Tehrani 301
Mohammad Soltan 164, 182, 213, 269, 289
Mohammad Soltan Alayinoghli 197
Mohammad Soltan Bayat 269
Mohammad Soltan b. Baba Elyas Bayat 182
Mohammad Soltan Chagani 182
Mohammad Soltan Chaghatay 290
Mohammad Soltan Chekani 303
Mohammad Soltan Dhul-Qadr 152, 175

Mohammad Soltan Dhul-Qadr-oghlu 295
Mohammad Soltan Esparlu 271
Mohammad Soltan Jagirlu 280
Mohammad Soltan [Khan] Tekkelu Sharaf al-Dinoghlu 158
Mohammad Soltan [Khan] Torkman 213
Mohammad Soltan Orumlu 273, 297
Mohammad Soltan Rumlu 289
Mohammad Soltan Shams al-Dinlu 296
Mohammad Soltan Tekkelu 261
Mohammad Taleb Khan 156
Mohammad Taqi Nasiri 10
Mohammad Tarka 235
Mohammad Yar Khan Imur 152
Mohammad Zahed Soltan 163
Mohammad Zaman Beyg 8, 213, 301
Mohammad Zaman Khan 156, 184, 217
Mohammad Zaman Khan Beygdeli Shamlu 84
Mohammad Zaman Khan Shamlu 203
Mohammad Zaman Soltan 190
Mohammad Zaman Soltan Shamlu 169
Mohanna Khan Arab Khazai 304
moharrer-e sarkar-e tofangchiyan 10
Mohebb Ali Soltan b. Bektash Khan 250
mohrdar 149, 216
mohr-e athar-e ashraf 308
mohr-e mehr-e athar 309
mohtarafeh-ye asnaf 308
Mokri 120, 125, 238, 247
Mokri or MakriQoli Khan 287
monajjem-bashi 55, 309
monshi al-mamalek 9, 10, 42, 48, 61, 62, 63, 64, 66, 73, 74
Montasha Soltan Ostajalu 154
Moqaddam 114, 125, 247
moqarrari 308
Morad Aqa 290
Morad Beyg Afshar 182

Morad Beyg Keroghlu 212
Morad Beyg [Khan] 195
Morad Khan Beyg b. Mehdi Khan Soltan Arab 181
Morad Khan Chapni 234
Morad Khan Kangarlu 248
Morad Khan Soltan Beybordlu 147
Morad Mirza 103
Morad Soltan 214
Morad Soltan Dhul-Qadr 281
Morad Soltan Timurlu 183
moraqqaban 309
Morghab 160
Morshedqoli Beyg 138
Morshedqoli Khan 206
Morshedqoli Khan Chavoshlu Ostajalu 241
Morshedqoli Khan Ostajalu 45
Morshedqoli Khān Ostājalu 20, 45
Morshedqoli Khan Yakan Ostajalu 220
Morshedqoli Khan Yakan Ostajalu b. Shahqoli 237, 304
Morshedqoli Soltan 182, 184
Morshedqoli Soltan Chavoshlu b. Yakkan Shahqoli 297
Morshedqoli Soltan Ostajalu b. Shahqoli Yakan 277
Morshedqoli Soltan Quchilu 295
Morshedqoli Soltan Shamlu 213, 264
Morsheqoli Soltan Jalayer 254
Morteza Pasha 172
Mortezaqoli Beyg 162, 218
Mortezaqoli Khan 162, 172, 198, 212, 248, 283
Mortezaqoli Khan Bijerlu 26, 216
Mortezaqoli Khan b. Mehrab Khan Qajar 246
Mortezaqoli Khan Gaskari b. Amireh Siyavosh 188
Mortezaqoli Khan Pornak Torkman 142, 152, 166, 168, 200
Mortezaqoli Khan Qajar 156, 242
Mortezaqoli Khan Sadlu 275
Mortezaqoli Khan Torkman 210
Mortezaqoli Khan Ziyadoghli 259

Mortezaqoli Soltan b. Mehrab Khan 262
Mortezaqoli Soltan [Khan] Pornak Torkman 241
mosaheb 30, 93, 213
Moshasha dynasty 142
moshref 308
moshrefan-e shotor-khan va havich-khaneh va sharbat-khaneh 80
moshref-e establ 79
moshref-e khazaneh-ye amereh 78
moshref-e qeychachi-khaneh 79
moshref-e qur-khaneh 80
moshref-e qush-khaneh 79
moshref-e zarrab-khaneh 80
Mosib Khan 148
Mosib Khan Sharaf al-Din-oghlu 266
Mosib Khan Sharaf al-Din-oghlu Tekkelu b. Mohammad Sharaf al-Dinoghlu 266
Mosib Khan Tekkelu 266
Mosib Soltan Ostajalu 240
Mostadam Soltan Hajjilar Ostajalu 210
Mostafa Beyg 139
Mostafa Beyg Kangarlu [Ostajalu] 298
Mostafa Beyg [Khan] 236
Mostafa Beyg Mahmudi [Kurdi] 237
Mostafa Beyg [Tekkelu?] 285
Mostafa Pasha 179, 293
Mostafaqoli Khan Beygdeli 121
Mostafaqoli Khan Qajar 275
Mostafa Soltan Chavoshlu 182
Mostafa Soltan Jastani 209
Mostafa Soltan Kangarlu 294
Mostafa Soltan Ostajalu 220
Mostafa Soltan Qajar 195
Mostafa Soltan Sadlu 142
Mostafa Soltan Shamlu 185, 273
Mostafa Soltan Varsaq 181
mostahfez 159
Mostang 130
mostowfi al-mamalek 23, 24, 26, 42, 56, 307
mostowfis 25, 39, 43, 56, 63, 66, 67, 78, 307

mostowfi-ye baqaya 72
mostowfi-ye khasseh 57, 307
mostowfi-ye mowqufat-e mamalek 77
Mosul 132, 248
motamed al-khavass 20
motasaddi 206, 269, 298
motavalli 13, 14, 27, 148, 158, 241, 248, 287, 308
Mowdudqoli Soltan Chaghatay 272
Mowjudqoli Khan 272
Mowla Sajjad b. Sayyed Badran 145
Mowredestan (?) 210
Mozaffar Hoseyn [Khan] 272
Mozaffar Hoseyn Mirza 256
Mozaffar Hoseyn Mirza b. Bahram Mirza 257
Mozaffar Soltan 175, 194, 265
Mozaffar Soltan Asayesh-oghlu Ostajalu 191, 229
mules 40
Musa Beyg 156
Musa Beyg [Soltan] Mowsellu 155
Musa Khan 30, 287
Musa Soltan 247

N

Nabi Hoseyn Khan 271
Nabik 126, 142
Nader Shah 8, 24
Nadr Khan Dhul-Qadr 138
Nafas Soltan Garrus 304
Nafas Soltan Sadlu b. Aliqoli Soltan 260
Nafsqoli Soltan 187
Nahababad (?) 248
Nahabad 128
Nain 133
Najaf 132, 248
Najafqoli Khan 172, 177
Najafqoli Khan b. Qazaq Khan Cherkes 287
Najafqoli Soltan 139, 255
Najm al-Din Masud II 166
Najm al-Din Soltan 249
Nakhjevan 126, 171, 248
Nakhud Soltan Torkman 211

Nakodaris 99
Namdar Soltan 254, 293
naqdeh 309
Naqdi Beyg Shamlu [Khan] 246
Naqdi Khan Shamlu 224
Naqdi Soltan 253
Naravandaqan 249
Naser Ali Khan 162, 272
Naseri 83
Nasiri 130
Natanz 133, 148, 249
Navab Beygom 274
navvab towbi-ashiyan 309
Nazar Ali Beyg [Khan] Suklan Dhul-Qadr 148
Nazar Ali Beyg Sarem Beyg Lor 231
Nazar Ali Soltan Shamlu 239
Nazar Beyg [Soltan] Ostajalu 292
Nazar Beyg Zik 257
Nazar Khan Tavakolli 241
Nazar Soltan 249
Nazar Soltan Asayesh-oghlu 220
Nazar Soltan Ostajalu 219
nazer 309
nazer-e boyutat 35, 37, 38, 40, 153, 173, 225, 308
nazer-e daftar-khaneh 60
nazer-e masjed-e Mashhad 18
Neh va Bandan 130, 249
Nelqas 116, 125, 249
Nematollah Malamiri 206
Nematollah Sufi 178
Nesa 129, 139, 157, 249
Neyriz 135, 205, 250
Nezam al-Molk 195
Nimruz 275
Nishapur 110, 129, 177, 250
Niyazabad 90
Niyaz Beyg b. Yadgar Beyg Pazuki 141
Nosrat Khan 277
Nowruz Beyg Inanlu 181
Nowruz Soltan 209
Nowshir Beyg Talesh 247
Nur 131, 251
Nur al-Din b. Ebrahim Khan 231
Nur al-Din Soltan Paydar 254
Nur Ali Khalifeh-ye Rumlu 149

Nur Ali Soltan Jamshidi 212
Nura Mohammada 301
Nur Mohammad Khan 139, 157, 246, 250
Nurollah Khan 163, 178, 233, 283

O

Obeh 298
Oghlan Budaghi Chegani 218
Oghurlu Beyg 153
Oghurlu Khan 259
Oghurlu Khan b. Mehdiqoli Khan Shamlu 224
Oghurlu Khan Shamlu 266
Oghurlu Soltan 177
Oghurlu Soltan Bayat 167, 169, 198
Oghurlu Soltan Chapni 185, 234
Oghurlu Soltan Chegini 194
Ologh [or Abu] Khan Shamlu 216
Olyar Khan 190
omara-ye janqi 25
ommal 308
Ommat Beyg [Khan] Dhul-Qadr 282
Ommat Beyg [Khan] Qarasarlu Köshek-oglu Ostajalu 241
Ommat Beyg Sarusheykhlu Dhul-Qadr aka Khalil Soltan 281
Ommat Soltan 196, 275
Ordubad 9, 61, 126, 251
Ordughdi Khalifeh 147
Ordughdi Khalifeh-ye Tekkelu 268, 300
Ordughdi Khan Alplu Afshar 182, 183
Ordughdu Khalifeh-ye Tekkelu 266
Orfah 132, 252
Orufah 252
Orufah-ye Diyarbekr 252
Orumi 113, 252
Orumiyeh 125
Otar Khan 149
Otuzayeki 209, 238
Oveys Beyg Pazuki 139
Owlash Beyg Ostajalu 209
Owliya Beyg 142

INDEX 331

Owtar Khan 170, 177, 257

P

Pahlavan Qamari 218
Pahlavan Qomari 214
Palangan 134, 227, 253
paludeh 99
Pambak 127
Panah Mohammad Khan Dhul-
    Qadr 152, 286
Panbak 93
Panjdeh 106, 128, 253
Parsi-badan 135
Parsi-Badan 253
parvancheh-ye bayazi va daftari
    307
parvanejati 309
Pasak 125, 254
Pasakuh 129, 254
Paydar 127, 254
Pa-ye Hesar 189
Pazuki 153
Persian Iraq 132
Pesand Khan 153
petroleum 92
Peykar [Beyg] Khan Ziyadoghlu
    286
Peykar Khan Igirmi-dört Qajar
    165
Peykar Soltan 258
Pir Budaq Khan 252
Pir Budaq Khan b. Shahbandeh
    Khan 156, 260
Pir Budaq Khan Pornak Torkman
    155, 162, 225
Pir Budaq Soltan b. Shahbandeh
    Khan Pornak 177
Pireh Mohammad Beyg Chavoshlu
    266
Pireh Mohammad Khan 295
Pireh Mohammad Khan Chavoslu
    Ostajalu 193
Pireh Mohammad Khan Ostajalu
    148, 219, 229
Pir Gheyb Khan Ostajalu 198,
    219, 295
Pir Gheyb Ostajalu 198
Pir Gheyb Soltan Ostajalu 297
Pir Gheyb Talesh 151

Piri Beyg Qajar 258
Piri Beyg Quchlu[y] or Pari Beyg
    Quchlu [Ostajalu] 266
Piri Soltan Rumlu 186
Pir Mohammad Khan 190
Pir Oveys 297
Pirqoli Kangarlu 274
Pirqoli Soltan Kangarlu 181
pishkesh 13, 103
pishkesh-nevis 78
Pordel Khan 186
Poshang 185
P.s.k 86
Pudeh 254
Pudeh-Someyram 133
Pushang 185
Pushanj 185

Q

Qabaleh 254
Qabanat 258
Qaban Soltan Beygdeli Shamlu
    272
Qadi Mohammad Kashi 281, 301
Qadi Mohammad Kashi Sadr 213
Qadi Soltan Torbati 206, 297
Qadurmish Khan 252
Qaen 129, 254
Qalamru-ye Ali Shükr 196
Qalandar Soltan Chuleh-ye
    Chaghatay 138, 293
Qalandar Soltan Kalehgir 211
Qalandar Soltan Tavakkoli 208
qalehdar 170, 172
Qaleh-ye P.s.k 86
Qalich Beyg b. Oveys Beyg Pazuki
    141
Qalich Beyg Pazuki 302
Qalich Khan b. Bayandor Khan
    150
Qalich Khan [b. Saru Khan] 150
Qalich Qurchi-ye Safi Mirza 225
Qalij Beyg Imur 152
Qalmaq 90
Qanbar Soltan Asayesh-oghlu
    Ostajalu 181
Qanbar Soltan [Khan] Shamlu
    191
Qanbar Soltan Zanganeh 168

Qandahar 83, 84, 128, 130, 255
Qanqara [Soltan] 289
Qansu Beyg 300
Qapan 258
Qapanat 117, 258
Qapan Khan Beygdelu 252
Qapan Soltan Beygdeli Shamlu
    189
Qappanat 125
qapuchi-bashi 233
Qara-aghach 258
Qara Aghaj 125, 127
Qara Alus 259
Qarabagh 126, 258
Qara Beyg [Khan] 180
Qara Beyg Qajar 193
Qarach 259
Qarachehdagh 48
Qaracheh-Elyas Beybordlu 171
Qaracheh Soltan 180
Qarachqay Soltan 177
Qaradagh 260
Qara Hasan Khan Chavoshlu
    Ostajalu 262
Qara Hasan Khan Ostajalu 198
Qara Hesar 260
Qarajehdagh 11, 12, 47, 118,
    125, 260
Qarajeh Soltan Tekkelu 197
Qara Khan 180
Qara Khan Bayat 141, 288
Qara Khan Söklen Dhul-Qadr
    216
Qara Khan Soltan 161
Qara Mostafa Pasha 146
Qara Shahverdi Soltan Dhul-Qadr
    177
Qara Soltan Shamlu 97, 294
Qarcahqay Khan b. Manuchehr
    Khan 242
Qarchaqay Khan 241
Qarenjehoghlu Ostajalu 296
Qarni-yaraq 126
qasab 308
Qasem 285
Qasem Ali Soltan 289
Qasem Khan 159, 251
Qasem Khan Afshar 248

Qasem Soltan Enanlu Afshar 222, 278
Qasem Soltan Inanlu Afshar 269
Qatenamish Beyg 164
Qazakh 173
Qazaq Khan b. Hoseyn Khan Shamlu 239
Qazaq Khan Cherkes 153, 173, 286
Qazaq Khan Tekkelu b. Mohammad Khan 202
Qazaqlar 127, 140, 141
Qazaq Soltan 98, 220
Qazeghman 260
Qazeqman 127, 260
Qazi Beyg [Khan] Tekkelu 201
Qazvin 134, 260
Qebchaq 128, 263
Qelich Beygh b. Ostajalu Mohammad Khan 265
Qepchaq 263
Qezel Aghaj 125
Qezel Ali Khan 280
Qezel Aqaj 148, 262
Qiyas Soltan Ostajalu 289
Qobad Khan 266, 272
Qobad Soltan [Khan] Qajar b. Budaq Khan 268
Qobeh 92, 128, 263
qol-beygi 309
Qolhan 128, 254, 255, 263, 284
Qoli Beyg Afshar 215
Qoli Khan Afshar 183
Qoli Khan Dhul-Qadr 184
Qoli Soltan Afshar 138, 167
qollar-aghasi 30, 156, 217, 225, 283, 308
Qom 133, 148, 184, 263
Qomisheh 133
Qorban Ali Beyg 139
Qorban Ali Mirza 285
Qorkhmas Khan 246
Qorkhmas Khan Rumlu 198
Qorkhmas Khan Shamlu 198
Quchan 218
Quch Beyg Rumlu 289
qurchi-bashi 22, 24, 28, 29, 31, 44, 138, 156, 167, 197, 216, 265, 307

qurchis 25, 27, 28, 33, 43, 49, 60, 64, 65
qurchi-ye khasseh-ye sharifeh 309
qurchi-ye rekab 52
qurchi-ye tir va kaman 266
Qur Hamzeh 169, 256, 257, 303
qur-khaneh 18
Qurkhmas Khan Shamlu 262
Qurkhmas Soltan Shamlu 148
quruqi 17, 31, 35
qushchi-bashi 152
Qushqan 98

R

Rahmatabad 210
Rais Mohammad Kerai 137
Rajab Ali Beyg 23
Ranekuh 131, 264
Rar 133
Rasht 131, 264
rasm al-vezarat 309
rayezan 308
rekab-khaneh 309
Rey 32, 147, 265
Rey-Tehran 134
Rezaqoli Khan 216
Rezaqoli Soltan 271
Rezaqoli Soltan Siyah-Mansur 169, 303
rezvan makan 14
rikas 309
Road (?) 210
Romahiyeh 267
Romamiyeh 132
Rostam Beyg 204, 299
Rostamdar 131, 267
Rostam Khan 156, 235, 242
Rostam Khan Afshar 224
Rostam Mirza 217, 256
Rostam Mirza b. Bahram Mirza 257
Rostam Mirza b. Soltan Hoseyn Mirza 169, 303
Rostam Mohammad Khan 176
Rostam Mohammad Khan Sadlu 153, 217
Rostam Soltan Arashlu 289
Rostam Soltan Soklan 160

rosumat 308
rosum-e hokmi 307, 308
Rowshan Soltan Legzi 208
royal secretariat 73
Rugad 189

S

Sabzavar 129, 268
Sadabad 133, 179, 270
Sadarak 126
Sadi 295
Sadlu 88
Sadlu Aghcheh 270
Sadmara 235
Sadmard 269
Sadmareh 134, 269
sadr 76
Sadr al-Din Khan Ostajalu b. Saru Pireh 151
Sadr al-Din Khan Safavi 148
sadr-e ammeh 28
sadr-e khasseh 28, 59
Safi Khan Lezgi 172
Safi Mirza b. Abbas 241
Safiqoli Beyg 165, 177, 178, 216, 225, 283, 302
Safiqoli Beyg b. Saru Soltan 292
Safiqoli Beyg [Khan] b. Rostam Khan 242
Safiqoli Khan 163, 198, 199, 203, 217, 233, 242
Safiqoli Khan b. Dhul-Feqar Khan 219
Safiqoli Khan b. Emamqoli Khan 231
Safiqoli Khan b. Karjasi Beyg 177
Safiqoli Khan b. Qurkhmas Samkhuti 158
Safiqoli Khan b. Rostam Khan 172
Safiqoli Khan Qolkhanchi-oghlu 161
Safiqoli Khan Soltan 178
Safiqoli Khan Torkestan-oghlu 203, 242
Safiqoli Khan Ziyad-oghlu Qajar 156
Safiqoli Soltan 162
Safiqoli Soltan Beygdeli 292

Safi Vali Khalifeh b. Sufiyan
    Rumlu 191
Saheb 268
Saheb-e ekhteyar 206
saheb-e towjih 67
saheb-qerani 14
Said Beyg Fumeni 188
Said Khan b. Haqqnazar Khan
    159
Sajavand 135, 270
Sakhar 270
Saleh Soltan 266
Salim Khan Shams al-Dinlu 140,
    236, 279
Salim Khan Shams al-Dinluy-e
    Dhul-Qadr 140
Saliyan 127, 160, 270
Salman Khalifeh Torkman 255
Salman Khan 195, 208, 241
Salman Khan Ostajalu b. Shah Ali
    Mirza 262, 298
Salman Soltan [Khan] Donboli
    Su-bashi 173
Salmas 117, 173, 270
Samireh 269
Sam Mirza 201
Sanjab Soltan Afshar 183
Sarab 116, 125, 148, 271
Sarakhs 111, 129, 208, 271
Saray Farhadjerd 103
sardar 26, 27, 30, 307
Sardar Beyg 165
sarkhatt-nevis 68, 74
sarreshteh-nevis 308
Saru Aslan 172
Saru Beyg 272
Sarufarqan 272
Saru Khan 28
Saru Khan Beyg 172
Saru Khan b. Qalich Khan 150
Saru Khan Sahandlu 199, 214,
    275
Saru Khan Soltan 161
Saru Khan Soltan Beygdelu 272
Saru Khan Soltan Salmasi 271
Saru Pireh 265
Saru-qargan 125
Saruqargan 272
Saruqazqan 272

Saruqurghan 272
Saruqurqan 272
Saru Soltan Beygdelu 204
sar-vazir-e azam 307
Sarvestan 135, 272
Savadkuh 131, 272
Saveh 134, 154, 272
Savokh-Bolagh 265
Savokh-Bulagh 134, 262
Sayyed Abdollah 146
Sayyed Abdollah b. Sayyed
    Farajollah 146
Sayyed Ahmad Khan 217
Sayyed Ali b. Mowla Sajjad 145
Sayyed Ali b. Sayyed Abdollah
    146
Sayyed Ali Khan 207
Sayyed Ali Khan b. Mowla Khalaf
    b. Abdol-Motalleb 146
Sayyed al-Sajedin Imam Zeyn al-
    Abedin 91
Sayyed Asadollah Khan 303
Sayyed Badran Shoja al-Din b.
    Sayyed Fallah 145
Sayyed Barakah b. Sayyed Mansur
    145
Sayyed Beyg 157, 204, 289
Sayyed Beyg b. Masum Beyg Safavi
    152
Sayyed Beyg b. Sayyed Masum
    Beyg 152
Sayyed Beyg Kamuneh 167, 206,
    274
Sayyed Elyas b. Mowla Sajjad 145
Sayyed Fallah b. Sayyed Mohsen
    145
Sayyed Farajollah Khan b. Sayyed
    Ali Khan 146
Sayyed Hasan Hazar Jaribi 200
Sayyed Heybatollah b. Mowla
    Khalaf 146
Sayyed Heydar Khan b. Sayyed Ali
    Khan 146
Sayyed Hoseyn Tobadkani 271,
    305
Sayyed Jamaz Arab 289
Sayyed Khan 287
Sayyed Mansur b. Mowla Abdol-
    Motalleb 145
Sayyed Mir Shahi 142

Sayyed Mobarak b. Abdol-
    Motalleb b. Heydar b. Soltan
    Mohsen b. Mohammad b.
    Falah 145
Sayyed Mobarak Khan b. Sayyed
    Motalleb 290
Sayyed Mohammad Arab 289
Sayyed Mohammad b. Sayyed
    Naser Ostajalu 250
Sayyed Mohammad Kamuneh
    204, 248
Sayyed Mohammad Khan b.
    Sayyed Farajollah 146
Sayyed Mohammad Khan b.
    Sayyed Mobarak 145
Sayyed Mozaffar Mortezai 244
Sayyed Naser b. Sayyed Mobarak
    145
Sayyed Naser b. Sayyed Mobarak
    Moshasha 273
Sayyed Nasir al-Din 142
Sayyed Qavam al-Din 244
Sayyed Rashed b. Salem b. Abdol-
    Motalleb 145
Sayyed Salameh 181
Sayyed Soleyman 157
Sayyed Zeyn al-Abedin 240
Sayyed Zonbur b. Mowla Sajjad
    179
Schorer 8, 24
seal 41, 44, 46, 48
Sejestan 275
Sekandar Soltan Banehi 164
selahdar-bashi 18, 309
Semnan 134, 153, 273
sepahsalar 26, 29, 31, 34, 44, 156,
    198, 216, 217, 257, 307
Sert 132
Sevanduk Beyg 271
Sevenduk Beyg Zanganeh 161
Sevenduk Soltan 158
Seyf Beyg 289
Seystan 84, 128, 130, 212, 275,
    276
Shabankareh 135, 205, 278
Shaberan 127, 160, 175, 278
Shaborghan 288
Shadidlu 126
Shadilu 278
Shaflan 107, 128, 278

Shaft 38
Shah Abbas I 9, 20, 25, 34, 42, 45, 47, 52, 58, 59, 71, 72, 120
Shah Abbas II 70
Shah Ali aka Evaz Soltan 157
Shah Ali Khalifeh-ye Dhul-Qadr 175
Shah Ali Soltan Afshar 297
Shah Ali Soltan Chegani 299
Shah Ali Soltan Khodabandehlu 199
Shah Ali Soltan Ostajalu 151
Shah Amir Khan 280
Shahbandeh b. Pir Budaq Khan Pornak Torkman 155
Shah Budaq 154
Shahmir Khan 280
Shah Mohammad Khodabandeh 9, 192, 291
Shahnavaz Khan 216, 257
Shahnavaz Khan Soltan 209
Shahnazar Soltan 220
Shahnazar Soltan [Khan] Tükeli Chaghatay 241
Shahnazar Soltan Köshek-oghlu Ostajalu 251
Shahnazar Soltan Tükeli Chaghatay 208
Shahqaqi 125
Shah Qobad Beyg [Soltan] Tekkelu 206
Shahqoli Beyg b. Ras Khan 174, 196, 274
Shahqoli Beyg Qarenchi-oghlu 241
Shahqoli Beyg [Soltan] b. Aras Khan 196
Shahqoli Khalifeh Dhul-Qadr 282
Shahqoli Khalifeh Dhul-Qadr Mohrdar 264
Shahqoli Khalifeh Mohrdar Dhul-Qadr 174, 282
Shahqoli Khalifeh-ye Dhul-Qadr 278
Shahqoli Khan 37, 162
Shahqoli Khan b. Khalil Khan Afshar 224
Shahqoli Khan Pornak 241

Shahqoli Khan Zanganeh 22, 27, 50
Shahqoli Qarancheh Ostajalu 223
Shahqoli Soltan 156, 167
Shahqoli Soltan Afshar 103, 208, 215
Shahqoli Soltan Afshar b. Mostafa Soltan 246
Shahqoli Soltan b. Morshedqoli Khan 237, 297
Shahqoli Soltan Chamesgezek 177
Shahqoli Soltan Kholafa Rumlu 174
Shahqoli Soltan Ostajalu 171, 240, 248
Shahqoli Soltan Piyadeh Torkman 273
Shahqoli Soltan Qamari 208
Shahqoli Soltan Qarancheh-oghlu Mahi-Faqihlu Ostajalu 295
Shahqoli Soltan Qarenjeh-oghlu 221
Shahqoli Soltan Qarenjeh-oghlu Ostajalu 208
Shahqoli Soltan Tabat-oghlu Dhul-Qadr 274
Shahqoli Soltan Tati-oghlu Dhul-Qadr 152
Shahqoli Soltan Yekan Ostajalu 202
Shahrabad 210
Shahr-e zur 134, 278
Shahrokh 19
Shahrokh Beyg Afshar 250, 268
Shahrokh Beyg [Soltan] Zanganeh 293
Shahrokh b. Farrokh Mirza 284
Shahrokh Khan 217
Shahrokh Soltan 218
Shahrokh Soltan b. Ali Beyg 293
Shahrokh Soltan Zanganeh 179, 221
Shah Rostam Abbasi 219, 235
Shah Rostam II 235
Shahryar 32
Shah Safi I 10, 26
shahsevan 164
Shahsevan 115, 125
Shah Soleyman 22, 27, 30, 34

Shah Soltan b. Hamzeh Soltan Qazaq Ostajalu 273
Shah Soltan Hoseyn 7, 10, 14, 18, 19, 22, 23, 27, 30, 31, 32, 35, 38, 39, 169
Shahsovar Beyg 234
shah-tabin 66
Shah Taher Khorasani 207
Shah Tahmasp 46, 96
Shah Tahmasp I 9, 73
Shah Tahmasp II 8, 23
Shahvali Soltan 152
Shahvali Soltan Jalaer 254
Shah Vali Soltan Tati-oghlu 241
Shahvali Soltan Tati-oghlu Dhul-Qadr 282
Shahverdi Abbasi 235
Shahverdi Beyg Chulehi 43
Shahverdi Beyg Ostajalu 103
Shahverdi Beyg [Soltan] Kachal Chavoshlu Ostajalu 151
Shahverdi Beyg [Soltan] Ostajalu 176
Shahverdi Khalifeh 179, 213, 270, 293
Shahverdi Khalifeh-ye Enanlu 184
Shahverdi Khalifeh-ye Shamlu 170, 198, 205, 249, 250
Shahverdi Khan 216, 236
Shahverdi Khan b. Khalifeh-ye Ansar 260
Shahverdi Khan b. Mohammadi Khan 235
Shahverdi Khan Kord Mahmudi 168
Shahverdi Khan Seyl-Sopor 283
Shahverdi Khan Soltan Ziyad-oghlu 258
Shahverdi Khan Zanganeh 218
Shahverdi Soltan 181, 258
Shahverdi Soltan Afshar 166, 168, 185
Shahverdi Soltan Kandazlu 290
Shahverdi Soltan Tati-oghlu Dhul-Qadr 274
shajarat 308
Shal 130, 278
Shal-e Mostan 278
Shal va Mostan 278
Shamakhi 127, 172, 278

Shamkhal Soltan Cherkes 280
Shamlu 249
Shams al-Din Khan 204
Shams al-Dinlu 95, 127, 173, 259, 279, 302
Shams al-Din Qazaqlar 140
Shamshi Khan Qazaqlar 175
Shamshir Ali 137
Shamshir Khan 302
Shamsi Khan Qazaqlar 140
Shaqaqi 115, 279
Shaqlan 204, 278
Sharaf al-Din Bedlisi 296
Sharaf al-Din Beyg 167
Sharaf al-Din Khan Bedlisi 184, 270
Sharaf Khan 296
Sharaf Khan Bedlisi 248
Sharaf Khan [Rudaki Kurdi] 168
Sharif Beyg Rudhaki Kord 296
Shebli Soltan Cherkes 290
Sheikh Afrasiyab 165
Sheikh Ahmad Aqa 262
Sheikh Ali Beyg [Khan] Zanganeh 180
Sheikh ʿAli Khan Zanganeh 27
Sheikh Ali Khan Zanganeh 22, 211, 218, 293
Sheikh Ebrahim II 284
Sheikh Fares 291
Sheikh Safi al-Din 47, 118
Sheikhshah 284
Sheikh Shehab al-Din 47, 118
shekar-bashi 225, 286, 287, 292
Shekari Soltan Esparlu 148, 271
Sheki 127, 279, 285
Shindand 182
Shir Ali 158
Shir Ali Soltan Baradust 294
Shiraz 135, 280
Shirazi Soltan 168
Shir-bachcheh 172
shirehchi-bashi 188, 216
Shir Khan Afghan 186
Shirvan 127, 284
Shirvanshah 284
Shoja al-Din Hamzeh Beyg 277
Shoja al-Din Mohammad Mirza b. Esmail II 282

showkat-panah 13
Shulestan 135, 288
Shurehgel 127, 141, 288
Shushtar 135
Silakhur 235
Simun Khan 196
singers 101
Siyavosh Beyg [Soltan] 176
Siyavush Khan 225
Sobhanverdi Beyg Ardalan 228
Sobhanverdi Khan 150
Soheyl Beyg 301
Sojas 125, 291
Soleyman Beyg b. Mirza Beyg 164
Soleyman Beyg Khonoslu [?] 204
Soleyman Beyg Qushchi 254
Soleyman Beyg Rumlu 147, 171, 266
Soleyman [Beyg] Soltan Qushchi 263
Soleyman Chelebi Chini [Chapni] 252
Soleyman Khalifeh-ye Shamlu 152, 292
Soleyman Khalifeh-ye Torkman 264
Soleyman Khalifeh-ye Torkman b. Sohrab Khalifeh 298
Soleyman Khan Ardalan 228
Soleyman Khan Ostajalu 286
Soleyman Mirza b. Tahmasp 282
Soleymanqoli Beyg 165
Soleyman Soltan 209
Soleyman Soltan b. Mohammad Hoseyn Soltan Tekkelu 299
Soleyman Soltan Dhul-Qadr 251
Soltan Abbas Mirza 202
Soltan Ali Afshar 103
Soltan Ali Betlich 227
Soltan Ali Beyg b. Sorkhab Beyg Ardalan 227
Soltan Ali b. Mohammad 145
Soltan Ali Khalifeh Shamlu 255
Soltan Ali Mirza 165, 258
Soltan Ali Qurchi 103
Soltan Ali Soltan Shamlu 255
Soltan Hasan 229
Soltan Hasan Mirza 241
Soltan Hoseyn b. Shah Rostam 235

Soltan Hoseyn Khan Shamlu 261
Soltan Hoseyn Mirza 244
Soltan Hoseyn Mirza b. Bahram Mirza 169, 256, 277
Soltaniyeh 121, 125, 219, 292
Soltan Mahmud b. Ghazi Beyg 284
Soltan Mahmud b. Mozaffar Soltan 195
Soltan Mahmud Mirza 193, 286
Soltan Mahmud Mirza b. Tahmasp 229, 285
Soltan Masum 148
Soltan Masum Khan 266
Soltan Masum Soltan Torkman 154, 210, 273
Soltan Mohammad Khan b. Soltan Morad Khan 244
Soltan Mohammad Mirza b. Tahmasp 202, 282
Soltan Mohammad Mirza Khodabandeh 103
Soltan Mohammad Shah 235
Soltan Mohsen b. Mohammad 145
Soltan Morad Khan Torkman 273
Soltan Morad Mirza b. Tahmasp 256
Soltan Mostafa Mirza 9, 249
Soltan Ostajalu 103
Soltan Qazaq 240
Soltan Soleyman Mirza 241
Somay 127
Someyram 293
Sonqor 134, 179, 211, 293
Sorkhab Beyg b. Mamun Beyg Ardalan 227
soyurghal 13, 309
Sufi 294
Sufi Soltan 103
Sufi Vali Rumlu 186
Sufiyan Khalifeh 222
Sufiyan Khalifeh Shamlu 201, 240
sufi-zadeh-ye qadim 32
Sulagh Hoseyn Tekkelu 227
Sulaq Hoseyn 170
Sulaq Hoseyn Tekkelu 179, 253, 293
Sumay 121, 164, 294

Sundar Beyg b. Qanqara Soltan 289
Surloq 294
Surlugh 294
Surluq 125
Syunik 258

T

Tabarestan 242
Tabas 100, 112, 129, 294, 298
Tabas-e Gilaki 294
Tabat Aqa Dhul-Qadr 208
tabinan 309
Tabriz 9, 29, 124, 154, 219, 252
TabTab 199, 249
Tafaroshi clan 74
Tahmasp Ali Khan Aghcheh-Qoyunlu Qajar 172
Tahmasp I 17
Tahmasp Khan Gholam 262
Tahmasp Mirza 7, 200, 201
Tahmaspqoli Beyg 179, 231, 236
Tahmaspqoli [Beyg] Khan 162
Tahmaspqoli Khan 8, 24, 235
Tahmaspqoli Khan Tarkhan Torkoman 216
Tahmaspqoli Soltan Areshlu Afshar 198
Tahmaspqoli Soltan b. Ali Khan 175
Tahmaspqoli Soltan b. Aliqoli Khan 175
Tahmaspqoli Soltan Dhul-Qadr 165
Tahmaspqoli Soltan Enanlu 269
Tahmasp Soltan b. Mohammad Soltan Chaghatay 290
Tahmurath Beg 24
tahvilat 308
taj 309
taj-e vahhaj 308
Tajiks 21, 36
talab 13
talab-e daftari 307
Taleb Beyg 162
Taleb Khan 162
Taleqan 274
Talesh 125, 149

ta'liqeh 307
tankhvah 13, 307
Tarom 126, 148, 219, 295
Tarom-e Khalkhal 295
Tarom-e Pain 295
Taromeyn 295
Tavakkol Khan 189
Tavakolli 208
Taviqun Soltan Qajar 280
Tavus Mirza 286
tax payers 57, 70, 72, 76
Tehran 265
Tergavar 127
Teymur Soltan [Khan] Ostajalu 277
teyul 270, 308
teyuldar 297
Teyuldar 138, 149, 150, 167, 174, 179, 195, 196, 197, 206, 213, 248, 252, 260, 270, 273, 275, 288, 292, 293
teyuls 19, 20, 25, 26, 27, 31, 32, 33, 36, 52, 56, 60, 63, 64, 65, 67, 68, 69, 72, 73, 74
Tianeti 295
Tiflis 127, 295
Timur Khan Ajarlu Shamlu 228
Timur Khan Ardalan 199
Timur Khan b. Montasha Soltan Sheykhler Ostajalu 266
Timur Khan Soltan Ali Beyg Ardalan 228
Timur Kord 181
Timur Soltan 294
tofangchi-aghasi 23, 29, 34, 36, 37, 38, 44, 138, 156, 178, 209, 293, 308
toghra 9, 26, 41, 43, 57, 62
Tonekabon 131, 296
Torbat 296
Torbat-e Heydari 129, 297
Torbat-e Heydariyeh 108
Torbat-e Zaveh 304
Tormak mountains 83
Torshiz 103, 129, 273, 297
tovachi-bashi 46, 261, 282, 307
towbi-ashyan 14
towhid-khaneh 307

towliyat 308
Tukret Beyg 237, 288
Tulak 298
Tun 112, 128, 129, 254, 298
tupchi-bashi 38, 203, 242
tupchis 25, 309
Turks 9, 20

U

Ubeh 128, 204, 298
Uhkhli 195
Ujarud 126, 299
Ukh 183
Ulameh Soltan Tekkelu 154
Uq 130, 299
Ushniyeh 252
Usmi Khan Qeytaq 175
Utar Khan 219
Utar Khan Dhul-Qadr 275
uzangu qurchi 177
Uzbegs 10, 138, 157, 160, 190, 196, 204, 211, 239, 245, 250, 255, 276, 299, 305

V

vajeb-e takhyiri 21
Vakhushtu Beyg [Soltan] [Khan] 290
vakil 8, 42, 45, 71
vakil-e divan-e a'la 308
vali 309
Vali Beyg Ostajalu 254
Vali Beyg [Soltan] Tekkelu b. Ali Soltan Sharaf al-Din-oghlu 197
Vali Beyg Tekkelu b. Ali Soltan 148
Vali Jan Khan Torkman 200, 213
Vali Khalifeh Evji Shamlu 241
Vali Khalifeh Rumlu 191, 229
Vali Khalifeh Shamlu 264
Vali Khalifeh-ye Rumlu 241
Vali Khalifeh-ye Shamlu 148, 202, 247, 251, 255
Vali Khan Afshar 216
Vali Khan Ostajalu 297
Vali Khan Sharaflu Ostajalu 220

Vali Khan Tekkelu 170, 198
Vali Khan Torkman 213
Vali Mohammad Khan 217
Vali Soltan Dhul-Qadr 252
Vali Soltan [Khan] Afshar 215
Vali Soltan [Khan] Qalkhanji-oghlu Dhul-Qadr 282
Vali Soltan Sufi 264
Van 126, 149, 299
vaqaye-nevis 9
Varamin 134, 299
Vargahan 116, 300
Varghahan 126
Vaset 132, 300
Vashnaveh-ye Qom 264
vazifeh 13
vazir-e boyutat 75
vazir-e divan 309
vazir-e divān-e aʻla 20, 308
vazir-e halal 76
vazir-e Isfahan 58
vazir-e mohr 47, 307
vazir-e mowqufat 309
vazir-e mowqufat-e chahardeh masum 59
vazir-e Qara Alus 75
vazir-e qurchiyan 64
vazir-e Sarhadd 76
vazir-e tofangchiyan 65
vazir-e tupchiyan 65
Vazvan 264
velvet 98
vozara-ye arbaʼeh 308

W

war council emirs 44
white eunuchs 17, 20

Y

Yadgar Beyg b. Zeynal Pazuki 141, 260
Yadgar Beyg Pazuki 141, 207, 260
Yadgar Mohammad Soltan Torkman 273
Yadgar Soltan [Mowsellu] 103
Yahya Khan 246, 272
Yahya Khan Bakhtiyari 291
Yahya Khan b. Yusof Khan 159

Yahya Khan Taleshi 150
Yakan Beyg Afshar 183
Yakan Beyg [Soltan, Khan] Afshar 182
Yamut 131
Yaqub Beyg [Khan] Dhul-Qadr 282
Yaqub Beyg [Soltan] 215
Yaqub Khan 103
Yaʻqub Soltan 163
Yaqub Soltan 217
Yaqub Soltan Qajar 258
Yar-Ahmad Khuzani 166, 205
Yar Ali Soltan Bayat 167
Yar Ali Soltan Tekkelu 103
Yasaq-kashi 119
yasavol 309
yasavol-e sohbat 309
Yazd 300
Yegan Beyg Ostajalu 197
Y.ki 130
Yoli Beyg Gholam 206
Yolqoli Beyg b. Aydin Aqa Dhul-Qadr 238
Y.saku 129
Yusof Ali Khan 239, 241
Yusof Beyg Afshar 138
Yusof Beyg Ziyad-oghlu Qajar 165
Yusof Khalifeh Ziyadoghlu 258
Yusof Khan 152, 278, 286
Yusof Khan Afshar 216
Yusof Khan b. Oghlan Bedagh Chega 241
Yusof Khan Soltan 269
Yusof Rais 242
Yusof Soltan 177, 188
Yusof Soltan b. Qoli Soltan Afshar 215
Yusof Soltan gholam 170
Yusof Soltan [Khan] Rumlu 298
Yutam Soltan Gorji 176

Z

Zabet 228
zabetan 307
zabet-e dushallok 71
zabeteh-nevis 71
Zabolestan 275, 277

Zadeh-ye Makhdum 261
Zagam 95, 127, 302
Zakariya Khan 163
Zakhur 128, 280, 302
Zakiyeh 143
Zalem 302
Zal Khan 172
Zaman Beyg 219
Zaman Khan 144, 221
Zaman Khan Abdali 204
Zaman Khan b. Qazaq Khan 225
Zaman Soltan 158, 178
Zamindavar 130, 169, 303
Zanganeh 52
zargar-bashi 283
zarrab-bashiyan 308
zarrabiyan 307
Zarrin-kamar 133, 187
Zaruzbil 126, 303
Zaveh 103, 129, 220, 304
Zenjan 125
Zeybadat 304
Zeydan 135, 304
Zeydanat 304
Zeynal Beyg [Khan] Beygdelu Shamlu 266
Zeynal Beyg [Khan] Mahmudi 173
Zeynal Beyg [Khan] Shamlu 224, 265
Zeynal Beyk [Soltan] 208
Zeyn al-Din Soltan Shamlu 151, 157, 181, 250
Zeynal Khan 162, 260
Zeynal Khan Shamlu 151, 201, 261, 274
Zeytunat 304
Zirabad 208
Ziya al-Din b. Sharaf Khan 296
Zohab 134, 304
Zonur 304
Zonuz 304
Zunuz 126
Zurabad 305
Zuri 106, 128, 305

www.ingramcontent.com/pod-product-compliance
Lightning Source LLC
Chambersburg PA
CBHW081149290426
44108CB00018B/2491